Soldiers of Democracy?

Soldiers of Democracy?

Military Legacies and the Arab Spring

Sharan Grewal

OXFORD
UNIVERSITY PRESS

Great Clarendon Street, Oxford, OX2 6DP,
United Kingdom

Oxford University Press is a department of the University of Oxford.
It furthers the University's objective of excellence in research, scholarship,
and education by publishing worldwide. Oxford is a registered trade mark of
Oxford University Press in the UK and in certain other countries

Published in the United States of America by Oxford University Press
198 Madison Avenue, New York, NY 10016, United States of America

British Library Cataloguing in Publication Data
Data available

Library of Congress Control Number: 2023932437

ISBN 978–0–19–287391–0
ISBN 978–0–19–887351–8 (pbk.)

DOI: 10.1093/oso/9780192873910.001.0001

Printed and bound by
CPI Group (UK) Ltd, Croydon, CR0 4YY

For Emma

Acknowledgments

I studied in Cairo in the fall of 2011. In those heady days of the Arab Spring, I could not help but be swept up in the emotion of revolution. The thrill of protests, the excitement of the country's first real election, the passion and polarization as the shocking results rolled in—each got me hooked on the study of revolution and democratization. I owe a tremendous debt to my professors at the American University in Cairo that semester—Gamal Soltan, Maye Kassem, and Gianluca Parolin—for kindling my early interest in these topics.

I returned to Egypt in the summer of 2012 for my first research trip, conducting interviews with the major political parties. Inspired by this trip, and with the encouragement of my Georgetown professors Erik Voeten, Samer Shehata, Judith Tucker, and Joseph Sassoon, I decided to apply for a PhD at Princeton University as a bright-eyed undergraduate senior. I do not know what Princeton saw in me, but I am enormously grateful they gave me the chance, and changed the course of my life.

The summer before I started the PhD, I was fortunate to serve as an intern at the US State Department, where I worked in the Bureau of Democracy, Human Rights, and Labor. It would prove to be an eventful summer. In July 2013, Egypt's military staged a coup, arresting the democratically elected president, and massacring his supporters in Rabaa and Nahda squares. With the support of my supervisor, Dan Mahanty, I drafted an internal memo covering those massacres for the State Department, and witnessed firsthand the seemingly arcane but incredibly consequential debate about whether to call the coup a coup.

When I arrived in Princeton in August 2013, therefore, I knew from the start that my dissertation would focus on Egypt, and why its transition to democracy had so rapidly been crushed. But I had not foreseen a comparison with Tunisia. For that I owe early discussions with Amaney Jamal, my wise and prescient PhD advisor, for introducing me to a more sound comparative methodology and to a country that has since become a second home.

I traveled to Tunisia first in January and June of 2014, before moving there in July 2015. Over the next year, I interviewed dozens of military and civilian leaders who had helped shepherd the country to democracy. I will be forever indebted for their time, generosity, and willingness to share their stories. No words can express my gratitude to Tunisia's retired military officers in particular, who spent countless hours making this project possible. Especially generous was retired Colonel Major Mahmoud Mezoughi, president of Tunisia's retired officers' association, who patiently answered my unending stream of questions, facilitated interviews with tens of other officers, and helped me to administer a survey to the association. I have returned to Tunisia every summer and every winter since 2014, in total conducting over 100 interviews there.

None of this fieldwork would have been possible without a stellar team of Tunisian research assistants. Foremost among them was Intissar Samarat, whose tenacity and personality opened so many doors over the course of my research. Safa Belghith, now a PhD student at Ghent, and Hamza Mighri, now in DC at the IMF, both provided invaluable research assistance as well. And Mohamed Dhia Hammami, now a PhD student at Syracuse, cannot be thanked enough, not only for his assistance, but also his incredible knowledge—and investigative skills—of all things Tunisia.

Over the course of the PhD, I was blessed to have a remarkable group of scholars to serve as my dissertation committee. Amaney Jamal was the advisor everyone dreams for, providing regular, thoughtful feedback, generous in her praise and kind in her criticism. Rory Truex took an early interest in the project, providing sharp feedback, good humor, and remarkable patience despite the tenure clock and a baby, even remarking that I did not bother him enough! Kris Ramsay was particularly helpful in pushing me to think through the theory in a more systematic and structured manner. And Tarek Masoud's vast knowledge of Egyptian politics was critical to piecing together that part of the story, and he has been a guiding light and champion for me in the profession. At Princeton, I also received invaluable feedback along the way from Chris Achen, Faisal Ahmed, Elizabeth Baisley, Gary Bass, Mark Beissinger, Carles Boix, Winston Chou, Rafaela Dancygier, Romain Ferrali, Joanne Gowa, Ashley Hill, Alisha Holland, Dayna Judge, Amanda Kennard, Alex Kustov, Helen Milner, Steve Monroe, Elizabeth Nugent, Tom Pavone, Grigo Pop-Eleches, Daniel Tavana, Leonard Wantchekon, Jennifer Widner, Keren Yarhi-Milo, and Deborah Yashar.

Initial findings from my research were published in the *Washington Post*'s Monkey Cage in 2015 and 2016, and in a report for the Carnegie Endowment for International Peace in 2016. I am indebted to Marc Lynch and Yezid Sayigh for these opportunities, and for their helpful edits and queries on my initial drafts. Early versions of the book were also presented at Oxford, Columbia, Georgetown, George Washington, NYU Abu Dhabi, William & Mary, Brookings, the Project on Middle East Democracy, and the APSA and MESA conferences. For insightful feedback at these venues, I thank Madiha Afzal, Holger Albrecht, Nate Allen, Lisa Anderson, Ben Ansell, Abdullah Aydogan, Zoltan Barany, Eva Bellin, Lindsay Benstead, Dina Bishara, Hicham Bou Nassif, Steven Brooke, Risa Brooks, Dan Byman, Matthew Cebul, Tamara Cofman Wittes, Erica de Bruin, Kim Guiler, Shadi Hamid, Kristen Harkness, Amy Hawthorne, Donald Horowitz, Stathis Kalyvas, Kevin Koehler, Bob Kubinec, Mirjam Künkler, Ellen Lust, Suzanne Maloney, Stephen McInerney, Rani Mullen, Phil Roessler, Natan Sachs, Naunihal Singh, Robert Springborg, Lisa Wedeen, Scott Williamson, Sarah Yerkes, A.Kadir Yildirim, and Sean Yom.

For financial support for my research, I am indebted to the National Science Foundation, the Smith Richardson Foundation, Princeton's Bobst Center for Peace and Justice, the Princeton Institute for International and Regional Studies, Princeton's Center for International Security Studies, the Project on Middle East Political Science, the Brookings Institution, and William & Mary's Global Research Institute and Government Department. For the time, space, and resources to write (and rewrite) the manuscript, I thank Steven Rathgeb Smith and Betsy Super at APSA's Centennial Center; Tarun Chhabra, Bruce Jones, Suzanne Maloney, and Natan Sachs at the Brookings Institution; and Paul Manna, Sue Peterson, and Mike Tierney at William & Mary.

Revising the dissertation into a book was a grueling task, doubling in length by expanding in every direction: new mechanisms, new dependent variables, new interviews, and new quantitative analyses. Three scholars in particular helped me get this manuscript over the finish line. Risa Brooks was indispensable in helping me think through both the details of Egypt and Tunisia's stories, and how they speak to the broader field of civil–military relations. Matthew Cebul was my sounding board at every step, patiently listening and reflecting on every proposed tweak to the theory. And Phil Roessler took the time to read the entire manuscript, providing invaluable feedback in helping me sift through reviews and consider how to revise the manuscript into its final version.

At Oxford University Press, I want to thank Dominic Byatt for seeing potential in the manuscript at an early stage, and for securing two fantastic anonymous reviews. I also thank Karen Bunn, Sam Augustin Durai Ebenazer, and Barbara Ball for their patience in awaiting the final version, and the speed and skill with which they turned it around.

Finally, I want to close by thanking my family, whose love and support has made this book possible. I owe immense gratitude to my parents, Parwinder and Sukhbir, who left rural India in pursuit of knowledge and opportunity, and who continually serve as my inspiration and example. My brother, Parry, took a keen interest in my work, routinely asking about my research and providing some of the most helpful questions. And my wife, Emma, has been my rock throughout this process. It is truly symbolic that we met on my first day of fieldwork in Tunisia, as she has nourished and nurtured this project from the start through her tireless optimism, unfailing kindness, and unending patience. It is for those reasons that I dedicate this book to her.

Contents

An online appendix is available at www.oup.co.uk/companion/Grewal

List of Figures

List of Tables

1

Introduction

In 2011, mass protests rocked the Arab world. In the Arab Spring, as the uprisings came to be known, millions of protesters mobilized across the region, rallying for bread, freedom, and social justice, and demanding an end to decades of dictatorship. For weeks they gathered in central squares and roundabouts, protesting, chanting, singing, dancing, clashing with police, and finally, celebrating, as they toppled their dictators in Tunisia, Egypt, Libya, and Yemen. For a brief moment, it appeared that in the Arab world—one of the last strongholds of dictatorship—democracy was about to take root.

Over the course of the next ten years, these hopes would fade. Egypt's attempt at democracy would collapse first, in a brutal military coup and massacre in 2013 that produced a renewed military dictatorship. Transitions in Libya and Yemen, meanwhile, descended into civil wars by 2014, devastating conflicts from which they are only beginning to emerge. Even Tunisia, the Nobel Peace Prize-winning model of democracy in the region, ultimately succumbed to an incumbent takeover by a populist president in 2021.

While each country's path to breakdown was unique and multifaceted, a critical element in every story was the role of the military. In Egypt, the military delivered the fatal blow to democracy in a military coup. In Libya and Yemen, militaries that had fractured along regional and tribal lines facilitated the descent into civil war. In Tunisia, the military ignored the calls for a coup in 2013, allowing the country to at first emerge as the region's one success story. And its democracy later collapsed when that military agreed to shut down the parliament and help the president consolidate power. Militaries were likewise paramount in explaining why other Arab Spring protests could not even initiate transitions in the first place, with dictators in Syria and Bahrain surviving even massive uprisings through the use of indiscriminate military repression.

The central role that militaries played in the Arab Spring is by no means unique to the region. Globally, the military has been the leading cause of democratic collapse. Military coups account for roughly 61 percent of all democratic breakdowns between 1789 and 2008.[1] Far from being a "third-world" phenomenon, military coups in fact caused many of Europe's democratic breakdowns after the first wave, including in France (1799), Spain (1923, 1936), Portugal (1926), Poland (1926), Greece (1909, 1925, 1935), Bulgaria (1923), and Lithuania (1926). Beyond coups, militaries commonly play supporting roles in the other forms of breakdown as well, helping elected

---

[1] Svolik (2015, p. 16). Incumbent takeovers accounted for another 30%, civil wars for 7%, and popular uprisings for 2%.

Soldiers of Democracy?. Sharan Grewal, Oxford University Press. © Sharan Grewal (2023).
DOI: 10.1093/oso/9780192873910.003.0001

leaders like Peru's Alberto Fujimori close the parliament in an incumbent takeover, or splintering to spark civil wars. Moreover, militaries often decisively shape whether a transition is initiated in the first place, making or breaking revolutions when they decide to either defect or defend the dictator during pro-democracy uprisings.[2] In short, if there is any one actor that is integral to the course of democratization, it is the military.

And yet, despite their centrality, militaries have been relatively neglected in the study of democratization. "The military has probably been the least studied of the factors involved in new democratic movements," observed Al Stepan (1988, p. xi). Decades later, Zoltan Barany (2012, p. 2) laments that "the situation has not changed drastically." In part because the military is difficult to penetrate, scholars of democratization have focused less on understanding militaries and their motivations and more on the underlying factors that might create an opportunity for a coup, such as poverty, recessions, lack of education, or polarization.[3] But it has been less clear why some militaries seize these opportunities, and others—"soldiers of democracy"— ignore them. Likewise, while we know that elites, particularly in highly unequal societies,[4] may want to use the military to repress the lower classes or to help them stage incumbent takeovers, it is less clear why the military sometimes obeys and other times does not. While scholars like Barbara Geddes (1999) have rightly highlighted the unique behavior of military juntas in processes of democratization,[5] these regime types are just the tip of the iceberg in exploring variation in militaries.

In this book, I leverage the cases of the Arab Spring to generate a broader theory about why militaries support or thwart democratic transitions. I develop a generalizable account of military behavior that helps explain not just which militaries stage coups during democratic transitions, but also which ones repress pro-democracy uprisings, facilitate incumbent takeovers, or fall to civil wars. I test each hypothesis globally through a statistical analysis of all countries between 1946 and 2010. I then tease out the mechanisms through detailed case studies of Egypt and Tunisia, drawing on over 140 interviews with civilian and military leaders and three surveys of military personnel. Overall, the book attempts to bring the military front and center to the study of democratic transition and consolidation.

The Argument in Brief

The argument in a nutshell is that how the military is treated under autocracy shapes how it behaves under democracy. Where autocrats *empowered* their militaries, securing their loyalty through a share of power and wealth, they create militaries that

---

[2] Chenoweth and Stephan (2011, p. 58) find that major security force defections make mass uprisings 60% more likely to succeed.

[3] See, e.g., Lipset (1959); Londregan and Poole (1990); Gasiorowski (1995); Haggard and Kaufman (1995); Przeworski and Limongi (1997); Boix and Stokes (2003); Maeda (2010); Tang, Huhe, and Zhou (2017).

[4] See, e.g., Moore (1966); Skocpol (1979); Boix (2003); Acemoglu and Robinson (2006); Svolik (2012).

[5] See, e.g., Geddes (1999); Geddes, Wright, and Frantz (2014); Svolik (2015); Debs (2016); Kim (2021).

fear that democratization will encroach upon their corporate interests. Empowered militaries are therefore more likely to repress mass uprisings, and if that fails, to stage coups against new democracies. By contrast, where autocrats *marginalized* their militaries, neglecting and counterbalancing them, they create militaries that view democracy as a chance to gain. While democratization is therefore easier with marginalized militaries, these militaries are also less able to prevent a descent into civil war, and are more easily co-opted into incumbent takeovers. How the dictator treated the military under autocracy thus generates important legacies that shape both the likelihood of democratization and the form by which it breaks down.

The theory, presented in more detail in Chapter 2, begins with one of the most important decisions each dictator must make: how to prevent a military coup. Historically, the vast majority of dictators that have been toppled, over 60 percent according to Svolik (2012), have lost power at the hands of their own soldiers. To prevent this fate, dictators cannot simply abolish their militaries: most need them for both external and internal security. How dictators solve this dilemma—how they choose to "guard their guardians"—is our point of departure.

I argue that dictators can "coup-proof"[6] their militaries through one of two "ideal-type" strategies: empowering the military or marginalizing it. Empowering the military refers to securing its loyalty by satisfying its corporate interests: granting the military such a high level of material wealth and political influence that it no longer sees any interest in staging a coup. Egyptian President Hosni Mubarak (1981–2011), for instance, afforded his military veto power over national security decisions, regular appointments as ministers, governors, and ambassadors, a bloated budget and salaries, and control over large sectors of the economy. With its corporate interests satisfied, the Egyptian military was "wedded to Mubarak."[7] Field Marshall Abd al-Halim Abu Ghazala, when asked why he did not stage a coup against Mubarak while his tanks were already on the streets crushing a police mutiny, replied: "I am happy where I am."[8]

While empowerment removes the military's will to stage a coup, an alternative strategy—marginalization—entails removing its capacity to. Starving the military materially, keeping it far from political power, and counterbalancing it with paramilitary forces makes a coup far more difficult, depriving the military of the strength and connections to carry one out. Tunisia's Zine El Abidine Ben Ali (1987–2011), for instance, privileged the presidential guard and national guard, relegating the military to a meager budget, outdated weapons, and little influence over policy. While such marginalization bred resentment, the military had no capacity to act on it. Their 30-year-old helicopters ("flying coffins"[9]) had become too risky to use even for field visits, let alone staging a coup. Overpowering the national guard and presidential guard was out of the question. "People who want a coup will [therefore] need both the

---

[6] Horowitz (1985, pp. 532–553); Brooks (1998); Decalo (1998); Quinlivan (1999); Talmadge (2015); Greitens (2016); Harkness (2018); de Bruin (2020).

[7] Bou Nassif (2013).

[8] Quoted in Kandil (2012, p. 179).

[9] Jebnoun (2014, p. 303). They gained the name after a helicopter crash killed the army chief in 2002.

army and security forces," observed Presidential Guard Chief Ali Seriati, an impossible task given their institutional rivalry and "political competition."[10] Neglected and counterbalanced, the Tunisian military could not oust Ben Ali.

Both of these coup-proofing strategies—empowerment and marginalization—can thus help a dictator survive, but they do so in two very different ways. Empowered militaries are strong and satisfied: they may have the capacity to stage a coup, but no will to do so. Marginalized militaries, by contrast, are weak and resentful: they may have the will to stage a coup, but no capacity to do so. The dictator can thus coup-proof the military when deciding how much political power and material resources to grant the military at the time of regime formation. A number of factors shape which strategy dictators choose, from their threat perceptions, to their mode of regime birth, to their personal preferences. But once chosen, these strategies tend to become "path-dependent,"[11] creating vested interests in their maintenance.

Over time, the two strategies then generate two additional differences between these militaries, beyond their satisfied or neglected corporate interests. The first is their political composition. By and large, dictators would prefer to stack their militaries with their political supporters, thereby producing a "protection pact"[12] with a shared aversion to the opposition. Empowering the military facilitates such stacking by helping to attract the in-group into its ranks. In Egypt, for instance, Mubarak could readily attract the secular elite into the officer corps, given its wealth and power. He could even raise educational requirements to make it virtually "impossible for an underprivileged man or the son of a petit-bourgeois family to be admitted."[13] But with a marginalized military, Tunisia's dictators could not similarly stack the officer corps with the secular elite, who held "a military career in low esteem."[14] Instead, Ben Ali had to settle for privileging the few in-group officers who did join to the top ranks, while the majority of the officer corps came to consist instead of out-groups. Probabilistically, then, empowered militaries are more likely to consist of the dictator's in-group, and marginalized militaries, of their out-groups.

The final difference that these strategies develop over time is the military's conception of professionalism. Empowered militaries come to justify their powerful role in the state as part of their professional mission, as their duty to be the guardian of the state or referee of politics. Marginalized militaries, by contrast, kept far from politics, are socialized into viewing *that* role as normal and desirable. Empowered militaries thus develop politicized worldviews, and marginalized militaries, apolitical ones. In a survey of Egypt and Tunisia's militaries, I find that Tunisian officers were three times more likely to rank "being apolitical" as a key part of professionalism. Beyond socialization, differential recruitment also shapes the politicization of each force, with empowered militaries attracting more politicized, power-seeking recruits. In Tunisia, "if you want to make politics, you don't go into the army," remarked one

---

[10] Interview with General Ali Seriati, Tunis, January 22, 2019.
[11] Thelen (1999); Pierson (2000).
[12] Slater (2010).
[13] Aclimandos (2011, p. 16).
[14] Ehrenreich (1988, p. 294).

officer. "You would do law or business administration . . . Maybe in Egypt or Algeria, but not in Tunisia."[15] "The army [here] has never been a path to political power," said another,[16] and thus never attracted power-seeking recruits. The political power of the military thus shapes what type of individual joins the officer corps and into what conception of professionalism they are socialized.

In short, the dictator's choice to either empower or marginalize the military has tremendous consequences for the military's corporate interests (satisfied or neglected), political composition (in-group or out-group), and professionalism (political or apolitical). Each of those factors, in turn, will shape the military's attitudes toward and behavior during processes of democratization.

Empowered militaries—privileged, politicized, and stacked with the dictator's in-group—fear democratization. On a political level, democracy will challenge their veto power and guardianship role in the state, as elected civilians are empowered as decision-makers and attempt to impose civilian control. On a material level, they are likely to see their bloated budgets cut, with the new democracy facing electoral incentives to "trim the fat" and redistribute the excess to their constituents. And where empowered militaries were stacked with the dictator's in-group, democratic norms will push for more open recruitment, threatening their identity. Fearing these losses, empowered militaries are more likely to repress pro-democracy uprisings. If that fails, they will then attempt to run the transition themselves, driven by their more politicized nature and greater stake in the outcome. The elected government during such a transition faces a difficult process of bargaining with the empowered military over what privileges it might retain in the new democracy. While strategically, new democracies know that moving too quickly against an empowered military may trigger a coup, balancing these competing incentives and finding the proper pace at which to curtail the military's power is a decision fraught with uncertainty and miscalculation. As a result, many new democracies inheriting empowered militaries make the fatal mistake of moving too quickly, sparking a coup.

In Egypt, for instance, a military empowered by successive dictators viewed democratization as a threat. When the Arab Spring protests erupted, the military attempted to repress the uprising, arresting and torturing dissidents throughout the 18 days. "The army here is loyal to this country and to the regime," noted a retired general at the time.[17] When that repression failed to quell the uprising, however, the military staged a coup to shepherd and constrain the subsequent transition. Democracy brought to power the Muslim Brotherhood's Mohamed Morsi, who attempted to bargain with the military, preserving some of its interests while encroaching on others. President Morsi asserted his role as commander-in-chief to try to impose security decisions the military disagreed with, including in the Sinai, Ethiopia, and Syria. "I don't want to count to you the number of times that the armed forces showed its reservations on many actions and measures that came as a surprise," Field

---

[15] Interview with retired Colonel-Major Mahmoud Mezoughi, Tunis, March 4, 2020.
[16] Interview with retired officer, Tunis, March 2020.
[17] Retired Army General Hosam Sowilam, quoted in Kirkpatrick (2011*b*).

Marshall Abdelfattah el-Sisi would later recall.[18] Morsi likewise attempted to limit the military's economic ambitions, denying them full control over the new Suez Canal Corridor Development Project, expected to generate billions in revenue. "The military of course thought that that would be a major reduction of their potential earnings if they don't get this project as a major contributor," explained former Minister Amr Darrag.[19] And Morsi also tried to open up the ranks of the secular elite military to Islamists. The reaction was fierce: we "will not allow infiltration!" exclaimed one general.[20]

These encroachments, however, were precisely what democracy entails for an empowered military. "Everyone who believes that Egypt needs to go through a democratic course led by elected civilians knows that that means curtailing the power of the military in the political domain," Darrag noted. "As a matter of fact, the role of the military is not to get into partnerships in economic contracts," either.[21] These encroachments were also what the Brotherhood believed the electorate wanted. "We are behaving according to the Egyptian people's choice and will, nothing else," President Morsi explained.[22] Morsi understood that moving too quickly would spark a coup, but ultimately miscalculated his level of domestic and international support. Aggrieved by democracy, the empowered military in 2013 staged a coup to end Egypt's democratic transition.

When inheriting a marginalized military, by contrast, the path to democratization is much easier. Their more apolitical outlook, out-group composition, and lack of vested interests in the regime will lead them to step aside and allow pro-democracy uprisings to succeed. During the transition, marginalized militaries should then see their fortunes improve. Having been sidelined by the dictator, they should now see an advisory role institutionalized under democracy. Underfunded and counterbalanced by the dictator, they should now enjoy a "rebalancing" under democracy, with more resources going toward the institution with greater need, the neglected military. And where the autocrat privileged his in-group in promotions even while out-groups formed the majority of the force, democracy will spell more meritocratic promotions. Apolitical, and gaining from the transition, these militaries are thus likely to act as "soldiers of democracy": ignoring any opportunity for a coup.

At the same time, these marginalized militaries may still carry risks of their own. Weak and neglected, marginalized militaries are less able to deter and defeat rebel challenges, and their rivalries with their counterbalancing forces might themselves spark civil wars. Likewise, while their neglect under autocracy makes them more easily co-opted into democracy, it also makes them more easily co-opted by elected leaders aspiring to consolidate their own control. During such incumbent takeovers, their apolitical nature may likewise lead them to obey orders rather than take a public, political position refusing the takeover. While the modal outcome should still be

---

[18] Quoted in Associated Press (2013).
[19] Interview with Amr Darrag, Istanbul, July 11, 2016.
[20] Quoted in Eleiba (2012).
[21] Interview with Amr Darrag, Istanbul, July 11, 2016.
[22] Quoted in Kirkpatrick and Erlanger (2012).

democracy, marginalized militaries thus also bring heightened risks of incumbent takeovers and civil wars.

In Tunisia, for instance, a military that had historically been neglected and counterbalanced under autocracy stepped aside during the Arab Spring uprising, having little interest in preserving Ben Ali. "We were not going to harm the population for the good of a King!" one general told me.[23] This military then saw its fortunes improve over the course of the transition. Politically, it gained representation in a national security council and appointments as presidential advisors, granting the military influence over security policy. Once sidelined, "the military is now at the center," praised one officer.[24] Materially, the military's budget increased more quickly than any other ministry's, and the newly elected governments courted an influx of foreign assistance, rebalancing the military vis-à-vis the counterbalancing forces. "Before the revolution, we would whisper we want to be like the police and national guard," one officer told me. "Now they whisper they want to be like us!"[25] Finally, while Ben Ali used to favor his in-group, the secular coastal elite, in promotions, democracy produced affirmative action, including a new army chief from the interior region of Sidi Bouzid. It "marked an important turning point," noted one officer,[26] breeding goodwill toward the transition. "Without a doubt, things have improved," confirmed the late Armed Forces Chief of Staff, Said El Kateb.[27] Apolitical, filled with out-groups, and gaining from democracy, the military ignored the secular elite's calls for a coup in 2013.

These gains were precisely what democracy entails for a marginalized military. "What I discovered was that Ben Ali was so afraid of the military that they were not equipped at all to fight terrorism," explained President Moncef Marzouki.[28] "They didn't have anything. So I began to discuss with them to bring some material from the US, to bring some helicopters and equipment. This was a real revolution in the army." These gains were likewise what the newly elected leaders believed voters wanted. "The image of the military was huge among the people," observed Prime Minister Hamadi Jebali. "Especially because of its role in the revolution. The people wanted this institution increased. It wasn't the same for the police and national guard."[29]

While these gains led Tunisian officers to support the transition, these same dynamics would also make them susceptible to President Kais Saied's incumbent takeover in 2021. After his election in 2019, Saied co-opted the military by enhancing its corporate interests even further. He quickly promoted all of the top officers and granted them regular access and input into policy decisions. He employed the military in responding to the COVID-19 pandemic, allowing the defense budget to increase further despite the health crisis, and securing "the good image of the army

<hr>

[23] Interview with retired General Mohamed Ali El Bekri, Tunis, November 28, 2015.
[24] Interview with retired Colonel-Major Mokhtar Ben Nasr, Tunis, August 27, 2015.
[25] Interview with retired Colonel Major Mahmoud Mezoughi, Tunis, January 8, 2019.
[26] Interview with retired Colonel Major Mohamed Ahmed, Tunis, October 17, 2015. Quoted also in Grewal (2016).
[27] Interview with retired General Said El Kateb, Tunis, November 6, 2015.
[28] Interview with former President Moncef Marzouki, Tunis, June 22, 2016.
[29] Interview with former Prime Minister Hamadi Jebali, Sousse, December 17, 2015.

among the population."[30] Saied also appointed two military doctors as ministers of health, the military's first ministerial positions in 30 years. Beyond these corporate interests, the military's out-group composition made it sympathetic to Saied's vision of radical reforms to the system. Finally, the military's apolitical professionalism also led it to obey Saied's orders: "To say 'no, this is unconstitutional' would have been intervention into the political arena. Is that acceptable? Would that have been better for the country?" one general asked me rhetorically.[31] In short, while the Tunisian military's corporate interests, composition, and professionalism made democratization easier, they also increased the risk of an incumbent takeover.

In sum, this book argues that an autocrat's choice to either empower or marginalize the military has important downstream consequences for democratization. Empowered militaries are more likely to repress pro-democracy uprisings, and if that fails, to stage coups against new democracies. Marginalized militaries, while permitting democratization, also bring heightened risks of incumbent takeovers and civil wars. These military legacies from autocracy thus shape whether democratic transitions occur, how they unfold, and the form by which they break down. Of course, political actors still have agency to resist these structural incentives, with new democracies occasionally succeeding in respecting the interests of an empowered military or failing to enhance a marginalized one. However, the contribution of this book is to highlight an understudied structural factor—military legacies—that shapes the chances that democracy takes root.

Structure of the Book

This book advances this argument through thirteen chapters. The remainder of Chapter 1 surveys the existing literature on democratization, noting the relative absence of the military and highlighting the ways in which the book fills this gap.

Chapter 2 lays out the theory of the book, showing how different coup-proofing strategies under autocracy shape the likelihood that the military accepts democracy. It shows how coup-proofing tactics fit one of two underlying logics: empowerment or marginalization. It discusses how dictators choose between them during the critical juncture of state formation, and how their decisions tend to set their country on a path-dependent trajectory. The theory then shows how this choice has important implications for the military's corporate interests, composition, and professionalism, and in turn, whether they support or oppose democracy. Those attitudes influence whether a transition is initiated, how it is run, and the likelihood that it falls to a military coup, incumbent takeover, or civil war.

Chapter 3 tests the theory globally through a cross-national analysis of all countries between 1946 and 2010. It first shows that dictators can indeed coup-proof their regimes by pursuing empowerment or marginalization, reducing the risk of a

---

[30] Interview with retired army officer, Email, August 18, 2021.
[31] Interview with retired army officer, Nabeul, June 2022.

coup four-fold when they keep the military's budget either small or large. It then explores how dictators choose between these strategies, showing how their threat perceptions, personal preferences, and most importantly, path-dependence, shape their choice. The rest of the chapter then examines the consequences of these coup-proofing strategies, showing that empowerment makes democratization far more difficult. When facing empowered militaries, pro-democracy uprisings are significantly more likely to face repression, less likely to see defections, and in turn less likely to succeed. Even if they do manage to democratize, the legacies of having empowered the military will continue to pose an obstacle. About 40 percent of transitions inheriting empowered militaries fall to military coups, compared to just 10 percent for marginalized militaries. Still, while the modal outcome for transitions inheriting marginalized militaries is democracy, they also come with significantly higher risks of incumbent takeovers and civil wars. The chapter thus shows that each of the hypotheses generated in the theory chapter indeed find empirical support cross-nationally.

The bulk of the book, Chapters 4 through 12, then return to the cases with which we began, illustrating the theory and its mechanisms through a detailed, comparative study of Egypt and Tunisia. Chapter 4 first introduces the two cases, highlighting how they are a useful comparison and qualifying several of the leading explanations for their divergent transitions. While the popular wisdom claims that Tunisia's transition (initially) succeeded due to its wealthier and more educated population, its more moderate Islamists, and the strength of its civil society, I show that these differences did not stop Tunisians from calling for democratic breakdown at a rate similar to Egyptians. Both countries in the summer of 2013 witnessed mass and elite support for a military coup. The central difference between them was how their militaries responded to these calls. The divergent responses of their militaries, I argue, were shaped by the coup-proofing strategies pursued by each country's previous autocrats.

To substantiate these claims, the book draws upon a wide range of original data.[32] The first are 141 interviews conducted with senior civilian and military leaders prominent in each country's democratic transition. In Tunisia, these interviews included a former president, three prime ministers, and eleven military generals. In Egypt, where most of the transitional government has been imprisoned or murdered, these culminated in a former minister, two former presidential advisors, and three former parliamentarians. I had the fortune of conducting interviews in Cairo and Luxor in August 2012, prior to the 2013 coup, and a second round in June 2014. But the quickly closing space for academic freedom meant the final interviews were conducted among activists in exile in the US, UK, Canada, and Turkey from 2014 to 2016. In Tunisia, the democratic transition made fieldwork far safer. Living in Tunis between 2015 and 2016 allowed me to build trust and rapport with my interlocutors, particularly the community of retired military officers. I then returned for shorter trips every year since.

---

[32] The interviews were approved through Princeton IRB #6749, and the surveys through #7866 and #10748.

Beyond interviews, I also consulted a number of other primary sources. The first were memoirs and autobiographies, to help flesh out historical coup-proofing patterns. These included new looks at well-traversed memoirs from Presidents Mohamed Naguib, Gamal Abdel Nasser, and Anwar Sadat in Egypt, as well as lesser known memoirs by General Habib Ammar, Colonel Boubaker BenKraiem, and Captain Moncef El Materi in Tunisia. Second, I explored a treasure trove of newly declassified US State Department cables and CIA analyses, particularly to shed light on the path-dependence of these coup-proofing strategies in the 1970s and 1980s. Third, I consulted a wide variety of decrees, laws, public speeches, and official statements in both countries, including the official testimonies submitted to military courts concerning the 2011 revolutions. Finally, in Tunisia, I was also fortunate enough to access a Ministry of Defense publication, "Registry of Retired Officers: Commanders and Senior Officers," that permitted me to create a dataset of all senior officers and in turn to trace out historical patterns of regional discrimination in promotions.

These data form the backbone of my structured comparison of Egypt and Tunisia, which proceeds in seven chapters (Chapters 5–7 on Egypt, 8–11 on Tunisia). For each country, I devote one chapter to the origins and path-dependence of each country's coup-proofing strategy since independence; a second chapter to how those strategies influenced the military's behavior in the 2011 revolution; and the remaining chapter(s) to how they shaped the military's behavior during the subsequent democratic transition.

Chapters 5–7 present the case of Egypt, showing how the coup-proofing strategies chosen by Egypt's previous dictators structured and ultimately terminated the country's democratic transition in 2013. Chapter 5 shows how the military was empowered by Presidents Gamal Abdel Nasser, Anwar Sadat, and Hosni Mubarak, a strategy that proved path-dependent despite changes in leadership, political assassination, and even defeat in war. Chapter 6 then shows how this empowered military responded during the 2011 revolution. While initial accounts claimed that the military resented Mubarak and thus was eager to oust him, this chapter instead shows that its calculations were far more hesitant. The military throughout the uprising engaged in low-level repression of the protesters, and only when that failed, begrudgingly decided to jettison Mubarak. Chapter 7 finally shows how this empowered military behaved during the democratic transition. It details how the military took an active role not only in running the transition, but in polarizing and dividing the revolutionary forces. Once its losses began to materialize, the military then actively organized counter-revolutionary protests and staged a coup to abort the transition.

Chapters 8–11 present the case of Tunisia, showing how the coup-proofing strategies chosen by Tunisia's dictators allowed it to initially emerge as the Arab Spring's one success story, only to then fall in an incumbent takeover. Chapter 8 first details how Presidents Habib Bourguiba and Zine El Abidine Ben Ali marginalized the military, a strategy that remained path-dependent despite changes in leadership, failed coups, and growing security threats. Chapter 9 shows how this marginalization shaped the military's behavior in the 2011 revolution. Resentful of Ben Ali, the military shirked rather than use force against protesters, leading Ben Ali to flee. Chapter 10 then details how the marginalized military gained from the democratic transition, leading it to ignore the calls for a coup. Without recourse to the military, civilian leaders had no choice but to compromise, putting the transition back on track. Chapter 11 finally examines why the military facilitated President Kais Saied's incumbent takeover in 2021, showing how the same legacies of marginalization also shaped how Tunisian democracy ultimately broke down.

The case studies of Egypt and Tunisia therefore show how the coup-proofing strategies pursued by previous autocrats structured the military's attitudes toward and behavior during democratization. To complement these qualitative accounts of the two transitions, Chapter 12 then moves to test the arguments quantitatively through three surveys of the Tunisian and Egyptian militaries. The first surveyed Tunisia's retired officers' association, reaching 72 retired senior officers in 2016.[33] The second and third surveys leverage an innovative methodology employing targeted advertisements on Facebook to reach 2,171 Egyptian and 271 Tunisian military personnel, both retired and active-duty, in 2018. While each methodology has unique pros and cons, the surveys paint a consistent story. The results show how the differing coup-proofing strategies in each country indeed produced militaries with differing corporate interests, political compositions, and conceptions of professionalism. Those three attributes, in turn, shaped whether they supported repressing the revolution in 2011 and ending the transition in a coup in 2013. Priming experiments embedded in each survey then confirm that the military's gains and losses from democracy had a causal effect, shaping their support or opposition to the transition.

Finally, Chapter 13 concludes by addressing two sets of lingering questions. First, how might countries with empowered militaries eventually escape their "coup trap"? The chapter first outlines certain factors that make democratic transitions still possible in these hard cases, such as when the military is thoroughly delegitimized by defeat in war or economic collapse. The chapter then outlines several policies the international community can pursue during transitions to help discourage military coups. The second extension is to consider how to mitigate the second major risk to democratic transitions: incumbent takeovers. What policies can domestic audiences and international community pursue to discourage militaries from cooperating with presidential aggrandizement? Here, the chapter derives some lessons from and for the United States, where a professional, apolitical military has likewise had to recently consider how it might respond to a potential incumbent takeover.

Democratic Transition and Consolidation

Before we proceed, several definitions are in order. A democracy is a "political system [in which the . . .] most powerful collective decision makers are selected through fair, honest, and periodic elections in which candidates freely compete for votes and

---

[33] I am indebted to retired Colonel Major Mahmoud Mezoughi for facilitating this survey.

in which virtually all the adult population is eligible to vote" (Huntington, 1991, p. 7). This definition "implies the existence of civil and political freedoms to speak, publish, assemble, and organize that are necessary to political debate and the conduct of electoral campaigns" (p. 7). While democracy is not necessarily the most orderly or efficient form of government, it is the most responsive and representative, most protective of political freedoms, and the most peaceful means of adjudicating disputes.[34]

A transition to democracy is a move from autocracy to democracy, and is complete when the first elected government assumes office. Democracy has consolidated once it has become "the only game in town; [. . .] when in the face of severe political and economic crises, the overwhelming majority of the people believe that any further political change must emerge from within the parameters of democratic formulas" (Linz and Stepan, 1996, p. 5), rather than, for instance, seeking a military coup or incumbent takeover.

A military refers to the state's forces responsible for external security, generally consisting of an army, navy, and air force. A coup is an "overt attempt by the military or other elites within the state apparatus to unseat the sitting head of state using unconstitutional means" (Powell and Thyne, 2011). A coup is distinct from an assassination in that the coup plotters, even if momentarily, assume executive power.[35] Incumbent takeovers, meanwhile, refer to democratically elected leaders undermining democracy from within: rigging elections, restricting freedoms, purging and packing courts, or dissolving parliaments. When performed rapidly, incumbent takeovers are often called "self-coups," *autogolpes*, or power grabs; when gradually, democratic erosion or backsliding.[36]

Military coups have traditionally been the primary cause of democratic breakdown. While they have become less frequent after the Cold War, they remain a major threat to democracy. In the last ten years, militaries have upended transitions in Guinea-Bissau (2012), Mali (2012, 2020), Egypt (2013), Thailand (2014), Myanmar (2021), Guinea (2021), Sudan (2021), and Burkina Faso (2022), among others. Yet despite being a major cause of democratic collapse, there have been few empirical tests of what actually motivates some militaries to stage coups against nascent democracies. In part because the military is one of the most difficult institutions to penetrate, the literature has focused less on why militaries choose to intervene and instead on what conditions may create an opportunity for them to intervene. Democratic transitions featuring greater disillusionment with democracy and political polarization, for instance, have been thought to produce elites and masses who are receptive to a democratic breakdown[37] and even who "knock on the door of the barracks" asking for a military intervention.[38]

---

[34] Dahl (1989); Schmitter and Karl (1991); Hamid (2022).

[35] What the coup-plotters do once in power is another matter. Of 208 coups since 1946, 23 can be classified as not power seeking, in which the coup plotters sought to a) immediately cede power to elected or appointed civilians and b) not to exercise power from behind the scenes. See Grewal and Kureshi (2019).

[36] Maeda (2010); Svolik (2015); Bermeo (2016); Levitsky and Ziblatt (2018); Waldner and Lust (2018).

[37] Sartori (1966); Sani and Sartori (1983); Bermeo (2003).

[38] Stepan (1971).

Several factors have been identified as creating these conditions of disillusionment and polarization. Democracies with lower levels of economic development are thought to be particularly susceptible, whether because the populace has not yet "modernized"[39] or because the elites are more likely to fear the redistribution of their wealth.[40] Economic recessions over the course of a transition have similarly been thought to contribute to disillusionment with democracy and thus the opportunity for a military coup.[41] Countries with presidential and plurality electoral systems, strong ethnic cleavages, or restrictions on political participation are thought to create a sizable group of marginalized individuals calling for the fall of democratic institutions that exclude them from power.[42] Countries with stronger civil societies and political parties, meanwhile, are thought to be better able to keep the public invested in democracy.[43]

Each of these theories point to factors that make the public or political elites less supportive of democracy, and thus create the opportunity for a military coup. They do not, however, explain whether the military would want to seize this opportunity. In passing, many scholars have acknowledged that the military may not always be loyal to the elites or opportunistic in this fashion. Skocpol (1979, p. 29) recognized that state apparatuses like the military "are at least potentially autonomous from direct dominant-class control." Similarly, Przeworski (1991, p. 31) observed that militaries may have preferences of their own, noting a difference between the Spanish and Argentinian militaries' preferences toward democracy.[44] Yet he was quick to note that these were "just seat-of-the-pants speculations" that merited further research.

Most of the literature on the military and democracy concerns transitions away from military rule. While military juntas generally seek to withdraw from the limelight, and therefore often initiate democratic transitions,[45] these transitions tend to be short-lived. As the literature on "pacted transitions" has observed, transitions away from military rule have trouble consolidating, as newly elected governments need to carefully negotiate with the outgoing military elite over the privileges they will retain under democracy in a context of uncertainty, mistrust, and time-inconsistency problems.[46]

While an important start, military rule is only the tip of the iceberg. Militaries are often powerful, even dominant, members of an authoritarian coalition from behind the scenes—"ruling but not governing" day-to-day in Cook (2007)'s famous

---

[39] Lerner (1958); Lipset (1959, 1960); Inkeles (1966).

[40] Boix (2003); Acemoglu and Robinson (2006).

[41] Londregan and Poole (1990); Gasiorowski (1995); Maeda (2010); Tang, Huhe, and Zhou (2017).

[42] Stepan and Skach (1993); Horowitz (1993); Linz and Valenzuela (1994); Wright (2008).

[43] Linz and Stepan (1996); Diamond (1999), though see also Jamal (2007).

[44] Przeworski (1991) observes that "in post-1976 Spain, the military [...] were so starved by Franco that even a nonpolitical life under democracy seemed satisfactory to them [while ...] the post-1983 Argentine military [...] knew that losing could mean long jail sentences for many of them" (p. 31).

[45] Geddes (1999); Debs (2016). This behavior is distinct from other empowered militaries, and reflects the fact that military rule is in fact "off-equilibrium" behavior (Svolik, 2012). Militaries would have preferred securing their interests without forming a junta and governing the country, and now initiate transitions only to get out of the limelight.

[46] Stepan (1971, 1988); O'Donnell and Schmitter (1986); Karl (1990); Huntington (1991); Linz and Stepan (1996); Cheibub (2007); Svolik (2015).

phrase. Such cases are not technically military regimes, yet their militaries should oppose democracy for similar reasons. Variation in militaries among what are considered party-based or personalist dictatorships may have important ramifications for democracy. The military in North Korea, which receives an enormous 25 percent of GDP as its budget, will likely respond much differently to democracy than Singapore's, which receives just 3 percent. Such variation in the military's privileges, I contend, is a critical piece of the puzzle of why some transitions fall to coups.

Moreover, such variation can be found even within military juntas. While military rule is generally correlated with what I call empowerment, this is not always the case. The "military-as-government" occasionally neglects the "military-as-institution," counterbalancing it with security forces. Stepan (1988) argues that Brazil finally democratized in the 1980s because the military had resented the rise of the National Intelligence Service and the decline of the military's budget under military rule. "Most military men expressed a preference for a progovernment civilian who would maintain the regime. By and large they felt this would be the best way to protect the interests of the military as an institution."[47] O'Donnell, Schmitter, and Whitehead (1986) explore similar variation in the level of "militarization" in the otherwise "military" regimes of Latin America and Southern Europe. In the military juntas in Argentina and Uruguay, the military was politically dominant and "institutionally responsible" for repression, and thus opposed democracy, fearing prosecutions and the loss of their institutional privileges. Such countries only democratized after poor governance or defeat in war led to a massive loss in the military's public support. By contrast, in the ostensibly military regimes of Franco's Spain, Salazar's Portugal, or even the juntas of Brazil and Chile, militaries played less of a political role, and repression was the duty of internal security forces or specialized army units, leading the majority of military officers to instead accept democratization.[48] In short, more important than whether the authoritarian ruler is a military officer or junta is the coup-proofing strategy they pursue vis-à-vis the military: do they empower their militaries or marginalize them?

In analyzing the third wave of democracy, Huntington (1991, pp. 252–253) suggests that new democracies should increase military spending and invest in weapons procurement to give the military new "toys" to play with during the transition.[49] While a sensible policy, I show the structural contexts in which new democracies are incentivized to pursue this strategy. When dealing with empowered militaries, new democracies instead face electoral pressure to cut military spending, not increase it. It is when new democracies inherit marginalized militaries that democratic pressures push toward enhancing them.

More recently, Gibler and Tir (2010) and Albertus and Menaldo (2012) argue that an autocracy's repressive or coercive capacity—as measured by the size of the military relative to the population—decreases the likelihood of democratization. My account

<hr>

[47] Stepan (1988, p. 57).
[48] O'Donnell and Schmitter (1986, pp. 28–29).
[49] Powell, Faulkner, Dean, and Romano (2018) provide empirical support for this recommendation.

is consistent with these findings in that empowered militaries are larger and stronger than marginalized ones. Yet, we differ importantly on the mechanism. I argue that as important as the military's capacity to block democratization is its will to do so. With the incredible lethality of military force as early as 1900,[50] rebellions and revolutions are unlikely to succeed unless the military experiences defections.[51] As Lenin astutely observed, "no revolution of the masses can triumph without the help of a portion of the armed forces that sustained the old regime."[52] It is generally the military's will and not its capacity that determines whether democratization can proceed.

My intervention builds off of pioneering work on how dictators control and coup-proof their militaries. Scholars have highlighted a dizzying array of measures that dictators can pursue to lessen the threat of a coup, from stacking the military with the dictator's in-group,[53] to funding and fostering professionalism,[54] to building up parallel militaries,[55] among other tactics. I unify and distill this expanding literature to show that these various tactics tend to cluster into two larger strategies: empowerment and marginalization. While scholars have begun to explore how coup-proofing shapes the military's response to mass uprisings,[56] I extend these studies to show how they also shape democratic transition and consolidation.

In bringing the military front and center, my aim is to refine our understanding of what shapes the military's attitudes toward democracy. I seek to put forth testable hypotheses and provide initial cross-national and case study evidence to demonstrate their plausibility. I am not claiming that the military is the only relevant factor in explaining democratization; far from it. My intent is simply to begin to rectify the scholarly neglect of the military, an institution that has played a critical role in the democratic transitions the world has experienced thus far.

Moreover, in contrast to popular perceptions that the era of military coups has passed, a look at the world's remaining autocracies would suggest that the military is likely to play an even larger role in future democratic transitions. Many of the world's remaining autocracies are countries with very powerful militaries, including Russia, China, North Korea, Thailand, Myanmar, Algeria, Syria, and the monarchies of the Persian Gulf. If and when these countries transition to democracy, the threat of a coup would be a real possibility. The importance of studying the military's attitudes toward democracy, therefore, is only likely to grow.

---

[50] Biddle (2004).

[51] Russell (1974); Pion-Berlin and Trinkunas (2010); Chenoweth and Stephan (2011); Nepstad (2011).

[52] Quoted in Lieuwen (1961, p. 134).

[53] Enloe (1980); Roessler (2016); Harkness (2018); Johnson and Thurber (2020); Allen and Brooks (2022).

[54] Huntington (1957); Janowitz (1960); Quinlivan (1999).

[55] Decalo (1998); Belkin and Schofer (2003); Belkin (2005); Greitens (2016); de Bruin (2018, 2020).

[56] McLauchlin (2010); Barany (2011, 2016); Bellin (2012); Brooks (2013, 2017); Makara (2013); Pion-Berlin, Esparza, and Grisham (2014); Bou Nassif (2015*b*), (2021); Koehler and Albrecht (2021).

2

A Theory of Military Behavior

> The soldiers, [. . .] being accustomed to live licentiously under Commodus, could not endure the honest life to which Pertinax wished to reduce them; thus, having given cause for hatred, [. . .] he was overthrown.
> —Niccolò Machiavelli (1515), *The Prince*, pp. 93–94

Introduction

The central argument of this book is that how militaries were treated under autocracy shapes whether they support or thwart democracy. Where autocrats *empowered* their militaries, allowing them to "live licentiously," militaries stand to lose their perks and privileges under democracy, sparking a coup. Where autocrats instead *marginalized* their militaries, they stand to gain from democracy, breeding support for a transition.

The following pages present this theory in more detail. The chapter begins by introducing the two general strategies autocrats pursue to coup-proof their militaries: empowerment or marginalization. Empowering the military grants it the material resources and political privileges it desires and thus removes its will to stage a coup, even if it grants it the capacity to do so. By contrast, marginalizing the military neglects it materially and keeps it far from power, generating the will to stage a coup, but depriving it of the capacity to do so. While both strategies might therefore keep the dictator safe from a coup, they produce two very different militaries: one powerful and satisfied; the other, weak and neglected.

The chapter then discusses how dictators choose between these strategies at the time of regime formation, showing how their choices are shaped by, among other factors, the level of security threats, colonial legacies, and their personal preferences. Once chosen, however, they tend to remain path-dependent, as any shift risks sparking a coup.

Over time, these two strategies then generate two additional differences between these militaries, beyond their satisfied or neglected corporate interests. The first is their political composition. By and large, dictators would prefer to stack their militaries with their in-group, so that they remain loyal and wedded to the status quo. Yet, doing so is difficult with a marginalized military, as the in-group will not find its low salaries and lack of political influence attractive. While empowered militaries might be stacked with the dictator's in-group, marginalized militaries are more likely to consist of out-groups.

Soldiers of Democracy?. Sharan Grewal, Oxford University Press. © Sharan Grewal (2023).
DOI: 10.1093/oso/9780192873910.003.0002

The final difference that these strategies develop over time is the military's conception of professionalism. Empowered militaries come to view their powerful role in the state as part of their professional mission, as their duty to be the guardian of the state or referee of politics. Marginalized militaries, by contrast, kept far from politics, come to view *that* role as normal and desirable. Empowered militaries thus develop politicized worldviews, and marginalized militaries, apolitical ones. In short, the dictator's choice to either empower or marginalize the military has tremendous consequences for the military's corporate interests (satisfied or neglected), political composition (in-group or out-group), and professionalism (political or apolitical).

The chapter then moves to outlining how these three mechanisms in turn produce divergent behavior during transitions to democracy. Empowered militaries oppose democratization, fearing it will encroach on their corporate interests and in-group identity. They are thus more likely to repress pro-democracy uprisings. If that fails, however, and the dictator is toppled, their politicized nature and interests to preserve will lead them to try to run the democratic transition themselves. They will then engage in a process of bargaining with the newly elected government over the privileges they seek to retain under democracy. While occasionally these bargains succeed, producing a tutelary democracy, more often, uncertainty and miscalculations in the bargaining process drive these militaries to stage coups and abort the transition entirely.

Marginalized militaries, meanwhile, are more likely to view democratization as an opportunity to enhance their corporate interests, and are not as wedded politically to the dictator. They are thus more likely to step aside during mass uprisings, allowing the dictator to be toppled. Apolitical, they are more likely to let civilians run the transition, rather than play a political role themselves. Gaining from democracy and shying away from politics, they are unlikely to stage coups against democratic transitions. While democratization is therefore more likely with marginalized militaries, they also come with heightened risks of incumbent takeovers and civil wars. Weak and neglected, these militaries are less able to deter and defeat rebel challenges, while their neglected interests make them more easily co-opted by elected leaders aspiring to consolidate their control. In short, a dictator's choice of empowering or marginalizing the military generates unique downstream legacies for democratic transition and consolidation.

How to Guard the Guardians

The point of departure for the theory is the motivating dilemma of civil–military relations: "how to guard the guardians." Empirically, more dictators are toppled by military coups (68%) than by popular revolutions (11%) or foreign takeovers (6%).[1]

---

[1] Svolik (2012).

How autocrats choose to "coup-proof"[2] their militaries is therefore one of the most consequential decisions for their survival.

In confronting this challenge, most dictators do not have the luxury of simply abolishing their militaries: they need an army for external (and often internal) security. But they can decide how strong to make the military. While many factors shape military power,[3] a crucial and universal decision all dictators must immediately make is the military's level of material resources: how much of the state's budget should the dictator allocate toward the military? With more resources, the military can recruit more personnel, can purchase better equipment, can provide better training and education, and can offer higher salaries that attract more talented recruits. In short, all else equal, the more material resources the autocrat provides the military, the more effective it will be in countering security threats.

However, the dictator also faces a fundamental dilemma: a military strong enough to counter security threats is also strong enough to oust the dictator.[4] This tension, which forms the basis of Feaver (1996, 1999)'s "civil-military problematique," Svolik (2012)'s "moral hazard of authoritarian repression," and McMahon and Slantchev (2015)'s "guardianship dilemma," implies that the way to coup-proof the military is to keep it weak. By depriving the military of the capacity to stage a coup, it may be less able to counter security threats, but it will also pose less of a risk to the dictator.

While true, this dilemma and this solution consider only half the story. The threat a military poses to a dictator is not simply a function of its capacity, but also its will. Coups are risky endeavors, and the anticipated gains to the military must be worth those risks.[5] If the dictator is already attending to the military's every wants, providing it all the resources it desires, then the military will have no interest in staging a coup, even if it has the capacity.

Put simply, I argue in this book that there are two "ideal-type" strategies of coupproofing the military: *marginalizing* it, which deprives it of the capacity to stage a coup, or *empowering* it, which removes its will to stage a coup. Indeed, the empirical record suggests as much. Figure 2.1, for instance, plots the level of military spending (from the Cross-National Time-Series data archive[6]) in every dictatorship[7] between 1946 and 2010, with the likelihood that that regime was overthrown in a military coup.[8] As can be seen, the data exhibit an inverted U-shaped curve: coups were less likely when the military was weak, but also when the military was strong.[9]

To see why, the next two sections unpack what exactly each strategy entails, and how they differentially protect the dictator from a coup.

---

[2] Horowitz (1985, pp. 532–553), Quinlivan (1999).

[3] See, e.g., Biddle (2004); Brooks (2008); Talmadge (2015); Pollack (2018); Lyall (2020).

[4] Janowitz (1964, p. 32).

[5] See, e.g., Finer (1962, p. 61), Thompson (1973, p. 5), and Nordlinger (1977, p. 64). See also Besley and Robinson (2010)'s formal model.

[6] Banks and Wilson (2017).

[7] Recorded in Geddes, Wright, and Frantz (2018).

[8] As recorded by Powell and Thyne (2011).

[9] The figure represents the predicted probability of a coup as generated by a survival analysis (Cox Proportional Hazards model) predicting coups with the level of military spending and its square.

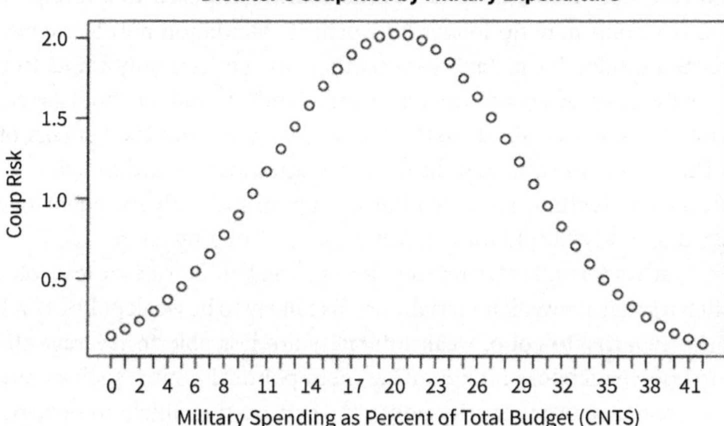

Figure 2.1 Predicted Coup Risk in Dictatorships by Military Expenditure, 1946–2010

Marginalizing the Military

One strategy of coup-proofing the military is marginalizing it: keeping it too weak to stage a coup. Although neglecting the military and starving it of resources might generate resentment and thus the will to stage a coup, it also deprives it of the capacity to do so.

Coups require a minimum level of military force. Coup-plotters must have enough troops and tanks to seize strategic locations across the country, including government buildings, airports, and radio and television stations. The military must also have sufficient training and materiel to do so quickly and efficiently. The secret of the coup's success is to project an image that the coup is a fait accompli[10] by seizing all of these locations simultaneously and efficiently—the weaker the military, the harder that is. "The need for maximum speed means that the many separate operations of the coup must be carried out almost simultaneously," writes Luttwak (1979, p. 49) in his coup handbook; "this in turn requires a large number of people."

Second, militaries also need the capacity to fight off any resistance to the coup, whether from the dictator's bodyguards, his police forces, or protesters that might mobilize in his defense. Dictators often increase this resistance further by militarizing their police forces, strengthening their presidential guards, or developing party militias, each of which would need to be overpowered in the event of a coup.[11] The weaker the military, the less able it is to overcome these potential counterbalancing forces.

Finally, while staging the coup, the military must at the same time retain sufficient force to fulfill its original function of ensuring the country's security. If diverting time,

---

[10] Singh (2014) calls this "making a fact."
[11] Decalo (1998); Belkin and Schofer (2003); Belkin (2005); de Bruin (2018, 2020).

energy, and resources into a coup leaves the country exposed to a foreign or rebel attack, then the coup may no longer be worth it. McMahon and Slantchev (2015, p. 302)'s formal model, for instance, shows that "the general only wants to take the risks and pay the costs of a coup when he is sufficiently confident about surviving the conflict with [the enemy], since survival is necessary to reap the benefits of ruling the state." The weaker the military, the fewer excess resources and time it will have to spend plotting, conducting, and defending a coup. In short, all else equal, neglecting the military materially should make it less capable of staging coups.

But there is also a second set of reasons for why weak militaries are less able to stage coups: militaries that are weak materially are also likely to be weak politically. Because they lack the capacity to coup, weak militaries are less able to leverage the threat of a coup to coerce dictators into granting them political power, such as ministerial positions or influence over security policy.[12] They are thus likely to be kept farther from governance, limited instead to military affairs.[13] Figure 2.2 lends credence to this claim, showing that weaker militaries are likely to have fewer positions in the cabinet.[14]

Their lack of political power further undermines their ability to stage coups. Militaries that are not involved in policy-making or governance may not have the confidence that they can run the state in the immediate aftermath of the coup.[15] One Tunisian general, for instance, told me that: "The first time I saw a minister I said 'Oh my God, that's a minister'! You're not used to it. Over time you get confidence

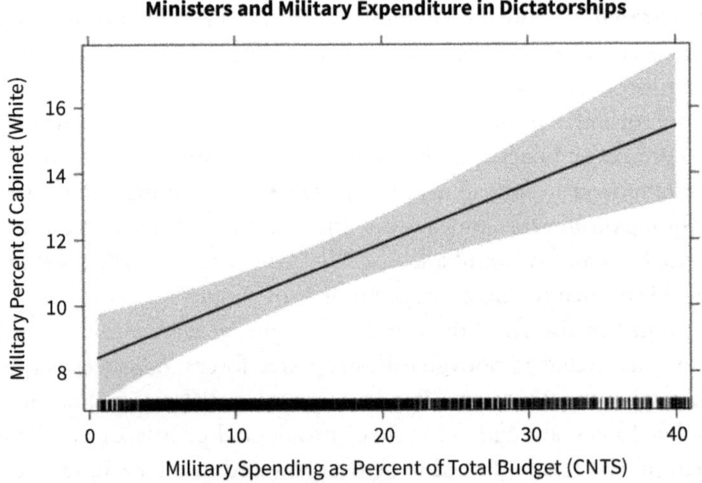

Figure 2.2 Military Ministers in Dictatorships by Military Expenditure, 1946–2010

---

[12] Svolik (2013).
[13] Brooks and White (2022) thus refer to this strategy as "containment."
[14] Data on active-duty officers in the cabinet come from White (2017).
[15] Janowitz (1964, p. 42) and Nordlinger (1977, p. 52).

in yourself, and say no Mr. Minister, you are wrong. But in the beginning it's difficult to say that"[16]—let alone, we might add, to oust the president or run the country themselves. Second, their absence on the political scene also deprives weak militaries of connections to the civilian political elite, who often play critical roles in legitimizing coups by showing they have public and political support.[17] In short, their lack of political power deprives weak militaries of the confidence and connections that facilitate coups.

One pattern of coup-proofing the military is thus to marginalize it: to keep it weak materially and politically. Starved of resources and lacking political experience, they are less able to stage coups. While these militaries may resent their marginalization, and thus harbor the will to stage a coup, they lack the capacity to act on those sentiments.

Empowering the Military

Marginalizing the military, however, is not the only way to coup-proof. Another pattern is instead to empower it: to wed it to the regime by granting it all the resources and privileges it desires. Although empowering the military might give it greater capacity to stage a coup, it will also remove its will to do so.

Decades of research into military coups find that a core driver is corporate interests. While scholars differ slightly in their definitions, universally included in the military's corporate interests are (1) its material resources (including its budget, weapons, and salaries) and (2) its political power (including autonomy over its own affairs and influence into civilian ones).[18] When dictators neglect or encroach upon these interests, it generates grievances that fuel support for military coups. In his analysis of 229 coups, Thompson (1973, p. 10) finds that a central driver was "corporate grievances . . . concerned with the position and resource standing of the military organization." Nordlinger (1977, p. 78) concurs: "The great majority of coups are partly, primarily, or entirely motivated by the defense or enhancement of the military's corporate interests."

While the first strategy, marginalization, heightens these grievances, a second strategy is instead to alleviate them: to empower the military in both its material resources and political influence such that it no longer sees any interest in a coup.[19] An autocrat could allocate to the military a large budget, veto power over security policy, regular appointments as ministers and governors, and even control over economic enterprises.[20] In Egypt, for instance, successive autocrats permitted military officers to staff thousands of civilian positions at every level of government, and to

---

[16] Interview with retired brigadier-general, Tunis, October 2015.
[17] Finer (1962); Stepan (1971); Kinney (2022).
[18] See, e.g., Thompson (1973, pp. 12–25), Nordlinger (1977, pp. 63–79), Horowitz (1980, pp. 179–200), and Stepan (1988, pp. 93–97).
[19] Janowitz (1964, 1977) calls this pattern a "civil–military coalition."
[20] On the latter, see Siddiqa (2007); Izadi (2022).

profit from a sprawling economic empire producing both military and civilian goods. The autocrat, by this strategy, satisfies such a high level of the military's corporate interests that it is content to remain behind the scenes.

One might ask: couldn't the military secure an even larger budget or even more ministerial positions if it staged a coup and ran the country itself? While yes, there comes a point where these marginal gains do not outweigh the risks and costs associated with a coup itself. The first is that coups themselves are risky endeavors: about half of all coup attempts fail, and often due to little more than chance.[21] The punishment for plotting a coup is typically death. Second, even when they succeed, coups come with significant legitimacy costs. Coups are generally viewed negatively at home and abroad, and if a military cannot successfully legitimize its takeover, it stands to see its domestic reputation tarnished, US military aid suspended, and the country reprimanded or ejected from regional organizations like the African Union.[22] Third, post-coup, the military will either need to stay in power to ensure its new privileges, which will invariably tarnish its reputation further, or entrust its interests to a new dictator, who may or may not give them a better deal than his predecessor. The 1943 coup in Argentina, for instance, eventually brought the consolidation of power by Colonel Juan Perón (r. 1946–1955), who to the officers' surprise counterbalanced the military with workers' militias.[23]

Given these risks and costs, there comes a point—an "equilibrium"—where the autocrat can keep the military sufficiently satisfied to avoid a coup. While a marginalized military might calculate that a coup is worth it, an empowered one, one that is already enjoying a high degree of political and material power, likely will not. The precise level of power and privileges the military enjoys under a strategy of empowerment can vary across countries and over time, as the dictator and his empowered military negotiate based on the credibility of the latter's threat to stage a coup.[24] In the extreme case, the president may be little more than a civilian façade for the military—think Algeria's Abdelaziz Bouteflika after a stroke left him paralyzed but still president from 2013–2019.[25] But despite variation in the privileges the military enjoys, what defines the strategy of empowerment is that the underlying logic remains the same: to please the military's interests so much that it is content to remain behind the scenes.

In short, while marginalized militaries are weak materially and politically, empowered militaries are strong materially and politically. To satisfy their corporate interests, they will enjoy not only material wealth, but political influence as well. In some cases, an empowered military may not want to be placed directly in the limelight

---

[21] Finer (1962), Nordlinger (1977, pp. 100–101), Luttwak (1979); Powell (2012); Singh (2014); Lachapelle (2020).

[22] Finer (1962, p. 18), Wiking (1983); Souaré (2014); Powell, Lasley, and Schiel (2016); Masaki (2016); Tansey (2017, 2018); Grewal and Kureshi (2019); Yukawa, Hidaka, and Kushima (2020); Grewal and Kinney (2022).

[23] See Nordlinger (1977, p. 84).

[24] Svolik (2013). Hence, this strategy has also been labelled a "grand bargain" (Brooks, 2019; Brooks and White, 2022) or "grand extortion" (Collier and Hoeffler, 2006; Collier, 2009, p. 151).

[25] Ghanem (2019); Zoubir (2019); Grewal (2021b).

through positions in the cabinet, wary of the damage it might do to their reputations. They may prefer to wield their political influence behind the scenes (a pattern Cook (2007) pithily terms "ruling but not governing"). But in most cases, an empowered military's political influence will manifest in positions in the cabinet, producing the correlation in Figure 2.2.

In sum, empowered militaries are at the center of the regime, enjoying wealth and power. They therefore see little interest in staging a coup, with their corporate interests already satisfied. While they may have the capacity to, they lack any will to do so.

Coup-Proofing Tactics

The dictator can thus coup-proof the military when setting its level of material resources and political power: either marginalizing or empowering it. However, in addition, I argue that these general strategies are often complemented by particular tactics that reinforce their underlying logics. Namely, I argue that marginalizing the military is often accompanied by *counterbalancing* it; while empowering the military is often accompanied by *stacking* it.

Scholars have identified a whole platter of tactics dictators can pursue to help keep their militaries in check, from stacking the military with the dictator's in-group,[26] to building up parallel militaries,[27] to initiating frequent purges and reshuffles,[28] to embedding commissars,[29] to privileging loyalty over merit in promotions.[30] Yet, as Brooks (2019, p. 383) astutely notes in her review of this literature, these "tactics are treated largely as a menu of interchangeable options," and pushes scholars instead to start "to identify the broader strategic logics that underpin" them.

I argue that some of these tactics seek to reduce the military's capacity to coup, and thus fit the broader strategy of weakening and marginalizing it, while others seek to reduce the military's will to stage a coup, and thus fit the broader strategy of empowering it. I focus in this book on the two tactics that have attracted the most scholarly attention: counterbalancing and stacking.

Counterbalancing refers to the creation of institutional rivals to the military, whether a presidential guard, a paramilitary force in the Ministry of Interior, or a militia tied to the ruling party. What is key for counterbalancing is that this second militarized force is both separate from and privileged over the regular military, ensuring that it defends the dictator in the event of a military coup.[31] Although

---

[26] Enloe (1980); Harkness (2016, 2018); Roessler (2016); Johnson and Thurber (2020); Allen and Brooks (2022).

[27] Decalo (1998); Quinlivan (1999); Belkin and Schofer (2003); Belkin (2005); de Bruin (2018, 2020).

[28] Sudduth (2017, 2021); Easton and Siverson (2018); Hassan (2020); Wong and Chan (2021); Goldring and Matthews (2021).

[29] Casey (2020); Matthews (2022).

[30] Biddle and Zirkle (1996); McMahon and Slantchev (2015); Talmadge (2015); Narang and Talmadge (2018); Mattingly (2022).

[31] Although recent scholarship on counterbalancing neglects this point, it was central to the original work on counterbalancing. See, e.g., Decalo (1998, pp. 21–22).

counterbalancing "infuriates"[32] military officers by diverting their resources to other, unnecessary apparatuses, any attempt to stage a coup is likely to be stopped by the privileged, counterbalancing force. The 1982 coup attempt by the counterbalanced Kenyan military, for instance, was violently stopped by the General Services Unit, a paramilitary wing within the police.[33] By increasing the resistance the military will face, counterbalancing deters—and if that fails, defeats—coup attempts from the military.[34]

The tactic of counterbalancing is thus consistent with the logic of marginalization. Just like starving the military of resources, counterbalancing generates resentment in the military toward the dictator, but inhibits its capacity to act on it.[35] Counterbalancing thus furthers the goal of marginalization, reducing the military's capacity to coup.

Beyond their shared logic, there are three additional reasons why marginalized militaries are more likely to be counterbalanced than empowered ones. First, because they are weak, marginalized militaries are less able to block the creation of a counterbalancing force. When dictators attempt to counterbalance already powerful militaries, on the other hand, they are often overthrown. Nigeria's military, for instance, staged a coup in 1993 to disband the National Guard, which President Ibrahim Babangida had created less than a year earlier.[36] Similar threats to counterbalance an empowered military have sparked coups in Venezuela in 1948, Syria 1951, Guatemala 1954, Honduras 1963, Algeria 1965, Indonesia 1965, Ghana 1966, Mali 1968, Chile 1973, Niger 1974, Bangladesh 1975, and Pakistan 1977.[37] Second, counterbalancing itself implies diverting funds that might otherwise have gone to the military, thus producing weaker militaries on average. Finally, once counterbalancing is implemented, the dictator can afford to neglect the military even further, knowing that he is protected by the counterbalancing forces. Thus, I argue that marginalization and counterbalancing should co-occur empirically.

Figure 2.3 provides strong support for this contention. To measure counterbalancing, it draws on data from Geddes, Wright, and Frantz (2018) recording whether a paramilitary force exists outside of the military's chain of command, either under the direct command of the dictator (like a presidential guard) or under the command of his ruling party (such as a party militia).[38] As can be seen, weaker militaries are far more likely to be counterbalanced. In short, not only does marginalizing the military sap its capacity to coup, but it also clusters with tactics like counterbalancing that further erode its capacity to coup.

---

[32] Horowitz (1985, p. 547), see also Nordlinger (1977, p. 49).

[33] N'Diaye (2002), Powell (2012, p. 1023).

[34] Belkin and Schofer (2003); Belkin (2005); de Bruin (2018, 2020).

[35] Like marginalization, counterbalancing also therefore inhibits the military's ability to fight wars (Biddle and Zirkle, 1996; Belkin and Schofer, 2003; Belkin, 2005; Brooks, 2008; Pilster and Bohmelt, 2011; Powell, 2014; Talmadge, 2015; Narang and Talmadge, 2018).

[36] de Bruin (2020, p. 9).

[37] Finer (1962, p. 55), Thompson (1973, p. 17), Nordlinger (1977, pp. 75–77), and de Bruin (2020, p. 9).

[38] I thus combine two variables: *paramil_pers* and *paramil_party*.

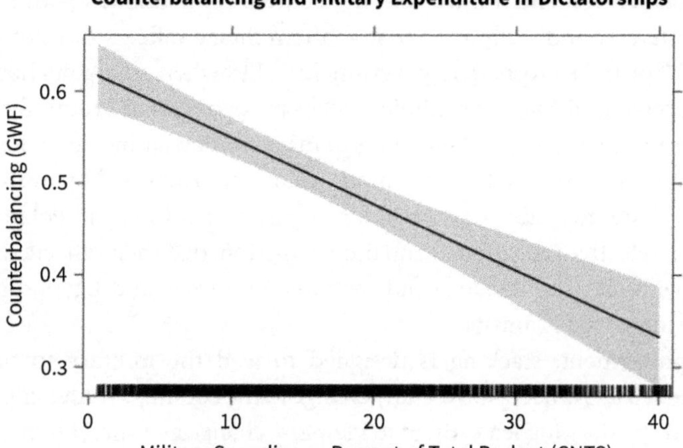

Figure 2.3 Counterbalancing in Dictatorships by Military Expenditure, 1946–2010

Empowered militaries may still encourage the creation of paramilitary forces, just not counterbalancing ones. After all, paramilitary forces can be quite useful, allowing empowered militaries to keep their hands clean of repression and thus maintain their image among the population. As Janowitz (1964, p. 37) observed, "The military [. . .] seeks, whenever possible, to withdraw from the continuous task of day-to-day policing and repression of political opposition." Thus, paramilitaries may still exist alongside empowered militaries, but they will be service to them, not sidelining them; likely under their command, not under the direct command of the dictator or ruling party. In short, as shown in Figure 2.3, empowered militaries are less likely to be counterbalanced.

By contrast, a second major coup-proofing tactic—stacking—is likely to co-occur with empowered militaries, rather than marginalized ones. While definitions vary,[39] I view stacking the military as over-recruiting the dictator's in-group into the military's officer corps.[40] Whether it is a class, ethnic, regional, or ideological group, stacking creates a "protection pact"[41] between the dictator and his officers, with a shared aversion or sense of threat toward the excluded group(s). The officers' shared identity with the dictator in turn breeds loyalty, reducing their will to stage a coup.

In the European monarchies of the seventeenth and eighteenth centuries, the military was effectively stacked along class lines. As Nordlinger (1977, p. 11) observed, "[T]he European aristocracy simultaneously constituted the civilian and military elite [. . .] Noble families with several sons often sent one in the army, another in

---

[39] Allen and Brooks (2022).

[40] In short, I am not concerned here with stacking the rank-and-file, or stacking the counterbalancing force. I consider the latter a counterbalancing tactic.

[41] Slater (2010).

governmental service, and a third into the church. [. . .] Imbued with similar values, [. . .] interests and outlooks," aristocratic military officers did not "challenge the monarch" or their brothers in government.[42] Elsewhere, dictators have ensured loyalty by over-recruiting their ethnic, sectarian, or regional group: Syria's Hafez al-Assad, for instance, recruited members of his own Alawi minority to form 90 percent of the officer corps.[43] Others promote "value congruence"[44] by over-recruiting officers who share their ideology: communist parties in China and Poland ensured, through both selective recruitment and indoctrination, that their officers shared their ideology,[45] while secular dictators did the same in Turkey and Egypt, producing a shared aversion to the Islamists.

Like empowerment, stacking is designed to wed the military to the regime. Empowerment leads officers to view any change to the country's leadership as a threat to their interests; stacking leads them to view any change as a threat to their identity. Both thus produce a loyal military that prefers the status quo, reducing their will to stage a coup.

Beyond their shared logics, there are two additional reasons why stacking is more likely in empowered militaries than marginalized ones. The first concerns how to attract the dictator's in-group into the military. Forcing them to serve defeats the purpose, as conscription often produces resentment and desertions rather than loyalty.[46] Yet the in-group is likely to have several more attractive career paths—they could leverage their connections or their identity to secure a cushy bureaucratic job or a lucrative private-sector one. How then, will the dictator attract them to pursue instead a demanding and dangerous career in the military, one that could cost them life and limb? Attracting enough of the in-group to form the majority of the officer corps is a tall task if the military is marginalized, with low salaries and no political influence.[47] But where the military is empowered, enjoying material wealth and political power, dictators will have an easier time over-recruiting their in-group into its ranks. Empowering the military should thus facilitate stacking.

Second, stacking should in turn facilitate empowerment. Once the military has been stacked with his in-group, the dictator is more likely to trust it. Sharing an identity, he will become more confident that the officers will not turn their guns on him. The dictator will thus become more willing to invest in the military, reinforcing the link between stacking and empowerment.

Figure 2.4 finds strong evidence that stacking and empowerment indeed co-occur. To measure stacking, it draws on data from Geddes, Wright, and Frantz (2018) recording whether "one or a few regions, ethnicities, or religions are overrepresented

---

[42] See also Janowitz (1964, p. 3).

[43] Bou Nassif (2015*b*), (2021).

[44] Stepan (1971, p. 58).

[45] Wiatr (1968, p. 238) and Nordlinger (1977, p. 16).

[46] Nepstad (2011); McLauchlin (2015); Barany (2016); Lutscher (2016); Cebul and Grewal (2022).

[47] In passing, Janowitz (1964, p. 52) makes a similar point in explaining why colonial powers struggled to form aristocratic militaries in their colonies. "Under colonial rule, the low status of the military profession, plus alternative opportunities of civilian education abroad and the possibility of a civil service career, meant that most sons of established families were uninterested in a military appointment."

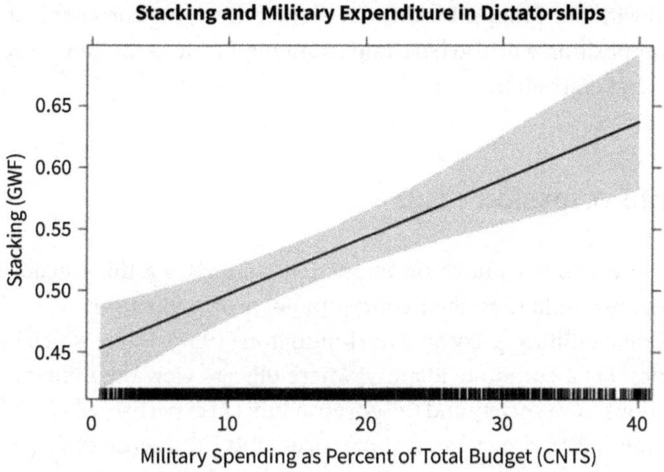

Figure 2.4 In-Group Stacking in Dictatorships by Military Expenditure, 1946–2010

in the officer corps" to the point of comprising most or all of the officers.[48] Here again, we find a strong correlation: empowered militaries are far more likely to be stacked than marginalized ones. In short, not only does empowering the military reduce its will to coup, but it also clusters with tactics like stacking that further remove its will to coup.

Although marginalization makes it difficult to stack the majority of the officer corps with the in-group, some members of the in-group will still join. The pattern that is likely to emerge in marginalized militaries is therefore what we might call *discrimination*: favoring the few in-group officers who do join in promotions to the top ranks, even if out-groups comprise the majority of the force. As we will see in Tunisia, Habib Bourguiba (r. 1956–1987) attempted at first to stack the officer corps with his in-group, the coastal elite. But coastal families did not view the neglected military as an attractive route to power or wealth, and Bourguiba accordingly had to settle for discrimination, privileging the few who did join in promotions to the top, while the majority of officers came from more impoverished families particularly from the interior regions. While the out-groups may resent the favoritism shown to the few in-group officers, those privileged officers at the top will weed out any coup plots from below, purging any potential threats. Empowering the military thus goes hand-in-hand with stacking, while marginalization fits better with discrimination.

In sum, empowerment and marginalization often have knock-on effects shaping the military's political composition. Probabilistically, empowered militaries are likely to be stacked with the dictator's in-group, while marginalized militaries are

[48] I thus combine two variables: *milethnic_hetero* and *milethnic_homo*; or alternatively, where *milethnic_inclusive*=0.

instead filled with out-groups. In addition to their diverging corporate interests, this diverging composition will also have important implications for how these militaries respond to democratization.

Origins of Professionalism

Yet there is also another knock-on effect that comprises a third major difference between these two militaries: their conception of professionalism.

A professional military, according to Huntington (1957), is one which boasts three characteristics: (1) a corporate identity, where officers view the military as distinct and autonomous from society and the government; (2) expertise, where officers value education, training, and meritocratic practices; and (3) a sense of responsibility to society, which drives their actions. For Huntington, such professionalism helped render civilian control possible, by keeping the military engaged in the military profession, and out of the civilian, political one. However, several scholars have questioned this hypothesis, arguing that professionalism might encourage, rather than discourage, military intervention into politics, whether by enhancing their capacity to intervene,[49] by helping develop corporate interests that fuel intervention,[50] or by fueling a mentality that they are superior to their corrupt civilian counterparts.[51]

Part of the difficulty in adjudicating between these hypotheses is that professionalism itself is a slippery concept.[52] Whether professionalism encourages intervention depends in part on whether officers view a role for the military in politics as professional or not. Indeed, officers may view the military as having a professional responsibility to defend the state against all enemies, foreign and domestic, and thus may view intervention as a professional duty to save the state from venal politicians. In other words, more important than whether officers identify as professional is whether their conception of professionalism includes a political or guardianship role for the military in the state.[53] These "role beliefs," as Fitch (1998) terms them, allow officers to even justify their interventions as professional actions.

It has been less clear, however, how these role beliefs arise. In this book, I argue that a dictator's coup-proofing strategy, empowerment or marginalization, helps determine whether officers come to define military professionalism as including a guardianship role or not. If a dictator chooses to marginalize the military, keeping it far from politics, officers are more likely to come to view professionalism as being apolitical. Meanwhile, dictators who choose to empower their military,

---

[49] Abrahamsson (1972), Kamrava (2000, p. 91), Savage and Caverley (2017), and Bohmelt, Escriba-Folch, and Pilster (2019).

[50] Finer (1962, p. 47), Janowitz (1964, p. 36), Nordlinger (1977, p. 53), Perlmutter (1977), Rodriguez (1994, p. xiii).

[51] Rouquié (1987, pp. 101–104), Decalo (1990, p. 3), Shah (2014, pp. 5–6).

[52] Finer (1962, p. 25).

[53] Similarly, other scholars have argued that whether professionalism encourages or discourages politicization boils down to whether officers view a political role as professional or instead fully accept civilian supremacy (Finer, 1962, p. 28) and embrace a "civilian ethic" (Nordlinger, 1977, p. 13).

granting them political appointments and veto power, in turn generate officers who view political involvement as professional. This connection results from two distinct mechanisms: recruitment and socialization.

First, empowerment and marginalization shape whether the military attracts politicized, power-seeking individuals into the military's ranks. When empowered, the military comes to be viewed as a pathway to wealth and power, with officers receiving high salaries and regularly being appointed as ministers and governors. In such an environment, where military service becomes "the most privileged route for recruitment into top ministerial and bureaucratic positions,"[54] individuals seeking an eventual political career will join the military. By contrast, where the military is neglected and kept far from politics, it will not be viewed as a pathway into the halls of power, and thus not attract the political elite. Those who join the officer corps will instead be those motivated by more apolitical considerations. By shaping the motivations by which officers join the military, the dictator's choice of coup-proofing strategy helps shape whether officers view political power as desirable or not.

The second effect concerns socialization.[55] As junior officers join the military's ranks, they look toward their senior counterparts to model their behavior and see what is appropriate. If the senior officers are not involved in politics, the junior ranks will come to see that as normal, even appropriate—how things should be. If, by contrast, the senior officers are the center of political power, receiving regular appointments into the government and helping determine security policy, *that* role will come to be viewed as normal and appropriate. In other words, whether the military is empowered or marginalized helps socialize the junior ranks into viewing political behavior as professional or not.

In short, through both recruitment and socialization, a dictator's choice of coup-proofing strategy will shape officers' role beliefs: whether professionalism includes or excludes a political role for the military. Marginalization, by encouraging an apolitical conception of professionalism, thus adds another element that further discourages military coups against the dictator. Empowerment, by contrast, creates officers who view a guardianship role as their professional duty.

Ideal-Types

The preceding discussion points toward two "ideal-type" strategies by which dictators can coup-proof their militaries, presented in Table 2.1. The first, marginalization, involves neglecting the military materially, keeping them far from political power, and counterbalancing them with security forces. This marginalization leads these militaries to be filled with out-groups, but the dictator discriminates in promotions to ensure his in-group forms the top ranks. While each of these elements generates

---

[54] Bou Nassif (2013, p. 513), referring to Egypt under Mubarak.
[55] Socialization is particularly strong for military organizations, which come closest to being a total institution. See Be'eri (1970, p. 294), Nordlinger (1977, p. 61).

Table 2.1 The Strategic Logic of Coup-Proofing

Strategy: Logic	Marginalize Will but no Capacity	Empower Capacity but no Will
<u>Tactics</u>		
Material Resources	Low	High
Political Power	Low	High
Counterbalancing	Yes	No
Stacking	No	Yes
Discrimination	Yes	No
<u>Consequences</u>		
Corporate Interests	Neglected	Satisfied
Composition	Out-group	In-group
Professionalism	Apolitical	Political

resentment among the majority of the officers, they will have no capacity to act on it, being too weak and facing resistance from the counterbalancing forces and loyal officers at the top. Moreover, kept far from politics, they will develop an apolitical professionalism, discouraging political activity like coups.

The second strategy, empowering the military, pursues the opposite approach. Here, the dictator pleases the officers by granting them material resources and political influence, and agreeing not to counterbalance them. Their power and wealth attract the dictator's in-group, allowing him to stack the military with his loyalists. These elements in turn generate a politicized worldview justifying their praetorian role. While their strength, homogeneity, and politicization might give these militaries the ability to coup, they will have no interest in it, wedded to the dictator through a share of power and shared identity.

As ideal-types, these two strategies are mutually exclusive. One military is overfunded and the other underfunded; one is politically powerful and the other weak; one is counterbalanced and the other not; one is dominated by in-groups and the other by out-groups; one politicized and the other apolitical. In subsequent chapters, I will show that Egypt and Tunisia fit these two ideal-types quite well, with dictators in Egypt choosing to empower the military and those in Tunisia choosing to marginalize it.

Globally, however, these strategies are likely to emerge more as gradations rather than distinct categories. Some dictators may not empower their militaries as well as Egypt's did, and others may not marginalize their militaries as well as Tunisia's did. Moreover, there are also cases of mixed strategies, where dictators attempt to pursue both strategies simultaneously, despite their competing logics. In Saudi Arabia, for instance, the monarchy appears to both counterbalance the military with the national guard, but, given its oil wealth, can still wed them both to the regime materially.[56] Other dictators may appear in the middle as a result of attempts to transition between

---

[56] Be'eri (1982, p. 78), Quinlivan (1999).

the two strategies. Sudan, for instance, long had an empowered military, but Omar al-Bashir attempted to counterbalance it with the Rapid Support Forces in the 2010s.[57]

Without dismissing this complexity, I will focus on the ideal-types in the remainder of this chapter, to show what exactly each strategy entails for the likelihood of democratization. As we will see, even these ideal-types will prove complex enough in their downstream consequences. However, in mixed cases, suffice it to say that we would expect both of the dynamics I outline later to play out, thus producing mixed outcomes as well.

It is worth clarifying two additional points at this stage. First, these strategies of controlling the military are distinct from regime type. Although many "military regimes" empower the military, some do not. Some military juntas in fact neglect the "military-as-institution," choosing to counterbalance it with security forces. Brazil's military junta (r. 1964–1985), for instance, privileged the National Information Service (housed in the presidency);[58] Spain's Francisco Franco (r. 1939–1975) privileged the *Guardia Civil* and *Policia Armada*;[59] Portugal's António de Oliveira Salazar (r. 1932–1968) privileged the secret police PIDE;[60] and Greece's Regime of the Colonels (r. 1967–1974) privileged the military police (ESA).[61] Conversely, while marginalization may correlate with personalist and party-based regimes,[62] several of these regimes—from North Korea to Communist China—also empower their militaries. While they may correlate, it is the treatment of the military, rather than regime type, that I will show influences democratization.

Second, these strategies tend to be chosen at the start of a dictator's rule, and then prove relatively sticky, as they create vested interests in their maintenance. Empowered militaries, as already discussed, tend to block the creation of counterbalancing forces, thus preventing a shift from empowerment to marginalization. Similarly, once stacked with the dictator's in-group, militaries tend to resist opening up their ranks, often sparking a coup when a future leader tries to alter its identity.[63] Empowered militaries thus tend to stay empowered. Likewise, although a marginalized military would not oppose its empowerment, other actors will attempt to resist the military's rise, particularly the privileged counterbalancing force. As we will see in Tunisia, early attempts by Bourguiba's successor, Zine El Abidine Ben Ali, to empower the military were met with opposition from the police and ruling party, who concocted a fake coup plot in the military to shake Ben Ali's trust in the army and push him to continue its marginalization instead. Likewise, attempts to purge the out-group to stack the military with the in-group may provoke a coup or civil war, deterring or preventing such a shift.[64] Short of a major shock to the system, such as defeat in war, a mass uprising, or a coup, these coup-proofing strategies should remain relatively path-dependent.

---

[57] Hassan and Kodouda (2019); Grewal (2021*b*).
[58] Stepan (1988).
[59] Stepan (1988); Zaverucha (1993).
[60] Gallagher (1979); O'Donnell and Schmitter (1986).
[61] Diamandouros (1986); Karakatsanis (1997).
[62] Geddes, Wright, and Frantz (2018).
[63] Harkness (2016, 2018); Allen (2019).
[64] Horowitz (1985); Roessler (2016).

Adopting a historical institutionalist approach, I thus argue that the coup-proofing strategies autocrats pursue are generally chosen during the critical juncture of regime formation, and then prove relatively sticky. How dictators chose between them at the start of their regimes is thus the first puzzle to explore.

Choice of Strategy

Why do some dictators empower their militaries, while others marginalize them? As with most political phenomenon, there is no one factor that influences which strategy dictators choose. Instead, a number of considerations, from personal preferences to security threats to colonial legacies, help to shape a dictator's decision.

All else equal, dictators would likely prefer to marginalize their militaries. Empowering their militaries requires sharing power and resources with them, which dictators might prefer to keep for themselves. If we assume, like most political scientists do,[65] that dictators want to maximize their own wealth and power, then they should have a general preference for marginalizing rather than empowering the military.

However, dictators are also constrained by their threat assessments. Greitens (2016), for instance, argues that dictators face three threats—elite coups, mass rebellions, and foreign wars—and structure their coercive apparatus according to whichever they perceive as the largest threat at the time they take office. Dictators who are most concerned about the threat of a coup will choose to coup-proof; yet, this does not tell us *how* they will coup-proof.

To some extent, the mix of threats dictators face can explain their choice. If mass and/or foreign threats are *also* salient at the time—in addition to the coup threat— then dictators may be more likely to choose empowerment. Empowering the military produces a strong, loyal military that can both crush the rebels and deter the foreign enemy, all while not staging a coup.[66] Marginalization, by contrast, would produce a weak, neglected military that would be less able to fight off external threats,[67] and less able to repress rebels.[68] As such, marginalization is more likely to be chosen when the elite (coup) threat is high but mass and external threats are low, while empowerment is likely to be chosen when the elite threat is high *and* the mass/external threats are high.

For instance, Ahmed (2013) and Shah (2014) attribute Pakistan's powerful, praetorian military to its long-standing rivalry with India. With external threats salient since independence, Pakistani leaders have preferred empowering to marginalizing

---

[65] See, e.g., Svolik (2012); Geddes, Wright, and Frantz (2018).

[66] Coup-proofing tactics associated with empowering the military, such as bribery and indoctrination (for ideological stacking), are argued by Reiter (2020) to actually improve military effectiveness. Still, over-involvement in politics or the economy might hinder empowered militaries' battlefield performance (Finer, 1962; Henry and Springborg, 2011; Narang and Talmadge, 2018; White, 2017).

[67] Biddle and Zirkle (1996); Belkin (2005); Brooks (2008); Pilster and Bohmelt (2011); Powell (2014); Talmadge (2015); Narang and Talmadge (2018); Lyall (2020).

[68] McLauchlin (2010); Bellin (2012); Kandil (2012); Brooks (2013); Lutterbeck (2013); Makara (2013); Albrecht (2015); Lee (2015); Bou Nassif (2015*b*); Barany (2016); Koehler (2016).

the military. Indeed, even in democracies, persistent international threats lead to fears of becoming a "garrison state" where the military would accumulate significant political influence.[69]

Although important, security threats are not determinative of a dictator's strategy.[70] Even when facing the "triple threat"—fearing elites, the masses, and foreign enemies – dictators do not always empower their militaries. Iraq's Saddam Hussein (r. 1979–2003), for instance, faced considerable mass and foreign threats, yet chose to neglect and counterbalance the regular military by privileging a Republican Guard. Despite the Iran–Iraq war (1980–1988), Saddam chose to double down on counterbalancing, investing further into the Republican Guard to fight the war, and then diverting additional resources to building up a Special Republican Guard as a second counterbalancing force.[71] Counterbalancing thus determined how he responded to security threats, rather than those threats shifting his strategy to empowerment. Saddam counterbalanced until the end, even in the face of a US invasion.

In other words, even when security threats are high, dictators have a choice of how to respond to them. One strategy is building up the military, but alternative strategies include building up the counterbalancing force, securing foreign alliances,[72] and making concessions to deflate internal rebellions. As we will see in both Egypt and Tunisia, how a dictator chooses to respond to their threat perceptions depends in part on their personal preferences.

Beyond their own threat perceptions and preferences, dictators are also constrained by their predecessors' choices. If they inherit empowered militaries, dictators will have a difficult time marginalizing them without sparking a coup. Even for a country upon its independence, leaders may still be constrained by two colonial legacies. The first is the *colonial inheritance*. Where colonial powers built a largely indigenous military, with local forces occupying the bulk of the officer corps and colonial officers staffing only the top ranks—such as in the Arab Legion in Jordan[73]— post-independence rulers had little choice but to keep these already established militaries happy. Marginalizing them would have risked sparking a coup. By contrast, where colonial powers simply conscripted indigenous soldiers to serve in their metropolitan military, denying the colony an officer corps of its own, these troops lacked the organization to pose a coup threat to the ruler, granting him greater flexibility in designing his military.

In Ghana, for instance, Kwame Nkrumah (r. 1960–1966) inherited the Gold Coast regiment of the UK's Royal West African Frontier Force, forming the core of his military upon independence. Nkrumah attempted to starve and counterbalance this military, detaching and lavishly outfitting the President's Own Guard Regiment

---

[69] Lasswell (1941); Friedberg (2000).

[70] Indeed, Bohmelt and Bove (2014) and Zielinski, Fordham, and Schilde (2017) find that international security threats are only weak predictors of military spending, if at all.

[71] Biddle and Zirkle (1996); Talmadge (2015).

[72] Many find "arms and allies" to be substitutes (Morrow, 1993; Sorokin, 1994; Kimball, 2010; Digiuseppe and Poast, 2018).

[73] Massad (2001); Jamal (2012); Jevon (2017). The initial influence of the military was so strong that Finer (1962, p. 2) even referred to Jordan as a "royal military dictatorship."

(POGR) in 1965, but the inherited military quickly ousted him in a coup in 1966.[74] In Tunisia, however, where Habib Bourguiba designed his coercive apparatus nearly from scratch, he had a much freer hand in counterbalancing the new military with a national guard.

The second colonial legacy is the *mode of independence*.[75] Countries which gained independence through war or military coup were more likely to produce powerful and popular militaries than countries which gained independence through a peaceful nationalist movement in which the military played little role. Wars of independence tend to grant the military vast legitimacy and an image as the founders of the nation.[76] In South America, for instance, the militaries' "institutional ethos is rooted in the early-nineteenth-century South American wars of independence, which accorded these forces a privileged status as founders of both nation and state."[77] In Indonesia, the military's role in the independence movement "conferred upon [it] a great deal of popular legitimacy."[78] "In Poland, as a result of the protracted struggle for national independence, the armed forces over the course of the nineteenth century became one of the nation's most celebrated and trusted institutions."[79] Similar accounts can be told for the Turkish and Algerian militaries.[80]

These powerful and popular militaries are difficult for autocrats to cast aside.[81] When Algeria's first president, Ahmed Ben Bella, attempted "to cut himself free from the influence of the army" by establishing popular militias to counterbalance the military, he was quickly ousted in a coup by Colonel Houari Boumédienne.[82] Boumédienne and each subsequent Algerian leader have sought to empower the military, affording it significant political and material power. Countries that secured independence through wars or military coups are thus more likely to see empowerment than marginalization.

Of course, neither colonial legacy is determinative, either. The United States, for instance, fought a war of independence, yet almost entirely disbanded the Continental Army in its aftermath.[83] That decision stemmed in part from threat assessments and personal preferences. The founding fathers perceived few security threats that

---

[74] First (1970, p. 197), Nordlinger (1977, p. 74). One coup-plotter, General Ocran (1969), would write that, "In all this plan to build a second Army one thing stood out prominently: and that was a plan gradually to strangle the Regular Army to death."

[75] For analysis of why some countries saw wars of independence while others saw peaceful liberation movements, see Spruyt (2005) and Lawrence (2013). For other ways in which the mode of independence shaped democracy, see García-Ponce and Wantchékon (2017).

[76] In a similar vein, Slater (2010); Lachapelle, Levitsky, Way, and Casey (2020); Levitsky and Way (2022); Meng and Paine (2022) argue that regional rebellions and violent social revolutions can cause militarization.

[77] Rial (1996, p. 50).

[78] Hernandez (1996, p. 67).

[79] Onyszkiewicz (1996, p. 101).

[80] Cook (2007, p. 28).

[81] Janowitz (1964, p. 15) likewise writes that "military formations born in the struggle for national liberation have maintained wide political involvements."

[82] Willis (2012, p. 88).

[83] The army was cut down to just 80 men: "twenty-five privates, to guard the stores at Fort Pitt, and fifty-five to guard the stores at West Point" (Huntington, 1957, p. 144).

would warrant a standing army, and had a heightened fear of a coup.[84] Their personal experience with the abuses of the British army likewise led them not to favor a strong army that could one day be used in repression.[85] The most complete explanations for how leaders choose their strategies during state formation thus come from combining each of these factors—colonial legacies, security threats, and personal preferences.

Coup-Proofing and Democracy

With the causes of these coup-proofing strategies outlined, let us now turn to their consequences. To review, dictators can coup-proof by either empowering or marginalizing their militaries, a decision which has important implications for the military's corporate interests (satisfied or neglected), political composition (in-group or out-group), and professionalism (politicized or depoliticized). Through those three characteristics, I contend that these coup-proofing strategies also shape the military's attitude toward and behavior during democratization.

I argue that empowered militaries are likely to oppose democratization, while marginalized militaries are likely to support it. To see how democratization will differentially affect these militaries, we must first describe what democracy implies for civil–military relations. I make three assumptions: (1) democracy means that political power is exercised by elected politicians, with the military subordinate to civilian decision-making but granted an advisory role; (2) democratization implies a shift away from pleasing the dictator's narrow "selectorate" to now a broader electorate, with important implications for the military's material resources; and (3) democratic norms imply that recruitment and promotion in the military are inclusive and meritocratic. Each of these aspects of democracy creates pressure on newly elected leaders to alter civil–military relations. Elected leaders of course have agency to resist these changes, which I explore further on; my aim here is simply to establish what structural pressures they will face under democracy.

Assumption 1: Political Power. The first assumption specifies that in a democracy, elected politicians wield political power, including over national security issues. The head of state, as commander-in-chief, has the final say over security policy, which must be obeyed by the military. "Regardless of how superior the military view may be," Feaver (1996, p. 154) writes, "the civilian view trumps it. [. . .] In other words,

---

[84] In the December 1782 "Newburgh conspiracy," Major General Alexander McDougall and Colonels John Brooks and Matthias Ogden, after having not received their salaries in months, approached Congress with a petition signed by soldiers in the Newburgh encampment threatening that "any further experiments on their [the Army's] patience may have fatal effects" (Kohn, 1970, p. 189). "When a congressman asked them what, specifically, the Army might do if not satisfied, one colonel replied that Congress could expect 'at least a mutiny' [and that. . .] 'any disappointment might throw them blindly into extremities," (Kohn, 1970, p. 194). With still no payments in March 1783, officers at Newburgh woke to a new petition to change "the meek language" and send Congress an ultimatum that if still not paid, "nothing shall separate them [Congress] from your arms but death" (Kohn, 1970, p. 207). Upon realizing the gravity of the situation, George Washington approached the officers and talked them out of it; but, fearing the army, the Congress disbanded it soon thereafter.

[85] Huntington (1957, pp. 156, 166).

civilians have a right to be wrong." Yet within a system of civilian control, the military still plays an important role: one that Huntington (1957, p. 16) describes as "the responsibility of expert advisor." The top brass has a critical role in informing and advising the elected leaders on national security issues, even if they must obey the civilians' final decisions. This advisory role is often institutionalized in positions such as a national security council or a military advisor to the president.

This assumption has important implications for both empowered and marginalized militaries. Empowered militaries, which had previously enjoyed veto power over national security decisions, will be forced to accept civilian control. Moreover, as civilians are empowered as decision-makers, officers will no longer routinely receive plum appointments as ministers and governors.[86] These losses not only encroach on the empowered military's corporate interests, but also its conception of professionalism, which includes a role for itself as the guardian of the state, deserving of veto power over at least security decisions. Marginalized militaries, by contrast, are set to gain politically from democracy. From once having no input into national security issues, marginalized militaries will gain an important advisory role, for instance, receiving membership in a national security council for the first time. By assumption 1, that is, the military's political power, democracy should thus make a empowered military worse off, while making a marginalized military better off.[87]

Assumption 2: Material Resources. The second assumption is an expansion of the winning coalition under democracy, and the policy and budgetary shifts that implies for the military. In autocracies, the winning coalition is a narrow group of (often) business elites, security officials, and party operatives—those individuals who are essential to the dictator's survival.[88] In such a set-up, the dictator will distribute private goods for the few members in that "selectorate." By contrast, in a democracy, the winning coalition expands to the much larger number of voters who are essential to an electoral victory. As such, the policies that a democratic leader will pursue are public goods for the benefit of the electorate. Moving from autocracy to democracy, therefore, should entail the redistribution of wealth from the pockets of the narrow autocratic selectorate to goods and services that benefit the masses. Insofar as security is also a public good, this assumption implies that democracy creates pressures to fund the military as much as—but no more than—what is needed to counter security threats. Moreover, it implies that democratization will incentivize efforts to alter the military's structure to make the most efficient use of its resources, thereby freeing up funds to use for other public goods.

---

[86] Moreover, given that involvement in politics and business tend to undermine military readiness and training (Finer, 1962; Henry and Springborg, 2011; Narang and Talmadge, 2018; White, 2017), democratization should also push militaries out of these sectors to make it more effective in its primary duty.

[87] Beyond security decisions, the military will also lose control of judicial decisions, opening themselves up to prosecution. Empowered militaries, having been co-opted in part to deal with mass threats, are often implicated in repression under the previous autocracy, and thus fear criminal prosecutions under democracy. Where autocrats had marginalized their militaries, by contrast, repression was primarily the task of the militarized police or specialized military units, "exempting the bulk of military officers from charges of direct responsibility" (O'Donnell and Schmitter, 1986, pp. 28–29).

[88] Bueno de Mesquita, Smith, Siverson, and Morrow (2003); Boix (2003).

Materially, empowered militaries are set to lose resources. Democratization will create electoral pressures to redistribute the budget away from lining the coffers of the military to instead funding public goods that benefit the masses, like health and education.[89] Insofar as the military had been overfunded relative to the level of security threats in order to buy their loyalty, excess military spending should be cut to leave just enough to counter security threats. In the Dominican Republic, for instance, the first democratically elected president, Juan Bosch (r. February–September 1963), refused the military's demands for new jets, arguing "the funds were needed for economic programs designed to benefit his lower-class supporters."[90] Bosch lasted mere months in office before being ousted in a coup.

Beyond redistribution, a second reason empowered militaries are set to lose funding is because a critical role the military played for the dictator—repression—is no longer needed. Democracies are far less likely to repress protests, let alone to use the military in that task.[91] As a result, the amount of funding a democracy needs to provide the military will be reduced.[92] Finally, beyond these "rational" considerations, newly elected governments often face electoral pressure to weaken empowered militaries as punishment. As O'Donnell and Schmitter (1986, p. 36) observe:

> During and immediately following the transition, there will be many competing claims for public funds and a generalized revulsion against materially rewarding the armed forces for what many are bound to feel is the mess they have made of civic life and, often, of the economy during the authoritarian period. It may even be tempting to disarm them or, at least, to scale down their salaries, perquisites, and equipment.

Indeed, some new democracies, as in Costa Rica, Haiti, and Panama, went so far as to eliminate their formerly empowered militaries altogether.

Marginalized militaries, by contrast, should see their fortunes improve under democracy. While they had been neglected and underfunded under autocracy, they should now see their budgets increase to match security threats. Where militaries had been counterbalanced, democracy should spell the "rebalancing" of these apparatuses, with more funds going toward the institution with greater need, the neglected military. Newly elected governments may likewise see rebalancing as a strategic opportunity to co-opt the neglected military into democracy and use them to counterbalance the previously privileged security forces. These forces may even be merged into the military or disbanded altogether, redirecting weapons and equipment back into the armed forces. In Malawi, for instance, President Hastings Kamuzu Banda (r. 1964–1994) had neglected and counterbalanced the army with the Malawi Young Pioneers (MYP) militia. Democratization, however, led to the forced disbanding of the MYP, an operation the army celebrated as "Bwezani": the "taking back" or

---

[89] Hunter (1997, pp. 9–11).
[90] Nordlinger (1977, p. 81), Lieuwen (1964, p. 61).
[91] Davenport (1995, 2007).
[92] Acemoglu, Ticchi, and Vindigni (2010).

"returning" of their weapons.[93] By assumption 2, therefore, democratization should create pressures to cut the material power of previously empowered militaries, while increasing the material resources of marginalized ones.

Assumption 3: Composition. Finally, democratic norms imply that the military should be inclusive and meritocratic in its recruitment, promotions, training, and educational opportunities. The struggle to open the doors of the military are often long and drawn out—the US did not end racial segregation in the military until 1948—but democratic norms inexorably push for inclusion and meritocratic practices. The recent pressure on the US military to include and promote women and LGBT individuals is similarly motivated by democratic norms of inclusion and equality.

By this assumption as well, empowered militaries stand to lose, while marginalized militaries stand to gain. A military that had been stacked with the dictator's in-group may see free and fair elections bring the out-group to power, whom they oppose on identity-based grounds. Moreover, this out-group may proceed to open up the doors of the military, due to both normative, democratic pressures and also self-interest. Existing officers may therefore face increased competition from newly recruited out-group officers, and some may even be purged to more quickly move toward an inclusive, balanced military. "Such restructuring," argues Harkness (2016, pp. 598–599) in her analysis of stacked African militaries, "threatens existing officers, who now face strong incentives to defend their positions of privilege." Latin America likewise saw recurrent coups after elections brought Communists to power and sparked fear of communist infiltration of the armed forces.[94]

By contrast, the majority of officers in marginalized militaries will benefit from greater inclusion. In the case of discrimination, where out-groups formed the majority of the officer corps but the autocrat favored his in-group in promotions to the top, democratic norms should push for more meritocratic promotions. Newly elected leaders may even pursue temporary affirmative action promotions in order to more quickly bring about a balanced, inclusive military. While the favored minority at the top ranks may be made worse off, the discriminated majority will benefit from these meritocratic or affirmative action promotions.

In sum, democratization, as defined by these three assumptions, should make an empowered military worse off, and a marginalized military better off. Table 2.2 summarizes the precise mechanisms by which this occurs. Empowered militaries will see a reduction in their political and material power, while inclusive recruitment will threaten the stacked officer corps. Marginalized militaries, by contrast, will see a rebalancing and enhancement of their power, while the discriminated majority of the officer corps will benefit from meritocratic promotions. In short, the majority of officers in an empowered military should oppose democracy, fearing the loss of their privileges, while the majority in a marginalized military should support democracy, anticipating a chance to gain.

---

[93] Newell (1995), Decalo (1998), Chirambo (2004).
[94] Needler (1964).

Table 2.2 Coup-Proofing and Democracy

Autocratic Strategy	Autocratic Tactic	Democratization	Attitude
Empowerment	Power Sharing Stacking	Reduction in Power Inclusive Recruitment	Oppose Democracy
Marginalization	Counterbalancing Discrimination	Rebalancing Meritocratic Promotions	Support Democracy

Take, for example, the experiences of Turkey and Benin. In Turkey, the military had been empowered since independence by Mustafa Kemal Atatürk (r. 1921–1938) and his successor, İsmet İnönü (r. 1938–1950), both former military officers. But when Turkey attempted to democratize in the 1950s, that military legacy would prove fatal. The newly elected prime minister, Adnan Menderes of the Democrat Party, was not only a civilian himself, but also reduced the proportion of military officers in the cabinet.[95] Menderes then cut the size of the army from 700,000 to 400,000 to focus on other priorities. "Many officers became convinced that the government was deliberately starving the army of resources. . . and felt robbed of the central role in Turkish political culture which they had traditionally enjoyed."[96] "The military felt they had lost access, not only to the pinnacle of power, but to social status and prestige as well."[97] Beyond those corporate interests, the military had historically been stacked ideologically with Kemalists, who felt Menderes had strayed too far from those secular, nationalist principles by re-Arabizing the call to prayer and reopening mosques and imam-hatip schools. The military accordingly overthrew Menderes in a coup in 1960, a pattern they would repeat in the country's three subsequent attempts at democratization.

In Benin, by contrast, the military's marginalization facilitated democratization. President Mathieu Kérékou (r. 1972–1991), despite having come to power in a military coup, neglected and counterbalanced the military by building up what had been a ceremonial presidential guard, and by creating the People's Militia.[98] Kérékou also discriminated in military promotions, privileging his in-group, officers from the north, in promotions to the top ranks, while resentful southerners made up the majority of the force.[99] Sensing these tensions, the opposition gave explicit guarantees to the military that it would reverse both the counterbalancing and the discrimination upon democratization. In the 1990 National Conference, which initiated the democratic transition, the opposition pledged to dismantle the paramilitary forces and redistribute their equipment into the military, and also to change the leadership

---

[95] Tachau and Heper (1983, p. 20).
[96] Hale (1994, pp. 98–99).
[97] Tachau and Heper (1983, p. 21).
[98] Morency-Laflamme (2018, p. 474).
[99] Decalo (1990, p. 131), Decalo (1997, p. 55).

of the army to favor marginalized (southern) officers. "These promises convinced disgruntled officers to rally to the anti-regime cause," writes Morency-Laflamme (2018, p. 475), facilitating democratization.

In short, how the military views democracy is shaped by how it had been treated under autocracy. When autocrats empowered their militaries, the officers are likely to view democracy as a threat to their interests. But where dictators marginalized their militaries, democracy is likely to enhance their interests. These anticipated gains and losses structure their attitudes toward democracy, leading them to support or oppose a transition.

The military's attitude toward democratization, of course, is but one among many factors that shape their actual behavior during it. To tease out the 'observable implications' of the military's attitudes, the next sections discuss four behavioral outcomes: (1) how the military responds to a pro-democracy uprising, (2) whether the military stages a coup during a democratic transition, (3) whether the military facilitates an incumbent takeover, and (4) whether the transition falls to a civil war.

The Military and Mass Uprisings

The first step in democratization is the initiation of a transition. While some transitions are fully "elite-led," others occur through public pressure, particularly pro-democracy demonstrations and strikes. In these democratic transitions (which Pinckney (2020) has termed "civil resistance transitions"), the military often plays a critical role in whether the protests succeed in initiating democratization. As the dictator's "repressive agent of last resort,"[100] the military is often called upon to help crush the uprising after protests overwhelm the police. How the military chooses to respond—to "defend or defect" from the dictator—often makes or breaks the revolution, determining whether a transition is initiated.[101]

I argue that empowered militaries should be more likely than marginalized ones to defend the dictator in these "endgame"[102] scenarios. Empowered militaries are invested in the regime, viewing any change as potentially threatening their interests and identity. There is no guarantee that a new leader who comes to power will respect the military's interests, and if that new leader is democratically elected and responsive to the assumptions we have outlined, they will likely curtail the military's interests. Accordingly, empowered militaries should be more likely to repress pro-democracy protesters.

Marginalized militaries, by contrast, should be more likely to step aside, allowing protesters to topple the dictator and initiate a transition.[103] Neglected and resentful of the dictator, they have little interest in preserving him, while they may well

---

[100] Svolik (2012, p. 127).
[101] Barany (2011, 2016); Chenoweth and Stephan (2011); Bellin (2012); Lee (2015).
[102] Croissant, Kuehn, and Eschenauer (2018); Bou Nassif (2021); Koehler, and Albrecht (2021).
[103] Brooks (2013); Makara (2013); Bou Nassif (2015a), (2015b); Lutscher (2016); Dworschak (2020).

gain from a new leader, particularly a democratically elected one, per the assumptions outlined. In some cases, these militaries may therefore openly refuse orders to repress protesters, siding with the protests instead. However, such public, top-level defections may not be the modal outcome. Indeed, the top officers in a marginalized military are typically loyal to the dictator, hailing from his in-group, and otherwise tend to have inculcated an apolitical professionalism, both of which militate against a public defection. Instead, a more likely outcome is one of shirking:[104] where the senior officers agree to deploy the military, but the junior officers and soldiers on the ground tend to shy away from using force, deserting or defecting instead. In some cases, the dictator may anticipate that the neglected military will shirk—or worse, turn their guns onto the regime—and thus may not even ask the military to fire, as we will see in Tunisia.

In short, on average, empowered militaries should be more likely to defend the dictator, blocking a transition, while marginalized militaries should be more likely to defect from the dictator, facilitating a transition. However, there are also additional variables at play that complicate both sides of this relationship.

First, although marginalization is likely to breed military defection, this does not guarantee the success of a pro-democracy uprising. While the dictator may not be able to rely on the neglected military for repression, he can still rely on the counter-balancing forces: the paramilitary, militia, or presidential guard. In some cases, those forces may be sufficient to put down an uprising, such as the Iranian Revolutionary Guard Corps and Basiji militias' crushing of the Green Revolution in Iran in 2009.

Similarly, while empowerment makes a transition less likely, other considerations may still produce a transition. The first concerns the protesters' composition vis-à-vis the military's.[105] Empowered militaries, often stacked with the dictator's in-group, should readily repress protests emanating from the out-group. In Bahrain in 2011, a largely Sunni military defended the Sunni monarchy against the majority Shia population. In Syria in 2011, a largely Alawi military defended the Assad regime against protests from the majority Sunni population. But if the protests are cross-cutting, including sizable numbers even of the dictator's in-group, repression becomes more difficult. In Egypt in 2011, although the military was largely stacked with secularists harboring an aversion to the Muslim Brotherhood, the Brotherhood was but one group among an otherwise secular uprising. The cross-cutting nature of the protests can thus dampen even empowered militaries' will to repress.

A second and related consideration concerns the legitimacy costs of repression.[106] If the protests are large, cross-cutting, peaceful, and garnering media attention, overt repression such as firing into the crowd will tarnish the military's reputation both at home and abroad. Empowered militaries, which try to cultivate a reputation as the defenders of the nation to justify their guardianship role in the state, may think twice

---

[104] Feaver (1998); Pion-Berlin and Trinkunas (2010); Koehler, Ohl, and Albrecht (2016).

[105] McLauchlin (2010); Bellin (2012); Lutterbeck (2013); Morency-Laflamme (2018); Grewal (2019*a*); Johnson and Thurber (2020).

[106] Bellin (2004, 2012); Pion-Berlin and Trinkunas (2010); Chenoweth and Stephan (2011); Nepstad (2013, 2015); Pion-Berlin, Esparza, and Grisham (2014).

about tarnishing that reputation with large-scale repression. Indeed, many empowered militaries have intentionally carved themselves out of internal security duties to maintain their clean reputations. Moreover, where militaries are tied to US or European military aid, tarnishing their reputations with repression may also have international consequences like aid suspensions.

A third variable concerns the method of recruitment of soldiers on the ground.[107] Where soldiers are conscripted, forced into service, they will on average be less loyal to the regime than soldiers who voluntarily opted into service. Beyond this difference in motivation, conscripts are also thought to be more representative of the people than volunteers, in turn leading them to identify with and share the same grievances as the protesters. Conscripts are thus susceptible to protesters' efforts to fraternize or appeal to the soldiers to defect.[108]

Although an empowered military may have incentives to defend a dictator, each of these factors may constrain its ability and will to use its full force to crush an uprising. As we will see in Egypt in 2011, an empowered military had to settle for low-level repression, arresting and torturing dissidents out of the limelight, in an attempt to save both Hosni Mubarak and the military's reputation and cohesion. Ultimately, some empowered militaries may not be able to put down mass uprisings.

Once it becomes clear that they cannot save the dictator, empowered militaries are likely to instead opt for staging a coup: jettisoning the dictator in the hopes that that might garner them a reputation as the savior of the revolution and in turn help them weather the subsequent transition. If they cannot stave off a transition, empowered militaries should therefore be more likely to engage in "conservative rollback coups"[109] designed to position the military to constrain and control the subsequent democratic transition.

Marginalized militaries, by contrast, should take a more passive approach. Driven by their apolitical professionalism, along with fewer interests to preserve, they are more likely to simply step aside and let protesters topple the dictator and run the subsequent transition themselves. Empowered militaries, driven by their more politicized role beliefs and having interests to preserve, should instead seize power to guide the subsequent transition. In short, even when empowered militaries cannot prevent a transition, and thus "defect" from the dictator, they do so in very different ways than a marginalized military.

Coups against Democracy

Assuming a transition to democracy begins, the next puzzle is whether the transition survives, or falls to a military coup. Empirically, about half of transitions break

---

[107] Binnendijk and Marovic (2006); Nepstad (2011); Lutterbeck (2013); Barany (2016); Brooks (2017); Cebul and Grewal (2022).

[108] Ketchley (2014); Anisin and Musil (2021); McCarthy (2022); Grewal (2022a).

[109] Koehler and Albrecht (2021).

down, and the majority of those breakdowns, 68 percent by my count, do so through a military coup.

I argue that empowered militaries are considerably more likely than marginalized ones to stage coups during democratic transitions. As outlined, democratic norms and incentives should lead new democracies to encroach upon the interests of a co-opted military. With elected civilians empowered as decision-makers, the military should be pushed out of ministerial positions and lose its veto power over security policy. With constituents to serve, elected governments should redistribute the military's bloated budget toward public services for the electorate. And pushed by meritocratic norms, elected governments should open the ranks of the military, reducing its stacking by the dictator's in-group. Democratization should thus provide grievance for a coup, fueling military interventions. With their politicized role beliefs, such militaries should likewise be driven to intervene by a sense that they deserve a more political role than what the new democracy has offered.

However, there are also two other sets of variables at play. First, whether these grievances actually translate into a successful coup against democracy depends on whether an opportunity for a coup exists.[110] Given the domestic and international legitimacy costs of staging a coup, militaries often wait until favorable conditions exist, particularly public disillusionment with democracy. This disillusionment allows them to frame their coups as simply responding to the will of the people, and not usurping power for themselves, mitigating the reputation costs of a coup.[111] Accordingly, empowered militaries are likely to intervene when their grievances for a coup coincide with disillusionment with democracy, for instance, during times of economic recession.[112] Put differently, if the new democracy is performing well, there may be no opportunity for an empowered military to stage a coup.

The second qualification is that although new democracies are incentivized to curtail the privileges of empowered militaries, they also have agency to resist these structural incentives. Knowing that moving too quickly against a military might spark a coup, they often attempt to strike bargains or "pacts" with empowered militaries, agreeing to respect some of their privileges while encroaching on others.[113] Some new democracies, for instance, continue to permit the military to hold veto power over declarations of war, and others permit them continued profits in the military–industrial complex.

The combination of these two qualifications is that when inheriting empowered militaries, new democracies will engage in a process of bargaining with the military over its prerogatives. The new democracy will weigh, on the one hand, the normative and electoral incentives it faces to rein in the military's privileges, with, on the other, the likelihood that those encroachments might terminate the entire democratic experiment. How quickly and to what extent it moves against the military thus depends on the credibility of the latter's threat to stage a coup, what O'Donnell and

---

[110] Finer (1962); Stepan (1971, 1988); O'Donnell and Schmitter (1986).
[111] Grewal and Kureshi (2019); Grewal and Kinney (2022).
[112] Londregan and Poole (1990); Singh (2014).
[113] O'Donnell and Schmitter (1986); Linz and Stepan (1996).

Schmitter (1986, p. 24) call "playing coup poker." To win, a new democracy will need to measure its encroachments according to its level of domestic and international support. Where there is high support for democracy at home and abroad, and thus no opportunity for a coup, a new democracy can get away with encroaching on the military's privileges. But where support for democracy falls, and there are fewer domestic and international repercussions for a coup, the new democracy will need to tread carefully, lest their encroachments spark military intervention.

In some cases, new democracies with empowered militaries may be able to thread this needle and avoid a coup. Particularly in cases where the economy is booming or the military has been thoroughly delegitimized, for instance through defeat in war,[114] new democracies may be able to consolidate against the threat of a coup. But in most cases, striking this bargain with an empowered military is a difficult task, riddled with uncertainty, mistrust, and miscalculations. New democracies have to accurately measure the level of domestic and international support for a coup, as well as the extent to which their encroachments are aggrieving the military, all the while performing the normal tasks of building a new democracy.

History is accordingly littered with examples of new democracies miscalculating, pushing too quickly and inadvertently sparking a coup. In South Korea, Prime Minister Chang Myon (r. 1960–1961) attempted to cut the budget of a military consuming nearly 50 percent of government expenditure, proposing to cut the military's size by 100,000 in his first year.[115] General Park Chung-hee swiftly ousted him from power. In Peru, the military justified their overthrow of elected President José Bustamante (r. 1945–1948) by noting that he had tried to weaken "the power, undermine the prestige, and destroy the unity of the Armed Institutions."[116] The military's statement criticized Bustamante for not having "built even one military base" and adopting "the inconceivable project of reducing the military forces by one-third, for economic reasons."[117] And in Algeria, the secular military did not even permit the elected Islamic Salvation Front (FIS) to take office, stepping in to halt the 1991–1992 elections out of fear that the FIS would Islamize the country and purge and prosecute army officers.[118]

Beyond bargaining with the military, new democracies inheriting empowered militaries also face a second bargaining problem: one with their opposition. When the military is a politicized actor, pitching itself as the guardian or arbiter of the system, it creates the possibility that either side—the government or the opposition—might ally with the military against the other. The opposition fears that the democratically elected government might renege on their commitment to democracy, instead working with the military to recreate a civil–military autocracy. Meanwhile, the government fears that the opposition might suss out the military for a coup. That outside option then makes bargaining between the government and opposition more difficult. If the opposition believes it can come to power through a military coup, for

---

[114] O'Donnell and Schmitter (1986), Barany (2012, p. 346).
[115] Woo (2011, p. 67).
[116] Quoted in Rozman (1970, p. 554).
[117] Quoted in Astiz (1969, pp. 138–139).
[118] Zoubir (1993, pp. 97–98), Willis (1997, pp. 245–247).

instance, then it has no reason to bargain and work with the government. And if the government believes it has the support of the military to repress the opposition, it has no incentive to compromise with the opposition. The mere presence of a politicized military thus exacerbates polarization between the government and opposition, in turn facilitating democratic breakdowns.[119]

New democracies that inherit marginalized militaries, by contrast, face a much easier time democratizing. First of all, the apolitical professionalism these militaries developed under autocracy will lead them to shy away from a coup. But in addition, a marginalized military will likely see its interests enhanced, not curtailed, by democracy. Democratic incentives push new democracies to strengthen the neglected military so that it has sufficient resources to counter security threats. Democratic norms likewise push new democracies to grant the marginalized military input into security policy, the advisory role they were deprived under autocracy. Finally, where autocrats had pursued discrimination in promotions, democratic norms should push for meritocratic ones, elevating the discriminated majority of the military.

These gains for the military, of course, come at the expense of the counterbalancing forces. The dictator's in-group that had been privileged in promotions will now have to compete on merit for those top positions. Meanwhile, seeing the military rise, the paramilitary or militia may feel their situation has become relatively worse off. In some cases, new democracies may even abolish or merge the counterbalancing forces into the regular military to eliminate duplication. But while the counterbalancing forces may now harbor grievances against democracy, *they* will now find themselves counterbalanced by the majority of the military that is gaining from and thereby wedded to democracy. Just as divergent preferences among a counterbalanced military kept it coup-proofed under autocracy, so too do diverging preferences keep it coup-proofed under democracy.

To illustrate, take the examples of Brazil and Spain. In Brazil, the military junta (r. 1964–1985) had counterbalanced the military with the National Information Service (SNI), housed in the presidency. "The rank and file of the SNI," according to Stepan (1988, p. 26), "often had special access to cars, planes, and personal budgets. . .—privileges that most of the active-duty military, as well as civilians, resented." Accordingly, while the SNI opposed democratization, fearing it "would curtail their privileged positions,"[120] most of the military welcomed it. "By and large they felt this would be the best way to protect the interests of the military as an institution."[121] As Stepan (1988, p. 80) continues:

In fact, the rank and file officers and soldiers in distant garrisons, and, indeed, many leaders of the military as institution, felt the authoritarian regime had rather neglected their needs; they did not perceive a major budgetary imperative to maintain the authoritarian regime, and some key leaders even thought they would fare better as a budgetary pressure group under a democratic regime. The first

[119] Rustow (1970); Linz and Stepan (1996); Svolik (2019); Nugent (2020).
[120] Stepan (1988, p. 26).
[121] Stepan (1988, p. 57).

two years of the New Republic proved them right as the military budget percentage of GNP rose somewhat, and all three services launched significant modernization programs.

While the military gained from democracy, the SNI would eventually be abolished and replaced by a weaker, civilianized intelligence system.[122]

In Spain, the military likewise saw its fortunes improve through the 1976 democratic transition. Francisco Franco, a military general in power since 1939, had marginalized the military by strengthening the *Guardia Civil* and *Policía Armada*, both militarized security forces, and fragmented the armed forces by creating eleven intelligence services and appointing separate ministers for the army, navy, and air force with no central minister of defense.[123] As Franco's "neglected cousin,"[124] "in post-1976 Spain, the military [. . .] were so starved by Franco that even a nonpolitical life under democracy seemed satisfactory to them."[125] When the democratically elected government in 1977–1978 centralized the intelligence services, appointed a minister of defense, and then demilitarized the *Policía Armada*, the military's funds and weapons were no longer squandered or diverted to the police. "The equipment of the military under Franco had been inferior and obsolete, and the democratic governments inaugurated major programs of investment and modernization."[126] When rogue elements of the now weakened *Guardia Civil* attempted a coup in 1981, large portions of the military refused,[127] defeating the coup with the help of the king and protesters.

Democratization in the United Kingdom was similarly facilitated by military legacies. After King Charles II restored the monarchy in 1660, he pursued two coup-proofing tactics to prevent another general like Oliver Cromwell from ousting the Crown. The first was to ensure that the aristocracy and landed elite were given preferential treatment in the officer corps. This was ensured by making officer commission and promotion dependent on a system of "purchase" rather than merit.[128] While the middle class staffed the junior ranks, the upper classes dominated the top. Second, the Crown set up a militia, not "as a complement to the standing army, but as a counter-balance to it."[129] Democratization in turn reversed both of these coup-proofing tactics. In 1871, the Liberal Party was pushed by its newly enfranchised middle-class electorate to abolish the system of purchase so that "the officer corps would become more representative of society as a whole."[130] The militia was in turn merged into the military as the Special Reserve in 1908. More generally, Moore (1966, p. 32) argued that "the repressive apparatus of the English state was relatively weak, a

---

[122] Hunter (1997, p. 8).

[123] Zaverucha (1993).

[124] Stepan (1988, p. 90).

[125] Przeworski (1991, p. 31).

[126] Huntington (1991, p. 250).

[127] The coup-plotters' plans unravelled when key generals decided to oppose the takeover (Agüero, 1995, pp. 163–165).

[128] Bruce (1980, pp. 66–69).

[129] Bruce (1980, p. 71). "The militia had an independent chain of command, was officered by the landed classes, and was responsible directly to Parliament."

[130] Bruce (1980, p. 156).

consequence of the civil war, the previous evolution of the monarchy, and of reliance on the navy rather than on the army. In turn the absence of a strong monarchy resting on an army and a bureaucracy, as in Prussia, made easier the development of parliamentary democracy."

In short, empowered militaries should see a reduction in their power through democratization, sparking a coup, while marginalized militaries should see an increase in their power, co-opting them into democracy. Structurally, democracies inheriting marginalized militaries should be unlikely to see military coups. Of course, agency still matters. Leaders may fail to take advantage of an opportunity to strengthen a marginalized military, or similarly could take care to respect the interests of a previously empowered military. Yet the structural advantage favors transitions with previously marginalized militaries.

Incumbent Takeovers

Coups, however, are not the only ways that democracies die.[131] Increasingly, democracies are falling to 'incumbent takeovers'—when the elected leader dismantles democracy from within. Takeovers can occur gradually and subtly, or overnight in a rapid 'self-coup' (*autogolpe*), coined when Peru's Alberto Fujimori in 1992 ordered the military to shut down the Congress and arrest opposition leaders. Similarly, in Nepal in 2005, King Gyanendra declared a state of emergency, dissolved the parliament, and deployed the military to enforce a curfew. And most recently, Tunisia's President Kais Saied in 2021 deployed the army to freeze the parliament and then hauled several opposition politicians in front of military courts. These examples of self-coups all call our attention to the important roles that militaries can play also in this second form of democratic breakdown. Even in coups initiated by the head of state, militaries often play supporting roles, facilitating the breakdown.

Counterintuitively, I argue that democratic transitions inheriting marginalized militaries are more likely to fall to incumbent takeovers. This is partly due to the fact that coups and incumbent takeovers are "competing risks":[132] the democracies with empowered militaries are likely to have already fallen to military coups before an elected leader has the chance to consolidate power. Given that the structural correlates of military coups and incumbent takeovers are similar—economic recessions, political polarization, disillusionment with democracy—these transitions may have already collapsed into coups. Moreover, initial moves toward incumbent takeovers, such as attempts to extend term limits, may serve as the spark for military coups, preventing incumbent takeovers.[133]

---

[131] For more, see Levitsky and Ziblatt (2018).
[132] See Maeda (2010).
[133] Carter (2016); Harkness (2017).

But even in those cases where democracies survive the threat of a coup, I argue that marginalized militaries are more likely than empowered ones to facilitate an incumbent takeover. Incumbent takeovers are typically constitutionally ambiguous affairs: the popular, elected leader, in order to maintain a veneer of constitutionality and legitimacy, often invokes a state of emergency clause in the constitution to justify shutting down the parliament and ruling by decree. While military officers know they are supposed to refuse illegal and unconstitutional orders, incumbent takeovers are intentionally less clear. Even in the United States, military officers are only supposed to refuse orders that are "manifestly unlawful"—orders that even an ordinary person with no legal training would understand to be illegal.[134] But in these scenarios, when the president has justified his takeover by invoking the constitution, the generals may be uncertain over whether the order is illegal. In these cases, other considerations may influence the military's calculations over whether to obey.

The first and most important is their level of support for the president. If they support the elected leader, they are more likely to trust his interpretation that the takeover is legitimate, and thus obey his orders. As we have already seen in the previous section, it is on balance easier for elected leaders to win the support of a previously marginalized military than an empowered one. Based on both their corporate interests and political composition, elected leaders can more easily secure the support of formerly neglected militaries—whether to advance democracy or their own takeovers.

Second, their apolitical professionalism likewise inclines marginalized militaries to obey orders during incumbent takeovers. Their desire to remain far from politics, as well as their subordination to civilian control, will lead them to shy away from taking the political stance of refusing the incumbent takeover. Risa Brooks (2020, p. 24), outlining the "paradoxes of professionalism," argues: "Military leaders may think that it is inappropriate for them to rebut publicly or otherwise challenge a president's or politician's statements or policy decisions if doing so could influence partisan debate–even when those political leaders are using the military's popular esteem or its resources to gain an advantage in that partisan competition." Applying this logic to an incumbent takeover, apolitical military officers may be hesitant to refuse the president's orders, fearing that that would constitute wading into politics. A related reason apolitical "military leaders may comply with politicians' requests," Brooks (2020, p. 24) continues, is "because they believe that staying apolitical requires deferring to civilian authority, whatever the request." By this logic as well, marginalized militaries, which have learned to be subordinate to civilian control, are more likely than empowered militaries to simply defer to the civilian leader's requests during incumbent takeovers.

In short, while marginalized militaries are unlikely to stage coups themselves, their corporate interests, political composition, and apolitical professionalism also increase the risk that they facilitate incumbent takeovers. Counterintuitively,

---

[134] See Hodges (2022).

although marginalization makes democracy more likely, it makes incumbent takeovers more likely as well.

Civil Wars

A third major threat to democratic transitions is a descent into civil war. The instability and uncertainty of transitions often slows economic growth, while the elections heighten political polarization, fueling the political and economic grievances that lead to violence. While civil wars are rare, I argue that they are more likely in democratic transitions inheriting marginalized militaries than those with empowered ones, for two reasons.

First, counterbalancing raises the specter of the security forces splintering, clashing with one another.[135] Particularly during mass uprisings, the various forces are likely to take different sides: the neglected military will prefer the opposition, while the counterbalancing forces will prefer to stick with the autocrat. In some cases, these divisions can lead to civil war. In Libya, for instance, Muammar Qaddafi had stacked certain units with tribes loyal to him, allowing them to counterbalance the rest of the military. When the Arab Spring uprising erupted, those units stuck by Qaddafi, fighting to defend him.[136] The neglected military units, meanwhile, defected to form the Free Libyan Army. This splintering of the counterbalanced military transformed the uprising into a civil war. Even Tunisia saw limited clashes between the military, presidential guard, and national guard in the wake of Ben Ali's ouster. Empowered militaries, meanwhile, are more likely to uniformly repress or defect, avoiding these divisions.

Second, marginalized militaries are on average weaker than empowered ones, having been neglected by the autocrat. They are also less able to coordinate with the security forces, having been rivals under dictatorship. As a result, marginalized militaries are less able to deter and defeat internal challenges. Take the example of Yemen after the Arab Spring. Under dictatorship, the Yemeni military had been counterbalanced by the Republican Guard and the Central Security Forces. In the wake of the Arab Spring revolution, two rebel groups—the Houthis and the Southern Transitional Council—both seized parts of the territory, in the north and south, respectively. The federal government, with its weak military and fragmented, rivalrous security forces, could not defeat either challenge, leading Yemen's transition to descend into civil war by 2014.[137]

In sum, an autocrat's decision to pursue marginalization is both a blessing and a curse for future democratic transitions. While military coups may be unlikely, transitions with marginalized militaries also carry heightened risks of incumbent takeovers and civil wars.

[135] See also de Bruin (2020); Arriola, Dow, Matanock, and Mattes (2021); McLauchlin (2023).
[136] Gaub (2013); Bou Nassif (2021, pp. 235–248).
[137] Knights (2013); Brownlee, Masoud, and Reynolds (2015).

Research Design

The theory thus generates four testable hypotheses:

1. During mass uprisings, empowered militaries should be more likely than marginalized ones to repress the protests.
2. During democratic transitions, empowered militaries should be more likely than marginalized ones to stage coups.
3. During democratic transitions, marginalized militaries should be more likely than empowered ones to facilitate incumbent takeovers.
4. During democratic transitions, marginalized militaries should be more likely than empowered ones to descend into civil war.

To test these hypotheses, this book takes a mixed methods approach. In the next chapter, I first explore the theory globally. I leverage data on all countries between 1946 and 2010 to examine how dictators choose between marginalization and empowerment, and then trace out the downstream consequences for democratization. I show that the more the dictator had empowered the military, the more likely it is to repress mass uprisings and to stage coups against new democracies. Yet, democracies inheriting marginalized militaries also come with heightened risks of incumbent takeovers and civil wars.

Having shown the broad, cross-national correlations, the remainder of the book then zooms in to two particular cases—Egypt and Tunisia—to process-trace the causal story, illustrating the precise mechanisms at work. Drawing on over 140 interviews with high-level civilian and military officials, as well as three surveys of military personnel, I show that in Egypt, a historically empowered military attempted to repress the 2011 Arab Spring uprising. When that failed, it attempted to control the democratic transition by running it itself. Yet, as the military began to see its interests and identity threatened by democracy, it staged a coup to end the transition entirely. In Tunisia, by contrast, a historically marginalized military stepped aside from the dictator in the 2011 revolution, and then allowed civilians to run the transition. As the military saw its corporate interests enhanced by democracy, it ignored calls for it to stage a coup in 2013. Yet, ultimately, its marginalization allowed it to be co-opted by elected president Kais Saied, who used the military to stage an incumbent takeover in 2021. The cases of Egypt and Tunisia thus allow us to vividly tell the full story of how dictators coup-proof their militaries and what long-term legacies those create for democratization.

3
Cross-National Analysis

Introduction

The thesis of this book is that how militaries are treated under autocracy shapes how they behave under democracy. Where autocrats empowered their militaries, securing their loyalty through power and wealth, they will perceive democracy as a threat to their privileged positions. By contrast, where autocrats marginalized their militaries, they will view democracy as a chance to gain influence and resources. Empowered militaries should therefore be more likely than marginalized ones to repress pro-democracy uprisings, and if that fails, to stage coups against new democracies. Democratization should thus be more difficult with empowered militaries. Yet, marginalized militaries may carry unique risks of their own, being less able to prevent a descent into civil war, and more easily co-opted into incumbent takeovers.

In this chapter, I explore these patterns worldwide, leveraging data on military expenditure in all countries between 1946 and 2010. I begin by showing that these two strategies—empowering and marginalizing the military—can both be effective at coup-proofing the military, helping dictators stay in power. I then explore how dictators choose between them in the early years of regime formation, showing how their initial threat perceptions and personal preferences, among other factors, shape this decision. But once chosen, these strategies tend to remain path-dependent.

The bulk of the chapter then moves to exploring the downstream consequences of these strategies on democratization, showing that empowered and marginalized militaries indeed behave differently. I first examine how the military responds to a mass uprising calling for regime change. I find that the more the dictator had spent on the military, the more likely it is that the military represses the mass uprising; the less likely it is that the military experiences defections; and the less likely it is that the uprising succeeds in toppling the dictator.

I then explore what happens if a transition to democracy is initiated. I find that transitions that inherit empowered militaries are significantly more likely to break down, and in particular through military coups. Empowered militaries stage coups in about 40 percent of transitions, compared to only 10 percent for marginalized militaries. Yet, transitions with marginalized militaries are not entirely without danger. While the modal outcome may be democracy, these transitions are about three times as likely to fall to incumbent takeovers and civil wars. In other words, even when the regime collapses and a transition to democracy begins, how the dictator had treated the military in the past creates institutional legacies that shape both the likelihood and form of democratic breakdown.

Soldiers of Democracy?. Sharan Grewal, Oxford University Press. © Sharan Grewal (2023).
DOI: 10.1093/oso/9780192873910.003.0003

These findings carry several important implications for the study of democratization. First, scholarship explaining why some transitions fall to coups has tended to focus on the opportunity for a coup,[1] typically created through economic recessions.[2] I argue that this neglects whether the military has the motive to seize that opportunity. Where marginalized militaries see their positions improve under democracy, I show that they are unlikely to intervene even when the conditions are ripe for a coup. Some transitions appear blessed with these "soldiers of democracy."

Second, when existing literature does try to capture the military's will to stage a coup, it often does so by controlling for transitions away from military rule. Yet, the data suggest that there is important variation within both military juntas and civilian regimes in how they coup-proof their militaries. What matters is not whether the dictator himself is a military officer or came to power in a coup, but how he treats the military. Whether military or civilian, dictators who empower their militaries create legacies that make democratization far more difficult.

The Dictator's Dilemma

I argue in this book that a dictator has two dominant strategies for coup-proofing the military: removing its capacity to coup by marginalizing it, or removing its will to coup by empowering it. A full measure of marginalization and empowerment would entail examining all of the military's corporate interests—its material resources, political power, autonomy, image, and so on—and collectively determining the extent to which the military is satisfied (giving it no reason to coup) or neglected (making it too weak to coup). Unfortunately, there are no available datasets that allow us to capture the military's corporate interests in their entirety, nor would it be easy to create one.

In this chapter, therefore, I will focus on one core element of the military's interests: its budget. Where the military's budget is high, its corporate interests are more likely to be satisfied, and it will have little interest in a coup. By contrast, where the military's budget is low, it will be too weak to stage a coup. Variation in the military's budget should thus allow us to capture the strategies of empowerment and marginalization.

The best measure of the military's budget comes from the Cross-National Time-Series (CNTS) Data Archive, run by Banks and Wilson (2017). I use the 2017 edition, which contains data on all countries between 1815 and 2016. The variable I choose records the military's budget as a percent of the country's total budget.[3] Such a ratio is

---

[1] Finer (1962); Stepan (1971); Norris (1998); Canache (2002); Booth and Seligson (2009); Rose, Mishler, and Munro (2011).

[2] Londregan and Poole (1990); Gasiorowski (1995); Maeda (2010); Svolik (2015).

[3] The variable in the CNTS dataset is called "revexp7" and it captures "the ratio of national defense expenditure to total national expenditure." The latter, however, is in $1000s, requiring users to divide by 10 to capture the military's percent of the total budget between 0 and 100 (%), or to divide by 1000 to transform it into a proportion between 0 and 1. For all figures in this book, I use the former, finding it easier to visualize a 0-100 percent scale. For all tables, however, I use the latter, in an effort to standardize all covariates between 0 and 1 to compare effect sizes.

preferable to logging military expenditure or scaling it per soldier or per citizen, since larger values on any of these measures might simply denote a richer country that has a larger overall budget. Computing the military's percent of the budget better captures whether it is marginal or central to the regime.

Our proxy for the dictator's coup-proofing strategy will thus be the military's budget, with lower values indicating a marginalized military and higher values indicating an empowered one. This measure captures the core, universal element of the two strategies—the military's material resources—and does so with the longest temporal coverage.

Still, there are two limitations to this measure. First, the military's budget is often just one element of its total material resources. Some militaries see their budgets augmented through foreign military assistance, and others through profits generated through their economic holdings. These additional revenue streams allow the dictator to empower the military even further. Using the budget alone might therefore make some (in reality) empowered militaries appear weaker than they really are—Egypt among them.[4] However, if anything, these biases should cut against the findings that follow. If a larger budget still correlates with poorer democracy outcomes even when it undercounts some of the most empowered militaries, results should be even stronger when placing them correctly.

A second limitation to using the budget is that it neglects other elements of the military's corporate interests, such as its political power. The military's power is much more difficult to measure quantitatively. The best available measure comes from White (2017), recording the number of active duty officers in the cabinet. Yet, not only does this cover a much shorter time frame (1963–2008), but it also does not capture retired officers, through whom the military can also generate political influence.[5] Moreover, many militaries prefer to exercise their influence from behind the scenes, "ruling but not governing" in Cook (2007)'s words. Still, we will use White (2017)'s data as a robustness check showing that results hold when capturing the military's political power, rather than material resources.

To determine which countries are dictatorships, I use the coding from Geddes, Wright, and Frantz (2014, 2018). While this limits our temporal scope to 1946–2010, their 2018 dataset includes several fascinating new variables on the military, such as the measures of counterbalancing and stacking I introduced in the previous chapter. Their 2014 dataset, meanwhile, has been a go-to resource for classifying dictatorships into military, party, or personalist regimes, and is thus useful for us to show that coup-proofing strategies are distinct from these regime types. Indeed, military regimes spent an average of 18 percent of the budget on the military, compared to 15 percent for both party and personalist regimes. The difference is marginal; there is considerable variation within each that I will show shapes military behavior more than regime type.

---

[4] Egypt in our dataset spent an average of just 21% of its budget between 1952 and 2010 on the military.
[5] See, e.g., Neto and Accorsi (2022); Grewal (2022*b*).

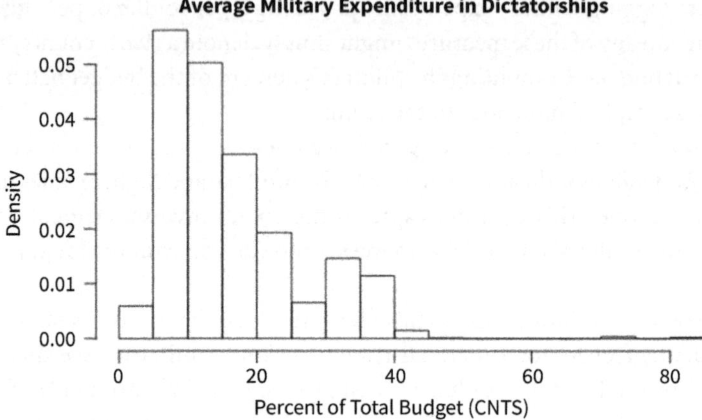

Figure 3.1 Histogram of Military Expenditure in Dictatorships, 1946–2010

For proof of concept, Figure 3.1 plots the average level of military spending in every authoritarian regime. Most dictatorships kept the military relatively marginal, at 5–15 percent of the budget. Yet, the data exhibit a noticeable second peak at 30–40 percent of the budget, reflecting regimes where the military was empowered.

Delving into these cases confirms our intuition. The regimes spending 30+ percent of the budget on the military include several commonly known to have powerful, praetorian militaries. Nigeria's military regime between 1966 and 1979, for instance, spent an average of 35 percent of the budget on the military; Pakistan's military regimes spent 29 percent between 1958 and 1971 and then 31 percent from 1977 to 1988; and Myanmar's military regime spent 32 percent from 1988 to 2010. On the other end of the spectrum are militaries that have clearly been marginalized. Malawi under Hastings Banda (r. 1964–1994), who counterbalanced with the Young Pioneers militia, spent just 5.7 percent on the military; Kenya (1962–2002), which counterbalanced with the General Services Unit, spent 8.5 percent; and Mexico under the PRI (1946–2000), which depoliticized the military and kept it weak and fragmented,[6] spent just 6.1 percent. In short, the budget data appear to be capturing the variation we intend it to.

Coup-Proofing

Do these coup-proofing strategies actually work? Are dictators less likely to experience coups if they pursue marginalization or empowerment? To find out, I merge in data on all military coups between 1950 and 2010 from Powell and Thyne (2011).

---

[6] Serrano (1995); Camp (2005).

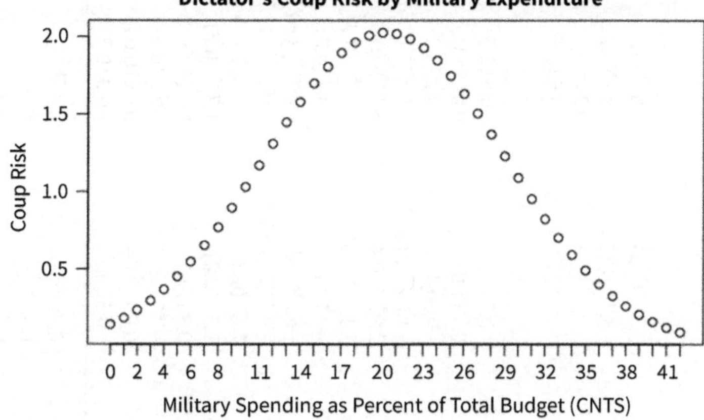

Figure 3.2 Predicted Coup Risk in Dictatorships by Military Expenditure, 1946–2010

I then conduct a survival analysis[7] that predicts the likelihood that a regime falls to a military coup in a given year based on its level of military spending in the previous year.[8] Because we anticipate that both low and high levels of spending will reduce coups, I model the effect with a polynomial, permitting a curvilinear relationship.

The results (Figure 3.2) are striking: both marginalization and empowerment significantly ($p < 0.001$) reduce the likelihood of a coup. Coup risk is low for regimes that neglect their militaries, steadily increases and then peaks for regimes that spend roughly 20 percent on the military, and then falls again for the empowered militaries receiving 30–40 percent of the budget. Indeed, pursuing either marginalization or empowerment appears to make coups 4–5 times less likely, dropping from roughly a 2 percent chance each year to less than a 0.5 percent chance. Both coup-proofing strategies thus appear to successfully coup-proof the military.

Table 3.1 shows that these patterns hold when controlling for a number of covariates that might otherwise confound this relationship. I control for civil wars and inter-state wars (from UCDP/PRIO[9]), to show that the link between military expenditure and coup risk is not due to higher security threats. I control for features of

---

[7] Here and throughout this chapter, I employ the Cox Proportional Hazards model (Cox, 1972), given that we are more interested in the effects of independent variables, rather than in the shape of the underlying hazard rates.

[8] I remove outliers on the military spending variable using Tukey's rule: values greater than 1.5 interquartile ranges above the third quartile (Tukey, 1977), or 41.25% of the budget. Results are similar when leaving them in, other than a longer right-tail.

[9] Gleditsch, Wallensteen, Eriksson, Sollenberg, and Strand (2002). For both, I code a "war" as having at least 1,000 battle deaths in a year.

Table 3.1 Dictator's Coup Risk (Cox Proportional Hazards)

	Dependent Variable: Military Coup					
	(1)	(2)	(3)	(4)	(5)	(6)
Coup-Proofing						
Military Budget	10.8*** (2.5)	7.1** (2.9)	6.8** (2.9)			
Military Budget^2	−11.0*** (2.7)	−7.7** (3.1)	−7.5** (3.1)			
Military Ministers				6.9*** (1.4)	3.9** (1.8)	4.0** (1.8)
Military Ministers^2				−5.7*** (1.8)	−4.7** (2.3)	−4.7** (2.3)
Counterbalancing			0.4 (0.3)			0.3 (0.3)
Stacking			−0.05 (0.3)			−0.4 (0.3)
Covariates						
Civil War		−1.1** (0.6)	−1.2** (0.6)		−0.7 (0.5)	−0.6 (0.5)
Foreign War		0.03 (1.0)	−0.1 (1.0)		0.1 (1.0)	0.01 (1.0)
Coup-Born		−0.7** (0.3)	−0.6* (0.3)		−0.3 (0.3)	−0.3 (0.3)
Rebel-Born		−2.0*** (0.7)	−2.0*** (0.7)		−1.6*** (0.6)	−1.6*** (0.6)
Military Regime		3.5*** (0.5)	3.7*** (0.5)		2.9*** (0.4)	3.1*** (0.5)
Personalist Regime		1.6*** (0.4)	1.5*** (0.4)		1.1*** (0.3)	1.1*** (0.3)
Conscription		−0.4 (0.3)	−0.4 (0.3)		−0.1 (0.2)	−0.2 (0.3)
Population, log		−7.0*** (1.8)	−7.3*** (1.8)		−6.7*** (1.6)	−7.0*** (1.7)
GDP per capita, log		−8.6*** (1.7)	−8.8*** (1.7)		−9.8*** (1.6)	−10.0*** (1.7)
Δ GDP per capita		2.8 (5.2)	3.2 (5.3)		7.8* (4.2)	7.9* (4.4)
Oil Production, log		2.0*** (0.7)	2.1*** (0.7)		1.5* (0.8)	1.7** (0.8)
Education, log		−0.9 (1.7)	−0.8 (1.7)		0.8 (1.6)	0.2 (1.6)
% Protestant		−0.6** (0.3)	−0.6** (0.3)		−0.5* (0.2)	−0.4 (0.3)
% Muslim		0.03 (0.04)	0.04 (0.04)		0.03 (0.04)	0.05 (0.04)
Post-Cold War		−0.5 (0.4)	−0.5 (0.4)		−0.3 (0.3)	−0.3 (0.3)
Observations	2,667	2,310	2,270	3,477	2,909	2,862
R^2	0.01	0.1	0.1	0.01	0.1	0.1
Max. Possible R^2	0.4	0.4	0.4	0.4	0.3	0.3
Log Likelihood	−619.9	−446.7	−445.8	−734.9	−513.3	−505.2

Note: *$p<0.1$; **$p<0.05$; ***$p<0.01$.

Note: Coefficients represent the log(hazard).

Note: The combination of the term and its polynomial shows that budget/ministers at first increases coup risk and then reduces it, producing the curvilinear relationship shown in Figure 3.2.

the regime that might shape both its military expenditure and its durability, such as whether it came to power originally in a coup or insurgency,[10] and whether it is a military or personalist regime,[11] all from Geddes, Wright, and Frantz (2014, 2018). I also control for whether the regime employs conscription (Toronto, 2014), which might shape military expenditure as well as coup risk.[12] Finally, I control for standard demographic and socioeconomic variables, including population size, percent with primary or secondary education, GDP per capita, and change in GDP per capita (all from CNTS), oil production (from Haber and Menaldo (2011)), percent Protestant and percent Muslim (from Brown and James (2018)), and post-Cold War. All variables are lagged one year to examine their impact on coups in the next year.

Despite these controls, both of the coup-proofing strategies continue to significantly reduce coup risk (model 2). Moreover, results are similar when measuring the military's political power (models 4–5), rather than material resources. In the final models (3 and 6), I show that the dictator's coup-proofing strategies are robust to controlling also for counterbalancing and stacking (from Geddes, Wright, and Frantz (2018)), two coup-proofing tactics that cluster with these overall strategies both empirically and theoretically (see Chapter 2). The fact that the military's material resources and political power remain significant predictors of coup risk suggest these effects are not driven solely by their correlated coup-proofing tactics, and instead reflect broader underlying strategies.

In short, both marginalization and empowerment appear to work, coup-proofing the military. How then do dictators choose which one to pursue?

Choice of Strategy

I hypothesized that a number of factors, from security threats to path-dependence to personal preferences, would shape how dictators decide between these strategies. To explore these hypotheses, Table 3.2 examines the correlates of military expenditure, while Figure 3.3 plots the most important variables.

The results are illuminating. First, fear of a coup alone does not shape their choice of strategy. Dictators who survived a coup attempt in the last year or who witnessed a successful coup elsewhere in the region, who might therefore have heightened fear of a coup, are no more or less likely to fund their militaries. After all, they could respond to the coup threat by either marginalizing or empowering their militaries—both are effective coup-proofing strategies. Instead, the mix of threats they face seem to shape

---

[10] Slater (2010); Lachapelle, Levitsky, Way, and Casey (2020); Levitsky and Way (2022); Meng and Paine (2022).

[11] Gandhi and Przeworski (2007); Gandhi and Lust-Okar (2009); Gandhi and Sumner (2020); Chin, Song, and Wright (2022)

[12] Cohn and Toronto (2016); Vasquez III and Powell (2021).

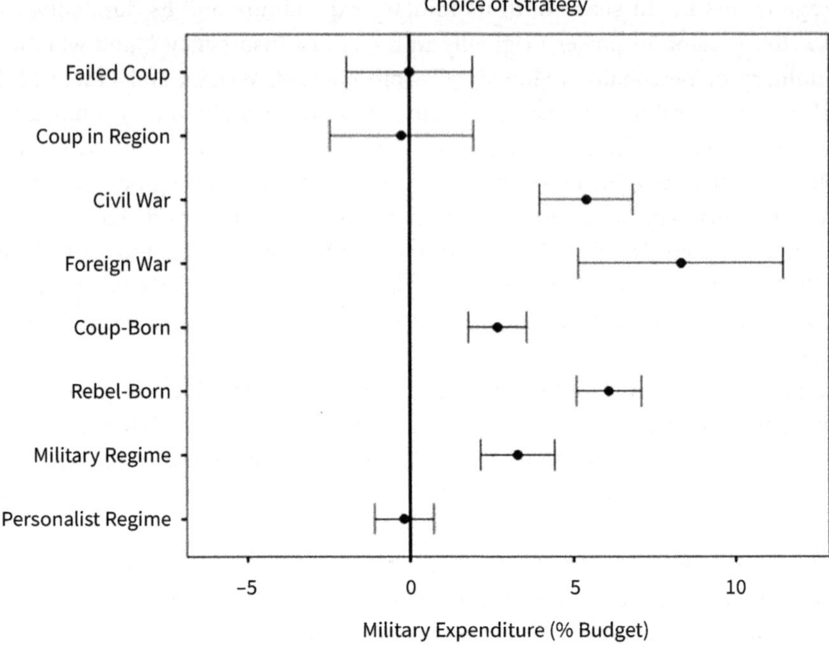

Figure 3.3 Choice of Coup-Proofing Strategy in Dictatorships, 1946–2010

their choice. Dictators who, while fearful of a coup, also need strong militaries to fight domestically or abroad are more likely to choose empowerment. Dictators who faced a civil war or foreign war the previous year spend 5–7 percent more of their budget on the military. The cocktail of threat perceptions thus shapes coup-proofing strategies.

At the same time, dictators are also constrained by how they came to power. Regimes born out of coups or insurgencies often develop highly powerful and popular militaries that are difficult to cast aside. Both types of regime birth are thus associated with higher military spending. Finally, the type of regime the dictator seeks to create—a rough proxy for their personal preferences—likewise shapes their expenditure. Dictators heading military regimes on average spend more on their militaries, though as we have noted there remains considerable variation within them.

Yet, by far the most important variable is path-dependence. To illustrate, Table 3.2 model 2 adds the military's budget in the previous year. Doing so makes all of the aforementioned effects disappear or weaken considerably. On its own, the military's budget in the previous year explains almost 90 percent of the total variation in the military's budget this year (model 3, see R^2). While threat perceptions may slightly alter the degree to which the dictator empowers or marginalizes the military, those strategies appear to be path dependent. Models 4–6 illustrate that these patterns are robust to examining the military's political power as well.

Table 3.2 Dictator's Choice of Coup-Proofing Strategy (OLS)

	Dependent variable:					
	Military Budget			Military Ministers		
	(1)	(2)	(3)	(4)	(5)	(6)
Path-Dependence						
Budget last year		0.38^{***} (0.003)	0.39^{***} (0.003)			
Ministers last year					0.77^{***} (0.01)	0.85^{***} (0.01)
Covariates						
Failed Coup	-0.0000 (0.01)	0.001 (0.003)		-0.002 (0.01)	-0.01 (0.01)	
Coup in Region	-0.002 (0.01)	-0.0001 (0.004)		0.06^{***} (0.02)	0.02^{*} (0.01)	
Civil War	0.05^{***} (0.01)	0.01^{***} (0.003)		0.02^{**} (0.01)	-0.001 (0.01)	
Foreign War	0.08^{***} (0.02)	0.02^{***} (0.01)		0.01 (0.02)	0.002 (0.01)	
Coup-Born	0.03^{***} (0.005)	0.003^{*} (0.002)		0.10^{***} (0.01)	0.02^{***} (0.004)	
Rebel-Born	0.06^{***} (0.01)	0.01^{***} (0.002)		0.03^{***} (0.01)	0.003 (0.004)	
Military Regime	0.03^{***} (0.01)	0.003 (0.002)		0.14^{***} (0.01)	0.03^{***} (0.01)	
Personalist Regime	-0.002 (0.005)	-0.003^{*} (0.002)		0.03^{***} (0.01)	0.01^{*} (0.004)	
Conscription	0.01^{***} (0.004)	0.001 (0.001)		0.01 (0.01)	0.001 (0.003)	
Population, log	-0.03 (0.02)	-0.01 (0.01)		-0.04 (0.03)	-0.01 (0.02)	
GDP per capita, log	0.06^{***} (0.02)	0.003 (0.01)		-0.03 (0.03)	-0.02 (0.02)	
Δ GDP per capita	0.01 (0.06)	0.005 (0.02)		-0.02 (0.07)	-0.0005 (0.04)	
Oil Production, log	-0.02^{***} (0.01)	-0.003 (0.003)		0.05^{***} (0.01)	0.02^{*} (0.01)	
Education, log	-0.09^{***} (0.03)	-0.02^{***} (0.01)		-0.17^{***} (0.03)	-0.04^{*} (0.02)	
% Protestant	-0.01^{***} (0.002)	-0.0003 (0.001)		-0.02^{***} (0.003)	-0.01^{***} (0.002)	
% Muslim	0.01^{***} (0.001)	0.0002 (0.0002)		-0.01^{***} (0.001)	-0.002^{***} (0.001)	
Post-Cold War	-0.01^{***} (0.004)	0.0004 (0.002)		-0.01^{**} (0.01)	-0.01 (0.004)	
Constant	0.17^{***} (0.04)	0.03^{*} (0.02)	0.01^{***} (0.001)	0.22^{***} (0.05)	0.05 (0.03)	0.02^{***} (0.002)
Observations	2,318	2,177	2,560	2,967	2,907	3,417
R^2	0.20	0.90	0.90	0.32	0.73	0.72
Adjusted R^2	0.20	0.90	0.90	0.32	0.73	0.72

Note: $^{*}p<0.1$; $^{**}p<0.05$; $^{***}p<0.01$

Having explored the causes of coup-proofing, let us now turn to their consequences. I theorized that empowered and marginalized militaries should behave differently during processes of democratization. The first observable difference is how they behave during pro-democracy uprisings.

Mass Uprisings

Empowered militaries should be more likely than marginalized ones to repress mass uprisings, more fearful of what regime change might mean for their corporate interests. To test this hypothesis, I turn to data collected by Chenoweth and Stephan (2011). Their Nonviolent and Violent Campaigns and Outcomes (NAVCO) dataset has been a remarkable resource providing country–year data on 384 resistance campaigns between 1945 and 2013. I subset to the 245 campaigns focused on regime change, as opposed to secessionist movements or independence struggles. I then merge in the data on military expenditure to trace out how the dictator's coup-proofing strategy shapes military behavior during times of revolution.

I first examine the probability that the military represses the mass uprising. NAVCO offers two variables in this regard, one capturing the severity of repression and the other the scope of it. The first, *Repression*, records whether the regime employed physical violence against the opposition.[13] The second, *Indiscriminate Repression*, records "widespread state violence against the [general] population," and not just the opposition. When militaries repress, they are likely to do so indiscriminately—for instance, firing into the crowd—given that they are often called upon as a last resort to fully crush the protests, and generally lack the non-lethal equipment and crowd-control training of the police.[14]

Table 3.3 presents the results. Military expenditure strongly correlates with both the use of repression and the use of indiscriminate repression. Regimes with more empowered militaries are significantly more likely to repress, even when controlling for a variety of covariates. I include variables related to the country context as well as specific NAVCO variables about the campaign itself, such as whether they are nonviolent, large, united, diverse, and enjoying international support. Regardless of these controls, military spending continues to exhibit a strong, positive effect on repression. Notably, this effect is distinct from having a military regime, which on its own exhibits little to no impact on repression.

---

[13] I thus dichotomize NAVCO's "repression" variable into those committing moderate or extreme repression v. those not employing repression or only mild repression (economic fees or threatening but not actually using violence).

[14] For neither variable does NAVCO specify whether it is the military repressing or just the police. The dependent variables therefore dilute the analysis by including as a "1" cases where the military does not repress but the police does. Indeed, almost 95% of country–years see repression. Only 62% of country–years, however, see indiscriminate repression. That variable should thus do a better job addressing this limitation.

Table 3.3 Coup-Proofing Strategy and Repression of Mass Uprisings (NAVCO)

	Dependent variable:					
	Repression			Indiscriminate Repression		
Military	(1)	(2)	(3)	(4)	(5)	(6)
Military Budget	0.11*** (0.04)	0.16*** (0.05)	0.18*** (0.07)	0.37*** (0.09)	0.33*** (0.12)	0.31** (0.14)
Military Regime		0.04* (0.02)	0.02 (0.03)		0.05 (0.05)	0.06 (0.06)
Conscription		−0.01 (0.02)	0.01 (0.03)		0.04 (0.05)	0.01 (0.06)
Counterbalancing			−0.03 (0.03)			−0.05 (0.06)
Stacking			0.10*** (0.04)			0.17** (0.08)
NAVCO Variables						
End Year of Campaign		−0.09*** (0.03)	−0.07* (0.04)		−0.18*** (0.07)	−0.16** (0.08)
Nonviolent		−0.10*** (0.03)	−0.06 (0.04)		0.02 (0.07)	−0.05 (0.08)
Campaign Size, log		−0.06 (0.08)	−0.09 (0.10)		0.37** (0.17)	0.55*** (0.21)
Hierarchal		−0.0003 (0.001)	−0.0004 (0.001)		0.004** (0.002)	0.005** (0.002)
United		−0.03 (0.02)	−0.01 (0.03)		−0.09* (0.05)	0.04 (0.07)
Ideological Diversity		0.01 (0.02)	0.03 (0.03)		−0.02 (0.05)	0.12* (0.07)
Class Diversity		−0.04 (0.03)	−0.05 (0.04)		−0.004 (0.06)	−0.12 (0.08)
Gender Diversity		0.03 (0.03)	0.02 (0.03)		0.01 (0.06)	−0.001 (0.07)
Foreign Support		0.001 (0.0005)	0.001 (0.001)		0.002** (0.001)	0.005*** (0.001)
Diaspora Support		−0.001 (0.0005)	−0.0002 (0.001)		0.001 (0.001)	0.0002 (0.001)
Foreign Media		−0.0000 (0.002)	0.01 (0.02)		−0.01 (0.005)	0.01 (0.04)
Domestic Media		0.0005* (0.0003)	0.001** (0.0004)		−0.001 (0.001)	0.001 (0.001)
Reliability		−0.25*** (0.08)	−0.17 (0.10)		−0.46** (0.18)	−0.45** (0.21)
Context						
Population, log		0.06 (0.12)	0.22 (0.20)		−1.23*** (0.27)	−0.50 (0.42)
GDP per capita, log		−0.27** (0.13)	−0.32* (0.17)		−0.78*** (0.29)	−1.02*** (0.36)
Δ GDP per capita		0.63 (0.38)	0.56 (0.45)		0.95 (0.86)	1.45 (0.92)
Oil Production, log		0.30 (0.19)	0.68** (0.27)		1.10*** (0.42)	2.35*** (0.55)
Education, log		0.16*** (0.06)	0.13 (0.08)		0.26* (0.13)	0.04 (0.16)
% Protestant		0.05*** (0.02)	0.01 (0.02)		0.08** (0.03)	0.03 (0.04)
% Muslim		−0.001 (0.004)	−0.003 (0.01)		−0.01 (0.01)	−0.01 (0.01)
Constant	0.91*** (0.02)	0.36 (0.29)	−0.02 (0.38)	0.47*** (0.04)	0.01 (0.64)	−1.82** (0.77)
Observations	732	500	344	732	500	344
R^2	0.01	0.17	0.17	0.02	0.19	0.23
Adjusted R^2	0.01	0.13	0.10	0.02	0.15	0.17

Note: *p<0.1; **p<0.05; ***p<0.01

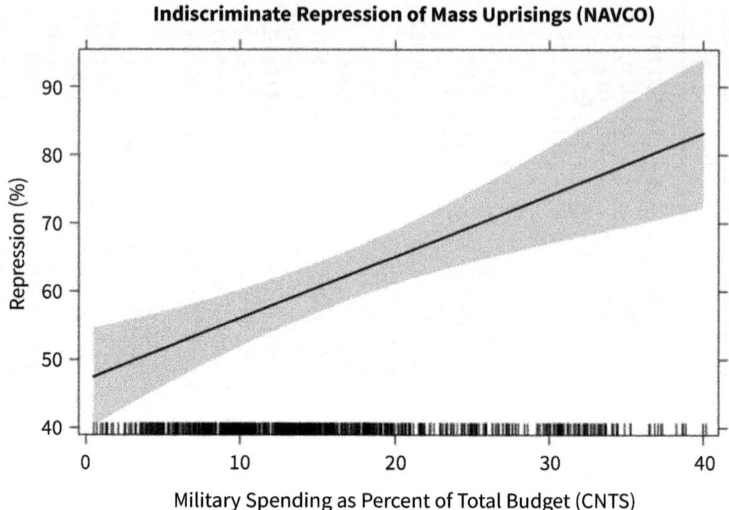

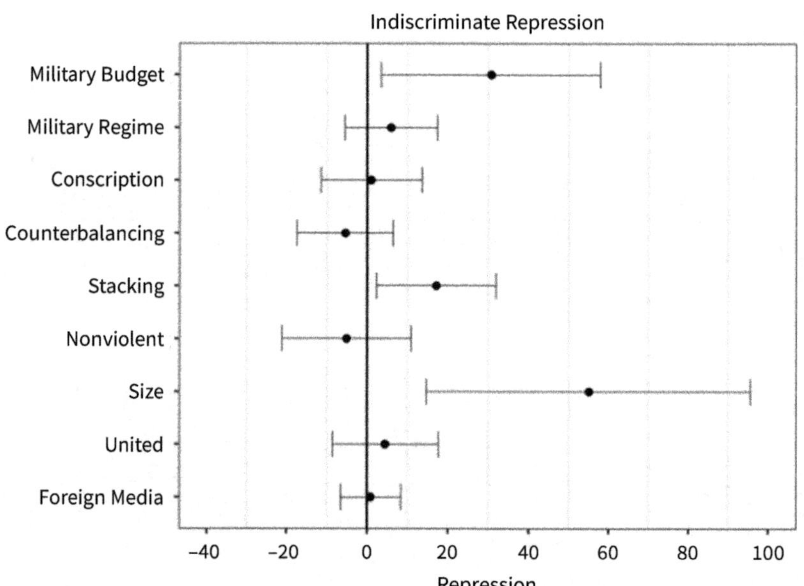

Figure 3.4 Indiscriminate Repression of Mass Uprisings, 1946–2010 (NAVCO)

Figure 3.4 visualizes the effect of military spending on indiscriminate repression. With empowered militaries, mass uprisings face an 80 percent chance of indiscriminate repression, compared to only 50 percent for marginalized militaries. Substantively, this effect size for military expenditure is greater than that of any other variable except the size of the protests. Larger protests, more threatening to the dictator, likewise provoke more indiscriminate repression, in line with Davenport (2007)'s "Law of Coercive Responsiveness."

Beyond repression, two additional NAVCO variables shed further light on the military's behavior during mass protests. First, Table 3.4 models 1–3 show that empowered militaries are also significantly less likely to see defections during mass uprisings. Empowerment creates a strong, loyal military willing to crush internal threats without major defections. Beyond the overall coup-proofing strategy, the two coup-proofing tactics that correlate with these broader strategies also see effects on defection. Like empowerment, stacking the military with the dictator's in-group produces more loyalty and fewer defections during times of revolution. By contrast, counterbalancing the military increases the chance of defections. Neglected and resentful, these militaries have little interest in preserving the regime. The two "ideal-types" of coup-proofed militaries—one marginalized and counterbalanced, the other empowered and stacked—thus create important legacies in how they respond to mass uprisings.

Existing literature suggests that how the military responds—repression or defection—is so important that it can make or break revolutions. Table 3.4 models 4–6 therefore explore whether the campaign succeeds in toppling the dictator. As expected, the stronger the military, the lower the chance of success. Figure 3.5 (top) illustrates this effect visually: with the most marginalized militaries, protesters have a roughly 15 percent chance of success in any given year, but with the most empowered militaries, this drops to nearly 0 percent. Here again, the dictator's coup-proofing strategy is among the most important variables shaping the success of mass uprisings, more important even than whether the protesters are nonviolent, united, and receiving foreign media coverage, and second only to the size of the protests.

In short, the dictator's coup-proofing strategy has tremendous downstream consequences for how those militaries behave during mass uprisings. Empowered militaries, wedded to the regime through a share of power and often a shared identity, are significantly more likely to repress the protests, and significantly less likely to see defections. In turn, uprisings against regimes with empowered militaries are significantly less likely to succeed.

Still, some uprisings do succeed in toppling the dictator and sparking a transition to democracy.[15] Even in these cases, however, the legacies of having empowered the military will continue to pose a major obstacle for democratization.

---

[15] This dynamic raises the possibility of selection effects regarding which empowered militaries allow for a transition to democracy to even occur in the first place, prior to our analysis in the next section about whether the transition succeeds. The cases that do experience transitions should be either the relatively weaker empowered militaries and/or relatively stronger pro-democracy movements. In either case, these selection effects should make it more difficult to uncover the effect we go on to do, where empowered militaries are more likely to undermine democratic transitions. If that effect obtains even when we are only observing the relatively "nicer" empowered militaries, effects would be even stronger were all countries to see a transition to democracy.

Table 3.4 Security Force Defections and the Success of Mass Uprisings (NAVCO)

	Dependent variable:					
	Defections			Success		
	(1)	(2)	(3)	(4)	(5)	(6)
Military Budget	-0.12^{*} (0.07)	-0.23^{**} (0.09)	-0.16 (0.11)	-0.17^{***} (0.05)	-0.13^{**} (0.06)	-0.15^{**} (0.08)
Military Regime		-0.06 (0.04)	0.03 (0.05)		-0.04^{*} (0.03)	-0.03 (0.03)
Conscription		0.03 (0.04)	-0.02 (0.05)		0.04 (0.03)	0.05 (0.03)
Counterbalancing			0.13^{***} (0.05)			-0.01 (0.03)
Stacking			-0.10^{*} (0.06)			-0.02 (0.04)
NAVCO Variables						
End of Campaign		0.08 (0.05)	0.01 (0.06)		0.40^{***} (0.04)	0.44^{***} (0.04)
Nonviolent		0.18^{***} (0.05)	0.23^{***} (0.06)		0.11^{***} (0.04)	0.11^{**} (0.04)
Campaign Size, log		0.29^{**} (0.13)	0.33^{**} (0.16)		0.37^{***} (0.09)	0.33^{***} (0.11)
Hierarchal		0.002 (0.001)	0.002 (0.001)		0.001 (0.001)	0.001 (0.001)
United		0.08^{**} (0.04)	0.05 (0.05)		0.04 (0.03)	0.07^{**} (0.04)
Ideological Diversity		-0.03 (0.04)	0.09^{*} (0.05)		-0.04 (0.02)	-0.02 (0.04)
Class Diversity		0.17^{***} (0.05)	0.01 (0.06)		0.07^{**} (0.03)	0.06 (0.04)
Gender Diversity		-0.14^{***} (0.04)	-0.10^{*} (0.05)		-0.04 (0.03)	-0.04 (0.04)
Foreign Support		-0.0000 (0.001)	0.0004 (0.001)		0.0000 (0.001)	-0.0002 (0.001)
Diaspora Support		0.002^{**} (0.001)	0.001 (0.001)		0.0005 (0.001)	0.001^{*} (0.001)
Foreign Media		0.001 (0.003)	0.03 (0.03)		0.004^{*} (0.002)	0.05^{**} (0.02)
Domestic Media		0.001 (0.0005)	0.0001 (0.001)		-0.0000 (0.0003)	-0.001 (0.0004)
Reliability		-0.04 (0.14)	-0.08 (0.16)		0.03 (0.10)	0.18 (0.12)
Context						
Population, log		-0.78^{***} (0.21)	-1.12^{***} (0.32)		-0.06 (0.14)	0.14 (0.23)
GDP per capita, log		-0.58^{***} (0.21)	-0.73^{***} (0.28)		-0.12 (0.15)	-0.15 (0.20)
Δ GDP per capita		1.06 (0.64)	1.41^{**} (0.71)		-0.26 (0.45)	-0.21 (0.51)
Oil Production, log		-0.43 (0.32)	-0.39 (0.42)		-0.06 (0.22)	-0.09 (0.30)
Education, log		0.02 (0.10)	-0.24^{*} (0.12)		-0.15^{**} (0.07)	-0.30^{***} (0.09)
% Protestant		-0.01 (0.03)	0.01 (0.03)		-0.04^{**} (0.02)	-0.05^{**} (0.02)
% Muslim		0.02^{***} (0.01)	0.03^{***} (0.01)		0.01 (0.005)	0.01 (0.01)
Constant	0.20^{***} (0.03)	0.46 (0.48)	0.44 (0.59)	0.15^{***} (0.02)	0.17 (0.34)	0.002 (0.42)
Observations	732	500	344	732	500	344
R^2	0.004	0.21	0.26	0.01	0.35	0.41
Adjusted R^2	0.003	0.17	0.21	0.01	0.32	0.37

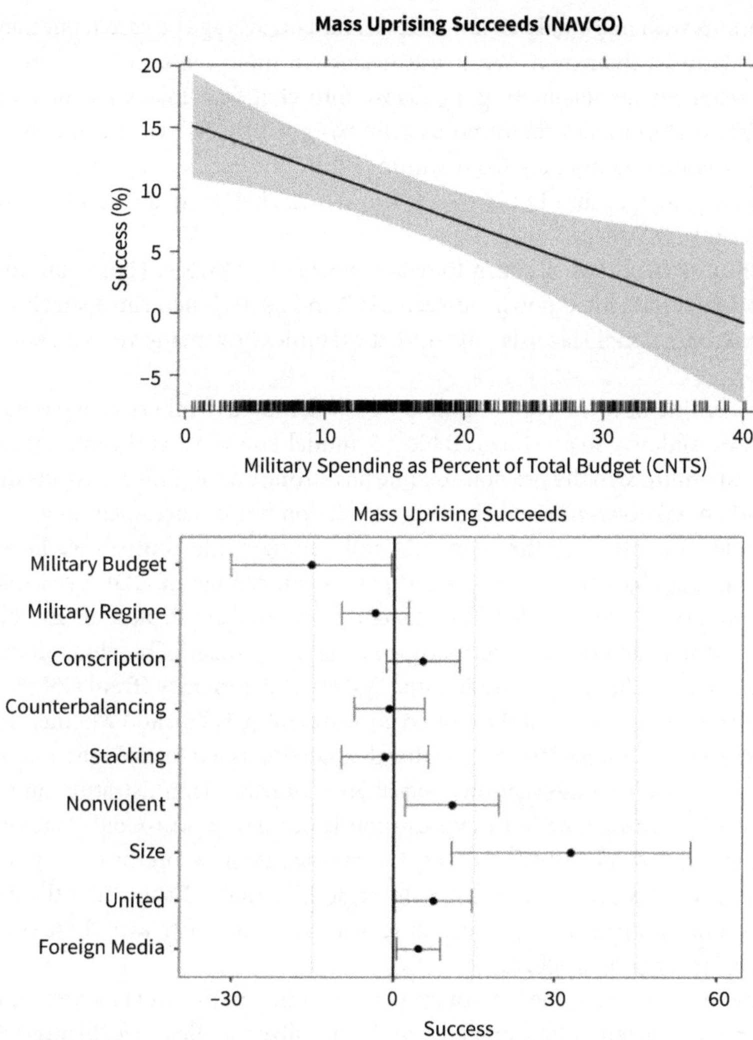

Figure 3.5 Success of Mass Uprisings, 1946–2010 (NAVCO)

Democratization

Assuming the country begins a transition to democracy, what is the chance that the transition survives? Here, I argue that the type of military each transition inherits from the previous regime will have important impacts shaping its likelihood of survival. The more the dictator had empowered the military, the more difficult democratization will be. Democracy creates normative and electoral pressures on the newly elected government to redistribute an empowered military's bloated budget toward public goods, and to exert civilian control over the military, curtailing its material and political power. As a result, empowered militaries should be more likely to end democratic transitions, particularly through military coups.

Transitions with marginalized militaries should on average be easier, but they may still carry risks of their own. Weak and neglected, these militaries are less able to fend off rebel threats, facilitating a collapse into civil war. Likewise, their neglect under dictatorship makes them more easily co-opted by elected incumbents seeking to undermine democracy from within. While the modal outcome should still be democracy, marginalized militaries will also bring heightened risks of incumbent takeovers and civil wars.

To test these hypotheses, I turn to data collected by Ulfelder (2010) on different forms of democratic breakdown between 1955 and 2010. I then run a survival analysis (Cox Proportional Hazards model) that examines how many years a democracy survives.

I first examine how the type of military each democracy inherits shapes its overall risk of breakdown, in any form. Table 3.5, model 1 shows that the average level of military expenditure in the previous regime has strong and significant effects making democratic breakdown more likely. This correlation holds when including a variety of covariates. I control for the economic and demographic controls we have used throughout this chapter, including GDP per capita, change in GDP per capita, oil production, population size, level of education, and percent Protestant and percent Muslim.[16] I then add political controls, including the number of previous attempts at democracy (from Ulfelder), a presidential system of democracy (from CNTS[17]), the occurrence of protests against the elected government (CNTS), and whether the previous regime was a military or personalist dictatorship (Geddes, Wright, and Frantz (2014)). I also include international variables capturing demonstration and diffusion effects, recording whether the transition is occurring post-Cold War, whether the country is a former British colony, the average Polity score in the region, and the occurrence of a coup elsewhere in the region.[18] Finally, I show that the effect is robust to controlling for the coup-proofing tactics that correlate with these strategies (counterbalancing and stacking).

Despite these controls, the level of military spending in the previous regime exerts a major impact on democratic breakdown. To visualize the effect size, Figure 3.6 plots the probability of survival over time by the level of military spending. The impact is considerable: when inheriting the most marginalized militaries, transitions have about an 85 percent chance of survival, but when inheriting the most empowered militaries, this falls to nearly 65 percent.

---

[16] For the importance of these variables for democracy, see Gasiorowski (1995); Przeworski and Limongi (1997); Fish (2002); Woodberry (2002); Boix (2003); Acemoglu and Robinson (2006); Maeda (2010); Svolik (2015); Tang, Huhe, and Zhou (2017).

[17] I code a presidential system as a democracy where the president governs as the sole (polit09=0) and effective (polit07=2) executive. For the importance of presidential systems, see Stepan and Skach (1993); Linz and Valenzuela (1994); Bernhard, Reenock, and Nordstrom (2001); Maeda (2010). Military legacies may shape the choice of a presidential system (Cheibub, 2007), but it is important to test for these institutional explanations even if they may weaken the effects of coup-proofing strategies.

[18] For the importance of these effects, see First (1970); Wejnert (2005); Brinks and Coppedge (2006); Gleditsch and Ward (2006); Levitsky and Way (2010); Miller (2020).

Table 3.5 Coup-Proofing Strategy and Democratic Breakdown (Cox Proportional Hazards)

	Dependent variable:			
	Breakdown (1)	Military Coup (2)	Self-Coup (3)	Civil War (4)
During Dictatorship				
Prev Military Budget	2.15** (1.02)	3.27** (1.37)	−3.65* (1.94)	−3.69*** (1.05)
Prev Personal Regime	0.72 (0.76)	1.21 (1.07)	0.16 (1.00)	1.24** (0.53)
Prev Military Regime	−1.09* (0.61)	0.05 (0.70)	−4.11 (3.43)	0.50 (0.39)
Prev Counterbalancing	−0.43 (0.56)	−2.02* (1.20)	−1.86* (1.03)	−0.05 (0.29)
Prev Stacking	−0.28 (0.49)	0.52 (0.70)	0.01 (0.62)	2.22*** (0.50)
Covariates				
GDP per capita	−14.13*** (3.41)	−10.19** (4.19)	−14.21*** (4.54)	6.39*** (1.98)
Δ GDP per capita	−4.13 (4.46)	4.26 (7.97)	−4.84 (4.99)	−1.15 (7.01)
Oil Production	0.34 (1.78)	0.07 (3.61)	−1.50 (2.49)	−4.19*** (1.11)
Population	−10.43*** (3.85)	−9.04 (6.05)	10.01 (7.35)	4.00 (2.51)
Education	0.94 (3.43)	0.94 (5.55)	−3.41 (4.76)	0.13 (2.56)
% Protestant	−0.21 (0.30)	0.46 (0.63)	−0.12 (0.47)	−2.60*** (0.46)
% Muslim	−0.20** (0.08)	−0.16 (0.10)	−0.16 (0.15)	−0.09 (0.07)
Post-Cold War	1.30*** (0.20)	1.58 (0.98)	−0.38 (1.07)	−1.30*** (0.49)
Prior Demo Attempts	−1.59*** (0.61)	1.29*** (0.20)	1.22** (0.53)	−0.63** (0.30)
Former British Colony	0.16 (0.14)	0.03 (0.68)	0.03 (1.33)	2.23*** (0.39)
Av Polity in Region	0.01 (0.72)	−4.85** (2.43)	6.79* (3.94)	−2.32* (1.39)
Coup in Region	0.76 (0.66)	4.12*** (1.26)	1.08 (1.02)	−1.37* (0.77)
Presidential System	−3.52** (1.78)	−0.30 (0.92)	−0.72 (0.89)	1.17** (0.56)
Anti-Gov Protests	1.32* (0.80)	−0.05 (0.24)	−0.11 (0.11)	0.01 (0.06)
Observations	909	909	909	909
R^2	0.18			
Max. Possible R^2	0.43			
Log Likelihood	−166.04	−108.98	−88.39	−298.18

Note: *p<0.1; **p<0.05; ***p<0.01
Note: Coefficients represent the log(hazard).
Note: Models 2-4 use a competing risks survival analysis.

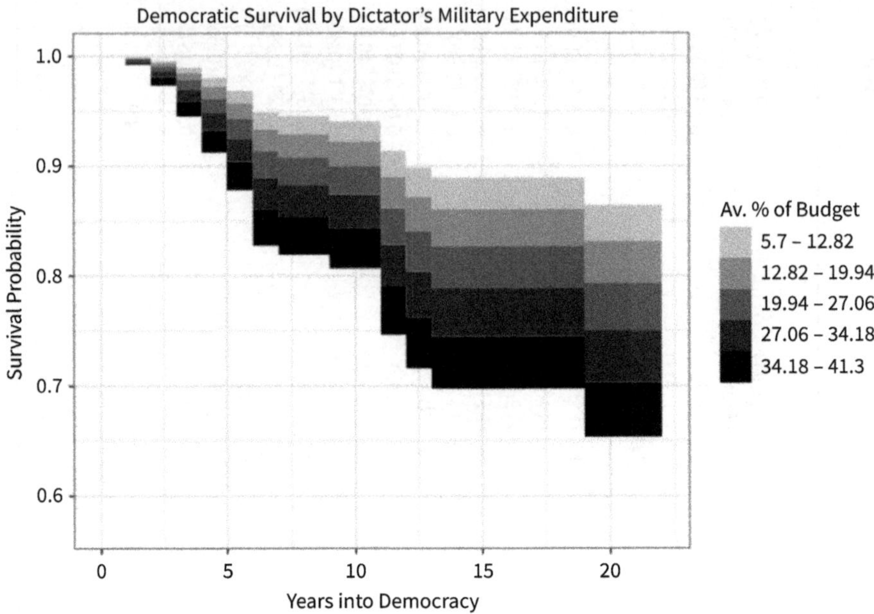

Figure 3.6 Military Empowerment and Democratic Breakdown, 1946–2010

Results are even more revealing when separating out how the democracy dies. The most common form of democratic collapse is a military coup, but democracies also die in incumbent takeovers and civil wars. Since these each represent competing forms of democratic breakdown, we cannot be sure whether a transition that collapsed in a coup might not have collapsed in some other way had the coup not occurred. To address this issue, I follow Maeda (2010) and Svolik (2015) in explicitly modeling a "competing risks" survival analysis.[19] The remainder of Table 3.5 presents those results, showing the effect of the previous dictator's military spending on the likelihood that a democracy collapses in a military coup (model 2), incumbent takeover (model 3), or civil war (model 4).

As hypothesized, empowered militaries are significantly more likely to stage coups. Figure 3.7 illustrates the effect size. The most empowered militaries have a roughly 40 percent chance of staging a coup against democracy, compared to less than 10 percent for the most marginalized militaries. In other words, even when controlling for these covariates, empowered militaries are about four times more likely to stage coups than marginalized ones. Given that coups account for the largest share of democratic breakdowns, this effect underscores why transitions with empowered militaries are less likely to succeed. Moreover, while existing literature tends to control for whether the previous dictatorship was a military regime, our results show that military regimes have no effect on the likelihood of coups once we control for the level

---

[19] Prentice, Kalbfleisch, Peterson, Flournoy, Farewell, and Breslow (1978); Fine and Gray (1999).

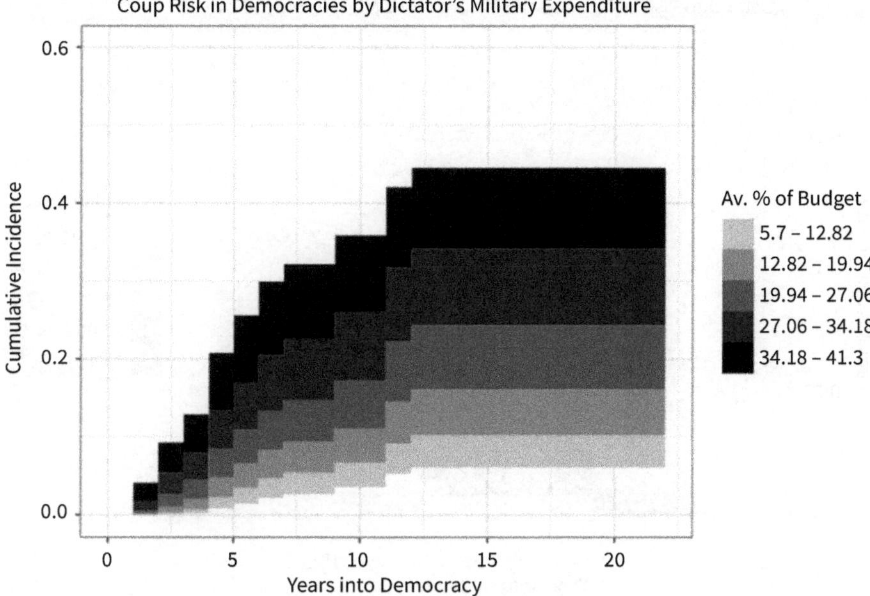

Figure 3.7 Military Empowerment and Coups against Democracies, 1946–2010

of military spending. What matters is not whether the dictator was a military officer, but how they treated the military. Empowered militaries make democratization more difficult.

However, marginalized militaries are not without their risks. The two less common forms of democratic breakdown—incumbent takeovers and civil wars—are comparatively more common with marginalized militaries. Table 3.5 models 3 and 4 present those results. Transitions with marginalized militaries are about three times more likely to fall to incumbent takeovers, increasing the rate from about 3 percent for empowered militaries to 10 percent for marginalized ones (Figure 3.8 top). In other words, while still rare, self-coups are significantly more likely with marginalized militaries.

Civil wars are likewise more common with marginalized militaries.[20] Figure 3.8 (bottom) shows that that the risk of civil war increases from roughly 10 percent for the most empowered militaries to 30 percent for the most marginalized ones. In short, marginalized militaries make civil wars significantly more likely.

How dictators treat their militaries under autocracy thus produces important legacies shaping military behavior under democracy. Where dictators had empowered their militaries, democratic transitions are more likely to break down, and to do so in

---

[20] Ulfelder (2010) had only coded three cases of democracies as falling to civil wars, insufficient to conduct statistical analysis. Instead, I examine the aforementioned data on civil wars from UCDP/PRIO, which finds that 24 democracies have faced civil wars (whether or not they collapsed as a result). However, this means the various forms of breakdown examined in Figures 3.7 and 3.8 do not add up to the overall breakdown count in Figure 3.6.

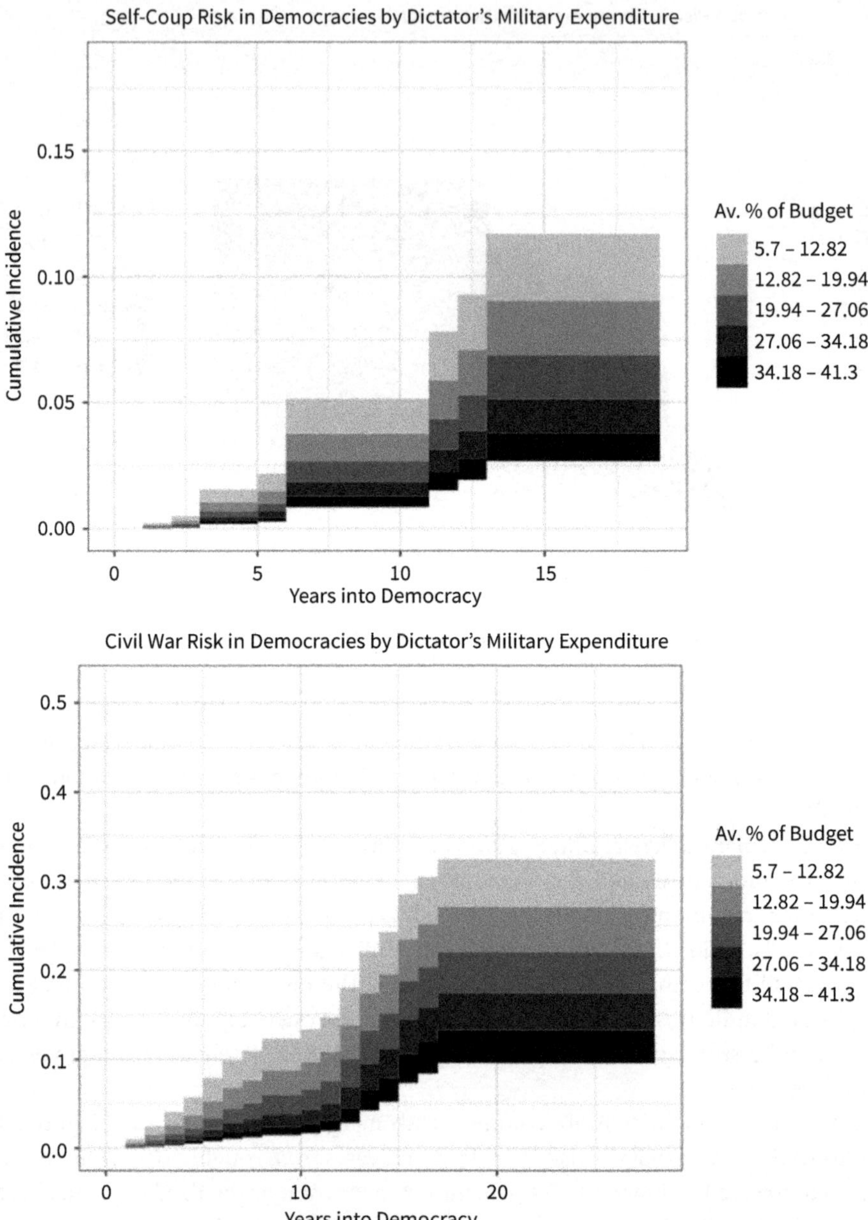

Figure 3.8 Incumbent Takeovers and Civil Wars in Democracies, 1946–2010

military coups. Where dictators had instead marginalized their militaries, democratization is comparatively easier, though still comes with relatively higher risks of civil wars and incumbent takeovers. These military legacies from autocracy thus shape both whether and how democracies break down.

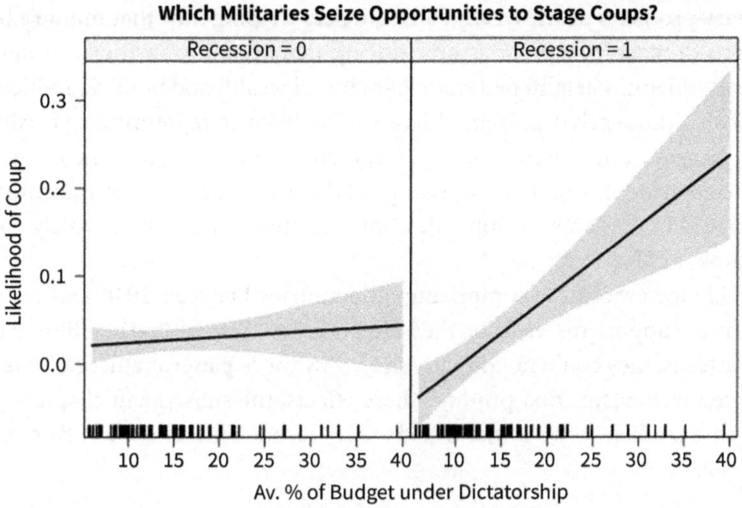

Which Militaries Seize Opportunities to Stage Coups?

Figure 3.9 Interaction of Military Legacies with Economic Recessions

Corollary: Economic Recessions

Traditional analyses of whether democracies fall to military coups have focused on the opportunity for the military to intervene, as proxied by economic recessions. Yet coups require both an opportunity and a motive: militaries must have grievance to seize that opportunity. To demonstrate even more directly that coups require both, Figure 3.9 interacts the level of military spending with an economic recession, coded as any negative annual change in GDP per capita.

As the panel on the left shows, without a recession, militaries have little opportunity to intervene. Even powerful, praetorian militaries will find it difficult to stage a coup when the government is popular. When a recession is present, however (right panel), *not all* militaries seize the opportunity to intervene. Coups come uniquely from empowered militaries, who have been aggrieved by democracy. Marginalized militaries, which gain from democracy, are seemingly wedded to the transition, ignoring the opportunity to overthrow it. These "soldiers of democracy" allow the transition to weather their "Brumairean" moments and live another day.

In short, democracies are most susceptible to military coups when both an opportunity and a motive are present. When a transition enters an economic recession with an empowered military, it is at grave risk of a coup.

Conclusion

This chapter sought to empirically test whether a dictator's coup-proofing strategy might create military legacies that shape the likelihood of democratization. In particular, it examined how a dictator's choice to either empower or marginalize the military produces downstream consequences shaping how that military behaves during pro-democracy uprisings and during democratic transitions. Empowered militaries, enjoying a heightened share of material wealth and political influence, are wary of losing those privileges, and thus are more likely to repress mass uprisings and stage coups against new democracies. Marginalized militaries, by contrast, are more likely to step aside during mass uprisings and support democratic transitions. Yet, they may also be less able to stop a descent into civil war and more easily co-opted into incumbent takeovers.

The evidence examined, comprising all countries between 1946 and 2010, provided strong support for each of these hypotheses. Yet, while they illustrated the overall patterns, they could not directly show why those patterns emerge. To tease out the precise mechanisms that produce these effects, the subsequent chapters present detailed case studies of two of the world's most recent democratic transitions: Egypt and Tunisia.

4
Case Selection: Egypt and Tunisia

Introduction

The focus of the next nine chapters are on Egypt and Tunisia. Why, after both populations toppled their dictators in the 2011 Arab Spring revolutions, did their paths so quickly diverge? Why did Egypt's democratic transition after just two years collapse in a military coup, while Tunisia's survived for over a decade, becoming the role model for the region?

The central argument of this book is that this divergence stemmed, first and foremost, from the nature of each country's military. In Egypt, a military that had been the center of power since 1952 saw democracy as a threat to its interests and identity, and once its losses materialized, it stepped in to end the transition. In Tunisia, by contrast, a military that had been neglected, marginalized, and counterbalanced under autocracy saw its position improve under democracy, producing support for the transition. How each military had been treated under autocracy thus shaped how they behaved under democracy.

I develop and detail this argument over the course of the next eight chapters. Chapters 5, 6, and 7 focus on Egypt, showing why the military became the center of power, and how that influenced the military both in the 2011 uprisings and in the 2013 coup. Chapter 8, 9, 10, and 11 then do the same in Tunisia, showing why the military was marginalized under autocracy and how that led it to shirk in the 2011 revolution, to ignore calls for a coup in 2013, and yet to facilitate the president's incumbent takeover in 2021. Chapter 12 then provides quantitative evidence of these hypotheses, drawing on original surveys conducted of each country's military.

This chapter, however, introduces the comparison between Egypt and Tunisia, demonstrating why they make for a fruitful comparison. I outline the similarities between them, showing how they "hold constant" factors like religion, culture, international context, mode of transition, and authoritarian legacies. I then refute six counter-explanations for their diverging transitions. I address the three major "mass-based" theories that claim that Tunisians were (1) more developed, (2) more culturally tolerant, or (3) more committed to democracy than Egyptians. I then address three elite-based theories that emphasize Tunisia's (4) more moderate Islamists, (5) more compromising secularists, or (6) stronger civil society. Refuting each in turn, the chapter instead puts forth the military as the primary cause of their diverging transitions. The chapter then contests and qualifies two common theories about their militaries: that Tunisia's military was simply (7) too small or (8) too professional

Soldiers of Democracy?. Sharan Grewal, Oxford University Press. © Sharan Grewal (2023).
DOI: 10.1093/oso/9780192873910.003.0004

to carry out a coup. Having addressed these counter-explanations, the subsequent chapters then turn to outlining and substantiating my theory.

The Puzzle

In the 2011 Arab Spring uprisings, Tunisians and Egyptians took to the streets en masse, rallying for the fall of the regime (*isqāt al-nizām*) and demanding bread, freedom, and social justice. In both cases, the protesters succeeded in toppling their long-time dictators. Tunisia's Zine El Abidine Ben Ali fled the country on January 14, 2011, while Egypt's Hosni Mubarak stepped down in turn on February 11.

The two countries then embarked on transitions to democracy, holding their first ever free and fair elections in the fall of 2011. In both cases, these historic elections propelled long-repressed Islamist movements out of the prisons and into the parliament. In Tunisia, the *Ennahda* (Renaissance) movement won the Constituent Assembly elections with 37 percent of the vote, while in Egypt, the Muslim Brotherhood (*Ikhwān al-Muslimīn*) won 37.5 percent of the vote in the elections for the People's Assembly.

The Islamists, however, lacked experience in governing, and faced monumental expectations from the revolutionaries. As the economy stagnated and security deteriorated, impatient populations quickly grew disillusioned with these newly elected governments. In both countries, protesters took to the streets once more. In the summer of 2013, mass protests now called for the fall of these elected governments, creating a "Brumairean moment" to overturn democracy. But here, the two transitions diverged.

In Egypt, the military, led by General Abdelfattah al-Sisi, seized the opportunity created by these protests to stage a coup and remove the elected President Mohamed Morsi. Sisi has since consolidated his control in Egypt, ending the short-lived democratic experiment and returning the country to a brutal military dictatorship.

In Tunisia, by contrast, the military did not intervene, ignoring the calls for it to follow the lead of its Egyptian counterpart. Without recourse to the military to topple the government, opposition elites eventually realized they had to negotiate with the Ennahda-led government. After two months of mass protests, Tunisia's political parties finally came together to negotiate a path forward under the auspices of four civil society organizations known as the Quartet. Subsequently, Tunisia held two additional rounds of free and fair presidential and parliamentary elections in 2014 and 2019, becoming the "success story" of the region. Although its democracy has since collapsed in an incumbent takeover in 2021, its survival for ten years made it the longest-lasting democracy in the region.

How do we explain these contrasting experiences? Why did Tunisia's transition to democracy survive for ten years while Egypt's failed in just two? Why, in particular, did Tunisia's military not follow Egypt's and stage a coup in 2013? As this contrast forms the central puzzle of this book, it is worth reflecting on how these two cases make for a fruitful comparison.

Similarities

The cases of Egypt and Tunisia help to "hold constant" a number of factors that might otherwise have shaped their likelihood of democracy. First, both transitions were sparked by the same wave of mass uprisings: the Arab Spring. The rate of success of a democratic transition has varied considerably by the wave in which it occurred,[1] whether as a result of diffusion effects during particular waves[2] or the global environment at the time. Occurring contemporaneously, Egypt and Tunisia's transitions thus hold constant structural factors of the international community, such as the post-Cold War dominance of the US alongside the steady rise of China and Russia, as well as diffusion effects from elsewhere in the region, like the collapse of neighboring Libya, Yemen, and Syria into civil war.

Second, both democratic transitions were initiated by mass revolutions, not top-down elite transitions. Observing the third wave, scholars highlighted that transitions were more successful when they formed pacts with soft-liners in the regime, resulting in elite-led transitions as opposed to unstable ruptures through mass uprisings.[3] However, more recently, scholars have argued that democratic transitions that begin through mass, nonviolent uprisings should be more likely to succeed.[4] Focusing on two cases of mass uprisings thus helps to hold constant these potential initiation effects.

Third, both Egypt and Tunisia are relatively homogenous countries, with Egypt 90 percent Sunni Muslim, and Tunisia, 99 percent. They thus avoid the sectarian and ethnic divisions that drove neighboring countries like Libya, Yemen, and Syria into civil war, and that generally make democratization more difficult.[5]

Fourth, despite that homogeneity, both transitions faced intense polarization along secular–Islamist lines. While both populations had been relatively united in toppling the former dictators, questions of identity then came to the fore as they tried to decide on what came next. Islamists offered one approach, arguing that religion should infuse the character of the state and inform its laws, pitting themselves against secular parties who tended to oppose a larger role for religion in politics. Election surveys show that attitudes toward religion and the state were by far the most important determinant of how both Egyptians and Tunisians voted in the founding elections.[6] With Islamists winning these elections and having a chance to input their beliefs into the constitutions, both countries quickly polarized along secular–Islamist lines.[7] Given that such cleavages are generally believed to be more polarizing than traditional, economic cleavages and hence more threatening to democracy,[8] the cases of Egypt and Tunisia are helpful for controlling for this factor, as well.

---

[1] Huntington (1991).
[2] Wejnert (2005); Gleditsch and Ward (2006); Weyland (2012).
[3] O'Donnell and Schmitter (1986); Huntington (1991); Linz and Stepan (1996).
[4] Chenoweth and Stephan (2011); Kadivar (2018, 2022); Pinckney (2020).
[5] Rustow (1970); Horowitz (1993).
[6] Ozen (2018); Dennison and Draege (2021).
[7] Hamid (2014); Ozen (2020).
[8] Rustow (1970).

Fifth, unlike most other countries in the region, neither Egypt nor Tunisia are resource-rich economies. Both do enjoy some resource rents: Egypt's oil reserves amount to 13.7 times its annual consumption, and Tunisia's about 12 times its annual consumption. Tunisia also boasts important phosphate reserves, with the state-owned *Compagnie de Phosphate de Gafsa* (CPG) the fifth largest phosphate company in the world. However, overall, natural resources amount to a very small fraction of each country's GDP: about 6.9 percent in Egypt and 3.3 percent in Tunisia.[9] Larger proportions of their GDPs are driven by their service sectors (54 percent and 64 percent of GDP, respectively), industry (34 percent and 26 percent), and agriculture (12 percent and 10 percent).[10] Neither country's democratic transition, therefore, could be expected to suffer from an oil or resource curse.[11]

Finally, both democratic transitions shared a similar authoritarian legacy. In both countries, the dictators ousted in the 2011 revolutions presided over dominant-party regimes with a history of autocratic elections. Egypt's Hosni Mubarak relied on the National Democratic Party (NDP) to win parliamentary super-majorities through rigged elections, while Tunisia's Zine El Abidine Ben Ali did the same through the Democratic Constitutional Rally (RCD). The NDP routinely received upwards of 70 percent of the vote in Egypt's parliamentary elections, and the RCD upwards of 80 percent in Tunisia's. Yet, both regimes still permitted a variety of opposition parties to split the remaining seats among themselves. Since a history of autocratic elections can bode well for democratic consolidation,[12] controlling for this legacy is another advantage of our case selection.

Existing Explanations

Given these similarities, it is only natural that much has already been written attempting to explain why Egypt and Tunisia's transitions diverged.[13] I review six of the most commonly cited explanations. I begin with the three "mass-based" theories, which argue that Tunisians are (1) more developed, (2) more culturally tolerant, and (3) more committed to democracy than Egyptians. In the next section, I then discuss three elite-based theories, which emphasize Tunisia's (4) more moderate Islamists, (5) more compromising secularists, or (6) stronger civil society.

Mass-Based Theories

Socioeconomic Explanations

Among the most common explanations for the divergence of Egypt and Tunisia's transitions is socioeconomic: that Tunisia is simply a more developed country, with a wealthier and better educated citizenry than in Egypt.[14] Given that globally, a

---

[9] Source: World Bank, 2018.
[10] Source: CIA World Factbook, 2017.
[11] Ross (2001).
[12] Miller (2013).
[13] For an excellent summary and analysis of the major theories, see Bellin (2018).
[14] Sanborn and Thyne (2014); Rapanos (2018).

Table 4.1 Socioeconomic Variables in Egypt and Tunisia, 2010

	Egypt	Tunisia
GDP per cap., PPP (2011 $)	9824	10121
% Literate	72	79
% University Education	30	35
% Unemployed	9	13
% under $1.90/day	3	2
% Gini coefficient	31.5	35.8
% Life expectancy	71	75

Source: World Bank Development Indicators, 2010

country's level of development is a standard correlate of democracy, it is widely assumed that this supposed difference in Egypt vs. Tunisia must also have played a role in these two cases, as well.

Putting aside the merit of these socioeconomic theories,[15] the data themselves do not quite support the assumed gap between Egypt and Tunisia. The World Bank's 2010 Development Indicators suggest that the two countries were actually more similar than different (Table 4.1). Tunisia enjoyed a slightly higher GDP per capita than Egypt ($10,121 v. $9,824 in 2011 international dollars),[16] but the difference is marginal, with both being classified as lower-middle income countries—middling countries for whom, statistically, democratization "could go either way."[17]

Likewise, each of the other socioeconomic indicators show more similarity than difference. Tunisia enjoys a slightly higher literacy rate (72 v. 79 percent) and proportion of citizens with a university education (30 v. 35 percent), and only a minor difference in the poverty rate (2 v. 3 percent) and life expectancy (71 v. 75 years). Moreover, some of the socioeconomic indicators in fact cut in the other direction: Tunisia actually had a higher unemployment rate (9 v. 13 percent) and greater inequality (Gini coefficient 31.5 v. 35.8) on the eve of the transition to democracy.[18]

A second socioeconomic explanation for democracy focuses less on the structural preconditions and more on the changes that occur during the transition itself. If economic recessions accompany democratic transitions, they tend to breed democratic breakdown.[19] Several have accordingly singled out Egypt's declining economy as the cause of its breakdown.[20]

However, the data likewise contradict this account. In PPP terms, Egypt's GDP per capita actually increased throughout its transition (Figure 4.1), rising from $9,686 in 2011 to $11,093 in 2012 and $11,221 in 2013.[21] Tunisia's GDP per capita, meanwhile, stayed stagnant, $10,576 in 2011 and $10,770 in 2013, such that Egypt even surpassed Tunisia.

---

[15] For critiques of the development–democracy nexus, see, e.g., Rustow (1970); O'Donnell and Schmitter (1986); Linz and Stepan (1996).

[16] See World Bank.

[17] Bellin (2018, p. 443).

[18] Both Gini indices likely underestimate the true rate of inequality. See Achcar (2020).

[19] Gasiorowski (1995); Bernhard, Reenock, and Nordstrom (2001).

[20] Cambanis (2015); Luciani (2017).

[21] Source: World Bank.

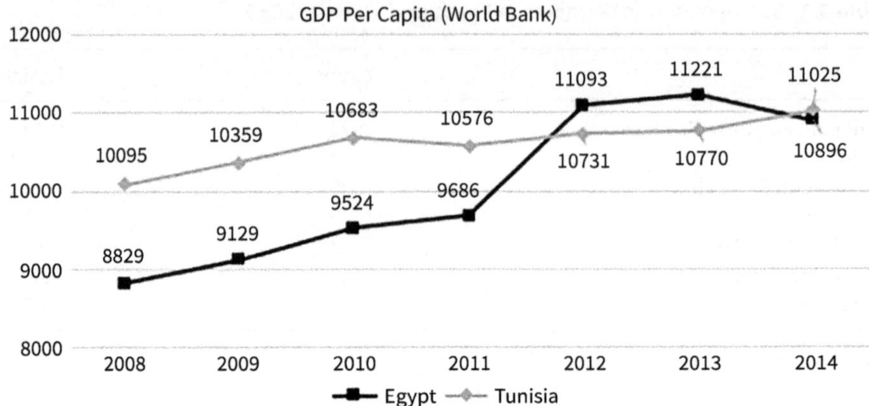

Figure 4.1 GDP Per Capita, PPP (Current International $), 2008–2014

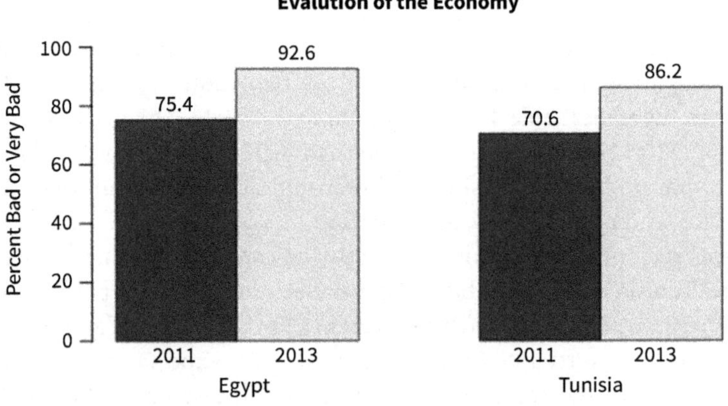

Figure 4.2 Evaluation of the Economy (Arab Barometer)

Survey data as well suggest that Tunisians were just as frustrated with the economy as Egyptians over the course of the transition. According to nationally representative surveys conducted by the Arab Barometer (Figure 4.2), almost 90 percent of both Egyptians and Tunisians rated the economy as "bad" or "very bad" in spring 2013, a 15-point increase from 2011.

In short, the data suggest that Egypt and Tunisia were more similar than different in terms of their socioeconomics, whether in their structural preconditions or their economic performance during the transition itself. Accordingly, while socioeconomic indicators may correlate with democracy globally, they have a more difficult time explaining Egypt and Tunisia's divergent transitions.

Culture

A second commonly heard explanation is cultural: that Tunisians for centuries had exhibited a more tolerant and consensual political culture than Egyptians. Stepan (2012) and Masri (2017), for instance, observe that Tunisia was the first Arab country to abolish slavery in 1846, and the first to write a constitution in 1861. They review the progressive writings of Tunisian thinkers Ibn Khaldun (1332–1406), Khayr al-Din (1820–1890), and Tahar Haddad (1899–1935), to argue that "Tunisia has a long intellectual and educational tradition that combines important secular and spiritual elements."[22] For Stepan, the roots of this cultural tolerance appear to lie in Tunisia's "links to the old Muslim kingdom of Andalusia in southern Spain and to the Ottoman Empire" (p. 97), while for Masri, the roots go back even further, to the Phoenician (and later Roman) city-state of Carthage, highlighting that "Tunisia has been non-Arab and non-Muslim longer than it has been either."[23] Accordingly, they imply that Tunisians' ability to compromise and make democracy work post-2011 reflects this more tolerant culture.

These cultural accounts have been critiqued on a number of grounds, not least of which for picking and choosing historical examples. Tunisia's more recent political experience, which would presumably be fresher in Tunisians' minds, was one of intolerance and repression under the dictatorships of Habib Bourguiba (1956–1987) and Zine El Abidine Ben Ali (1987–2011). Stepan tries to dismiss these decades—the entirety of Tunisia as an independent state—as simply an aberration, "lost decades" in this civilization's otherwise progressive march, but it is hard to believe that contemporary Tunisian political culture was influenced solely by Ibn Khaldun and Tahar Haddad, and not also by Bourguiba and Ben Ali. Tahar Haddad, we might add, was not embraced by Tunisian society, but banished and discredited as a heretic to live out his days in solitude.[24] These accounts also struggle to explain how Tunisia emerged as one of the largest exporters of foreign fighters to ISIS despite this tolerant culture.

Meanwhile, others have criticized these cultural explanations for neglecting important reformist movements and intellectuals in other Arab countries. Egypt, for instance, boasted reformist scholars with far greater influence and impact. As Tarek Masoud (2018, pp. 170–171) observes in his critique of Masri's book, "Masri even describes how, in the late-nineteenth and early-twentieth centuries, Tunisian reformers benefited from traffic with Egyptian intellectual giants including Muhammad Abduh, who argued for modernizing education (p. 148); Qasim Amin, who called for the empowerment of women (p. 160); and Taha Hussein, who argued for greater intellectual engagement with the West (p. 159)." We would be hard pressed to say that a reformist intellectual tradition distinguishes Tunisia from Egypt, when it may well have been influenced by Egypt's.

Moreover, the implication of these cultural arguments is that Tunisians are more tolerant and willing to compromise with one another than Egyptians, and that that is why its transition succeeded. Yet while Tunisia's *elites* may have found common ground (see next section), the masses were less eager to compromise. Public opinion data at the time suggests that Tunisians were as polarized as Egyptians during the transition.

---

[22] Stepan (2012, p. 97).
[23] Masri (2017, p. 104).
[24] Masri (2017, p. 225).

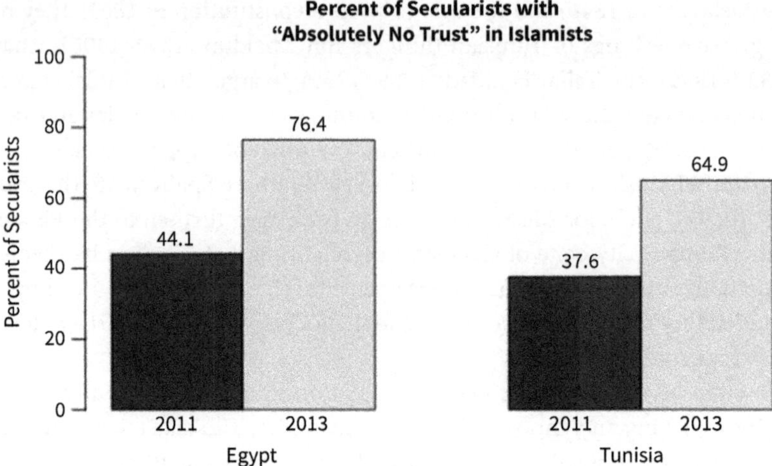

Figure 4.3 Secularists with "Absolutely No Trust" in Islamist Party (Arab Barometer)

Both Egypt and Tunisia's transitions polarized along secular–Islamist lines as the founding elections brought Islamists to power. Survey data from the Arab Barometer, a nationally representative poll conducted in 2011 and 2013,[25] help to illustrate the extent of polarization over the course of each country's transition. Figure 4.3 plots the percent of secularists[26] expressing "absolutely no trust" in their country's ruling Islamist party, the Egyptian Muslim Brotherhood or Tunisia's Ennahda. The survey data suggest that by 2013, a large majority of secularists in both countries—about 70 percent—had "absolutely no trust" in the Islamists. In both countries, that figure represented nearly a doubling of the percent of secularists reporting no trust since 2011.

In short, contrary to these cultural arguments, Tunisians appear to have become as polarized as Egyptians during their respective transitions.

Democracy

A final mass-based theory extends from the previous two, arguing that because of their culture and higher level of education, Tunisians were simply more committed to democracy than Egyptians. But the reality is that Tunisians became just as disillusioned as Egyptians.

[25] The 2011 survey was conducted between June 16 and July 3 in Egypt, and September 30 and October 11 in Tunisia, in both cases prior to the parliamentary elections. The 2013 survey was conducted between March 31 and April 7 in Egypt, and between February 3 and 25 in Tunisia, in both cases prior to the "Brumairean" moments of summer 2013.

[26] Secularists are coded as those who disagree or strongly disagree that "the government and parliament should enact laws in accordance with Islamic law." Despite advocating for a lesser role of religion in politics, this side of the spectrum tends not to refer to itself as "secular," given the atheistic connotations this word carries in Arabic.

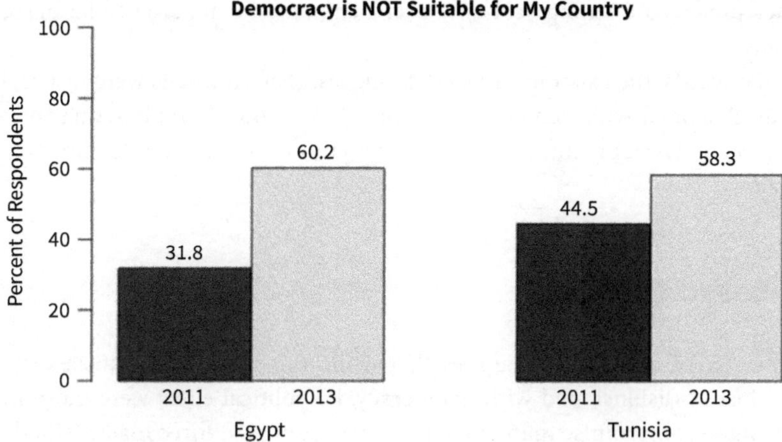

Figure 4.4 Democracy Is NOT Suitable for My Country (Arab Barometer)

With the economy stagnant and security deteriorating, Tunisians increasingly soured on democracy. Arab Barometer data reveal that by 2013, about 60 percent of Tunisians no longer felt that democracy was suitable for their country (Figure 4.4).[27] This level of disillusionment was similar to that in Egypt, where a similar 60 percent no longer supported democracy.[28]

The Arab Barometer also offers six other measures of support for democracy, and by each of these, Tunisians actually became *more* disillusioned with democracy than Egyptians. By 2013, Tunisians were more likely than Egyptians to say that "under a democratic system, the country's economic performance is weak" (36 v. 20 percent), that "democratic regimes are indecisive and full of problems" (50 v. 23 percent), that "democratic systems are not effective at maintaining order and stability" (41 v. 20 percent), that "a democratic system is not better than other systems" (15 v. 13 percent), that "the citizens in your country are not prepared for a democratic system" (60 v. 44 percent), and that "democracy negatively affects social and ethical values in your country" (45 v. 22 percent).

These results are not unique to the Arab Barometer. Survey data from the Pew Research Center likewise suggest that Tunisians by 2013 were more disillusioned with democracy than Egyptians.[29] In their 2013 survey, 72 percent of Tunisians said they were "not too satisfied" or "not at all satisfied" with democracy, while only 56 percent of Egyptians said the same. Similarly, 56 percent of Tunisians said they preferred stability over democracy, compared to only 43 percent of Egyptians, and 66 percent

[27] The Arab Barometer asked respondents whether democracy was suitable for their country on a 10 point scale. I code as suitable those ranking democracy above 5, the neutral category.

[28] For more on *who* became disillusioned with democracy in Egypt and Tunisia, see Grewal and Monroe (2019); Ketchley and El-Rayyes (2021).

[29] See Pew Global Attitudes Project, Spring 2013. The Egypt survey was conducted between March 3 and 23, 2013, and the Tunisia survey between March 4 and 19, 2013.

said they preferred a strong economy over democracy, compared to 52 percent of Egyptians.

In other words, the existing survey data suggest that Tunisians were just as, if not more, disillusioned with democracy. Contrary to accounts emphasizing their culture or level of development, Tunisians were no more committed to democracy than Egyptians.

Elite-Based Theories

A second set of explanations argues that while the masses in Tunisia may have become just as disillusioned with democracy, its political elites were more mature and willing to compromise than in Egypt. There are at least three major "elite-based" theories: that compared to Egypt, Tunisia boasts more moderate Islamists, more compromising secularists, or a stronger civil society. I respond to each in turn.

More Moderate Islamists

Among the most prominent elite theories is that Tunisia's Islamists were more moderate than Egypt's. There is no doubt that Ennahda is more liberal and relatively more secular than the Muslim Brotherhood, in part because Tunisia is a more secular country and many of Ennahda's leaders also lived in exile.[30] However, it is more difficult to make the case that Ennahda's more moderate nature was the reason Tunisia's transition succeeded, or even that it meant that polarization was any less severe. As Sharqieh (2013) astutely observed, while Ennahda was more moderate, Tunisia's secularists were more extreme than in Egypt:

> Tunisia also faces at least one kind of polarization that is more extreme than in other Arab cases: the vast (and growing) divide between Tunisia's secularist liberals and its ultraconservative Salafi Islamists. Tunisian secularism is vibrant and unparalleled in the Arab world; under Bourguiba and Ben Ali, Tunisia was the only Arab country to ban the hijab in state institutions. [. . .] Tunisia is a sharp contrast with Egypt, for example, where there was basic consensus on the establishment of Islam as the state religion; in Tunisia, the sheer distance between these two cultural extremes makes the chance that they will coalesce around one vision for the state rather slim.

Indeed, Tunisia's secularists, unlike Egypt's, actually opposed mentioning *shari'a* in the constitution, making this a contentious issue on which Ennahda's hardliners eventually had to concede. Likewise, Tunisia's secularists also more strongly championed women's rights, rallying against a clause Ennahda had inserted into a draft constitution making women "complementary," rather than equal, to men. And they succeeded in pushing a clause guaranteeing not just freedom of belief as in Egypt but

---

[30] Sharqieh (2013); Cavatorta and Merone (2013); Wolf (2017); Grewal (2020*a*).

freedom of conscience—permitting atheism as well. In short, even though Tunisia's Islamists were more moderate, its secularists were more "extreme." Hence, the ideological distance between the Islamists and secularists in Tunisia was as large as in Egypt.

In fact, nearly every accusation lobbed at Egypt's Muslim Brotherhood was also lobbed at Tunisia's Ennahda. In Egypt, the Brotherhood was accused of harboring a secret apparatus responsible for beating up protesters in the December 2012 *Ittihadiyya* protests. In Tunisia, Ennahda was likewise accused of harboring a secret apparatus responsible for assassinating two secular politicians in 2013. In Egypt, the Brotherhood was accused of turning a blind eye to militancy in the Sinai; in Tunisia, Ennahda was criticized for pursuing a lenient policy toward Ansar al-Sharia even after they attacked the US Embassy in September 2012, not declaring them a terrorist group until August 2013. In Egypt, the Brotherhood was accused of encouraging Egyptians to go on jihad in Syria; in Tunisia, Ennahda likewise was accused of facilitating the flow of foreign fighters and ultimately making Tunisia one of the top exporters of ISIS fighters. In short, despite its moderation, it is quite likely that had the Tunisian military intervened, we would be blaming Ennahda's radical policies just as we do the Brotherhood's.

Finally, the strongest critique of this argument is that it ultimately did not matter. Despite Ennahda's moderation, Tunisians still took to the streets demanding Ennahda's ouster just as Egyptians did for the Brotherhood. As Hamid (2014, p. 205) persuasively argues, attitudes toward Islamists seem almost inelastic: "[W]hat[ever] Islamists did or didn't do would have little effect on how their staunchest opponents viewed them. What frightened secularists wasn't what Ennahda had already done, but what it might do."

Indeed, this fear of and hostility towards Ennahda still runs deep today, long after the 2013 crisis. In a nationally representative survey I conducted in September 2019,[31] only 32 percent of Tunisians believed that Ennahda accepts democracy, with 43 percent saying it does not. Similarly, only 31 percent of Tunisians said that cohabitation with Ennahda was beneficial to the country, with 48 percent saying it was not. Most strikingly, 43 percent of Tunisians even said that Ennahda should be dissolved. Yes, Ennahda may have been more moderate and inclusive than the Brotherhood, but that did not breed much goodwill.

Secularists

A second elite theory argues that the difference lies not with the Islamists, but with the secularists. Tunisia's secular elites were simply more willing to cooperate and accept democracy than in Egypt. Masoud (2014), for instance, argues that Islamists and secularists were more evenly balanced electorally in Tunisia, such that secularists there felt they had a chance in elections. Yet with Morsi down to a 32 percent approval rating by June 2013, secularists in both countries should have thought they could

---

[31] The face-to-face survey of 1013 Tunisians was conducted by One to One for Research and Polling between September 10 and 14, 2019.

win the next elections. A second version of this argument emphasizes that Islamists and secularists in Tunisia had a longer history of working together, which built trust heading into the Arab Spring.[32] Many scholars have highlighted the October 2005 *collectif*, wherein Islamist and secularist leaders had come together to agree on several principles they wished to see under democracy.[33] But this account neglects the fact that Egypt had a similar history, with the Muslim Brotherhood forming an electoral alliance with the secular *al-Wafd* Party in 1984, participating in the Kefaya movement in the 2000s, and even collecting signatures for Mohamed ElBaradei in 2010.[34]

The most important critique of both of these arguments, however, is that the secularists in Tunisia, despite their electoral strength or trust in Islamists, still preferred to have Ennahda ousted and dissolved. Several of the secular leaders who signed the *collectif* still sided with the protesters in 2013: Mustapha Ben Jaafar, for instance, suspended the constituent assembly, and Hamma Hammami led many of the protests calling for the fall of the troika government. As I document in Chapter 10, secular leaders from across the spectrum praised Egypt's coup and called for it to be repeated in Tunisia. Even within the National Constituent Assembly, there was little solidarity with Ennahda beyond CPR and Ettakatol. A full 75 of the 79 remaining MPs signed on to a petition calling for Ennahda's dissolution in October 2012—even prior to any of the 2013 assassinations.[35]

Even Beji Caid Essebsi, the leader of the secular opposition who began the negotiations with Ennahda in 2013, did not do so out of some firm belief that Ennahda deserved a place in politics. On the contrary, Essebsi tried hard to get Ennahda forcefully ejected from power like the Brotherhood was in Egypt. As late as September 2013, after dialogue had begun, Essebsi was still threatening an Egypt-scenario. Essebsi was asked explicitly by NPR's Leila Fadel (2013): "[C]ould Tunisia become Egypt, with the Islamists forced from power and persecuted by a military-backed regime?" Essebsi answered, "Now, no . . . But . . . if we don't go forward, maybe yes." Likewise, as late as December 2013, Essebsi was threatening Ennahda with prosecutions, telling Weymouth (2013a) that: "They [Ennahda] are scared because of what happened during their time, but nonetheless we cannot give them any guarantees [of immunity]. The only guarantee is that there will be a process of justice."

Moreover, once his marriage of convenience with Ennahda unraveled, then-President Essebsi once again threatened Ennahda with judicial dissolution. In November 2018, Essebsi legitimized rumors that Ennahda harbored a secret apparatus responsible for the 2013 assassinations by instructing his national security council to investigate the matter.[36] Meanwhile, he met with the lawyers filing that accusation in the counter-terrorism judicial pole to dissolve Ennahda on that basis. Despite Ennahda's moderation, despite any shared history, despite an even balance

---

[32] Stepan (2016); Hassan and Kodouda (2019); Kilavuz (2019); Nugent (2020).

[33] Many secularists, however, doubted Ennahda's commitment to the *collectif*, and denied it made any difference in the transition (Saati, 2018).

[34] Browers (2007); Shorbagy (2007); Egypt Independent (2010); Magued (2020).

[35] See Le Monde (2012).

[36] al Ghanmi (2018).

of power—still Ennahda was not viewed as a legitimate political actor even in the eyes of the secularists who negotiated with them.

Instead, I argue that the main reason that secularists came to the negotiating table in Tunisia but not in Egypt was that *they had no other choice* in Tunisia. In Egypt, the secularists knew that the military would help them, that the generals were eager to jump in and force Morsi out of power as soon as possible. By contrast, in Tunisia, there was no such "outside option." After two months of protests, secularists had no choice but to come to the table.

Civil Society

A final elite theory argues that Tunisia's transition succeeded due to its stronger civil society. These scholars in particular highlight the role played by the Nobel Peace Prize-winning Quartet, especially the Tunisian General Labor Union (UGTT), in bringing Islamists and secularists to the table and mediating the National Dialogue in the fall of 2013.[37]

But the first issue is that the UGTT was also partly responsible for the crisis in the first place. It had been spearheading many of the protests and strikes against the troika, both in the wake of Belaid's assassination and after Brahmi's. It was openly calling for the fall of the democratically elected government, and eventually succeeded in securing it, so much so that the UGTT is often considered the Tunisian equivalent of Egypt's military, and UGTT leader Houcine Abassi as Tunisia's Sisi.

Still, there is no doubt that the role the Quartet played starting in September 2013 was unique and contributed to resolving the crisis, regardless of who caused it. But those negotiations did not begin until two months after Brahmi was assassinated. At that point, the secularists had already given up on a military coup, and resorted to the Quartet's offer of dialogue as a second best. In other words, had Tunisia's military been like Egypt's, and seized the opportunity to stage a coup in August 2013, there would have been no National Dialogue to speak of.

Likewise, if Egypt's military's had not intervened immediately after June 30, it is not inconceivable that Morsi and the NSF might have had to sit down for negotiations. If the outside option of the military was not available, it is quite possible that the NSF leaders would have eventually resigned themselves to dialogue, maybe even in the presence of civil society mediators. In both countries, the military's decision to intervene or not was temporally prior to the involvement of civil society, making it the key variable to explain.

The Military

For these reasons, I argue that the most important difference in explaining Egypt and Tunisia's divergent transitions was the behavior of their militaries. Egypt's military staged a coup to end the transition; Tunisia's did not. But the differences do not end

---

[37] Netterstrøm (2016); Yousfi (2018); Hartshorn (2019); Bishara (2020).

there. Egypt's military had also taken an interest in the transition from the start, running the show directly through the Supreme Council of the Armed Forces (SCAF), while Tunisia's instead retreated behind the scenes. Egypt's military likewise played each political party off against each other, polarizing and breeding mistrust between them, while Tunisia's played no such role. Even in the 2011 revolution, the Egyptian military only begrudgingly abandoned Mubarak, while Tunisia's more readily shirked in favor of the protesters.

Scholars have thus far put forth two primary explanations for why the Egyptian and Tunisian militaries behaved so differently during the revolution and transition: that Tunisia's military was too weak to stage a coup, or too professional to do so. I do not deny that capacity and professionalism played important roles. Indeed, I incorporate them in my account, showing how a dictator's coup-proofing strategy shapes the military's capacity and professionalism. Tunisia's military, I argue, became weak and apolitical as a result of Bourguiba and Ben Ali's decision to marginalize it. Yet, I argue that these factors are secondary to each military's corporate interests in explaining their divergent behavior during the Arab Spring.

Capacity

The first possible explanation for why Tunisia's military did not stage a coup in 2013 is that it was simply too weak to do so, boasting neither the size nor strength to carry one out. On average, a military's capacity is an important determinant in whether it can stage a coup. But in any particular case, one must consider the military's capacity relative to the potential resistance to the coup. If there is no resistance, even a small military could stage a coup.

Egypt's military, after all, had been quite weak when it staged its first coup in 1952. At the time, it had been "understaffed, unequipped, and trained for little more than parade ground marches."[38] It numbered just 36,000 out of a population of 21 million, half the size per capita of Tunisia's today.[39] Yet, such a military was able to overthrow Egypt's despised monarchy because there was little resistance. Indeed, Nasser would go on to boast that just "ninety officers with only small arms" were all that were needed "to take over a nation" as big as Egypt.[40]

Tunisia's military, by contrast, could never stage a coup against Bourguiba or Ben Ali because it was certain to face armed resistance from the national guard and presidential guard. Such forces kept the military in check under dictatorship. But in 2013, each of these counterbalancing forces would likely have been *supportive* of a coup, having been made worse off under democracy. Had the military wanted to stage a coup, these counterbalancing forces would have gone along with the attempt, rather than blocked it.

---

[38] Kandil (2012, p. 7).
[39] Tunisia's in 2013 numbered 36,000 in a population of 11 million.
[40] Quoted in Be'eri (1970).

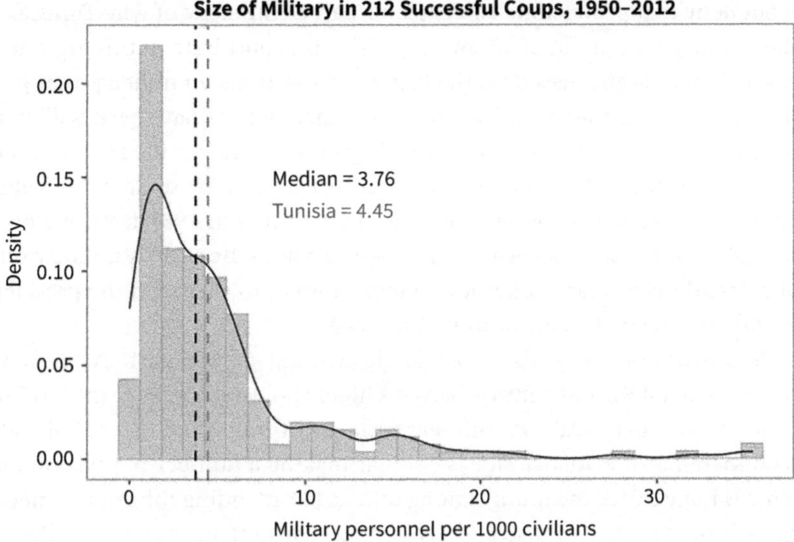

Figure 4.5 Tunisian Military's Capacity to Coup in Comparative Perspective

And together, the Tunisian military, national guard, and presidential guard would have had more than enough firepower to carry out a coup and run the country in 2013. Figure 4.5 places Tunisia in comparative perspective, relative to all 212 successful coups between 1950 and 2012 (from Powell and Thyne (2011)). In these coups, the median size of the military (from the Correlates of War, Singer, Bremer, and Stuckey (1972)) was 3.76 soldiers per 1,000 civilians. Figure 4.5 shows that Tunisia comes in above the median, at 4.45 soldiers per 1,000 civilians, when including the national guard, and just under the median, at 3.27 soldiers, when not.

The data thus suggest that in combination with the national guard and presidential guard, Tunisia's military would likely have been able to stage a coup in 2013. Had it wanted to, it would have been supported by the national guard, presidential guard, and the majority of the population. The key variable is thus not its capacity, but its will: as I will show in subsequent chapters, it did not have any interest in staging a coup.

Professionalism

Beyond capacity, a second commonly heard explanation is professionalism. Almost every scholar who has posited the importance of Tunisia's military has argued that it did not stage a coup because it is thoroughly professional.[41] Bou Nassif (2015a, p. 80), one of the most impressive scholars of the Tunisian military, claims that "putsches are anathema to its institutional culture." Likewise, almost all of the military officers and civilians I interviewed in Tunisia also paid lip service to this idea of the Tunisian military being a "republican" institution far from politics.

---

[41] See, e.g., Bou Nassif (2015a); Bellin (2018).

I do not deny that professionalism explains part of the story of why Tunisia's military did not stage a coup in 2013. But I qualify and contribute to this argument in three ways. First, I argue, based on the history of the Tunisian military, that professionalism is not the full story. At least some Tunisian officers have been willing both to plot and carry out coups. As I show in Chapter 8, Tunisian military officers have plotted at least three coups: (1) a foiled coup plot by Youssefists in 1962 featuring seven military officers; (2) a foiled coup plot by Islamists in 1987 featuring 66 military officers; and (3) the successful "bloodless" coup by Ben Ali, a military officer, who dispatched his military colleague, Habib Ammar, to surround the presidential palace while he declared a constitutional succession.

This "politicization" was also not simply a thing of the past. As I show in Chapter 10, General Rachid Ammar played a highly political role after the 2011 revolution. Despite his rhetorical commitment to the constitution and to professionalism, the preponderance of evidence shows Ammar making a number of political moves between 2011 and 2013, including among others, (1) attending ministerial meetings in 2011 as if he were the minister of defense; (2) shirking in response to President Marzouki's order to defend the US embassy in September 2012; (3) advising the troika to resign in the wake of Chokri Belaid's assassination in February 2013; and (4) criticizing the troika government while in uniform in a 3-hour live TV interview in June 2013.

Of the nearly 50 interviews I conducted with Tunisian military officers, only 1 officer refused adamantly to discuss political topics. All the rest were open to it, even to discuss taboo topics such as military coups. One retired brigadier-general argued that he would support a coup if the country was headed toward civil war:

> "I can understand the intervention of the armed forces in the case that everything collapsed. It would be necessary. It would be a crime if the armed forces did nothing. We cannot be sitting here while people are killing each other. It would not be aiming for power, but aiming for the security of population, to stabilize the situation in coordination with civilian powers. And if the civilian power collapses, we can temporarily take power to stabilize and then quickly give back power. I can accept and support such a move."[42]

Another retired Brigadier-General supported the notion of a "democratizing coup," one that restores democracy:

> "The military coup is not a taboo. In some democracies, we'll say it's absolutely forbidden. But others will say there is a possibility for a military coup when the situation is getting worse, and the aim of the coup is to reform."[43]

These statements are not unlike statements we hear from the Egyptian military, who argued that their intervention in July 2013 was also to restore democracy, prevent

---

[42] Interview with retired officer, Tunis, December 2015.
[43] Interview with retired officer, Tunis, March 2020.

civil war, and stabilize the country. In short, the historical record reveals that at least some Tunisian officers were willing to get involved in politics and even plot coups. While most officers may be professional, it cannot explain the full story. After all, if the Tunisian military had been thoroughly professional, why did every Tunisian president until that point—Bourguiba, Ben Ali, and Marzouki—all fear a military coup? Why did they go to such great lengths to coup-proof the military?

The second qualification I make of the professionalism argument is to observe that what matters is not whether an officer identifies as professional, but how they conceive of professionalism. Egyptian military officers, after all, also adamantly claim that they are fully professional. Sadat (1977, p. 234) explicitly embarked on a policy of professionalizing the armed forces upon coming to power in 1970, and officers and observers alike credit that policy with the military's improved performance in the 1973 war.[44] "We are not a political army—we are professional," observed one senior officer proudly. "That is why we achieved the crossing of the Suez Canal in 1973."[45] By 1982, the CIA was even concluding that "the Egyptian officer corps is by far the most professional in the Arab Middle East," explaining that: "Its professionalism is enhanced by a system of promotion by merit and a by a large and diversified education and training program. These have instilled expertise, discipline, and a sense of national accountability in the officer corps to a degree unequaled by any other professional group."[46]

Many scholars have likewise argued that the Egyptian military is professional. Eva Bellin (2012, p. 134), for instance, argues that the Egyptian military did not fire on protesters during the 2011 revolution because it was professional, in the sense of "not linked by blood or ethnicity to Hosni Mubarak and his family." Abdul Aziz and Hussein (2001, p. 85) likewise argued that if Hosni Mubarak had attempted to follow Hafez al-Assad's lead in appointing his son Field Marshall, "the move would be clearly rejected on the basis of the professionalism of the military." For Harb (2003, p. 282), the military's "professionalism was evident in recruitment, equipment acquisition, and training."

However, it is clear that the professionalism of the Egyptian military is different than that of the Tunisian military. They may both be professional in the sense of having (relatively) meritocratic recruitment and promotion practices, routinized organizational procedures, and an emphasis on training and education. Yet they very clearly differ in their conceptions of professionalism as it relates to the role of the military in the state. For the Tunisian military, professionalism means staying out of politics. Even a public statement like the Egyptian military made in 2011 saying that they would not fire on protesters would be considered by Tunisian officers as an inappropriate incursion into politics (even if they agree with that sentiment). But for the Egyptian military, being the guardian of the state, "ruling but not governing,"[47] is part of its professionalism. It is the role that it must play, and deserves to play, in the

---

[44] See, e.g, Harb (2003); Brooks (2008); Hashim (2011*a*).

[45] Quoted in Views from Abroad, "Sadat's Power Base," *Journal of Palestine Studies* 7:2 (1978), p. 160.

[46] CIA, "Egypt: The Roots, Values, and Attitudes of the Officer Corps," Reading Room, March 1982.

[47] Cook (2007).

state. That guardianship role is not perceived as contradicting professionalism, but instead is viewed as part of its professional mission.

Indeed, Egyptian officers see no contradiction between professionalism and the political role they play. Defense Minister Abd al-Halim Abu Ghazala (1981–1989), for instance, saw no problem with himself being an active-duty officer as defense minister. There was still, in his mind, civilian control over the military since "[t]he armed forces are always under the control of the government. We receive orders, execute them, do our duty as best we can and then return to our barracks—that is all."[48] Likewise, current President Abdelfattah al-Sisi continues to view the military as professional despite his toppling of the elected president Mohamed Morsi: "The Egyptian military does not make coup d'états," he told Weymouth (2013*b*) after his coup. "The last coup was in the fifties." The conflation of politics and professionalism in the Egyptian military had led it to not even view its very political actions as unprofessional.

In short, what matters is not whether the military believes itself to be professional but how it conceives of or defines professionalism. If being professional means being apolitical, then professionalism may well produce an aversion to coups. But if one's conception of professionalism includes the military serving as the guardian of the state, then it may even legitimize or help justify a coup.

In turn, the third and most important contribution of this book to professionalism is understanding how these differing conceptions of professionalism arise in the first place. I argue that the Tunisian military came to see professionalism as being apolitical, while the Egyptian military came to see it as being political, due to their dictators' coup-proofing strategies. As I demonstrate in the chapters that follow, in Egypt, where the military was elevated to be the center of power, officers became socialized into seeing that role as appropriate and professional. Meanwhile, politicized, power-seeking individuals came to enroll into the army, viewing it as the most promising route to political power. Both of these mechanisms, recruitment and socialization, instead produced the opposite result in Tunisia. Where the military was marginalized and kept far from politics, officers were socialized into seeing *that* role as appropriate and professional, while its marginal status meant it did not attract individuals seeking fame or fortune, only those seeking to serve their country or simply make a living. In short, the third contribution of this study is to show where the Tunisian military's apolitical conception of professionalism originated, showing that it stems first and foremost from the dictator's coup-proofing strategies.

Conclusion

In this chapter, I addressed several of the most common hypotheses for explaining why Egypt and Tunisia's transitions diverged. Among the masses, I showed that Tunisians were no more developed, tolerant, or committed to democracy than

---

[48] Quoted in Satloff (1988, p. 15).

Egyptians. Among the elites, I showed that despite Tunisia's more moderate Islamists, more compromising secularists, and stronger civil society, Tunisia still entered its "Brumairean" moment in 2013, with the secular opposition knocking on the door of the barracks asking the military to follow the lead of its Egyptian counterpart. With mass protests, institutional paralysis, and severe security threats, Tunisia seemed ripe for a coup in 2013.

But the Tunisian military did not intervene, allowing the transition a second chance. Only then, after it became clear that the military would not intervene, did Tunisia's political parties and civil society come together to hold a national dialogue. The military's behavior, therefore, is at the heart of understanding why Tunisia's transition avoided Egypt's path to democratic breakdown. In the following chapters, I present my argument, showing how the military's behavior was shaped, first and foremost, by the coup-proofing strategies pursued by each country's previous autocrats.

5

Egypt: Empowering the Military

Introduction

The central argument of the next three chapters is that the failure of Egypt's 2011–2013 democratic transition stemmed first and foremost from the nature of its military. To understand its nature, we must first return to its origins.

Our story begins with the Free Officers coup of 1952, which toppled the monarchy of King Farouk and initiated the military-led republic that rules the country to this day. Having come to power through a coup, the Free Officers were acutely aware that the military could make or break their rule. Free Officer Gamal Abdel Nasser, who served as Egypt's president from 1954 to 1970, decided that his best strategy for coup-proofing the military was to empower it, investing it into his regime. His choice to empower the military, rather than marginalize it, was influenced in part by structural factors and security threats, but also in large part due to his personal belief that the army was the only force capable of implementing the political and social transformations he sought.

Nasser accordingly secured the military's loyalty through two tactics: power-sharing and stacking. First, he granted the military almost complete autonomy over its affairs, and lavished it with a large budget and a steady stream of weapons from the Soviet Union. Politically, he permitted the military to claim the plurality of cabinet positions, as well as thousands of posts throughout the bureaucracy, initiating what Sayigh (2012) would later call the "Officers' Republic." Alongside power-sharing, however, Nasser also attempted to stack the military with like-minded officers, infusing his ideology of secular pan-Arabism into the military, while purging communists and Islamists from its ranks. Combined, the two strategies allowed Nasser to survive in power until his death in 1970. More importantly, they would set Egypt on a path-dependent course for the next half-century.

Nasser's successor, Anwar Sadat (1970–1981), tried his best to maintain both strategies—power-sharing and stacking—but with some modifications. The military continued to claim the most powerful political positions, including the president, vice-president, and defense minister, and to enjoy a bloated budget and a growing role in the economy. However, the military's humiliating defeat to Israel in 1967 also led to a shift away from a direct, "ruler praetorianism" to an indirect or "moderator praetorianism,"[1] with the military preferring to nurse its reputation by ruling increasingly from behind the scenes. The war with Israel would also lead Sadat to

---

[1] Stepan (1971), Perlmutter (1974); Nordlinger (1977); Cook (2007).

Soldiers of Democracy?. Sharan Grewal, Oxford University Press. © Sharan Grewal (2023).
DOI: 10.1093/oso/9780192873910.003.0005

modify Nasser's stacking of the military, attempting to shift its pan-Arabism towards an Egyptian nationalism, in order to facilitate the 1979 peace treaty. Most importantly, Sadat also loosened the stacking of the military with secularists by allowing Islamists to enter the officer corps. That loosening of Nasser's strategies would end up proving fatal for Sadat, who was assassinated by an Islamist Lieutenant in 1981.

Sadat's successor, Hosni Mubarak (1981–2011), in turn reinstated and indeed strengthened both coup-proofing strategies. The military under Mubarak exercised what amounted to veto power over both security and economic policy, and thoroughly populated the bureaucracy from top to bottom. The military also became heavily involved in the civilian economy, developing a formidable economic empire that Springborg (2011) terms "Military, Inc." Crucially, Mubarak also reinforced the stacking of the military with secular Egyptian nationalists, banning even those with distant relatives in the Muslim Brotherhood. Notably, the two strategies also began to reinforce one another, with the political and material wealth of the army helping to attract the secular elite to the officer corps.

In short, each of Egypt's autocrats after the 1952 coup chose to coup-proof the military through a share of power and shared identity, strategies intended to empower and invest the military into the regime. These strategies remained relatively path-dependent despite changes in leadership, political assassination, and even defeat in war. The chapter thus sets the scene for showing how the military's empowerment would in turn shape its behavior in the 2011 revolution (Chapter 6) and subsequent transition (Chapter 7).

The Coup of 1952

The stirrings behind the momentous revolution of 1952 began decades earlier, when frustration with the British occupation swelled into popular mobilization. Among those taking to the streets in 1935 was a high school student named Gamal Abdel Nasser, who recalled "shout[ing] from my heart for complete independence [. . . and] demand[ing] that the leaders of Egypt unite to agree upon a single policy."[2] Politicians were spurred into action, but the agreement they reached—the Anglo-Egyptian Treaty of 1936—"dealt a severe blow to my expectations,"[3] Nasser wrote, for it continued to permit over 10,000 British troops to remain on Egyptian soil. The episode confirmed to Nasser that Egypt's political class could not achieve the independence he sought.

The Treaty, however, lowered the entrance requirements into the military academy, permitting lower-middle-class men like Nasser to enroll. Nasser thus joined the army in 1937, but would soon be frustrated by how powerless it also was to defend Egypt's sovereignty. In 1942, British troops surrounded the Al-Abdeen Palace, declared King Farouk "a prisoner of the British Army,"[4] and forced him to appoint

[2] Nasser (1955, pp. 50–51).
[3] Ibid, p. 51. See also Neguib (1955, pp. 72–73)'s discussion of the treaty.
[4] Neguib (1955, p. 86).

a prime minister more friendly to the Allies' war efforts in World War II. Some 400 officers, including Nasser, offered to fight back, but were told to stand down.[5] "I am ashamed that our army has not reacted against this attack," Nasser would write to a friend.[6] "We accepted what happened on our knees in surrender."[7]

Nasser's frustrations with King Farouk would only escalate further in 1948, when the king sent the Egyptian army to war with the new state of Israel against the advice of the military leadership, who knew they were not prepared.[8] To make matters worse, King Farouk had purchased defective weapons from European powers, resulting in an embarrassing defeat.[9] Nasser would write that Egypt "has been deceived and forced into a battle for which she was not ready, her fate the toy of greed, conspiracy, and lust, which left her without weapons under fire."[10] That Nasser was sent as part of the delegation to negotiate the truce only added to his humiliation.

Upon their return to Egypt, the officers were then tasked with domestic repression to prevent Egyptians from attacking British installations. To ensure the military's loyalty,[11] the king appointed his brother-in-law as war minister, and other loyalists as chief of staff and commander-in-chief. But their use in domestic repression, especially when they supported the people's nationalist cause, did not sit well with the officers. Nasser observed that: "We have been used by the Despot as a bogey[man] to give the people nightmares; now it is high time that the bogey[man] be turned against the Despot to shatter his own dreams."[12]

Indeed, since their 1949 defeat in Palestine, Nasser had begun to assemble a group of officers, self-styled the Free Officers, to seize power and abolish the monarchy.[13] On July 23, 1952, they struck, arresting the military leadership and exiling the king. A 14-member Revolutionary Command Council (RCC) was then set up to govern the country, with Nasser at its core.

Gamal Abdel Nasser

From 1952 to 54, Lt. Colonel Nasser led the RCC behind the higher-ranking and initially better-known Major General Muhammad Neguib. With the abolition of the monarchy, Neguib was appointed Egypt's first president in 1953, with Nasser as his minister of interior.

---

[5] Kandil (2016, p. 231).

[6] Quoted in Aburish (2004, p. 18).

[7] Nasser (1955, p. 25). This was the "breaking point" for Neguib (1955, p. 14) as well.

[8] Neguib (1955, pp. 15–16) claimed a guerilla war would have been more effective.

[9] For details, see Neguib (1955, pp. 16–17).

[10] Nasser (1955, p. 23).

[11] The King was also afraid that if deployed, the military might stage a coup against him. He only agreed to use the military for repression after receiving assurances from the US Ambassador that "he would use the power, the might, the majesty of the United States to make sure the military would withdraw" afterwards. See Dee (2012).

[12] Nasser (1955, p. 31).

[13] Neguib (1955, pp. 98–99) claims they were not planning on revolting until 1955, but they were encouraged by their success in the January 1952 officers' club elections, when Neguib won 276 of 334 votes for president, and other Free Officers won as well.

But friction between them would soon emerge, in part due to disagreements over whether the military should stay in power or hand over the reins to civilians.[14] Neguib favored a retreat to the barracks, advocating in 1954 for "demilitarizing the Government, creating a constituent assembly, and holding a referendum to prepare the Egyptian people for a free election."[15] Nasser, however, viewed political parties and civilian experts as self-serving and divisive, and perceived the military's role to be more transformational: as the only force capable of completing both a political revolution (independence) and a social one (addressing class inequalities).[16] Nasser accordingly wrestled power from Neguib, becoming Egypt's president from 1954 to 1970.[17]

Nasser was acutely aware of the political importance of the military, having come to power through a military coup and having relied on the support of the military to sideline Neguib. He could not afford to let the military oust him, as well. Yet, like every leader, Nasser faced a choice over how to coup-proof the military. One approach would have been to marginalize and counterbalance the military, removing it from political and material power and instead building up a paramilitary or militia force to protect him from the army. The other approach, the one which Nasser pursued, was instead to empower the military: to maintain its loyalty through a steady stream of material perks and political appointments, and to stack it top to bottom with his supporters.

In making this decision to empower rather than marginalize the military, Nasser was influenced both by structural factors and by his personal preferences. On the one hand, structurally, the military had just staged a coup to popular acclaim, with its officers now expecting a growing role for themselves in the state. Sidelining it after it brought Nasser to power would have been a difficult endeavor. Contrast Nasser's situation with that of Habib Bourguiba in Tunisia: when Bourguiba came to power in 1956, the Tunisian military did not even exist yet, giving him a freer hand in deciding how to coup-proof. In that sense, Nasser was constrained by preexisting structures, namely the existence, popularity, and politicization of the military.

Security threats also played a role in convincing Nasser to empower the military. Part of the spark behind the 1952 coup was the military's devastating loss to Israel in 1948. Restoring Egypt's pride was an important mission for Nasser, and that would require, if necessary, military force to oust the British and defeat Israel. As the late Egyptian scholar Anouar Abdel-Malek observed, "[I]f we take into account the geopolitical vulnerability of Egypt, the need to build a strong army was a logical consequence."[18] Nasser was therefore more predisposed to investing into the military than marginalizing it.

Finally, and most importantly, Nasser also personally wanted the military to play a larger role in politics. In his mind, as already alluded to, the military was the only

---

[14] See Be'eri (1970, p. 114), Kandil (2016, p. 235).
[15] Neguib (1955, p. 233).
[16] Nasser (1955, pp. 34–42).
[17] For more on their power struggle, see Vatikiotis (1978, pp. 138–151).
[18] See Abdel-Malek (1968, p. xxiii).

force capable of completing the political and social transformations he desired. As he wrote in 1955:

> The situation demanded the existence of a force set in one cohesive framework, far removed from the conflict between individuals and classes, and drawn from the heart of the people: a force composed of men able to trust each other; a force with enough material strength at its disposal to guarantee a swift and decisive action. These conditions could be met only by the Army.[19]

In short, Nasser preferred to empower, rather than marginalize, the military. Accordingly, his coup-proofing strategy became one of empowerment: keeping the officers happy through a share of power and a shared identity.

The first part of this strategy meant investing into and empowering the military, granting it a dominant share of both material resources and political power. The military's budget skyrocketed, rising from 3.9 percent of gross national product in 1950 to 12.3 percent in 1965.[20] A larger budget meant higher salaries across the board, and more funds to invest into equipment and weapons. The military also began to develop its own arms industry, setting up the National Organization for Military Production in 1954. Nasser likewise courted massive increases in military aid from the Soviet Union. The military swelled from 80,000 troops in 1955 to over 180,000 by 1965.[21]

That this empowering of the military was designed to buy its loyalty was not lost on observers at the time. Miles Copeland, the CIA station chief in Cairo, observed that:

> Nasser made it quite clear to our ambassadors that his regime relied on the military for its insurance, and that he regarded a "shabby army as a potentially disloyal army." [. . . The officers'] loyalty could be ensured by catering to their healthier wants: prestige, a few harmless privileges, a few inexpensive perquisites, and, above all, a service of which they could be proud.[22]

But salaries and weapons were not the only ways Nasser bought the military's loyalty. A related element was granting it autonomy over its own affairs.[23] The defense minister (at that point called war minister) was always an active-duty military officer, preventing any civilian oversight over the military's activities. "Egypt's generals did not want to answer to a civilian minister of defense, and Nasser was keen on keeping them loyal."[24] The military in 1956 was also exempted from any external audit or inspection of its finances and assets.[25] That autonomy and lack of oversight in

---

[19] Nasser (1955, p. 42).
[20] Bou Nassif (2021, p. 68).
[21] See Hurewitz (1969, Table 2).
[22] Copeland (1969, p. 101).
[23] Kandil (2012) even claims the military had so much autonomy as to mobilize for war with Israel in 1967 without Nasser's consent.
[24] Bou Nassif (2021, p. 59), relying on the memoirs of Defense Minister Amine Huweidi (1992).
[25] Decree 263 of 1956; see Sayigh (2019, p. 26).

turn provided opportunities for corruption, most notably during the War in Yemen (1962–1967).[26]

The Defense Ministry was not the only political office monopolized by the generals. All of the most important political positions, including Nasser's vice-presidents,[27] prime ministers,[28] and interior ministers,[29] were staffed exclusively by military officers, particularly his co-conspirators from 1952. About 35–45 percent of each cabinet under Nasser were military officers, and this shot up to 55 percent in 1966 and 66 percent on the eve of the 1967 war.[30] About 60 seats in parliament were reserved for military officers, including the speaker and deputy speaker.[31] Sharing political power with the military was viewed by observers as yet another way of satisfying the officers' interests and thus keeping them loyal.[32]

Notably, the appointment of military officers into political positions did not stop at the top levels. Thousands of military officers were appointed throughout the bureaucracy, providing officers with cushy post-retirement careers, or for the more politicized, a route into the halls of power. Abdel-Malek (1968, p. xxiii) estimates that 1,500 military officers were "appointed to the upper ranks of the nonmilitary establishment [. . .] between 1952 and 1964." According to Be'eri (1970, p. 427), in 1962, 25 of the 58 Egyptian ambassadors (43 percent) were former officers; by 1964, 48 of the 73 (66 percent) were officers. Hurewitz (1969) claims that in 1961 "more than 3400 of the 4100 employees in the ministry of interior were either active military officers or men who had resigned their commissions after transfer from the armed forces." Officers were likewise appointed into various state-owned companies. "The armed forces became involved in land reclamation, housing, the national transport system, state security [. . .] and many other activities," noted Field Marshal 'Abd al-Ghani al-Gamasy in his memoirs.[33] According to President Anwar Sadat (1977, p. 161), officers under Nasser were appointed "as board chairmen in civilian establishments, as chairmen of town councils, and in all the civic institutions throughout Egypt. The army officers even had a say in the renting of government-owned apartments."

In short, the military under Nasser had become the new ruling elite, enjoying a dominant share of both material and political power. With their interests satisfied under Nasser, there was no need for the officers to stage a coup. There was no

---

[26] Vatikiotis (1978, p. 162) notes that: "Vast profits from a rampant black market in imported luxury goods accrued to those officers who could transport them back to Egypt at government expense and free of customs duties. Favourable treatment regarding housing and services for these veterans compounded the corruption and became a national scandal." See also Sadat (1977, p. 161).

[27] These include Abdelhakim Amer (1958–1965), Abdel Latif Boghdadi (1958–1964), Kamal el-Din Hussein (1961–1964), Zakaria Mohieddin (1961–1964, 65–68), Hussein el-Shafei (1961–1965, 68–70), Anwar Sadat (1964, 69–70), Hassan Ibrahim (1964–1966), and Ali Sabri (1965–1968).

[28] These include Nasser himself (1954–1962), Ali Sabri (1962–1965), Zakaria Mohieddin (1965–1966), Mohamed Sedki Sulayman (1966–1967), and then Nasser once again (1967–1970).

[29] Zakaria Mohieddin from 1954 to 67, then Sharawy Gomaa (1967–1971).

[30] See Cooper (1982, p. 205), Brooks (2008, p. 119), and Faksh (1976, p. 143).

[31] Sadat (1977, pp. 149–150).

[32] Hurewitz (1969) claims that "[I]t was part of 'Abd al-Nasir's genius that he managed to preserve the loyalty and the cooperation of his colleagues in later years, for he continued taking all basic decisions only after consultation with his colleagues and his staff." For power-sharing with Amer in particular, see Brooks (2008, p. 76).

[33] El-Gamasy (1993, p. 85). For more on land reclamation, see Springborg (1979).

shortage of riches to be made already. Officers who wanted political power, likewise, did not need to seize it by force; military service itself had become "the most privileged route for recruitment into top ministerial and bureaucratic positions."[34] As Perlmutter (1974, p. 182) put it: "The military establishment's major source of support was obviously the praetorian regime. Thus, to turn against their praetorian-in-chief [would have been] a monumental and unwise course of action." Power-sharing was thus the first major component of Nasser's coup-proofing strategy.

The second approach to maintaining the military's loyalty was through a shared identity. Nasser attempted to stack the military with officers who shared his revolutionary, pan-Arabist agenda. The first step in this regard was to purge the military of officers espousing rival ideologies, namely, communists and Islamists. During the 1952 coup itself, all generals, brigadiers, and colonels who opposed the Free Officers were cashiered. Nasser then tasked infantry aide Salah Nasr with preparing a list of 'independent-thinking' officers who might challenge their rule. Out of the 3,500 officers on the list, 800 were retired, 2,300 reassigned to administrative duties within the army, and the rest appointed to civilian positions.[35]

Having eliminated rivals, Nasser then sought to indoctrinate the remaining officers into sharing his ideological mission of social transformation and liberation from colonialism. Nasser in 1953 created the Office of the Commander-in-Chief for Political Guidance (OCC) to infuse his ideas into the officer corps. War Minister Mohammed Fawzi (1968–1971) observed in his memoirs that the military academy focused not just on technical training, but on elevating cadets' "national and political awareness" to create "revolutionary officers" who shared Nasser's worldview, and would therefore act as an "executive tool for achieving revolutionary goals."[36] To build nationalist sentiment further, the military was also heavily involved in industrialization projects, public transportation plans, and the building of the Aswan High Dam, and played a key role in defending the nationalization of the Suez Canal in the 1956 Suez Crisis. These attempts at indoctrination constituted a second element of Nasser's coup-proofing strategy: stacking the officer corps with like-minded individuals who would feel ideologically invested in the regime, and thus be loyal to it.

1967 Defeat

The 1967 defeat to Israel in just six days delivered a major blow to the regime, shattering Nasser's image as a strong, pan-Arab hero. Nasser initially tendered his resignation, but an outpouring of popular support into the streets led him to remain as president until his death in 1970. In these final years, Nasser's coup-proofing strategy of pleasing the officer corps remained the same, though the tactics slightly changed.

[34] Bou Nassif (2013, p. 513)
[35] Nasr (1999, pp. 156, 186). See also Kandil (2012, p. 16).
[36] See Imam (2001, pp. 17, 31). See also Bou Nassif (2021, p. 64).

The first noticeable shift was the (relative) demilitarization of the cabinet. From a high of 66 percent on the eve of the war, the percent of the cabinet being military officers went back down to its usual levels, reaching 39 percent in March 1968 and 42 percent in October 1968.[37] While military officers remained as president, vice-president, prime minister, and ministers of defense, interior, and foreign affairs (among others), the military withdrew from several traditionally civilian roles. This demilitarization, however, did not represent a curtailment of the military's interests or a move to marginalizing it. Instead, the officers themselves had sought to withdraw from politics.

One lesson the officers had learned from their defeat was that to be effective on the battlefield, they needed to return to their original mission of national defense. As Field Marshal al-Gamasy remarked in his memoirs: "The growing power and presence of the armed forces in civilian life was detrimental to its main responsibility, which was to be a fighting force, ready for battle."[38] "A critical mass within the armed forces saw clearly how the politicization (and straightforward corruption) of the military had hurled their institution to the abyss."[39]

The military's defeat had also tarnished its public image, with Egyptians blaming the officers for their loss. "People spit at them, taxi drivers refused to carry them," reported one journalist.[40] Frustration with the military then turned into critiques of its privileges: "Ordinary men and women [. . .] began to ask why army officers had expensive automobiles [. . .] and why some of them had three apartments, two of which they sublet at handsome profits."[41] Protests against the military even erupted in February 1968 "after light sentences had been passed on the air force commanders" for negligence during the war.[42] The demilitarization of the March 1968 cabinet "was a direct response to the riots of February 1968,"[43] offering the officers a way to withdraw from the limelight, nurse their reputation, and demonstrate to Egyptians that they were taking national defense seriously.

The second major shift post-1967 was the establishment in 1969 of the Central Security Forces (CSF), a paramilitary force housed in the Ministry of Interior. While some interpret this move as an attempt to counterbalance the military,[44] this instead also reflected the military's interests. The regime had sought to repress those protests that erupted in February and November 1968.[45] Soldiers initially took on this task, but officers quickly realized such repression was tarnishing their reputation further. "Use your army against [Israeli Defense Minister] Dayan, not against us," chanted the protesters.[46] To avoid any further damage to their image, the top brass sought

[37] Brooks (2008, p. 119).
[38] El-Gamasy (1993, p. 85). See also Brooks (2008); White (2017).
[39] Kandil (2012, p. 90).
[40] Carthew (1967, p. 85). See also Be'eri (1970, p. 325); Brooks (2008, p. 113).
[41] Brady (1967).
[42] Sadat (1977, p. 195).
[43] Cooper (1982, p. 205); Abdalla (1988, p. 1,455).
[44] Kandil (2012); Bou Nassif (2021).
[45] For more on these protests, see Kandil (2012, p. 96).
[46] Vatikiotis (1978, p. 196).

to create a force outside of the military—the CSF—that could do the dirty work of repressing protesters instead.[47]

Two pieces of evidence help support the notion that the CSF was not intended to counterbalance the army. The first was that army officers controlled it from the start: the minister of interior remained Free Officer Sharawy Gomaa. Second, as late as 1965, Nasser was warning other countries not to counterbalance their militaries. When Algerian President Ahmed Ben Bella threatened to build up a militia, Nasser warned, presciently, that: "Having two militaries in one country will bring about disaster."[48]

In short, the final years of Nasser's reign saw a continuation of empowerment. Observers at the time agreed that the military "remained the central constituency" of Nasser's regime,[49] and "continued to wield a monopoly of political power."[50] "Needless to say, the Egyptian army is the bulwark of Nasser's repressive base."[51] The slight demilitarization of the cabinet and the formation of the CSF were in the service of the military's interests, allowing them to nurse their reputation. While the precise manifestation of empowerment had thus shifted, the underlying strategy remained the same: pleasing the officers' interests.

Anwar Sadat

Nasser passed away in 1970, and the generals decided to elevate his vice president, retired Colonel Anwar Sadat, as Egypt's next president. Sadat's "basic task", according to his autobiography, "was to wipe out the disgrace and humiliation that followed from the 1967 defeat."[52] Sadat claims the armed forces told him "that Egypt was passing through a difficult and very critical period, that the armed forces had a mission to accomplish, and that they therefore needed a supreme commander under whom they could achieve this objective."[53]

Following Nasser's lead, Sadat therefore allowed the military to withdraw further from politics to focus on warfare. The military's presence in the cabinet was reduced from 42 percent in 1968 to 33 percent in November 1970 and 31 percent in May 1971.[54] The prime minister, notably, was no longer a military officer, but a veteran diplomat (Mahmoud Fawzi). As Sadat explained:

> In the 1967 War we lacked neither training, good tactics, weapons, nor fighting ability, thank God. It was all a question of negligence on the part of the command. [. . .] Politicians had been actual commanders of the armed forces in Egypt with

---

[47] Springborg (1989, p. 101), Tartter (1991, p. 340), Human Rights Watch (1992, p. 29).

[48] See "Minutes of the First Meeting between Premier Zhou Enlai and President Nasser," June 22, 1965. Available at the Wilson Center's Digital Archive. Ben Bella would in turn be ousted by the military.

[49] Vatikiotis (1978, p. 158).

[50] Abdel-Malek (1968, p. xv).

[51] Copeland (1969, p. 100).

[52] Sadat (1977, p. 215).

[53] Sadat (1977, p. 205).

[54] Cooper (1982, pp. 206–207).

disastrous results for us—in the 1956 War, the Yemeni War, and finally in the 1967 War. The armed forces, I insisted, should be professional and should be kept out of politics.[55]

Sadat was not alone in this thinking. "The officer corps was resolutely against reentering the political fray, especially while it was still trying to remedy the disasters brought about by the politicization of the military."[56] That the core of the officers preferred to focus on Israel rather than politics was made clear in April 1971, when the war minister, Mohammed Fawzi, began plotting to remove Sadat from power. But the chief of staff, Mohammad Sadeq, vehemently opposed it, telling Fawzi: "If you want to resign, you can. But the army is not going to move [...] Are the armed forces of Egypt prepared to get themselves mixed up in politics at a time when we are preparing for the battle?"[57] General Sadeq then warned Leithy al-Nasser, the head of the Republican Guard, that "if the guards betrayed Sadat, he would mobilize the military to rein them in even if it led to a bloodbath."[58]"Sadeq, along with the rest of the armed forces, simply wanted to win the war, and believed that political bickering only postponed it."[59]

Accordingly, the bulk of the officers corps agreed with Sadat on the need to focus on war, not politics. The size of the military nearly doubled once again from 233,000 troops in 1970 to 423,000 in 1975, and Sadat invested heavily in their equipment and training. This focus on war and not politics was then vindicated in the 1973 war, when Egypt succeeded in crossing the Suez Canal and pushing Israel further back into the Sinai. The 1973 war restored the military's pride and shored up its reputation among the public. "We are not a political army—we are professional," one senior officer noted proudly. "That is why we achieved the crossing of the Suez Canal in 1973. We will not return to being a political army."[60]

With this new strategy vindicated, Sadat moved to further civilianize the cabinet after the war. The percentage of cabinet positions allocated to military officers fell to 20 percent in 1974 and then to 9 percent in 1976.[61] It slightly ticked up to 18 percent again in 1980, when Sadat himself assumed the prime ministership and appointed General Kamal Hasan Ali as foreign minister.

This demilitarization of the cabinet under Sadat did not reflect a marginalizing of the military's position. It is better viewed as the military voluntarily disengaging from politics, rather than being sidelined from it.[62] After all, retired officers continued to serve in the most important positions—president (Sadat) and vice-president (Hosni Mubarak, 1975–1981)—therefore determining the regime's overall strategies.

---

[55] Sadat (1977, p. 185 and p. 234).
[56] Kandil (2012, p. 102).
[57] Heikal (1983, p. 41).
[58] Kandil (2012, p. 103).
[59] Ibid.
[60] Quoted in Views from Abroad, "Sadat's Power Base," *Journal of Palestine Studies* 7:2 (1978), p. 160.
[61] Figures compiled from Cooper (1982, pp. 206–207), Brooks (2008, p. 119), and CIA, "Egypt: The Roots, Values, and Attitudes of the Officer Corps," Reading Room, March 1982.
[62] Be'eri (1982); Brooks (1998); Harb (2003). For contrasting takes, see Springborg (1989, pp. 96–97).

Moreover, active-duty officers retained control of the Ministry of Defense, preventing any civilian oversight over its activities. However, the withdrawal of officers from the limelight allowed the military to avoid public scrutiny and focus instead on national defense, and increasingly, as we will see further on, on its defense and civilian industries. That the military was not aggrieved by this civilianization of government is confirmed by its continuation under Sadat's successor, Hosni Mubarak, and even under Abdelfattah al-Sisi today. This period is therefore best described as the military moving from what scholars term a "ruler" or "governor" model of military praetorianism to the more stable "moderator" model, controlling the state from behind the scenes.[63]

Likewise, this demilitarization should not be viewed as the Egyptian military becoming an apolitical force like Tunisia's. While it withdrew from high-profile positions, it still viewed its rightful place as the center of the regime, "ruling but not governing."[64] It continued to view a military background as a prerequisite for positions like president and vice president, and continued to perceive the military as deserving regular appointments throughout the bureaucracy. While its notion of professionalism came to emphasize being a "behind the scenes" political power, it continued to emphasize a role in governance nonetheless.

Material Interests

While Sadat satisfied the military's political interests, he was increasingly unable to meet his end of the bargain materially. In large part due to Sadat's foreign and economic policies, military officers began to see their economic position decline in the late 1970s.

The first difficulty concerned Sadat's shift from the Soviet to US orbit. Sadat expelled Soviet military advisors in 1972, and when the Soviets stalled in re-building the Egyptian military's arsenal after the war,[65] Sadat abrogated the Soviet–Egyptian Treaty of Friendship and Cooperation in 1976 and turned instead to the United States. That process, however, was equally slow, and US weapons and aid did not materialize until the signing of the Egyptian–Israeli Peace Treaty in 1979. In the meantime, however, grievances began to accumulate in the military over their deteriorating arms inventory, with officers starting to questioning whether Sadat was right to place so much faith in the United States.

Indeed, the director of the CIA, Enno Knoche, warned in February 1977 that: "The situation in Egypt is becoming critical and Sadat's future depends on what the US does. He needs to be able to demonstrate the wisdom of tying himself to Washington. There are dangers in Sadat's own relationships with the military."[66] That same month,

---

[63] Stepan (1971); Perlmutter (1974); Nordlinger (1977).

[64] Cook (2007).

[65] See Sadat (1977, pp. 247, 267, 278, 284–287, 292) for his frustrations with the Soviets.

[66] "Minutes of a Policy Review Committee Meeting," Washington, February 4, 1977. In: Foreign Relations, 1977–1980, Volume VIII, pp. 15–16.

Egypt's foreign minister, Ismail Fahmy, sent the same message to Secretary of State Cyrus Vance, noting that while the army is not a problem now, "we don't want it to develop into one. [. . .] The military aspect is a matter of life and death for countries like Egypt."[67]

Beyond the delay in weapons, a second difficulty Sadat faced in his relations with the military concerned his liberalizing of the economy beginning in 1974. These *"infitah"* policies had the effect of increasing inflation, making it harder for Egyptians—including low and middle-ranking military officers—to make ends meet. Secretary of Defense Harold Brown in 1979 noted that "former MOD Gamasy told me privately he is worried about the effects on Army morale and attitudes of an eroding economic position military personnel experience in their personal lives."[68] "The regime's chief prop, the military establishment, is also increasingly affected by the economic squeeze," observed the CIA in 1977. "During 1976, there were several demonstrations of dissatisfaction by individual military units, most centering on economic problems, and military officers repeatedly made their grievances known to government leaders."[69]

Despite this low-level grumbling, however, the military's senior leadership downplayed any concerns. In May 1976, an anonymous senior leader "stated that the morale of the armed forces was good, that they are considered totally reliable, and that the impact of shortages of spare parts had been blunted by efforts to acquire parts and new equipment from other sources. Although there were some troubling problems with inflation and the cost of living, he pointed out that the officers still did considerably better than their civilian counterparts."[70] The CIA therefore concluded, presciently, that "short of an assassin's bullet, or another heart attack, we see no immediate threat to Sadat."[71]

Moreover, to rectify these economic grievances, Sadat allowed military officers to seek profits elsewhere: through the production and sale of weapons, and ultimately, civilian goods. In the 1970s, the National Organization for Military Production expanded from manufacturing small arms and ammunition to assembling more advanced weapons systems. Among its manufacturing plants were the Abu Zaabal Tank Repair Factory, which overhauled and repaired tanks and would eventually produce Egypt's main battle tank; the Hulwan Company for Machine Tools, which produced mortars and rocket launchers; and the Heliopolis Company for Chemical Industries, which produced bombs and missile warheads.[72]

In 1975, Egypt, Qatar, Saudi Arabia, and the United Arab Emirates jointly founded the Arab Organization for Industrialization (AOI), combining the Gulf's oil money (an initial deposit of $1 billion) with Egypt's conscript labor force to manufacture

---

[67] "Memorandum of Conversation," Cairo, February 17, 1977. In: Foreign Relations, 1977–1980, Volume VIII, p. 58.

[68] "Memorandum From Secretary of Defense Brown to President Carter," Washington, February 19, 1979. In: Foreign Relations, 1977–1980, Volume XVIII, p. 66.

[69] CIA, "National Intelligence Estimate: Egypt-1977," Reading Room, February 3, 1977.

[70] CIA, "Egypt: Sadat's Domestic Position," Reading Room June 1, 1976.

[71] Ibid.

[72] Tartter (1991, pp. 328–329).

weapons and military equipment. Exempted from Egyptian taxes and business restrictions, the AOI at first consisted of nine companies. The five wholly owned by Egypt produced missiles, rockets, aircraft engine parts, and armored personnel carriers, among other items. The four joint ventures produced French Gazelle combat helicopters and engines, British Swingfire antitank guided missiles, and American Chrysler jeeps.[73]

Beyond its defense industry, the military under Sadat also began to enter the civilian economy. In 1978, the government set up the National Service Project Organization (NSPO), which allowed the military to produce goods for both its consumption and for sale to civilians. These activities at first focused primarily on agricultural products and clothing, but increasingly focused on other activities. By the early 1980s the NSPO was manufacturing "doors, window frames, stationery, pharmaceutical packaging, and microscopes," and "was involved in a number of infrastructure projects, [. . .] construct[ing] power lines, sewers, bridges, and overpasses in Cairo and elsewhere."[74]

Sadat also allegedly permitted officers to benefit from corruption, most notably in the shipment of US military aid. After the signing of the Peace Treaty, the Egyptian-American Transport and Services Corporation (EATSCo) received the Egyptian contract to ship US arms to Egypt, and charged $51 million between 1979 and 1981 to ship roughly $300 million worth of arms to Egypt. Under criticism that this figure was "unusually high" and included $30 million for a middleman company, both the US Justice Department and Egypt's government began investigating whether Egyptian officers may have improperly received a cut. The *Washington Post* in 1982 reported that these officers included "Kamal Hassan Ali, then defense minister and now foreign minister of Egypt; Gen. Mohammad Abu Ghazala, then Egypt's military attache here and now defense minister, and Gen. Mounir Sabet, chief of military procurement and the brother-in-law of President Mohamed Hosni Mubarak."[75]

Other than corruption, Sadat also offered military officers reduced prices and other preferential treatment to help ease their economic situation. "During religious holidays in October 1980, for example, lamb was sold to officers at 30 percent below the normal government-controlled price. Such reduced prices apparently are available to the officer corps on a regular basis."[76] In 1978, "5,000 apartment units were allocated to junior officers" who had been struggling to afford housing, while "three million Egyptian pounds" were "earmarked to purchase motor bikes for soldiers and officers to make up for the lack of public transportation."[77]

But while the military may have had access to these opportunities to help make ends meet, everyday citizens did not. Frustration with Sadat's economic reforms peaked in 1977, when a cut in subsidies sparked massive bread riots. With the police

---

[73] Tartter (1991, p. 329).

[74] Tartter (1991, pp. 325–327).

[75] Kamen and Armstrong (1982). Egypt's investigation declared those three innocent. The US investigation led EATSCo's founders, Egyptian officer Hussein K. Salem and CIA officer Thomas S. Clines, to plead guilty, but did not target the others.

[76] CIA, "The Egyptian Military: Political Attitudes and Involvement," Reading Room, February 1981.

[77] CIA, "Egyptian Military Discontent," Reading Room, September 26, 1978.

and CSF overwhelmed, the army was asked to deploy to help ensure security. Notably, the army complied, helping to repress the protesters, and did not instead oust Sadat. Despite any reduction in their material interests, the senior leadership still calculated that their interests were best preserved under Sadat.

However, while preserving Sadat, the military also made clear that it held veto power over Sadat's policies. Its condition for repressing protests was that Sadat reinstate the subsidies.[78] According to the CIA, the military also vetoed efforts to curb "military spending as an alternative to civilian austerity."[79]

The bread riots also led the generals to push Sadat to strengthen the CSF further. In order "to obviate the need to call upon the armed forces [again] to deal with domestic disturbances,"[80] the CSF was expanded to 100,000 troops,[81] with its arsenal upgraded from batons and rifles to tear-gas canisters and armored vehicles. In 1979, the US supplied the CSF with 153,946 tear-gas bombs, 2,419 automatic weapons, and 328,000 rubber bullets.[82] This was not to counterbalance the military, but instead to help the military's reputation by keeping it out of domestic repression.

Ideational Stacking

Sadat also attempted to implement two changes to Nasser's stacking of the officer corps with secular pan-Arabists. First, in preparation for the eventual peace treaty with Israel, Sadat attempted to convert the Arab nationalists into Egyptian nationalists, emphasizing that Egypt had born the brunt of the wars with Israel and that it was time to think of "Egypt first." Bou Nassif (2021, p. 99) documents how Sadat "over and over again […] in [his] speeches to the military […] systematically lashed out at radical Arabs supposedly conspiring against Egypt." Such efforts were relatively successful in shifting the attitudes of the officer corps. After Sadat traveled to Israel to speak in the Knesset, one senior officer observed that: "What Sadat has done should have been done years ago. […] We have died enough for the Palestinians […] I am an Egyptian first and an Arab second. I support the Palestinian need to get back its homeland, but I am no longer willing to die for them."[83]

But it was Sadat's second change to Nasser's stacking that would eventually prove more important—and indeed, fatal—to his rule. Sadat loosened the strategy of stacking to permit Islamists into the ranks of the officer corps as well. In order to counter the growing influence of the leftists, who were critical of Sadat's *infitah* policies, Sadat self-styled himself the 'Believer President' and attempted to co-opt the support of the Islamists. He released the Muslim Brotherhood from prison, and allowed them to proselytize and mobilize in universities and trade unions. Most importantly, he also allowed some Islamists to enter the military academies.

---

[78] Cooper (1982, p. 272), Kandil (2012, p. 169); and Taylor (2014, p. 122).
[79] CIA, "Egypt: Widespread Rioting", Reading Room, January 19, 1977.
[80] Tartter (1991, p. 340).
[81] Human Rights Watch (1992, p. 31).
[82] Kandil (2012, p. 170).
[83] Quoted in Views from the Ground, "Sadat's Power Base," *Journal of Palestine Studies* 7:2 (1978), p. 160.

These Islamist junior officers were not as easily persuaded into accepting Sadat's negotiations with Israel, nor in accepting his secular rule. Already in 1974, Palestinian activist Saleh Sarieh had collaborated with Islamist cadets in Egypt to seize the Technical Military Academy in Heliopolis in an attempt to "use the arsenal of heavy weapons stacked within to occupy the parliament [. . .] and declare the Islamic Republic of Egypt."[84] In 1977, military officers affiliated with the Islamist group *Takfir wal-Hijra* kidnapped and killed the former minister of religious endowments; "Egyptian authorities found the *Takfir* in possession of military vehicles, uniforms, and training manuals."[85] The number of Islamist officers and soldiers was apparently so high already in March 1975 that "senior Egyptian security officers [. . .] had doubts about the dependability of the army for action against the [Muslim] Brotherhood," particularly because two former Free Officers, Kamal al-Din Husayn and Husayn al-Shafi'i, had allegedly joined forces with the Islamists.[86]

Sadat's loosening of stacking to allow Islamists into the military's ranks would end up proving fatal. One first lieutenant, Khaled al-Islambouli, who was affiliated with the Egyptian Islamic Jihad, had by now accumulated a number of grievances with Sadat: "The first was that the existing laws in the country were not consistent with Islamic law and in consequence Moslems were suffering. The second was the peace [treaty . . .], and the third the recent arrest of Moslem leaders, their persecution and humiliation."[87]

On October 6, 1981, at a military parade celebrating the 1973 war, Islambouli and his colleagues struck, assassinating Sadat. How they were able to avert the gaze of the military and civilian intelligence agencies remains unclear, with some observers, including Sadat's descendants[88] and the sociologist Hazem Kandil (2012, p. 172), insinuating that the military may have been complicit in the assassination.[89] Others, however, call such claims "conspiracy theories."[90] It is certainly possible that beyond the Islamist officers, some committed Arab nationalists might also have been frustrated with the peace treaty, or that their material grievances may have led some officers to look the other way. But until further evidence comes to light, all we can conclude for now is that Sadat's weakening of ideational stacking, permitting Islamists into the armed forces, contributed to his assassination.

Hosni Mubarak

With Sadat's assassination, his vice-president, air chief marshal and 1973 war hero, Hosni Mubarak, assumed the presidency. Given what happened to Sadat, Mubarak

---

[84] Bou Nassif (2021, p. 92), see also Satloff (1988, p. 29).

[85] CIA, 'Egypt: The Roots, Values, and Attitudes of the Officer Corps," Reading Room, March 1982.

[86] CIA. Egypt: Sadat's Domestic Position, Reading Room, June 1, 1976.

[87] Heikal (1983, p. 246).

[88] Farahat (2011, p. 20).

[89] Bechir Ben Aissa, who attended the parade as the Tunisian military attache in Egypt, recently claimed that he "noticed that Hosni Mubarak was looking at the clock, he and Field Marshal Abu Ghazaleh, and they were puzzled, as if they were waiting for something to happen that was delayed. Then the disaster occurred."

[90] Heikal (1983, p. 268) and Springborg (1989, p. 97).

first moves were to reinstate the stacking of the military. Mubarak began by ordering a purge of the armed forces aimed at rooting out Islamist sympathizers.[91] He then re-applied Nasser's ban on Islamists entering the military academies. In practice, Mubarak banned not just Islamists, but even those with Islamist relatives. If military intelligence discovered that "a candidate, or any of his family members, [was] even remotely associated with the [Muslim] Brothers, he [would be] immediately and irreversibly disqualified."[92] Though less successful, even among the rank-and-file, "military intelligence carefully monitor[ed] conscripts to prevent the growth of militant Islamic or extremist groups in the armed forces."[93]

These limits on recruitment into the officer corps, and to a lesser extent the soldiers, produced a relatively "secular" military. I use that word in quotes because Egypt in general had become a fairly conservative society. Egyptian "secularists" still often cite religious verses, and tend to accept the constitution's stipulation that laws should be in accordance with sharia. However, what secular in this context means is anti-Islamist, particularly anti-Muslim Brotherhood. "Loathing of the Muslim Brotherhood runs very deep in the officer corps," observed Bou Nassif (2021, p. 112), highlighting that the armed forces magazine "ran several articles in the 1990s pertaining to religious extremism and how to fight it [. . . including] maintaining that 'terrorist,' not 'fundamentalist,' was the accurate word to designate Islamist activists. [. . .] According to an Egyptian journalist close to the Supreme Council of the Armed Forces (SCAF), military officers '[do] not consider the Brothers to be Egyptians at all ("*mush masriyyin*").'"

Beyond recruitment, the regime's decade-long battle with Islamist insurgents from *al-Gama'a al-Islamiyya* in the 1990s had the effect of further indoctrinating the military with an anti-Islamist ideology, especially as casualties and regime propaganda mounted. Women in *niqab* and men in *gallabiyya* were banned from military clubs,[94] while military personnel were not permitted to pray during military exercises. Accordingly, through a combination of selective recruitment and indoctrination, Mubarak was able to stack the officer corps with secular, anti-Islamist forces.

Political Power

Beyond stacking, Mubarak also strengthened the other major coup-proofing tactic: power-sharing. The military under Mubarak remained "Egypt's single strongest institution, the ultimate arbiter of political power, and the key to the regime's survival."[95] It commanded the dominant share of political power, "ruling but not governing" from behind the scenes.[96]

---

[91] Publicly, 30 officers and 100 soldiers were removed, but Satloff (1988, p. 31) estimates that the true figure was "far larger."

[92] Bou Nassif (2017, p. 165).

[93] CIA, "The Egyptian Military: Its Role and Missions Under Mubarak," Reading Room, July 8, 1987. See also Hashim (2011*b*, p. 107).

[94] Sayigh (2012, p. 20).

[95] CIA, "The Egyptian Military: Its Role and Missions Under Mubarak," Reading Room, July 8, 1987.

[96] Cook (2007).

At first, Mubarak appeared to also elevate the military into high-profile positions, tapping General Kamal Hassan Aly to serve as prime minister in 1984. Defense Minister Abd al-Halim Abu Ghazala (1981–1989) was also a strong personality who received considerable media attention.[97] But with this heightened profile came increased public scrutiny over the military, its financing, and its assets. Abdalla (1988, pp. 1456–1460) documents how in the 1980s, opposition politicians and the media were increasingly criticizing the military's lump-sum budget, calling for it to be dis-aggregated, inspected by the Central Auditing Agency, and reduced by half a billion pounds or more.[98] They also called for the position of defense minister to be separated from army commander (to facilitate civilian control), and to reduce the army's influence over the presidency and ruling party.

Mubarak repeatedly defended the military and its prerogatives, noting for instance that the "budget has already been reduced to the maximum" and that any further reduction "would serve an Israeli interest not an Egyptian interest."[99] However, despite his efforts, the officer corps eventually realized that they would need to continue staying out of the limelight in order to retain their privileges. For the rest of Mubarak's tenure, military officers would generally stick to four ministerial positions: defense, military production, civil aviation, and local development.[100] Moreover, unlike Abu Ghazala, Defense Minister Hussein Tantawi (1991–2012) intentionally "abstained from conspicuous politicized public appearances."[101]

"We believe the military prefers to remain above politics," the CIA estimated in 1987. "The military [is] largely content with its role of a 'behind-the-scenes' power."[102] Indeed, from behind the scenes, the military exercised what amounted to veto power over security policy. "The formulation of defence and national security strategy seems to be the preserve of the military establishment," noted Abdalla (1988, p. 1,458). Even over internal security matters, the military was able to both carve itself out of crowd control duties, allowing it to keep its hands clean, but also to supervise the police and CSF in these missions. Satloff (1988, p. 15) describes how the armed forces oversaw the police and CSF's crushing of a textile strike in 1984, despite soldiers not being deployed.

The military also exercised a veto over economic policy. In the 1990s and 2000s, the regime began to increasingly liberalize the economy, privatizing state assets. But throughout this period, the military was able to carve out exceptions for its companies. Defense Minister Hussein Tantawi "wields significant influence" in the cabinet, assessed the US in 2008, "oppos[ing] both economic and political reforms" beyond strictly military affairs.[103]

In addition to this veto power, the military also dominated the lower levels of government, which remained outside the limelight. Taylor (2014, p. 135) writes that on

---

[97] For more on Abu Ghazala, see Springborg (1989, pp. 98–100).
[98] See also Satloff (1988, pp. 19–25) and Springborg (1989).
[99] Abdalla (1988, p. 1461); Satloff (1988, p. 20).
[100] Sayigh (2012, p. 11).
[101] Abul-Magd (2017, p. 115).
[102] CIA, "The Egyptian Military: Its Role and Missions Under Mubarak," Reading Room, July 8, 1987.
[103] Quoted in Alexander and Stewart (2011).

the eve of Mubarak's ouster, "retired or active duty officers [. . .] served in the three most senior posts in the General Intelligence Directorate, four of 29 cabinet posts, 14 of 27 governors, 11 of the 13 key leaders in the Ministry of Civil Aviation, 15 of the 19 leaders in the Ministry of Military Production, nine of the ten Chairmen of the Arab Organization for Industry, the CEO of the Suez Canal Authority, and all 13 of the key posts of the Seaport Authority in the Ministry of Transportation." Bou Nassif (2013, p. 517) calculates that during Mubarak's 30-year tenure, military officers assumed 63 of 156 governorship appointments (40 percent), compared to just 22 percent for the police and 38 percent for civilians. Below the level of governor, Sayigh (2012, p. 14) estimates that military officers occupied some 2,000 civilian posts in local governments.

Given the military's dominant role behind the scenes, there was little reason to oust Mubarak. Ruling behind a nominally civilian government allowed the military to enjoy autonomy, veto power, and a steady rate of political appointments throughout the bureaucracy. In Abul-Magd (2017, p. 153)'s words, the "generals were the invisible, de facto rulers of the country." As Taylor (2014, p. 135) concludes, "In sum, few incentives existed to lead the military to pursue greater prestige through supporting an overthrow of the regime."

Material Interests

Beyond its political power, the military under Mubarak also enjoyed a vast share of material resources. Military officers continued to be an elite class, among the most privileged in the nation. The military's material wealth was derived from at least four different sources.

The first and arguably least important source was the budget. While Sadat had let the budget stagnate once negotiations with Israel began, Mubarak undertook a massive increase in the budget in his first years in office, tripling it between 1980 (LE 1 billion) and 1986 (LE 3 billion).[104] It roughly tripled again by 1997 (LE 8.7 billion), and once again by 2010 (LE 25.4 billion).[105] Notably, these official figures for the defense budget are widely viewed by experts as an underestimate of the military's actual budget.[106] It is therefore especially striking that despite this underestimation, the official figure for the Defense Ministry was still larger than almost all other ministries, including the Ministry of Interior, throughout Mubarak's tenure. Moreover, starting in 1991, a portion of the national budget set aside for disaster management and emergency response also routinely went to the officer corps, typically on retirement, in direct cash installments known as "loyalty allowances" ('alawat wala').[107]

A second source of material wealth not included in the budget was US military aid, amounting to roughly $1.3 billion each year since 1979, second only to Israel.

---

[104] Satloff (1988, p. 9).
[105] Sayigh (2012, p. 7).
[106] See, for instance, Kuimova (2020).
[107] Sayigh (2012, p. 4) and Bou Nassif (2013, p. 527).

Through this aid, Egypt's military gained access to some of the world's most advanced weaponry from US defense companies. But less well known is that the aid also created opportunities for additional accrual of wealth. US foreign military financing must be spent on weapons and equipment from US companies, but *which* companies are left up to the Egyptian military to decide. This arrangement created a perverse market for US defense contractors to compete for these funds, leading some US companies to pay off Egyptian generals in exchange for promises to secure a contract.

Kechichian and Nazimek (1997, p. 135) write that: "In 1993, the Wall Street Journal uncovered several cases of payoffs from U.S. defense contractors to the Egyptian military. The perks ranged from expense-paid weekends in New York to $1.1 million in 'fat' that was added to a defense contract 'to make every Egyptian officer happy.'" These payoffs did not stop after their exposure. In 2009, the US Securities and Exchange Commission issued a cease-and-desist order against United Industrial Corporation after it discovered that its subsidiary, ACL Technologies, had paid a retired Egyptian air force general LE 3.38 million ($564,000) to act as its middleman between 1997 and 2002 to help it secure contracts.[108] One retired general claimed that Mubarak, Tantawi, and others in the top brass "took cuts in every deal the Egyptian military signed," storing those millions in bank accounts abroad.[109]

A third source of wealth was the Egyptian military's arms industry, which began to boom under Defense Minister Abu Ghazala in the 1980s. Spurred in part by increased demand from Iraq in its war with Iran, Egypt exported somewhere between $340 million to 1 billion worth of military equipment in 1982 alone.[110] These profits accrued directly to the military, offering another off-the-books source of funds. In 1987, the CIA estimated that "about two-thirds of [Egyptian] military profits from arms deals support military housing, maintenance, and purchases of spare parts."[111]

The final and most well-known source of wealth is the Egyptian military's involvement in civilian enterprises, what Springborg (2011) has termed "Military, Inc."[112] The Egyptian Government estimated that the armed forces were involved in some 300 civilian projects between 1980 and 1987.[113] In 1985, the military's NSPO produced 18 percent of the total food produced in Egypt that year.[114] Over the next two decades, the military penetrated nearly every civilian sector, producing everything from cars to computers to pesticides, and building hotels, bridges, apartments and even entire cities.[115] In these endeavors, military enterprises enjoyed several advantages over civilian ones, including cheap, conscript labor; exemptions from import taxes since 1986, sales taxes since 1991, and income taxes since 2005; and political connections for securing contracts and winning lawsuits—in turn, allowing them to crowd out the market. By the 2000s, experts estimated that the military through the

---

[108] See SEC filing: Securities Exchange Act of 1934, Release No. 60005, May 29, 2009.
[109] Quoted in Bou Nassif (2013, p. 528).
[110] Springborg (1989, p. 108),Tartter (1991, p. 330).
[111] CIA, "The Egyptian Military: Its Role and Missions Under Mubarak," Reading Room, July 8, 1987.
[112] Springborg appears to have borrowed the term from Siddiqa (2007)'s book on Pakistan.
[113] CIA, "The Egyptian Military: Its Role and Missions Under Mubarak," Reading Room, July 8, 1987.
[114] Springborg (1989, p. 113).
[115] Springborg (1987); Abul-Magd (2013); Bou Nassif (2013); Marshall (2015); Abul-Magd and Grawert (2016); Abul-Magd (2017).

Ministry of Military Production (MOMP), the Arab Industrial Organization (AIO), and the National Service Projects Organization (NSPO) reportedly controlled some 15–30 percent of the Egyptian economy.[116] The military's economic empire satisfied not just its own needs, but also generated a billion-dollar-a-year export business,[117] all of which operated outside of parliamentary control or executive oversight.

These sources of wealth allowed Mubarak and the top brass to lavish new privileges onto the officer corps beginning in the 1980s. The military constructed new apartment buildings on army-controlled land outside of Cairo, selling them to officers at highly subsidized prices. For many, "this becomes a second, third, or fourth source of rental income."[118] These new military cities came complete with nurseries, primary, preparatory, and secondary schools, as well as their "own supermarkets, consumer cooperatives, and petrol stations, where military personnel and their families may buy consumer goods at discounted prices."[119] "Officers and their families also benefit from military hospitals that serve their health needs, a chain of military resorts providing for their holidays, and a military travel service operating in Egypt and overseas."[120] "Military officers enjoyed life inside a unique military subculture—a 'little Disney World' including theaters, playgrounds, and officer clubs."[121]

The material perks afforded to military officers did not stop at retirement. Officers who had remained loyal throughout their careers could expect that upon reaching the retirement age they would receive a loyalty allowance of roughly LE 40,000,[122] as well as a cushy, post-retirement position, whether in the civil service or in one of the many military companies. These positions offered retired officers a second salary in addition to their military pension. Combined, the most well-placed retired officers could expect to receive salaries upwards of $83,000 to $166,000 USD per *month*.[123]

This extravagant material wealth was designed to buy the military's loyalty. "Mubarak's incorporation of the senior officer corps [. . .] assured him of their loyalty and quiescence," argued Sayigh (2012, p. 8). Junior officers as well were incentivized to stay loyal, knowing that "their turn could come," observed Bou Nassif (2013, p. 516). "If [they] remained loyal [. . .] they could rise in the hierarchy and join the circle of privileged senior officers."

Attracting the Secular Elite

This strategy of co-opting the military through a share of power and resources in turn also reinforced Mubarak's other strategy of stacking the military with secular, elite loyalists. The material riches and social esteem earned through a career in the

[116] Kurtzer and Svenstrup (2012).
[117] Kandil (2012, p. 182).
[118] Springborg (1989, p. 105)
[119] Sayigh (2012, p. 20).
[120] Springborg (1989, p. 105). See also Sayigh (2012, p. 20).
[121] Taylor (2014, p. 134).
[122] Sayigh (2012, p. 5).
[123] Sayigh (2012, pp. 5, 19).

army meant that the Egyptian military had little difficulty recruiting new officers from the elite classes. While Tunisia's autocrats had to give up on a strategy of stacking the officers with elites (see Chapter 7), in Egypt, such a strategy remained feasible— so much so that the military even increased its entrance requirements to privilege elite applicants. In particular, a candidate's *family's* "educational attainment [became] an additional filter. Applicants whose parents do not both hold university degrees are barred from military college," noted Sayigh (2012, p. 21), skewing the officer corps towards well-educated families. Moreover, "those securing higher scores on the entrance exams tend increasingly to come from families that can afford private schools or extra tutoring,"[124] exacerbating these trends.[125] The Egyptian historian Tewfik Aclimandos (2011, p. 16) thus concludes that under Mubarak:

> It has become almost impossible for an underprivileged man or the son of a petit-bourgeois family to be admitted to the Military or Police Academies. Nasser, Sadat and Mubarak would probably not be admitted today.

The elite families who populated the officer corps under Mubarak tended to be wealthier, more socially liberal, and more secular than the average Egyptian. They accordingly also tended to be more politically conservative, fearful that any shock to the system like a revolution or coup might alter their cushy lifestyles by bringing the Muslim Brotherhood or other Islamists to power. Attracting such elite families into the officer corps thus produced a naturally more loyal military, eager to preserve the status quo and viewing the Islamist alternative as an existential threat.

In short, the political and material empowerment of the Egyptian military also reinforced the second strategy of stacking the military with secular, elite loyalists. Combined, the two strategies meant that Mubarak could rely on a highly loyal army.

Counter-explanations

In the wake of the 2011 revolution, several scholars have inferred from the Egyptian military's eventual "defection" that they must have been disgruntled with Mubarak. Perhaps searching for a similarity with the Tunisian military, many have claimed the Egyptian military had also felt neglected relative to the police and CSF, or that they feared the rise of Mubarak's son, Gamal, a businessman who might privatize the military's economic assets.[126]

While plausible, neither of these accounts are quite convincing. In Chapter 6, I examine the Egyptian military's behavior in 2011, showing how it was actually quite

---

[124] Sayigh (2012, p. 21).

[125] Springborg (1989, p. 105) likewise claims that: "Entrance into this neoMamlukian, autonomous military world is regulated by an increasingly separate and exclusive educational system."

[126] Albrecht and Bishara (2011); Barany (2011, 2016); Masoud (2011); Kandil (2012); Marshall and Stacher (2012); Stacher (2012); Abul-Magd (2013); Makara (2013, 2016); Taylor (2014); Albrecht (2015); Bou Nassif (2015*b*); Koehler (2016).

different from Tunisia's, and demonstrating how neither resentment towards the police nor Gamal Mubarak—had those existed—could fully explain its actions. In the remainder of this chapter, however, I question whether the Egyptian military truly felt resentful towards either the police or Gamal Mubarak at all.

Counterbalancing

There is no denying that the size and funds of the ministry of interior grew rapidly under Mubarak.[127] Its forces grew exponentially from 150,000 to 1 million,[128] compared to the military's 450,000. The police's budget likewise skyrocketed, but notably never eclipsed the military's budget, despite now having twice as many troops to pay. Even towards the end of Mubarak's rule, "at every comparative level, the military generals received more from the regime than their peers in the police."[129] Beyond budget and salaries, the military also enjoyed considerably more political appointments: Bou Nassif (2013, p. 517), for instance, calculates that the military received nearly twice as many governorship appointments than the police (22 percent v. 40 percent). As one police general admitted, "[W]e have our own slice of the cake, but the armed forces have the cake itself."[130]

Most importantly, the military also staffed key positions within the Ministry of Interior. Sayigh (2012, p. 6), in refuting the notion that a police state had relegated the Egyptian Armed Forces (EAF) to the background, notes that: "The EAF also provides active-duty officers to fill a significant number of command and senior administrative positions in the Interior Ministry and General Intelligence Directorate." It is hard to see how a Ministry of Interior staffed in key places by military officers could serve as a counterweight in stopping a military coup.

The case of the Central Security Forces (CSF) is emblematic. As a paramilitary force in the Ministry of Interior, it could have plausibly served as a counterbalance to the military, much like Tunisia's national guard did for its military. Egypt's CSF more than tripled under Mubarak, increasing from 100,000 to 325,000 troops. But despite this increase, the CSF was very clearly second-tier. Its conscripts themselves were "composed of men called up for Egypt's obligatory military service but who—usually because of a lack of education qualifications or vocational skills—fail to make the cut for the army."[131] Its weapons and equipment likewise "never became a match for the armed forces in terms of firepower."[132]

Moreover, the CSF was relatively neglected and ill-treated. The military "did not favor resources being allocated to another barracked force," leaving the CSF with "outrageously inadequate" wages, roughly $10/month in 1987.[133] CSF commanders,

---

[127] Sayigh (2012).
[128] Kandil (2012, p. 194).
[129] Bou Nassif (2021, p. 161).
[130] Quoted in Bou Nassif (2021, p. 162).
[131] Adam (2012).
[132] Bou Nassif (2021, p. 118).
[133] Springborg (1987, p. 7).

meanwhile subjected their troops to "incessant humiliation and abuse in already bleak living conditions."[134]

These material grievances in the CSF in turn produced a major mutiny of CSF forces in February 1986. Incensed by a rumor that their term would be extended another year, 17,000 CSF conscripts rioted in the streets, burning down buildings and looting throughout Cairo. If the CSF troops had no motivation to even serve Mubarak an extra year, how could they be expected to defend him in a coup attempt?

Instead, the military was brought in to crush the CSF mutiny, reinforcing who was boss. Had the military truly been upset with Mubarak, it would have seized power at that moment, when its tanks were already in the streets crushing the CSF. Indeed, Defense Minister Abu Ghazala was reportedly egged on by one of his commanders to continue on and stage a coup.[135] It would have been a simple affair, Abu Ghazala admitted, "requir[ing no] more than dispatching one officer [. . .] to the television and radio studios to deliver a communique on my behalf. The whole story would have been over in five minutes."[136] But ultimately, Abu Ghazala decided not to oust Mubarak: "I am happy where I am." As Kandil (2012, p. 179) explains, "[H]e did not need to stage a coup [. . .] to have his way with the regime."

Indeed, the army's crushing of the CSF mutiny itself revealed the true power dynamics at play: the military had never been counterbalanced by the police. As Satloff (1988, p. 16) remarked: "The army's role in suppressing the police conscript riots removed any doubt about the military's preeminent position and wiped away any pretense to a balance among the various security agencies." Had it been otherwise, Mubarak after the mutiny might have invested into the CSF, to make sure it did not feel neglected and hence might have been able to serve as a counterbalance to the army moving forward. But instead, "The government did not learn much from the CSF revolt. Very little was done to improve quality of life, pay or skill levels."[137] By 2011, the salaries of CSF conscripts remained a meager LE230 ($40) a month.[138] While military conscripts were not particularly well treated either, they "still made four times as much as" the CSF troops.[139] Unsurprisingly, another rebellion of CSF troops emerged in Camp Mubarak in November 2008, and several more emerged in the wake of the 2011 revolution.[140]

If the military remained the dominant force, why then did the generals allow the police to balloon in size? A large police force, including the paramilitary CSF, was useful for the military in two regards. First, they allowed the military to keep its hands clean of domestic repression. As Taylor (2014, p. 137) writes: "From the military's standpoint, the MoI served a useful function as a foil for favorable perceptions of the military. In general, the military saw the MoI as doing the 'dirty work of black ops,

---

[134] Adam (2012).
[135] See former PM Kamal Ganzouri's memoirs (Al-Ashwal, 2013).
[136] Kandil (2012, p. 179).
[137] Hashim (2011*b*, p. 108).
[138] Adam (2012).
[139] Bou Nassif (2021, p. 161).
[140] Adam (2012).

torture, interrogation, and spying internally on Egyptians' while the military could focus on polishing its image as defenders and champions of the Egyptian people."

But avoiding domestic repression was not only useful for maintaining its reputation at home. Equally important was keeping the military's hands clean for international consumption. Since 1998, US military aid has been subject to the "Leahy Law," preventing assistance from going to military units involved in human rights abuses. To maintain its $1.3 billion in aid each year, the Egyptian military had to present clean hands to the United States, as well. And that required a strengthened police force to commit abuses on its behalf. Defense Minister Tantawi reportedly made this case so often to US officials that an embassy cable ahead of his visit in March 2008 warned DC that: "He will also state that the military is not behind human rights problems in Egypt and that U.S. Congressional human rights conditionally [SIC] is mis-targeted."[141]

In short, whatever level of strength the police achieved under Mubarak was in service of the military. The Ministry of Interior never became a rival power that counterbalanced the military's hegemony. In the wake of the CSF mutiny, the CIA assessed that: "The Egyptian military is the country's strongest institution and is the only force that alone can replace the regime or protect it against internal opposition groups."[142] Henry and Springborg (2011) concurred: "By contrast [to Tunisia], former President Hosni Mubarak's Egypt was a military state to which the police were subordinate, [. . .] under-equipped, [and] poorly paid."

Gamal Mubarak

While there is little evidence to support the notion that the military was counterbalanced, there is comparatively more truth to the argument that the military opposed Gamal Mubarak, Hosni's younger son and heir apparent. If he succeeded to the presidency, Gamal would have become the first president with a civilian background since the 1952 coup. Moreover, Gamal Mubarak, a private-sector businessman, had championed neoliberal reforms throughout the 2000s. If he continued to do so as president, Gamal might have posed a potential threat to the military's economic empire.

My critique of this argument proceeds in two parts. The first, which follows, is that despite some tensions between them, a Gamal Mubarak presidency was still preferable to the military than a democratic transition that might bring the Muslim Brotherhood to power. Though he might reduce their profits, Gamal at least understood the importance of the military in the regime, and shared their aversion to an Islamist takeover. The second critique, which I make in the next chapter, is that

---

[141] US Embassy Cairo, "Scenesetter for MINDEF Tantawi's Visit to the U.S. March 24-28," March 16, 2008, 08CAIRO524_a.

[142] CIA, "Egypt: Threats to the Regime and to the Foreign Presence," Reading Room, May 16, 1988.

Gamal Mubarak was out of the picture relatively soon into the January 2011 protests, and thus cannot fully explain the military's later defection.

Hosni Mubarak appeared to groom his son Gamal for the presidency in the 2000s, appointing him assistant secretary-general of the National Democratic Party in 2000. Gamal then appeared to wield considerable influence over Egypt's economic policies with the appointment of Prime Minister Ahmed Nazif in 2004, helping to accelerate neo-liberal reforms and strengthen the private sector. However, as mentioned earlier, even at the height of this push for privatization, the military was able to carve out exceptions for its own enterprises. Without any coercive power of his own, it is difficult to see how Gamal Mubarak could have removed the military's effective veto power or privatized its assets.

Moreover, the military enjoyed two important levers to pressure the private sector. First, as one Egyptian professor told the US Embassy, "the defense minister can put a hold on any contract for 'security concerns.'"[143] Second, and relatedly, "the armed forces possess the legal power to confiscate public land at any time for purposes of national security."[144] Combined, the ever-present threat that the military might confiscate their land or cancel their contract meant that the private-sector businessmen that emerged in the 1990s and 2000s often did so in collaboration with the military. As Roll (2013, p. 10) observes: "Over the decades close networks had grown between the generals and various leading entrepreneurs, with the latter functioning for example as advisers and service providers in connection with arms deals. [. . .] The private sector is heavily dependent on the military when it comes to buying land, for example to build new factories or tourist resorts."

Much of the private sector thus emerged in symbiosis with Military Inc., not in competition with it. Still, the rise of the private sector did introduce some competition to the military's companies. Although the military retained important advantages over the civilian sector (conscript labor, tax breaks), the military reportedly had to "improve the quality" of its services in order to compete,[145] perhaps cutting into their bottom line. The military accordingly felt "threatened by the business community," observed retired General Mohamed Kadry Said.[146]

Although the military might have preferred a military officer as president, almost all observers agreed that the military would have accepted Gamal as president. The same General Kadry Said just quoted also said that the military would accept Gamal if he won an election, and that a military coup is "not an option."[147] The oft-cited US Embassy cable that quotes Egyptian academics discussing the threat posed by Gamal to the military also notes that all the "analysts agreed that the military would allow Gamal to take power through an election if President Mubarak blessed the process

---

[143] US Embassy Cairo, "Academics see the military in decline, but retaining strong influence," September 23, 2008, 08CAIRO2091_a.

[144] Roll (2013, p. 10).

[145] Ibid.

[146] Quoted in Cambanis (2010).

[147] Ibid.

and effectively gave Gamal the reigns of power."[148] Finally, the US Embassy itself in its assessment observed that:

> While there are economic and political tensions between the business elite and the military, the overall relationship between the two still appears to be cooperative, rather than adversarial. [...] We agree with the analysis that senior military officers would support Gamal if Mubarak resigned and installed him in the presidency, as it is difficult to imagine opposition from these officers who depend on the president and defense minister for their jobs and material perks.[149]

After all, the military and Gamal Mubarak saw eye-to-eye on the most existential issues: sharing power between them and not permitting the Muslim Brotherhood and other political parties to come to power and interfere in the military's affairs. While the military would not use force to oppose a Gamal Mubarak presidency, it would step in "with force if necessary" to stop the Muslim Brotherhood from coming to power, according to retired Army General Hosam Sowilam.[150] "We will not accept any interference by the political parties into our military affairs."

In short, while a Gamal Mubarak presidency may not have been the military's first preference, they likely preferred it to a democratic transition that might end up empowering the Muslim Brotherhood. Had there been a smooth transition to Gamal, without any protests, the military would likely have consented. But that is not what ended up happening—instead, mass protests emerged in 2011 against Hosni Mubarak's rule, forcing the military to begrudgingly choose between tarnishing its reputation with large-scale repression, or entering the unknown.

Conclusion

Since the 1952 coup, the Egyptian military has effectively governed the country. Each of its presidents—Nasser, Sadat, and Mubarak—decided that their best coup-proofing strategy was to keep the military invested in their regime. They each shared considerable political power and material resources with the military, buying their loyalty. They also each attempted to mold the military ideationally to fit their regime, producing a relatively secular, anti-Islamist force that viewed the rise of the Muslim Brotherhood as an existential threat. These two strategies—power sharing and stacking—would in turn shape how the military reacted to the protests in 2011 and to the subsequent democratic transition.

---

[148] US Embassy Cairo, "Academics see the military in decline, but retaining strong influence," September 23, 2008, 08CAIRO2091_a.
[149] Ibid.
[150] Quoted in Cambanis (2010).

6

Egypt: Repression and Revolution

> If [Mubarak had been] able to succeed, nothing would have happened.
> We would have pulled our people back to the barracks.
> —**Egyptian General (in Weymouth, 2011)**

Introduction

In January 2011, the world watched in awe as millions of Egyptians took to the streets, toppling their 30-year-dictator, Hosni Mubarak, in just 18 days. The military's response to these protests proved critical to Mubarak's fall, with the generals declaring on January 31 that they would not fire on protesters, and eventually stepping in to topple Mubarak themselves on February 11.

Several scholars have inferred from the Egyptian military's eventual "defection" that it must have been disgruntled with Mubarak. Perhaps searching for a similarity with the Tunisian military, many have claimed the Egyptian military had also felt neglected relative to the police, or that they feared the rise of Mubarak's son, Gamal, a private-sector businessman who might push for privatizing the military's economic assets.[1]

The Egyptian military's behavior in 2011, however, belies these resentment hypotheses. On the contrary, the military tried its best to preserve Mubarak. After deploying into the streets on January 28, the military helped to repress protesters, detaining and torturing demonstrators even after its January 31 pledge not to use force. Having been the center of power under Mubarak, the military remained loyal throughout nearly all of the uprising.

However, while the military could repress protesters out of the limelight, it could not afford to engage in large-scale, public repression such as firing on the protesters in Tahrir Square. Such a massacre would severely tarnish the reputation of the military at home and abroad. Even if the military managed to preserve Mubarak, such repression would make it harder to justify its privileged position in the state and the economy. Moreover, a massacre might prompt the suspension of US military aid, cutting into the military's bottom line.

The military therefore engaged in a wait-and-see approach, hoping that its low-level repression combined with Mubarak's concessions might allow it to preserve

---

[1] Albrecht and Bishara (2011); Barany (2011, 2016); Masoud (2011); Kandil (2012); Marshall and Stacher (2012); Stacher (2012); Abul-Magd (2013); Makara (2013, 2016); Taylor (2014); Albrecht (2015); Bou Nassif (2015*b*); Koehler (2016).

Soldiers of Democracy?. Sharan Grewal, Oxford University Press. © Sharan Grewal (2023).
DOI: 10.1093/oso/9780192873910.003.0006

both Mubarak and its image. After 18 days, however, the generals realized this strategy would not work. The only way to clear the square would be to topple Mubarak and initiate a transition.

However, the military also could not afford to let a transition get out of hand, given the institutional interests it needed to preserve. Accordingly, the military decided to seize power itself, forcing Mubarak to resign and hand over power to the Supreme Council of the Armed Forces. Contrary to the Tunisian military's more passive and apolitical approach, Egypt's military staged a coup, driven by its greater material and political interests. It also actively manufactured an image that it had sided with the people and saved the revolution, an image that it hoped would help it weather the coming democratic transition.

In sum, the military's behavior in 2011 reflected the way in which Mubarak had treated it. Due to his efforts to empower them into his regime, the officers were reluctant to let Mubarak fall. Once they finally realized they had no choice, those same interests then led them to stage a coup, hoping to preserve their privileged position moving forward.

The 2011 Revolution

Protests against Hosni Mubarak began on Tuesday, January 25, which since 2009 had become National Police Day, meant to celebrate the police's resistance of British colonialism in 1952. Instead of celebrating, activists had called for a demonstration outside of the Ministry of Interior to protest police brutality—in particular, their gruesome murder of Khaled Said in June 2010. Organized by Wael Ghonim's Facebook page, "We are all Khaled Said," over 200,000 protesters showed up, far exceeding Ghonim's hopes of 50,000.[2]

Just 11 days earlier, Egyptians had gotten an unexpected boost from watching the experience of Tunisia, where protesters had succeeded in ousting President Zine El Abidine Ben Ali on January 14. "What happened in Tunisia is a model," said one Egyptian prior to January 25. "It shows that . . . we can do it [too]."[3] As protesters took to the streets on the 25th, another activist told *Al-Jazeera* that the protests are meant "to send a message to the Egyptian regime that Mubarak is no different than Ben Ali and we want him to leave too."[4]

Protests continued over the next two days, led primarily by young activists from the National Association for Change and the April 6 Youth Movement. However, the fourth day, January 28, had the advantage of coinciding with a Friday, when the masses could be mobilized after Friday prayers at the mosque. Labeled the "Day of Rage," protesters numbered into the hundreds of thousands, encompassing young and old, men and women, Muslims and Christians, secularists and Islamists.

[2] Kirkpatrick and Sanger (2011).
[3] Quoted in Trager (2011).
[4] Quoted in Al-Jazeera (2011).

The police and Central Security Forces (CSF) tried their best to prevent protesters from reaching the iconic Tahrir Square, coming out in full force with tear gas and rubber bullets. But Egyptians had learned from Tunisians how to deal with the police: "We pulled out all the tricks of the game—the Pepsi, the onion, the vinegar," noted Ahmed Maher, leader of the April 6 movement, "who wore cardboard and plastic bottles under his sweater, a bike helmet on his head and a barrel-top shield on his arm."[5] "The strategy was the people who were injured would go to the back and other people would replace them. We just kept rotating."

After more than five hours of battling the police, the protesters emerged victorious, occupying Tahrir Square as the police, exhausted and dejected, withdrew. While most protesters celebrated in Tahrir, others took the battle further. As Abul-Magd (2012, p. 571) notes, "Protesters attacked police forces in every province in the country, stormed into police stations, and burned many of them down."[6]

As Interior Minister Habib al-Adly would later admit, "None of us foresaw the size or persistence of the demonstrators, we never thought we might be outnumbered . . . We had no plan to deal with such events . . . the troops did not have the know-how and training to conduct a multiple-day operation . . . I decided to inform the president that we must resort to the armed forces."[7]

The Military Deploys; Supports Police

With the police overwhelmed, Mubarak turned to the military for help. The commander-in-chief, Field Marshal Hussein Tantawi, recalled: "Meetings between us were held to know the stance of the armed forces, especially on January 28 when the military was ordered to go down and support the police in fulfilling its duties."[8]

Notably, the military obeyed, deploying in force that evening, January 28, to defend vital institutions such as government buildings, police stations, foreign embassies, and even major private businesses.[9] Even more importantly, as Tantawi alludes to, the military "supported the police in their duties," resupplying them with ammunition and according to some witnesses, attacking protesters themselves. Maikel Nabil Sanad (2011), a protester who was later imprisoned for his blog post "The army and the people wasn't ever one hand," witnessed "military police jeeps passing through demonstrators to provide live ammunition to the police so they start firing again." Said (2012, p. 408) likewise confirms "many incidents" of "army members giving weapons to police." In her research, Holmes (2012, p. 399) finds that: "Some witnesses also observed soldiers shooting protesters on January 28. One of my interviewees said he saw a soldier kill approximately twelve people that night."

---

[5] Quoted in Kirkpatrick and Sanger (2011).
[6] For violence against the police, see also Ketchley (2017).
[7] See Adly's testimony to the military court. Quoted in Kandil (2012, p. 236).
[8] Tantawi's testimony to the military court, September 24, 2011. Quoted in Holmes (2012, p. 399).
[9] See Marshall and Stacher (2012).

Other accounts support the claim that the military helped the police in repressing protesters. The International Crisis Group (2011, p. 5) personally observed that "police and soldiers jointly detained and assaulted protesters" on January 28 and 29. Egyptian journalist Ashraf Khalil (2012, p. 193) describes a soldier detaining and "aggressively interrogat[ing]" a protester at the Egyptian Museum, "slapping him hard across the face." Taylor (2014, p. 123), citing interviews with US government officials, writes: "In the Ma'adi quarter of Cairo, reports surfaced that army tanks had used their machine guns to repulse successive waves of demonstrators seeking to overrun a police station."

In short, as soon as the military deployed on January 28, it began to support the regime by helping the police repress demonstrators. This was not the behavior of a military that resented Mubarak and felt counterbalanced by the police. Instead, as shown in the previous chapter, the military had become invested in the regime. It was the center of power, running the show from behind the scenes. As retired General Hosam Sowilan told *The New York Times* that day, "The army in Tunisia put pressure on Ben Ali to leave. We are not going to do that here. The army here is loyal to this country and to the regime."[10]

Mubarak's "Concessions"

Any doubt that the military was the center of Mubarak's regime would vanish the next day, January 29, when Mubarak announced his first "concessions" in response to the protests. First, Mubarak appointed a vice-president for the first time in his 30-year reign. Given that both Sadat and Mubarak had been vice-president before assuming the presidency, this appointment was widely viewed as selecting a successor. Notably, Mubarak did not choose his son Gamal. Instead, he appointed ex-army general Omar Suleiman, who had led the General Intelligence Directorate. If there had been any resentment from the military towards Gamal, he was now out of the picture: instead, a retired general was now set to become the next president.

Second, Mubarak also fired the prime minister, Ahmed Nazif, and replaced him with Ahmed Shafik, a retired air force chief (1996–2002) who had since served as the minister of civil aviation. In other words, not only was Gamal out of the picture, but his neo-liberal ally, Nazif, was as well. In their place came the military.

Mubarak's elevation of Suleiman and Shafik was "an attempt to secure the loyalty of the military," observed Holmes (2019, p. 56). "What concerns us now is this is clearly a military takeover," noted Egyptian political scientist Emad El-Din Shahin that day.[11] Egyptian economist Ragui Assaad concurred: "Suleiman was the military's candidate forever . . . this is a way of paving the way for a military-led regime," noting also that "Gamal is clearly off the table. He would be unacceptable now."[12]

---

[10] Quoted in Kirkpatrick (2011*b*).
[11] Quoted in Slackman (2011).
[12] Quoted in Slackman (2011).

At this point, in the evening of January 29, it was clear that the military—not the police or private sector—was dominant. The military was set to succeed Mubarak when he resigned, and was heading the government in the meantime. If there had been any question of who was running the show, it was now plain to see.

The military's actions the next day in turn reflected continued loyalty. On January 30, Suleiman, Tantawi, and Chief of Staff Sami Anan met with Mubarak, and appeared to agree on taking further steps to disperse the protesters. Minutes before the curfew, the military presented a show of force to try to scare demonstrators into going home. Fighter jets roared over Tahrir Square, flying "menacingly"[13] low several times over the crowds. As one protester observed, "The planes are out there to scare the people. It's time for the curfew and no one is going home. It's clear to me that the army is here to protect Mubarak."[14]

The "Defection"

Although the military had thus far been helping to repress protesters, the military made a major public statement the next day that many interpreted to be a "defection" from Mubarak. On January 31, the military released a video statement saying: "To the great people of Egypt, your armed forces, acknowledging the legitimate rights of the people . . . have not and will not use force against the Egyptian people."[15]

There are two primary challenges with interpreting this statement as a defection. The first is explaining its timing. For those arguing that defection stemmed from the military's resentment of Gamal Mubarak, Gamal at this point was out of the picture, making it unclear why the military would defect now. Likewise, for those claiming the military was upset by having been sidelined by the police or the party, the military had now been elevated into the highest positions, claiming president, vice-president, and prime minister. Why would it repress at first when it was (in this narrative) threatened and marginalized, only to defect once it had regained its central position in the regime?

The second challenge with the "defection" narrative is that the military's statement was false. The military *had* been repressing protesters thus far, and would continue doing so until the very end of the uprising. Throughout the protests, soldiers were arresting, detaining, beating up, and torturing protesters. While there were also some individual defections, the military was engaged in low-level repression throughout the uprising.

At the same time, there was also some truth to the military's statement. Although it had been engaged in low-level repression, it could not afford to engage in large-scale, public repression. Massacring protesters in the streets was simply out of the question, for the same reasons that the military had stayed out of domestic repression for the past three decades: it could not afford to tarnish its domestic and international image.

---

[13] Bou Nassif (2021, p. 167).
[14] Quoted in Reuters Staff (2011*a*). See also Khalil (2012, pp. 209–210).
[15] Quoted in BBC (2011*a*).

Domestically, the military had worked assiduously to build back its reputation after the 1967 defeat, by exiting the political limelight, propping up the Interior Ministry, and providing public goods and services. While a massacre might succeed in preserving Mubarak, the military would come under increasing criticism by the opposition, questioning its prerogatives like they did in the 1980s. In order to preserve its corporate interests, it needed to maintain a popular image in the Egyptian psyche.

Internationally as well, a massacre would have had enormous consequences. US President Barack Obama on January 28 had already drawn a clear red line: "I want to be very clear in calling upon the Egyptian authorities to refrain from any violence against peaceful protesters."[16] White House spokesman Robert Gibbs even more explicitly threatened that America's "assistance posture" would depend on events "now, and in the coming days."[17] "We are watching very closely the actions of the government, the police and all of those in the military," Gibbs noted.[18] Secretary of Defense Robert Gates also made his first call to Tantawi on January 30, in which he "urged him to ensure that the army would exercise restraint in dealing with the protesters."[19] The message at this stage was clear: a massacre of protesters might cost the military its $1.3 billion in US aid.

Critical to both the domestic and international calculations was the composition of the protesters. Had the protesters primarily represented the Muslim Brotherhood, as they did during the August 2013 Rabaa massacre, the military could paint them as terrorists and traitors, and thereby avoid or at least mitigate the reputation costs. But in 2011, the military simply could not paint them as such. The hundreds of thousands of protesters assembled on the ground were everyday Egyptians from all walks of life.

Indeed, the Muslim Brotherhood had been intentionally downplaying its role in the revolution precisely to avoid such a framing. While the Brotherhood endorsed the protests on January 23,[20] and several leaders such as Mohamed Beltagy and Gamal Heshmat participated on January 25, they did not instruct the rank and file to join until January 28. Conscious that "the government uses us to scare people here and abroad,"[21] the Brotherhood also made sure the rank and file did not chant Islamist slogans.

In short, although the military could engage in low-level, out-of-the-limelight repression, it could not afford to fire on the protesters directly. A massacre of protesters would have been political suicide: spelling the end of its image at home and abroad to such an extent as to threaten its corporate interests. The most the military could do to preserve Mubarak was to engage in low-level repression and facilitate repression from other actors like the police.

---

[16] Obama (2011*a*). In his memoirs, Obama (2020, p. 645) would write that: "[T]he Mubarak regime had received billions of U.S. taxpayer dollars; we supplied them with weapons, shared information, and helped train their military officers; and for me to allow the recipient of that aid, someone we called an ally, to perpetrate wanton violence on peaceful demonstrators, with all the world watching–that was a line I was unwilling to cross."

[17] Quoted in Landler (2011).

[18] Quoted in CNN Wire Staff (2011).

[19] Gates (2014, p. 505).

[20] See IkhwanWeb (2011*c*).

[21] Brotherhood leader quoted in Kirkpatrick (2011*b*).

However, even those actions might now invite increased scrutiny. Now that the military had been elevated into the spotlight through the appointment of Suleiman as vice president and Shafik as prime minister, it might be publicly blamed for any repression of protesters, even that emanating from the police. Accordingly, in order to preserve its image, the military needed to take action now to create the fiction of distance between itself and the regime.

The January 31 statement that the military would not use force against protesters should thus be viewed in this light: as political theater designed to improve the military's image. Indeed, as part of this play, "the backdrop of the military's public announcement showed a film of protesters cheering the soldiers."[22] The video statement was an attempt to ingratiate the military with the protesters, to create the fiction that it was on the protesters' side, and to pretend that there was daylight between it and the regime so as to deflect responsibility for any repression that was and would continue to occur.

In other words, rather than representing a defection, the military's statement should instead be viewed as the military hedging its bets. If its low-level repression worked, this statement would allow the military to have its cake and eat it too: to preserve Mubarak and its image. Meanwhile, if its repression did not work, and Mubarak was toppled, the statement would help the military portray itself as the savior of the revolution, a reputation that might help it avoid the revolutionary justice that was sure to come.

In short, rather than siding with the people, the "Army took the side of the Army," in the words of CENTCOM Commander John Abizaid.[23] That the military was hedging, not defecting, would become increasingly clear over the next ten days. Rather than protecting the people, the military would continue to facilitate and engage in repression and try to preserve Mubarak from behind the scenes.

The Battle of the Camel

From February 1 to February 10, the military pursued what we might call a "wait-and-see" approach, seeing if its low-level repression combined with Mubarak's concessions might be able to stem the protests. As one senior general told Weymouth (2011), "we gave the presidential institution the full opportunity to manage events. If it were able to succeed, nothing would have happened. We would have pulled our people back to the barracks."

Mubarak began with a major speech on February 1, his second of the uprising. Mubarak pledged to step down once his term ended in September, and promised a revision of the constitution in the meantime. Such "concessions," however, did little to please the protesters, who wanted Mubarak gone now, not in six months.

---

[22] Taylor (2014, p. 123).
[23] Quoted in Taylor (2014, p. 127).

On February 2, Mubarak attempted to organize pro-regime protests. About 700 men showed up outside the Ministry of Information, allowing the state television to film them chanting "six months isn't enough, we want you until the end."[24] Another 1,000 were marching from the Pyramids to Tahrir, with several riding on horses and camels.

Those forces would turn out to be thugs intent on beating up the protesters. As they approached Tahrir around 2:30 p.m., the military withdrew from their positions surrounding the square, allowing them to enter. The thugs then proceeded to attack the protesters with clubs and swords, killing 13 and wounding 1,200. For 14 hours the military simply stood by, watching the thugs clash with the protesters.[25] For some, the military's behavior revealed that it had not actually sided with the protesters. "I had a bit of [a] nervous breakdown," noted the Revolutionary Socialist Tarek Shalaby. "I couldn't believe they were just filming us killing each other."[26]

"It wasn't just that they weren't doing anything," argued activist Mohamed El Dahshan. "They were complicit. They let these guys through."[27] Dahshan even confronted the army, asking a colonel, "Why aren't you doing anything?" The colonel retorted: "Aren't you expressing your opinion? They're here expressing their opinion as well."[28]

By that evening, the thugs had made their way to nearby rooftops, pelting the protesters from above with rocks and molotov cocktails. Protesters eventually drove them from those rooftops, but the thugs re-grouped on the nearby October 6 bridge. The battle continued until the early morning of February 3, when the thugs appeared to be supplemented by plainclothes police officers firing live ammunition. "Unable to break the protesters' discipline or determination, the Mubarak forces resorted to guns, shooting 45 and killing 2, according to witnesses and doctors interviewed early that morning."[29]

Until now, the government could deflect blame for the clashes, saying the thugs were simply everyday citizens passionate for Mubarak. But now, with the use of live fire, it was clear that their side also included at least the police, making it more difficult to deny responsibility. With its image now hanging in the balance, the military finally, 14 hours later, stepped in, firing into the air to separate the two sides.

Military Repression

The military in these days was not just a passive actor, facilitating repression by the police and armed thugs. Instead, the military between February 1 and February 10 also threatened and even engaged in repression itself. Although it could not afford to publicly use force to clear Tahrir Square, that did not stop the military from trying.

---

[24] Khalil (2012, p. 219).
[25] Shahin (2012, p. 67), Kirkpatrick (2018a, p. 49).
[26] Quoted in Khalil (2012, p. 223).
[27] Quoted in Khalil (2012, p. 225).
[28] Quoted in Khalil (2012, p. 226).
[29] Kirkpatrick and Sanger (2011). See also Khalil (2012); Kortam (2013).

The army commander in Cairo, General Hassan al-Roweny, repeatedly went down to Tahrir to try to cajole and intimidate the protesters into going home. "End this silly business," he pleaded with the protesters on February 5, urging them to at least allow traffic through the square. "We can't use violence, but we can be very tough with people," he warned. "You all have the right to express yourselves, but please save what is left of Egypt." When the crowd responded that Mubarak should leave, Roweny turned around and left, saying, "I will not speak amid such chants."[30]

Another lieutenant colonel sent the same message. "You guys are taking it too far. [. . .] You have delivered the message, but now you are going to rip the country apart." Ignoring protesters' attempts to fraternize by offering him water, he added: "I want to know where all this stuff is coming from. Where is the money coming from? In whose interest is all this?"[31]

On February 6, General Roweny ordered the tanks surrounding Tahrir to close in, hoping to pack in the protesters and push them into leaving. But protesters laid down in front of their tracks, deterring them from moving further.[32] The military also tried to barricade the square. "Each day brought several new military truckloads of waist-high concrete barriers that were unloaded and assembled across the perimeter," noted Khalil (2012, p. 208). "It was as though they were trying to physically cut Tahrir Square off from the rest of Egypt."

While the military shied away from using force under the cameras of Tahrir Square, it did so repeatedly outside of the limelight. Both the military police, led by General Hamdi Badin, and military intelligence, led by General Abdelfattah al-Sisi, detained, interrogated, and tortured protesters even after the military's promise not to use force on January 31. On February 9, Human Rights Watch (2011) verified that:

> Army officers and military police arbitrary detained at least 119 people [. . .] and in at least five cases tortured them. [. . .] Since January 31, Human Rights Watch has documented the arbitrary arrest by military police of at least 20 protesters who were leaving or heading to Tahrir Square. [. . .] Military police [also] arrested at least 37 human rights defenders and activists since January 31 and held them from periods ranging from 12 to 48 hours. [Finally . . .] Human Rights Watch has compiled a list of 62 Egyptian and international journalists arrested by the military police since February 2.

Military intelligence likewise detained, disappeared, and even tortured to death protesters, journalists, and activists. The lawyer Osama Abdel Hamid, for instance, was tortured and murdered by Military Intelligence Group 75 at the military prison at Heikstep base (east of Cairo). When his father found his body 12 days later, it had been "misshapen" by torture and had a fractured skull.[33] Nermeen Yousry, who founded the organization "We Will Find Them" to help search for the disappeared,

---

[30] Quoted in Steavenson (2011).
[31] Quoted in Steavenson (2011).
[32] Steavenson (2011) and Awad and Zayed (2011).
[33] Hill and Mansour (2013).

noted that: "Actually me, myself, I used to chant: 'The army and the people are one hand,' but now, yes, maybe we will realize that the army was never on our side [. . .] they were trying to break down the revolution [. . .] make people scared, terrify people from going to the square."[34]

In other words, although the military did not shoot protesters, it did engage in repression throughout the uprising, even after its January 31 pledge not to. As one Western diplomat observed, Field Marshall Tantawi is "a product of the regime and he's perfectly happy to arrest people."[35] Observing that the military "was responsible for most cases of torture during the Egyptian uprising, not the interior ministry," Bou Nassif (2021, pp. 168–170) thus concludes that: "The SCAF did whatever it could to help the embattled president, short of ordering a full-scale massacre of protesters."

Continued US pressure

A massacre, after all, was still out of the question. The United States in particular was continuing to apply pressure on the Egyptian military not to crack down on protesters. As President Obama (2020, p. 646) recalled in his memoirs:

> Once or twice a day, we had Gates, Mullen, Panetta, Brennan, and others quietly reach out to high-ranking officers in the Egyptian military and intelligence services, making clear that a military-sanctioned crackdown on the protesters would have severe consequences on any future U.S.-Egyptian relationship. The implication of this military-to-military outreach was plain: U.S.-Egyptian cooperation, and the aid that came with it, wasn't dependent on Mubarak's staying in power, so Egypt's generals and intelligence chiefs might want to carefully consider which actions best preserved their institutional interests.

President Obama, however, was also calling for Mubarak to step down. "An orderly transition must be meaningful, it must be peaceful, and it must begin now," Obama (2011*b*) said publicly on February 1. But unlike with the US's call for it to exercise restraint, the Egyptian military could sense some daylight between Obama and his staffers on his call for Mubarak to leave now.

In fact, the senior members of his administration—Vice President Joe Biden, Secretary of State Hillary Clinton, and Secretary of Defense Robert Gates, among others—were wary of abandoning Mubarak, and had tried to push Obama to say that Mubarak should go "sooner rather than later" instead of "now." But "the president overrode the unanimous advice of his senior-most national security advisers, siding with the junior staffers in terms of what he tells Mubarak and in what he would say publicly," recalled Secretary Gates (2014, p. 506).

---

[34] Quoted in Hill and Mansour (2013).
[35] Quoted in Steavenson (2011).

These divisions became public when after Obama's call for a transition to begin now, Frank Wisner, who Obama had just days previously sent as an envoy to Mubarak, said at the February 5 Munich security conference that "President Mubarak's continued leadership is critical." Hillary Clinton at the same conference reiterated that "we are supporting" the transition process led by the new vice president, Omar Suleiman.[36] Obama "took me to the woodshed" for these comments, Clinton (2014, p. 289) would later write, but it was too late: it had become public knowledge that Obama and his advisors were not in lockstep.

Secretary Gates (2014, p. 507) recalled that "Crown Prince Mohamed bin Zayed of the UAE [. . .] gave me an earful, saying that he was getting mixed messages from the United States, that the message from the vice president and me was not the same as what he was hearing from the White House or the media."

In light of these mixed messages from the United States, the Egyptian military knew that the most important calls, in terms of US military aid, were those coming from the Department of Defense. All "the other calls were considered noise," observed former US ambassador to Egypt Daniel Kurtzer.[37] The hesitance that Secretary Gates, as well as top US military leaders, were expressing to the Egyptian military convinced it that it did not need to pressure Mubarak to leave immediately. It could instead embark on its wait-and-see approach between February 1 and 10.

Sussing out the Opposition

Over time, however, the military began to realize that its low-level repression was not going to work. The protests were continuing to overwhelm the police, and the regime could not seem to turn the tide. Accordingly, the military began to suss out the opposition, to examine what reforms might get them to leave the square.

On February 6, Vice President Omar Suleiman held talks with a number of opposition groups, including the Muslim Brotherhood and Wafd Party. The opposition representatives demanded a full democratic transition, and not just partial reforms. "But Suleiman responded, 'Democracy comes in stages,'" recalled Mustafa al-Naggar, coordinator for Mohamed ElBaradei's National Association for Change.[38]

After all, the military was wary about what a democratic transition might mean for its privileged position in the state. True democratization might mean weening the military out of the economy and politics, and relegating it to military affairs. Retired General Mahmoud Zaher, in a conversation with Steavenson (2011), "emphasized that the role of the Army in Egypt was not confined to the military sphere, that it was 'politically influential and politically involved and politically distinct.'" The army, according to General Zaher, could only tolerate a democracy with "limitations" that preserved the military's prerogatives, including a stipulation that the president must

---

[36] Kirkpatrick (2018a, p. 50).
[37] Quoted in Taylor (2014, p. 126).
[38] Quoted in Awad (2011b).

have a military background, admitting that this "may cause some outsiders to say that our democracy is different from their democracy."

In short, the military was unwilling to side with the protesters' demands and initiate a full transition to democracy. Unlike in Tunisia, the military could not afford to let these opposition parties come to power or help run a transition, for fear of what that might spell for its interests. The military's best hope lay instead with convincing Mubarak to delegate his powers to Vice-President Suleiman, leaving himself in a simple caretaker position.[39] That delegation might satisfy some of the protesters' demands, as well as allow Suleiman to manage a transition in a way that respected the military's interests.

Mubarak's Last Speech

On February 10, Mubarak complied with the military's wishes, delegating power to Suleiman. In what would become the final speech of his presidency, Mubarak reiterated his earlier concessions: that he would step down after elections in September and that the constitution would be revised in the meantime. He now also added—toward the end of the speech—that he had "delegated to the vice president some of the powers of the president," though which ones were not made clear. After all, Mubarak also implied that he would not be a mere figurehead: "I have declared my commitment [...] to carrying out my responsibility in protecting the constitution and the people's interests until power and responsibility are handed over to whoever is elected next September."[40]

Mubarak's muddled speech ended up fumbling the new concession, which anyway would not have been enough at this point. Protesters swelled in Tahrir, booing the speech, and demanding Mubarak's immediate resignation. The next day, February 11—another Friday—saw renewed protests numbering over a million, confirming that the concession had not worked. Protest leaders were also threatening to make their way from Tahrir to the presidential palace in Heliopolis, which might force the military's hand into using violence to defend the palace. That "would destroy the relationship between the soldiers and people," observed General Roweny.[41] The only way to end the protests and preserve its image, the military finally realized, would be for Mubarak to resign. "We gave Mubarak a chance to fix the deteriorating situation, but he could not," said one SCAF general. "So we had to intervene."[42]

President Obama (2011c), for his part, likewise condemned Mubarak's final speech. "The Egyptian people have been told that there was a transition of authority, but it is not yet clear that this transition is immediate, meaningful or sufficient.

---

[39] This proposal came originally from the "wise men," a group of statesmen, scholars, activists, and businessmen, on February 3.

[40] Quoted in BBC (2011b).

[41] Quoted in Sidney Blumenthal's email to Hillary Clinton, "Intel Report and Options: What really happened and what should happen now," February 12, 2011, Wikileaks.

[42] Quoted in International Crisis Group (2012, p. 20).

Too many Egyptians remain unconvinced that the government is serious about a genuine transition to democracy, and it is the responsibility of the government to speak clearly to the Egyptian people and the world. The Egyptian government must put forward a credible, concrete and unequivocal path toward genuine democracy, and they have not yet seized that opportunity."

While some in the administration were still wary of abandoning Mubarak, worrying it would only give rise to the Muslim Brotherhood, the tide had turned. There were no more mixed signals coming from the US government: Mubarak had to go. The Brotherhood, for its part, had tried to reassure the West in the final days of the uprising. Brotherhood leaders penned a series of op-eds—including by Mohamed Morsi (2011) in *The Guardian* on February 7, by Essam El-Erian (2011) in *The New York Times* on February 9, and Abdel Moneim Aboul-Futouh (2011) in *The Washington Post* on February 10—each designed to convince the West that they wanted democracy, not an Islamic theocracy.

Two other factors beyond US pressure were also pushing the generals to intervene. First, the military's low-level repression was increasingly becoming public. After the Human Rights Watch report on February 9, "NPR's Lourdes Garcia-Navarro said protesters had become increasingly concerned in recent days of a 'stealthy crackdown' by soldiers. [. . .] 'Some of the people that have been trying to get in supplies to the square have disappeared only to re-emerge later with allegations that they have been mistreated by the army,' Garcia-Navarro said."[43]

Second, the officers were beginning to see defections in the lower ranks. On February 10, after Mubarak's speech, Major Ahmad Shuman, who had until that point been guarding the western entrance to Tahrir, took off his uniform and joined the protesters. Speaking live on *Al-Jazeera*, he also called for both Mubarak and Tantawi to resign.[44] The next day, Shuman was joined by 15 of his colleagues ranging from captain to lieutenant colonel. "The armed forces' solidarity movement with the people has begun," he said.[45] Fearing that this wave of defections might cascade further, the generals decided to step in and nip this in the bud.

The Coup

At 6 p.m. on February 11, Vice President Suleiman at long last read out the statement protesters were waiting for: "President Muhammad Hosni Mubarak has decided to step down from the office of president of the republic." Tahrir Square exploded in jubilation: after 30 years in power, Mubarak had been toppled.

Notably, Mubarak did not announce his resignation himself, leading to rumors that it may not have been voluntary: that the military may have forced him from office behind the scenes. Such speculation of a coup then gained further momentum

---

[43] Quoted in NPR Staff and Wires (2011).
[44] See Mekay (2011).
[45] Quoted in Awad (2011*a*).

from the second half of Suleiman's statement: in his absence, Mubarak "instructed the supreme council of the armed forces to manage the affairs of the country."

Constitutionally, the speaker of the parliament was supposed to succeed the president in the case of resignation.[46] The military, however, was taking no chances on Fathi Sorour, the civilian politician who had served as speaker since 1990. Instead, the military took power itself. Given the vast political and economic interests it needed to preserve, the military could not afford to entrust the process to civilians. Unlike in Tunisia, it could not simply step aside and let the constitutional procedure play itself out.

Seizing power in contradiction of the constitution, of course, was a coup d'etat, and risked inviting the wrath of Tahrir Square. Protesters might feel that if anyone had the right to run the country now, it was them—not the military. Major General and member of the SCAF Mamdouh Shahin admitted as much in an interview with *Al-Masry al-Youm* on March 17: "What happened in 1952 in fact had been revolutionary legitimacy, because the Free Officers [. . .] carried out the revolution and seized power. [. . .] Now we have a different situation, where those who revolted on January 25, 2011 were not the ones who seized power."[47]

To prepare the ground for their intervention, the military needed to make it seem like it was on the side of the people, not staging a coup but simply fulfilling a revolution. In the days prior to the coup, it therefore began a concerted effort to cement its image as the "savior of the revolution." Building off its January 31 statement that it would not use force against the people, the military in the final days of the uprising took pains to stress that it had defended the people (notwithstanding its actual repression). Vice President Suleiman, for instance, in his speech following Mubarak's on February 10, emphasized that the army "has protected the revolution of the youth and protected the nation and the legitimacy of the constitution."[48]

The military also sought to exploit and re-package a slogan that protesters had begun to chant as early as January 28, when the military was first deployed. Protesters that day introduced the chant: "The army and the people are one hand" (*al-geysh wal-sha'ab iyd wahda*). For some, this chant reflected a genuine belief that the army would be on their side, since the army was conscripted and thus came from the people. For others, this slogan was a strategic move to fraternize with the army and make sure it would be on their side.[49]

Either way, the slogan helped to create the image of the military as distinct from the Mubarak regime, something the generals now sought to use to their advantage. Particularly in the wake of Mubarak's ouster, the military began to market the slogan itself, posting it onto billboards across the country, often accompanied by a picture

---

[46] See Article 84. The article also says that the speaker himself cannot run for president, making clear that his assumption of the office is temporary.

[47] Quoted in Osman (2011).

[48] Quoted in Reuters Staff (2011*b*).

[49] See International Crisis Group (2011, p. 16), Said (2012, p. 408), Ketchley (2014, pp. 162–172). In this regard, one protest organizer told Arrow (2011) that: "One of the main points which we used was Sharp's idea of identifying a regime's pillars of support. If we could build a relationship with the army, Mubarak's biggest pillar of support, to get them on our side, then we knew he would quickly be finished."

of a soldier cradling a baby – not quite "one hand" as equals, but with the military as the father defending the people.[50]

The military's efforts succeeded, at least temporarily, in creating the image of the army as the savior of the revolution. Cementing that image required deposing Mubarak themselves. As Taylor (2014, p. 133) astutely observes: "Military elites, seeing a unique opportunity to remake the national myth, decided to force Mubarak to step down. With the narrative of the military's glory from the 1973 war fading due to generational turnover, the Armed Forces saw their 'guardian of the uprising' role as a means to secure both their status in society and renew it for another generation."

In short, the military's response to the 2011 revolution was driven first and foremost by its corporate interests. Having been the center of power under the Mubarak regime, it had major political and economic interests to preserve. It therefore remained loyal for nearly all of the uprising, engaging in low-level repression, facilitating repression from other actors, and attempting to intimidate and threaten the protesters into dispersing. At the same time, it could not afford to engage in more public repression, for instance, massacring protesters in the streets. Such repression would have had tremendous consequences for its image at home and abroad, threatening to undermine its corporate interests. Ultimately, given the scale and persistence of the demonstrators, the military begrudgingly decided that to preserve its interests, it had to jettison Mubarak.

Counter-explanations

There are at least four counter-explanations for the military's behavior in 2011. For some, the generals were envious of the power and resources being accumulated by either (1) the police or (2) businessmen, and so eagerly seized the opportunity to give Mubarak and his regime the velvet shove. For others, the source of the military's defection is found lower down in the military's ranks. Bou Nassif (2012, 2015*b*, 2021), for instance, argues that the junior officers did not enjoy the privileges of their more senior counterparts, leaving the generals with no other choice but to defect. Barany (2011, 2016) and Holmes (2012, 2019) make similar arguments about the conscripts, who they argue were more likely to identify with the protesters than fire upon them.

While there is truth to each of these arguments, none fully captures the military's behavior in the 2011 revolution. With regards to the first two (the "resentment" hypotheses), the top generals were not, in fact, very eager to get rid of Mubarak, and instead agonized over the decision for 18 days. As shown, the military was initially loyal to the regime, even helping to resupply the police—not behavior we would expect from a military feeling resentful of them. Throughout the 18 days, the military engaged in low-level repression on behalf of Mubarak.

The military's behavior in the aftermath of the revolution also belies both of these explanations. Had the military been resentful of the police and businessmen, it would

---

[50] See, e.g., Ketchley (2014, p. 180)

have tapped into the revolutionary demands of the people and gone after both institutions after Mubarak's ouster. It would have purged and weakened the police—and if it truly felt threatened by the paramilitary force, the Central Security Forces, it would have either dissolved or incorporated them into the military. But despite the major calls for security-sector reform, none of this materialized.[51] On the contrary, as even Kandil (2012, p. 230) admits, the SCAF "quickly directed its troops to protect police stations and the Interior Ministry, and authorized [only] limited security purges, which stuck to the letter of the law."

Likewise, the military after the revolution did not seize the opportunity to prosecute businessmen and confiscate their assets. As Roll (2013, p. 11) observed: "Those who maintained good relations with the military had little to fear, and even those who did not enjoy its protection were still able to leave the country. Numerous private jets transported wealthy families and their assets out of the country. The Bank for International Settlements estimates that foreign banks' liabilities to Egyptian citizens increased by more than $6 billion during the first quarter of 2011 alone." While the military had to prosecute a handful of the most notoriously corrupt businessmen, such as Ahmed Ezz, in order to satisfy popular outrage, most were left untouched. In some cases, the military even protected the facilities of business partners, as in the case of the Kharafi Group.[52]

There is comparatively more truth to the arguments about the military's lower ranks being less supportive of Mubarak. Junior officers received fewer perks than their senior counterparts, and conscripts none at all. Protesters repeatedly fraternized with the soldiers and junior officers stationed around Tahrir Square, on occasion securing pledges that they would not fire on them even if ordered.[53] That Egypt had a conscript army, in particular, was a major constraint that inhibited the senior leadership from ordering a massacre of protesters. It could have risked a cascade of defections. As we will see in the survey (Chapter 12), conscripts were in fact significantly less likely to say that they would have followed orders to fire on protesters in 2011.

However, the senior leadership could still comfortably order low-level repression, despite these constraints. The junior officers and soldiers had fewer qualms about arresting dissidents out of the limelight, or about facilitating repression from other actors. The oft-cited Captain Majed Boulos was the exception that proved the rule. Hailed as the "Lion of Tahrir Square", Boulos helped protect protesters from thugs during the Battle of the Camel, firing warning shots their way. Yet Boulos was but "one minor exception"[54]: the vast majority of officers and soldiers stationed around Tahrir that day simply looked the other way, allowing the protesters to get killed. Likewise, while Major Shuman and 15 other officers defected, they did so only at the very end, after 14 days of the military repressing protesters. Notably, they were the

---

[51] Sayigh (2015).
[52] Marshall and Stacher (2012).
[53] See, e.g., the January 30 episode described by Steavenson (2011).
[54] Said (2012, p. 410).

first military officers to defect in the entire uprising. All in all, as Said (2012, p. 405) notes, "very few incidents of army defections took place during the 18 days."

Some scholars even go so far as to argue that the junior officers were on average *more* supportive of repression. Taylor (2014, p. 128), for instance, argues that:

According to [former US Ambassador] Kurtzer's discussion with two members of the SCAF, support for the regime versus the street broke down along generational lines. Contrary to popular wisdom, the older generation of officers, led by Field Marshal Tantawi, was "scared" about the outcomes of the popular unrest and, therefore, was more willing to entertain the demands of the demonstrators; the younger generation of military officers, on the other hand, headed by the leaders of the Second Army Division and Military Intelligence, advocated a hard-line military response to reassert control. Despite the personal relationship the older generation of officers enjoyed with Mubarak, they also remembered the immense difficulties faced by the army when it intervened in politics in the 1970s as a result of the instability of Sadat's rule. The younger generation, however, believed it was easy to govern the masses because of the relative stability Egypt had enjoyed for the past several decades.

The military's behavior after Mubarak's ouster provides further evidence in this regard. Over the course of 2011–2012, Tantawi, Anan, and the Supreme Council of Armed Forces (SCAF) made repeated concessions to protesters each Friday they mobilized. However, a junior officer quoted by Galey (2012) argued that although "[t]here are some good people [in the SCAF . . .] most of them don't understand what it is they are doing. They panic and they give into protesters' demands. Giving in every time people gather in Tahrir Square is not how democracy works."

As for the conscripts, there is no doubt that they received almost none of the privileges afforded to the officer corps, and thus had little material interest in sticking with Mubarak. That said, some conscripts were still willing to help detain and arrest protesters, and could have been selectively utilized based on their perceived loyalty. Moreover, the regime could, and did, make use of units less reliant on conscription, such as the military police, military intelligence, and the republican guard. In short, while conscription was a major constraint on why the senior officers could not engage in a massacre, it posed less of a constraint when conducting low-level repression.

Conclusion

In sum, the military's behavior during the 2011 uprising should be largely characterized as loyalty, rather than defection. For most of the 18 days, the military was engaged in low-level repression of protesters, trying to preserve Mubarak from behind the scenes. This loyalty stemmed first and foremost from Mubarak's efforts to empower and invest the military into his regime. The political and economic interests that the military had built up since 1952 were best preserved by keeping Mubarak in power.

But eventually, the military realized that it would not be possible to preserve both Mubarak and their interests. The protests were simply too large and too determined, persevering through whatever repression the regime could muster. Accordingly, after 18 days, the military decided to jettison Mubarak in order to preserve the system he had presided over.

Those same interests in the system led the military to not just oust Mubarak, but to seize power themselves, wary of what a transition might spell for its perks and privileges if it was not running the show. But as we will see in the next chapter, despite the generals' efforts, the transition would soon get out of hand, leading them to have to seize power a second time in 2013.

7

Egypt: A Coup against Democracy

Maybe we could have avoided a coup, but we would also have aborted the revolution. The people rose up to achieve a modern state where they have a say in governing their country, not to turn around and give everything to the military.

—Former Egyptian Minister Amr Darrag[1]

Introduction

After the success of the Egyptian revolution in toppling Hosni Mubarak, expectations ran high that Egypt might transition to democracy. Over the course of the next two years, Egypt held its first free and fair parliamentary and presidential elections, both of which were won by the Muslim Brotherhood. The election of the Brotherhood's Mohamed Morsi as president of Egypt was a historic moment, given the decades of repression it had faced at the hands of Egyptian autocrats.[2] But just as quickly as it began, Egypt's transition came to a crashing halt. On July 3, 2013, General Abdelfattah al-Sisi ousted Morsi in a military coup, ending the young democratic experiment. Why did Egypt's democratic transition fail?[3]

Existing explanations highlight Egyptians' disillusionment with democracy as a result of an economic recession and political polarization, driving the masses to take to the streets again on June 30, 2013 to demand military intervention.[4] Other explanations emphasize the Brotherhood's inability to govern effectively or compromise with other political parties, ostensibly driven by the Brotherhood's insular internal organization, Islamist ideology, or the temptations of power.[5] Still others argue that the Brotherhood's opposition had lost faith that they could win parliamentary elections, and therefore asked the military to intervene.[6]

These explanations, while undoubtedly important, tend to portray the military as a disinterested or reactive actor, obliged to intervene by the demands of the disillusioned masses and opposition political parties. This narrative is reinforced by a

---

[1] Interview, Istanbul, July 11, 2016.
[2] For more on the history of the Brotherhood, see Wickham (2013).
[3] For a helpful overview of the dominant theories, see Bellin (2018).
[4] For economics, see Hubbard (2013), Abul-Magd (2017), and Luciani (2017); for polarization, see Lynch, Freelon, and Aday (2017), Fahmy and Faruqi (2017), Hassan, Lorch, and Ranko (2020), Hatab (2020), and Nugent (2020).
[5] See Hamid (2014), al Anani (2015), Kandil (2015), and Trager (2016).
[6] See Masoud (2014); Brownlee, Masoud, and Reynolds (2015).

Soldiers of Democracy?. Sharan Grewal, Oxford University Press. © Sharan Grewal (2023).
DOI: 10.1093/oso/9780192873910.003.0007

perception that President Morsi had been respecting the military's interests, appointing military officers as governors, and codifying their privileges in the constitution.[7]

By contrast, this chapter highlights the active role the military played to undermine and ultimately terminate the democratic transition. With interests to preserve, it directly managed the transition, and played each party off against each other to polarize and divide the revolutionary forces. When the Brotherhood came to power, it attempted to bargain with the military, respecting some of its interests, but also encroaching on others. Morsi challenged the military's privileges in the constitution, removed its veto power over national security policies, and limited its control over major economic contracts.[8] Morsi also tried to reverse the military's ban on officers from Islamist families, threatening the military's secular identity.

This "at times confrontational approach"[9] was calibrated to Morsi's assessment of his own level of domestic and international support vis-à-vis the military's. But Morsi ultimately miscalculated each of these factors, unaware the military was helping to orchestrate the June 30 protests and oblivious to the private messages the United States was sending Sisi. As a result, Morsi pushed the military too far, sparking a coup.

Beyond providing a new explanation for the collapse of Egypt's transition, this chapter also demonstrates how certain military legacies shape the outcomes of democratic transitions. The Egyptian military had historically been empowered by its autocrats, enjoying a secret budget, vast economic holdings, a monopoly over national security decisions, and a cohesive, secular identity. These legacies made democratization more difficult, as the newly elected government had incentives to curtail these privileges and bargain with the military over them. Such bargains are fraught with uncertainty and miscalculation, more often than not resulting in military coups.

The Military Council

Although the Egyptian military eventually abandoned Hosni Mubarak, it was not particularly keen on democratization. By definition, democracy would entail the reduction of the military's role in politics, as elected civilians are instead empowered as decision-makers. True democratization might therefore entail the loss of the military's veto power over national security and economic policy, and fewer appointments as governors and local administrators. Materially, democracy could also bring the reduction of the military's budget, as an elected government might seek to redistribute funds to its constituents. Moreover, an elected government in the spirit of the revolution might seek transparency over the military's economic empire,

---

[7] See, e.g., Stacher (2012); Eskandar (2013); Hamid (2014); Masoud (2014); al Anani (2015); Ashour (2015); Trager (2016), and Abul-Magd (2017).

[8] The latter two are also discussed by Bou Nassif (2017) and Marshall (2015), respectively.

[9] Interview with Brotherhood leader Abdullah al-Haddad, London, July 14, 2015.

especially since observers increasingly viewed its management of civilian enterprises as a hindrance to its training and readiness.[10]

But the military also could not avoid a transition, just as it could not save Mubarak. The popular and international pressure on the military was too great. Any attempt to simply install a military general like Defense Minister Hussein Tantawi as the new Mubarak might provoke another round of mass protests in Tahrir, not to mention international condemnation by Western leaders like President Barack Obama who had publicly committed to a transition.

Cognizant of these competing threats, the Egyptian military decided to directly manage a democratic transition so as to preserve its interests. After Mubarak's ouster, the military ruled the country directly through the Supreme Council of the Armed Forces (SCAF). Rather than letting civilians run the transition, the military took it upon itself to make sure the transition did not run out of hand.[11]

To legitimize its shepherding of the transition, the military drew upon the impression that it had intentionally created during the revolution: that it had defected from Mubarak and protected the revolution. Billboards sprung up across the country portraying a soldier holding a baby with the revolutionary chant, "The army and the people are one hand."[12] Beyond propaganda, the military council also attempted to intimidate and censor both public and private news media, reminding them on multiple occasions not to publish anything about the military without prior approval from the SCAF.[13]

In addition to increasing its own popularity, the military council also needed to demobilize the street. The military had been unable to publicly repress the united front of protesters during the 2011 uprising. Moving forward, it was therefore critical that the military divide-and-rule the revolutionaries, in case it ever needed to deploy large-scale repression to preserve its interests. On the one hand, the revolutionaries were bound to divide, with ideological differences between Islamists and secularists already salient before the revolution. But through its actions, the military council also stoked this polarization, undermining the brief unity Islamists and secularists enjoyed during the revolution.

Dividing the Revolution

At first, the SCAF, led by Defense Minister Hussein Tantawi and Chief of General Staff Sami Anan, appeared to privilege the Islamists. Its first actions were to create an eight-member committee to propose constitutional amendments and a roadmap

---

[10] As Henry and Springborg (2011) noted at the time: "The Egyptian army is not the tight professional force that many consider it to be. It is bloated and its officer core is indulged, having been fattened on Mubarak's patronage. Its training is desultory, maintenance of its equipment is profoundly inadequate, and it is dependent on the United States for funding and logistical support."

[11] See Albrecht and Bishara (2011).

[12] See Ketchley (2017, pp. 72–73).

[13] Kirkpatrick (2018a, p. 59) describes one such reminder in March 2011, and Cambanis (2015, p. 118) in September 2011.

that would guide the transitional period. While Tunisia's corresponding commission included representatives from all political parties,[14] the Egyptian military's committee instead appeared catered to Islamists.

Of the eight members of the commission, at least two were viewed as Islamists: Subhi Saleh, a former member of parliament from the Muslim Brotherhood, and Tareq el-Bishri, the chairman of the committee who had been an advisor to the Kefaya movement but was widely considered a moderate Islamist. The remainder were independents: no political movement other than the Muslim Brotherhood was represented. While the secular revolutionaries went along with the commission, the seeds of doubt were sown. At the time, Walid Rachid of the secular April 6 youth movement observed that some members were indeed concerned about Bishri's Islamist leanings.[15]

Those seeds of doubt sprouted further when the Bishri committee recommended, and the SCAF approved, that elections be held first, followed by the drafting of a new constitution. Like in Tunisia, this sequence was viewed as privileging the Islamists, who were better organized and thus likely to have the upper hand in elections and in turn in drafting the constitution. The secularists, instead, preferred to draft the constitution first, ensuring it would enshrine liberal norms and freedoms before the Islamists got a chance to govern.

But unlike in Tunisia, the SCAF was in charge, meaning that the proposal to hold elections first was coming not just from the Islamists but also from the military, sparking fears among secularists that the Islamists had formed a pact with the military. Mohamed El-Ashkar, general coordinator of the Kefaya Movement, accused the Brotherhood of opportunistically dealing with the generals: "The Muslim Brotherhood have turned the revolution from a patriotic responsibility into an opportunity to seize bounty."[16] The novelist Alaa Al Aswany (2012) opined that this betrayal was intrinsic to the Brotherhood, who could not be trusted: "The Muslim Brotherhood has always broken with the national consensus and allied itself with despotic authority against the will of the people."

Both the military and the Muslim Brotherhood, of course, deny that there was any pact, merely a temporary convergence of interests. As one retired general explained:

> They [the Muslim Brothers] may have wanted to guarantee a quick win for the group and a chance to write a new constitution. The SCAF's goal at the time was to calm down the streets, and with the Brothers being the most organised and numerous group, they naturally felt it made sense to let them have a critical say.[17]

---

[14] See Stepan (2012, p. 92)

[15] Quoted in Kirkpatrick (2011*a*). Later, Al Aswany (2012) argued that "Bishri wanted to ensure the political dominance of the Muslim Brotherhood, to which he belongs."

[16] Quoted in Tarek (2011).

[17] Quoted in International Crisis Group (2012, p. 4).

True or false, the impression of a pact contributed to feelings of betrayal among the secularists towards the Islamists, dividing up the revolutionaries. As Brotherhood leader Amr Darrag later realized:

> "The military since day 1 was working to dismantle the revolution, to drive a wedge between the Muslim Brotherhood and other political and social movements. So they tried to appear to be responding to the interests of the Brotherhood, pushing for early elections that would give an advantage to the Brotherhood. [. . .] It was natural for *us* to go for that. But the military pushed for that too, and that was start of the wedge driven between the Brotherhood and others."[18]

Moreover, the presence of the SCAF as manager of the transition also meant that Islamists and secularists did not have to find consensus on the transitional roadmap. While in Tunisia, all political parties eventually agreed on holding elections first, in Egypt, the military council instead moved forward with the constitutional amendments and put them up to a public referendum in March 2011. The secular camp, both the revolutionary youth and more established figures like Amr Moussa and Mohamed ElBaradei, rejected the amendments. But over their opposition, the referendum passed with 77 percent of the vote.

In short, the SCAF's approach to creating the transitional roadmap—seemingly siding with the Islamists and then moving forward without the consent of the secularists—fueled the secularists' fears that they were being sidelined, and in turn fueled their mistrust of the Islamists. But as the Brotherhood would soon find out, this was simply the opening salvo in a concerted effort by the military to "utilize each group against the other, first using the Islamists against the liberals, and then using the liberals against the Islamists."[19]

Supra-Constitutional Principles

Like the military, the Muslim Brotherhood was also conscious of its domestic and international support. The Brotherhood had seen what had happened to other Islamist groups who pushed too quickly: the West backed a military coup against the Islamic Salvation Front (FIS) in Algeria, and imposed a blockade after Hamas' victory in Gaza. Accordingly, the Brotherhood at the outset declared, in the words of its General Guide Mohamed Badie, that it "will not dominate, only participate."[20] It pledged not to run for more than one-third of parliamentary seats, and to endorse a consensus candidate for president rather than field their own. As Badie explained:

---

[18] Interview with Amr Darrag, Istanbul, July 11, 2016.
[19] Interview with Brotherhood MP AbdulMawgoud Dardery, October 11, 2020.
[20] See Badie's interview with al-Ahram, March 21, 2011 (IkhwanWeb, 2011*b*).

> We are determined to have for Egypt a consensus president to comfort and reas-
> sure everyone, domestically inside Egypt, and externally on the international
> level, bearing in mind the economic blockade on Gaza because of Hamas's rise to
> power.[21]

The Brotherhood knew that the best path to warding off a Western-backed military coup was for the revolutionary forces to remain unified. Accordingly, the Brotherhood attempted to corral all of the pro-revolution parties into one electoral coalition, the Democratic Alliance for Egypt. At its announcement on June 14, 2011, the Democratic Alliance boasted 28 parties, from the secular al-Wafd Party to the Salafi Nour Party.[22]

But the Democratic Alliance would soon fall apart, in no small part due to actions taken by the SCAF. On July 3, 2011, the SCAF floated the idea of "supra-constitutional principles" that would govern the drafting of the new Egyptian constitution.[23] In what seemed to be an attempt to ally with the secularists, the military proposed 10 principles that would bind the future (Islamist) parliament and constituent assembly as it drafted the constitution. Eight of the 10 principles enshrined the rights and freedoms that the secularists desired, and feared the Muslim Brotherhood would not pursue. Article 1 called Egypt a "civil" (rather than religious) state, article 2 provided non-Muslims the right to worship, and article 4 banned parties formed on a religious basis.

But articles 9 and 10 created the Faustian bargain. In return for these liberal values, the principles would codify the privileges that the military sought to preserve under democracy. The military's budget would be listed as one figure, without any meaningful civilian oversight into its usage. All legislation related to the military, as well as national security decisions, would require the consent of the SCAF.[24] In short, the military sought to retain veto power over all matters related to the armed forces, not allowing democracy to encroach upon its budget, economic empire, or security policy.

The supra-constitutional principles divided the secularists. The revolutionary youth, committed to true democratization, opposed the principles, rejecting any privileged status for the military. Others, however, like Mohamed ElBaradei, were more supportive: "Today, we have a nascent democracy in a region that swarms with old ideas dating back to medieval times," ElBaradei observed. "Hence, we need the military to protect the constitution and the civil nature of the state during this phase of incipient democracy." While the military should not be "running affairs of state," ElBaradei added, it should enjoy "some kind of autonomy" in handling its own

---

[21] See Badie's interview with Amr Laithi on December 5, 2011 (IkhwanWeb, 2011*d*).

[22] See Ahram Online (2011).

[23] In July, they were proposed by the vice president of the Court of Cassation, Hisham al-Bastawisy (El-Gallad, 2011). When they were later proposed again in November, they were proposed by Deputy Prime Minister Ali el-Selmi, ultimately becoming known as the Selmi principles.

[24] See this first iteration of the supra-constitutional principles at El-Gallad (2011).

affairs.[25] While others remained silent, the outside option the military was dangling would become increasingly tempting in the following weeks.

In protest of the supra-constitutional principles, the Muslim Brotherhood took to the streets on July 29, their first protest since the revolution. That protest, dubbed the "Friday of Unity," brought together all the forces that opposed the military's principles, from the hardline Salafis to the revolutionary youth. The protests were massive, far eclipsing any of the protests that the revolutionary youth had on their own staged thus far. But the Salafis moved beyond the agreed-upon slogans, chanting in addition for an Islamic state. The size of the protests, and the explicit calls for Islamic rule—quickly re-dubbed the "Friday of Kandahar"—led secularists to become more fearful of the Islamists, and in turn, more supportive of the military's Faustian bargain.[26]

On August 16, leaders from the Wafd, Tagammu, and Nasserite parties, up until that point part of the Brotherhood's Democratic Alliance, broke with the coalition[27] and met with Deputy Prime Minister Ali el-Selmi to sign on to the supra-constitutional principles.[28] The 22 principles they agreed to, which ultimately became known as the Selmi principles, once again codified the military's prerogatives. Article 9 stipulated that:

> The Supreme Council of the Armed Forces—without any other—is in charge of handling all the affairs of the armed forces and discussing its budget. Such a budget should be set as one item and one figure in the State budget. The Supreme Council of the Armed Forces—without any other—is also concerned with the approval of any legislation relating to the armed forces before issuing it. [. . .] The President of the Republic declares war after approval of the Supreme Council of the Armed Forces and the People's Assembly.[29]

The next day, Army Chief of Staff Sami Anan reaffirmed his end of the bargain. Anan declared his support for the principle of Egypt as a civil state, stating, "We must insist on this clause" in the constitution as a matter of national security.[30]

Through these supra-constitutional principles, the military succeeded in breaking apart the Democratic Alliance.[31] It offered the secular parties a guarantee of preserving liberal values, rather than taking the risk of what the Islamists might do once

---

[25] Quoted in El-Hennawy (2011).

[26] The Brotherhood's criticism of the Salafis for chanting Islamist slogans at the July 29 rally also prompted the Salafis to leave the Democratic Alliance (Ketchley, 2017, p. 95).

[27] Indeed, just the day prior, the Democratic Alliance announced that all 34 of its member parties opposed the supra-constitutional principles. See IkhwanWeb (2011a).

[28] See Egypt Independent (2011).

[29] See full text at IkhwanWeb (2011f).

[30] Quoted in Mosalem (2011).

[31] A common alternative explanation is that the Brotherhood was dominating the alliance, refusing to give secular parties a sufficient number of slots on the joint electoral lists. The Wafd party, for instance, was demanding 40%, while they were only afforded 20% (in the end, they would win less than 10% of the vote). Amr Darrag acknowledged as much, observing that "they seemed to be looking for a bigger proportion of seats than their capabilities," but argued that ultimately, "the most important reason is that some of the parties in the coalition really sided with the military to overthrow the democratic transition because they knew they didn't have chance to get anything through elections. [. . .] I cannot ignore what was realized later that there was a lot of coordination between the Wafd and other forces who wanted to overthrow the revolution. They were working with the counterrevolutionary forces" (Interview, Istanbul, July 11, 2016).

in power, undermining the unity of the political parties. It also signaled to all sides what privileges the military sought to preserve under democracy, setting the stage for future negotiations.

Down, Down with Military Rule!

However, the military was ultimately forced to rescind the Selmi principles. While the military had succeeded in wooing the established secular parties, most of the revolutionary youth remained firmly in the anti-military camp. The April 6 youth movement and the Revolutionary Youth Coalition, among other groups, had been protesting almost every Friday after Mubarak's ouster for a continuation of the revolution. Increasingly, their demands took on an anti-militaristic character.

After the SCAF subjected female demonstrators to virginity tests in March, the revolutionary youth mobilized for an end to the practice, and in turn, for the SCAF to immediately hand over power to civilian authorities. Activists declared May 23, 2011 to be a "Day to Criticize the SCAF." Using the #NoSCAF hashtag, "thousands of people posted critical comments on this day, effectively breaking the taboo of deference toward the SCAF."[32]

In response, the SCAF increasingly cracked down on these protesters, by September subjecting nearly 12,000 civilians to military trials—far more than in Mubarak's entire 30 years.[33] Activists formed the No to Military Trials group, protesting and securing the endorsements of several presidential hopefuls. Anger towards the SCAF escalated further in October 2011, when soldiers appeared to fuel Muslim–Christian riots at Maspero.[34] As Kirkpatrick (2018a, p. 100) observed, by "that fall, [even] the talk show hosts were turning on the generals. One program broadcast footage of a soldier shooting a man in the back."

In that climate, Deputy Prime Minister Selmi's revival of the supra-constitutional principles once again on November 3 sparked a major backlash. Islamists coordinated with the April 6 and Revolutionary Youth movements to hold a protest on November 18.[35] These calls prompted the largest demonstrations since the revolution, with both Islamists and secularist youth joining forces to demand that "the army go back to its barracks and return our nation to civilian rule."[36] "*Yasqut, yasqut, hukm al-askar* [down, down, with military rule]," the protesters chanted.

The message was clear. The SCAF might have succeeded in getting the secular establishment on its side, but a relatively unified front against military rule remained between the Islamists and the revolutionary youth. The SCAF did not yet have the public support to secure its interests through the supra-constitutional principles.

---

[32] Holmes (2019, p. 86).
[33] See Human Rights Watch (2011).
[34] As activist Asmaa Mahfouz observed, "Look to the SCAF. We were together, Muslims and Copts, marching to Maspero. Suddenly we felt the attack. Why? To divide us, to make us forget about the SCAF and instead have Muslims and Christians fight against each other." Quoted in Cambanis (2015, p. 140).
[35] See Ketchley (2017, p. 95) and Khazbak (2011).
[36] April 6 activist Ramy el-Swissy, quoted in Shenker (2011).

The next day, the SCAF rescinded the Selmi principles, and the Brotherhood accordingly withdrew from the protests, focusing instead on the upcoming parliamentary elections.

The revolutionary youth, however, continued to mobilize, believing that now was the time to demand a complete handover to civilian rule. For the next five days, the youth faced off against the police in the infamous Battle of Muhammed Mahmoud Street. That decision to keep protesting rather than campaign in the final week before the elections was emblematic of the protesters' approach throughout the year. They had taken to the streets almost every Friday, rather than organize into political parties and campaign for the elections.

While it is easy to blame the youth for that fateful decision, it was in some ways a rational response to the SCAF's behavior. As Kirkpatrick (2018*a*, p. 58) observed:

> Whenever the transition faltered, the organizers behind Police Day called for another Friday afternoon *millioneya*—a million-man march. And each Thursday night the generals caved in, just in time to appease the protesters. The generals removed prime ministers, shook up cabinets, jailed Mubarak, put him and his interior minister on trial for murder, scheduled elections, repealed the so-called emergency law suspending due process rights, and more—all to defuse impending *millioneyas*. "The only thing that works is going back to Tahrir, but then they back down," one of the organizers, Shady el-Ghazaly Harb, told me. The "Thursdays of concessions," some Egyptians called them.

Cambanis (2015, p. 163) was even more explicit:

> Whatever its motives, the SCAF had created a Pavlovian cycle. The generals changed course only in response to huge crowds or violent clashes in Tahrir. They taught the revolutionaries that protest was the only tool that worked, and therefore the revolutionaries returned to Tahrir in response to every crisis. [. . .] All that time [. . .] was time *not* spent appealing to everyday Egyptians. Whether that was the SCAF's plan or merely a collateral benefit, it was in any case to the SCAF's advantage.

Seeing rewards from protests, the revolutionary youth never organized into parties or campaigned, resulting in a tremendous defeat in the 2011–2012 parliamentary elections. The "Revolution Continues" Alliance won just 2.8 percent of the vote, and 1.8 percent of seats. Despite their large street presence, the youth, shaped by the SCAF's Pavlovian cycle, could not translate that momentum into the polls, and thus handed the assembly to the Islamists. The imbalance of power between Islamists and secularists that many highlight as the cause of Egypt's democratic breakdown, may thus ultimately have had its roots in the military's behavior. Either way, with little representation in the assembly, the revolutionary youth had little attachment to it, and thus had few qualms when it turned out to be powerless.

The Toothless Parliament

The parliamentary elections were won decisively by Islamist parties. The Muslim Brotherhood came in first with 37.5 percent of the vote, followed in turn by the Salafi Nour Party with 27.8 percent. The elections were held over six rounds across three months,[37] giving observers ample time to fret over the Islamist victory before results were finalized.

The elections, both in process and in result, held echoes from Algeria in 1991, when a similar, multi-round election was on the verge of being swept by the Islamic Salvation Front (FIS). In that case, the Algerian military stepped in to cancel the elections before the run-offs could occur. In Egypt, despite fears that the military might do the same, the election was allowed to proceed as scheduled. Part of the reason is that there were fewer domestic calls for the parliamentary elections to be nullified halfway through in Egypt. But part of it also was the clear signal given by the US to the SCAF to stay out of the electoral process.

On November 25, on the eve of the elections, the White House made clear its support for a handover of power to civilians: "We believe that Egypt's transition to democracy must continue, with elections proceeding expeditiously," the White House (2011) said in a statement. "The United States strongly believes that the new Egyptian government must be empowered with real authority immediately," calling for "the full transfer of power to a civilian government" to take place "as soon as possible."[38] After the Muslim Brotherhood won the first round, the US also began a series of almost-weekly talks with Brotherhood leaders, sending Senator John Kerry and Ambassador Anne Patterson on December 10, Deputy Secretary of State William Burns and Ambassador Patterson on January 11, former President Jimmy Carter on January 12–14, Ambassador Patterson and Foreign Service Officer Donald Blome on January 18, and Assistant Secretary of State for Democracy, Human Rights, and Labor Michael Posner and Ambassador Patterson on January 26–27.[39] Unlike in Algeria, the US was keen to signal that it would support democratic elections, no matter the outcome.

Constrained by this domestic and international support for the transition, the SCAF had no choice but to let the elections proceed. But it had no intent of allowing the new Islamist parliament to actually govern. As SCAF General Mokhtar el-Mulla, the assistant defense minister, told a group of journalists after the first round, "Whatever the majority in the People's Assembly, they are very welcome, because they will

---

[37] The first stage took place on November 28–29, with a run-off on December 5–6; the second stage was then held December 14–15, with a run-off on December 21–22, and the final round occurred on January 3–4, with a run-off on January 10–11.

[38] Notably, this clear statement actually masked internal divisions already emerging in the Obama administration. As Kirkpatrick (2018*a*, p. 101) reveals, the Thanksgiving-weekend statement was crafted solely by Ben Rhodes and Denis McDonough, angering officials who were reticent to abandon the SCAF, like NSC director Steven Simon.

[39] Each meeting was in turn publicized by the Muslim Brotherhood, as if to signal to the military that the US supported the democratic process. See IkhwanWeb (2011*e*), (2012*d*), (2012*c*), (2012*f*), (2012*b*), (2012*a*), and IkhwanWeb (2012*e*).

not have the ability to impose anything."[40] On the eve of the parliament's first session, Tahani el-Gebali, vice-president of the Supreme Constitutional Court, noted that since the SCAF was acting as the president, it would have the right to ratify or veto any bill passed by the parliament.[41]

That veto would prove critical to preserving the military's interests. The parliament's first law, passed in March 2012, was to provide LE 100,000 to all families of protesters killed in the 2011 revolution,[42] rejecting the SCAF's suggestion to simply provide a martyr medallion.[43] The next month, the parliament approved in principle an amendment to the Code of Military Justice to remove the president's right to refer civilians to military tribunals under the state of emergency, ignoring SCAF General Mamdouh Shahin's plea to at least provide an alternative to enable the president to handle potential security threats.[44] That same week, a parliamentary committee approved a draft law setting a maximum wage for government employees of LE 50,000 a month, notably including salaries and all bonuses, incentives, and allowances, potentially restricting the perks and privileged enjoyed by military officers.[45] Meanwhile, Muslim Brotherhood leader Mohamed Badie threatened that the military's budget "must be reviewed and studied and scrutinized by the People's Assembly."[46]

But as the MPs quickly realized, none of the laws they passed in the parliament would be enacted, let alone implemented, without the consent of the SCAF. Nor could the newly elected parliament exert any meaningful check on the SCAF-appointed prime minister, Kamal Ganzouri, or his government, let alone withdraw confidence from that government and form their own. The parliament was toothless.

With the legislative body powerless, the Brotherhood looked toward the executive. Presidential elections were set for May 2012, with a run-off the following month. The Brotherhood had pledged in early 2011 that it would not field one of its own for president and would instead endorse a consensus candidate. At first, it was serious about that pledge, expelling Abdel Moneim Aboul-Futouh when he announced his candidacy in June 2011. But several developments led it to shift gears in spring 2012.

First, the Brotherhood observed, correctly, that the SCAF was trying to undermine the transition. As one Brotherhood parliamentarian explained: "The SCAF was taking a series of steps to circumvent the will of the people, prevent[ing] us from forming a government, prevent[ing] parliament from playing its role, undermining the constituent assembly. We had no choice but to react."[47] Meanwhile, two military generals—Ahmed Shafik and Omar Suleiman—had announced they were running for president. If the military won the presidential elections, the Brotherhood

---

[40] Quoted in Kirkpatrick (2018a, p. 113).
[41] Quoted in El-Hennawy (2012a).
[42] See Egypt Independent (2012d).
[43] See Al-Masry al-Youm Staff (2012).
[44] See Egypt Independent (2012a).
[45] See Al-Masry al-Youm (2012c).
[46] Quoted in Reuters Staff (2012).
[47] MB parliamentarian quoted in International Crisis Group (2012).

calculated, the transition would be over. "The revolution was going to go right into the hands of the soldiers," noted Brotherhood MP Abdul Mawgoud Dardery.[48]

Second, the Brotherhood had trouble finding a consensus candidate willing to work with it. Part of the reason stemmed from political polarization and the Brotherhood's insularity, but part of it also was due to behind-the-scenes maneuvering by the SCAF. For instance, Wafd leader El Sayyid el-Badawi, who had initially been part of the Brotherhood's Democratic Alliance, had considered seeking the Brotherhood's endorsement for a presidential run. But he was dissuaded by a call from an intelligence officer in spring 2012 telling him not to work with the Brotherhood. "The Brotherhood will witness their worst days in the coming period," the intelligence officer warned Badawi in a leaked recording. "We will take revenge [on] the Brotherhood and anyone who took part in a revolution to topple the state."[49]

Unable to find a consensus candidate that in its mind would be able to beat the SCAF in elections, the Brotherhood decided to break their promise and field their own candidate on March 31. That decision was internally contentious, passing in the Shura Council with 56 votes in favor to 52 against. The Brotherhood in fact nominated two candidates, in case something happened to the first: Khairat al-Shater, the Brotherhood's chief strategist, and Mohamed Morsi, the head of the Freedom and Justice Party.

The SCAF's reaction to the Brotherhood's bid for the presidency confirmed that it was not eager to let the Brotherhood come to power. On April 16, the elections commission disqualified the Brotherhood's charismatic first choice, Khairat al-Shater, on account of being imprisoned under Mubarak, leaving their awkward, "spare tire" candidate, Mohamed Morsi (who, we might add, had also been imprisoned under Mubarak).[50] Meanwhile, just days earlier, an administrative court had dissolved the constituent assembly that the parliament had created to draft the constitution.[51]

Nevertheless, the Brotherhood was confident that it still enjoyed more popular support than the SCAF. As one Muslim Brother observed:

The SCAF hopes to remain a key political player which has the upper hand in all the vital decisions. They are mistaken, however, to think they can play that role moving forward. The balance of power is decidedly not in their favour. They can sense their own weakness, which is why their demands are suddenly growing, and their attempts to dominate the political process are becoming more desperate.[52]

---

[48] Interview with AbdulMawgoud Dardery, Skype, September 30, 2019.

[49] See Ibrahim (2015) and Kirkpatrick (2018*a*, pp. 198–199).

[50] Nine other candidates were also disqualified, including General Omar Suleiman, leaving the deep state to unite around the remaining general, Ahmed Shafik. While Suleiman may have been a stronger personality, he was also much less palatable to the revolutionaries than Shafik, who had at least served as the transition's first prime minister from February to March 2011.

[51] While the composition of the constituent assembly matched the results of the elections, the court ruled that it did not take into account the country's diversity. Notably, the case to dissolve the constituent assembly had been filed by the secular liberals—showing, once again, how the presence of outside options (in this case, a court) inhibits compromise. There was little reason to try to negotiate with the Brotherhood and work through the constituent assembly when the assembly itself could simply be dissolved.

[52] Quoted in International Crisis Group (2012).

In the short term, the Brotherhood's calculations were right. Its candidate, Mohamed Morsi, won the first round of the presidential elections with 25 percent of the vote, just ahead of General Ahmed Shafik at 24 percent. Likewise, in the run-off elections, Morsi narrowly bested Shafik 52 percent to 48 percent. The Brotherhood also enjoyed just enough support from the revolutionary youth and from the West to survive what would become the SCAF's most flagrant attempt yet to abort the revolution.

The Constitutional Coup

On June 17, after the run-off elections indicated a victory for Morsi, but before the results were officially announced, the SCAF issued a supplementary constitutional declaration amending the 2011 constitution that was governing the transition. These amendments stated that the SCAF, and the SCAF alone, is "responsible for decisions on all issues related to the armed forces, including appointing its leaders and extending [their] terms in office," and that the "head of the SCAF is to act as commander-in-chief," leaving the new president a mere figurehead on security matters.[53] The SCAF also created a National Defense Council for the future president, in which military officers held 10 of 17 seats, an absolute majority.[54] To preserve its prerogatives in the new constitution, the amendments also granted the SCAF the right to revise any clause that in its opinion "conflicts with any principle in all of Egypt's former constitutions."[55] As if that were not enough, having dissolved the democratically elected parliament two days previously, the SCAF now also appropriated for itself all legislative powers in the absence of a parliament.[56]

As with the supra-constitutional principles, the secular establishment largely supported this power grab. Representatives of the Free Egyptians and Democratic Front parties defended the amendments, with MP Mohamed Abou Hamed explaining that "the declaration protects the constitution from control by religious groups and fortifies the decision of war against [their] jihadi illusions."[57] Representatives from 10 secular parties—including Wafd, Tagammu, and the Egyptian Social Democratic Party—were even rumored to have helped draft the amendments.[58] With that political support, many speculated that the SCAF might even declare Shafik the winner of the presidential elections and end the transition outright.

However, once again, many of the revolutionary youth put aside their differences with the Brotherhood to jointly protest against the supplementary constitutional declaration. The April 6 youth movement and the Revolutionary Socialists joined the

---

[53] See article 53 of the declaration (Ahram Online, 2012*f*). According to articles 53/1 and 53/2, the president would also have to obtain the SCAF's permission prior to declaring war or deploying the military domestically.

[54] See list of members at Ahram Online (2012*d*).

[55] See article 60 B1.

[56] See article 56 B.

[57] Quoted in Al-Masry Al-Youm (2012*e*).

[58] See Al-Masry Al-Youm (2012*d*).

Brotherhood, Salafis, and other Islamists in taking to the streets on June 19, chanting once again, "*yasqut, yasqut, hukm al-askar.*"[59]

Two days later, soon-to-be president Mohamed Morsi met with revolutionary youth leaders at the Fairmont Hotel to further solidify their united position. In this "Fairmont agreement," Morsi secured the support of the leader of the April 6 movement, Ahmed Maher, the administrator of the "We are all Khaled Said" Facebook page, Wael Ghoneim, and the novelist Alaa Al-Aswany, among others,[60] in exchange for promises to cancel the supplementary declaration, end military trials of civilians, and create an inclusive government.[61] "We should all unite against the military council's rule," argued Maher.[62]

The size of the protests on Tuesday, June 19 and again on Friday, June 22 give some indication that at this point, the general public might have sided with the Islamist and revolutionary forces against the military's power grab. Available survey data likewise confirm this insight. In March 2012, a Pew poll asked 1,000 Egyptians: "How important is it that the military is under the control of civilian leaders?" Overall, 65 percent of Egyptians surveyed agreed that civilian control of the military was "very" or "somewhat important." While the poll did not ask explicitly about the supplementary declaration, these results suggest that a majority of Egyptians might have opposed the military assuming such powers.

The United States was equally united in opposing the SCAF's power grab. Both the State Department and the Pentagon voiced their concern with the SCAF's actions, and implicitly threatened the suspension of military aid. State Department spokesperson Victoria Nuland warned that the SCAF's actions "in this crucial period are naturally going to have an impact on the nature of our engagement with the government and with the SCAF moving forward."[63]

Given this domestic and international pressure, the SCAF could not completely abort the transition by altering the presumptive election results and announcing Shafik as the winner—though they did consider it. They would have to declare Morsi the victor and hand over power.

But the SCAF also calculated that they did not need to rescind the supplementary constitutional declaration. On the domestic front, they calculated, correctly, that inaugurating Morsi as president would at least demobilize the Brotherhood, leaving just the revolutionary youth and salafists in the street. On the international front, meanwhile, the SCAF had learned from a recent episode that the US was not serious about its threats to withdraw military aid. After repeated threats to do so over the trial of US-funded NGO workers (including Sam LaHood, the son of the transportation secretary), the Obama administration instead paid over $4 million to bail them out of the country. "If the generals concluded [from this episode] that American threats

---

[59] See Al-Masry Al-Youm (2012*h*).
[60] Others in attendance included Shady El-Ghazaly Harb, Hamdi Qandil, and Sekina Fouad. For full list of attendees, see Ahram Online (2012*i*).
[61] See list of promises at Shukrallah (2012).
[62] Quoted in Egypt Independent (2012*b*).
[63] See Quinn and Alexander (2012).

to cut the military aid were only bluffs, they were correct," Defense Secretary Leon Panetta later told Kirkpatrick (2018*a*, p. 143). "The generals 'knew that, when push comes to shove, little was going to happen.'"

As a result, while the SCAF agreed to declare Morsi the winner, they kept their supplementary declaration in place. Just as the generals had permitted the parliamentary elections but tolerated only a toothless parliament, so too did it now seek just a figurehead president. The stage was thus set for the country's first democratically elected president to try to wrest power back from the military.

President Mohamed Morsi

President Morsi attempted to strike a balance with the military, respecting some of its interests but limiting others. The initial bargain[64] allowed the SCAF to choose the leaders of the "sovereign ministries"—defense, interior, foreign affairs, and finance[65]—and approved the 2012–2013 budget the SCAF had already prepared, despite the Brotherhood previously criticizing it for failing to redirect funds toward "revolutionary objectives, such as social justice."[66] However, Morsi denied the military the ministries of information[67] and justice,[68] and also created two fact-finding commissions to investigate the killing of protesters in the 2011 revolution[69] and the detention of civilians by the military since then.[70]

The negotiations with the military were an ongoing process, subject to change given improvements in either side's bargaining power—their level of domestic and international support. After an August 5 attack on the Rafah border crossing killed 15 soldiers, the military was put on the defensive, and Morsi seized the opportunity to increase his authority. On August 8, Morsi replaced the GIS intelligence chief, head of the republican guard, head of Central Security Forces, and the governor of North Sinai.[71] He also attempted to fire the chief of military police, but as a member of the SCAF, this removal according to the supplementary declaration required the approval of Tantawi.

Three days went by without any action from Tantawi. "So on [August] 11, the presidential team confronted the president and said that this was insubordination," claimed Presidential Aide Wael Haddara. "That if Morsi was willing to tolerate this, there would be no future for this government."[72] On August 12, Morsi therefore fired Tantawi and Military Chief of Staff Sami Anan, appointing SCAF members

---

[64] See Khazbak (2012).

[65] See Tarek (2012).

[66] See Ahram Online (2012*b*).

[67] The SCAF wanted to maintain Major General Ahmed Anis as minister of information, but Morsi appointed a journalist and fellow Muslim Brother, Salah Abdel Maqsoud. See Al-Masry Al-Youm (2012*g*).

[68] See El-Din (2012*b*).

[69] See Ahram Online (2012*c*).

[70] See Al-Masry Al-Youm (2012*b*).

[71] See El Gundy (2012).

[72] Interview with Wael Haddara, London (Canada), May 20, 2014. Haddara claimed Morsi had not informed anyone from his team in advance about his August 12 decision.

Abdelfattah Sisi and Sedki Sobhy in their place.[73] More importantly, Morsi cancelled the supplementary declaration, legally becoming the commander-in-chief and no longer requiring SCAF approval for his actions.[74]

President Morsi, in explaining why he decided to exert authority over the military by canceling the declaration, underscored that it was what democracy entailed, and what the people wanted:

> No, it is not that they [the military] decided to [exit politics]. This is the will of the Egyptian people through the elected president. [. . .] The president of the Arab Republic of Egypt is the commander of the armed forces, full stop. Egypt now is a real civil state. It is not theocratic, it is not military. It is democratic, free, constitutional, lawful, and modern. We are behaving according to the Egyptian people's choice and will, nothing else.[75]

At this stage, the domestic balance of power was firmly in Morsi's favor, permitting him to wrest control from the military. "We are talking now about seventy percent popularity," Morsi gloated in the same interview. "That is what is going on! That is what they are telling me!"[76] Indeed, a Baseera poll 50 days into his presidency estimated Morsi's public approval at 76 percent, an approval rating he would continue to enjoy for the next three months.[77]

Abdelfattah al-Sisi

Morsi's replacement for Tantawi, General Abdelfattah al-Sisi, was until then a little-known member of the SCAF. His only public appearance during the transition thus far had been to defend the virginity tests conducted on female demonstrators in spring 2011. But Sisi, as chief of military intelligence, had been the point person in meeting political parties, including Morsi as head of the Brotherhood's Freedom and Justice Party.

However, Morsi's decision to choose Sisi stemmed not just from personal familiarity. Morsi truly believed "Sisi was their man"[78]—a closet Islamist in an otherwise secular military. In 2006, while at the US Army War College, then Brigadier-General Sisi had written a thesis entitled "Democracy in the Middle East," where he laid out the case that "for democracy to be successful in the Middle East," it must show "respect to the religious nature of the culture" (p. 2). El Sisi (2006) goes on to say that the Middle East needs to be reunited "so that the earliest form of El Kalafa

---

[73] Tantawi and Anan were "promoted" to presidential advisors, and awarded the Nile and State medals, respectively. See Egypt Independent (2012c).

[74] Morsi in the meantime appropriated some of those powers to himself, including the power to legislate and to choose members of the constituent assembly. See Trew (2012).

[75] See Kirkpatrick and Erlanger (2012).

[76] Kirkpatrick (2018a, pp. 163–164).

[77] See all Baseera polls on Morsi at Baseera (2013).

[78] Springborg (2014).

[the caliphate] is reestablished," which in its initial form was "considered the ideal form of government" (pp. 4–5). Much like the Brotherhood, Sisi advocated that "the legislative, executive, and judicial bodies should all take Islamic beliefs into consideration when carrying out their duties," and that "the major tenets of the Islamic faith [. . .] should be represented in the constitution." Most importantly, Sisi appeared to advocate for Islamists to have the right to participate in a democracy:

> This includes allowing some factions that may be considered radical, particularly if they are supported by a majority through a legitimate vote. The world cannot demand democracy in the Middle East, yet denounce what it looks like because a less than pro-Western party legitimately assumes office. For example, the Palestinians recently elected members from the Hamas group. This group is not on favorable terms with the U.S. and other Western countries, yet they have [been] legitimately elected. [. . .] It is important that even though significant differences exist, particularly with respect to the status of Israel, that legitimately elected parties be given the opportunity to govern. (p. 5)

Beyond his thesis, Sisi and his family were personally more pious than other generals. Kirkpatrick (2018*a*, p. 220) notes that while at the War College in Carlisle, Pennsylvania, "the local mosque lacked a full-time imam, and Sisi himself sometimes led Friday prayers. (So did one of his sons, who enrolled at Dickinson College)." Before Morsi's election, he "would turn up for meetings with the Muslim Brothers with rolled-up sleeves and wet hands, as though from the ablutions before prayers."[79] Springborg (2014) claimed that:

> [Sisi] still fasts twice weekly, prays five times daily, and regularly punctuates his speech with religious references. Unlike many of his fellow officers, he also avoids social settings where alcohol is served and women are "inappropriately" dressed. Also unusual for an Egyptian military officer, he has ensured that all of the women in his family—including sisters, wife, daughters, and daughters-in-law—wear a hijab.

Perhaps most importantly, Sisi appeared to go out of his way to help Morsi after he won the elections. Sisi reportedly warned Morsi of an assassination plot at the military funeral for those killed in the August 5 attack (hence Morsi skipped it).[80] Sisi also gave Morsi a file documenting corruption in the army, which Morsi then used as justification for firing Tantawi and Anan.[81]

In sum, Morsi, and for that matter, most observers at the time,[82] believed that Sisi was on the side of the Islamists. Even ousted President Hosni Mubarak thought so as

---

[79] See Kirkpatrick (2018*a*, p. 221).
[80] See Kirkpatrick (2018*a*, p. 160).
[81] Interview with Abdullah al-Haddad, London, July 14, 2015.
[82] See, e.g., Springborg (2013) and Wenig (2014).

late as spring 2013, telling his doctor in a leaked recording that "the defense minister, I think, is to their liking."[83] He would later admit that Sisi "turned out to be devious."[84]

The View from Washington

With a soaring approval rating and a seemingly loyal defense minister, Morsi's only remaining challenge was to convince Washington. After Morsi was slow to condemn the attack on the US Embassy on September 11, 2012, President Obama, off-the-cuff, seemed to waffle in his support for Egypt: "I don't think that we would consider them an ally, but we don't consider them an enemy."[85]

But Morsi's handling of the flare-up between Israel and Hamas in November 2012 would remove any doubts in the relationship. After five days of fighting, Obama called Morsi on November 19 to help resolve the crisis. Immediately, Morsi brought Hamas to the table.

"Morsi effectively had the Hamas guys on the other line," exclaimed Ben Rhodes, Obama's deputy national security advisor. "We were talking to people who were one degree removed from Hamas. This was a whole new world. [. . .] The cease-fire talks had been going nowhere before Morsi stepped in."[86] Even the skeptics in Washington were now singing Morsi's praise. "It was a litmus test for Morsi, and he passed with flying colors," Steven Simon of the National Security Council told Kirkpatrick (2018*a*, p. 174). "He was indispensable."

In Cairo, Secretary of State Hillary Clinton met with Morsi on November 21 and publicly thanked him "for his personal leadership to de-escalate the situation in Gaza and end the violence. [. . .] Egypt's new government is assuming the leadership that has long made this country a cornerstone of regional stability and peace."[87]

In short, by mid-November 2012, Morsi was basking in the glory of a 70 percent approval rating, and strong gratitude and support from the West. He had wrestled back power from the military and appointed a seemingly loyal defense minister. But when all seemed to be going well, Morsi would make the most fateful blunder of his presidency.

The New Constitution

Morsi had much to fear from the judiciary. Senior judges who had been appointed by Mubarak bore no secrets about their distaste for the Brotherhood. Ahmed al-Zend, the head of the Judges' Association, had publicly argued that with the Brotherhood coming to power, "Egypt is falling. We won't leave matters for those who can't

---

[83] See Kirkpatrick (2018*a*, p. 222).
[84] See Kirkpatrick (2012*e*).
[85] See Chadbourn (2012).
[86] Quoted in Kirkpatrick (2018*a*, p. 174).
[87] Quoted in Hendawi (2012).

manage them, with the excuse that we're not people of politics. No, we are people of politics."[88] Tahani el-Gebali, Vice-President of the Supreme Constitutional Court (SCC), had likewise urged the SCAF in 2011 to delay parliamentary elections, fearing they "would bring a majority from the movements of political Islam."[89] Moreover, the president of the SCC, Farouk Sultan, had been catapulted into his position by Mubarak for having effectively convicted scores of Muslim Brothers in military courts.

The judiciary had already dissolved the lower house of the parliament, the People's Assembly, in June, and had overruled Morsi's attempts to revive it in July. In April, the judiciary had also dissolved the first constituent assembly chosen to draft the constitution. Now, senior judges were threatening to dissolve the second constituent assembly and the upper house of parliament (the Shura Council) as well.

Amr Darrag, the secretary-general of the second constituent assembly, noted at the time that "if these [dissolution] verdicts are handed down, we will be left only with a president, and without a Parliament or a Constituent Assembly," leaving the transition in limbo. "It is such a situation that could lead to the return of the generals."[90]

Paranoid that the judiciary would dissolve these institutions, Morsi on November 22 issued a new constitutional declaration stating that "no judicial body can dissolve the Shura Council or the Constituent Assembly." But Morsi's declaration did not stop there. Article 2 declared that in addition, *all* of Morsi's "constitutional declarations, laws, and decrees" since his election and until both a new constitution is approved and a new parliament is elected are "final and binding and cannot be appealed in any way or to any entity."[91] Morsi put not just the assemblies above judicial review, but everything he had ever done or would do in the coming months. For good measure, the declaration also concluded with a vague clause that: "The President may take the necessary actions and measures to protect the country and the goals of the revolution."

The reaction was rightfully fierce. ElBaradei slammed Morsi as Egypt's "new pharaoh," having "usurped all state power" in "a major blow to the revolution."[92] Amr Hamzawy called it a "complete assassination of the democratic transition,"[93] while Amr Moussa called it a "massacre of the judiciary."[94] Hamdeen Sabbahi warned Morsi that "the revolution will not accept a new dictator."[95] In turn, the four of them, along with al-Wafd's El Sayyid El Badawi, among others, united for the first time into the National Salvation Front (NSF), and spearheaded mass protests against Morsi's

---

[88] Quoted in Kirkpatrick (2012*b*).

[89] Quoted in Kirkpatrick (2012*c*).

[90] Quoted in El-Hennawy (2012*b*).

[91] See full text of Morsi's decree at Ahram Online (2012*e*). The declaration also ordered a retrial of Mubarak and other officials for killing protesters during the revolution, and fired and replaced the prosecutor-general.

[92] Ahram Online (2012*g*).

[93] Ibid.

[94] See Al-Masry Al-Youm (2012*f*).

[95] Ibid.

decree.[96] Meanwhile, about one-fourth of the 100-member constituent assembly withdrew in protest.[97]

But Morsi calculated that he still had the support of the majority—both in the assembly and in the street. He accordingly pressed ahead, riding roughshod over the secularists' objections. Over the course of the next week, amidst daily protests, the remaining members of the Constituent Assembly finalized the constitution, and then held a marathon, 14-hour overnight session to vote on each article. With the text approved on November 30, Morsi then canceled his problematic declaration. He then put the constitution up to a public referendum on December 15, where it passed with 64 percent of the vote.

The constitution had some flaws, but it was neither autocratic nor theocratic. It was a significant improvement over Mubarak's. The text, while imperfect, was not the problem. Indeed, most of the NSF leaders had no major qualms with the text, nor, apparently, did the general public. At the time, Baseera estimated that Morsi's popularity had fallen from 78 percent to 57 percent, a significant drop, but still enjoying majority support.[98]

The issue was with the process: rushed, exclusionary, and majoritarian. The constitution could have been an opportunity for consensus like it was in Tunisia. But Egypt boasted a powerful deep state—both the military and the judiciary—eager to dissolve the constituent assembly and roll back the gains of the revolution. In a major blunder, Morsi abandoned process for outcome, rushing to the finish line of having a new constitution. "This could have reflected consensus rather than the imposition of control by the majority," noted Amr Moussa, the first constituent assembly member to withdraw.[99]

The Army and the Constitution

But the secularists were not the only ones displeased with the constitution-drafting process. The military was also not fully satisfied with Morsi's constitution. On the one hand, the constitution did enshrine many of the military's desired privileges: a National Defense Council (NDC), which oversaw the military's budget and draft laws pertaining to it; no declaration of war without the NDC's approval; a stipulation that the minister of defense be a military officer; and military trials of civilians accused of

---

[96] See Ahram Online (2012*h*).

[97] 11 of the 26 withdrawn members were replaced by reserve candidates, largely Islamists. Hence in the final session, 85 of 100 members were present. 67 votes were needed for an article to pass in a first vote, and 57 in a second pass (Ahram Online, 2012*a*).

[98] See Baseera (2013).

[99] See El-Din (2012*a*). Amr Darrag claims that Moussa in fact told him "in person that they [the NSF] don't have any problem with the constitution other than the transitional article related to the continuation of Dr. Morsi as president during the transitional period. But the president was just elected, it did not make sense to have new elections." Interview, Istanbul, July 11, 2016.

"harming" the armed forces. These clauses led many observers to think the military's interests were fully respected.[100]

But Amr Darrag, Secretary General of the Constituent Assembly, noted the final document was the outcome of a conflictual negotiation with the military. The two military representatives, Mamdouh Shahin and Mohamed Magdy El-Din Barkat, had been pushing for additional powers. "Whenever the subcommittee had discussions, they always gave a hidden threat that the assembly could be dissolved, that another could be formed. They were quite stubborn. They used this threat to try to push for a lot of things they have been trying to achieve like those in the Selmi document."[101]

Darrag in particular mentioned four arenas where the military was forced to compromise. The first was in the respective powers of the president v. the SCAF. In the SCAF's supplementary declaration in June 2012, they had stripped the president of his title of commander of the armed forces, and gave the SCAF full control over all military appointments. In Morsi's constitution, by contrast, the president was named the "supreme commander of the armed forces" (article 146), and was empowered with appointing and dismissing military personnel (article 147). Though the defense minister must be a military officer, he would be chosen by the president, not the SCAF.

That loss of autonomy was not lost on the generals. At the time, General Ali Bilal criticized the constitution for allowing the Brotherhood to choose the defense minister: "When a particular identity tries to interfere or meddle in the army, this is unacceptable. It is for this reason that many military experts have cautioned against the day when the minister of defence could be polarised by a political force [. . .]. Unfortunately, such a possibility has been embedded into the new constitution in the article pertaining to the minister of defence."[102] Another officer was still hung up on the president's title: "Every time [Morsi] says 'I am the supreme commander of the armed forces,' I want to hit him with something."[103]

The second disagreement concerned the defense budget. In an earlier draft (and in Sisi's constitution today), the defense budget would be "incorporated as a single figure in the state budget," so that civilians would have no say—or even knowledge— over how the defense budget is allocated. But this clause was removed in the final draft, "which leaves open the possibility that the parliament may be able to review the military's budget" in more detail.[104] Moreover, the National Defense Council, which included among its membership the president, prime minister, finance minister, foreign minister, and speakers of both houses of parliament, would be explicitly tasked with "discussing" the armed forces' budget, suggesting greater civilian scrutiny of the budget than had previously been the case.

---

[100] See, e.g., Sayigh (2013); Hamid (2014); Masoud (2014); al Anani (2015); Ashour (2015); Trager (2016); Abul-Magd (2017), and Holmes (2019).

[101] Interview with Amr Darrag, Istanbul, July 11, 2016.

[102] Quoted in Eleiba (2012).

[103] Quoted in Ashour (2015, p. 21).

[104] See Al-Ali (2012). Al-Ali also notes that while the national defense council is tasked with reviewing the budget, "there is no indication that the council is exclusively competent to discuss the matter."

The third area of conflict was military trials of civilians. The final draft stated that: "Civilians cannot stand trial before military courts except for crimes that harm the armed forces,"[105] to be defined by law. The military, according to Darrag, had wanted more specificity in the constitution to explicitly permit "military courts for civilians for issues other than threatening facilities."[106] Sisi's constitution, for instance, permits military trials of civilians not just for "crimes that represent a direct assault against military facilities, military barracks, [. . .] equipment, [or] vehicles," but also for those against "documents, military secrets, public funds, or military factories; or crimes related to conscription."[107]

Finally, the most controversial article of the constitution was the composition of the National Defense Council (article 197), which discussed the defense budget and was to be consulted on all draft laws related to the armed forces. Prior to Morsi's election, the SCAF had created an NDC with 10 of 17 members, an absolute majority, coming directly from the military (see Table 7.1).[108] In Morsi's constitution, the military attempted to maintain this majority. While they still had the upper-hand (pre-August 12), General Shahin had threatened that: "If you put one of yours, I'll put one of mine!"[109]

The military "wanted to have the majority of the council from military backgrounds," explained Darrag. "But we reached the conclusion that it would be half and half and chaired by the president, who [at the time was] civilian. So if the division was civilian v. military, they would not win."[110] Accordingly, the constituent assembly

Table 7.1 SCAF's National Defense Council

Military	Security	Civilian
1. Defense Minister	1. Interior Minister	1. President
2. Armed Forces Chief of Staff	2. General Intelligence Service Chief	2. Prime Minister
3. Navy Commander		3. Foreign Minister
4. Air Force Commander		4. Finance Minister
5. Air Defense Commander		5. Speaker of Parliament
6. Chief of Operations		
7. Chief of Military Intelligence		
8. Chief of Military Judiciary		
9. Military Production Minister		
10. Assistant Defense Minister		

[105] See Morsi's constitution at the Constitute Project.
[106] Interview with Amr Darrag, Istanbul, July 11, 2016.
[107] See Sisi's constitution at the Constitute Project.
[108] See Ahram Online (2012*d*).
[109] Quoted in Roll (2016, p. 32).
[110] Interview with Amr Darrag, Istanbul, July 11, 2016. Darrag's interpretation requires considering the minister of interior and chief of the general intelligence service as civilians, since, in Darrag's words, "they report to the president," and not to Sisi through the military chain of command. The subcommittee at the time likewise referred to it as a half civilian, half military composition (Afify, 2012).

Table 7.2 Morsi's National Defense Council

Military	Security	Civilian
1. Defense Minister	1. Interior Minister	1. President
2. Armed Forces Chief of Staff	2. General Intelligence Service Chief	2. Prime Minister
3. Navy Commander		3. Foreign Minister
4. Air Force Commander		4. Finance Minister
5. Air Defense Commander		5. Speaker of Parliament
6. Chief of Operations		6. Speaker of Shura Council
7. Chief of Military Intelligence		

removed three military members from the SCAF's NDC—the chief of the military judiciary, the military production minister, and the assistant defense minister—and added one to the civilian's tally, the speaker of the Shura Council (see Table 7.2). If a vote were to break down on military v. non-military lines, therefore, the split would be 7 to 8 against the military. The constitution thus represented an encroachment on the military's historic veto power over national security decisions. Notably, in Sisi's 2014 constitution, the military re-gained an absolute majority.[111]

In short, while the 2012 constitution did preserve certain prerogatives for the military, it also pushed back on others. "This is where granularity is important," noted Morsi's Presidential Advisor Wael Haddara. And now that the military's losses began to materialize, "the presidential team got its first indications that Sisi was orchestrating something."[112]

The Clashes at Ittihadiya

The National Salvation Front's protests against Morsi's decree increasingly took on a violent character, with some agitators burning down dozens of Muslim Brotherhood offices across the country, and others storming the presidential palace. Ahmed Said of the Free Egyptians Party, who led one of the marches to the Ittihadiya Palace, found that the police and soldiers did nothing to stop him as he scaled the palace walls and toured the grounds. "It was clear that the police and the army and the judiciary and all the institutions were not with Morsi. He had no control."[113]

Dina Ezzat (2012*a*), from the state-owned *Al-Ahram*, described the scene from within the presidency:

---

[111] In Sisi's constitution, the split is 8–6, as the Shura Council has been abolished and the president is from the military.

[112] Interview with Wael Haddara, London, Ontario, May 20, 2014.

[113] Quoted in Kirkpatrick (2018*a*, p. 184). See also Ashour (2015, p. 15) on the police and military's refusal to secure the Ittihadiya Palace.

> Also shrinking is the president's faith in the uncontested support that he would have from the army and police should the demonstrations against him expand or turn into a state of civil disobedience. An army general told Ahram Online that the army for the most part never really welcomed the idea of a civilian president, especially one from the Muslim Brotherhood, and that Morsi's constitutional declaration had only increased this sentiment. [. . .] Worse, Morsi, according to the same [presidency] sources, received reports suggesting that some police and army officers had openly expressed support for the anti-Morsi demonstrators.

Without the military or police to defend the presidential palace, Morsi made yet another blunder, asking his supporters to come down and defend it ahead of a major protest scheduled for December 5. Not surprisingly, the move led to clashes, fueling fears of a civil war and accusations that the Muslim Brotherhood was harboring a secret militia.

Morsi in turn withdrew his supporters, rescinded the decree, and called for a dialogue. But curiously, Egypt's military simultaneously put out a call for dialogue: "Dialogue is the best and only way to reach consensus. The opposite of that will bring us to a dark tunnel that will result in catastrophe and that is something we will not allow."[114] The cryptically worded statement suggested that while the military would give political leaders a chance to work out their issues, it would not hesitate to intervene if a solution was not found. "The military is saying, 'Do not let things get so bad that we have to intervene,'" Moataz Abdel-Fattah, a political advisor close to Sisi, told the *New York Times*. "In the short term it is good for President Morsi, but in the long run they are also saying, 'We belong to the people, and not Mr. Morsi.'"[115]

That daylight between Sisi and Morsi became even more clear on December 11, when Sisi called for his own dialogue initiative to be held at the Air Defense Hall, even summoning Morsi through a formal invitation. Sisi inserted himself into the political fight as an arbiter between the political forces, sending an even stronger signal to the opposition that Sisi was not necessarily loyal to the president. "Why was there a need for such a statement to begin with?" one Brotherhood leader exclaimed. "Why was there no reference to support for the legitimate authority as embodied in the president?"[116]

The NSF accepted Sisi's invitation, but Morsi snubbed it, forcing him to cancel the dialogue. "It was a veiled message to stay out of politics, and we got it," noted an army colonel after the coup. "We understood that Morsi was an elected leader and [it] would be hard to defy that. But it was clear by then where his rule was driving the state."[117]

But at this point, all Sisi could do was send this signal to the opposition. He did not yet have the support, domestically or internationally, to stage a coup. Morsi still

[114] Quoted in Hussein (2011).
[115] Quoted in Kirkpatrick (2012*a*).
[116] Quoted in Eleiba (2012).
[117] Quoted in Alsharif and Saleh (2013).

enjoyed the support of the majority of Egyptians, even if that majority was increasingly limited to the Brotherhood, Salafis, and other Islamists. As presidential advisor Wael Haddara observed, the threat of a coup in December 2012 was still low given the "presence of a fairly large and at that point in time, solid, unified, Islamist bloc."[118]

Likewise, the international community still seemed to be backing Morsi. On December 5, the day of the clashes outside Ittihadiya Palace, President Obama met with Essam al-Haddad, Morsi's foreign policy advisor, at the White House. While Obama reportedly urged Haddad to compromise and govern inclusively, "the meeting itself sent another message: forty minutes with the president. Obama had their back, the Morsi team thought."[119]

The military felt the same. On December 11, the day Sisi called for a dialogue, the US had finalized a deal to send F-16 fighter jets to Egypt's military. The timing of that deal was seen a signal of support for Morsi, argued retired Brigadier General Safwat Al-Zayat:

> [I]t is obvious that the finalisation of the deal on 11 December, which happened to be at the height of the mass demonstrations in Tahrir Square against Morsi, conveyed a political message. Between the lines, Washington was sending a message to three parties. The first was to Morsi and it stated, "We support you. Move ahead." The second was to the army and it said, "We are encouraging this man," meaning Morsi. The third was to the opposition forces and it said the same thing. We need to bear in mind that Morsi had been put to the test during the last [Israeli] war against Gaza and passed with flying colours from the US perspective.[120]

Without the support of the US, Sisi was hesitant to stage a coup, unwilling to risk the suspension of US military aid. Retired General Hossam Kheirallah explained at the time that: "The army is aware that it needs the US in light of [. . .] various mutual arrangements and coordination in armaments."[121] Without their support, Sisi could not yet intervene.

The Brotherhood Confronts the Army

Despite seeing Sisi's signals to the opposition, Morsi's presidential team remained confident heading into spring 2013 that the threat of a coup was low. They believed that Morsi enjoyed sufficient public and international support to prevent Sisi from intervening. They accordingly continued their conflictual bargaining with the military over its privileges.

---

[118] Interview with Wael Haddara, London (Canada), May 20, 2014.
[119] Kirkpatrick (2018a, p. 183).
[120] Quoted in Eleiba (2013).
[121] Quoted in Eleiba (2012).

National Security Decisions

In addition to removing the military's monopoly over security policy in the constitution, Morsi also clashed with the military on several national security decisions, further reinforcing the loss of the generals' veto power over this domain. The first concerned the Sinai. Like Tunisia's Ennahda vis-à-vis Ansar al-Sharia, the Muslim Brotherhood preferred to negotiate with, rather than fight, militants in the Sinai. "The strategy of Morsi and our government—and also of most intellectuals and political parties—was that the only approach to end terrorist threats in Sinai is a comprehensive approach that is not just based on security and oppression," Amr Darrag explained. "Dr. Morsi and our government had a strategy made up of four points. One is security, but the other three are development, dialogue, and control of the borders. It is a comprehensive strategy in order to really achieve progress, it's not just a matter of military action."[122]

Accordingly, Morsi on a number of occasions prevented the military from attacking militants in the Sinai. In November 2012, Morsi halted a planned offensive the day before it was to be launched, reportedly telling Sisi: "I don't want Muslims to shed the blood of fellow Muslims."[123] In May 2013, after mediation freed six policemen and a soldier, Morsi ordered Sisi not to pursue the kidnappers. "I don't want to count to you the number of times that the armed forces showed its reservations on many actions and measures that came as a surprise," Sisi told his fellow officers after the coup.[124]

"The influence of the jihadist Salafists" increased under Morsi, Sisi said in another post-coup interview. "The security procedures that were in place to prevent terrorist elements and weapons from entering the country disappeared with President [Morsi]. So they found a very free and fertile environment to work in."[125]

Morsi's preference not to attack jihadists in the Sinai also soured relations with the Pentagon. Derek Chollet, Assistant Secretary of Defense, noted in his memoir that while Israel and Egypt under Mubarak "had regular contacts and coordinated security efforts in Sinai, Morsi ended that dialogue, and whenever we pressed him to do more to control the situation, he dismissed the problem as overblown."[126]

The Muslim Brotherhood pursued a similarly lenient strategy toward Hamas in neighboring Gaza. When the military revealed that Gazan militants were involved in the August 2012 attack that killed 16 Egyptian soldiers, Morsi rejected Sisi's request that he ask Hamas to hand them over.[127] Morsi also attempted to block the military's efforts to destroy tunnels connecting Egypt and Gaza, but was forced to back down

---

[122] Interview with Amr Darrag, Istanbul, July 11, 2016.
[123] See Associated Press (2013).
[124] Ibid.
[125] See Weymouth (2013*a*).
[126] See Chollet (2016, p. 119).
[127] See Associated Press (2013).

by March 2013.[128] Likewise, the Brotherhood allegedly proposed selling land in the Sinai to generate revenue for Palestine, but was quickly shot down.[129]

"Many of us [officers and soldiers] died to retrieve this land; we did so not knowing that Morsi would one day compromise the country's right to Sinai," one officer claimed. "Whatever the reason, Sinai is a red line. We will support our Palestinian brothers in every way possible but Sinai is not for sale."[130]

In a post-coup interview, Sisi went further. "The idea that gathers them [the Muslim Brothers] together is not nationalism, it's not patriotism—it is an ideology [Islamism] that is totally related to the concept of the organization. [. . .] Hamas is part of the Muslim Brotherhood. The Brotherhood looked at Hamas as part of the family."[131]

While too friendly toward militants in the Sinai and Gaza, the Brotherhood was also too aggressive for the military's taste in its foreign policy toward Ethiopia and Syria. As tensions flared with Ethiopia over its Nile dam, Morsi's language grew increasingly belligerent, noting publicly that "all options are open" and that "if [the Nile] loses one drop, our blood is the alternative."[132] Earlier, politicians assembled by Morsi—unaware they were on live TV—threatened to go to war, back rebels in Ethiopia, or, as a last resort, instruct Egyptian spies to destroy the dam entirely.[133] "You cannot imagine the reactions I got for [that] conference," Sisi would recall two years later.[134]

Morsi pursued a similarly aggressive posture toward Syria. In June 2013, Morsi severed diplomatic relations with Syria, while encouraging Egyptians to go on jihad to fight Bashar al-Assad's forces. After an Islamist conference in Cairo entitled "The Position of the Nation's Scholars on the Developments in Syria" decided to endorse jihad, Brotherhood spokesman Ahmed Aref announced that they "fully support and endorse the outcome of the conference."[135] Meanwhile, a presidential aide, Khaled al-Qazzaz, confirmed that Egyptians would be able to freely return to Egypt after fighting in Syria.[136] From the military's point of view, however, these actions represented a major security threat, raising the specter of experienced jihadists returning to Egypt.

In short, on each of these national security issues—Sinai, Hamas, Ethiopia, Syria—the Brotherhood pursued policies the military disagreed with, highlighting the generals' loss of control over Egypt's security policy. As one retired general proclaimed two days before the coup: "This guy [Morsi] lost his mind. He thinks he can declare jihad against Syria, threaten Ethiopia with war, and surround himself with

---

[128] See Omer (2013).
[129] See Ezzat (2012*b*).
[130] See Ezzat (2012*b*).
[131] Weymouth (2013*a*).
[132] See Al-Jazeera (2013).
[133] See Reuters Staff (2013*a*).
[134] Quoted in Nader (2015).
[135] See Mohsen (2013).
[136] See Kortam (2013).

militants who have kidnapped and killed our soldiers in Sinai. This is Egypt. We cannot be ruled by ignorant amateurs."[137] The military was not yet ready to give up its historic monopoly over national security decisions.

But for the Brotherhood, removing their monopoly was precisely what democracy entailed. As Darrag explained:

> [Morsi's] position according to the constitution indicates that he is the supreme leader of the military. This is the case in almost every democratic country. Who says that the methods of national security are only to be discussed and decided by the military alone? Actually, it should be the other way around! The representative of the people is the president elected by the people—and the ultimate chairman of the military establishment.[138]

Economic Contracts

A second source of friction between the Brotherhood and the military was over economic contracts. One month after Morsi's election, Brotherhood leader Gehad al-Haddad publicly threatened the military's empire: "The problem with the army is that they get natural resources for free, such as conscripts as labor, land and state contracts. We won't tell them to stop their product lines, but you will abide by the same market rules."[139]

While Morsi's team continued to award military-owned companies several small-scale contracts, they were more hesitant with regards to the massive Suez Canal Corridor Development Project. This initiative, designed to convert the Suez Canal into a major logistics hub and center for heavy manufacturing, would have amounted to "the largest infrastructure project in decades,"[140] and was expected to bring in $100 billion in revenue each year.[141]

"The army wanted to take [full control over] the project in the Suez Canal, but Morsi stood against that," explained Muslim Brotherhood leader Abdullah al-Haddad.[142] Morsi attempted to relegate the army "to just one among many government bodies involved in the effort."[143] "Morsi wanted to give them a chance to earn these contracts, but not to let them dominate [the process]," said al-Haddad. "This made the army start to feel like they are not as influential as before."[144]

Darrag concurred. "The Suez Canal project was an overall project of development, a series of programs to achieve a major development of the area. It was not for the military to take care of alone, but rather for the state to plan and organize. The military

---

[137] Interview cited in International Crisis Group (2013).
[138] Interview with Amr Darrag, Istanbul, July 11, 2016.
[139] Quoted in Marroushi (2012).
[140] Marshall (2015, p. 12).
[141] See Werr (2012).
[142] Interview with Abdullah al-Haddad, London, July 14, 2015.
[143] Marshall (2015, p. 12).
[144] Ibid.

of course thought that that would be a major reduction of their potential earnings if they don't get this project as a major contributor."[145]

Indeed, for the military, these economic contracts were a red line. Major General Mahmoud Nasr, SCAF member and assistant defense minister for financial affairs, had earlier warned that: "We will fight for our projects and this is a battle we will not leave. We will not allow anyone to destroy the labor that we have put in for 30 years. We will not allow anyone else to approach the projects of the armed forces."[146]

But for the Brotherhood, this was again what democracy entailed. "As a matter of fact, the role of the military is not to get into partnerships in economic contracts," noted Darrag. "This is not the role of the military anywhere in the world. [. . .] The main role of the military should have gradually moved to guardian of national security rather than an economic company."[147]

"Brotherhood-ization"

A final conflict between Morsi and the military concerned its composition. While the military had historically been stacked with secular, anti-Islamist forces, President Morsi sought to make it more inclusive of Islamists. First, he attempted to encourage any Islamists already in the military, but who had been hiding their true identities, to be more open about their religiosity. Soon after his appointment by Morsi, Defense Minister Sisi overturned Mubarak's ban on praying during military exercises, telling the military, "Pray as you please."[148]

Second, President Morsi sought to introduce new Islamists into the military's ranks, opening military recruitment to the Muslim Brotherhood for the first time. In November 2012, the director of the Military Academy in Cairo, Major General Esmat Mourad, announced that the academy would no longer automatically disqualify applicants with family ties to the Brotherhood. Accordingly, Morsi's nephew was included among this first cohort of more inclusive recruits in March 2013.[149]

It is unclear how many Islamists entered the military or revealed their identities during this time, though events post-coup suggest the number was small. In 2015, 26 officers were imprisoned for allegedly plotting an Islamist coup against Sisi.[150] "A handful" of army officers also left the military post-coup to join the Islamist insurgency in the Sinai.[151]

Despite the number being small, Morsi's efforts to introduce Islamists into a historically secular military led to fears of Morsi "Brotherhood-izing" ("*akhwānāt*") the

---

[145] Interview with Amr Darrag, Istanbul, July 11, 2016.
[146] See Jamaal (2012).
[147] Interview with Amr Darrag, Istanbul, July 11, 2016.
[148] Quoted in Wenig (2014).
[149] See Al-Masry Al-Youm (2013*a*).
[150] See MEE Staff (2015).
[151] See Reuters Staff (2018) and Bayoumy (2015). While some of them likewise received military training under Morsi, the most high-profile of these officers, Hisham Ashmawy and Emad al-Din Abdel Hamid, actually served in the military under Mubarak and were discharged in 2006 and 2007.

military. When Morsi's nephew was admitted into the military academy, military expert Robert Springborg predicted that "there is going to be dissatisfaction of a very major sort about this."[152] General Ali Bilal's reaction was emblematic: we "will not allow infiltration!"[153]

Responding to this pushback, Defense Minister Sisi moved to limit Morsi's push for inclusion in March 2013. First, Sisi introduced a new oath at the military academy, obliging cadets to pledge allegiance to Egypt and the military, which an anonymous military source revealed was "implemented to reaffirm the students' loyalty to the country and the military, and not to any political or religious movement or organization."[154] Two weeks later, Sisi then reiterated the military's ban on growing beards.[155] Opening the ranks of the military to all Egyptians came as a major affront to a military historically stacked by secularists.

In sum, whatever temporary marriage of convenience the Brotherhood and the military enjoyed in 2011 quickly ended in divorce. During Morsi's short tenure, the Brotherhood encroached upon a number of the military's interests, including its constitutional prerogatives, its monopoly over national security decisions, its economic interests, and its secular identity. These corporate grievances fueled the military's desire to oust Morsi.

The Road to June 30

However, Sisi still needed to obtain the domestic and international support for a coup. After all, lesser attempts to undermine the transition—the supra-constitutional principles and the supplementary constitutional declaration—had received blowback from both Islamists and the revolutionary youth, not to mention condemnation from the US. Ending the transition entirely through a military coup might well provoke the suspension of US military aid, and a massive, united protest in the streets that the troops might be unwilling to repress.

Sisi therefore needed to assemble a larger coup-coalition. The first step was to secure the support of the secular establishment, the high-profile politicians who had coalesced into the National Salvation Front (NSF) after Morsi's decree. Sisi had already signaled to this camp that the military might not be loyal to Morsi when he stepped in to call for a dialogue in early December. If that indirect signal had not been enough, the military then made direct contact with the NSF.

According to Kirkpatrick (2018*a*, p. 216), two senior generals of the SCAF began regular contacts with the NSF in December 2012. The message they sent was clear:

Members of the alliance told me that they knew by early 2013 that the intelligence agencies were working covertly to bring Morsi down. "We are not alone,"

---

[152] Quoted in Kingsley (2013).
[153] See Eleiba (2012).
[154] See Al-Masry Al-Youm (2013*b*).
[155] See Mohamed (2013).

businessmen and party leaders like [El Wafd's] Badawi would say at the meetings, using familiar Egyptians euphemisms for the *mukhabarat*. "The state institutions are with us." "You would get people in the meetings who knew what the security agencies wanted, what the security agencies were pushing," Khaled Dawoud, the journalist acting as spokesman for the group, later said. "We were the nice civilian faces," but the spy agencies were "doing things to lay the groundwork."[156]

Amr Hamzawy, one of the few dissenters in the NSF, said that by April 2013, "the plan was spelled out quite clearly—popular mobilization, followed by tanks, followed by early presidential elections. I sensed that the National Salvation Front was dead set on its decision to call on the army to intervene."[157] When Hamzawy objected, ElBaradei shot him down: "Without the army, we stand no chance."[158]

Laila Amiry, a co-founder of ElBaradei's Constitution Party, told me the same: that by April, they knew they could count on the military to remove Morsi. "Three months before the 30th, I found myself in a meeting [where] the plan for the 30th became very clear. The Brothers were not going to stay. The end was there." Notably, the NSF was told that the US had come on board, as well. "The main thing I heard in that meeting was that the Pentagon said that if your people want it, fine—all they care about is the peace treaty."[159]

But while the NSF moved firmly into the military's camp, the Muslim Brotherhood thought little of it. The NSF "didn't have much power on the street, and this is how we judged them," noted Abdullah al-Haddad. "We can gather thousands of people on the ground everyday, you can only get hundreds, be fair. We should get what we deserve. But we didn't judge the international aspect. We didn't realize their ability to communicate with European and American policymakers."[160]

Sisi's second task was to pull the Salafis off from the Brotherhood. If not, the Brotherhood might be able to mobilize half the voting population against the coup, and salafis in particular might be prone to retaliate violently. It was thus critical to get them on board.

Doing so was easier than expected. As soon as interlocutors hinted that the military was ready to move against Morsi, the Salafis weighed the costs and benefits. If they stuck by Morsi, all of the Islamists would be repressed. They would lose the freedom to worship and proselytize that they had won with the revolution. "We calculated that if this representative [Morsi] failed in the political spectrum, that the whole Islamic stream would be damaged," explained Nader Bakkar, spokesman for the Nour Party. "This is why we chose to take the side of the state by July 3. There was no benefit here, we were just managing our losses, minimizing the losses to the whole Islamic stream."[161]

---

[156] Kirkpatrick (2018*a*, p. 199).
[157] Quoted in Kirkpatrick (2018*a*, p. 216).
[158] Quoted in Kirkpatrick (2018*a*, p. 216).
[159] Interview with Laila Amiry, Cairo, June 5, 2014.
[160] Interview with Abdullah al-Haddad, London, July 14, 2015.
[161] Interview with Nader Bakkar, Cairo, June 3, 2014.

Wael Haddara, Morsi's advisor, said the Salafis told him the same thing: "By February, the Nour Party became acutely aware that there was going to not only be a coup, but that it would be violent and repressive. They felt that someone had to stake out a claim for Islam in the public space by appearing to be pro-regime, so that they could secure some measure of personal safety for the millions of self-identifying Islamists out there. In their words, they made the supreme sacrifice to play that role."[162]

In anticipation of a coup, the Nour Party thus broke with the Brotherhood, with chairman Younis Makhyoun on March 5 even threatening to publish a report documenting Morsi's 'Brotherhoodization' of the state. But even after the Nour Party defected, many in the Brotherhood continued to believe that Morsi would enjoy the support of the salafi base. The base had not followed the Nour Party leadership in voting for Abdel-Moneim Aboul-Fotouh in the presidential elections, so it stood to reason that they might not follow the leadership in supporting a coup, either.[163] The Brotherhood also made a conscious effort to shore up the support of its remaining Islamist allies, appointing a minister from *al-Wasat* in May and a governor from *al-Gama'a al-Islamiyya* in June.

Third, Sisi needed the support of the revolutionary youth and other protesters. The secret services first approached Ahmed Maher of the April 6 movement in February 2013 to lead the protests against Morsi.[164] When he refused, they approached the leaders of a new, grassroots movement called *Tamarod* ("Rebel"). Founded by five young men who had been part of the Kefaya movement against Mubarak, they had announced a campaign in April to collect 15 million signatures calling for Morsi's resignation, and to begin a campaign of civil disobedience on June 30, the anniversary of Morsi's inauguration.

Walid al-Masry, one of the five co-founders, recalled that they were soon approached by a group of retired military officers, who said they were reaching out on behalf of the military's current leadership. "We didn't ask them for help. They just offered it. And we welcomed that."[165]

Receptive, the Tamarod leaders coordinated directly with both former and current army officers, including meeting with Sisi.[166] The military and security forces provided funds and helped distribute Tamarod's petition,[167] which allegedly received 22 million signatures (which if true would amount to one-fourth of Egypt's population).

"How did we go from such a small thing, five guys trying to change Egypt, to the movement which brought tens of millions to the street to get rid of the Brotherhood?" asked Moheb Doss, another of the Tamarod co-founders. "The answer is we didn't. I understand now it wasn't us, we were being used as the face of what something bigger than us wanted. [. . .] The leaders of Tamarod let themselves be directed by others. They took orders from others."[168]

---

[162] Interview with Wael Haddara, London, Ontario, May 20, 2014.
[163] Interview with Abdullah al-Haddad, London, July 14, 2015.
[164] See Maher (2014).
[165] Quoted in Giglio (2013*a*).
[166] See Frankel and Atef (2014).
[167] See Alsharif and Saleh (2013).
[168] Quoted in Frankel and Atef (2014).

Indeed, as June 30 approached, Tamarod leaders began to provide political cover for a military coup. Hazem el-Zohery declared it would be a "success" if the military intervened.[169] Mahmoud Badr, Tamarod's official spokesman, "began making statements to the media that were in direct contradiction to what the group had earlier discussed, Doss said, and appeared to increasingly support the army."[170] When protests finally erupted and Sisi gave Morsi a 48-hour ultimatum, Badr then praised the military's involvement: "We salute the Army! We salute them! They have shown that they are with the people."[171]

Leaked audio recordings later revealed further links between the military and Tamarod. One leak revealed that General Abbas Kamel, Sisi's office manager and now spy chief, and General Sedky Sobhy, military chief of staff, were channeling funds from the United Arab Emirates to the Tamarod leadership.[172] Badr, who stood on stage with Sisi as he announced his takeover, reportedly received land from the military as a reward for his help in legitimizing the coup.[173]

"The Egypt that came out on June 30th had a backbone—and that was the deep state," argued Laila Amiry of ElBaradei's party. "They had all of the intelligence services behind them. To have imagined that Tamarod alone could do all that in the time that it did would be living a fantasy. [...] We were played in the worst way."[174]

A final step Sisi took was to get the general public on board. Just as they had refused to defend the presidential palace in December, the military and police largely refused to ensure security in spring 2013, as well.[175] When the military was tasked with enforcing a curfew in Port Said following riots by soccer fans, the soldiers refused. "People at night were playing football with the army which was supposed to be imposing the curfew!" exclaimed Ahmed Mekky, Morsi's justice minister.[176] The resulting chaos and crime contributed to the general public begging the military to come back and ensure security.[177] Indeed, by March, residents of Port Said were already protesting explicitly for a military coup.[178]

Beyond insecurity, Sisi also appeared to coordinate with the military's economic empire and other business elites to foment an economic crisis. In May and June 2013, Cairo was rocked by regular electricity blackouts and major fuel shortages. The week before the coup, lines at gas stations went on for miles, contributing to

---

[169] Quoted in Giglio (2013*b*).

[170] Quoted in Frankel and Atef (2014).

[171] Quoted in Frankel and Atef (2014).

[172] See Kirkpatrick (2012*d*).

[173] Ketchley (2017, p. 113). As these associations were revealed, Tamarod was quickly discredited, with one of its co-founders assaulted in October 2013 by secular activists and denounced as a "a pimp of the intelligence services."

[174] Interview with Laila Amiry, Cairo, June 5, 2014.

[175] See Alsharif and Saleh (2013), Ketchley (2017, pp. 113–116)

[176] Quoted in Blair, Taylor, and Perry (2013). The Associated Press (2013) notes that El-Sisi refused to get tougher on rioters in Port Said, noting, "The people have demands."

[177] See also Abadeer, Blackman, Blaydes, and Williamson (2022), who find in the March 2013 Afro Barometer survey that Egyptians who said they were concerned about crime were more supportive of "the military coming in to govern the country."

[178] See Kirkpatrick (2018*a*, pp. 204–205).

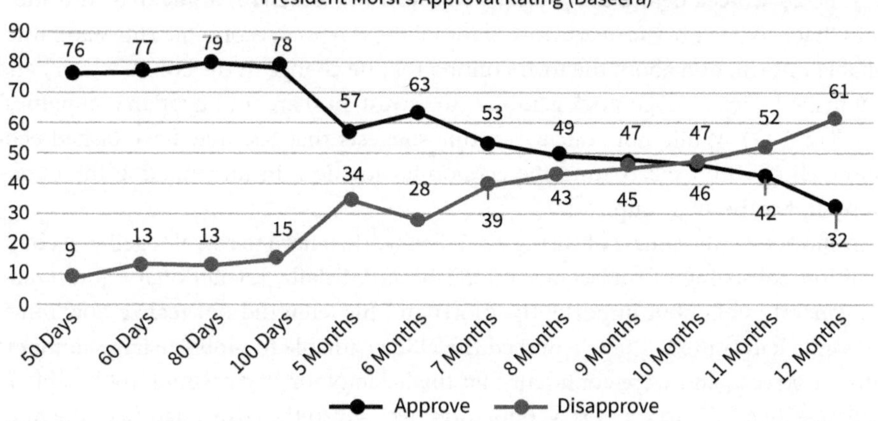

Figure 7.1 Morsi's Popularity over Time (*Source*: Baseera)

considerable frustration with Morsi.[179] Accordingly, ahead of the June 30 protests, Baseera estimated that Morsi was down to just a 32 percent approval rating (see Figure 7.1).[180]

But magically, the economic and security crises simply disappeared after the coup. As the *New York Times* reported:

> Gas lines have disappeared, power cuts have stopped and the police have returned to the street. The apparently miraculous end to the crippling energy shortages, and the re-emergence of the police, seems to show that the legions of personnel left in place after former President Hosni Mubarak was ousted in 2011 played a significant role—intentionally or not—in undermining the overall quality of life under the Islamist administration of Mr. Morsi.[181]

Laila Amiry was even more explicit:

> "The [Brotherhood's] biggest lie was to themselves—to not come out to the country and admit that I am not [actually] governing. The judiciary, intelligence, military, police—no one is with me. I can't even control gas lines. On the 30th gas lines disappeared miraculously. Train crashes stopped, buildings stopped falling."[182]

While it is difficult to conclusively prove coordination between Sisi and economic elites, Korotayev, Issaev, and Shishkina (2016) uncover suggestive evidence. In the lead-up to major political unrest, the stock market typically falls, plagued by uncertainty over the crisis. But in Egypt, the stock market in fact began growing starting

---

[179] One Egyptian waiting in line for gas told Hubbard (2013): "God willing, Morsi will fall and the army will take control."

[180] See Baseera (2013).

[181] Hubbard and Kirkpatrick (2013).

[182] Interview with Laila Amiry, Cairo, June 5, 2014.

on June 24, a week before the protests. Korotayev et al. (2016) argue that "this indicates that even before the overthrow of Morsi the Egyptian economic elite had rather reliable information about the forthcoming regime change in the country [. . .] and that helped to encourage stock gamblers to 'invest' in shares of Egyptian companies" (pp. 342–343). While not conclusive, this suggests that Sisi may have tasked economic elites with exacerbating the economic situation, in turn making the public more supportive of a coup.

In short, over the course of spring 2013, Sisi worked hard to corral together a coup-coalition consisting of the secular establishment, Salafis, revolutionary youth, and the general public. But importantly, Morsi and his team did not realize how much the sands had shifted. They dismissed the NSF as unable to mobilize large numbers into the streets, and were confident that the Salafi Nour Party would not be able to convince their base to support a coup. Moreover, given the covert nature of the military's support for Tamarod, they did not foresee just how large the June 30th protests would turn out to be.

"No one expected that June 30 would be that big," exclaimed Abdullah al-Haddad.[183] Wael Haddara concurred: "Why did protests grow so much by June, when the constitution was the main rallying point and nothing much happened since? I don't know. On paper, and subsequently confirmed by all Central Bank numbers, the economy was actually getting better. But what we did not know was that [the protests] were not organic—we did not know that Tamarod was heavily subsidized and supported by the army. We did not know about this concerted effort to choreograph things on June 30."[184]

Accordingly, as the country geared up for the June 30 protests, the leadership of the Brotherhood remained confident that they could mobilize as many supporters as the opposition. "The leaders sent messages to the ground level that nothing would happen," recalled Haddad. "This would just be a normal protest. Have your counter-protest, and the army will not intervene. Many Muslim Brotherhood leaders were convinced of that."[185]

International Support

Developments on the international front tell a similar story. While Sisi steadily gained the consent of key US policymakers to stage a coup, the Brotherhood remained oblivious.

While publicly, the US continued to express its support for democracy in Egypt, key players within the administration, particularly from the Pentagon, were privately telling the Egyptian military the opposite. General James Mattis, CENTCOM commander, had met Sisi in February, while General Michael Flynn, head of the

---

[183] Interview with Abdullah al-Haddad, London, July 14, 2015.
[184] Interview with Wael Haddara, London (Canada), May 20, 2014.
[185] Interview with Abdullah al-Haddad, London, July 14, 2015.

Defense Intelligence Agency, was speaking regularly with Sisi and other military officials. Both apparently "agreed with their Egyptian [. . .] counterparts that Morsi was a danger."[186]

On March 2, Secretary of State John Kerry met both Morsi and Sisi in separate meetings. Sisi reportedly hinted at the prospect of a military coup: "I will not let my country go down the drain." Kerry, rather than objecting, agreed: "This is a dangerous time," realizing then that "Morsi was cooked."[187]

On April 24, Secretary of Defense Chuck Hagel arrived in Egypt. Publicly, Hagel announced that he was there to "reaffirm American commitment to Egypt's emerging democracy, [and] encourage the democratic and economic reforms that are underway here."[188] That was the message Morsi and his team heard. But separately, Hagel also met with Sisi. Kirkpatrick (2018*b*) describes the scene:

> The White House was sending Secretary of Defense Chuck Hagel talking points intended to warn General Sisi that Washington would punish a coup. [. . .] But the message Mr. Hagel delivered "was totally, totally different," [said] a senior official on the National Security Council who read transcripts of the calls later. [. . .] "The White House wanted the message to be 'Democracy is important,' and Hagel wanted it to be 'We want to have a good relationship.' We never could get him to deliver stern talking points." [. . .] "I don't live in Cairo, you do," Mr. Hagel said he had told General Sisi. "You do have to protect your security, protect your country."

These mixed messages were compounded by internal disagreements within the Obama administration. While Mattis, Flynn, Kerry, and Hagel were telling Sisi to do what he saw fit, the officials that Morsi interacted with—President Obama and Ambassador Anne Patterson—were publicly and privately assuring him that the US supported the democratic process and would not condone a coup.[189] Accordingly, while Sisi believed he had a green light from the US, Morsi believed the US was sending Sisi a red light.

"It sounds so bloody naïve, but we really did think that the international community would not countenance a coup in 2013," said Presidential Aide Wael Haddara. "We really thought that that was just not possible."[190]

"We were really excluding the possibility of a military coup because we thought that the approach we adopted in running international relations was assuring and comforting the international powers," explained Amr Darrag, who served as minister of planning and international cooperation in Morsi's final months. "All of the statements coming from the US were that they are supporting the choice of the people. [. . .] Maybe they don't like us, fine, but they know we are a good factor in stabilizing the country, would not foolishly get into conflicts, and very clearly stated that

---

[186] Kirkpatrick (2018*a*, p. 211)
[187] Kirkpatrick (2018*a*, p. 212)
[188] Quoted in Alexander (2013)
[189] See, Ahram Online (2013).
[190] Interview with Wael Haddara, London (Canada), May 20, 2014.

we would abide by international commitments, meaning the peace treaty with Israel. We thought that because it is the 21st century, and that this is Egypt—not a banana republic—that the US and the West in general would not support [a coup], and that would be a safeguard against it."[191]

In addition to believing that the US was uniformly warning the Egyptian military not to stage a coup, Morsi's team also believed that such a "red light" from the US could stop a coup. "The U.S. has a lot of influence on the military," Darrag insisted. "The SCAF is very well connected to the U.S. They could have prevented it."[192] This confidence in the US's leverage may have been misplaced. An Obama administration official observed that given that Russia and the Gulf states were waiting in the wings, even a unified threat to suspend aid might not have deterred Sisi from staging a coup.[193] President Obama told Morsi as much in his final phone call with him on July 1: "The fact is, if the Egyptian military thinks the country's stability is at risk, they are going to make their own decision. They are not taking direction from the United States."[194]

The Military's Grievances

A final miscalculation concerned the extent to which the Brotherhood's actions were aggrieving the military. The Brotherhood, and President Morsi in particular, believed until the end that Sisi did not actually have sufficient motive to stage a coup. Sisi had "cultivated Mr. Morsi and other leaders, [. . .] including going out of his way to show that he was a pious Muslim."[195] Sisi, moreover, had admitted Morsi's nephew into the military academy and earlier provided Morsi with data on corruption in the army to sack Tantawi and Anan.

Ayman Nour, a secular leader who in April was offered but ultimately refused the prime ministership, recalled Morsi's strong faith in Sisi at the time. "I told [Morsi that . . .] one of my terms is that he does not intervene in choosing the ministers. I told him I will appoint this person and that, all of whom were not on good terms with him. He replied, do whatever you want, except one, Sisi."[196]

To Morsi, "Sisi kept saying 'I will not engage, I will not engage,'" said Abdullah al-Haddad. "He told Morsi that June 30 will be normal, like before."[197] Even after Sisi on June 23 publicly announced that the military would be compelled "to intervene" if Morsi did not solve the crisis within a week, he was still sending mixed signals privately. As the *New York Times* reported:

---

[191] Interview with Amr Darrag, Istanbul, July 11, 2016.
[192] Interview with Amr Darrag, Istanbul, July 11, 2016.
[193] Interview with Obama administration official who did not wish to be named, Washington, July 27, 2017.
[194] Kirkpatrick (2018*a*, p. 234)
[195] See Kirkpatrick and El Sheikh (2013).
[196] Quoted in Al Desoukie (2014).
[197] Interview with Abdullah al-Haddad, London, July 14, 2015.

When Mr. Morsi called the general, General Sisi told the president that "it [the statement] was to satisfy some of his men" and that "it was nothing more than an attempt to absorb their anger," one of Mr. Morsi's advisers said. "So even after that first statement, the president didn't think a coup was imminent.[198]

In sum, the Brotherhood ultimately miscalculated each of the factors affecting the threat of a coup: the military's will, the level of domestic support, and the level of international support. Accordingly, Morsi in the spring of 2013 pushed the military farther than the conditions permitted, sparking a coup.

The Coup

The protests on June 30th were massive, on par with the 2011 revolution. But unlike 2011, the atmosphere was festive from the start: there was no fear that the police or military would try to repress the protests. Sisi had already pledged on June 23 to stand by "the will of the people." And the protesters welcomed the army's involvement. As one retired general gloated: "The people have chanted 'the people and the army are one hand' again on 30 June, after they used to chant 'down with military rule'!"[199]

The next day, Sisi publicly issued Morsi a second ultimatum: meet the people's demands in 48 hours, or the army will intervene. "The armed forces warns everyone that if the demands of the people are not met during this set time period, it will be obliged, due to its national and historic duties, out of respect for the demands of the great Egyptian people, to announce a roadmap and measures for the future, which it would oversee in collaboration with all the loyal national factions and movements."[200]

But at this point, there was little more Morsi could do. NSF leaders Hamdeen Sabbahi and Mohamed ElBaradei had already turned down positions as vice-president and prime minister the previous summer,[201] and had been refusing since December to even have a dialogue. Even Aymen Nour turned down the prime ministership in April. After Sisi's ultimatum, Morsi offered again to bring in a new government, hold parliamentary elections, and even form a committee to revise the constitution. But the opposition would not budge. After all, there was little incentive to accept a share of the pie under Morsi, when they anticipated receiving the lion's share of the pie after the coup. The NSF was convinced that the army would hand them the reins after toppling Morsi, thinking the generals had learned from the 2011–2012 experience not to stay in power. Sisi, after all, had pledged repeatedly, including in his July 1 ultimatum, that "the armed forces will not take part in the political or governing arena,"[202] suggesting it would instead appoint civilians and retreat back to the barracks.

---

[198] See Kirkpatrick and El Sheikh (2013).
[199] Quoted in International Crisis Group (2013).
[200] See full text here: Reuters Staff (2013*b*).
[201] See Aboulenein (2012) and Al-Masry al-Youm (2012*a*).
[202] Quoted in Reuters Staff (2013*b*).

"They knew that their share [under Morsi] would be small, so they opted to cooperate with the military to overthrow Morsi instead," Darrag claimed. "They thought that by siding with the military they would have part of the cake. They did not realize that the military would use them and then kick them out."[203]

Indeed, the secularists even believed that if the military did try to stay in power, they would simply topple the generals, too. "The youth said who cares, we will bring down the SCAF as well!" Laila Amiry recalls. "They believed they were going to get rid of Sisi, just as they got rid of Mubarak and Morsi. At least know your power! They didn't realize they were just a small minority."[204]

There was likewise little Morsi could do to coax the military to back down. His administration's actions throughout the spring of 2013 had thoroughly aggrieved the officer corps. When Sisi made his first ultimatum on June 23, "two Morsi aides called the commander of the 2nd Field Army, Maj. Gen. Ahmed Wasfi, based in the Suez Canal region, and sounded him out about installing him in el-Sissi's place."[205] But Wasfi declined and immediately informed Sisi of the call.

With Morsi unable to please either the military or the opposition, Sisi intervened when the 48 hours were up. On July 3, the military arrested Morsi and other senior Brotherhood leaders. Sisi appeared on live TV, flanked by senior military officers and the coup coalition he assembled, including NSF's ElBaradei, Tamarod's Mahmoud Badr and Mohamed Abdelaziz, and Salafi Nour's Galal Murra,[206] and declared that Adly Mansour, the head of the Supreme Constitutional Court, would serve as interim president until new elections were held. ElBaradei would in turn be appointed vice-president.

Sisi's calculations turned out to be correct. Only the Brotherhood and a few smaller Islamist groups stood up against the coup, and the military and police had no issues brutally repressing these so-called "terrorists," including by massacring protesters at Rabaa and Nahda Squares on August 14. The US, meanwhile, expressed its disapproval of the military's actions, but stopped short of labeling it a coup. After the massacres, the US would partially suspend military aid, but restore it in full roughly a year later.[207]

Sisi in turn ran for the presidential elections, winning a farcical 97 percent of the vote in 2014 and again in 2018. He soon turned on the NSF leaders and revolutionary youth, imposing a military dictatorship even more brutal than under Mubarak. Egypt's brief democratic experiment, 2011–2013, thus began and ended at the hands of the generals.

---

[203] Interview with Amr Darrag, Istanbul, July 11, 2016.

[204] Interview with Laila Amiry, Cairo, June 5, 2014.

[205] Associated Press (2013), citing military officials.

[206] Halawa (2015) of *Al-Ahram* claims it was Bassam El-Zarqa, Nour's VP, rather than Murra, the secretary-general. Other civilians in attendance were: former Morsi advisor Sekina Fouad, Al-Azhar's grand imam Ahmed El-Tayeb, the Coptic Pope Tawadros II, and head of the Supreme Judicial Council, Hamed Abdullah. The military was represented by General Mohamed El-Assar, SCAF member; General Younes El-Masry, Commander of the Egyptian Air Force; General Ossama El-Gendy, the then Commander of the Egyptian Navy; and General Abdel-Moniem Altras, Commander of the Egyptian Air Defence Force.

[207] See Grewal and Kureshi (2019).

Reflections

Egypt's democratic transition failed, first and foremost, because of the type of military it inherited from previous autocrats. The Egyptian military had been governing the country for the past 60 years, and had come to not just enjoy but believe it deserved a dominant share of political and economic power. It was determined to fight tooth-and-nail to preserve its veto power over security policy, to shield its budget and economic empire from civilian oversight, and to maintain complete autonomy over its affairs.

But democratization, by definition, meant reining in these privileges. Democracy empowers an elected government to exercise civilian control over the military, allowing the commander-in-chief to make national security decisions, to determine recruitment policies and appoint the military's leadership, and to alter and oversee the military's budget.

Accordingly, whether it was the Muslim Brotherhood or anyone else elected into office, the pursuit of democratization would have encroached on the military's terrain. In the words of AbdulMawgoud Dardery, a member of the now-dissolved parliament:

> "The military was frustrated with democracy, not [just] with Morsi's foreign policy. I think even if we had a Christian president [but] who was democratically elected and was going to do what the people of Egypt wanted, the military would have been frustrated. The military did not want a democracy because democracy for the military means a sense of transparency and accountability. They did not want to be transparent about their budget, and they did not want to be held accountable. You see there is a saying that every country has an army, except Egypt. It's an army that has a country. So it is that type of comfort that they have had since 1952. They believe they are the ones who are supposed to run the country, not a democratically-elected president."[208]

Amr Darrag concurred:

> "Everyone who believes that Egypt needs to go through a democratic course led by elected civilians knows that that means curtailing the power of the military in the political domain. Maybe we could have avoided a coup, but we would also have aborted the revolution. The people rose up to achieve a modern state where they have a say in governing their country, not to turn around and give everything to the military. This is the point. If you just give everything to the military, you made the coup yourself by handing over power from the people to the military."[209]

That fundamental tension between the military and democracy underlies why Egypt's transition failed. It explains why the military sought to polarize and divide the

---

[208] Interview with AbdulMawgoud Dardery, Zoom, October 11, 2020.
[209] Interview with Amr Darrag, Istanbul, July 11, 2016.

revolutionaries through the constitutional referendum and the supra-constitutional principles. It explains why the military sought to strip both the parliament and the president of any powers before they took office. It explains why the Brotherhood encroached on the military's domain, and ultimately why the military bankrolled mass protests and staged a coup against Morsi.

This is not to say that the Brotherhood and the NSF, or the revolutionary youth and the Salafis, did not have agency. Yes, the Brotherhood could have done more to reach out to the secularists, and could have more accurately assessed the situation with the military. And yes, the secularists could have been more willing to cooperate with Morsi and not come knocking on the door of the barracks.

But structurally, their choices were fundamentally shaped by the military. The military actively sowed mistrust and polarized each side, playing one off against the other. It actively dangled in front of the secularists the option of overthrowing the Islamists by force. While Tunisia's military retreated behind the scenes, Egypt's military played the revolutionary forces like a grandmaster on a chessboard.

8

Tunisia: Marginalizing the Military

Introduction

The initial success of Tunisia's transition to democracy rests in large part with its military. Tunisia's "soldiers of democracy" stepped aside as the country's dictator was toppled in 2011, and subsequently chose to ignore calls in 2013 to end the democratic transition in a military coup. However, years later, the military would facilitate the president staging an incumbent takeover to end Tunisia's democratic era. To understand this seemingly contradictory behavior, we must begin with the military's origins.

In this chapter, I outline the patterns of civil–military relations that have characterized Tunisia since independence. Tunisia's founding father, Habib Bourguiba (r. 1956–1987), had a relatively blank slate on which to design the country's coercive apparatus. There was no military to inherit from the colonial era, and armed resistance played only a marginal role in the independence movement. Although Bourguiba faced both internal and external security threats, his personal preferences drove him not to empower the military, but instead to marginalize it, starving it of material resources and keeping it far from political power.

Cognizant that marginalizing the military might provide grievance for a coup, Bourguiba also pursued two coup-proofing tactics. First, he counterbalanced the military with the national guard, a militarized force that he placed in the Ministry of Interior. Second, he attempted to stack the military with loyalists, producing a largely secular military recruited primarily from Tunisia's economically developed coastal areas.

But stacking the military with the secular, coastal elite was unsustainable in the long run. As this marginalized, neglected military was not a pathway to power or wealth, it struggled to attract the elite. Over time, as poorer officers from the interior regions filled the lower ranks, the strategy shifted to privileging the coastal elite in promotions to the top ranks. By the 1970s, less than half of entering officers came from the coast, and yet the coast continued to dominate 92 percent of the top brass until Bourguiba's last days. The Tunisian case thus exemplifies how some coup-proofing strategies fit together better than others: the marginalization of the military made stacking give way to discrimination in promotions.

Over time, a third factor emerged that helped to coup-proof the military further: a professional, apolitical ethos. As the military was not a pathway to power like in Egypt, politicized, power-seeking individuals decided to seek employment elsewhere, leaving the military's ranks to be filled with more professional cadres. Moreover, with

Soldiers of Democracy?. Sharan Grewal, Oxford University Press. © Sharan Grewal (2023).
DOI: 10.1093/oso/9780192873910.003.0008

few of their superiors becoming ministers or governors, officers by the 1970s became socialized into thinking that being far from politics was not just normal, but healthy. Through these recruitment and socialization effects, the oft-cited professionalism of the Tunisian military was born.

As Bourguiba's health deteriorated, his prime minister, Zine El Abidine Ben Ali, ousted him in a palace coup. Ben Ali, a former military officer, appeared to roll back Bourguiba's strategies at first, appointing several military officers as ministers. And yet, Bourguiba's coup-proofing had produced path-dependent effects, creating vested interests in its maintenance. As the police and ruling party saw the military rise, they struck back, concocting a fake coup attempt in the army that shook Ben Ali's confidence in the military.

As a result, Ben Ali then chose to double down on Bourguiba's coup-proofing strategies. He neglected the military relative to the Ministry of Interior, and carved out the presidential guard—placed in the presidency itself—as yet another counter-balancing force. He continued to promote coastal officers at disproportional rates and allowed them to monopolize the top ranks. Finally, as the military was once again kept far from politics, the entering junior officers tended to be more apolitical, viewing the military not as a means of seizing power but of serving their country.

In short, this chapter offers three contributions. It (1) outlines the coup-proofing strategies employed by Bourguiba and Ben Ali; (2) describes their origins, and the structural and personal factors that led to their rise; and (3) shows their path-dependent effects allowing them to remain despite a change in the presidency. The chapter thus sets the scene for Chapters 9, 10, and 11 to show how each of these characteristics of the military—its marginalization, political composition, and professionalism—will in turn contribute to the military's behavior in the 2011 revolution, the crisis of 2013, and the 2021 incumbent takeover.

The Birth of the Army

After negotiating independence from France on March 20, 1956, Tunisia's founding father, Habib Bourguiba, had to make a series of decisions about how to set up his new regime. Foremost among these decisions was how to organize the regime's coercive apparatus. At the time, Bourguiba saw military coups peppering the region, including in Syria (1949, 1954), Egypt (1952), Iraq (1958), Turkey (1960), Yemen (1962), and throughout sub-Saharan Africa. As a result, Bourguiba was wary of the military, and sought ways to "coup-proof."

"Bourguiba did not like the military," noted the late armed forces chief of staff, General Said El Kateb. "And he had every right not to. In the 1950s, 60s, and 70s, there was a coup attempt every day!"[1]

In deciding how to coup-proof, Bourguiba had relatively free rein, as he created the military himself. There was no Tunisian military to inherit from the colonial era. There were about 3,000–4,000 Tunisian conscripts in the French army, but few

---

[1] Interview with retired General Said el Kateb, Tunis, November 6, 2015.

Tunisian officers and no fully Tunisian units. Separately, there was a small, ceremonial Beylical Guard, but it was considered more Ottoman than Tunisian. Moreover, neither played a major role in the independence movement, which relied primarily on demonstrations and negotiations rather than force. Accordingly, neither the Beylical Guard nor the Tunisian troops in the French army had the legitimacy to demand a political role or to make claims on state resources upon independence.

"Our independence movement was different from other nations," noted retired Colonel Major Mahmoud Mezoughi, head of the retired officers' association. "In Algeria, in Egypt, etc., there was an army. In Tunisia, there wasn't. During the colonial period, we had only the French army—which we considered an enemy—and the Beylical Guard—which was not considered a national army. Therefore the national movement did not center on the army but rather on the people. And the order that was created was not a military one, but a political one."[2] A former defense minister likewise observed that "we got our independence without a lot of military action, compared to Algeria, or compared to the coup and revolution in Egypt. We had some resistance fighters [*fellagha*], but the fighting with the French authorities was more political."[3]

With civilians dominant and with no real military inheritance, Bourguiba had a blank slate on which to design the new military. In this decision, Bourguiba was shaped in part by his family's personal experience with the brutality of the Ottoman military. As retired Colonel Boubaker BenKraïem (2012, p. 224) notes in his book: "It was said that Bourguiba had been, from an early age, allergic to the army to such an extent that he became an 'antimilitarist.' This would not be surprising on his part: he, who, since his early youth, often heard about the exactions, the bullying, the punishments inflicted on the populations of the Sahel, therefore on his family, by the troops of General [Ahmed] Zarrouk that the Bey sent to these regions to collect taxes and fees." Lisa Anderson (1986, p. 69) recounts in particular the uprising of 1864 and its subsequent repression by General Zarrouk: "In 1864, the Bey's military representative in the Sahil, Ahmad Zarruq, who was known as al-Jazzar ('the butcher'), crushed the rebellion there with such brutality that its memory could be invoked a century later by the Tunisian president, Habib Bourguiba. [. . .] In a speech delivered in 1966, President Bourguiba recalled, "I come from the Sahil, from a modest family that toiled and suffered . . . After Zarrouk's punitive expedition in the Sahil, my family was ruined."[4] That personal experience with military repression drove Bourguiba to be wary of a powerful military.

Accordingly, Bourguiba decided to create a small army with little power or resources. On June 30, 1956, Bourguiba combined 850 troops from the Beylical Guard with 24 officers,[5] 250 non-commissioned officers (NCOs), and 1250 soldiers from the French army to create the Tunisian military. Bourguiba did not even use

---

[2] Interview with retired Colonel Major Mahmoud Mezoughi, Tunis, October 9, 2015.
[3] Interview with an anonymous defense minister, Tunis, October 2015.
[4] Bourguiba's father subsequently served for 19 years in the Ottoman army, and ensured that his sons would not also have to serve.
[5] Five were later removed for having been trained in the Middle East (Iraq and Syria).

all the Tunisian conscripts who were serving in the French army, taking only those serving in French bases in Tunis, Bizerte, Sousse, and Sfax.[6] With an initial size just over 2,300, the Tunisian military was born.

Over the next five years, Bourguiba allowed the military to grow to a force of just 20,000—the smallest in the Arab world – and to command only modest equipment, primarily outdated French and American hardware. The military's salaries were low, not only in comparison to the private sector, but even compared to what Tunisian officers were making while part of the French army. The 24 officers held over in fact saw their salaries cut: "For example, a captain and father of three children received in the French Army a monthly salary of 185,000 francs, while in the Tunisian army he received only 139,000 francs; a shortfall equivalent to almost a quarter of the salary."[7]

In addition to neglecting the military in salaries and weapons, Bourguiba sought to keep the military far from politics and political power. Bourguiba in January 1957 banned the military from voting or joining political parties, and none were appointed into political positions like minister or ambassador until the late 1970s. Even over its own affairs, civilians, not military men, were in charge. Bourguiba himself served as the first minister of defense (1956–1957), before appointing his trusted deputy prime minister, Bahi Ladgham (1957–1966), a public servant who helped Bourguiba negotiate with the French. Abdelhamid Chelbi, a primary school inspector, was appointed as the ministry's secretary-general. In practice as well, the top brass had little influence over policy, even over matters of war. When Tunisian troops were ordered to attack French forces in the 1961 Battle of Bizerte, officers complained that they had not even been consulted beforehand.[8]

This material and political neglect of the military fit not only with Bourguiba's anti-militarism, but also with his policy priorities. As General El Kateb observed: "The military did not have capabilities, because Bourguiba had different priorities. Economic growth, education, health—these took up 80 percent of the budget!"[9] And this was no exaggeration. Table 8.1 shows Bourguiba's first budget in 1956. The military received just 4.5 percent of the budget, compared to a combined 72 percent allocated toward health, education, public works, finance, and agriculture.

Subsequently, from independence up through 1979, the defense budget generally did not reach more than 5 percent of the total budget, while "combined government expenditures on health and education normally accounted for more than five times the amount spent on defense."[10] With those spending priorities, "there was nothing left in the budget to develop the army," Mezoughi noted. "We couldn't even buy planes from the US and France. And when [US President John F.] Kennedy asked [Bourguiba] how he could help, Bourguiba said, 'provide milk for our schools.' Bourguiba asked for milk instead of military equipment!"[11]

---

[6] Cherif (2017, p. 138).
[7] Cherif (2017, pp. 136–137).
[8] BenKraïem (2012, p. 174).
[9] Interview with retired General Said el Kateb, Tunis, November 6, 2015.
[10] Ehrenreich (1988, p. 292).
[11] Interview with retired Colonel Major Mahmoud Mezoughi, Tunis, October 9, 2015.

Table 8.1 Tunisia's 1956–1957 Budget

Ministry	Amount	Percent
Defense	1,826,680,000	4.5
Interior	5,179,900,000	12.7
Health	3,665,060,000	9.0
Education	7,584,210,000	18.5
Public works	4,385,820,000	10.7
Finance	12,463,920,000	30.5
Agriculture	1,307,620,000	3.2
Other	4,486,790,000	10.9
Total	40,900,000,000	100

Source: Decret du 30 juin 1956 portant fixation du budget ordinaire pour l'exercice 1956-57, p. 899.

The small size and limited resources of the Tunisian military is often attributed to the lack of security threats at independence. On the contrary, Tunisia was attacked no less than seven times by France between 1956 and 1958, including on military outposts in Mareth-Gabés (October 27, 1956), Aïn Draham (May 21, 1957), Fum al-Khanga (January 2, 1958), Remada (May 1958), Djebel al-Kusha and Gafsa (May 1958),[12] as well as a massacre of 68 civilians in the bombing of Sakiet Sidi Youssef (February 8, 1958). But Bourguiba preferred to respond to these security threats with diplomacy and negotiations, rather than force. The 1961 Battle of Bizerte, the one instance when the Tunisian military attacked France, is emblematic. Bourguiba had no intention of winning militarily—indeed, one-third of the career military personnel were abroad at the time in a UN peacekeeping mission in Congo,[13] and were not brought back until after the French defeated the Tunisian troops and overran Bizerte.[14] Instead, Bourguiba's goal was to bring France to the table to negotiate their eventual full withdrawal from Tunisia in 1963.

Similarly, as threats with neighboring Algeria and Libya heated up,[15] Bourguiba continued to prefer diplomacy and alliances over war. "At the time, Tunisia had some problems with Algeria and Libya, but Bourguiba used diplomacy to solve crises," observed a former director of military intelligence. "The result is that he didn't need the army. [. . .] He would have dismantled it if he could."[16] "Bourguiba knew that as a small country we couldn't match the strong armies of our neighbors [Libya and Algeria] anyway," observed another retired brigadier-general. So he chose diplomacy. "He knew he could count on our allies France and the US when the moment came."[17] In

---

[12] See de la défense nationale (2012).

[13] See FM (2020).

[14] The battle was fought from July 19 to 23, 1961, while the Tunisian forces in Congo were repatriated between July 24 and August 1. See BenKraiem (2020).

[15] Grimaud (1995).

[16] Interview with retired officer, Tunis, October 2015.

[17] Interview with retired officer, January 2016.

short, Bourguiba was determined to keep the military marginalized—far from power, far from resources, and rarely let out of the barracks.

Coup-Proofing

However, Bourguiba also knew that the political and material neglect of the military could itself provide grievance for a coup. Even if the military was small, it could still overpower the unarmed civilian leaders. Accordingly, to complement this marginalization of the military, Bourguiba pursued two coup-proofing tactics, both of which were designed to ensure there would be armed resistance to a coup attempt were one to occur.

First, Bourguiba counterbalanced the military with the national guard, a paramilitary force that he placed in the Ministry of Interior rather than defense. "Bourguiba was clever to put the national guard in the ministry of interior," recalled former National Guard Commander General Habib Ammar. "It allowed him to have the army in one hand, and the national guard in the other."[18] A national guard colonel major observed:

> "It was from the beginning a political issue. At the time of independence, 1956, the national guard was supposed to be put in the MOD, as in most countries, like France, Spain, and Belgium. But during that time there were a number of coups d'état in African countries especially. Bourguiba wanted to prevent a coup and was scared of the military, so he placed the national guard in the MOI to create a balance in force between the MOD and MOI. Two different ministers, two different commanders. It was designed to prevent coups."[19]

The institutional separation of the military and national guard generated friction between them, clashing over jurisdiction and over resources—bureaucratic battles that the national guard tended to win. The national guard was privileged materially, receiving higher salaries than their counterparts in the military, with guard officers often receiving government cars and other perks.[20] As Table 8.1 indicated, the Ministry of Interior's initial budget was nearly triple that of the military's.

Moreover, from the start, the national guard was designed to be closer to politics and political power. About 80 percent of the national guard was initially recruited from those *fellagha* (resistance fighters against the French) who had demonstrated their loyalty to Bourguiba by laying down their weapons in 1954, ahead of Bourguiba's negotiations with France.[21] The choice to incorporate the (Bourguibist) *fellagha* into the national guard rather than military "had the advantage of extracting

<hr>

[18] Interview with retired General Habib Ammar, Tunis, July 13, 2018.
[19] Interview with retired national guard officer, January 2018,
[20] Interview with retired Colonel Major Mahmoud Mezoughi, Tunis, January 9, 2018.
[21] Interview with retired national guard officer, Tunis, February 2018.

the army from a certain historical legitimacy of those who fought against colonial-ism,"[22] and placing that legitimacy instead in the national guard. Its greater usage by Bourguiba likewise brought it closer to the regime: operating primarily in rural areas, "the National Guard had become, in a way, the militia of the ruling Party to get into the depths of the villages."[23]

Bourguiba's favoritism for the national guard was designed to earn its loyalty, ensuring it would defend him against a coup attempt from the military. While the national guard could not necessarily overpower the entire military[24]—it numbered just 5,000 troops under Bourguiba—the specter of armed resistance was expected to deter most coup-plotters, as bloodshed would tarnish the coup plot even if it suc-ceeded.[25] "People who want a coup will [therefore] need both the army and security forces," observed General Ali Seriati, a tough task given their institutional rivalry and "political competition."[26]

In addition to counterbalancing the military with the national guard, Bourguiba also attempted a second coup-proofing tactic: stacking the military with loyalists. At the time, Bourguiba was particularly concerned about supporters of his political rival, Salah Ben Youssef, a fellow Neo-Destour co-founder who criticized Bourguiba for negotiating independence from France and allowing French forces to remain on Tunisian soil, rather than bolstering the *fellagha* in their fight for full independence. More generally, Bourguiba and Ben Youssef were ideological rivals, with Bourguiba championing a more Francophone, secular, modernist agenda, and Ben Youssef rep-resenting a constituency that was more religiously conservative and Arab nationalist. As a result, Bourguiba's supporters tended to come from the Francophone elite families particularly in the more developed, coastal cities, while "Ben Youssef had strong regional support from the south, where the [*fellagha*] resistance was active and where the tribesmen and peasants have felt neglected by the concentration of [. . .] economic development in the coastal and northern regions."[27]

While Bourguiba had incorporated the Bourguibist *fellagha* into the national guard, the problem remained about what to do with the Youssefist *fellagha*, who had refused to disarm. He could not dare leave them as a rival militia, nor incorpo-rate them into the military for fear of an Arab nationalist coup inspired by Egypt's Gamal Abdel Nasser. He accordingly sought France's help to repress the Yousse-fists. In the months after independence, Bourguiba coordinated with French forces

---

[22] Cherif (2017, p. 236).

[23] Cherif (2017, p. 236).

[24] That said, national guard officers interviewed were confident they would be able to stop a coup attempt from the military, as they had actual combat experience, unlike the military that was simply train-ing in the barracks. For what it's worth, even their soldiers were better trained and experienced than the military's, as they were recruited from the top military conscripts following the completion of their year of service (see Ehrenreich (1988, p. 313) and article 4 of the *Statut particulier du Corps de la Garde Nationale*, Official Gazette, October 12, 1956).

[25] The larger numbers of the military do not necessarily mean a military coup would succeed. As Singh (2014) has observed, officers often bandwagon towards whoever appears to be winning during a coup attempt. Even minor resistance could undermine the coup-plotters' projection of dominance and fracture the coup coalition.

[26] Interview with former Head of Presidential Guard Ali Seriati, Tunis, January 22, 2019.

[27] Ashford (1965, p. 217).

to attack the Youssefists in the interior regions of the country. As the Truth & Dignity Commission concluded: "France assisted Bourguiba's wing from the Destour party to liquidate his opponents through bloody repression, intimidation, and 'pacification' operations which culminated during the summer of 1956 and led to the death of more than 1100 people between those killed under the shelling of the mountains of the southwest, the southeast and northwest (735) and extrajudicial liquidations (35), executions (28), and arrests (315)."[28]

In this context, Bourguiba sought to ensure that the military was dominated by his coastal, Francophone supporters at the expense of the remaining Youssefists. Bourguiba carefully vetted the 24 officers transferred from the French army, ultimately removing five of them "who had trained in the Middle East and who might therefore have been expected to sympathize with the militant Pan-Arab policies of Egypt's Nasser."[29] Even among the soldiers and NCOs, Bourguiba only incorporated those who had served in French bases in the coastal areas: Bizerte, Tunis, Sousse, and Sfax.[30]

Likewise, in training the new officer corps, Bourguiba was equally careful to stack it with loyalists. The Bourguiba Promotion, the first 100 officers sent to Saint Cyr, France in 1956 to form the nucleus of the new Tunisian army, were each vetted by the Neo-Destour party "not to belong to the Youssefist clan."[31] Moreover, the mere logistics of the entrance exam—in Tunis and testing French proficiency—selected for Francophone officers from Tunis and well-connected coastal cities. Most of the Bourguiba Promotion—73 percent—thus hailed from the coast, including 31 percent from Tunis, 30 percent from the Sahel, and 12 percent from Sfax and Djerba,[32] despite these areas only accounting for 45 percent of Tunisia's population at the time.[33] Subsequent cohorts as well were recruited primarily from the coast, and trained almost exclusively in Western countries, primarily France, out of fear that training in the Middle East might make them susceptible to Arab nationalism.

Into leadership positions as well, Bourguiba favored officers from the coast, much like he did in his civilian ministerial appointments.[34] The first (and only) commander in chief of the armed forces (1956–1962) was Mohamed El Kefi, a French army-holdover hailing from Sousse.[35] Habib Tabib, from Monastir, oversaw the creation of the land army, while Mohamed Habib Essousi, from Sousse, oversaw the creation of the air force.[36]

---

[28] IVD (2019, p. 138). See also Anderson (1986, p. 233) and Ehrenreich (1988, p. 285).

[29] Ehrenreich (1988, p. 289).

[30] Cherif (2017, p. 138).

[31] Cherif (2017, p. 203).

[32] Cherif (2017, p. 201).

[33] See 1956 census (Poncet, 1959, p. 247).

[34] Buehler and Ayari (2018).

[35] El Kefi in fact was not the most senior-ranking officer at the time. By seniority, the post should have gone to battalion commander Mohsen Sakka, from Monastir. Bourguiba, knowing the Sakka family well, instead chose to send him out of the country as military attaché to Paris (Cherif, 2017, p. 256). El Kefi, meanwhile, had demonstrated his loyalty by helping to funnel French arms to the *fellagha*

[36] The creation of the navy, meanwhile, was entrusted to the (civilian) secretary general of the Defense Ministry, Abdelhamid Chelbi.

As a result of these recruitment and promotion policies, the military, particularly the officer corps, was stacked with Bourguiba's loyalists. The regional bias, specifically, was not lost on observers at the time: "For the most part the officer corps is drawn from the coastal Sahel and its two centers of political and commercial importance, Sousse and Monastir, and the environs of Tunis, which include Bizerte and Cape Bon," observed Ware (1985, p. 38). Ehrenreich (1988, p. 289) concurred:

> The Tunisian officer corps took on a very homogenous character that only began to break down in the 1970s. Senior officers have been generally representative of Tunisia's economically and politically dominant families from the north, the coastal areas, and the major cities. Although military men have been kept from operating major business ventures or holding political office while in uniform, it has been common for family members to be prominent in business or in the Destourian political movement. Generally Western and Francophile in outlook, tied by kinship to the country's upper socioeconomic stratum, and personally familiar with leading figures in the PSD, high-ranking Tunisian officers must be classed as part of the national elite.

In short, to complement the marginalization of the military, Bourguiba pursued two coup-proofing strategies: (1) counterbalancing the military with the national guard, and (2) stacking the officer corps with perceived loyalists. While many officers may have felt that Bourguiba neglected and excluded the military from power and wealth, these two coup-proofing tactics were designed to ensure that any attempt at a coup would be resisted by the national guard and loyalists within the military. These coup-proofing strategies would soon be put to the test in 1962.

The Foiled Coup of 1962

The disastrous Battle of Bizerte of July 1961 did not sit well with some in the military. With 630 Tunisians killed compared to 24 for France, several officers blamed Bourguiba for the loss, arguing he had not invested into the military nor even consulted them ahead of time. Colonel BenKraïem (2012, p. 174) noted that many were "displeased with the way in which Bourguiba decided to wage war against France without first having warned the military command and without asking their technical opinion on the matter." Bourguiba's mobilization of "young destouriens without weapons and without military training" to simultaneously attack French forces "was catastrophic for the conduct of the fighting and [. . .] even prevented the soldiers from fighting" (ibid.). Others were disaffected by "the unwillingness of the ruling elite to accord confidence [. . .] or devote the attention and resources needed to satisfy the Army officer corps."[37] Former defense spokesman, retired Colonel Major Mokhtar Ben Nasr, for

---

[37] [Declassified] Leo G. Cyr, Counselor of U.S. Embassy Tunis, "The Neo-Destour and the Tunisian Army," August 23, 1963. National Archives at College Park, Maryland.

instance, noted that: "The biggest difference between the officers and Bourguiba was the Battle of Bizerte—he sent them in without weapons."[38] Some even questioned Bourguiba's intentions, with Colonel Noureddine Boujellabia (2004) suggesting that Bourguiba attacked the French not to win, but only to remove the reputation that he was the "valet for Western imperialism," sacrificing hundreds of lives to improve his image. The humiliating defeat at Bizerte thus catalyzed the military's existing feelings of marginalization and neglect into resentment toward Bourguiba—and for some, into a coup plot to remove him from power.

"The idea of the [coup] plot began to germinate in the minds of a few as early as September 1961, after the Battle of Bizerte," noted Borsali (2016, p. 183). "It was during this period that the first contacts were made." Among the ringleaders of the plot was Amor Bembli, a Lieutenant with unique experience in a coup d'etat. From Bembla in Monastir, Bembli had left Tunisia at a young age "to enlist in the Syrian troops fighting against the Jews in Palestine. After the ceasefire imposed by the UN, he enlisted in the Syrian national army [. . . where] he took part in Husni al-Zaim's *coup d'état* in 1949" (El Materi, 2014, p. 53). He subsequently joined the Lebanese army, but in 1956 was invited back to Tunisia to help form the new Tunisian army. Although "his enthusiasm for Arab nationalism and his tumultuous past certainly made him a suspect and undesirable man for the Tunisian government" (ibid.), he found his way to become the deputy chief of military police.

Over the course of a year, Bembli recruited the following military officers into the plot:

- **Major Abdel Sadok Ben Nasr Ben Said,** in charge of armored vehicles at Al-Aouina barracks in Tunis. Sadok Ben Said was an officer in the French army before being transferred to the Tunisian military upon independence. His brother, Naceur Ben Said, was minister of town planning and housing under Prime Minister Tahar Ben Ammar, the last Tunisian government before independence (El Materi, 2014).
- **Captain Kebaïer El Maherzi,** aide-de-camp to President Bourguiba (i.e., head of the presidential guard). Originally from La Marsa, he was transferred to the Tunisian army from the Beylical Guard.
- **Captain Salah Hachani,** commander of the Gafsa garrison. Originally from Menzel Bourguiba, Bizerte, he was transferred to the Tunisian army from the Beylical Guard.
- **Captain Moncef El Materi,** in charge of artillery at the Menzel Bourguiba barracks. Originally from Tunis, he was a member of the Bourguiba Promotion sent to St. Cyr in 1956. His uncle, Mahmoud El Materi, was a co-founder and the first president of the Neo-Destour Party.
- **Captain Mohamed Ben Belgacem Guiza,** in charge of heavy anti-tank artillery at the Bouficha barracks. "Hamadi" ben Guiza was a member of the Bourguiba Promotion sent to St. Cyr in 1956. Prior to joining the military, he served as secretary general of the Bab El Khadra cell of the Neo-Destour Party.

---

[38] Interview with retired Colonel Major Mokhtar Ben Nasr, Tunis, August 27, 2015.

- **Captain Mohamed Habib Barkia,** engineer. Barkia was a member of the Bourguiba Promotion sent to St. Cyr in 1956.

As these brief biographies indicate, the military officers involved in the 1962 coup plot were part of the coastal elite, with many having close relatives in politics. They therefore could be expected to sympathize with Bourguiba. Indeed, Captain Moncef El Materi (2014, p. 56), one of two who were pardoned and therefore could live to tell the tale, recounts that: "Often, I supported the regime. [. . .] I had a lot of consideration for President Bourguiba, who for me embodied power." Likewise, Captain "Hamadi Ben Guiza tells me that in his youth he had always lived in a nationalist environment where Habib Bourguiba was worshiped as a mythical god" (El Materi, 2014, p. 73).

Why then did they turn on Bourguiba, and begin to plot a coup? According to El Materi (2014, p. 46), they were inspired by the Arab nationalism of Gamal Abdel Nasser:

> As with all the young people of this turbulent period, the ideals inculcated in us were rather leftist with a fairly pronounced tinge of Arab nationalism [. . .] Gamal Abdel Nasser actively supported the national liberation movements and he became the idol of a whole youth who fought the foreign occupation. [. . .] We young free officers, living these events without effective participation, were very influenced.

El Materi in particular highlights three episodes that fueled discontent with Bourguiba: (1) The Battle of Bizerte, (2) The repression of the Youssefists, and (3) The lavish lifestyle of Bourguiba and his coterie. "The reality was obvious: Bourguiba was a dictator. He had just had Salah Ben Youssef executed" (p. 73). "Bourguiba, his ministers and leaders took a taste for sumptuousness and indecent luxury: official cars, villas, receptions and parties formed a stark contrast to the sacrifices [they] demanded of the people" (p. 38)—and, we might add, they demanded of the military.

As these grievances festered in the military, so too did they among the population. After the July 1961 Battle of Bizerte and August 1961 assassination of Salah Ben Youssef, at least two groups of civilians had also begun discussions of toppling Bourguiba—one based in Gafsa, and the other in Bizerte. The three groups—the Gafsa group, the Bizerte group, and the military officers—found each other through the networks of Hedi Gafsi[39] and Lt. Amor Bembli. They came to the conclusion that if they were to succeed, they must all work together. As Captain El Materi (2014, p. 70) explained:

> Without our help, the civilians could not do anything. The operation itself could degenerate into a civil war which would quickly be quelled and lead to their inexorable downfall. They were aware of this situation. On the other hand, a coup fomented only by the military would not succeed either. The civil and political

---

[39] Gafsi, whose family origins are from Gafsa, was born and raised in Menzel Bourguiba, Bizerte, and lived in Tunis, connecting him to all three groups.

element was very important for the change to go smoothly, especially since we
did not have a seasoned politician among us.

But coordination was no easy task. They could agree on the broad contours of the
plan: Captain Salah Hachani, commander of the Gafsa garrison, would provide
weapons to re-arm the *fellagha* fighters. The coup-plotters would then secure strategic
locations in Tunis, such as "telecommunications, radio, the Ministry of the Interior,
the National Guard, the headquarters of the Syndicate, the headquarters of the Party,
etc." (El Materi, 2014, p. 81). Captain Kebaïer El Maherzi, of Bourguiba's presidential
guard, would lead the seizing of the presidency.[40] The civilian and military plotters
also appeared to agree on what would happen after the coup: they would set up a transitional government led by civilians—including Mongi Slim, Mahmoud El Materi,
and Mohammed Masmoudi, among others[41]—who would shepherd the country to
democracy.

Among the major sticking points, however, was what would happen to Bourguiba. Many of the civilians, including Lazhar Chraiti, Abdelaziz Akremi, and
Mohamed Salah Baratli, wanted Bourguiba executed. "Cut off the head to dry out
the veins," Chraiti is quoted as saying.[42] But the more elite, coastal officers were
more sympathetic to Bourguiba, with all of them, according to El Materi (2014,
p. 80), opposing the killing of Bourguiba or the shedding of any blood whatsoever.
El Materi (2014, p. 56) at one point even suggested that the grievances they had with
the regime were not the fault of Bourguiba but of "his entourage" and that "it was
enough for Bourguiba to eliminate them to remedy the situation."

The thorny issue of Bourguiba's assassination, among others,[43] ultimately delayed
the plot and led to its failure. On December 18, 1962, the military officers refused to
attend the meeting of the civilians in Ezzahra (a suburb of Tunis), holding instead
their own separate meeting at the Bouchoucha barracks. At that meeting, Lt. Bembli
informed the officers that the civilians wanted to initiate the coup on December 20,
but the officers refused, and instructed Bembli to tell the civilians they would not

---

[40] According to the civilian plotter Temim Hamadi Tounsi, the Bizerte group had also "thought of proceeding to the neutralization of the Head of State in the farm of Aïn Ghelel where Bourguiba, in search
of a few moments of relaxation, sometimes spent his weekend" (quoted in Borsali (2016, p. 183)). Others believe El Meherzi was to share the night password to the presidential palace to allow Mohamed Salah
Baratli to kill Bourguiba. See IVD (2019, p. 295). At the time, the US Embassy likewise noted that the coup-
plotters had recruited a "member [of Bourguiba's] household who intended to afford the assassins access
to Bourguiba's private quarters." See: [Declassified] Francis Henry Russell, U.S. Ambassador in Tunisia,
December 26, 1962, National Archives at College Park, Maryland.

[41] Other names mentioned by El Materi (2014, p. 82) were Béchir Ben Yahmed, Tahar Amira, and Fathi
Zlitni, while other names mentioned by Tounsi were Taïeb Mhiri and Fadhel Ben Achour (Borsali, 2016,
p. 183).

[42] See Tounsi's account in Borsali (2016, p. 184).

[43] The civilians and military also disagreed on the level of foreign involvement in the coup. The civilians,
through Mohamed Gara, secretary general of the Bizerte municipality, had made plans to involve a student opposition group in France, while Cheikh Ahmed Rahmouni had connected with the Algerian Aissa
Soltani to try to secure the support of Ahmed Ben Bella and Houari Boumédiène. The military officers,
however were less sanguine about foreign involvement (El Materi, 2014, pp. 79, 80, 83). Even prior to this,
Lazhar Chraiti allegedly approached "the Egyptian ambassador in Tunisia [. . .] to examine the possibility of having weapons from the Egyptian regime. The Ambassador rejected the request" (El Materi, 2014,
p. 68).

meet until "a new agreement with the group of civilians" was reached, one in which "the practical aspect of the coup d'etat" was left to the exclusive "responsibility of the military" (El Materi, 2014, p. 80). That "disagreement between the soldiers and the civilians during the last meeting of December 18 [. . .] ended in failure [. . .] and left the project in abeyance."[44]

That delay, however, proved fatal. The next day, December 19, a non-commissioned officer, Amor Toukabri, reported the plot to his superiors.[45] Consistent with a counterbalancing approach, Bourguiba upon discovery of the plot tasked the Ministry of Interior with stopping the coup and arresting the conspirators, involving "massive National Guard formations [that] surrounded Bizerte [. . . and] placed heavy machine guns on principal access streets."[46] Between 200 and 400 people were arrested before Bourguiba found the 25 coup-plotters.[47] After a summary military trial from January 12 to 17, 1963, 13 of the defendants—including all seven of the military officers—were sentenced to death. Bourguiba's wife, Wassila, intervened on behalf of two officers, El Materi and Ben Guiza, allegedly due to their familial connections to the Neo-Destour, and managed to have their sentences commuted to life in prison.[48] The rest, however, were executed on January 24 by the national guard at Bir Bouragba.[49]

The Aftermath of the 1962 Coup

The 1962 coup plot failed largely due to Bourguiba's two coup-proofing tactics. On the one hand, the plotters were only able to recruit one officer from the national guard (Hassan Marzouk,[50] sentenced to two years in prison), permitting Bourguiba to use this more loyal apparatus to defeat the coup and arrest the plotters. Second, Bourguiba had almost perfectly stacked the military with his loyalists. The plotters only managed to recruit seven military officers, and even they were more sympathetic to Bourguiba than the civilians, which ultimately led the plot to fail. Colonel BenKraïem (2012, p. 176) likewise attributes the failure of the plot to the military officers, particularly those from the carefully vetted Bourguiba Promotion, for slowing down the coup plot enough for it to be discovered:

These [officers], although active members of the conspiracy, wanted to change the regime according to defined, sensible and civilized rules. On the other hand, they noted the in-existence of a sense of responsibility among the leaders of the civilian group. The latter with an indescribable feeling of hatred sought the bloodbath.

[44] Borsali (2016, p. 184).

[45] Borsali (2016, p. 177).

[46] [Declassified] Francis Henry Russell, U.S. Ambassador in Tunisia, January 7, 1963, National Archives at College Park, College Park, MD.

[47] Borsali (2016, p. 176). A 26th, the ex-*fellaga* fighter Mostari Ben Said Ben Boubaker, managed to flee to Algeria after being provided an Algerian passport, which appears to be the extent of Algerian involvement in the plot (Safi, 2020, p. 171).

[48] El Materi was subsequently pardoned and released in 1973.

[49] Abid (2019).

[50] Marzouk directed the tire training school at Bir Bouragba. See IVD (2019, p. 295).

> They wanted to kill, murder and sow terror in the country. Our comrades of pro-
> motion have, thanks to their civic sense, to their love for the fatherland at their
> political and intellectual level, dissociated themselves from the civil group and
> made the plot fail by interrupting, at least temporarily, all contact with it.

The failure of the coup plot therefore convinced Bourguiba to double-down on his strategy of marginalizing and counterbalancing the military. He reduced the size of the military from 20,000 in 1960 to 17,000 in 1965[51] to achieve "rough parity with other security forces."[52] Bourguiba also created the directorate of military security, a new branch in the military designed to monitor personnel to snuff out future coup plots. The first director of military security was Zine El Abidine Ben Ali, a member of the Bourguiba Promotion who hailed from Hammam-Sousse and who was the son-in-law of Commander in Chief Mohamed El Kefi. Ironically, the 1962 coup-plotters had considered recruiting Ben Ali into their plot, before concluding that he "was a die-hard fan of the regime and venerated Bourguiba."[53]

Bourguiba also sought to fragment the military to make a coup more difficult. From 1956 to 1962, the military had one active-duty officer—El Kefi—to coordinate the army, navy, and air force. In 1962, however, El Kefi became the first inspector general of the armed forces, and his former position was left vacant. Instead, the military developed three separate chiefs of staff for the army, navy, and air force, with no superior officer to coordinate between them.[54] Without an armed forces chief of staff, the military might be less effective, but it might also be less able to coordinate a coup. Moreover, while the military was fragmented, the internal security forces were centralized. In 1967, the Ministry of Interior saw the creation of a directorate general of national security to help coordinate the national guard, police, and newly formed Public Order Brigade.[55]

Having strengthened the system of counterbalancing, Bourguiba felt comfortable neglecting the military further. The military continued to receive no more than 5 percent of the budget, permitting little modernization of its outdated weapons. As Tunisia faced growing external threats from Algeria in the 1960s and Libya in the 1970s, the US embassy in 1974 assessed that Tunisia's equipment was "almost entirely obsolete. Most of it is World War II or Korean War vintage and as such compares

---

[51] Banks and Wilson (2017).

[52] [Declassified] Francis Henry Russell, U.S. Ambassador in Tunisia, January 15, 1963, National Archives at College Park, College Park, MD.

[53] El Materi (2014, p. 74). Other officers that they considered reaching out to were "Captain Hamadi Chebbi, along with Smail Bey and Bouattour" (El Materi, 2014, p. 72).

[54] The one exception was General Abdelhamid Escheikh in 1979–1981. Yet, this was a purely ceremonial position with no operational command, and was in fact designed to sideline him. In 1979, then army chief Escheikh had been asked by Minister of Defense Abdullah Farhat to help organize the Neo-Destour Party congress. Furious at this political involvement, Bourguiba refused to attend the party congress (Ehrenreich, 1988, p. 290), and demoted Escheikh through a promotion to this honorific position. He was subsequently pushed out of the country as Ambassador to Sudan (1981–1986) and then West Africa (86–87). Interview with Boubaker BenKraiem, Tunis, 2015.

[55] With trusted civilians as director general of national security (Fouad Mebazaa and then Tahar Belkhodja), Bourguiba felt comfortable briefly appointing military officers as commander of the national guard: Salem Sabbagh (1967–1969) and then Boubaker El Bekri (1969–1972). These would be the only two military officers appointed to the national guard until Habib Ammar in 1984.

unfavorably with sophisticated weapons being acquired by Tunisia's neighbors."[56] The same cable subsequently notes "recent reports that a number of Tunisian officers are complaining [. . .] they are unhappy with equipment obsolescence [. . . and] yearn for the shiny, new weaponry recently introduced into the inventory of the Libyan army."[57] The CIA likewise assessed in 1969 that Tunisian officers "complain that they get second-class treatment from the government,"[58] later noting that "there has been substantial disgruntlement over inadequate salaries and lack of promotion opportunities."[59]

Indeed, the military was increasingly facing a backlog in promotions. As retired Colonel-Major Mezoughi observed: "The highest rank in the army was [effectively] colonel (*'aqid*), as Bourguiba absolutely refused to let anyone become a general until the very end. He felt that if he let them become a general, they will gain the ambition to leave the army [and take power]."[60]

Bourguiba likewise continued to keep the military far from politics and political power. Officers "receive little publicity, and exert virtually no influence on government policy."[61] The defense minister was always a civilian, and few military officers were appointed as governors or ambassadors. The two exceptions in this period—Zine El Abidine Ben Ali, appointed ambassador to Poland in 1980–1984, and Abdelhamid Escheikh, appointed ambassador to Sudan 1981–1986—in fact prove the rule, as both received these positions not as a reward, but as a means of pushing them out of the country as Bourguiba grew wary of their intentions.[62]

The military felt marginalized, not just in terms of resources and power, but increasingly in terms of its social status and public image. While the national guard took the lead in securing the nation's borders and responding to most security threats, the military was instead confined to the barracks—"imprisoned" in the barracks as one officer put it.[63] "We worked exclusively in the barracks," noted Mezoughi. "We had no relations with society at all. The only time the army left the barracks was for fires or natural disasters. In public life, the army was absent."[64] There were few military parades, and no glorification of the army. "The military's role was marginalized," agreed Mokhtar Ben Nasr, former Defense Ministry spokesman. "In the time of Bourguiba and Ben Ali, the Tunisian people never knew their army. The military

---

[56] [Declassified] Telegram 7659 From the Embassy in Tunisia to the Department of State, Tunis, December 13, 1974, 1220Z, FOREIGN RELATIONS OF THE UNITED STATES, 1969–1976, VOLUME E–9, PART 1, DOCUMENTS ON NORTH AFRICA, 1973–1976.

[57] Ibid.

[58] [Declassified] C.I.A. Directorate of Intelligence, "Tunisia's Problems," Weekly Summary: Special Report, November 7, 1969.

[59] [Declassified] C.I.A. National Foreign Assessment Center, "Tunisia: Cautious Liberalization," Intelligence Assessment, February 1981.

[60] Interview with Mahmoud Mezoughi, Tunis, October 9, 2015.

[61] [Declassified] C.I.A. Directorate of Intelligence, "Tunisia's Problems," Weekly Summary: Special Report, November 7, 1969.

[62] Interview with retired Colonel Boubaker BenKraiem, Tunis, October 2015.

[63] Interview with retired Colonel Major Hedi Kolsi, Sfax, September 21, 2015. That greater involvement in countering security threats also meant that the national guard was eligible for danger pay and other supplementary funds, exacerbating the pay differential.

[64] Interview with retired Colonel Major Mahmoud Mezoughi, Tunis, October 9, 2015.

didn't have its real worth appreciated by the people."[65] Not only was the military not a path to wealth or power, it was not even a path to social status or esteem.

From Stacking to Discrimination

Over time, this multidimensional marginalization of the military made it more difficult to sustain Bourguiba's second coup-proofing strategy: stacking the military with loyalists. While at first, the vast majority of officers came from coastal, elite families, this proportion dwindled over time. As Tunisians began to realize that the military was not a path to power, wealth, or social status, it was no longer attractive to the elite families in the coast. "The Tunisian people—especially educated citizens from the prosperous northern and coastal areas—have normally held those who volunteered for a military career in low esteem," noted Ehrenreich (1988, p. 294). "In addition to the relatively low status of the job, engineers and technically trained Tunisians found the pay and benefits of the military to be less than what they could expect to attain in civilian life." Accordingly, Ehrenreich (1988, p. 289) observed in the 1970s and 1980s:

> a growing number of younger officers from the less privileged segments of the society. Many of these young officers, along with enlisted men who have long been characterized as coming from the margins of society, have not been insulated from the political debate and social turmoil that has gripped Tunisian society since the 1970s. It is thought by observers of Tunisian affairs that many of the younger officers and enlisted men are more sympathetic than their leaders to the government's critics, including Islamists, leftists, and those opposed to the concentration of political power in the top echelons of the PSD [Socialist Destourian Party].

In other words, the marginalization of the military meant that the regime could no longer recruit the officer corps primarily from the coastal elite, and instead had to fill its ranks increasingly with officers from more impoverished regions, who might not be as loyal to Bourguiba. To measure this regional shift more systematically, I collected biographical data on officers who entered the military between 1956 and 1977.[66] Their biographies were available in a June 2009 Ministry of Defense publication, "Registry of Retired Officers: Commanders and Senior Officers." While the registry only includes senior officers (from the rank of major and up),[67] the data confirm a major shift in their regional backgrounds over time. Figure 8.1 plots the percent of new officers that hail from the coast by entrance year. While roughly 70 percent of officers who entered in the 1950s came from the coast, that proportion fell to 45 percent by the late 1970s.

---

[65] Interview with retired Colonel Major Mokhtar Ben Nasr, Tunis, August 27, 2015.

[66] I stop at 1977 as most officers who joined after that were still in service in 2009, and hence not included in the MOD publication.

[67] The data thus likely underrepresent the true percentage of officers from interior regions, as many of them did not even make it to the rank of major given Bourguiba's favoritism for coastal officers in promotions (see later in chapter).

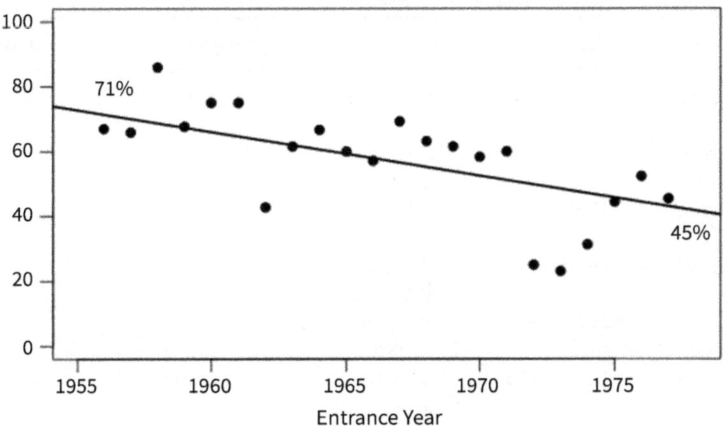

Figure 8.1 Regional Background of Entering Officers, 1956–1977

This regional shift was even more stark among the lower ranks—non-commissioned officers (NCOs) and soldiers—who very quickly shifted to coming predominantly from impoverished areas, particularly the interior regions, due to the military's low pay and prestige.[68] Ware (1985) observed that "the composition of the rank and file [. . .] by virtue of national conscription, tends to reflect the more depressed areas of the country, as it is young men without other means of livelihood or ways to perform alternative service who are caught up in the draft" (pp. 38–39). Ehrenreich (1988, p. 295) likewise notes: "Exemptions allowed to potential draftees were extremely liberal, and consequently a preponderance of illiterate young men were inducted for training and service."

In other words, Bourguiba's marginalization of the military made it less attractive to the elite coastal families that supported the regime. He could no longer recruit the majority of the military from these areas. However, he could still promote the loyal officers coming from the coast to the leadership positions. As Ehrenreich (1988, p. 289) observed: "His exclusive power to promote military officers has been among the strongest components of Bourguiba's control over the armed forces."

Indeed, Bourguiba continued the strategy of favoring officers from coastal regions in promotions to the top ranks. Table 8.2 lists each officer who assumed one of the military's top positions under Bourguiba: the chiefs of staff of the armed forces, army, navy, and air force, the director general of military security, and the inspector general of the armed forces.[69] About 92 percent (22 of 24) of these military leaders under Bourguiba came from the coast. Despite the officer corps becoming increasingly diverse, the top positions continued to be monopolized by coastal officers.

[68] Interview with former director of military security, Tunis, November 2015.
[69] Data on hometowns were found in the Ministry of Defense publication, "Registry of Retired Officers," 2009. Years determined through interviews with retired General Said El Kateb, Colonel Boubaker BenKraiem, and Colonel Major Mahmoud Mezoughi, among others.

Table 8.2 Military Leadership under Bourguiba, 1956–1987

Position	Years	Name	Origins	Coast
Commander in Chief	1956–1962	Mohamed El Kefi	Sousse	✓
Armed Forces Chief of Staff	1979–1981	Abdelhamid Escheikh	Tunis	✓
Army Chief of Staff	1962–1967	Habib Tabib	Monastir	✓
Army Chief of Staff	1967–1975	Mohamed Habib Essousi	Sousse	✓
Army Chief of Staff	1975–1979	Abdelhamid Escheikh	Tunis	✓
Army Chief of Staff	1979–1983	Mohamed Gzara	Monastir	✓
Army Chief of Staff	1983–1987	Youssef Barakat	Beja	
Navy Chief of Staff	1970–1978	Bechir Jedidi	Tunis	✓
Navy Chief of Staff	1978–1987	Habib Fedila	Mahdia	✓
Air Force Chief of Staff	1959–1967	Mohamed Habib Essousi	Sousse	✓
Air Force Chief of Staff	1967–1975	Azzeddine Talbi	Tunis	✓
Air Force Chief of Staff	1975–1985	Touhami Machta	Tunis	✓
Air Force Chief of Staff	1985–1986	Abdelhamid Fehri	Kairouan	
Air Force Chief of Staff	1986–1987	Ahmed Na'man Bouzgarrou	Tunis	✓
Dir. Gen. Mil. Security	1964–1974	Zine El Abidine Ben Ali	Sousse	✓
Dir. Gen. Mil. Security	1974–1984	Boubaker Balma	Tunis	✓
Dir. Gen. Mil. Security	1984–1986	Ammar Kheriji	Tunis	✓
Dir. Gen. Mil. Security	1986–1987	Youssef Ben Slimane	Djerba, Medenine	✓
Inspector General	1962–1964	Mohamed El Kefi	Sousse	✓
Inspector General	1967–1971	Habib Tabib	Monastir	✓
Inspector General	1974–1975	Mohamed Habib Essousi	Sousse	✓
Inspector General	1975–1984	Mohamed Salah Moqaddam	Tunis	✓
Inspector General	1984–1987	Mohamed Said El Kateb	Djerba, Medenine	✓
Total				22/24 (92%)

Bourguiba's favoritism of the coast thus had the effect of vertically fragmenting the military, with the top ranks coming primarily from elite families in the coast, but the lower ranks—junior officers, NCOs, and soldiers—increasingly hailing from impoverished interior regions. That imbalance fed into perceptions that coastal officers were receiving preferential treatment in promotions, while officers from the interior were discriminated—perceptions that fostered resentment toward Bourguiba and could be conducive to a coup. Yet, with loyalists continuing to staff the top brass, Bourguiba hoped that the senior officers would detect and terminate any coup plots emanating from below. In short, the original coup-proofing strategy of stacking the military with loyal coastal officers shifted over time to privileging them in promotions, a more sustainable tactic given the military's marginalization.

The Origins of Professionalism

The marginalization of the military not only shaped its regional composition, but also contributed to its depoliticization. At first, some of the initial officers came from notable, political families, as evidenced by the number of 1962 coup plotters who had familial links to the Neo-Destour Party.[70] Some may have even joined thinking the military would become a vehicle to political office, like in Egypt where hundreds of military officers serve as governors, ministers, and ambassadors. But in Tunisia, as these families started to realize the military was not a route to political power, they stopped joining.

"In my career, my colleagues and I have never met anybody who came to the army because he wants a political career," noted Mezoughi, who joined in 1967. "Maybe in Egypt or Algeria, but not in Tunisia. You would go somewhere else. You would do law or business administration. All the ministers come from the ENA [*École nationale d'administration*]. If you want to make politics, you don't go to the army, you go to the ENA!"[71]

Other officers agreed that the separation of the military from politics in turn shaped who chose to join. "The army has never been a path to political power."[72] "We went to the army to become officers, not to become ambassadors."[73] "Whoever puts on the uniform and enters the Tunisian National Army believes that his one and only job is to protect the nation and that he mustn't be involved in politics."[74]

The marginalization of the military thus contributed to fewer politicized, power-seeking individuals joining the military, and instead attracted more apolitical professionals. Their subsequent experience in the military then reinforced that apolitical ethos. The new directorate of military security, created in 1964, actively monitored

[70] Moncef El Materi, for instance, was the nephew of Neo-Destour's co-founder Mahmoud El Materi. His son, Sakher El Materi, later married President Ben Ali's daughter, Nesrine, and became one of the country's wealthiest businessmen.

[71] Interview with retired Colonel-Major Mahmoud Mezoughi, Tunis, March 4, 2020.

[72] Interview with retired officer, Tunis, March 2020.

[73] Interview with retired Colonel Boubaker BenKraiem, Tunis, 2015.

[74] Interview with retired Brigadier-General Jamal Boujah, Tunis, 2018.

officers for political statements or behaviors, setting the bounds of appropriate behavior. When Defense Minister Abdullah Farhat in 1979 involved military officers in organizing the logistics for the PSD party congress, he was fired, confirming the line between the military and politics. Bourguiba's oft-cited remark that Tunisia's "military is in the barracks," not in politics, both reflected the reality and contributed to norms about what the proper role of the military should be.[75]

Moreover, with very few of their superiors becoming ministers or turning political, junior officers came to see being apolitical as not just normal, but professional and even *desirable*. Officers internalized politics as something to actively avoid, something that might undermine the military's effectiveness. Mezoughi, for instance, insisted that keeping the military and politics separate "helps the military to become operational and not to have other thoughts rather than defending the country."[76] With the military kept separate from politics, officers over time were socialized into accepting that that was how things should be.[77] The marginalization of the military thus contributed to the development of a professional, apolitical mindset, what Tunisian officers often refer to as a "republican" ethos.[78]

In short, Bourguiba's strategy of keeping the military far from politics had a self-reinforcing element, recruiting and socializing officers into an apolitical mindset. Over time, Tunisia thus developed a third element—military professionalism—that helped to avoid a coup, complementing the counterbalancing and favoritism of coastal officers.

From Bourguiba to Ben Ali

For 20 years, these three factors helped Bourguiba avoid another military coup. But in the 1980s, internal and external threats escalated in a way that upset this balance and ultimately terminated Bourguiba's rule.

Relations with Libya's Muammar al-Qaddafi, who came to power in a coup in 1969, deteriorated considerably after Tunisia pulled out of a proposed merger of the two countries in 1974 (the Djerba Declaration). Qaddafi reportedly sought to overthrow Bourguiba, and acted on this intention in 1980. On January 27, 1980, some 30 to 60 Tunisian leftist[79] guerrillas trained and armed by Libya stormed the interior town of Gafsa, simultaneously attacking the army, national guard, and police outposts.[80] "As

---

[75] Interview with retired officer, Nabeul, June 2022.

[76] Interview with retired Colonel-Major Mahmoud Mezoughi, Tunis, March 4, 2020.

[77] Although she disagrees that the ethos was apolitical, Brooks (2013) also claims that the military's "de facto relegation to the periphery of the regime helped sustain a corporate ethos in which officers appeared to identify with the institution itself" (p. 208).

[78] Several military officers also highlighted that their training in Western democracies helped instill this apolitical, professional ethos. However, the two officers who later conducted a coup, Ben Ali and Habib Ammar, also received Western training, and I do not find evidence of Western training having a depoliticizing effect in either survey.

[79] The guerrillas called themselves the Progressive Nationalist Front, and the Gafsa incident was commemorated by the Popular Front coalition in 2014.

[80] See BenKraiem (2015).

they scrambled to respond, the Tunisian armed forces suffered from serious shortfalls in mobility and logistics and were forced to rely on the rapid injection of Moroccan and French support."[81] It took Tunisian forces two days "and several dozen casualties before they overwhelmed the guerrillas,"[82] exposing a major weakness were Libya's Qaddafi to attack more forcefully.

The Gafsa incident "shocked Bourguiba out of his complacency"[83] and led him to briefly invest into the military. Within days he secured 30 armored personal carriers and six transport helicopters from the US,[84] and considerably increased the military's budget. But for military officers who had felt starved by Bourguiba for decades, this increase was viewed as too little, too late:

> Since the late 1970s the army in particular has begun to consider itself disadvantaged vis-à-vis the civilian bureaucracy. This perception touches deeply the military sense of self-esteem. Called on to defend the nation against Qadhdhafism, the military has not received sufficient materiel from its point of view to carry out its mandate successfully and considers that what is now being absorbed comes too late and too little.[85]

Those sentiments were then compounded by Israel's airstrike against the Palestinian Liberation Organization (PLO) office in Hammam-Lif in October 1985, which killed 45 Palestinians as well as 22 Tunisian bystanders. Notably, the Tunisian military had not been able to even detect the Israeli F-15s coming, let alone stop the incursion. "Not more than one F-5 was able to scramble, and this did not occur until the Israeli aircraft had left the area."[86] "The undetected Israeli airstrike [. . .] humiliated the officer corps and did their image no good with the public."[87]

At the same time, growing internal threats were fueling further grievances among the military. The Tunisian General Labor Union (UGTT)'s general strike of January 1978 and the bread riots of January 1984 were the first major domestic challenges to Bourguiba's rule. In both cases, thousands of Tunisians took to the streets, clashing with police officers and burning down public and private establishments. In both cases, the army was called in to supplement the police and national guard, and in both cases they complied, helping to repress the protesters. "Untrained in crowd control, the troops on both occasions used what observers considered to be an excessive force to put down demonstrators."[88] According to the government's accounts, 42 protesters were killed in 1978 and 89 in 1984.

---

[81] Wehrey (2020, p. 1).

[82] Wright (1982, p. 120).

[83] Ware (1988, p. 594).

[84] "Memorandum From Secretary of State Vance to President Carter," Washington, February 2, 1980. In: Foreign Relations of the United States, 1977–1980, Volume XVII, Part 3, North Africa, pp. 497–498.

[85] Ware (1985, p. 39).

[86] Ehrenreich (1988, p. 300).

[87] [Declassified] C.I.A. Directorate of Intelligence, "Tunisia: Politicization of the Military," January 31, 1986.

[88] Ehrenreich (1988, p. 298).

This repression was not necessarily intended to defend Bourguiba, whom many officers felt had neglected and counterbalanced the military. Instead, the repression stemmed from a professional duty to defend state institutions and uphold law and order. "They were looting, they were destroying, lighting things on fire!" exclaimed retired Colonel-Major Mohamed Ahmed. "Many soldiers did not want to shoot, but the situation obliged them to do so."[89] As retired Colonel Major Mokhtar Ben Nasr insisted: "We must stabilize the situation, even if it involves firing shots. We had to protect the institutions."[90] As another retired Colonel Major put it, "we do not pick sides—we defend institutions."[91] The decision to repress in these two instances was not a political decision to defend Bourguiba, but rather stemmed from the army's professionalism.

Yet Bourguiba's use of the military for internal security frustrated the officers. As Ware (1985) observed at the time: "The military has resented having to assume a police function which belongs to other organs of security under civilian control. [. . .] The military does not believe it is receiving either added benefits or recognition for the new burden the civilians have laid on its shoulders" (p. 39). A couple of officers *were* elevated to new, high-profile positions: after the 1984 bread riots, Colonel Zine El Abidine Ben Ali was brought back from his ambassadorship in Poland to serve as director general of national security, minister of interior, and then prime minister, and Colonel Habib Ammar was appointed as the commander of the national guard. But for most officers, their situation barely improved. Even the loyalist senior officers began to doubt whether their subordinates would follow through if asked to fire again: "Senior officers were concerned that soldiers might hesitate to act during similar crises in the future. Presumably they were also concerned about [. . .] the changing character of the conscripts and junior officers, whose views tend to reflect those of the population, not the establishment."[92]

Some in the CIA assessed that "such sentiments increasingly are creating a climate conducive to coup plotting by junior and midlevel officers."[93] In 1983, 19 air force cadets were found guilty of plotting to overthrow the regime alongside the Islamist group Hizb al-Tahrir.[94] In December 1985, "about a dozen or so officers and non-commissioned personnel" were involved in an aborted coup attempt apparently foiled by Ahmed Na'man Bouzgarrou, a senior air force officer from Monastir and related by marriage to Bourguiba, who was then quickly promoted to air force chief of staff.[95] The favoritism in promotions that was producing a top brass from the elite coastal areas was successfully coup-proofing the military by creating resistance from above.

---

[89] Interview with retired Colonel Major Mohamed Ahmed, Tunis, October 17, 2015.

[90] Interview with retired Colonel Major Mokhtar Ben Nasr, Tunis, August 27, 2015.

[91] Interview with retired officer, Tunis, October 2015.

[92] [Declassified] C.I.A. Directorate of Intelligence, "Tunisia: Politicization of the Military," January 31, 1986.

[93] [Declassified C.I.A. Memo] Director of Central Intelligence, C.I.A., "Prospects for Tunisia," National Intelligence Estimate, December 1984.

[94] Ehrenreich (1988, p. 290).

[95] [Declassified] C.I.A. Directorate of Intelligence, "Tunisia: Politicization of the Military," January 31, 1986.

But those senior officers, while sharing Bourguiba's secular, coastal orientation, also began to view Bourguiba as a liability. As early as 1971, Bourguiba had been diagnosed with "involutional depression and 'mild but definite arterial brain damage.'"[96] By October 1987, the 84-year-old Bourguiba's dementia had reached an advanced stage, to the point of forgetting about ministerial appointments he had made the previous day.[97] According to military colonel-turned-national guard commander Habib Ammar (2011, p. 93), "the idea of 'change' [removing Bourguiba] began to germinate in our minds" on October 26, 1987, when he and Prime Minister Ben Ali were discussing "the deterioration of the old leader's health status and his inability to lead the country lucidly."

In particular, Bourguiba in this mental state was hell-bent on executing the leader of the Islamic Tendency Movement (MTI), Rached Ghannouchi. After a court sentenced Ghannouchi to life in prison on September 27, Bourguiba ordered a retrial demanding his execution, and as the weeks passed was on the verge of firing Ben Ali for not bringing him Ghannouchi's head. But Ben Ali and almost all of Bourguiba's advisors knew that would be a step too far. "Concern was reigning in all circles," noted Ammar (2011, p. 90), that executing Ghannouchi would spark retribution, leading to "anarchy, or even the beginning of a civil war." They decided that to preserve Bourguiba's regime, Bourguiba had to go.

Ben Ali and Ammar's coup-plotting then took on an added element of urgency on November 5, 1987, when they gained wind of a simultaneous plot against Bourguiba led by the Islamists and scheduled for November 8.[98] But this "November 8 group" had been detected, in large part due to Bourguiba's coup-proofing strategies. "Bourguiba was very strategic," explained one of the Islamist coup leaders, former air force sergeant Said Ferjani. "Wherever you had a military base, next to it is a national guard or police office."[99] This counterbalancing had forced the Islamists to recruit from every security apparatus, not just the marginalized military. Moreover, with the top brass largely secular, the plotters had to instead recruit a broad swath of low-ranking personnel. Moncef Ben Salem (2013, p. 45), another Islamist coup leader, noted that among "the most important deficiencies in the plot [was] the absence of senior officers [. . .] which made us build our plan horizontally, i.e., relying on the base, which increases the chance of exposure."

Indeed, the Islamist coup leaders were forced to assemble a massive coup coalition of 219 individuals, including 66 in the military and 62 in the Ministry of Interior.[100] That large number increased the risk of human error and ultimately led their plot to be discovered on November 5, when a low-ranking police officer in the MOI's Public

---

[96] [James] Relph, US Embassy Tunis, to Secretary of State, "Subject: Illness of President Bourguiba," January 3, 1971, telegram no. 0200Z, Foreign Relations of the United States, 1969–1976, vol. E-5, part 2, Documents on North Africa, 1969–72 (published digitally, 2007).

[97] Paul Delaney, "Senile Bourguiba Described in Tunis," *New York Times*, November 8, 1987.

[98] Interview with one of the three leaders of the group, Said Ferjani, Tunis, February 2, 2018, and four military officers in the group, Tunis, November 2, 24, and 25, 2015, and January 27, 2017. For more on the Islamist plot, see Grewal (2020*b*).

[99] Interview with Said Ferjani, Tunis, February 2, 2018.

[100] Grewal (2020*b*, p. 58).

Order Brigade left his wife a will, raising suspicions from his father-in-law, a master sergeant in the police.[101] He had the son-in-law arrested and tortured, revealing the 2–3 other coup-plotters he knew. Tipped off that something was afoot, Ben Ali and Ammar moved up their coup to preempt the Islamist plot. "We were subject to a real race against the clock."[102]

On November 7, 17 hours before the scheduled Islamist coup, Ben Ali sent Ammar to surround the presidential palace with 80 national guard commandos. Doctors assembled by Ben Ali then declared Bourguiba medically unfit to govern, invoking article 57 of the constitution and transferring power to Ben Ali. Now-President Ben Ali then arrested the members of the Islamist plot, torturing and killing Major Mohamed Mansouri—the highest ranked military officer involved—on December 1.

Coup-Proofing under Ben Ali

The ascendance of Ben Ali—a former military officer—to the presidency raised expectations among members of the officer corps that their time had finally come. Within weeks of taking office, Ben Ali promoted four officers to the rank of general[103] and created a new rank of colonel major to ease the backlog of colonels seeking promotions.[104] He elevated General Youssef Baraket to chief of staff of the (joint) armed forces, the powerful, centralized position that Bourguiba had denied the military for most of his tenure. Ben Ali then created a National Security Council (NSC) that included two military officers as permanent members,[105] giving the military for the first time regular input into security policy.

Over the next three years, Ben Ali also appointed a number of military officers to high-profile political positions. Under Bourguiba, only one military officer—Ben Ali—had ever become a minister. Now, Ben Ali appointed Habib Ammar as minister of interior (1987–1988), Abdelhamid Escheikh as minister of youth and sports (1988), foreign affairs (1988–1990), and then interior (1990–1991), and Mustapha Bouaziz as minister of justice (1989–1990) and then state domains (1990–1999). General Abdelhamid Escheikh even ran in the 1989 parliamentary elections as the head of the ruling RCD party's list for Tunis 1. Meanwhile, Boubaker BenKraiem was appointed as the governor of Sidi Bouzid (1990–1991) and then Kef (1991–1992).

---

[101] Ben Salem (2013).

[102] Ammar (2011, p. 94).

[103] These were Youssef Barakat (who became chief of staff of the armed forces), Said el-Kateb (who became chief of staff of the land army), Ridha Attar (who became chief of staff of the air force), and Youssef Ben Slimane (who remained as director general of military security). See decrees 87-1289 through 87-1295 issued in November 1987.

[104] See law 87-82 of December 31, 1987 modifying the 1967 general statute of the military.

[105] The chief of staff of the armed forces and the director general of military security. See decree 87-1297 issued on November 27, 1987 (amended by decrees 88-251 and 90-1195). The other members of the National Security Council stipulated by law were the president; the prime minister; the ministers of defense, the interior, and foreign affairs; and the director general of national security.

In the early 1990s, Ben Ali also allowed military officers to take over several of the security forces that had counterbalanced them under Bourguiba. He appointed Ali Seriati as director general of national security and then head of the presidential guard, Sadek Gmati as head of the intervention units and later commander of the national guard, Fethi Jarraya as commander of the Public Order Brigade, Abdelkader Ammar as director general of customs, and Mahmoud Lajnef as the MOI's head of general intelligence, directing the RCD party's network of informants.

These appointments meant that military officers between 1987 and 1991 held a plurality in the NSC, a dominant voice in policymaking, and "a higher degree of visibility and influence than ever before."[106] "The precedent has already been set for the entry of military men into important ministries," Ware (1988, p. 601) warned at the time. "It is not improbable that the officers who supported Ben Ali's coup will coalesce into a shadowy junta to bolster the regime."

Yet the decades-long strategy of marginalizing and counterbalancing the military had created vested interests in its maintenance. Threatened by the military's rise, the security forces and the RCD party searched for ways to put the military back in its place:

> Party apparatchiks believed that Bin Ali's bestowment of positions on the military's top brass was only the start of a potentially disastrous course. [. . .] In their drive to block the much-feared rise of the generals, they were able to count on the backing of the security establishment. [. . .] The police resented Bin Ali's appointment of senior military officers to commandership positions within the security establishment [. . .] They perceived the generals to be encroaching on a realm that should naturally remain the preserve of elites within the police.[107]

The police and the party realized that while Ben Ali was elevating military officers, he was also paranoid of them. "He was afraid that I would do against him what we did together," observed Habib Ammar, Ben Ali's right-hand man in the 1987 coup, who had been appointed minister of interior. "All the people around Ben Ali told him everyday, 'be careful of Habib, he is very strong, he will do a coup.' He was influenced by the people around him."[108] Just a year after appointing Ammar interior minister, Ben Ali forced him out of the country as ambassador to Austria (1988–1995).

Having succeeded in pushing out Ammar, the police and the party then moved to shake Ben Ali's confidence in the military as a whole. On May 22, 1991, the new minister of interior and RCD leader, Abdallah Kallel, publicly claimed to have discovered a coup plot within the military. Airing the testimony of army captain Ahmed Amara, Kallel claimed that military officers met with Islamists from Ennahda on January 6, 1991 in the small coastal hamlet of Barraket Essahel to plot Ben Ali's overthrow. In what became known as the *Barraket Essahel* affair, the Ministry of Interior rounded

---

[106] Ware (1988, p. 593).
[107] Bou Nassif (2015*a*, pp. 69–70).
[108] Interview with Habib Ammar, Tunis, July 13, 2018.

up, tortured, and purged from the military 244 of the most promising officers, NCOs, and soldiers, including three of six assistants to the army chief of staff.[109]

But in reality, there had been no such coup plot. Amara's "confession" had been extracted under torture, and one of the judges involved in the case confirmed the defendants were innocent but that the judges faced pressure to issue a guilty verdict.[110] A former director of military security argued that while roughly 80 of the 244 individuals may have been sympathetic to Ennahda, a meeting at Barraket Essahel as described in Amara's confession would have been impossible given the small size of the suspected house and the presence of a national guard office next to it.[111] Even Ali Seriati, the head of the presidential guard who is now on trial for Barraket Essahel, insisted that while *some* of the accused were guilty, he admitted it was "no more than 12."[112]

Despite the fabrication, the Ministry of Interior succeeded in purging 113 officers, 82 NCOs, and 49 soldiers from the military. In the words of then-Defense Minister Habib Boularès (2011), the military had been "decapitated." But even more importantly, the security forces had shaken Ben Ali's trust in the military. "The minister of the interior at the time, Abdallah Kallel, wanted to drive a wedge between the president and the armed forces, and to prove to Ben Ali that the security establishment was the true defender of his regime," noted one retired colonel.[113] "Ben Ali was not at the origin of Barraket Essahel [but] he believed the lies of the security establishment."

Shaken by this apparent coup plot, Ben Ali forced those military officers he had previously named ministers into retirement or out of the country as ambassadors. General Escheikh, who had enjoyed three ministerial positions, was pushed out as ambassador to France in 1991. General Said El Kateb, who had become chief of staff of the armed forces after Youssef Barakat, was made ambassador to West Africa (1991–1996) and then Southeast Asia (1996–1998). Noureddine Boujellabia was sent out as ambassador to Czechoslovakia in 1992, and Bechir Ben Aissa as ambassador to Eritrea in 1994.

For the rest of Ben Ali's rule, members of the military would receive just four new civilian or security posts.[114] The centralized position of armed forces chief of staff, last held by General El Kateb, was left vacant from 1991. Ben Ali stopped calling on the NSC, depriving the military of input into national security policy. To make a coup more difficult, Ben Ali redeployed a tank field regiment (the 32nd Armored Regiment) into the countryside, to move it farther from the capital.[115]

---

[109] Interviews with retired Colonel Major Hedi Kolsi, Sfax, September 21, 2015; retired Colonel Major Mohamed Ahmed, Tunis, October 17, 2015; retired Colonel Major Ali Hajji, Tozeur, October 24, 2015; and retired Colonel Amor Ben Romdhane, Tunis, November 4, 2015.

[110] Interview with anonymous military judge, Tunis, July 2018.

[111] Interview with a retired officer, Tunis, October 2015.

[112] Interview with Ali Seriati, Tunis, January 22, 2019.

[113] Quoted in Bou Nassif (2015*a*, p. 71).

[114] The four exceptions were (1) Habib Ammar, who was brought back briefly as minister of communications (1995–1997), (2) Mahmoud Lajnef as governor of Gafsa (1994–1994), (3) Ali Seriati, as head of the presidential guard (2001–2011), and (4) Muhammad al-Hadi Ben Hassine, who after serving 11 years as army chief of staff became director general of national security from 2002 to 2005. Mustapha Bouazizi retained his earlier appointment as minister of state domains until 1999.

[115] Jebnoun (2014, p. 302).

Ben Ali also made sure that the military remained "imprisoned" in the barracks, while the Ministry of Interior developed units to take the lead on security threats. The Anti-Terrorism Brigade (BAT) and the National Guard Special Unit (USGN), both in the Ministry of Interior, became the elite fighting forces, comparable to—and training with—the US military's special forces. The MOI also stepped up its surveillance of the armed forces, monitoring even routine military drills to the point of counting used cartridges to verify the number of shots fired.[116] When the military in December 2006 was asked to fight alongside the BAT and USGN against a jihadist group in Soliman, Ali Seriati of the presidential guard was put in command of the operation and tasked the intelligence services with monitoring "the distribution of live ammunition to every [military] combatant, regardless of rank or position, for fear that the military might use this ammunition against the regime."[117]

In addition to this institutional marginalization, Ben Ali began to further neglect the military materially, lavishing new weapons and higher salaries instead on the Ministry of Interior. As Figure 8.2 shows, the budget of the Interior Ministry, which had been roughly equal to the defense budget during the 1980s, was subsequently prioritized by Ben Ali. As the late General Said El Kateb—the last Armed Forces Chief of Staff under Ben Ali—observed: "Under Ben Ali, the budget allocated to the police was higher than the military's; the number of police officers increased dramatically. We could feel our marginalization."[118]

By the time Ben Ali was ousted in 2011, the Ministry of Interior's budget had grown to 165 percent of the defense budget.[119] The size of the national guard grew by over 70 percent during Ben Ali's reign, while the size of the military actually decreased from

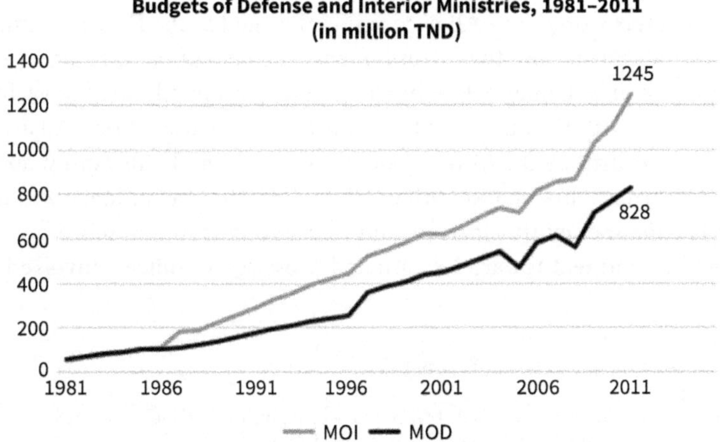

Figure 8.2 Budgets of Defense and Interior Ministries, 1981–2011

[116] Bou Nassif (2014, p. 120).
[117] Jebnoun (2014, p. 303).
[118] Interview with retired Armed Forces Chief of Staff General Said El Kateb, Tunis, November 6, 2015. Quoted also in Grewal (2016).
[119] Bou Nassif (2015*b*); Lutterbeck (2015).

38,000 to 35,800 during this time.[120] The Ministry of Interior as a whole, encompassing the national guard, state security, national police, and intelligence agencies, numbered 50,000–100,000 strong, dwarfing the military.[121] Tunisia had become a police state.

"Our secondary role became even worse than under Bourguiba," exclaimed Mezoughi. "It became a police state. Under Ben Ali, the police monitored everything, including the military."[122] "Ben Ali was even more concerned about the army than Bourguiba," claimed a national guard officer. "So he gave the national guard more than the military."[123]

Beyond the police and national guard, Ben Ali also built up a new counterbalancing force: the presidential guard. In 1988, Ben Ali carved the presidential guard out of the Ministry of Interior and placed it directly in the presidency.[124] He then doubled its size from 1,500 to 3,000, and transformed it into a militarized force complete with its own intelligence service.[125] The presidential guard was reportedly the best paid apparatus,[126] with the Tunisian presidency's budget skyrocketing from 1 million TND in 1988 to 311 million TND in 2010.[127]

With money redirected to the Ministry of Interior and presidential guard, the military languished with limited funds, menial salaries, and outdated equipment. Cordesman and Nerguizian (2010) found that the air fleet had not undergone any modernization since the 1980s. When an old, improperly maintained helicopter crashed in 2002, killing three generals including the army chief of staff, senior officers began to drive to field visits to avoid what they called "flying coffins."[128] Salaries, meanwhile, were paltry: a first lieutenant received 750 dinars a month, and a colonel-major 1,500. By comparison, an assistant professor in a public university would make 1,800.[129]

To make matters worse, Ben Ali used funds allocated to the Defense Ministry for his and his family's own gain. Investigations after the revolution have discovered that Ben Ali built the presidential palace in Hammamet and purchased the yacht *Alyssa* (for $1.2 million) with the budget of the Ministry of Defense.[130] Ben Ali also transferred property owned by the Ministry of Defense to himself, his family, and senior military officers for below-market prices.[131] The fact that the military was not only neglected but the money was instead funneled into corruption and other security services bred resentment toward Ben Ali and those senior officers involved in such transfers.

---

[120] See 1987 and 2010 in the IISS Military Balance.

[121] Lutterbeck (2015).

[122] Interview with retired Colonel Major Mahmoud Mezoughi, Tunis, October 9, 2015.

[123] Interview with retired national guard officer, Tunis, February 2018.

[124] Ben Ali's takeover in 1987 was in part facilitated by the fact that he, as minister of interior, was in command of Bourguiba's presidential guard (Ammar, 2011).

[125] Lutterbeck (2015, p. 823).

[126] Makara (2016, p. 218).

[127] Lutterbeck (2015, p. 816).

[128] Jebnoun (2014, p. 302-3).

[129] Bou Nassif (2015*a*, p. 85).

[130] Jebnoun (2014, p. 313).

[131] See, e.g., Kapitalis (2017).

Coastal Favoritism

Beyond marginalization and counterbalancing, Ben Ali also continued Bourguiba's other coup-proofing tactic: favoring officers hailing from Tunisia's wealthy coastal regions, especially Tunis, Bizerte, Djerba, and the Sahel, in promotions to the top ranks. Like for Bourguiba, this favoritism was partly a function of personal networks, as Ben Ali—who hailed from Hammam-Sousse—tended to know these officers or at least their families. More generally, Ben Ali, like Bourguiba, privileged these regions in economic development and political appointments, and hence viewed them as potentially more loyal to the regime.

Table 8.3 lists each of the officers Ben Ali appointed to the top military positions. Like with Bourguiba, the majority came from the coast. While the coast made up roughly 45 percent of Tunisia's population under Ben Ali,[132] they received 72 percent (18 of 25) of the top military posts under Ben Ali.

Moreover, coastal officers tended to stay in these positions for considerably longer than officers from the interior regions. In the army, for instance, two coastal officers monopolized the position of chief of staff for about a decade apiece: Mohamed al-Hadi Bin Hassine (1990–2002), from Bizerte, and then Rachid Ammar (2002–2011), from Monastir. In the air force as well, Ridha Attar from Tunis served as chief of staff for an outlandish 16 years (1987–2003). On average, the 18 coastal officers listed in Table 8.3 stayed in these top positions for three times longer than their counterparts from the interior regions (average of 6 years v. 2 years).

The preponderance of coastal officers at the top of the military contributed to perceptions that Ben Ali, like Bourguiba before him, was privileging officers from the coast in promotions. Retired Colonel Major Mohamed Ahmed, for instance, observed that: "If you are from Kairouan, Gafsa, or Kef, you are just an average officer. But if you are from the Sahel, you have a big chance of being promoted more quickly."[133] Another senior officer claimed that he "personally heard [Defense Minister] 'Abd al-Aziz Ben Dhia [. . .] refusing to sign a list of promotions [. . .] because it did not contain enough people from the Sahel."[134] A director of internal security, in charge of vetting officers for promotion, noted that "the officers from the Sahel were more privileged. [. . .] Among those at the same rank and same qualifications, if there is one from the Sahel in the list of those potential promotions, he will be chosen."[135]

However, a minority of officers, particularly senior officers from the coast, tended to refute this narrative, claiming their colleagues were simply looking for an excuse for why they were not promoted. It is difficult to determine for certain whether systematic coastal favoritism occurred under Ben Ali, and ultimately what is important are the widespread perceptions that it did. In a survey I conducted of 72 retired senior officers (see details in Chapter 12), 59 percent agreed that Ben Ali privileged the

---

[132] 2004 census. I summed Bizerte, Mahdia, Monastir, Nabeul, Sfax, Sousse, and Tunis.

[133] Interview with retired Colonel Major Mohamed Ahmed, Tunis, October 17, 2015. Quoted also in Grewal (2016).

[134] Quoted in Bou Nassif (2014, p. 108).

[135] Interview with retired officer, Tunis, October 2015.

Table 8.3 Military Leadership under Ben Ali, 1987–2011

Position	Years	Name	Origins	Coast
Armed Forces Chief of Staff	1987–1990	Youssef Barakat	Beja	
Armed Forces Chief of Staff	1990–1991	Mohamed Said El Kateb	Djerba, Medenine	✓
Army Chief of Staff	1987–1990	Mohamed Said El Kateb	Djerba, Medenine	✓
Army Chief of Staff	1990–2002	Mohamed al-Hadi Bin Hassine	Bizerte	✓
Army Chief of Staff	2002–2002	Abd al-Aziz Skik	Kairouan	
Army Chief of Staff	2002–2011	Rachid Ammar	Monastir	✓
Navy Chief of Staff	1987–1997	Chadli Cherif	Tunis	✓
Navy Chief of Staff	1997–2003	Ibrahim Barrak	Kairouan	
Navy Chief of Staff	2003–2010	Tarek Faouzi El-Arbi	Bizerte	✓
Navy Chief of Staff	2010–2011	Mohamed Khamassi	Tunis	✓
Air Force Chief of Staff	1987–2003	Ridha Attar	Tunis	✓
Air Force Chief of Staff	2003–2008	Mahmoud Ben Mohamed	Nabeul	✓
Air Force Chief of Staff	2008–2011	Taieb Laajimi	Tunis/Monastir	✓
Dir. Gen. Mil. Security	1987–1990	Mohamed al-Hadi Bin Hassine	Bizerte	✓
Dir. Gen. Mil. Security	1990–1991	Ali Seriati	Kairouan	
Dir. Gen. Mil. Security	1991–2001	Mohamed Hafiz Farza	Kerkennah, Sfax	✓
Dir. Gen. Mil. Security	2001–2002	Rachid Ammar	Monastir	✓
Dir. Gen. Mil. Security	2002–2009	Mohamed Meddeb	Nabeul	✓
Dir. Gen. Mil. Security	2009–2011	Ahmed Chabir	Gabes	
Inspector General	1987–1995	Mahmoud Gannouni	Monastir	✓
Inspector General	1995–1997	Hassen Jebli	Kef	
Inspector General	1997–2001	Chadli Cherif	Tunis	✓
Inspector General	2001–2002	Abd al-Aziz Skik	Kairouan	
Inspector General	2002–2010	Mansour Haddad	Djerba, Medenine	✓
Inspector General	2010–2011	Tarek Faouzi Larbi	Bizerte	✓
Total				18/25 (72%)

Sahel in promotions, and only 22 percent disagreed. In a second survey of 253 junior officers and soldiers, 69 percent agreed that Ben Ali did so, and only 12 percent disagreed. These perceptions, whether grounded in truth or not, are what reduced support for Ben Ali and later bred support for the transition.

But the data certainly suggest systemic favoritism by region. The aforementioned Registry of Retired Officers proves useful here, providing biographies for all 662 senior officers (major and above) who had retired by 2009. Based on this data, Figure 8.3 maps the birthplaces for all army officers between the rank of major and colonel-major (left) and for generals (right).[136] The maps speak for themselves: while mid-level officers came from all around Tunisia, generals hailed primarily from the coast. Though we only have data on senior officers, the difference would be even more stark for junior officers, most of whom come from the interior regions.[137]

Still, these patterns may not be evidence of favoritism. It could be that coastal officers were more likely to speak French, and therefore more readily sent out for foreign training, which enhanced their promotion prospects. Alternatively, this pattern could be a function of entrance year, or the Bourguiba Promotion in particular, which was largely recruited from the coast and subsequently privileged by their colleague Ben Ali.

To test for these counter-explanations, Table 8.4 presents an ordered logistic regression on the same dataset of retired officers. The power of this regression is that it allows us to calculate the effect of being from the coast on an officer's odds of being promoted, while controlling for a number of other variables that could also affect promotion, such as foreign training or being from the Bourguiba Promotion. I include controls for every variable that could be gleaned from the biographies:

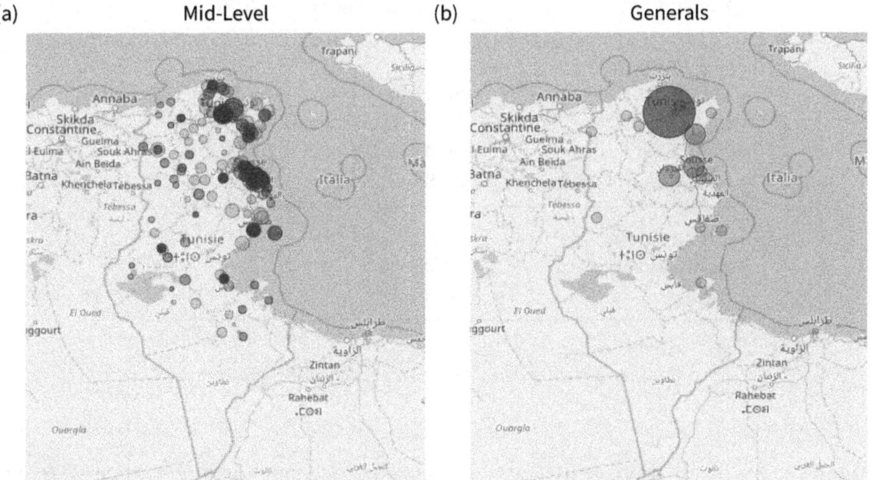

Figure 8.3 Senior Officers (army) by Birthplace

---

[136] Maps created through OpenStreetMap (CC-BY-SA).
[137] Interview with former director general of military security, Tunis, November 2015.

Table 8.4 Coastal Favoritism in Military Promotions (Ordered Logit)

	Dependent Variable: Rank	
	Coefficient	Odds Ratio
From Coast	0.40 (0.17)**	1.50
Branch		
Army	0.57 (0.16)***	1.76
Air Force	0.25 (0.21)	1.28
Entrance		
Entrance Year	0.03 (0.00)***	1.03
Bourguiba Promotion	−0.30 (0.26)	0.74
Foreign Training		
Cadet-France	−0.07 (0.21)	0.93
Cadet-Other West	1.76 (0.22)***	5.83
Cadet-Nonwest	−0.43 (0.02)***	0.65
Additional-West	2.01 (0.17)***	7.50
Additional-Nonwest	2.15 (0.14)***	8.58
Military Experience		
Served in War	−1.60 (0.06)***	0.20
Served in PKO	−0.72 (0.22)***	0.49
Number of Medals	0.81 (0.06)***	2.24
Demographic		
Died in service	0.28 (0.31)	1.32
Female	−2.33 (0.01)***	0.10
Cut-Points		
Major | Lt. Col	56.41 (0.01)***	
Lt. Col | Col.	57.92 (0.11)***	
Col. | Col. Major	59.93 (0.17)***	
Col. Major | General	61.83 (0.27)***	
Observations	625	
Residual Deviance	1388.654	
AIC	1426.654	

*Note: *p<0.1; **p<0.05; ***p<0.01*
Note: Odds ratio greater than 1 means higher chance of promotion.

branch (army or air force, with navy as the reference category); entrance year, and Bourguiba Promotion; foreign training, including where they did their initial offi-cer candidate school and where they did additional courses; combat experience (served in war, served in peacekeeping operation, and number of medals earned); and finally demographic variables including gender and whether they died while in service.

The results suggest that even when controlling for all these variables, officers from the coast had a significant advantage in promotions,[138] with an odds ratio of 1.50. In other words, on average, the odds of promotion were about 50 percent higher for an officer from the coast than one from the interior.[139] While we cannot definitively prove systemic favoritism of the coast, the data are hard to deny.

True or false, the perceptions of discrimination bred resentment not only toward Ben Ali but also towards senior officers believed to have secured their position through loyalty rather than merit. For instance, Ben Ali's final army chief, Rachid Ammar, had been head of the military's disciplinary council in 1991, and is accused of complicity in the purge of officers in the Barraket Essahel affair.[140] In 2002, after the helicopter crash that killed Army Chief of Staff Abdelaziz Skik, then-Colonel Ammar was chosen as the new army chief of staff over many qualified colonel majors, a promotion attributed to Ammar having been from the Sahel.[141] Ammar was then permitted to remain army chief of staff for 11 years, despite reaching the retirement age after just five. Ammar also stands accused of profiting from corruption—in particular, of securing a flat in the posh neighborhood of La Marsa for below-market value—while the rest of the military languished through meager salaries and poor working conditions. As a result, Ammar was widely vilified by retired officers as a sell out and puppet of Ben Ali.

Professionalism

While many officers harbored resentment toward the regime, most knew better than to show it. The professionalism that had developed in the 1960s and 1970s strengthened further in the 1990s and 2000s as the military was again kept far from politics and political power. It was not just that the police and military security were actively monitoring officers for political sentiments. The officer corps was also internalizing politics as something to consciously avoid. One of Ben Ali's defense ministers recalled that:

> "Even those in the army who were not necessarily favorable to the government or the president do not show it. During my time, there was maybe one or two officers who made a comment that was political. This doesn't mean they don't have things to say, but they are very prudent, very careful. They have been trained with that. [. . .] It is a very disciplined, professional army."[142]

Even those who resented Ben Ali knew it was inappropriate to express those sentiments, let alone act upon them by staging a coup. Kept far from the regime,

---

[138] As in Tables 8.2 and 8.3, officers are considered as being "from the coast" if they were born in the governorates of Bizerte, Tunis, Nabeul, Sousse, Monastir, Mahdia, or Sfax, or on the island of Djerba.

[139] Among covariates, foreign training and more medals tended to improve the odds for promotions, while women were significantly less likely to be promoted.

[140] Interview with retired Colonel Major Hedi Kolsi, Sfax, November 16, 2015.

[141] Interview with retired Colonel Major Mohamed Ahmed, Tunis, October 17, 2015.

[142] Interview with Kamel Morjane, Tunis, October 13, 2015.

the military under Ben Ali further internalized the "republican ethos"—the idea that the military exists to defend the country, not to take sides for or against the regime. One Brigadier-General argued that: "The role of the army is not to defend the regime, but to defend the country, to defend and protect the republican institutions. [. . .] The army was not against Ben Ali, nor against the people. It does its job, and that's it."[143] "When we speak of the neutrality of the Tunisian military," another brigadier-general explained, "it comes from the army's history and development: it has never been involved in politics."[144] Jamal Boujah, the former inspector-general of the armed forces, claimed that "the culture of the army in general leans towards absolute impartiality. It does not care about politics or political parties. [If asked to deal with protests,] the army intervenes in a very neutral way regardless of politics."[145]

That neutrality was on display in 2008, when the military was asked by Ben Ali to defend state institutions in Gafsa. For six months, police had been clashing with protesters in Gafsa, leading Ben Ali to bring in the army on June 7 to impose a curfew and protect public institutions in Redeyef. Unlike in the previous deployments of 1978 and 1984, the military in 2008 did not engage in repression itself,[146] and instead reportedly strove to deescalate tensions between police and protesters. Brigadier-General Boujah claimed that: "That is one of the reasons why the Tunisian army is loved and appreciated by the population. Because whenever tensions mount between the police and the people, the army always intervenes to make the police back off, which calms down the turmoil."[147]

Kamel Morjane, the defense minister at the time, claimed that:

"The army was really well received in these events. The people were happy to see the army intervening, because they knew the army was not there to deal with people. They were confident that the army would not treat them badly. When you put a soldier in front of a bank, as long as you don't touch the bank they won't touch you. When the military was deployed in Oum El Araies near the end of the day, around 6pm, they were very well received. The bakers even opened their doors and brought bread to the army!"[148]

Retired Colonel Major Mokhtar Ben Nasr, the defense ministry spokesman, noted the similarities between the 2008 Gafsa protests and the 2011 revolution:

"If the ex-president had been clever enough, he would have seen the revolution coming. He had deprived the interior regions and stripped them of their natural resources. Many Tunisians had higher education but were still unemployed. The

---

[143] Interview with retired director general of military security, Tunis, 2015.

[144] Interview with officer, Tunis, January 2016.

[145] Interview with Armed Forces Inspector General Jamal Boujah, Tunis, January 9, 2018.

[146] On the contrary, Amnesty International (2009) reports that: "All these forces committed serious human rights violations, including excessive use of force resulting in the deaths of two protesters and injuries to others." However, when detailing the precise violations, all concern the police and other internal security forces, not the military.

[147] Interview with Armed Forces Inspector General Jamal Boujah, Tunis, January 9, 2018.

[148] Interview with Kamel Morjane, Tunis, October 13, 2015.

most important point in 2008 [. . . is that] the military did not fire upon civilians, but intervened just to calm things down. [. . .] It was the first sign of the coming revolution."[149]

Conclusion

Since independence, the Tunisian military was marginalized politically and materially. Tunisian dictators Bourguiba and Ben Ali preferred to counterbalance the military with internal security forces, deterring, and on occasion, defeating coup attempts from the army. Meanwhile, within the military, they privileged a minority of officers hailing from the wealthy coastal regions, using them to weed out coup plots from below. Over time, the military's marginalization contributed also to the development of an apolitical professionalism. Those three characteristics—the counterbalancing, regional favoritism, and professionalism—would go on to create important legacies shaping the military's behavior in the Arab Spring, the topic of the next chapter.

---

[149] Interview with Mokhtar Ben Nasr, Tunis, August 27, 2015.

9
Tunisia: Shirking in the Revolution

> The Tunisian army in 2011 would not shoot other Tunisians. We were not going to harm the population for the good of a King!
> —Brigadier General (R) Mohamed Ali El Bekri[1]

Introduction

Protests erupted against President Zine El Abidine Ben Ali on December 17, 2010 in the interior town of Sidi Bouzid. That day, Mohamed Bouazizi, a street vendor whose vegetable cart had been confiscated by police, lit himself on fire, unintentionally sparking a revolution. Protests spread gradually, at first in the interior regions, and then reaching the capital on December 27. By January 9, the protests had escalated into a nationwide mass uprising, leading Ben Ali to flee the country on January 14.

An initial myth, published widely in both domestic and foreign press, claimed that Ben Ali's fall was precipitated by a defection from the army chief of staff, General Rachid Ammar, who in this narrative refused Ben Ali's order to fire on protesters. This account was plausible, given that, as shown in the previous chapter, the military had been neglected by Ben Ali, and hence may have been eager to give him the "velvet shove."[2]

But that account was quickly debunked, by, among others, Ammar himself, who revealed in his official testimony in April 2011 that this was "a false rumor": Ben Ali never asked him to fire, and thus he never refused.[3] The military was asked only to defend vital institutions, and Ammar complied, including to help secure the route to the presidential palace on January 13 and even the Ministry of Interior on January 14. That Ammar was until the end one of Ben Ali's most trusted soldiers was made clear on January 14, when in the face of a police mutiny Ammar was tasked with overseeing the Ministry of Interior's operations. As a result, a revisionist reading of the 2011 revolution claims that there was not military defection, but rather military loyalty.[4]

The truth is somewhere in between. The senior officers, having been stacked with coastal elite, were loyal to Ben Ali until the end, and were anyway too professional

---

[1] Interview, Tunis, November 28, 2015.
[2] Gaaloul (2011); Barany (2011, 2016); Bellin (2012); Brooks (2013); Lutterbeck (2013); Makara (2016).
[3] Ammar (2011, p. 304).
[4] Pachon (2014); Jebnoun (2014); Gallopin (2019); Holmes and Koehler (2020).

Soldiers of Democracy?. Sharan Grewal, Oxford University Press. © Sharan Grewal (2023).
DOI: 10.1093/oso/9780192873910.003.0009

to openly disobey an order, let alone push out the president. The junior officers and soldiers, on the other hand, felt marginalized and counterbalanced by Ben Ali, and those from the interior regions also resented Ben Ali's preference for the coast. Close observers thus believe that Ben Ali never asked the military to fire because he already knew the lower ranks would refuse—or worse, might turn their guns onto the regime. One effect of Ben Ali's coup-proofing strategies was thus to breed resentment within the lower and middle ranks of the military, leaving him unable to call upon the troops to help put down the uprising.

But Ben Ali's strained relations with the military not only left him without their help. Indirectly, they also contributed to the weakening and hollowing out of the internal security forces, and thus to his toppling. They did so in at least four ways. First, paranoid of a coup, Ben Ali was slow to deploy the military, in the meantime overextending and depleting the security forces. The military was not deployed until January 8, not permitted in Tunis until January 11, and not permitted to bring tanks into the capital until January 13.

Second, once the military was deployed, Ben Ali diverted the attention of the security forces away from the protesters and instead toward monitoring the military. Ben Ali wasted crucial resources of the national guard and presidential guard in embedding within military units in Tunis to prevent a coup.

Third, although the senior officers agreed to deploy the military to defend vital institutions, the junior officers on the ground often shirked in this mission. Particularly in the interior regions, military units stepped aside as protesters destroyed government buildings and burned down police stations. With police equipment and weapons looted and destroyed, the military's shirking further undermined the capacity of the police.

Finally, and most importantly, amid the military's shirking, (false) rumors of its defection became credible. In the final days of the uprising, the security forces themselves believed that the military had already abandoned Ben Ali. These rumors dampened the morale of the security forces, producing in them not just desertions but eventually a mutiny that forced Ben Ali to flee the country. In other words, even though the military did not actually defect, the rumors that it did produced actual defections in the security forces, ultimately leading Ben Ali to flee.

In sum, not only did Ben Ali's coup-proofing strategies leave him without the help of the military, but they also initiated the chain of events that would lead to his downfall. To empirically validate this account, this chapter draws upon unique interviews with many of the key players during the uprising, including the leader of the police mutiny, Samir Tarhouni; the head sof the presidential guard, Ali Seriati; and the originator of the rumor that the military defected, Yassine Ayari. The chapter also supplements these interviews with the official, Arabic-language testimony of each of the actors at the military court in 2011. Overall, it provides a new look at how Ben Ali's coup-proofing left him vulnerable to a mass uprising.

Paranoia of the Military

From the start, Ben Ali tried to keep the military far from the uprising. While the police, Public Order Brigade (BOP), national guard, and presidential guard were deployed early on, the military was left in the barracks until January 8—three weeks after the protests began, and about two weeks after they reached the capital. Not only was the military not mobilized, but its leaders were not even involved in discussions about the protests until January 9. While the heads of each of the internal security forces had been meeting regularly in a Crisis Cell since December 20, the military leaders were not invited until January 9.[5]

In reflecting on why Ben Ali fell, Ali Seriati, the head of the presidential guard, argued that: "The main problem was the lack of interaction with the military before January 9. We needed to have a joint meeting before then, but Ben Ali did not want to [involve them]."[6]

Throughout his rule, Ben Ali's management style had been to silo off the military from the other security forces, ensuring they would not collude against him. As Seriati continued:

> "The President collected intelligence from a number of sources: the ministry of interior, the army, the ruling party, and so on. But each sent their intelligence directly to the president. There was no intermediary. This was not good. [. . .] This was an error. If there had been a staff—security or military—for coordination, our response [to the revolution] would have been much better. Who coordinated between military and security? No one!"[7]

While the Crisis Cell could have served that purpose during the uprising, Ben Ali chose not to involve the military until late. He did not, after all, want the military to deploy. While he trusted Rachid Ammar and the other coastal, senior officers, the same could not be said about the lower ranks who would actually be deployed on the ground. He had kept them "imprisoned"[8] in the barracks for the last two decades for a reason: he feared that these forces might join the protesters, or even turn their guns onto the police, if they were to deploy.

After weeks of the police and BOP depleting their stockpiles of tear gas and rubber bullets, they turned to more lethal methods on January 8, firing live bullets for the first time in Kasserine and Thala.[9] As the death toll climbed,[10] protests actually escalated, spurred on by videos of police brutality. It was only then, after the police were depleted and overwhelmed, that Ben Ali finally called upon the military. The

---

[5] IVD (2019, pp. 343–344).
[6] Interview with Ali Seriati, January 22, 2019.
[7] Interview with Ali Seriati, Tunis, January 22, 2019.
[8] Interview with retired Colonel Hedi Kolsi, Sfax, September 21, 2015.
[9] See Ryan (2011).
[10] Bou Nassif (2015a, p. 81) estimates that police had killed 9 protesters between December 17 and January 7, and 71 between January 8 and January 14.

soldiers were tasked with defending vital institutions in Kasserine and Thala, including both government buildings and major factories, freeing up police to deal with protesters.

The next day, Army Chief of Staff Rachid Ammar joined the Crisis Cell for the first time to discuss the regime's response. At that January 9th meeting, the Cell agreed on a list of vital institutions across the country that the military would defend, notably including police stations and RCD party offices.[11] The military then deployed across the country that day.

But Ben Ali refused to let the military enter the capital, Tunis, until January 11, nor to bring in tanks into the capital until January 13. As Jebnoun (2014, p. 306) observed: "Ben Ali was reluctant to hand over the capital to heavily armed forces, which he feared might join the protest movement." Yet his delay only served to further deplete the energies and stockpiles of the internal security forces.

Samir Tarhouni, the chief of the anti-terrorism brigade, who would play a major role in Ben Ali's ouster, recalled that: "The tear gas was nearly finished by the end of January 13th. We didn't have more than 200 [canisters] on the 14th. We didn't have any equipment left, no water tanks, nothing, just a few canisters of tear gas."[12] Notably, a shipment of 10,000 tear gas grenades from France was due to arrive on January 15, the day after Ben Ali fled.[13]

And yet, despite this shortage in police resources in the final days of the uprising, Ben Ali's paranoia of the military made matters even worse. Once the military was permitted in the capital, Ben Ali asked the security forces to waste additional resources in monitoring the troops:

> The first [army] units given the task of maintaining security in Tunis were the Special Forces [. . . But] Ben Ali deployed armoured vehicles belonging to the National Guard alongside the Special Forces, which boasted an armoured personnel carrier in their possession that gave them superior mobility, manoeuvring, and firepower. [. . .] It becomes clear that the regime was trying to prevent the army from staging a coup.[14]

Likewise, when the military was asked to help defend the routes leading up to the presidential palace on the evening of January 13, members of the presidential guard were embedded within the military units (even wearing the army's uniforms).[15] By diverting the attention of the internal security forces to monitoring the military, Ben Ali further undermined their ability to defend him from protesters. His paranoia

---

[11] Interview with Ali Seriati, January 22, 2019. According to Seriati, also decided at that January 9 meeting was that the RCD party would attempt to infiltrate the protests and guide them away from confrontations with the police, and that the police in Thala and Kasserine would be replaced with national guard units.

[12] Interview with Samir Tarhouni, Tunis, January 18, 2018.

[13] See Seriati's testimony quoted in Mandraud (2011). Reportedly, 1,500 canisters were also due to arrive from Libya on January 14.

[14] Jebnoun (2014, p. 306).

[15] Ammar (2011, p. 306).

of a military coup thus left him more vulnerable to an overthrow by the masses by depleting and diverting the resources of the police.

Military Shirking

From January 8 to 14, the military was deployed across the country to defend sensitive locations, such as government buildings, police stations, RCD party offices, water and electricity plants, and embassies. These were not orders to fire on protesters per se, but they would entail doing so if protesters attacked these locations and refused to cease and desist despite the firing of warning shots.[16]

The military leadership complied with these missions, even heeding the call for additional reinforcements to defend the routes to the presidential palace on January 13 and the Ministry of Interior on January 14.[17] However, while the senior officers did not refuse, the junior officers on the ground did on occasion shirk in fulfilling these missions, particularly in the interior regions of the country. When protesters attacked these institutions, military units on the ground typically looked away rather than engage them with force.[18]

For instance, despite the military's deployment in Kasserine on January 8, soldiers stepped aside as protesters on January 9 attacked "several government buildings [...] and destroyed three banks, a police station, and a filling station."[19] A local resident of Kasserine noted in this regard that: "From the beginning, [the army was] against shooting at people. That is what prevented an even higher death toll."[20]

In Thala as well, protesters set fire to a government building on January 9 despite the military's deployment there the night before.[21] And throughout the country, protesters burned down tens of police stations—looting or damaging their weapons and equipment. The military's shirking in its duties thus had the effect of further undermining the capacity of the police, and reportedly led Ali Seriati to presciently warn on January 13 that "if the army continues to drag its feet as it does, tomorrow there will be no one in the presidential palace!"[22]

While the military may have had a professional duty to defend these sensitive locations, the marginalization of the military led the soldiers to look the other way. For some, it was the contrast of their neglect with the opulence of the regime: "Ben Ali's corruption was made through the military by using our planes and budget," noted retired Colonel Major Mokhtar Ben Nasr. "We knew a lot about their corruption. That's why we stood by the side of the people."[23]

---

[16] Interview with Brigadier-General Mohamed Ali El Bekri, Tunis, November 28, 2015.

[17] *Jeune Afrique* (2012).

[18] In some cases, the military also actively stepped in to defend protesters from security forces. See January 13, 2011 in Sfax: https://www.youtube.com/watch?v=ubFGeQbemug.

[19] BBC (2011c).

[20] Quoted in Ryan (2011).

[21] Rifai (2011).

[22] The quote by Seriati was reported by Defense Minister Grira. See *Jeune Afrique* (2011b).

[23] Interview with Mokhtar Ben Nasr, Tunis, August 27, 2015.

For others, it was their counterbalancing with the police: "We shed no tears when the people attacked police stations. The police were corrupt and arrogant vis-à-vis the population and the armed forces. That the military should kill civilians in order to protect the police was out of the question; whatever happened to the police, they asked for it."[24]

Even the professional officers ultimately sided with the people. "The problem for us, the dilemma, is that from one side you should defend [sensitive locations], because it's your mission," explained retired Colonel Major Mahmoud Mezoughi. "But on the other side, defend against whom? Against the Tunisian population. Whether they are rioting, or angry, they are our souls. The decision is very difficult. [. . .] And so far, we in the army haven't used hard means to defend these institutions. Another big example of that is what happened in El Kamour, Tataouine [in 2017]. The army was responsible for defending the oil pump, but the army let the young people go in, and didn't shoot."[25] A brigadier-general likewise observed that although the military is professional and neutral, "of course it is more with the population than the regime."[26]

The military's shirking was facilitated in part by its distance from the Ben Ali regime. Not implicated in repression under Ben Ali, and not viewed as part of the regime, protesters tended to treat soldiers more respectfully than the hated internal security forces. As a brigadier-general remarked, "The country was lucky that no one attacked the soldiers. What would have been the reaction? Imagine if a soldier reacts violently, then another who didn't know how it started, will also react . . . it could have initiated a chain of violence. We are lucky that all over the country people didn't provoke the army."[27]

Seeing the military shirking, the regime on at least three occasions attempted to provoke a military response. On January 10, the minister of defense, Ridha Grira, ordered the military to wear the blue uniforms of the Interior Ministry's intervention units. The irregular order, given to the defense minister by the interior minister, Rafik Belhaj Kacem,[28] was designed to make the soldiers look like the internal security forces, seemingly so that protesters might attack them and thus provoke the military into using force in self-defense. But Ammar, according to Defense Minister Grira (2011, p. 293), "persuaded him not to implement such instructions, stressing that the National Army has its own uniform and that it must practice its activities of all kinds while wearing its distinctive uniform." Ammar also sent an administrative telegram reminding the soldiers of the protocol for defending state institutions, underscoring that any live fire should only occur after "consultations and direct orders by the [military] leadership."[29] Such a reminder, although routine,[30] suggests that Ammar

---

[24] Retired colonel-major (army) quoted in Bou Nassif (2015*a*, p. 86).

[25] Interview with Mezoughi, Tunis, March 4, 2020. For more on the military's shirking in El Kamour, see Grewal (2019*a*).

[26] Interview with retired officer, Tunis, October 2015.

[27] Interview with retired officer, Tunis, October 2015.

[28] Grira (2011, p. 293),

[29] Ammar (2011, p. 304).

[30] Colonel Major Mokhtar Ben Nasr noted that a similar reminder was given during the military's deployment in Gafsa in 2008. Interview, Tunis, August 27, 2015.

was trying to avoid a provocation that might lead the military to fire without his permission.

The regime tried again the next day to provoke the military. On January 11, Defense Minister Grira told Ammar that he had instructions directly from Ben Ali for the soldiers to take off their helmets. Doing so would make them appear like the national guard, which also wore green uniforms but no helmets. Ammar claims he "was surprised by these instructions," and "felt that other parties [*atrāf ukhra*] were seeking to throw the National Army units into the reflections of the [. . . other] units deployed in the field and wearing green uniforms,"[31] such as the national guard. Ammar complied with the order, but told soldiers to instead wear their red berets to distinguish themselves from these other units.

Finally, on January 12, Ammar received word that national guard units, wearing the same green uniforms as the army, had taken positions next to the soldiers defending the Central Bank in Kasserine. Realizing that the soldiers might be blamed for the national guard's abuses,[32] Ammar "gave instructions to expel those security units from the location of the military units, to avoid confusion, to ensure unity of command, and to determine responsibility in the event of an emergency."[33]

Each of these three incidents suggests that the regime was attempting to trick protesters into attacking the military. Having seen the soldiers on the ground shirking, the regime appears to have been trying to provoke a military response: to force the troops to finally use their weapons, if only in self-defense. That Ammar each time took steps to avoid this eventuality could suggest an unwillingness on his behalf to repress protesters, at least without his permission, or simply reflect concern for the safety of his troops. At the same time, none of these incidents constitutes a defection per se: Ammar never publicly or privately refused to defend the regime. Contrary to the rumors, he was not fired or placed under house arrest, and instead maintained the confidence of Ben Ali until the end.

Would the Military Have Fired?

Although Ben Ali never ordered the military to repress protesters, it is worth considering what might have happened if he had. While we cannot know for sure, officers believed that the military would have responded just as it did to the order to defend vital institutions: compliance from the leadership, but shirking from the lower ranks.

Almost every officer I interviewed argued that Rachid Ammar would have complied with an order to fire on protesters. "Rachid Ammar is a myth," exclaimed one colonel-major. "He was in the pocket of Ben Ali, with an apartment in La Marsa! He would never say no."[34] Ammar and other coastal, senior officers, privileged by Ben Ali, had personal, career interests in sticking with him. Moreover, others claimed

[31] Ammar (2011, p. 304).
[32] Jebnoun (2014, p. 305).
[33] Ammar (2011, p. 304).
[34] Interview with retired officer, Tunis, October 2015.

that their professionalism would have led these senior officers to obey. "If they were ordered, they would have obeyed," argued a former defense minister. "[Refusing] would have been a coup! The military doesn't play with that. That would be a political decision."[35]

And yet, while the senior officers may have wanted to preserve Ben Ali, they knew that the officers and soldiers below them would not fire. "Ben Ali and Ammar knew that such an order wouldn't have been obeyed," argued retired Brigadier General Mohamed Ali El Bekri. "The Tunisian army in 2011 would not shoot other Tunisians. We were not going to harm the population for the good of a King!"[36]

A former navy chief of staff highlighted Ben Ali's neglect of the military:

> "The officers would not have opened fire on the protesters. [. . .] The overwhelming majority in the officer corps was unhappy with the regime. Ben Ali had marginalized the armed forces, just as Bourguiba had done before him. The officers were not going to risk their lives, and the lives of others, for the sake of a regime that had offered nothing to the armed forces."[37]

A former air force chief of staff instead pinpointed his counterbalancing of the military with the police:

> The armed forces would not have followed orders. I don't have a single doubt about that. In 1991, the regime humiliated the armed forces; 2011 was payback time for us. After Barakat Essahel, we were silent but resentful. Our attitude vis-à-vis the 2011 uprising was simple: good riddance, Ben Ali. His was the regime of the police, which had become like the Eastern German Stasi. The armed forces were not going to defend the regime of the security establishment, which had humiliated the military institution. Why should they have?[38]

In the end, Ben Ali never asked the military to fire, perhaps anticipating that the lower ranks would refuse. His coup-proofing strategies—neglecting and counterbalancing the military—had left him without their support in the 2011 revolution.

The Rumor Heard around the World

But it is a fourth and final effect of Ben Ali's coup-proofing that ultimately proved fatal to his rule. The common knowledge that the military had been neglected and marginalized, combined with its shirking during the uprising, fed into fears among the security forces that the military might not back them up in defending the regime. Those expectations then led them to latch on to and believe rumors that the military

---

[35] Interview with former defense minister, Tunis, October 2015.
[36] Interview with Mohamed Ali El Bekri, Tunis, November 28, 2015.
[37] Quoted in Bou Nassif (2015*a*, pp. 79–80).
[38] Retired air force chief of staff quoted in Bou Nassif (2015*a*, p. 80).

had defected, undermining their morale and leading key figures in the security forces to defect "as well." The military's rumored defection, even though it was untrue, thus initiated a cascade of defections that ultimately terminated Ben Ali's rule.

The rumor that Ammar said no to Ben Ali's order to fire was invented by Yassine Ayari, a blogger and cyber-activist who later became a member of parliament. In an interview, Ayari explained the backstory to his "rumor heard around the world":

> "On January 5–6, there were protests close to where my father [the late army Colonel Tahar Ayari] worked. I worried, what if my dad is killing those people? [. . .] But my father said: 'It's a police affair, we in the army have no orders to interfere with this.' So I thought, how do I push this information? I had to package it—we need a name to make the news. Tunisians need a hero. So I told [Nawaat, a popular blog, on January 7] that 'General Rachid Ammar refused to give the order for the army to interfere.' I knew Ben Ali doesn't need Ammar to give an order. He can give the order directly. And I know Rachid Ammar would not ever dare to say no. But I was happy—the news went around the world. Rachid Ammar was in the front page of every newspaper: the man who says no."[39]

For three days the rumor circulated around social media, before being picked up by newspapers starting on January 11.[40] On his blog on July 19, 2011, when Ayari came clean about this rumor, he explained that:

> It was a trick to destabilize the regime of ZABA [Zine el-Abidine Ben Ali], to encourage everyone to go out onto the streets, and to push everyone to fraternize with the army, something I did not doubt, me, the son of a military [officer], who knows the military ethics, and which was confirmed later. And it worked, it helped to get rid of ZABA, it encouraged the BAT (Anti-Terrorism Brigade) to do something that made ZABA flee (but that you'll know when Seriati or Tarhouni talk . . .)[41]

Samir Tarhouni, the head of the BAT, agreed with Ayari's assessment: "The media knows what they were doing. [This rumor] was a signal to the people, don't worry about the military, they are with the people."[42] But importantly, it was believed not just by the protesters, but by many in the security forces as well. "The lower ranks believed the rumor," Tarhouni continued. "They did not know the full truth. There is a certainly a percent of them who believed it."[43]

---

[39] Interview with Yassine Ayari, Tunis, June 20, 2018.

[40] The first newspaper to publish the rumor, according to a Google search for "Rachid Ammar" by date, appears to be *Doualia*, a Paris-based Arabic-language newspaper, on January 11. It was subsequently published on January 12 by *France24*, *Hespress*, and *Guinee-Plurielle*, and then *Al-Akhbar* on January 13. It only made English language newspapers after the revolution, see, e.g., the *New York Times* on January 16.

[41] Ayari (2011).

[42] Interview with Samir Tarhouni, Tunis, January 18, 2019.

[43] Interview with Samir Tarhouni, Tunis, January 18, 2019.

Even Ali Seriati, the head of the presidential guard, found the rumor credible enough to confront Ammar about it. On January 10, even before the rumor hit the newspapers, Ammar (2011, p. 304) recalled:

> I received a phone call from General Ali Seraiti informing me of the existence of a rumor on the social network Facebook stating that I had submitted my resignation from the national army, and this was prompted by the fact that I refused to provide orders to shoot at the demonstrators, to which I answered that it is a false rumor and that I have not received any instructions to shoot the demonstrators.[44]

Though Ammar denied the rumor, the seeds of doubt that the military might not defend the regime had been sown. Those seeds then sprouted further on January 13, when a new rumor spread among the security forces that the military was withdrawing from the capital. As Ammar (2011, p. 305) recounted:

> On January 13, Brigadier General Ahmed Chabir, the Director of Military Intelligence, informed me that there was a rumor spreading among the security forces [claiming] that the National Army units deployed in the capital had withdrawn from their stationing points [. . .] I was concerned about the effect of that rumour on the morale of the security forces, which would have considered that they were operating alone, and which would push them to withdraw in turn.

Ammar, loyal to the regime, attempted to counter these rumors and dissuade the security forces from withdrawing by ordering the military units in the capital to firmly announce their presence. But despite his efforts, the morale of the security forces had plummeted, and many began to give up. "On the evening of January 13, some security personnel from the police, the National Guard and the customs handed over their individual weapons to the military barracks," noted Ammar (2011, p. 305).[45] The rumors that the military was withdrawing and not defending the regime had begun to produce actual defections in the security forces. As Yassine Ayari put it: "The police thought the army was not going to help them, so they chose to abandon Ben Ali."[46]

Heading into January 14, therefore, Ben Ali's neglect and fear of the military had four major effects, contributing to: (1) his reluctance to deploy the military, depleting

---

[44] Importantly, this incident also increased Ammar's distrust of Seriati, as he believed Seriati had reported to Ben Ali the administrative telegram that he sent earlier that day: "I was surprised at how quickly that telegram was sent to Ben Ali, as I realized that the former president was informed of the content of that military administrative cable" (Ammar, 2011, p. 304). Jebnoun (2014, p. 305) writes: "Ammar assumed from this phone call that Seriati distorted the content of Ammar's military cable (issued to troops on 10 January) in order to undermine Ben Ali's trust in Ammar's loyalty to the regime."

[45] When Ammar reported this to Defense Minister Grira, he was suspicious, thinking "that Ammar intended to disarm the security forces, which in turn could pave the way for the army to seize power" (Jebnoun, 2014, p. 313). The paranoia of a military coup was widespread, affecting the defense minister as well. Ammar complied and stopped the collection of weapons, as Grira asked Ben Ali, who in turn allowed the collection to resume on the morning of the 14th.

[46] Interview with Yassine Ayari, Tunis, June 20, 2018.

the security forces, (2) wasting police resources in monitoring the military, (3) the military shirking and allowing police stations to get looted and destroyed, and (4) the police starting to give up, thinking the military had already defected. In other words, Ben Ali's coup-proofing of the military had the unintended consequence of hollowing out the massive and feared police force. Seeing the writing on the wall, some in the security forces then decided to take matters into their own hands.

January 14

The protests on January 14 were massive, fueled by Ben Ali's refusal to resign in a stubborn speech the night before. Some 30–40,000 protesters amassed outside the Ministry of Interior on Habib Bourguiba avenue in downtown Tunis.

Stationed on the balconies of the ministry was the Anti-Terrorism Brigade (BAT), deployed for the first time the night before in anticipation of armed resistance after protesters had looted police stations. In an interview with the author, the head of the BAT, Samir Tarhouni, explained what happened next:

> "The situation had worsened more and more. On the 14th, we had already sent all reinforcements into Tunis. There was nobody in the regions. Police stations were empty. Everyone was on Bourguiba [Avenue]. At 10 a.m., 1 kilometer away there was an attack on a police station; we didn't even intervene. There was no resistance when police stations were being attacked. And we were running out of tear gas. We didn't have the four stages of dealing with protesters.
>
> Around 2:25 p.m., my captain told me that [General Jalel] Boudriga ordered us to cock and load our weapons. But I told them no, just use the remaining tear gas (there were maybe 50 canisters left).
>
> Moments later I learned that the Trabelsis were at the airport trying to leave the country. I thought, if they leave, there would be no solution left. We were already at the point of no return. If they leave, and take out all their money, what would happen once the people found out? It would have been a catastrophe. They would attack everything—the airport, the ministries. The police already had a bad reputation, this [letting them go] would only confirm it."[47]

In Tarhouni's assessment, the regime was already on its last legs. The police were overextended, there was a shortage of ammunition, and as he noted earlier, some police had already given up. At this point, with the police depleted and exhausted, Tarhouni believed that there was only "a 5 percent chance" that the regime could "win" by killing protesters.[48] And if the Trabelsis left, protests would escalate, and the regime—including the police—would be finished. Tarhouni therefore decided to seize the opportunity, head to the airport, and stop the Trabelsis from leaving. "The plan was to broadcast this live to say that we have this group as hostages as

---

[47] Interview with Samir Tarhouni, Tunis, January 18, 2019.
[48] Gallopin (2019, p. 18).

a final gesture of being on the side of the people, and to exert pressure at these final moments."[49] "If the Tunisian people realize what I was doing, there would be a million people at the airport supporting me."[50]

Conveniently, Tarhouni's wife, an air traffic controller, had been able to delay the Trabelsis' flight long enough for Tarhouni and 11 of his men to arrive at the airport around 2:50 p.m. and capture them.[51] Learning of what Tarhouni had done, Ben Ali issued a state of emergency at 3 p.m., which put the military in charge of the country's security. Army Chief Rachid Ammar, who enjoyed the trust of Ben Ali, was thus placed at the head of the operations room of the Ministry of Interior.

The minister of defense, Ridha Grira, sought to free the hostages by force. At 3:55, he ordered the air force chief, Taieb Laadjimi, to fly in the army special forces from Bizerte, and at 4:43 ordered Ammar to kill Tarhouni if needed. Ammar replied that a firefight in the airport would be too dangerous and that he would try to negotiate instead.

At this point, Tarhouni's rebellious band of 12 had grown to 170. He had called in reinforcements from the BAT, reaching 60, and then secured the defection of Colonel Zouheir El Ouefi, the head of the rapid intervention brigades (BNIR), who brought another 50. Upon hearing the arrival of the army special forces at the Aouina barracks, Tarhouni realized he would need additional support.[52] He thus convinced Colonel Larbi Lakhal, the head of the national guard special unit (USGN), to abandon their posts outside the presidential palace and also join his rebellion. It is no coincidence that even during a mutiny, the fault lines that emerged pitched the military on the one hand and the top units of the Ministry of Interior on the other—the regime's counterbalancing structured even how it broke down in its final hours.

At 5 p.m., Jalel Boudriga, the head of the MOI's intervention units and Tarhouni's immediate superior, was sent to mediate. Boudriga confirmed that Ouefi and Lakhal had joined Tarhouni, but that they would hand over the Trabelsis to the army in the presence of the media. Ammar then reported to Seriati that "it is indeed a mutiny by the police and the national guard."[53]

In light of the mutiny, and fearing clashes between the mutineers and the army,[54] Seriati concluded to Ben Ali, "Mr. President, I am now unable to ensure your security in Tunisia." At 5:47 p.m., Ben Ali decided to flee the country, thinking he would return once the situation stabilized. As further evidence that Ammar had remained loyal until the end, Ben Ali from the plane at 8:20 p.m. called Ammar once more, inquiring whether the situation was now safe enough for his return. "I can't tell you anything yet, Mr. President. The situation is not clear."[55] Ben Ali would remain in exile in Saudi Arabia until his death in 2019.

[49] Tarhouni (2011).
[50] Interview with Samir Tarhouni, Tunis, January 18, 2019.
[51] Tarhouni (2011).
[52] Nawaat (2011).
[53] Ammar (2011).
[54] Gallopin (2019, p. 20).
[55] Ammar (2011, p. 310).

Aftermath

In short, the marginalization and counterbalancing of the military contributed to the military's shirking during the uprising, the overextension of the security forces, the credibility of the military's rumored defection, and ultimately Ben Ali's collapse. The immediate aftermath of the 2011 revolution sheds further light on these dynamics, reinforcing that it was indeed marginalization and counterbalancing, and not just, for instance, conscription or culture, that had shaped the military's behavior during the uprising.

First, although the military had shirked in defending sensitive locations under Ben Ali, with the lower ranks refusing to use force against civilians, the military did use force to ensure security in the wake of his ouster. The Bouderbala Commission found that the army killed 32 people in the days after Ben Ali fled, compared to none during the uprising itself.[56] That 32 was in fact more than the police, national guard, or presidential guard. While the military may have shirked during Ben Ali's regime, they did not immediately afterwards, suggesting that resentment toward Ben Ali may have indeed been shaping their behavior.

Second, the decades of counterbalancing the military likewise manifested itself after the revolution in several cases of clashes between the military and other security forces. At the presidential palace, the military reportedly fought off Ben Ali loyalists in the presidential guard in the days after the revolution. In addition, the *New York Times* reported on January 16 that "the military had called in reinforcements as it battled other security forces in the southern part of the country."[57] *The Guardian* on the same day reported soldiers clashing with loyalist police officers at the Interior Ministry and the Central Bank.[58]

Beyond these clashes, there are also a number of more isolated incidents of military personnel killing members of the security forces, seemingly out of revenge. In their final report, the Truth and Dignity Commission documented at least four such incidents, the first of which I reproduce in full below:

- **January 15, 2011:** After finishing their duty, and on their way back to the National Guard station of Fouchana, the national guard patrol was met with a military patrol that included officers Mohamed Fazzani, Bachir Mzoughi, Aymen Nouri, Mehrez Harrathi, Mohamed Amdouni, and Aymen Chihi. The national guards noticed that the military patrol proceeded to arrest the pickup belonging to Badreddine Jebassi and forced its passengers to lie down. So the national guards decided to stop and get out of their Mitsubishi car in order to inform the military patrol that they already checked these people, but four soldiers came to them and pointed their weapons towards them, despite the fact that they have identified themselves as national guards. However, the military officers deliberately harassed them, forced them to lie down, and assaulted them. A few moments later, another military officer, Colonel Abdelaziz Tlili, came

<hr>

[56] Bouderbala (2012).
[57] Kirkpatrick (2011*a*).
[58] Chrisafis (2011).

up and continued to harass them, then Sergeant Aymen Nouri and Colonel Abdelaziz Tlili deliberately fired live bullets at them, resulting in the injury of Mohamed Rezgui with gunshot wounds that caused his death, and the injury of Captain Khalid Sandid and Chief Warrant Mouldi Dridi with gunshot wounds at the level of their right thighs. Additionally, both agents Sahbi Doula and Moqded Ouerghmi were assaulted with extreme violence.[59]

While this and other attacks by the military on the national guard and police may have been isolated incidents, the number of clashes between them in the wake of Ben Ali's ouster suggests that these forces were competing for dominance or even airing out grievances built up over decades of counterbalancing. In short, the military's behavior immediately after Ben Ali's ouster, during which it used force against other security forces and against civilians, suggests that its counterbalancing and marginalization under Ben Ali were indeed driving its lack of desire to defend his regime during the revolution.

Counter-explanations

While the preponderance of evidence lends support to Ben Ali's coup-proofing being the cause of the military's shirking, there are at least two counter-explanations worth considering. First, a number of observers have argued that it was the Tunisian military's foreign training, primarily in Western countries, that led it to stand by the people.[60] This narrative is occasionally echoed by Tunisian officers themselves. As one brigadier-general explained:

> "It was a Tunisian political decision that the training of the Tunisian Army takes place in the West. That has given a certain spirit to the Tunisian Army which does not take any training in any other countries like Russia, etc. This choice made the Tunisian Army save the revolution. Most of the officers do their training depending on their respective specialties in France, Germany, European countries as a whole, and in the US. That is what has given the Tunisian military and the officers a democratic thinking since the dawn of independence."[61]

A second argument made by both scholars and officers is that their extensive participation in UN peacekeeping missions may likewise have imbued a sense of professionalism.[62] As another brigadier-general argued:

> "The most important part is our involvement in peacekeeping. We learned how to react and how to behave in tense moments, like in times of revolution. In certain moments, like 2011, when you see military [personnel] standing in the street,

[59] IVD (2019, p. 352).
[60] Blair (2012); Brooks (2013, 2016); Taylor (2014).
[61] Interview with retired Brigadier-General Jamal Boujah, Tunis, January 9, 2018.
[62] Albrecht (2020).

not under anyone's supervision, they are responsible for their reactions. When we speak of the neutrality of the Tunisian military, their education, their ethics, it comes from their missions all over the world, especially from PKOs. We learned a lot about how to stabilize the situation."[63]

These arguments, however, have a difficult time explaining the behavior of the Tunisian military. First, they are both constants, and so cannot explain why the Tunisian military was more willing to use force to ensure security following Ben Ali's ouster. Second, the police and national guard also received a considerable degree of Western training as well as engagement in UN peacekeeping operations, and yet were more willing to repress protesters. Finally, two of the most high-profile individuals who were ordering the repression of protesters—President Ben Ali and head of the presidential guard Ali Seriati—were both ex-military officers who had received years of training in the West. As Ware (1988, p. 593) recounts: "Ben Ali attended Saint-Cyr and the French Artillery School at Chalons-sur-Marne. In the course of his career he perfected his studies in artillery at Fort Bliss, Texas, and graduated from the Intelligence and Military Security course at Fort Holabird, Maryland, eventually earning a degree in electrical engineering." Ali Seriati likewise did his initial military education at Saint-Cyr, and returned later to France to obtain a degree in military engineering.[64] While we cannot rule them out entirely, it is difficult to claim that Western training or involvement in peacekeeping is why the Tunisian military did not fire.

Conclusion

The Tunisian military's behavior during the 2011 revolution is one of the most misunderstood aspects of the country's transition. Contrary to early reports of the military's defection from Ben Ali, as well as revisionist readings of the military's loyalty to Ben Ali, this chapter argues that the truth is in between. While senior officers like Rachid Ammar were loyal until the end, the junior officers and soldiers on the ground instead shirked in their duties to defend vital institutions, refusing to use force to defend elements of a regime that had neglected, counterbalanced, and discriminated against them. At the same time, the military's professionalism led these disgruntled officers and soldiers not to openly refuse orders or seek to topple Ben Ali themselves, but simply to step aside as protesters did the job for them.

Ben Ali's relations with the military not only left him without their help, but also indirectly contributed to the hollowing out of his feared police forces. His delay in deploying the military sapped the energies of the police, while his diversion of police resources to monitoring the military undermined their capacity to deal with protesters. As the military shirked, the police saw their stations destroyed by protesters and their equipment damaged or stolen. With the military shirking,

[63] Interview with officer, Tunis, January 2016.
[64] Interview with Ali Seriati, Tunis, January 22, 2019.

rumors of its defection became credible, breeding desertions and eventually a mutiny in the security forces that ultimately led Ben Ali to flee.

In short, even though the military did not give Ben Ali the velvet shove, its unwillingness to defend the regime contributed in multiple ways to his collapse. His choice of coup-proofing strategy had left him vulnerable to an overthrow by the masses. Those same coup-proofing strategies would subsequently shape the military's willingness to defend the democratic transition.

10
Tunisia: Supporting the Transition

What I discovered was that Ben Ali was so afraid of the military that they were not equipped at all to fight terrorism. They didn't have anything. So I began to discuss with them to bring some material from the US, to bring some helicopters and equipment. This was a real revolution in the army.
—**President Moncef Marzouki (2011–2014)**[1]

Introduction

After decades of a "democratic deficit" in the Middle East, Tunisia after the Arab Spring emerged as a success story. It was the only revolution in the region to survive the volatile, transitional years, find consensus over a new constitution, and begin to practice democracy. For ten years, its progress was praised as a "beacon of hope" and "model for the Arab world," even earning the country a Nobel Peace Prize in 2015. While its democracy would later be rocked by an incumbent takeover, its ten years of progress still stands as an exception to the region. How did Tunisia break the mold?

Existing explanations for the success of Tunisia's initial transition to democracy (2011–2015) emphasize its modestly high level of development,[2] education,[3] homogenous population,[4] strength of civil society,[5] and culture of compromise and reform.[6] These accounts, while undoubtedly important, tend to romanticize the Tunisian transition as inclusive and consensual. In this rosy narrative, the Tunisian people, highly educated, well-off, and culturally predisposed to compromise, remained committed to democracy and the success of their transition.

The reality, however, is a bit more complex. Two years into the transition, a majority of Tunisians had actually grown disillusioned with democracy, seeing it bring only economic crisis, political polarization, and growing insecurity. After a military coup reversed Egypt's democratic transition, Tunisia faced widespread calls demanding a repeat of the Egyptian scenario in Tunisia. Despite their level of development, education, and political culture, opposition elites and protesters even made direct contact

---

[1] Interview with former President Moncef Marzouki, June 22, 2016.
[2] Rapanos (2018).
[3] Sanborn and Thyne (2014).
[4] Brown (2014).
[5] Netterstrøm (2016); Yousfi (2018); Hartshorn (2019); and Bishara (2020).
[6] Stepan (2012, 2016); Masri (2017).

Soldiers of Democracy?. Sharan Grewal, Oxford University Press. © Sharan Grewal (2023).
DOI: 10.1093/oso/9780192873910.003.0010

with the military asking for a coup. Tunisia in the summer of 2013 seemed ripe for following Egypt's path.

But the Tunisian military chose not to intervene. Without the help of the military, the opposition was unable to overthrow the elected government and was forced to instead come to the negotiating table, facilitating a grand bargain that put the transition back on track. The behavior of the military during Tunisia's transition is therefore one of if not the critical element to explaining why the Tunisian transition succeeded. Why didn't the Tunisian military intervene in the summer of 2013?

I argue that the military's refusal to overthrow democracy in a military coup was driven by its corporate interests, its political preferences, and its professional norms. First, since independence, the Tunisian military had been marginalized and counterbalanced by the internal security forces. Democratization, however, incentivized transitional governments to invest into the neglected military and grant it an advisory role in security decisions, generating support within the military for the transition. Second, previous autocrats Bourguiba and Ben Ali had privileged a minority of military officers who hailed from the coastal regions in promotions. Democratization incentivized the end of this regional discrimination, elevating for the first time discriminated officers from the interior regions to head the armed forces. Finally, the apolitical professionalism that the Tunisian military developed while marginalized under dictatorship likewise discouraged it from staging a coup. While the counterbalancing forces that previous autocrats had privileged—the national guard, presidential guard, and coastal military officers—may have had sufficient support for a coup from the public, *they* now found themselves counterbalanced by the majority of the military who were gaining from and thus supportive of democracy. The coup-proofing strategies chosen by previous dictators therefore had important authoritarian legacies shaping the success of Tunisia's transition.

Beyond providing a new explanation for the Tunisian success story, this chapter also helps generate a broader theoretical argument about the effects of autocratic coup-proofing strategies on subsequent democratization. While empowerment undermined democracy in Egypt, the case of Tunisia suggests that marginalization—including tactics like counterbalancing and discrimination—may be more conducive to democratic survival. Both tactics lead the majority of the military to resent autocracy, and both can easily be—and often naturally will be—reversed over the course of a transition. Democratization creates normative, electoral, and strategic incentives to strengthen a marginalized military and to move toward meritocratic promotions. As a result, militaries that have historically been subject to marginalization should be readily co-opted into the new democratic order.

General Rachid Ammar

The rumor that General Rachid Ammar had refused to fire on protesters made him a hero overnight. In the wake of Ben Ali's ouster, Rachid Ammar became, in the words of *The New York Times*, "the most powerful and the most popular figure in Tunisia."[7]

---

[7] Kirkpatrick (2011*a*).

He was lionized in Tunisian media as the "hero of the revolution," while popular rappers who had been the anthem of the uprising even called on him to take power.[8]

Politicians reportedly did the same. "I was consistently and repeatedly offered the presidency," Ammar would later tell *Ettounsiya* in a live TV interview. "Everyone [asked me]: [prime minister] Mohamed Ghannouchi, [interior minister] Hamed Friaa, [defense minister] Ridha Grira [. . .]. Yet I said no. I refused not because I did not want to become president, but because I was afraid for Tunisia. [. . .] I believed that the right path to secure the country and its future was to follow the clauses of our constitution."[9]

Accordingly, the presidency transferred, constitutionally, to the speaker of the parliament, Fouad Mebazaa, while Ben Ali's prime minister, Mohamed Ghannouchi, remained in his post. However, as protests continued against these remnants of the Ben Ali regime, these interim rulers asked Ammar to diffuse the crisis by publicly lending them his support. In recognition of Ammar's role as the key powerbroker, they asked Ammar "to use his popularity to clear the square," explained one colonel-major.[10] Addressing the protesters in the Kasbah on January 24, Ammar pleaded with them to "let this government work," while promising them that the army would protect the revolution. "Our revolution is your revolution . . . [The army is] the guarantor of the youth revolution and will ensure that it arrives safely."[11]

That promise to defend the revolution would later be invoked by protesters in 2013 to beg Ammar to take power. But for now, Ammar continued to work behind the scenes. After all, there was no need to assume an official political position. For all intents and purposes, Ammar had become the center of power. "For any problem, everyone would refer to Rachid Ammar," explained one politician. "He was governing the country."[12]

"After the revolution the army was very well-positioned," admitted a retired brigadier-general who was serving alongside Ammar. "Most of the politicians from the period of Ben Ali had gone. Rachid Ammar was the only figure that knew how to run the government. And at the time, the problems were security matters: how to confront the deteriorating situation in the south, what to do with Libyan refugees, how to respond to a large strike or protest. In practice, though not legally, Rachid Ammar was the man calling the shots."[13]

Belying his stated commitment to the constitution, Ammar took on a much larger role than prescribed by law. Ammar informally acted as the minister of defense, regularly attending ministerial meetings. "Everybody knew that the real minister of

---

[8] The rapper Guitoh in his song *A5er tanbih* [The last warning] proclaims: "I demand that the army organize a coup d'état. [. . .] We need men in power like Rachid ben Ammar [sic]." He even warns interim rulers Mebazaa and Ghannouchi of a "scenario 87," referring to Ben Ali's removal of Bourguiba. See https://www.youtube.com/watch?v=jt3HrX1mgos.

[9] Rachid Ammar's interview with *Ettounsiya*, June 24, 2013. See https://www.youtube.com/watch?v=Pf3dvxdhm-s.

[10] Interview with retired Colonel-Major Mahmoud Mezoughi, Tunis, October 9, 2015.

[11] Quoted in *Jeune Afrique* (2011a). Watch his speech here. https://www.youtube.com/watch?v=5RA5EEKvckk.

[12] Interview with CPR co-founder Fethi Jerbi, Tunis, September 17, 2015. Quoted also in Grewal (2016).

[13] Interview with a retired officer, Tunis, November 2015. Quoted also in Grewal (2016).

defense was Rachid Ammar, and not Mr. Abdelkarim Zbidi," noted the at-the-time inspector general, General Mohamed Ali El Bekri.[14]

Beyond the Ministry of Defense, Ammar also exerted considerable influence over the Ministry of Interior, working closely with the newly appointed minister Farhat Rajhi. "After Ben Ali left, I spent roughly 52 days going every day to the Ministry of Interior, as Mr. Farhat Rajhi kept calling me every day to go there and discuss the situation," Ammar recalled. "At that period, I spent most of the time in the Ministry of Interior instead of Defense!"[15]

With this influence over both ministries, Ammar began to rebalance the military vis-à-vis its former rivals. With revolutionary fervor raging in the streets, the interim government moved against the police and national guard, which had earned the ire of protesters for having employed repression under Ben Ali. On February 2, five days into office,[16] Interior Minister Rajhi purged 42 senior security officials, including all 26 members of the General Directorate of National Security.[17] In their place, Rajhi brought in the military: Brigadier-General Ahmed Chabir, former director of military security, was installed as the MOI's new director general of national security (DGSN), and was reportedly given "orders to purge stalwarts of Ben Ali's regime" from key positions.[18] By the end of the month, Army Colonel Moncef Helali was also appointed commander of the national guard. One month after the revolution, military officers were now in direct command of their former rivals in the Ministry of Interior.

Military officers were likewise elevated to civilian positions formerly out of reach. In Ben Ali's entire 23-year reign, only two military officers ever became governors.[19] Already in February 2011, six active-duty officers were appointed as governors, primarily in restive regions that were experiencing continued protests: Hassen Ftouhi in Sidi Bouzid, Omar Ben Haj Slimane in Kasserine, Mohamed Sahraoui in Kairouan, Mohamed Fawzi Jaoui in Sousse, Mondher Yedas in Gabes, and Salah Sebai in Kebili.[20]

On the ground as well, it was the military that was taking the lead in ensuring security. After having been "imprisoned" in the barracks under Ben Ali, rarely used for security, now the military was taking over most police functions, including in the capital. On a number of occasions this even meant clashing with rogue elements of Ben Ali loyalists in the police and former ruling party who were attempting to wreak havoc across the country.[21]

---

[14] Interview with retired Inspector General of the Armed Forces General Mohamed Ali El Bekri, Tunis, November 28, 2015. Quoted also in Grewal (2016).

[15] Rachid Ammar's interview with *Ettounsiya*, June 24, 2013.

[16] Rajhi's decision to purge the ministry came soon after he was attacked by a mob of 3,000 people, allegedly disgruntled police officers, on January 31, narrowly escaping only with Ammar's help. See El Fekih (2011) and Amara (2011).

[17] See Agence France-Presse (2011) and Sayigh (2015).

[18] Agence France-Presse (2011). Chabir would be sacked on March 1 due to disagreements with Rajhi.

[19] Boubaker BenKraiem, who served as governor of Sidi Bouzid (1990–1991) and then Kef (1991–1992); and Mahmoud Lajnef, who briefly served as governor of Gafsa in 1994.

[20] See La Presse (2011) and Kapitalis (2012).

[21] See, e.g., Amara (2011).

This trend of elevating the military relative to the security forces would continue over the next several months. In March, the interim government dissolved the most notorious police forces: the directorate of state security [*amn al-dawla*] as well as the inspection superior and the university security [*amn jamai'i*]. While the police were weakened, the military was further strengthened. In April, Rachid Ammar was promoted from army chief of staff to armed forces chief of staff, a powerful, centralized position that Ben Ali had denied the military for 20 years and that now gave Ammar command over the navy and air force, as well.

Military officers, meanwhile, continued to be appointed into senior civilian positions. In June, Brigadier General Faouzi Aloui became the director general of prisons and rehabilitation in the Ministry of Justice. In July, Colonel Major Mohamed Abdennaceur Belhaj was appointed the director general of customs in the Ministry of Finance—the second military officer ever in that position.[22] In August, two additional military officers were appointed as governors: Bechir Bedoui in Kasserine and Nejib El Ghali in Tataouine.

Not surprisingly, these developments did not sit well with the police and national guard. "After the revolution, there was a marginalization of the security forces," lamented one retired national guard colonel-major. "It was an opportunity for revenge. The intent was to weaken the Ministry of Interior."[23] Rachid Ammar "is a cardboard hero," claimed a police officer, Issam Dardouri. He "tried to demonize the security forces."[24]

Their rapid reversal from a position of power to one of weakness led the security forces over the course of 2011 to form unions to try to defend themselves from further security sector reform.[25] Several of these unions attempted to push back against their newly appointed military leaders. In September, national guard officers organized by the National Union of Internal Security Forces demanded the resignation of their commander, army Colonel Moncef Helali, among other reasons due to his "status as a soldier."[26] Helali was in turn sacked on December 1 and replaced by one of their own, national guard inspector-general Montasser Al-Skouhi. Separately, hundreds of police officers also protested in September against Rachid Ammar, calling for his immediate resignation and claiming that he sought to seize power.[27]

In short, the transitional year following Ben Ali's ouster saw the start of a rebalancing between the military and security forces. While the military was gaining from democracy, the security forces were being made worse off. These trends of rebalancing the military and reversing its marginalization would then be continued by Tunisia's first democratically elected government.

---

[22] The first was Abdelkader Ammar in the early 1990s. See Leaders (2011).

[23] Interview with retired national guard officer, Tunis, February 2018.

[24] Quoted in Tuniscope (2015).

[25] See more on the unions, see Grewal (2018*b*).

[26] See *Espace Manager* (2011).

[27] See AFP (2011). This incident prompted the interim prime minister, Beji Caid Essebsi, to ban police unions, but he soon reversed his decision.

The Troika Government

Like in Egypt, the 2011 elections were won by an Islamist party, *Harakat Ennahda* (the Renaissance movement). And like in Egypt, the expectation that Ennahda might win had prompted fears of an 'Algerian scenario'—that the military might step in to cancel the elections. In May 2011, interior minister Farhat Rajhi, who had worked closely with Ammar, warned that "if Ennahda takes power, there will be a coup d'etat."[28] Rajhi in particular warned that a clique of "Saheliens"—those hailing from the wealthy coastal regions—would ask Ammar (who also hailed from the Sahel) to step in should the Islamists win.[29]

Like in Egypt, however, the elections were allowed to proceed, which Ennahda then swept with 37 percent of the vote, winning 41 percent of seats. But while Egypt's military council denied the parliament the right to form the government, in Tunisia, the military did not have such vested interests to preserve. Ennahda was therefore permitted to form a government, and thus, unlike the Muslim Brotherhood, had to secure a formal alliance to reach a majority.

Ennahda formed a coalition government with two secular parties, the Congress for the Republic (CPR) and Ettakatol. In this "troika" government, as it came to be known, Ennahda's Hamadi Jebali became the prime minister, CPR's Moncef Marzouki assumed the presidency, and Ettakatol's Mustapha Ben Jaafar headed the constituent assembly.

Going into office, the leaders of the troika government did not have a prepared strategy for dealing with the military and police. But their perceptions were much more positive towards the former. "Our image of the police was very negative," noted Prime Minister Hamadi Jebali. "We had been victims of the police. Our image of the army was much better. It did not engage in torture, etc. like the Egyptian army or others. And it did not take over when there was vacuum of power."[30]

The leaders of the troika thus trusted the army more than they trusted the police. In addition, they were also conscious of how Bourguiba and Ben Ali had intentionally weakened the military. Jebali continued:

> "We had an institution that was weak, did not have much ability, and was far from politics. This is a result of its history. The army did not have a big role during the opposition to colonialism, before colonialism, or after colonialism. There was also a policy of Bourguiba [. . .] Bourguiba did not like the military. He wanted to weaken the military. He weaponized the police and the national guard—the national guard was in the Ministry of Interior! [. . .] Ben Ali was from the army, but he arrived at the same conclusion to keep the army far. He undertook a coup, and then feared a coup. So he used the security [forces] to fend off the army—and [to fend off] the opposition!"[31]

---

[28] Quoted in Ryan (2011).
[29] In a 2021 *Al-Jazeera* documentary, Hamadi Jebali also revealed that Ammar told him that several people called him on election day and asked him to act.
[30] Interview with former Prime Minister Hamadi Jebali, Sousse, December 17, 2015.
[31] Interview with former Prime Minister Hamadi Jebali, Sousse, December 17, 2015.

Cognizant of these dynamics, the leaders of the troika knew they needed to substantially reform the security sector. On the one hand, the police needed to be weakened and kept far from political power: "We could not keep it as it was before, as a political police," Jebali argued. The military, meanwhile, needed to be strengthened after what Bourguiba and Ben Ali had done to it. That, moreover, was what the troika believed the people wanted: "The image of the military was huge among the people," Jebali observed. "Especially because of its role in the revolution. The people wanted this institution increased. It wasn't the same for the police and national guard."[32]

Accordingly, the troika continued the policies that began in 2011 of rebalancing the military vis-à-vis the security forces. The military was largely given autonomy over its sphere, with Prime Minister Jebali leaving Defense Minister Zbidi in his post and granting General Ammar wide latitude in the military's affairs. By contrast, the troika took a much more interventionist role with the security forces. Ennahda's Ali Laarayedh assumed the post of interior minister, and attempted at least initially to shake up the ministry, forcing into early retirement between 80 and 130 security officials.[33] Laarayedh most notably dismissed the director general of the intervention units, Colonel Moncef Laajimi, who was at the time on trial for killing protesters during the 2011 revolution.[34]

Indeed, while the police tended to be the target of transitional justice, the military was largely unaffected, due to its lack of involvement in Ben Ali's repression. In some cases, military officers were even the beneficiary. A major push was made by the troika government to rectify Ben Ali's purge of 244 military personnel in the 1991 Baraket Essahel affair (see Chapter 8). On June 23, 2012, on the armed forces' fifty-sixth anniversary, President Moncef Marzouki delivered an official state apology for the affair, clearing them of any wrongdoing, and symbolically elevating their ranks by 2–3 promotions.[35] Separately, Ennahda also elevated a handful of the expelled military officers who had been involved in the November 8th group—the Islamist coup plot planned for 1987. Mohamed Sidhom, who had been an army captain at the time, was appointed governor of Jendouba in February 2012, and subsequently governor of Kasserine from August 2012 to February 2014. Others were incorporated elsewhere into the civilian bureaucracy or municipal governments.[36]

Beyond transitional justice, the troika government also elevated active-duty officers in two major ways. First, the troika continued the post-revolution trend of appointing military officers into senior civilian positions. Brigadier-General Mohamed Meddeb, for instance, was appointed as the new director general of customs in September 2012. The same month, Colonel-Major Brahim Ouechtati was appointed as a presidential advisor. These appointments marked a stark contrast from

---

[32] Interview with former Prime Minister Hamadi Jebali, Sousse, December 17, 2015.

[33] See International Crisis Group (2015, p. 12).

[34] After pushback from police unions, Laarayedh was forced to transfer Laajimi to a consultant position. See Grewal (2018b, pp. 3–4).

[35] While they were not reinstated into the military, their pensions were made commensurate with their new ranks. See law 2014–28 of June 2014.

[36] Second Lieutenant Sifi Tlili was appointed delegate (*mu'tamid* or *délégué*) of Sijoumi in Tunis and then Hebira in Mahdia, and Navy First Lieutenant Fathi al-Hafsi was appointed delegate of Bir Mcherga in Zaghouan and then Kondar in Sousse. Captain Sassi Bettayeb became head of the Ministry of Transportation's regional transport company in Medenine. See also Grewal (2020b, p. 68).

the Ben Ali era, and suggested that the military's gains in 2011 might continue even after that exceptional year.

The second and perhaps most important way the troika government elevated the army was by granting it a role in policy deliberations. Under Ben Ali, most security decisions were made by Ben Ali alone or in consultation with the head of his presidential guard, Ali Seriati. It was a top-down, "personal rule," said one army officer.[37] Ben Ali had rarely called upon the National Security Council, denying the military a channel for providing input into policy deliberations.

That absence of the military in security policy shifted immediately under the troika, where the military gained the political role Huntington (1957, p. 16) described as "the responsibility of expert advisor." Prime Minister Jebali consulted weekly with a security council featuring the ministers of defense, interior, and foreign affairs; the top security officials; and the top two military officers—the chief of staff of the armed forces (Rachid Ammar) and the director general of military security (Kamel Akrout).[38] By fall 2012, President Moncef Marzouki had likewise reactivated Ben Ali's National Security Council, meeting with it about monthly, and often inviting the top five officers, including the chiefs of staff of the navy (Mohamed Khamassi) and air force (Mohamed Nejib Jelassi) as well as the inspector-general (Taieb Laajimi). As already mentioned, Marzouki in September 2012 also appointed for the first time a military advisor to the president (Brahim Ouechtati), institutionalizing a role for the military in the presidency itself.[39] The top military officers could thus now routinely provide their advice and judgment to civilian policymakers through these institutionalized channels. Such a role for the military is normal in a democracy, but given the legacy of Ben Ali, represented a relative elevation in the military's influence.

The Salafist Challenge

This new system of managing the military gave senior officers direct and regular input into national security policy. But the top generals and the troika government did not always see eye to eye, prompting the troika to fear the potential for a coup. A major sticking point was over how to deal with Ansar al-Sharia, a salafist group that had emerged in the wake of the revolution.

The troika believed that Ansar al-Sharia would moderate over time if given space and allowed to participate freely in political and religious activities. But the military and security forces thought otherwise. Rafik Abdessalem, foreign minister in the troika from Ennahda, noted that: "The intelligence information from the military and MOI were saying to the civilians you have to be careful, not just about their religious activities, but that they have a strategy of violence, [. . .] making trainings and getting military equipment from Libya. The military institutions and security forces were very aware at the time of the dangerous aspects of Ansar al-Sharia."[40]

---

[37] Interview with retired officer, Tunis, October 2015.
[38] Interview with former Prime Minister Hamadi Jebali, Sousse, December 17, 2015.
[39] For more on the intra-troika dynamics that produced these decisions, see Grewal (2016, pp. 6–7).
[40] Interview with former Foreign Minister Rafik Abdessalam, Tunis, February 10, 2018.

Indeed, in April 2012, Ennahda leader Rached Ghannouchi had warned the salafists that if they moved too quickly, they'd risk provoking an Algerian scenario. "Secularists still control the economy, the media and the administration," Ghannouchi told salafi youth in a leaked video. "The army and police also are not guaranteed [*madmūn*]."[41]

These fears of a potential coup would escalate further on September 14, 2012, when Ansar al-Sharia attacked the US embassy in Tunis, just three days after its Libyan counterpart had killed the US Ambassador Chris Stevens in Benghazi. Up until this point, the troika had not taken seriously the security threat posed by the salafists, and had accordingly deployed only a small contingent of police officers to defend the US embassy. Those agents were quickly overwhelmed.

"We had expected just demonstrations," noted Foreign Minister Abdessalem. "But when people reached the embassy and targeted it, it was quite clear it is becoming quite dangerous, bearing in mind what happened in Benghazi."[42]

Ali Laarayedh, the minister of interior, ordered additional police reinforcements. But they were slow to respond, prompting the troika to believe that the police were intentionally conspiring to undermine the government. "The security forces were very slow," said Abdessalem. "How to explain this? A lack of professionalism? Psychological aspects of the security forces becoming more passive after the collapse of the Ben Ali regime? Or was it calculated by certain forces of the MOI?"[43]

As the situation escalated, US Secretary of State Hillary Clinton called President Marzouki after having been unable to reach Prime Minister Jebali, and pressed him to send in reinforcements. Marzouki in turn ordered the military to defend the embassy. But General Ammar "began to procrastinate," Marzouki would later tell *Al-Jazeera*. "I asked him where the army was, he told me that it took time . . . and then he asked for a written authorisation that I sent him and during that time things evolved quickly at the embassy."[44] Faced with what he termed "military disobedience," Marzouki then deployed the presidential guard, who finally succeeded in repelling the salafists.[45]

But friction with the top brass would not end there. Even after the attack, the troika continued to prefer dialogue with the salafists, and Marzouki invited several leaders of Ansar al-Sharia to the presidential palace in October.[46] Ammar and other secular, coastal officers vehemently disagreed. "Marzouki accepted in Carthage people who are terrorists!" exclaimed a former director general of military security. "During that period Ammar saw some contradictions [between Marzouki's words and deeds].

---

[41] See Amara (2012), and watch the video at: https://www.youtube.com/watch?v=5aFECUkDyug.

[42] Interview with former Foreign Minister Rafik Abdessalam, Tunis, February 10, 2018.

[43] Interview with former Foreign Minister Rafik Abdessalam, Tunis, February 10, 2018.

[44] Quoted in *Middle East Monitor* (2017). As Marzouki's chief of staff, Adnen Manser, emphasized, "The Aouina barracks are only 2 kilometers from the US embassy! [Ammar] didn't refuse, but he obeyed slowly. It was clear he didn't want to do it. [. . .] The tanks only arrived after the situation was resolved!" (Interview, Sousse, July 14, 2018).

[45] One army colonel major argued that Ammar refused because the troika had not taken the threat seriously and not asked the military to defend the embassy from the start. Interview, Tunis, October 2015.

[46] Marzouki now regrets this invitation, describing it as a mistake. See F. K. (2019).

Some generals believed that Marzouki, his party, and Ennahda, by their conduct, helped terrorism grow."[47] The civilians at the time could sense that disagreement with the military leaders. Marzouki observed that Ammar "was complaining all the time that we are not fighting sufficiently against terrorism, that we are accepting to discuss with salafists and so forth."[48]

These disagreements, and the resulting fear of a coup, intensified further after salafists assassinated the leftist politician Chokri Belaid in February 2013. The opposition held Ennahda responsible, and staged large protests during Belaid's funeral calling for the fall of the troika government. At the time, Defense Minister Zbidi, without Marzouki's consent, lent military helicopters to a private television station, Nessma TV, to help film the service.[49] As Nessma had been fervidly anti-troika, Marzouki interpreted this move as the beginning of a Zbidi-Ammar coup. As he later told *Al-Jazeera*, this appeared to be a "cinematic" attempt to dramatize and inflate the number of protesters, much like the Egyptian military's choreographing of June 30.[50]

But Zbidi was not the only one making implicitly political moves. General Ammar likewise entered the political fray to try to push the troika out. In the wake of the assassination, Jebali had formed a "Council of Elders" to discuss their options. Ammar, controversially part of the council, said he advised Jebali to have the troika step down and allow the formation of a technocratic government.[51] Ammar later justified his intervention by saying that while "the army should be totally separate and independent from politics," it also "has a commitment to protect the country."[52]

Concerned by these signals, the troika complied in part, reshuffling the cabinet to make Ennahda's Ali Laarayedh the new prime minister and bringing in a number of technocrats, for instance to run the Ministry of Interior. Marzouki also pushed Ennahda to replace Defense Minister Zbidi. His replacement, Rachid Sabbagh, a specialist in Islamic jurisprudence who previously headed the Higher Islamic Council, was a much less active defense minister. Indeed, when I interviewed Laarayedh in 2015 and Marzouki in 2016, neither could even remember his name. Marzouki said: "At that time, I decided that the minister would play no role, and that I would play the role [of defense minister]."[53] "A ministry can walk without a minister," Laarayedh told me.[54]

[47] Interview with former director general of military security, Tunis, November 5, 2015. Quoted also in Grewal (2016).

[48] Interview with President Moncef Marzouki, Tunis, June 22, 2016.

[49] Interviews with Presidential Spokesman Adnen Mansar, Tunis, September 22, 2015, and a retired brigadier-general, Tunis, November 5, 2015.

[50] Quoted in Kardi (2017). For June 30, see Chapter 7.

[51] Ammar later claimed: 'The assassination of Chokri Belaid could have signed the death certificate of the Tunisian state. Hamadi Jebali's initiative to form a government of technocrats was my idea to save the country from chaos." See Dahmani (2013).

[52] Rachid Ammar's interview with *Ettounsiya*, June 24, 2013.

[53] Interview with former President Moncef Marzouki, Tunis, June 22, 2016.

[54] Interview with former Prime Minister Ali Laarayedh, Tunis, December 7, 2015.

Recalibration

The new Laarayedh government made important changes in their strategy vis-à-vis the military to alleviate friction with the generals. First, the troika increasingly conceded to the generals' viewpoint that the salafists posed a major security threat. Already in December 2012, the troika tasked the military with rooting out Katiba Ukba Ibn Nafaa, a local branch of Al-Qaeda in the Maghreb (AQIM) who had set up camp in the Chaambi mountains. After the assassination of Chokri Belaid, the troika also began to crack down on Ansar al-Sharia. In May 2013, the troika deployed 11,000 soldiers and police officers in Kairouan to prevent Ansar al-Sharia from holding its third annual conference, calling the group "a threat to security and public order."[55]

Under Ben Ali, these counter-terrorism operations would have fallen primarily under the jurisdiction of the police and national guard—in particular, the Anti-Terrorism Brigade (BAT) and the National Guard Special Unit (USGN). The military would have been left "imprisoned" in the barracks, or if deployed, heavily monitored by the presidential guard like in the 2007 operation in Soliman. But now, under the troika, the military was playing a leading role, particularly in the Chaambi mountains.

According to Foreign Minister Abdessalam, this was an intentional policy of rebalancing the military vis-à-vis the security forces:

> "The military was not happy with the regime of Ben Ali. He used the military [only] as a tool under the umbrella of the security forces. [. . .] We [the troika government] gave more space for the military institutions. Even in fighting terrorism, I think the military played a vanguard role. This was not the case under the regime of Ben Ali."[56]

But deploying the military also required investing in it. As Marzouki recalled:

> "What I discovered was that Ben Ali was so afraid of the military that they were not equipped at all to fight terrorism. They didn't have anything. So I began to discuss with them to bring some material from the US, to bring some helicopters and equipment. This was a real revolution in the army."[57]

Indeed, the troika invested heavily into the military. In 2012, 2013, and 2014, the military's budget increased more quickly than any other ministry's. Table 10.1 reports the budget of the Ministry of Defense from 2011 to 2015, revealing that the defense budget on average increased by a staggering 24 percent each year after the revolution, about doubling in both absolute terms and as a share of the government's total

---

[55] See Ben Bouazza (2013*b*).
[56] Interview with former Foreign Minister Rafik Abdessalam, Tunis, February 10, 2018.
[57] Interview with former President Moncef Marzouki, Tunis, June 22, 2016.

Table 10.1 Ministry of Defense (MOD) Budget, 2011–2015 (in million TND)

Year	MOD	% Change	Share
2011	807	-	3.8
2012	1,046	30	4.1
2013	1,233	18	4.5
2014	1,564	27	5.7
2015	1,921	23	6.9
Average	-	**24**	-

budget.[58] "It is the ministry that has increased most since the revolution," Laarayedh said.[59]

Beyond this larger budget, the troika government also courted an influx of military aid, weapons, and joint trainings from foreign powers. Military aid from the US, for instance, jumped from $17.1 million in 2011 to $29.5 million in 2012, an increase of 73 percent. The troika also strengthened military ties with both Turkey and Qatar, signing security cooperation agreements with them in April and December 2012, respectively.[60]

"President Marzouki and the troika were very helpful," noted Air Force Chief of Staff Bechir Bedoui. "When we started fighting terrorism, we didn't have the equipment or armament. We needed goggles for night operations, helicopters—they cost millions of dollars. But they [the troika] invested! We bought Sikorsky [helicopters] for 700 million! I could not imagine they would do this. They gave us everything we asked for."[61]

The military's increasing involvement in counterterrorism not only bought the troika goodwill, but also provided Marzouki the opportunity he needed to maneuver Ammar out of his post. On June 6, 2013, two soldiers were killed and two others wounded by a roadside bomb in the Chaambi mountains. Parliamentarian Mohamed Abbou, President of the Democratic Current (a splinter party from Marzouki's CPR), held Ammar responsible, and publicly called for his resignation, arguing "it is inconceivable for the official to remain in his position when he failed in it."[62] As Marzouki began to hint at retiring the general, Ammar himself chose to resign on June 23 to avoid the image of being fired.

However, the fear of a coup would not dissipate with Ammar's resignation–indeed, it was just beginning. The day after he resigned, Ammar went on live TV to conduct

---

[58] In these years Tunisia passed both a standard annual budget in December the year prior, as well as a supplementary budget mid-year through. The figures in Table 10.1 reflect the entire year's funding, i.e., including the supplementary increase.

[59] Interview with former Prime Minister Ali Laarayedh, Tunis, December 7, 2015.

[60] For Turkey, see subsequent ratification by the Constituent Assembly (organic law 2013–38 of 7 October 2013), and for Qatar, see subsequent presidential decree (2013–3178 of July 31, 2013).

[61] Interview with retired Brigadier General Bechir Bedoui, Tunis, March 5, 2020.

[62] See Business News (2013).

a three-hour interview with *Ettounsiya*. Although he had submitted his resignation the day before, he showed up to the interview in military uniform, and criticized the troika government. Ammar claimed that the government was not doing enough to counter terrorism, and warned that Tunisia was accordingly at risk of becoming another Somalia. "The Somalisation of our country cannot be ruled out."[63]

Ammar's interview alarmed the troika government. Intentionally or not, it had sent a signal to the opposition that the military might be on their side, critical of the government. Marzouki believes that Ammar was trying to lay the groundwork for a De Gaulle-esque return to politics:

> "I think that Rachid Ammar was waiting for something. I think he knew that there would be a lot of trouble that summer, and that maybe they would call on him to restore order. He would appear like De Gaulle in France."[64]

Marzouki also claimed that he received an intelligence report stating that when Rachid Ammar was leaving the presidential palace after submitting his resignation, he was "very upset," and vowed to a presidential guard that "this is not goodbye—I will be back!"[65]

Knocking on the Barracks

The pivotal moments for Tunisia's transition then took place between July and September of 2013. One week after Ammar's interview, protests began in Egypt against President Mohamed Morsi. Three days later, the Egyptian military intervened to remove Morsi from office. Immediately afterwards, Tunisia faced widespread calls at both the mass and elite levels demanding a repeat of the Egyptian scenario in Tunisia. In a mirror image of how Tunisia's Jasmine Revolution diffused to Egypt, Egypt's military coup now emboldened the opposition in Tunisia to think that their military might also intervene.

Copycat groups of the Tamarod movement, which organized the June 30 protests in Egypt, began to form in Tunisia, while opposition elites coalesced into a National Salvation Front (NSF) as they had in Cairo. Popular Front Secretary-General Ammar Amrousi noted that "the victory of the Egyptian people [in ousting the Muslim Brotherhood] provides Tunisians with optimism and a high spirit to carry on with their struggle."[66] Emboldened by Egypt, opposition groups called on the troika government to resign and for the constituent assembly to be dissolved.

Politicians across the opposition spectrum expressed implicit support for military intervention. A review of the newspapers *al-Maghreb*, *al-Chorouk*, and *al-Tunisiyya* in the days after Egypt's coup finds representatives of every major opposition party

---

[63] Quoted in Dahmani (2013).
[64] Interview with former President Moncef Marzouki, Tunis, June 22, 2016.
[65] Interview with former President Moncef Marzouki, Tunis, June 22, 2016.
[66] Quoted in Parker (2013).

on record praising the toppling of Morsi and calling for a repeat of the Egyptian scenario.[67] These include: Mohamed Ali Nasri (Nidaa Tounes), Mohamed Brahmi (People's Movement), Zied Lakhdar (Democratic Patriots' Movement), Slim Riahi (Free Patriotic Union), Mohamed al-Hashmi Hamdi (Current of Love), and the executive bureaus of both the Socialist Party and the Workers Party. Indeed, as late as September 2013, Beji Caid Essebsi, the leader of the National Salvation Front, was threatening an Egypt-scenario if Ennahda did not step down.[68]

The media likewise appeared to be egging on a coup. The front page of the newspaper *Al-Maghreb* on July 5, two days after Egypt's coup, read: "The second wave of the Arab Revolutions: After Egypt, Tunisia Prepares . . ." On page 3, the newspaper then reports on "the General in third place," highlighting a poll that showed General Rachid Ammar third in voting intentions, with over three times as much popular support as President Marzouki.

The assassination of opposition politician Mohamed Brahmi on July 25—Tunisia's second political assassination in 2013—then added fuel to the fire, sparking massive protests and labor strikes across the country demanding the fall of the democratically elected troika government. The NSF and the Tunisian general labor union (UGTT) jointly staged a sit-in outside of the National Constituent Assembly in Bardo demanding its dissolution. These events prompted a major defection from the troika, with Mustapha Ben Jaafar, the speaker of the assembly, deciding to suspend its activities, paralyzing the sole elected institution. With mass protests, a second assassination, and an institutional vacuum, Tunisia in August 2013 seemed ripe for following Egypt's path.

Political elites also made direct contact with members of the military asking for a coup. A former inspector general of the armed forces—the third highest position in the military—recounted how two prominent leaders of Nidaa Tounes had begun courting him after Belaid's assassination, and asked openly after Brahmi's assassination about the possibility of a military takeover.[69] Similarly, the lawyer Nacer Laouini, speaking at Brahmi's funeral, publicly singled out the new army chief, General Mohamed Salah Hamdi, saying, "The head of the army is here [at the funeral]. We ask the army to be on the side of the people as it always has been and protect Tunisians against Ennahda."[70]

Beyond opposition elites, support for a coup ran high among the Tunisian public as well. On the day of the coup in Egypt, crowds gathered outside of the Egyptian embassy in Tunis and chanted: "Oh Rachid, oh Ammar, where is your promise to the revolutionaries?,"[71] referring to Armed Forces Chief of Staff Rachid Ammar's promise in January 2011 to "protect the revolution"—the same "justification" Egypt's military used to legitimize its coup. General Ammar was well aware of this public support

---

[67] Archives found in the National Documentation Center, Tunis.

[68] Essebsi was asked explicitly by NPR's Leila Fadel (2013) in September 2013, "Could Tunisia become Egypt, with the Islamists forced from power and persecuted by a military-backed regime?" He answered, "Now, no. But if we don't go forward, maybe yes."

[69] Interview with retired officer, Tunis, December 2015.

[70] See Ben Bouazza (2013a).

[71] See, e.g., https://twitter.com/Souihli/status/352535134739763202.

for an intervention. Videos show that during the funeral for Chokri Belaid, demonstrators surrounded Rachid Ammar in his car, calling Ghannouchi a killer, begging Ammar to rid the country of Ennahda, and chanting: "Oh Mr. Rachid, the people are with you!"[72]

Survey data suggest that this sentiment was shared by a wide swath of the public. Both the Afrobarometer, conducted in January 2013, and the World Values Survey, conducted in December 2013, found that 33 percent of Tunisians openly rated "having the military rule" as a "good" or "very good" way of running the country. Notably, this level of support for military rule should be seen as a lower bound of the true level of support, given that the Afrobarometer was conducted prior to the assassinations, and the World Values Survey was conducted long after protests had subsided.

Cross-nationally, Tunisia's 33 percent comes in above the average (31 percent) for the six countries for which survey data is available in the two years prior to a successful military coup. As Figure 10.1 demonstrates, Tunisia's level of public support for military rule was similar to Thailand before its 2014 coup (at 34 percent), and above Turkey before its 1997 coup (at 24 percent). Moreover, it is well above failed coups, for which the average level of public support was only 16 percent, suggesting that a coup in Tunisia in 2013 may have had sufficient public support to succeed.

Perhaps the most important evidence that there were sufficient calls for a coup was that the military itself felt pressure to intervene. Retired Colonel Major Mokhtar Ben

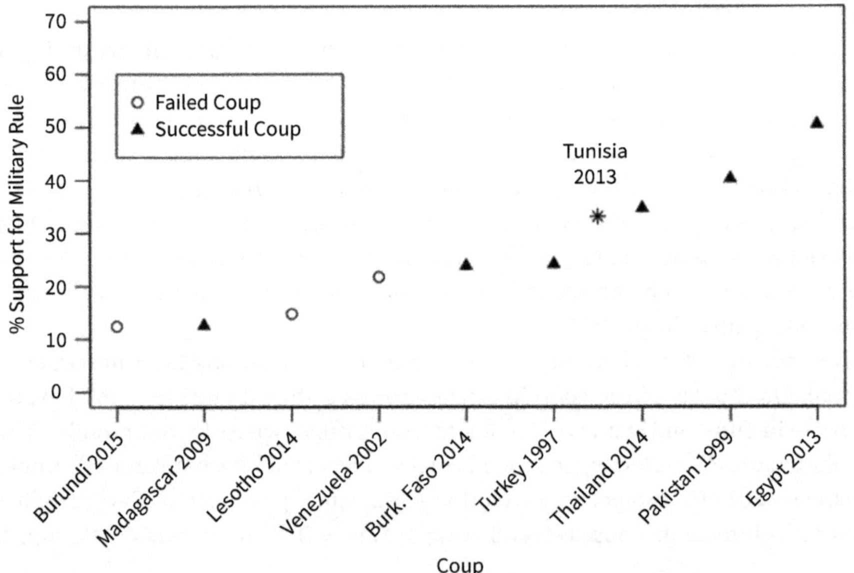

Figure 10.1 World Values Survey / Afrobarometer within 2 years before Military Coup

[72] https://www.youtube.com/watch?v=xP21dXw3j7w.

Nasr, who served as the Defense Ministry spokesman after the revolution, observed that:

> The street and conditions were calling for a coup. The people feared Ennahda would install a new type of dictatorship. They wanted a coup, and events in Egypt sent a message that maybe it is possible that our army would do the same.[73]

A former director general of military security, the second highest position in the military, agreed, noting that the warnings by opposition politicians to "look at Egypt" were an implicit "call for the military to intervene."[74] Brigadier-General Bechir Bedoui, the air force chief of staff in August 2013, noted that "we saw it on Facebook, and we heard it in person. Our families even—people would say take it, take the power, what are you waiting for? [...] Also on TV! When they [protesters] went close to the parliament, they said very clearly: we are waiting for 'communiqué No. 1,' meaning the army takes power!"[75]

With the exogenous shock of Egypt's coup galvanizing Tunisians to knock on the door of the barracks, the window for a coup had opened.

Positive Discrimination

Heading into summer 2013, the troika government had been fairly confident that the military would not seize this opportunity and stage a coup. Despite the signals they had received from General Ammar, they were confident that the majority of officers were professional and apolitical. And moreover, they had been enhancing the military's corporate interests: granting it autonomy and a larger budget, and allowing it to take the lead in counter-terrorism. But with the increasing calls for a coup, they pursued a series of additional steps to "guarantee the professionalism" of the military.[76]

The first order of business was choosing a replacement for Rachid Ammar. In this decision, President Marzouki was influenced by his recent discovery of the regional dynamics at play within the army. His military advisor, General Brahim Ouechtati (appointed in September 2012), had explained to Marzouki that while the officer corps hailed from all corners of Tunisia, the top brass under Bourguiba and Ben Ali almost always came from the coast. "In this country, there was a tradition that the major officers are all from the Sahel," Marzouki noted. "If you are from the South, forget it, you would never be chief of staff."[77]

---

[73] Interview with retired Colonel Major Mokhtar Ben Nasr, Tunis, August 27, 2015. Quoted also in Grewal (2016).

[74] Interview with retired officer, Tunis, October 2015. Quoted also in Grewal (2016).

[75] Interview with retired Brigadier General Bechir Bedoui, Tunis, March 5, 2020.

[76] Interview with Presidential Chief-of-Staff, Imed Daimi, Tunis, September 22, 2015. Quoted also in Grewal (2016).

[77] Interview with President Moncef Marzouki, Tunis, June 22, 2016.

Accordingly, in choosing Ammar's replacement, Marzouki pursued what we might call "positive discrimination" or "affirmative action": intentionally looking to elevate someone from outside of the historically privileged regions. This was not only what he believed a democracy should strive to do, but also what was strategic at the time: an officer from the interior regions, he believed, would be less likely to work with Ammar in a potential coup.

Mindful of the symbolism, Marzouki on July 9 chose as Ammar's replacement Colonel Major Mohamed Salah Hamdi of Sidi Bouzid, where the revolution began. Hamdi's appointment sent a signal, Marzouki claimed, that "for the first time, you could become a high officer wherever you come from. This was very new in the Tunisian army."[78] Hamdi had also led the army's special forces during the 2007 Soliman operation, and thus brought important counter-terrorism experience. In 2011, General Ammar had tasked Hamdi with the unenviable role as military attaché to Libya, which Marzouki's team interpreted as a "punishment" and thus a signal that he would be unlikely to work with Ammar.[79]

As the calls for a coup escalated, Marzouki would make further changes to the military's leadership that would mirror this pattern of positive discrimination, bringing in officers from "the regions" to replace those from the coast. In mid-August, Marzouki received troubling reports that the number 2 military officer, the director general of military security (Kamel Akrout), was allegedly "providing intelligence to the media."[80] Marzouki thus decided to make further changes to the military leadership to ensure their loyalty, and ensure they would not collaborate with Ammar. As Marzouki explained:

> "I was extremely suspicious. I never thought that the Egyptian scenario would be easy to replicate here in Tunisia, but I said to myself I cannot take the risk. And at that time I decided to remove all the people close to General Ammar—all from the Sahel—and replace them with those coming from the South and from the Interior. [...] The best officers from the South and Interior had been sent out [of the country] as military attachés in Egypt and Libya, so I asked them, would you come back, and would you defend the republic, defend the revolution?"[81]

Having secured positive responses, Marzouki then shuffled the top brass on August 21. He fired Akrout,[82] who hailed from Bizerte, and replaced him with Nouri Ben Taous (from Sfax), who had been the military attaché in Libya after Hamdi. He likewise fired the inspector general of the armed forces, Taieb Laajimi (from Tunis), and put in his place Mohamed Nafti (from Gafsa), who had been military attaché

---

[78] Interview with President Moncef Marzouki, Tunis, June 22, 2016.

[79] In the view of the presidential team, officers that Ammar favored were sent to Paris or DC, while those he disliked were sent to Libya or Egypt.

[80] Interview with Presidential Spokesman Adnen Mansar, Tunis, September 22, 2015.

[81] Interview with former President Moncef Marzouki, Tunis, June 22, 2016.

[82] Akrout was appointed as military attaché to the United Arab Emirates. While a potentially puzzling decision given the UAE's support for counter-revolutions, Marzouki explained that he believed Akrout "would already be in touch with" the UAE, and that this way maybe they would receive some information about what the UAE was up to from others in the embassy (Interview, Tunis, June 22, 2016).

Table 10.2 Elevating the Interior Regions in Military Promotions

Position	Old	New	Date
Military Advisor	—	Ouechtati (Beja)	Sep 2012
Army Chief of Staff	Ammar (Monastir)	Hamdi (Sidi Bouzid)	Jul 2013
Military Security	Akrout (Bizerte)	Ben Taous (Sfax)	Aug 2013
Inspector-General	Laajimi (Tunis/Monastir)	Nafti (Gafsa)	Aug 2013

in Egypt. Military officers from the "regions" thus now claimed 4 of the 6 top positions, including the army chief of staff, director general of military security, inspector general, and the newly created military advisor to the president (see Table 10.2).

While elevating the interior regions, President Marzouki and Prime Minister Laarayedh both insisted that they were keen on maintaining a "balance" between the regions, hoping not to antagonize those from the coast. Hence they maintained in his position the navy chief of staff, Mohamed Khamassi (from Tunis), and although they fired the air force chief (Mohamed Nejib Jelassi from Monastir), he was replaced with another officer from the coast, Bechir Bedoui (from Bizerte).[83] Notably, each appointee was also highly qualified, with most having played a role in the counterterrorism operations in Soliman in 2007: Bedoui at the time had been chief of operations in the air force, Khamassi had been chief of operations in the navy, Hamdi the director of the army special forces, and Nafti his deputy.[84]

The troika's elevation of officers from the interior regions bred considerable goodwill from officers who had felt discriminated. These appointments "marked an important turning point," noted retired Colonel Major Mohamed Ahmed. "Now it doesn't matter if you're from the Sahel or from the center, south, or north. It was a very personal position of Marzouki to mark a difference with the past."[85]

"The promotion of the generals from the regions was like transitional justice in the army," argued Marzouki's chief of staff, Imed Daimi. "The goal was not to make a gap between the regions, but rather because the officers from the interior regions were deprived of or banned from the high ranks. Marzouki gave them their deserved ranks, and when Hamdi was appointed, all of the mid-level officers from the interior regions said finally, the end of the privileging of the Sahel!"[86]

In short, for both normative and strategic reasons, democratization had reversed one of Ben Ali's coup-proofing strategies—regional discrimination—and in turn bred goodwill towards the transition. In August–September 2013, the troika also doubled down on their reversing of Ben Ali's other major coup-proofing strategy: the marginalization and counterbalancing of the military.

---

[83] Bedoui also has family origins from the Sahel.

[84] Interview with Bechir Bedoui, Tunis, March 5, 2020.

[85] Interview with retired Colonel Major Mohamed Ahmed, Tunis, October 17, 2015. Quoted also in Grewal (2016).

[86] Interview with former Presidential Chief-of-Staff, Imed Daimi, Tunis, September 22, 2015. Quoted also in Grewal (2016).

Rebalancing the Military

Already, the troika had elevated the military's political influence, budget, and jurisdiction vis-à-vis the internal security forces. Now, as protests continued to heat up, the troika took three additional measures to cement the military's support. First, the troika government conceded fully to the military's viewpoint that the salafists were a security threat. On August 27, the government officially labelled Ansar al-Sharia a terrorist organization, following its earlier ban on the organization's activities in May. While the troika had been slow to come around, they eventually fully endorsed a military crackdown on the salafists.

From the perspective of the military, this meant that their representation in the various security councils was not just descriptive representation. They had gained actual, substantive policy influence, the power to shape the government's decisions. "At the beginning of the revolution, the government lacked awareness about military issues," argued retired Colonel Major Mokhtar Ben Nasr, the former Defense Ministry spokesman. "Today, it has changed. The military is now at the center."[87]

That influence over security policy, something the military had been denied under Ben Ali, thus represented a major gain from the revolution. Notably, almost the exact same sequence of events in Egypt represented a loss: in Egypt, the Muslim Brotherhood likewise had been lenient at first towards militants in the Sinai, but eventually conceded to the military's approach. But there, the military had not started from a marginalized position: for Egypt's military, these events did not represent a victory of pushing the civilians to act, but rather represented an encroachment on their historic monopoly over security policy. Military legacies thus shaped whether the advisory role democracy prescribed for the military was viewed as a gain or a loss.

Second, the troika also further reversed the military's counterbalancing by the internal security forces. On August 29, the troika government at the advice of military officers in the NSC established military buffer zones along Tunisia's southern borders with Libya and Algeria. In these zones, any police, national guard, or customs officers would now be "subject to the command of the military, who ensures the coordination of all field missions, patrols, and movement within the area."[88] In other words, with this decree, the military was given not just autonomy over its sphere, but also command over its former rivals.

"Without a doubt, things have improved," observed retired Armed Forces Chief of Staff General Said El Kateb. "Ben Ali relied on the police. Now, each institution has seen its capabilities enhanced. The military has importance, the police has importance, the national guard has importance. Each has a unique mission to fulfill."[89]

The internal security forces, however, did not view the military's rise—or for that matter the democratic transition—in the same positive light. The internal security

---

[87] Interview with Mokhtar Ben Nasr, Tunis, August 27, 2015.
[88] See article 5 of decree 2013–230 issued on August 29, 2013.
[89] Interview with retired Armed Forces Chief of Staff General Said El Kateb, Tunis, November 6, 2015. Quoted also in Grewal (2016).

forces had been purged, senior leaders had been put on trial, and the military's budget was steadily outpacing theirs. They had not only lost their monitoring powers over the military, but were now even subject to the military's command in the border zones.[90] This frustration with the troika was no secret: police officers were repeatedly criticizing the government in the media, and even staged protests against them.[91]

Accordingly, the troika had considerable fear that the internal security forces might conspire against them. The most real scare came towards the end of the crisis. In late September 2013, President Marzouki said he received a call from Ennahda head Rached Ghannouchi warning him about a potential threat to his life from Sami Sik Salem, the head of the presidential guard.[92] While Ghannouchi did not specify the precise threat, Marzouki's chief of staff, Adnen Manser, claimed that they feared an assassination attempt whereby the presidential guard would step aside and allow "commandos from the sea to come and kill [Marzouki],"[93] referring to the national guard special unit. Manser noted that Sami Sik Salem in private conversations had become increasingly critical of Marzouki's statements. He also recalled one night in July 2013 when Marzouki was leaving the presidential palace and there happened to be no presidential guards, when normally there would be 6–8 to escort him. Accordingly, they took Ghannouchi's tip seriously. On September 28, upon Marzouki's return from the UN General Assembly, he fired Sik Salem and replaced him with Taoufik Guesmi, who was chosen because he had been demoted out of the presidential guard by Sik Salem in January 2012.[94] The troika on October 4 likewise fired the head of the national guard, Montasser al-Skouhi, and put in his place Mounir Ksiksi.

Despite this scare from the internal security forces, the troika at the same time appeared to double down on its strategy of elevating the military. On September 25, the troika announced a pay increase of 110 dinars/month for all ranks in the military,[95] continuing a trend of pay increases since the revolution. "Since independence, the police and national guard had been much better paid than the military. We were miserable," claimed retired Colonel Major Mahmoud Mezoughi. "After the revolution, [. . .] our pay was doubled, and steadily became larger than [theirs]. Before the revolution we would whisper we want to be like the police and national guard! Now they whisper they want to be like us!"[96]

Once counterbalanced by the security forces, the relationship between Tunisia's coercive apparatuses was being recalibrated under democracy. "Now when I meet a soldier or officer, the first thing he says is that 'we are very thankful for Mr. Marzouki

---

[90] That the national guard was upset by this is reflected in their union's repeated pleas to "reassess" the military zones after each terrorist attack. See, e.g., S (2018).

[91] See, e.g., AFP (2013).

[92] Interview with President Moncef Marzouki, Tunis, June 22, 2016. Asked whether it was true that he called Marzouki with this tip, Ghannouchi neither confirmed nor denied, simply stating: "I . . . forget." (Interview with Rached Ghannouchi, Tunis, February 8, 2018).

[93] Interview with Presidential Spokesman Adnen Manser, Sousse, July 14, 2018.

[94] Interviews with President Moncef Marzouki (Tunis, June 22, 2016) and Adnen Manser (Sousse, July 14, 2018).

[95] See decree 3797 of 2013 dated September 25.

[96] Interview with retired Colonel Major Mahmoud Mezoughi, Tunis, January 8, 2019.

for improving our situation,'" claimed Marzouki's chief of staff, Imed Daimi. "We hear the opposite among the police—they say Marzouki cared for the military and not for us!"[97]

In short, from a marginalized position prior to the revolution, the military had begun to become a priority, witnessing increased material and political power. Democratization had thus reversed both of Ben Ali's hated coup-proofing strategies: a marginalization relative to the security forces, and a regional discrimination that privileged coastal officers.

At the time, military officers also believed that these gains from democracy would be best preserved by continuing the democratic path. It was only now under democracy that retired officers had gained a voice in civil society,[98] and thus could help lobby and guide the government on how to deal with the military. "The best thing we got after the revolution is the liberty of expression," praised retired General Said el-Kateb. "Sometimes I write articles for [the magazine] *Leaders*, sometimes I am invited to conferences at the Temimi Foundation [for Scientific Research and Information]. We were not permitted to do this under the regime of Ben Ali."[99] With this voice, retired officers could help inform the public and the government about "the institution of the military, the needs of this period, and how to transform an institution that traditionally occupied a very marginalized role in the country to the risks and challenges for the military today," noted another colonel-major.[100]

That voice could also serve to defend the more meritocratic promotions post-revolution. Retired Colonel Major Mohamed Ahmed affirmed: "If all appointments come from the Sahel, for instance, nobody will stay silent–we will say something about it! With the new constitution, new parliament, and new liberty of the press, things have changed, and we will at least denounce a reversion to the old ways."[101]

Professionalism

Beyond the reversal of Ben Ali's two coup-proofing strategies, a third factor also helps to explain the military's lack of interest in a coup in 2013: its professionalism. Brigadier-General Bechir Bedoui, who became the air force chief of staff in August 2013, argued that: "Tunisians discovered after the revolution that the military was more democratic and patriotic than the rest. There's no doubt about that. You wouldn't find anyone for a coup d'etat."[102]

As argued in Chapter 8, this professionalism had its origins in the military's marginalization, which shaped both recruitment and socialization in a way that

---

[97] Interview with presidential chief-of-staff Imed Daimi, Tunis, September 22, 2015. Quoted also in Grewal (2016).

[98] For a list of civil society organizations led by retired officers, see Grewal (2016).

[99] Interview with retired General Said El Kateb, Tunis, November 6, 2015. Quoted also in Grewal (2016).

[100] Interview with retired officer, Tunis, October 2015. Quoted also in Grewal (2016).

[101] Interview with retired Colonel Major Mohamed Ahmed, Tunis, October 17, 2015. Quoted also in Grewal (2016).

[102] Interview with Bechir Bedoui, Tunis, March 5, 2020.

privileged staying out of politics. Many officers began to view politics as something detrimental to the military, as a distraction to its training and effectiveness. Moreover, in this worldview, politics might also undermine the military's public esteem. Retired Colonel-Major Mahmoud Mezoughi argued that:

> "The population in Tunisia has big confidence in the military. If one of us becomes a minister, and is involved in politics, he may make mistakes, and that may alter the confidence of the people in the military. So myself, and my colleagues, we don't want any military [officer] as minister of defense, for instance."[103]

The military's lack of involvement in politics over the past decades also had one other effect that inhibited a coup: reducing officers' confidence that they would be able to run the government. A retired brigadier-general, who served in a political role post-revolution, noted that:

> "The first time I saw a minister I said 'oh my god, that's a minister'! You're not used to it. Over time you get confidence in yourself, and say no Mr. Minister, you are wrong. But in the beginning it's difficult to say that. [...] Very few [officers] in Tunisia have been ambassadors, and we've only had two ministers, both from the same promotion as Ben Ali (because they helped him make a coup). That's it. Maybe once every 10 years [Ben Ali] asked an officer for a special role. [...] And most of the officers who came after 2011 didn't get [enough] time to get these experiences. [...] But Egypt is much different. It's a question of culture."[104]

Mezoughi agreed that most officers don't have the confidence to "make politics":

> "We as military, in our career, we were not involved in politics. But as a minister, you need someone who has experience with the parliament, the president, other ministers. If you put some general, of course he knows politics, foreign relations, and everything in schools. But we as military, it's difficult for us, not to understand, but to make politics."[105]

A Coup Deterred?

In short, the military's professionalism, as well as its gains from democracy, help to explain why most officers opposed a coup in 2013. But although most of the military was gaining from democracy, a minority of officers—such as Rachid Ammar and other senior officers from the coast—were made relatively worse off. The internal security forces, as mentioned earlier, likewise held grievances toward the troika. Why didn't these previously privileged forces stage a coup?

---

[103] Interview with Mahmoud Mezoughi, Tunis, March 4, 2020.
[104] Interview with retired officer, Tunis, October 2015.
[105] Interview with Mahmoud Mezoughi, Tunis, March 4, 2020.

The most important reason is that they feared resistance from the majority of the military gaining from and thus supportive of the transition. "The dictatorship was built on the security forces, they were the face of the regime," noted Presidential Spokesman Adnen Mansar. "The biggest supporter of Ben Ali, and the biggest opposition to Ennahda, was the Ministry of Interior. [. . . In 2013,] we feared that the security forces would take the side of the protesters. But we had trust that the military would be the fastest in protecting us. Our trust in the military was much stronger than our trust in the Ministry of Interior. [. . . If it came to it,] the military could have stopped a coup."[106]

Having previously been the ones doing the counterbalancing, now the security forces found *themselves* counterbalanced by the military. Members of the national guard and presidential guard explicitly acknowledged this inability to coordinate with the military. "The division of force [between the military and national guard] certainly inhibited it [a coup]," noted one national guard officer. "Maybe it would have been possible to think about a coup if we had been unified or had been one entity."[107] A former commander of the national guard's special unit—the unit that carried out Ben Ali's coup in 1987—similarly argued that the lack of a coup was because the "left hand" (referring to the Ministry of Interior) and the "right hand" (referring to the Ministry of Defense) were unable to cooperate:

> "In 2011, 2012, 2013, there were several opportunities. It could have happened in 2013, with the simplest of things. I wouldn't call it a coup—if the operation of 1987 was an operation of 'change,' then an operation of 'saving' could have come in 2013—an operation to save the Tunisian people, to save the state! But all the people, all the sectors, would need to coordinate, to put 'hand' in 'hand.' And this, in my opinion, led to a difficulty for certain things to happen."[108]

Ali Seriati, the former head of the presidential guard, concurred: "The separation had a big effect. If you put all these units together, there's no guarantee that at some point someone with certain ideas won't think about that."[109]

Military officers agreed as well, emphasizing their new strength to resist a coup: "The coup attempt did not happen in Tunisia, and will never happen despite all odds and pressures, because everyone knows his fields and powers and authorities. I wouldn't say fear, but there is a huge respect for the Tunisian Army, for its training and ammunition, that everyone knows about. The national guard is trained at the military academies. Therefore, everyone knows his abilities compared to the Tunisian Army."[110]

With military force divided between paramilitary forces that opposed the transition and a military supportive of it, there was certain to be resistance, deterring a

---

[106] Interview with Adnen Mansar, Tunis, September 22, 2015.
[107] Interview with retired national guard officer, Tunis, January 2018.
[108] Interview with retired national guard officer, Bouficha, July 2018.
[109] Interview with former Presidential Guard Head Ali Seriati, Tunis, January 22, 2019.
[110] Interview with retired officer, Tunis, January 2018.

coup. The formerly counterbalancing forces under autocracy were now themselves counterbalanced under democracy. The civilian leadership acknowledged as much: "We [the troika government] benefited from the competition between the security forces and the military institution," noted Foreign Minister Abdessalem.[111]

"The clear determination of the army was crucial in deciding the fate of all things," noted Tarek Kahlaoui, the head of the presidential think tank. "The army is the most powerful, most lethal force. If the army is clearly against any coup, it would be difficult for the police to coup."[112]

After all, the army in the summer of 2013 was not only passively supporting the transition by not staging a coup. It had also actively obeyed the troika's orders to defend vital institutions during the protests. President Marzouki argued that due to these various factors—its professionalism, its gains from the revolution, and his reshuffling of the top brass—the military remained loyal during the protests. "I remember that in 2013, there were calls to occupy state buildings. [General Hamdi] told me you can be sure nobody would enter any office building. The army at that time was ours, for sure."[113]

Similarly, the coastal military officers such as General Rachid Ammar knew they would face resistance from the rest of the military if they were to stage a coup. A former inspector general of the armed forces observed that "even if a certain group of the Army will attempt a coup, the other 99 percent will absolutely be against it, and will intervene to stop it."[114] Another brigadier general who worked closely with Ammar concurred:

> "Why didn't Rachid Ammar take power? Let me start from good to worse. The good: that he is republican, believes in the law. That's the good one [Laughs]. It's very easy to hide behind 'I'm republican, I follow the law.' It's very easy to say that afterwards. But probably he was afraid, he didn't know if people would go with him, he wasn't entirely in control."[115]

The civilian leadership sensed the same. "I think even if the generals were tempted, I'm not sure the army would follow them," claimed Imed Daimi, the president's chief of staff. "Even though some generals had contact with the opposition and desired the government to go, it's not clear that mid-level officers would follow. [. . .] Maybe Rachid Ammar understood that the situation had changed. He understood that he has no base in this new climate. He was very contested in the army from mid and low-level officers. He felt that he lost his sovereignty and domination over the army."[116]

Marzouki concurred. "During that summer a lot of people were asking the army to intervene. Even beyond the radio and TV. [General] Hamdi told me that a lot of people were trying to discuss with officers and saying, 'hey, we are expecting you to

[111] Interview with former Foreign Minister Rafik Abdessalam, Tunis, February 10, 2018.
[112] Interview with Tarek Kahlaoui, Tunis, June 9, 2014.
[113] Interview with Moncef Marzouki, Cambridge, Massachusetts, September 9, 2022.
[114] Interview with a retired officer, Tunis, January 2018.
[115] Interview with officer, Tunis, December 2015.
[116] Interview with Imed Daimi, Tunis, September 22, 2015.

do something.' [. . .] But General Ammar was not popular within the army. He had been faithful to the [Ben Ali] regime. And all the high ranking officers were coming from the Sahel. When I moved his friends, when I removed all the people who were close to Ammar and replaced them by those coming from the South and from the Interior, everyone sighed. [. . .] I cannot say they [the Sahelien officers] were ready to undertake a coup. But if there was trouble, they would not have been as faithful as the others I decided to appoint. This I'm sure of."[117]

With the majority of the military gaining from democracy, Ammar could not secure a large enough coup coalition. While he may have had support from the public, he lacked the support of a military now gaining from democracy.

As the weeks passed, the opposition increasingly began to realize that the military was not going to intervene, that a coup was not in the cards. Accordingly, they switched gears, hoping to bring down the government instead through negotiations. They continued protesting, but entered into dialogue with the troika, mediated by the Quartet, on the pre-condition that the troika step down from power afterwards. As Marzouki put it: "When the counterrevolution realized that there would be no coup like in Egypt, they decided to change their strategy to harassment leading to technocratic government."[118] That strategy eventually succeeded in finding consensus over a new grand bargain, putting the transition back on track.

Conclusion

In the summer of 2013, Tunisia appeared ripe for a military coup. Opposition politicians and protesters, emboldened by the coup in Egypt, came knocking on the door of the barracks. With mass protests, institutional paralysis, and severe security threats, the Tunisian military had the opportunity to intervene.

The Tunisian military, however, chose not to follow the lead of its Egyptian counterpart. In this chapter, I argued that this decision was shaped by the coup-proofing strategies pursued by Tunisia's previous autocrats. During the critical juncture of state formation, Habib Bourguiba had decided to counterbalance the military with a powerful Ministry of Interior, and to privilege a minority of officers who hailed from wealthy, coastal areas. These coup-proofing strategies had produced resentment among the majority of the military toward autocracy and toward senior officers complicit in these strategies. Democratization, however, created incentives for Tunisia's new leaders to reverse these hated coup-proofing strategies. This reversal of fortune bred considerable goodwill within the military towards the transition, giving the officers little incentive to stage a coup. Moreover, the apolitical professionalism they had inculcated under authoritarianism similarly discouraged a coup. While coastal elite officers like General Ammar may therefore have had the support of the public for a coup, they lacked the critical support of the military.

[117] Interview with President Moncef Marzouki, Tunis, June 22, 2016.
[118] Interview with President Moncef Marzouki, Tunis, June 22, 2016.

Tunisia therefore survived its "Brumairean moment" in 2013, allowing it to remain on the democratic path. The underlying challenges, however, continued. The economy struggled to recover, perceptions of corruption were growing,[119] and Tunisians remained relatively disillusioned with democracy and the political process.[120] While a military coup was unlikely for the reasons described in this chapter, these grievances eventually fueled the rise of a populist president, Kais Saied, who leveraged this public support to stage an incumbent takeover—the topic of the next chapter.

[119] See Yerkes and Muasher (2017).
[120] See Grewal (2019*b*).

11
Tunisia: Facilitating the Takeover

To say "no, this is unconstitutional" would have been intervention into the political arena. Is that acceptable? Would that have been better for the country?

—Retired Brigadier General[1]

Introduction

The lack of a military coup in 2013 allowed Tunisia's democracy to survive those volatile, transitional years. It gave political parties the opportunity to find consensus over the drafting of the 2014 constitution, in turn permitting the country to hold two subsequent rounds of free and fair parliamentary and presidential elections in 2014 and 2019. For many observers, Tunisian democracy by then had passed the "two-turnover test" and seemed on the verge of consolidation.

However, the underlying grievances that had led the general public and secular elites to push for a military coup in 2013 had not gone away. Tunisians remained frustrated with democracy for not delivering economically, and increasingly blamed not just the Islamists but all political parties, viewing the political class writ large as corrupt and self-serving. The grounds were thus still fertile for an overthrow of Tunisia's democracy—but this time, hope would be placed not in the military, but in the populist president.

On July 25, 2021, Tunisia's president, Kais Saied, staged an incumbent takeover. Flanked by the top military and security officials, Saied ordered the army and police to shutter the parliament and allow him to rule by decree. Capitalizing on the public's frustration with the parties, Saied put a number of politicians on trial in both civilian and military courts, and then rewrote the constitution to grant himself hyper-presidential powers. Tunisian democracy, at least temporarily, had collapsed.

While the causes of Saied's presidential coup are beyond the scope of this book, this chapter addresses the role of the military in his power grab. Why did Tunisia's military obey Kais Saied's order to close the parliament, thereby facilitating his takeover of power? Why didn't the officers refuse Saied's orders, in defense of democracy and of the constitution?

It is worth noting at the outset that even without the military's support, Saied's incumbent takeover might still have succeeded, given that the police could have

---

[1] Interview, June 2022.

Soldiers of Democracy?. Sharan Grewal, Oxford University Press. © Sharan Grewal (2023).
DOI: 10.1093/oso/9780192873910.003.0011

closed the parliament on their own. However, the generals' refusal would have deprived the president's coup of the legitimacy and popularity brought by the military, and emboldened his opposition to take a stronger stance against it. It is thus worth questioning why the army obeyed.

I argue that the same three factors that led the military not to stage a coup in 2013 now shaped their decision to facilitate Saied's takeover. First, while their notion of professionalism—apolitical and subordinate to the civilian president—made them averse to a coup in 2013, it also led them to obey Saied's orders in 2021. Their subservience to the president led them to defer to his interpretation that the order was legal, while their desire to remain far from politics convinced them that following orders was less political than refusing. Second, the military's political composition, unlike in 2013, now aligned with the coup attempt. Having seen politics up close, military officers—like the general public—had become disillusioned, even disgusted, by the political class, leading them to support Saied's populist mission of cleaning up the political system. And third, Saied effectively co-opted the generals, convincing them their personal and corporate interests would be best enhanced by facilitating his takeover of power. In short, the military's interests, politics, and norms all aligned in support of Saied's presidential coup.

The Takeover

Kais Saied, an austere law professor, was elected president in 2019 in a landslide victory with a populist mandate to clean up the system. Without a political party and untainted by the politics of the last eight years, Kais Saied was viewed as the clean, honest, rule-of-law candidate, who would finally hold the corrupt elites accountable and deliver power and prosperity to the people. But upon assuming the presidency, Saied found himself constrained by the 2014 constitution, which envisions a relatively weak presidency that shares power with a prime minister tied to the parliament. Frustrated with what he called these "locks" in the 2014 constitution, Saied searched for a way to amass more power.

In July 2021, Saied was given a prime opportunity, with the country reeling from a number of crises. The Delta variant had caused a massive spike in COVID-19 cases—at the time the second highest in the world per capita—and the government had just botched the roll-out of its first vaccines.[2] The pandemic had likewise increased inflation and poverty, with the percent of Tunisians saying the economy was getting worse doubling from January 2020 to January 2021.[3] The polarized and fractured parliament was not only struggling to find consensus, but heated disagreements were elevating into fistfights. Meanwhile, long-standing antipathy towards the Islamist party Ennahda, the largest in parliament, was catalyzed by the election of

---

[2] See Grewal (2021*a*).
[3] See polls by Emrhod Consulting quoted in Grewal (2021*a*).

its president, Rached Ghannouchi, as speaker of parliament, reigniting the polarization of summer 2013. In this context, Saied enjoyed widespread support for moving against the widely despised government and parliament.

Kais Saied struck on July 25, seizing complete power in an incumbent takeover. Flanked by the top military and security officials, Saied dismissed the prime minister, froze the parliament, and announced that he would rule by decree. He also lifted the immunity of parliamentarians, so that they could be prosecuted on allegations of corruption and treason.

Saied attempted to grant his presidential coup a veneer of constitutional legitimacy by claiming to activate article 80 of the 2014 constitution. That article grants the president the ability to temporarily assume exceptional powers after consulting with the prime minister and speaker of parliament, neither of which occurred in this case. Article 80 goes on to state that the parliament must remain in "a state of continuous session throughout such a period" (not frozen), and that the president cannot even present a motion of censure against the government, let alone unilaterally dismiss it. By most readings, therefore, Saied violated the constitution on July 25. However, there was no constitutional court in place yet to rule against him, as political parties had for six years been unable to agree on its membership, and Saied had blocked attempts to lower the parliamentary threshold needed.[4] Moreover, there were enough constitutional law professors (beyond Saied) who publicly came out in support of the move that sufficiently muddled its unconstitutionality. These professors argued that if the government and parliament were the cause of the crisis, then the president is permitted to move against them, regardless of what the article says.[5]

Saied announced his coup while flanked by the top military and security officials, creating the impression that they supported his move. That impression would then solidify when both the military and security forces obeyed Saied's orders to station tanks and troops in front of the parliament to ensure it stayed frozen. Their loyalty would be put to the test just hours later, when the speaker of parliament, Rached Ghannouchi, and deputy speaker, Samira Chaouachi, attempted to enter the assembly.

Approaching the parliament's gates, Chaouachi said she "found a soldier there, and I told him '*As-salāmu alaykum*,' but he didn't reply to me. So I told him, our values and morals tell you that when someone says hello you should reply with the same. I [then] introduced myself and the speaker of the parliament. I told the soldier that we are here to perform our duties since we had swore to protect the constitution." But the soldier denied them entry. "I told him he swore as well to protect the constitution, but he said, 'No, I swore to protect the homeland (*al-watan*).'"[6] She and Ghannouchi soon left, not wishing to cause a confrontation with the security forces.

---

[4] For more details, see Grewal and Hamid (2020) and Jrad (2021).

[5] These professors also pointed to article 72 of the constitution, which says that the president "ensures respect for the constitution." They interpreted this to mean that in the absence of a constitutional court the president is the one who determines if an action is constitutional—an interpretation that in effect would allow the president to do whatever he wants.

[6] Interview with Deputy Speaker Samira Chaouachi, Tunis, June 29, 2022.

For the next year and a half, the military would continue to surround the parliament, facilitating Saied's incumbent takeover. Why did it do so? Why did the Tunisian military, long hailed for its pro-democracy stance, obey Saied's orders to freeze the democratically elected parliament? I argue that the same three factors—its professionalism, political composition and corporate interests—can help explain this decision as well.

Professionalism

Professional soldiers are taught to obey all orders except those that are illegal. Tunisia's military is no exception. The oath Tunisian officers swear during their commission is to obey orders "within the limits of the laws of the state and military regulations (*qanūn al-dawla wa taratīb al-jaysh*)." Moreover, while not discussed extensively, officers had received "education at different levels of the military [making] clear that if your boss gives you an illegal order, you just tell him: 'No, this is not legal, so I cannot execute,'" noted one retired brigadier-general.[7]

However, officers had never had to apply this principle in practice, having never been given an unconstitutional order by a president. Even during the 2011 revolution, army chief Rachid Ammar never said no to a direct order from Ben Ali (see Chapter 9). Moreover, officers had never had formal discussions during their education over what types of orders from a president might be unconstitutional, nor formally studied the 2014 constitution or article 80, to know those particular limits. While they were aware they should refuse illegal orders in general, in practice "it's not always so black and white," noted a brigadier-general. "Sometimes what is legal and is not legal is difficult to say."[8]

Likewise, military officers had never formally studied the principle of neutrality. Article 18 of the 2014 constitution stated that the military "is required to be completely impartial." Today, post-July 25, some officers are realizing that that means staying neutral during political battles between different branches of government. As Brigadier-General Mohamed Meddeb publicly noted in February 2022, the military must not be used "in support of a branch of power against other branches."[9] But, "neutrality is a new rule for us, and this [July 25] was the first case where the army needed to apply this rule," an army general told me. "Until this moment, we didn't talk about neutrality in the military, because neutrality means there are at least two different parties. But until 2011, there was always just one party . . . the question of neutrality, we didn't even think about that, to be frank with you."[10]

Not only did the military not have formal training or experience to draw upon on July 25, there was also no one to consult. There was no constitutional court, and in addition, Tunisia's military had no internal channels, either: it lacked the equivalent

---

[7] Interview with retired officer, June 2022.
[8] Interview with retired officer, June 2022.
[9] See Meddeb (2022).
[10] Interview with retired officer, June 2022.

of the US military's Office of General Counsel to weigh the constitutionality of an order, nor were the military courts competent in that regard. With no one to consult, the senior command had to decide for themselves.

In their decision, the military leadership was guided by two longstanding principles of their professionalism: (1) to stay far from politics, and (2) to be subservient to the commander-in-chief. Both of these principles, instilled as a result of Bourguiba and Ben Ali's coup-proofing strategies (see Chapter 8), pushed the Tunisian military to obey Saied's orders.

The first principle of professionalism was the military's apolitical nature. The military leadership was inclined to ignore the thorny question of constitutionality, viewing it as a political question that they should stay far away from. "To say 'no, this is unconstitutional' would have been intervention into the political arena," one general told me. "Is that acceptable? Would that have been better for the country?"[11] Put in this unfortunate position, the officers calculated that obeying the order would be less political, as simply 'following orders.'

Moreover, as an apolitical military, officers preferred to judge the legality solely of the narrow mission they were assigned ('secure the parliament') and ignore the broader political or constitutional ramifications of that action (that that would freeze parliament's activities). On a technical level, Saied's order to secure the parliament fell within the military's mission of supporting the internal security forces in securing vital institutions. As one colonel-major explained, "the army obeyed the order of the President [because . . .] the requested action falls within the framework of the secondary mission of the Armed Forces, which consists in supporting the forces of the police in the defense of sensitive points and state agencies. So, in the eyes of the military command, the president's order was not unconstitutional."[12] In that sense, the officers viewed the parliament as any other vital institution, like an embassy or water facility, and deployed troops to secure it. "Since the Iraq War in 1991, we have always done that: protect '*points sensibles*,'" noted one general. "So, let's assume that the President called them and he told them, as we have always done: 'The Parliament is a sensitive point, so you have to protect it.' Protect it, what does that mean? That means also to prevent someone from entering."[13]

But treating the parliament like a water facility ignores that it is also a constitutional body, and that closing it has major political implications, freezing the activities of an elected institution. It ignores that the parliament, unlike a water facility, is a co-equal branch of government, and that the military must be neutral in any turf battle between the president and parliament. In other words, the military's desire to be apolitical by focusing on the narrow task it was assigned ("securing a vital institution") blinded the military to the broader political ramifications of following that order. As Brooks (2020, p. 17) has noted in the US context, "the reflexive self-identification

---

[11] Interview with retired officer, June 2022.
[12] Interview with retired officer, Email, August 18, 2021.
[13] Interview with retired officer, June 2022.

of military officers as apolitical can encourage blind spots such that they fail to rec-ognize the political content or impact of their actions." In Tunisia, apolitical officers obeyed the precise order they were given without considering or engaging with the political ramifications of that action.

A second principle of professionalism that likewise pushed the military to obey Saied's orders was its subordination to civilian control. On both the constitutional and technical levels, the military was inclined to defer to the commander-in-chief, rather than question him. On the technical level, if we view the order as simply "securing" the parliament, it raises the question of what threat the parliament is being secured from. But historically, the military has always deferred to the president in his judgment of threat. "At the technical level, we don't care," explained one general. "You're supposed to assume that there is a danger. We don't discuss if there is a *real* danger, no. You just obey the order."[14] The Tunisian military had internalized following such orders without question, and not to evaluate whether the threat was real.

Likewise, if we view the order as instead freezing the parliament's activities, the military was likewise inclined to simply defer to the president's interpretation that that was constitutional. The president, after all, was a constitutional law professor; the officers had no training or expertise in this field. "I am not better qualified than him!" one general exclaimed.[15] Retired General Bechir Bedoui, the former air force chief, made a similar remark on Radio IFM: "The interpretation of Article 80 requires the opinion of a specialist. There was a whole polemic between the renowned experts in constitutional law—even they could not reach an agreement on Article 80. Imagine people with different specialties, with operational and military expertise."[16] Unable and unwilling to ascertain the constitutionality themselves, the officers deferred to the president's interpretation.

In addition, the president is the commander-in-chief, and the officers had no his-tory or experience of questioning, let alone refusing, a president's orders. For 70 years, Tunisia's officers had deeply ingrained the principle of civilian control, and subordi-nation to the presidency. As a brigadier-general noted, "Saied's role is the supreme commander of the armed forces. That's his legal position . . . To say that the military should have refused—things here don't go in the way that you think. [At most,] they might discuss a question or an issue [with the president] and, when asked for their opinion, would say this is not our job or this is not our priority, or maybe we can do this another way, etc."[17] But once the commander-in-chief has decided and given them a direct order, the military must simply execute. Having learned to be sub-servient to civilians, the Tunisian military found it difficult to say no to Saied during his incumbent takeover.

In short, the Tunisian military obeyed Saied's orders not just because it was not pro-fessional enough, and had not fully internalized what neutrality entails in a moment

---

[14] Interview with retired officer, June 2022.
[15] Interview, June 2022.
[16] See Bedoui's intervention here on March 19, 2022. See also Hammami (2022).
[17] Interview with retired officer, June 2022.

like this. On the contrary, it was precisely the two principles of professionalism they had learned—to be apolitical and subordinate to civilians—that led them to facilitate the president's coup.

Political Composition

Although for some officers it was their apolitical professionalism that led them to obey, for others, it was their political preferences. By 2019, the dominant political cleavage had shifted towards a pro-system v. populist divide. And on that cleavage, the military and Saied found themselves seeing eye to eye.

The military post-2011 had become increasingly attuned to politics. Part of this development was natural: the result of Tunisia simply having more politics for officers to be exposed to post-2011 than under dictatorship. Democracy brought dozens of political parties, competitive elections, real parliamentary activity—and free media coverage of each—making it difficult for officers to ignore politics.

But civilian politicians made matters worse, occasionally dragging the military into politics. As covered in Chapter 10, opposition politicians in 2013 openly called for and met with military officials asking for a coup against the troika. In 2017, President Beji Caid Essebsi deployed the military to secure an oil facility in Tataouine from protesters, inserting the troops into his political battle. In 2019, when Essebsi's health took a turn for the worst and doctors had to place him in an artificial coma, the minister of defense, Abdelkrim Zbidi, reportedly threatened to send the army to surround the parliament to prevent the assembly from declaring a presidential vacancy.[18] Zbidi in his presidential campaign that year also attempted to give the impression that the military supported him, featuring blown-up pictures of himself with the military leadership during his rallies,[19] and being advised by esteemed retired General Rachid Ammar.

These attempts by civilian politicians to involve the military in politics not only set the stage for Kais Saied to do the same in 2021, but also began to politicize the officer corps. One brigadier-general, who retired in 2012, observed: "I am sure that the new Captain who joined the army after 2011, his thinking is completely different than mine . . . Before, we really didn't discuss democracy or politics. Now, I'm sure that if someone in office raises a political issue which has to do with the army, our officers are not surprised. Now, even to discuss what happened on the 25th of July, I am sure that is a normal thing."[20] Prime Minister Youssef Chahed singled out the 2019 elections: "The military began to accept politics when Zbidi campaigned with pictures of generals behind him."[21]

Another contributor to the politicization of the Tunisian military was democracy granting it suffrage. Denied the vote for 60 years, parliament granted the military

---

[18] See Business News (2019).
[19] See, e.g., https://twitter.com/Selim_/status/1170630760149258241.
[20] Interview with retired officer, June 2022.
[21] Interview, Cambridge, Massachusetts, September 9, 2022.

the right to vote in the 2018 municipal elections.[22] About 33 percent of military and security forces registered to vote, but only 12 percent of those showed up on election day,[23] due in part to the lack of attractive candidates (civilian turnout was also low at 36 percent). For some, this process of even considering who to vote for might have politicized some officers: "Voting is the best explanation of the politicization [of the military]," noted one General. "If you ask me to choose between these [parties], the first time I will choose with reasoning and logic, with my head. But the second time I will choose with my heart . . . so doing this two, three times—finally, I will be with that guy, leftist or liberal or Islamist. That is politicization."[24]

Retired officers, for their part, also began to wade into politics.[25] At least five retired officers ran and won in the 2018 municipal elections, with one even becoming a mayor. Retired officers then formed two political parties to contest the 2019 parliamentary elections (Act for Tunisia and the Five Star Movement), while retired Army Chief General Muhammad al-Hadi Bin Hassine attempted to run for president. The Act for Tunisia Party website declared that: "Its members were soldiers, they were apolitical, but by necessity they were pushed to be politicized . . . They firmly believe that staying out of the political sphere is equivalent to treason." The actions of these retired officers likewise contributed to shifting norms about what political behavior was appropriate for officers to engage in.

But once attuned to politics, military officers began to dislike what they were seeing. Like the general public, military officers became disillusioned, even disgusted, with the political class, viewing them as corrupt and self-serving, bickering amongst themselves while the country headed towards financial ruin. In 2020, I routinely heard retired officers complain about the political parties. "The political class after the revolution has been really down, low quality," said one general. "Everyone now can become a deputy or minister, people who never went to school. We come across [politicians] who can't even write a paragraph!"[26] "I have no confidence in them because they only want power and money," said another.[27] A third retired general–who ran (unsuccessfully) for parliament in 2019–told me that he witnessed corruption and vote-buying during the campaign, and claimed that "many smugglers" were elected to parliament.[28]

In this context, it is likely that many officers bought into the populist rhetoric of President Kais Saied, who lambasted the political class for their corruption and vowed to clean up the system and bring order and discipline back to the country. Rather than stay neutral in political affairs, many of the politicized officers came to identify with and support the president's anti-system politics. Particularly in 2021, when the political parties bickered amongst themselves, unable to solve the country's looming

---

[22] Many retired officers opposed the granting of suffrage, see Grewal (2017). US-trained officers tended to be more supportive Grewal (2022*b*).

[23] See Grewal (2018*a*).

[24] Interview with retired officer, June 2022.

[25] For more, see Grewal (2019*b*) and Grewal (2022*b*).

[26] Interview with retired officer, March 2020.

[27] Interview with retired officer, Tunis, March 2020.

[28] Interview with retired officer, March 2020.

economic and health crises, retired officers began to publicly turn to the president. Two months prior to Saied's coup, six prominent retired military officers, including Brigadier-General Mohamed Meddeb and Colonel-Major Mokhtar Ben Nasr, publicly urged President Kais Saied to take decisive action to end the country's malaise. "Our country is at a crossroads. The state has disintegrated and its authority has vanished. Corruption has spread and violence has spread in all its forms, and we are on the brink of a real economic collapse." Criticizing the political parties, their petition observed that "success will not be conferred to any democratic system in which all the actors do not enjoy a minimum level of integrity and devotion to the country."[29]

That political support for the president and opposition to the parties then served as "partisan blinders" justifying the president's violation of the constitution. As one retired colonel-major told me soon after the president's coup:

> Like the majority of the Tunisian people, the military were not comfortable with the chaotic situation in the country before July 25. They were even angry with the politicians who drove the country into this situation. I even think they were frustrated that they couldn't do anything to save the country. So, I can say that the military community strongly supports the President like the rest of the population . . . It is also true that there is a violation of the constitution somewhere. But I think that the Army, like the majority of Tunisians who expressed their joy on the night of July 25, felt that there was no other alternative to save the country than to take these measures . . . The people had a feeling of relief. They had felt very uneasy before July 25 because of the constitutional blockage that would lead the country to bankruptcy . . . It was better to violate the constitution than to starve."[30]

In addition to populism, two other political cleavages also pushed military officers to support the president's coup. The first was anti-Ennahda sentiment. In interviews, several retired officers, particular secular ones from the coast, expressed an antipathy, even hatred, towards Ennahda, legacies of their time serving under Bourguiba and Ben Ali. "Under Bourguiba, we believed in Western values . . . we've lost freedom since then. Now there is social pressure to fast [during Ramadan], to not wear the bikini," lamented one retired admiral.[31] "Ennahda just wanted to get their hands on everything," claimed a retired general.[32] Former President Moncef Marzouki explained that: "Ben Ali had destroyed everything in the army related to any kind of Islamism. The army is political Islam-free. Many officers even hate Ennahda."[33]

In 2013, Marzouki had attempted to resolve this friction between the military and the Ennahda-led troika by bringing in officers who, while not Islamist, were at least from social classes and regions more supportive of the revolution. "But when I left office," Marzouki said, "the first thing that President [Beji Caid] Essebsi did was to

---

[29] See petition here.
[30] Interview with retired officer, Email, August 18, 2021.
[31] Interview with retired officer, June 2016.
[32] Interview with retired officer, Tunis, March 2020.
[33] Interview with Moncef Marzouki, Cambridge, Massachusetts, September 9, 2022.

Table 11.1 President's Essebsi's Military Appointments

Position	2015–2017	2017/18 –
National Security Advisor	Kamel Akrout (Bizerte)	
Army Chief of Staff	Ismail Fathali (Beja)	Mohamed El Ghoul (Mahdia)
Military Intelligence	Taoufik Rahmouni (Tunis)	Habib Dhif (Tunis)
Inspector-General	Jamal Boujah (Kairouan)	Abdelmoneim Belaati (Bizerte)
Air Force Chief of Staff	Mohamed Fouad Aloui (Sfax)	Mohamed Hajjam (Tunis)
Navy Chief of Staff	Abdelraouf Atallah (Kairouan)	

remove all of my appointees."[34] Essebsi's initial appointees were still relatively diverse by region (see Table 11.1), but he would reshuffle the brass once again in 2017 after the military shirked in repressing protesters in Tataouine. This time, Essebsi brought in officers exclusively from the coast. Mohamed El Ghoul (from Mahdia) replaced Ismail Fathali (Beja) as chief of staff of the land army, Abdelmoneim Belaati (Bizerte) replaced Jamal Boujah (Kairouan) as inspector-general, and Mohamed Hajjam (Tunis) replaced Mohamed Fouad Aloui (Sfax) as chief of staff of the air force. After these changes, all but one of the top officers hailed from the coast, harkening back to the coastal favoritism of Essebsi's former bosses, Bourguiba and Ben Ali.

Essebsi's new generals "were chosen on the fact that they are from a particular region, a particular social class, more supportive of the counter-revolution," claimed Marzouki. "And these new guys are now supporting the dictatorship . . . When [Saied] organized his constitutional coup, he was supported by these officers."[35] In short, the secular, coastal officers who had returned to the top of the military under Essebsi may have supported Saied's coup in the hopes that it would dislodge Ennahda from power.

But at the same time, Saied's moves also appealed, for different reasons, to officers from the interior regions. While he did not touch the coastal generals Essebsi placed at the top of the military, respecting instead the military's autonomy, Saied still signaled his proclivity towards addressing regional discrimination through his appointments as national security advisor. He first chose as his advisor Mohamed Salah Hamdi, the same general from Sidi Bouzid that Marzouki had appointed as army chief of staff to replace Rachid Ammar in 2013. Hamdi later resigned, but he was replaced by another officer from the regions—Abdelraouf Atallah from Kairouan, the one military chief inherited from Essebsi who was not from the coast. More generally, Saied's vision of a decentralized, bottom-up system where regions would have greater political power likely appealed politically to officers from these regions.

In short, the officers' political preferences—their political support for the president rather than neutrality—led them to justify the president's power grab. Some shared his populism, others his anti-Ennahda sentiments, and others still his empowerment

---

[34] Interview with Moncef Marzouki, Cambridge, Massachusetts, September 9, 2022.
[35] Interview with Moncef Marzouki, Cambridge, Massachusetts, September 9, 2022.

of the regions. These political preferences served as "partisan blinders" that led some officers to ignore the violations of the constitution out of support for the president's politics.

Corporate Interests

A third factor that led the military to obey Saied's presidential coup was his co-optation of the officers through their corporate interests. As discussed in the previous chapter, between 2011 and 2015, the military saw its material and political interests enhanced, reversing their marginalization under Ben Ali. The military's budget increased more quickly than any other ministry's; it began a modernization of its weapons systems through increased foreign aid; and it saw political influence through the appointment of a military advisor to the president and two permanent representatives in the National Security Council. Each of these gains invested the military into the transition, leading them to ignore the calls for a coup in 2013.

However, these gains slowed under President Essebsi (2014–2019). Essebsi, an elderly statesman who had served under both Bourguiba and Ben Ali, had been influenced by their anti-militaristic attitudes. As soon as security threats receded, Essebsi began to curtail the military's budget and influence. After increasing by roughly 21 percent each year between 2011 and 2016, the defense budget in 2017 was cut for the first time since the revolution, despite it not yet having caught up to that of the Ministry of Interior. In addition, Essebsi in January 2017 removed the two military representatives from the National Security Council, depriving the military of regular input into policy decisions. Retired officers at the time viewed their removal as a major grievance, an "unfortunate" move that "doesn't help the country handle defense and security issues."[36]

As I have argued elsewhere,[37] Essebsi's curtailment of the military's corporate interests in 2017 deprived him of their full support that year. In May 2017, Essebsi ordered the military to defend an oil valve in El Kamour, Tataouine after protesters had halted its activity with a sit-in. While the military leadership obeyed the order to deploy, the soldiers on the ground shirked rather than use force, ultimately allowing the protesters to enter the site and shut off the oil valve. In explaining the military's behavior, retired officer Fathi Aouadi emphasized the lack of budget and material investment: "Our army is reputedly loyal . . . but it has been exhausted in all directions . . . Its staff is worn down . . . [now] it has just been ruled that it would be responsible for [production sites] throughout the country. Is it with the same staff?,"[38] he asked

---

[36] Interview with retired officer, Email, May 13, 2017. However, Essebsi's national security advisor, retired Admiral Kamel Akrout, defended this move as active-duty officers in his view should only comment on technical and operational matters, not the broader political and strategic discussions of the security council. Interview, Tunis, February 8, 2018.

[37] See more in Grewal (2019a).

[38] See Aouadi (2017).

rhetorically, implying it would need more funds and troops if it were to repress on Essebsi's behalf.

Frustrated by the military's shirking, Essebsi would take three further measures against the military in his final years in office. First, because he had to rely on the national guard instead of the army to clear the protesters in Tataouine, Essebsi began to privilege the guard politically. In September 2017, Essebsi promoted the national guard commander, Lotfi Brahem, to minister of interior, the first time in 26 years that the interior minister did not have a civilian background. As for the military, despite public calls from retired officers for military personnel to also serve in ministerial positions,[39] Essebsi refused such demands. Essebsi did, however, continue the trend of appointing retired officers to non-ministerial positions, including retired Admiral Kamel Akrout as national security advisor (2015–2019), retired Colonel Elyes Mnakbi as head of TunisAir (2016–2020), retired Colonel-Major Mokhtar Ben Nasr as head of the counter-terrorism commission (2018–2019), and Brigadier-General Jamal Boujah as head of the environment police (2017–2018), but none as ministers.

Second, Essebsi also refused the military (and NATO)'s request to create a national intelligence center that would have collected and analyzed intelligence from all agencies—military, police, national guard, and presidential guard. Such a fusion center, according to Essebsi's advisor Admiral Akrout, would have helped to "break down the barriers between these departments and strengthen cooperation" between them.[40] However, "Essebsi did not want this," Akrout complained.[41] Essebsi's monopoly over intelligence from the presidential guard, and to some extent the military, was too important for remaining politically relevant in Tunisia's divided system. "Intelligence is a very useful tool," Akrout continued. "Every decision-maker does everything to have it as a lever within his or her reach, especially with the political system that currently exists in Tunisia."[42]

Finally, as discussed in the previous section, Essebsi also meddled in promotions. After the military shirked in Tataouine, Essebsi fired several of the top officers—without promotion—and brought in new officers he thought would be more loyal to him. This meddling in the top brass undermined the military's autonomy, and frustrated the officers further. In short, while the Tunisian military continued to see some gains under Essebsi, he also on occasion thwarted its growing appetite. Although democracy had advanced the military's interests during the transition, it now became less clear whether it was the best path for advancing them even further.

President Kais Saied, on the contrary, would considerably advance the military's corporate interests along multiple dimensions, in turn securing their support for his incumbent takeover. From the start, Saied cultivated a close relationship with the military brass, giving them regular access to the president. Saied routinely summoned the National Security Council, and typically invited all five of the top generals. He

---

[39] See in particular articles in *Leaders* magazine by retired Colonels Mohamed Kasdallah (2017) and Boubaker BenKraiem (2017).

[40] Quoted in *Arab Weekly* (2020). See also Wehrey (2020).

[41] Quoted in Haddad (2019).

[42] Quoted in Arab Weekly (2020).

likewise met those five regularly through the Superior Council of the Armies (CSA). Unlike Essebsi, Saied also met with individual generals, particularly Habib Dhif, the director of military intelligence (*Agence Nationale de Renseignement, de Sécurité et de Défense*). Classmates in high school,[43] Saied and Dhif met individually in November 2019 soon after Saied's assumption of office, and again in January 2021, when they discussed "the readiness of the armed forces to . . . protect the state and its institutions,"[44] a phrase that takes on new meaning when considering July 25. Saied likewise took every opportunity to visit the troops, so much so that the national guard felt jealous. "Saied has been bouncing from one barracks to another for months," lamented a retired national guard colonel major after the coup. "He was always trying to get closer to the officers."[45]

At the same time that Saied granted the officers access, he also granted them autonomy. Rather than follow the approach of Marzouki and Essebsi and reshuffle the top brass, Saied simply left Essebsi's appointees in place. Instead, he co-opted these generals by promoting them earlier than expected. Every June, on the anniversary of the army's founding, Saied announced major promotions. In 2020, he promoted Dhif from brigadier-general to divisional general, his national security advisor Abdel Raouf Atallah from rear-admiral to vice admiral, and the head of military justice Marouane Bougerra, from colonel-major to brigadier-general. In 2021, Saied promoted to divisional general the army chief, Mohamed El Ghoul, the air force chief, Mohammed Hajjam, the inspector-general of the armed forces, Abdelmoneim Belaati, and the director general of military health, Mustapha Ferjani. While Bourguiba and Ben Ali had been hesitant to promote officers to these senior ranks, Saied elevated them relatively quickly, with each member of the CSA serving 3–4 years as brigadier-general prior to becoming divisional-general. These quick and regular promotions sent a signal to military officers that if they stick with Saied, additional promotions might follow.

And they would prove to be right. Post-coup, he would promote Dhif in 2022 to army corps general, the highest rank in the military. Only four officers before him had ever reached that rank: Abdelhamid Escheikh, Youssef El Baraket, Said El Kateb, and Rachid Ammar. Since each of those officers had become the joint chief of staff of the three armies, observers believe Dhif may soon receive that senior-most position as well.[46] Left vacant since Ammar's resignation, filling that position has been a major demand of the military, one that Saied seems on track to fulfill. In 2022, Saied also promoted several other senior officers, including the navy chief, Adel Jhen, from rear admiral to vice admiral; Mohamed Ben Jemaa to rear-admiral; and Lamjed Hammami and Salah Ben Abdessalem to brigadier-general. In August 2022, Divisional General Mustapha Ferjani, who had led the COVID-19 response, was appointed as a minister-adviser to the president.

---

[43] See Jebnoun (2022).
[44] See Agence Tunis Afrique Presse (2021).
[43] Quoted in Lafrance (2021).
[46] See, e.g. Beau (2022).

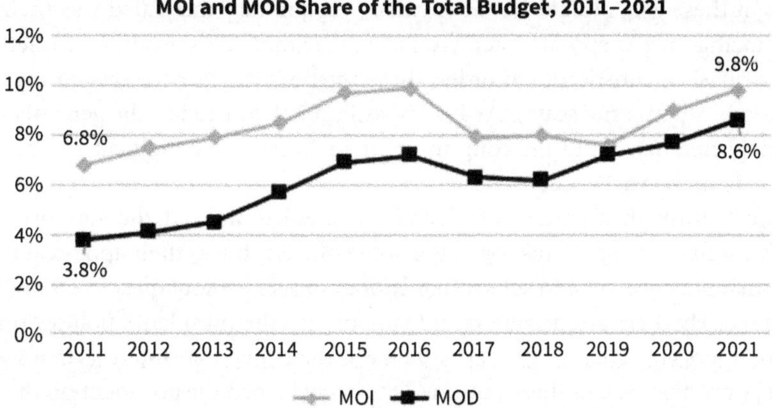

Figure 11.1 Defense and Interior Ministries' Share of the Total Budget, 2011–2021

Beyond promotions, Saied also advanced the military's material interests. Soon into Saied's tenure, the COVID-19 pandemic hit, and we might have expected budgetary priorities to shift towards the Ministries of Health and Social Affairs, rather than Defense. Instead, the defense budget continued to grow in 2020 and 2021, in part because Saied tasked the military with responding to the health crisis. The military set up mobile testing centers throughout the country, particularly in remote, rural areas, and later took the lead in administering vaccines. In 2021, on the eve of the president's coup, the defense budget had grown to 8.6 percent of the total budget, more than double the 3.8 percent it was back in 2011 (see Figure 11.1). The increase sent a message that Saied, unlike Essebsi, would prioritize the military moving forward. Indeed, post-coup, Saied would decree the creation of the Fidaa Foundation, which will provide the military and security forces a retirement grant equivalent to their salary in the event of death or retirement."[47]

The military's involvement in responding to COVID-19 also brought it additional goodwill from the people. The director general of military health, Mustapha Ferjani, was widely praised for the military's efficient response, reinforcing, in the words of one officer, "the good image of the army among the population."[48]

Finally, and perhaps most importantly, Saied also elevated the military's political influence. Saied appointed two military doctors, Colonel-Majors Faouzi Mehdi and Ali Mrabet, successively as minister of health in 2020 and 2021. Subsequently, post-coup, Saied would appoint Divisional General Belaati as Minister of Agriculture in January 2023. For the first time since the 1990s, military officers under Saied were appointed as ministers. The proverbial glass ceiling had been broken.

---

[47] Quoted in D. (2022).
[48] Interview with retired officer, Email, August 18, 2021.

Each of these gains might have convinced the military that Saied was their man for advancing their corporate interests. Put in the ambiguous position of whether to follow a quasi-unconstitutional order, these interests might have seeped into their calculations, tipping the scales. As Bou Nassif (2022) concludes, the generals might have supported Saied and his coup in order to "consolidate political and resource gains made in the past decade."

In short, through a variety of mechanisms, Saied secured the support of the military for his incumbent takeover. For some officers, it was their apolitical professionalism that drove them to subserviently obey orders without question. For others, it was precisely their politicization and support for the president's politics that led them to support the coup. For others still, it was their corporate interests that secured their support. For each of these reasons, "the army helped the president on the night of July 25 by closing the doors of Parliament."[49]

Aftermath

At the time of writing (February 2023), the military is continuing to support Saied by blocking the entrance to the parliament. Military justice has likewise put a number of opposition politicians, journalists, and activists on trial. However, over the past two years, we have also seen signs that the military is hesitant to become too associated with the president, fearing that that politicized image might tarnish its reputation at home and abroad. This dynamic suggests that although facilitating an incumbent takeover comes with fewer reputation costs than staging a coup themselves, the officers still have some PR challenges to deal with.

Immediately after Saied's coup, retired officers took pains to frame it as a neutral, rather than political, action. Retired Colonel-Major Mokhtar Ben Nasr explained that the military "must execute [the president's] orders, while remaining neutral."[50] Retired Colonel-Major Mahmoud Mezoughi, head of the retired officers' association, likewise clarified that "the confidence of the National Army in the person of the President of the Republic or the closeness of a number of leaders to him has nothing to do with following his orders or instructions, but based on what is required by the doctrine of the military institution."[51]

In my own conversations, retired officers expressed regret over how Saied created the image that the military supported him politically. One brigadier-general, for instance, told me that even if the soldiers had to follow orders and deploy around the parliament, they should not have spoken with Chaouachi and Ghannouchi that night, and instead left that public element to the police. "I wish that the soldier didn't react. If she or he asked him, 'Hey! Soldier, I am talking to you! Let us go through.' At most, he should have said, 'I have nothing to do with the door. That's not my mission.'

---

[49] Interview with retired officer, Email, August 18, 2021.
[50] Quoted in Quillen and MacDiarmid (2021).
[51] Quoted in Diwan FM (2021).

And he goes away. People who try to enter or to leave the Parliament . . . it's not a military job. It's the security's job. He does not have to respond to people . . . But, unfortunately, the President is happy with that. For him, it's a show of support."[52]

This general felt similarly about the ongoing military trials of civilians. The 2014 constitution noted that military courts are competent only to deal with "military crimes," but whether that includes insulting the military as well as serious state crimes like treason remains a question of interpretation. Until parliament resolves that question with amendments to the code of military justice, the original code applies, permitting such trials.[53] But while legal, this general was concerned that the rush of military trials under Saied were undermining the military's image: "It's legal. But now the question is, is it opportune? Does this harm the military institution? I wish that the military justice did not have these cases, but unfortunately it's not the case."[54]

Some believe that this dynamic encouraged the military by spring 2022 to start rejecting the president's cases. Ghazi Chaouachi, secretary-general of the Democratic Current, claimed that "we have internal information that the military is taking distance from Saied . . . Military justice started refusing the referral of personalities to the military courts, since what he was doing started to defame the military and started to show it as a dependent institution."[55]

Likewise, some commentators claimed military officers refused to assume political positions offered by Saied. "There are limits to how much the military will adhere to the president's plans," reported *Africa Intelligence*. "According to our sources, the army refused to appoint officers to replace governors ousted by Saied. Likewise, the project to place military officers at the head of strategic public entities, such as the port unit STAM and railway company SNCFT, has so far not led anywhere. The army does not believe it is its place to take on these roles, made all the more tricky to handle by the economic crisis and pandemic. More importantly, the army does not want to damage its popularity, something that was hard won by Ben Ali's overthrow in 2011 and then its fight against terrorism."[56]

Finally, the military is also concerned that the image that it supports Kais Saied might undermine its relations with the United States. In the aftermath of the president's coup, the US Senate in its appropriations bill mandated the Secretary of State submit a report on the Tunisian military's role in the country's "democratic backsliding" and on whether Tunisia's government was "using or relying on the military to reinforce its autocratic actions." Projecting an image that it was not in lockstep with Saied was therefore important for maintaining its military assistance from the United States.

Still, as of writing, none of these costs have been severe enough to change the military's overall calculus. The military has continued to block the parliament despite

[52] Interview with retired officer, June 2022.
[53] See Grewal and Mighri (2019).
[54] Interview with retired officer, June 2022.
[55] Interview with Ghazi Chaouachi, Tunis, July 6, 2022.
[56] See African Intelligence (2021).

the president's more overt violations of the constitution, such as dissolving the parliament, reshuffling the supreme judicial council, and suspending the 2014 constitution. Without sustained domestic and international pressure on the military, it is likely to continue to support Saied's coup.

Conclusion

The type of military Tunisia's democracy inherited helps explain why it obeyed Saied's orders and went along with his incumbent takeover. Apolitical and subservient, it did not question, let alone refuse Saied's orders. Long marginalized, it was relatively easy to co-opt through its corporate interests. And long aloof from politics, it became disillusioned with the chaos and bickering of actual democratic politics, embracing Saied's populist, anti-system rhetoric.

Saied's deployment of the military into domestic political battles risks setting a dangerous precedent for Tunisia moving forward. As one general warned: "If today you can do these things because you have the power, tomorrow someone else can say exactly the same thing, saying the country is in danger. All the people who have done coups, military especially, have said the same thing: that the country is in danger, that he alone can solve it. We cannot accept that."[57]

Simultaneously, the more visible role of the Tunisian military in politics today has led some civilians to call for it to play an even larger role, breaking taboos instilled since Bourguiba. For instance, the July 25 movement, a group in favor of Saied's power grab, called on him in August 2022 to reshuffle the cabinet and replace poor-performing ministers with senior military officers. "Military leaders showed ability to accomplish their mission during hard times," they explained.[58]

To avoid falling into the coup trap moving forward, Tunisia will need to develop an active commitment from both civilian and military circles. On the civilian side, politicians moving forward will need to recommit to keeping the military out of politics. That may require a national dialogue convincing the elites of the long-term dangers of involving the military, as well as a public campaign to strengthen public opinion against such uses of the troops. On the military side, it is important for Tunisian officers to have frank, internal discussions about the professionalism of obeying orders on July 25, and more generally on how to respond when given an unconstitutional order. It should develop internal channels for assessing the legality and constitutionality of orders, either creating an office composed of legal and constitutional experts or a mechanism for quickly referring orders to the constitutional court. Through these reforms to both the civilian and military circles, Tunisia's military may be able to regain its historic legacy in the region as the exception: soldiers of democracy that stay far from political intrigue.

---

[57] Interview with retired officer, June 2022.
[58] Quoted in Agence Tunis Afrique Presse (2022).

12
Surveying the Military

Introduction

The Egypt and Tunisia chapters provided detailed accounts of each military's behavior during the Arab Spring based on interviews with many of the officers involved. But there were hundreds of military personnel who could have altered the course of history in these moments, whether by firing on protesters during the 2011 revolutions, or by plotting or opposing a coup in 2013. We must therefore grapple with the question of how representative those interviews were of the military as a whole. Would we find the same results if we were to reach larger numbers of military personnel?

This chapter addresses this question directly, presenting the results of three original surveys of military personnel. The first surveyed Tunisia's retired officers' association in 2016, reaching 72 retired senior military officers in Tunisia. The latter two were online surveys in 2018, reaching 271 Tunisian and 2,171 Egyptian military personnel, both active-duty and retired. While each survey carries unique advantages and disadvantages, together they reveal a consistent story about how each military's corporate interests, composition, and professionalism shaped their responses to the 2011 revolution and the crises of 2013.

The two surveys in Tunisia confirm that the military felt marginalized under Zine El Abidine Ben Ali. About 80 percent of the military personnel in each survey felt that Ben Ali had neglected the military and had favored the police and national guard over the military. These sentiments strongly correlated with lower support for Ben Ali, as well as a lower willingness to repress protesters on his behalf in the 2011 revolution. Likewise, about 65 percent in each survey felt that Ben Ali had favored officers hailing from the coastal regions (the Sahel) in promotions, a sentiment that likewise bred resentment towards Ben Ali and left him without the military's support in 2011. Pluralities in each survey then confirm that the military's situation improved during the transition, with the Troika government enhancing the military's budget, weapons, and salaries, granting them greater input into security decisions, and ending the favoritism of the Sahel. Those improvements strongly correlated with higher support for democracy, and lower support for a hypothetical military coup in 2013. In short, the two Tunisia surveys confirm each part of the story, demonstrating how Ben Ali's coup-proofing strategies inadvertently laid the groundwork for democracy.

The third survey then shows the opposite dynamic in Egypt. Unlike in Tunisia, officers in Egypt showed no signs of being neglected or counterbalanced by Hosni Mubarak, and were significantly more likely than Tunisian officers to say they would have fired on protesters in 2011 if ordered by their superiors. Majorities surveyed

Soldiers of Democracy?. Sharan Grewal, Oxford University Press. © Sharan Grewal (2023).
DOI: 10.1093/oso/9780192873910.003.0012

then say the military saw its interests encroached upon by the elected president Mohamed Morsi, who they say overruled the military on security decisions, denied them important economic contracts, reduced their powers in the constitution, and tried to "Brotherhoodize" the military. Each of these sentiments strongly correlate with support for the 2013 military coup against Morsi, a finding that is robust to using a list experiment to mitigate social desirability bias. Likewise, priming experiments embedded in all three surveys confirm that these gains and losses during the transition shaped officers' support for democracy and for a coup in 2013.

Beyond corporate interests, the surveys also show how Ben Ali and Mubarak's coup-proofing strategies altered the military's composition and professionalism. Egyptian officers were six times as likely as Tunisian ones to identify as upper class, and four times as likely to say they joined the military due to its high salaries, sentiments that correlated with higher support for both firing on protesters in 2011 and staging a coup in 2013. Meanwhile, Tunisian officers were three times as likely to define professionalism as "being apolitical," a sentiment that reduced support for firing on protesters in 2011 and staging a coup in 2013.

In sum, the survey results provide fascinating insight into how these militaries viewed the 2011 revolutions and the crises of 2013. They provide important empirical support for each facet of the theory, complementing the interview evidence presented in earlier chapters. Together, they reveal a consistent story of how corporate interests, composition, and professionalism shaped the military's attitudes during the revolution and transition.

Methods

In an ideal world, we would conduct our surveys through the Ministry of Defense or a military academy, and thereby reach a representative sample of active-duty officers. However, as a foreigner, even Tunisia's Ministry of Defense viewed my proposal with suspicion. At the same time, an official survey may also suffer certain constraints: it may limit the types of questions one could ask, and may also skew results if officers believe their answers will be viewed by their superiors. Accordingly, in this chapter, I detail two alternative routes for surveying military personnel.

The first approach was to survey Tunisia's retired officers' association, the Association of Former Officers of the National Armed Forces (AAOAN). Established in 2011, the association was home to 174 members at the time of the survey. After building trust and rapport through a year of interviewing its members, the association allowed me to conduct a survey in fall 2016.[1] Sixty-two members completed paper copies of the survey at the association between August and December 2016, and ten others completed an online version in August 2016, resulting in 72 surveys total, or a 41 percent response rate. The questionnaire was in Arabic, but an English translation can be found in the Online Appendix.

---

[1] I am indebted to the kindness and generosity of AAOAN president, retired Colonel Major Mahmoud Mezoughi, for facilitating the survey.

The survey sample consisted entirely of senior officers. Sixty-seven of the 72 officers (93 percent) were colonels or colonel-majors (a unique rank created in Tunisia between colonel and brigadier general). The remaining five were lieutenant colonels and majors. The officers surveyed had retired between 2001 and 2015, with 46 percent retiring after the 2011 revolution. Survey 1 thus succeeded in capturing senior officers who had likely served in key roles during Tunisia's revolution and transition, granting it the highest degree of external validity.

At the same time, we should be cognizant of the limitations of surveying a retired officers' association. First, they are all retired, and may therefore hold different opinions than those who are active-duty. In theory, such differences should be minimal: senior officers who spend their entire careers in the military likely continue to be attuned to the military's corporate interests and its professional ethos well after retirement. Moreover, now retired, they have the liberty to speak freely and critically of the governments they served. A more serious limitation is that the officers' association had to approve the questionnaire. We were therefore not able to ask directly about more sensitive topics, such as whether they would have fired on protesters had Ben Ali asked them to in 2011, and whether they would have supported General Rachid Ammar in staging a coup had he pursued one in 2013. A final limitation is that the survey sample is relatively small (72), limiting the number of covariates we can examine.

To address each of these limitations, I pursued a second approach for the latter two surveys: recruiting respondents through targeted advertisements on Facebook. Facebook advertisements have become increasingly common for recruiting convenience samples for academic surveys, particularly given their low cost.[2] However, Facebook ads also boast an under-utilized advantage: the ability to target advertisements to specific groups. Facebook classifies its users into having certain interests based on information they report in their Facebook profile (such as their employment history) as well as their activity on Facebook (such as liking certain Facebook pages). These algorithm-determined interests have been shown to be fairly accurate for most users.[3] By targeting advertisements just to users with a particular interest, Facebook can oversample hard-to-reach populations. Social scientists have used targeted advertisements to oversample American Catholics, Polish migrants, and German far-right party supporters.[4]

Building off this scholarship, I used Facebook advertisements to oversample Tunisian and Egyptian military personnel. I purchased ads on Facebook that were shown between July 7 and August 19, 2018. The ad itself (see online appendix) featured a picture of the country's military and invited Facebook users to take "a survey about security in the Middle East." Clicking on the ad took users out of Facebook

---

[2] i.e., Cassese et al. (2013); Samuels and Zucco (2014); Zhang et al. (2020); Guiler (2020).

[3] In a representative Pew survey in the US, 59 percent said their Facebook-assigned interests "somewhat" or "very accurately" represented them, while only 27 percent said they were "not very" or "not at all" accurate. The remaining 14 percent either refused to answer or were not assigned interests by Facebook due to lack of activity. See Hiltin and Rainie (2019).

[4] See Bhutta (2012); Potzschke and Braun (2017) and Jager (2017), respectively.

and into Qualtrics, a survey platform, where they filled out a consent form and then answered the survey.[5] Crucially, the advertisement was not shown to all 7 million Tunisians and 35 million Egyptians on Facebook, but only to the 440,000 and 5 million, respectively, that Facebook has classified as having an interest in the military. Not everyone interested in the military would have actually served, but this targeting allows us to oversample the number of military personnel who see the advertisement.

Indeed, the results bear this out. In Tunisia, 1,653 people clicked on the advertisement and filled out the questionnaire. Of these, 271 (or 16 percent) reported in the survey that they have military experience, including 150 who said they were active-duty, and 121 who said they were former military personnel. In Egypt, a much larger country with a much larger military, 6,855 people filled out the survey. Of these, 2,171 (32 percent) said they have military experience, including 496 active-duty and 1,675 former military personnel. Both rates are considerably higher than in the actual population,[6] suggesting that the targeted advertisement indeed succeeded in oversampling military personnel, and in turn in producing sizable samples of military personnel (271 Tunisians and 2,171 Egyptians).

These military personnel were primarily soldiers and junior officers, complementing the first survey of senior officers. Figure 12.1 presents their ranks (among those who revealed them). Like the actual militaries, many of the respondents in surveys 2 and 3 were soldiers (34 percent in Tunisia and 39 percent in Egypt) and non-commissioned officers (NCOs; 34 percent in Tunisia and 44 percent in Egypt), with smaller proportions of junior officers (19 percent and 9 percent, respectively), and senior officers (13 percent and 8 percent).

This diversity across ranks is especially useful for our study. The soldiers and NCOs are the ones who would directly repress protesters, and thus are some of the most important for considerations about the 2011 revolution. Meanwhile, the junior and senior officers can order more large-scale defection and repression, and are the primary actors behind coups. Each level is therefore important in explaining the behavior of these militaries.

There are two primary limitations to these online surveys. The first is that all respondents are self-identified military personnel; there is no way to independently verify their military status.[7] However, the survey created no structural incentive to lie. All Egyptians and Tunisians were allowed to take the survey, whether military or civilian. The survey was not presented as being only for military personnel, and indeed the majority of respondents (excluded in this chapter) were civilians.

---

[5] There are important ethical considerations about the data Facebook collects on its users. Because the survey is conducted on a separate platform, Facebook does not learn their answers to any of the questions. A second concern with Facebook-assisted surveys is whether the respondents are actually "real" people, or potentially bots. The online appendix presents a number of verification checks: (1) geo-locating respondents to show that they were indeed located in Egypt and Tunisia, (2) showing their time to completion, to demonstrate they were taking the survey seriously and not zipping through like a bot, and (3) showing that there were no duplicate surveys, and only 2 percent of surveys were even 85 percent the same.

[6] The military makes up less than 1 percent of these countries' overall populations.

[7] For the sake of anonymity, no names could be recorded; nor, for that matter, is there a public list of names in the military to cross-check with.

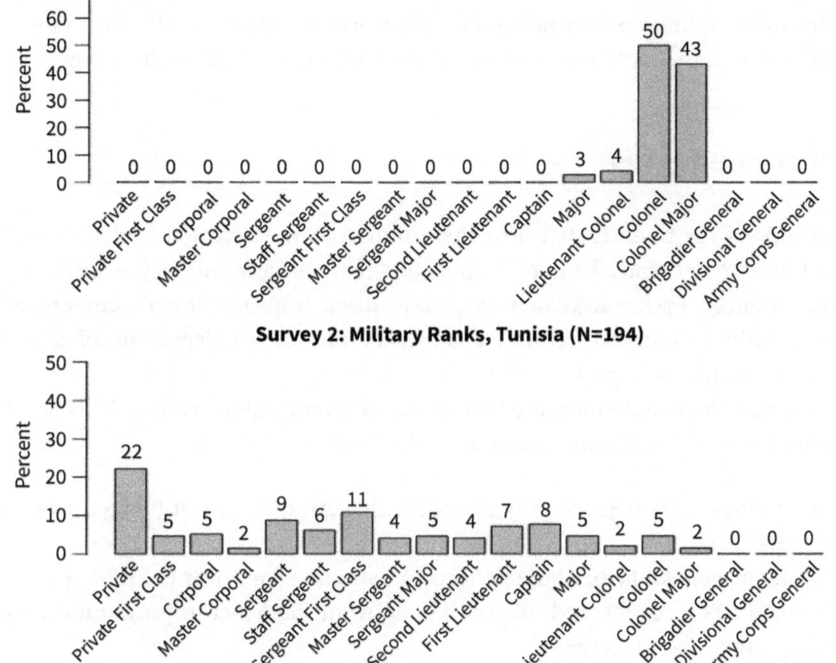

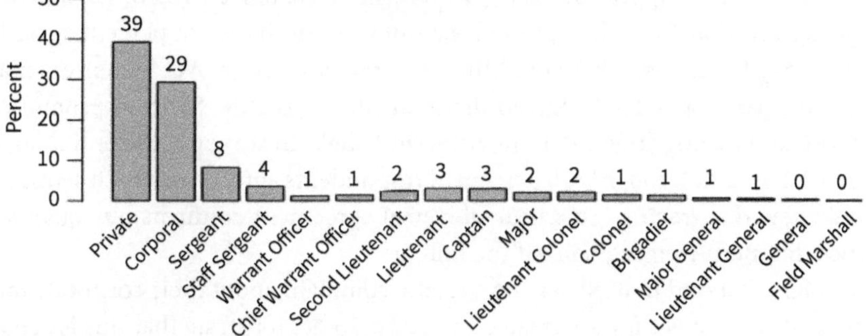

Figure 12.1 Military Ranks in Each Survey

Moreover, the results in the Tunisia sample are consistent with our survey of the retired officers' association.

The second limitation is that at best, the survey is representative only of the military personnel who are on Facebook, a sample that likely skews younger, wealthier, and better educated than the average military personnel (for demographic comparisons, see online appendix). While we do not have data for the military, only about 35 percent of Egyptians and 55 percent of Tunisians have Facebook accounts. While representative samples of the military would be the gold standard, they are near impossible in this context. In short, the military personnel surveyed in surveys 2 and 3 are self-reported, and by no means representative of either military. Despite these limitations, these surveys provide us with the first large-scale survey samples of active-duty military personnel in the Arab world, and provide a look into some of the taboo topics we could not address with the officers' association in survey 1.

Military Legacies

The theory of the book is that how these militaries were treated under autocracy shaped how they behaved under democracy. In Tunisia, a military neglected and counterbalanced under autocracy saw its position improve under democracy. In Egypt, a military empowered under autocracy saw its privileges curtailed under democracy, sparking a coup.

To capture these dynamics, the two Tunisia surveys gauged respondents' level of agreement with the following questions:

1. "The military was neglected by President Ben Ali in terms of budget, weapons, and salaries."
2. "President Ben Ali favored the police and national guard over the military."
3. "President Ben Ali favored officers hailing from the Sahel in promotions, especially to the rank of General."

There was overwhelming agreement with all three statements. In the survey of the officers' association (Figure 12.2, top), 88 percent of the officers (63 of 72) agreed or strongly agreed that Ben Ali neglected the military. Similarly, 92 percent agreed or strongly agreed that Ben Ali favored the Ministry of Interior over Defense. Finally, 59 percent agreed or strongly agreed that Ben Ali favored the Sahel in promotions, with those disagreeing largely coming from the Sahel.[8] In survey 2, the online survey (Figure 12.2, middle), roughly 70 percent of respondents agreed with each sentiment, with very few disagreeing. This near-universal agreement confirms our qualitative evidence that Ben Ali marginalized the military.

One might respond that officers universally complain about their corporate interests, regardless of how they are treated in reality. To demonstrate that this is actually not the case, in the survey in Egypt I asked almost identical statements:

1. "The military was neglected by President Mubarak in terms of budget, weapons, and salaries."
2. "President Mubarak favored the police and central security forces over the military."
3. "Gamal Mubarak represented a threat to the military's economic interests."

---

[8] Among the 35 officers who grew up in the coast, 44 percent agreed that Ben Ali privileged the Sahel. Among the 37 officers not from the coast, 73 percent agreed that Ben Ali favored the Sahel, a significant difference (p=0.008). Notably, even among the Sahelien officers, more agreed than disagreed (44 v. 34 percent) that Ben Ali favored the Sahel (the remaining 22 percent from the coast answered neutral).

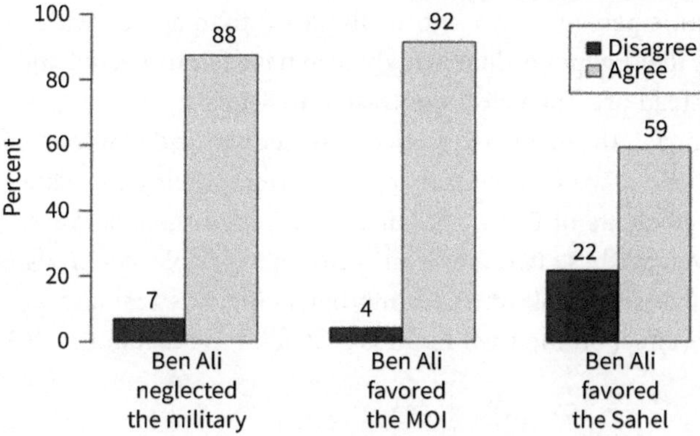

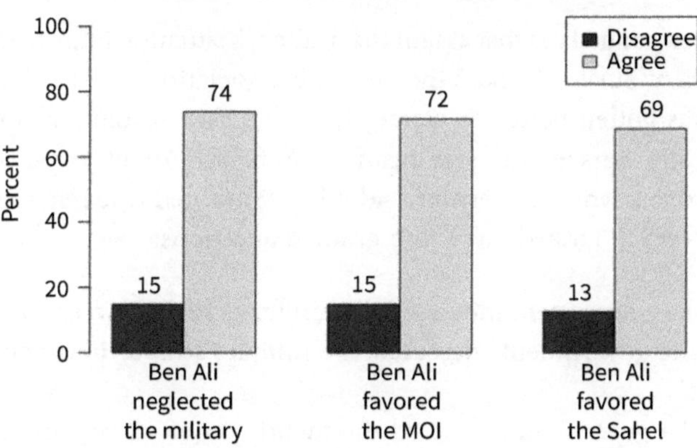

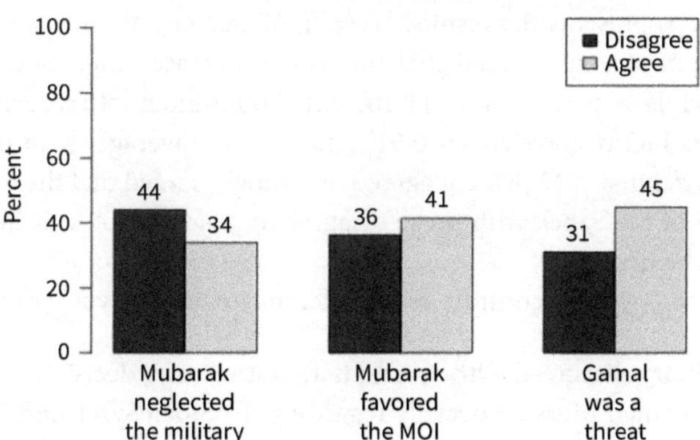

Figure 12.2 Coup-Proofing under Ben Ali and Mubarak, Surveys 1–3

In Egypt (Figure 12.2, bottom), we do not see the same overwhelming agreement. Roughly the same percent, if not more, disagreed than agreed with each statement. Despite claims that Egypt's military might also have felt neglected and marginalized, the surveys instead present a clear contrast with Tunisia.

In both countries, the first two questions—whether the dictator neglected the military and whether he favored the Ministry of Interior—highly correlate, with Pearson's correlation coefficients of 0.69, 0.56, and 0.55 in the three surveys, respectively. I accordingly average these two questions into one variable, *counterbalanced*, for the regression analyses that follow. If counterbalancing was real and salient, it should have a negative effect on their willingness to defend the dictator in 2011.

The Transition

The surveys then gauged to what extent the military's situation improved or worsened under democracy. Survey 1 asked the Tunisian association whether "the position of the military has gotten better or worse since the 2011 revolution" on a 1–5 scale from significantly worsened to significantly improved. About 35 percent said their situation improved, while 15 percent said it had worsened (the remainder answered neutral). In survey 2, I asked more fine-grained questions:

- "The troika government increased the military's budget, weapons, and salaries."
- "The troika government increased the military's input into national security decisions."
- "The troika government reduced the favoritism of officers from the Sahel in promotions."

Figure 12.3 (top) presents the results. Overall, 65 percent of Tunisian military personnel agreed or strongly agreed that the troika increased their budget, weapons, and salaries, while 49 percent agreed it increased their input into security policy. The two statements highly correlate (r=0.51), and hence I average them into one variable, *rebalanced*. Finally, 42 percent agreed or strongly agreed that the troika reduced the favoritism of the Sahel, with those disagreeing tending not to believe there was favoritism in the first place.

The results in Egypt, by contrast, tell a different story. In Egypt, I asked whether:

- "The military disagreed with several national security decisions made by President Mohamed Morsi, especially regarding the Sinai, Syria, and Ethiopia."
- "President Mohamed Morsi denied the military important economic contracts, such as the Suez Canal Corridor Development Project."
- "President Mohamed Morsi limited the military's prerogatives in the constitution."
- "President Morsi attempted to Brotherhoodize ('*ikhwanat*') the military."

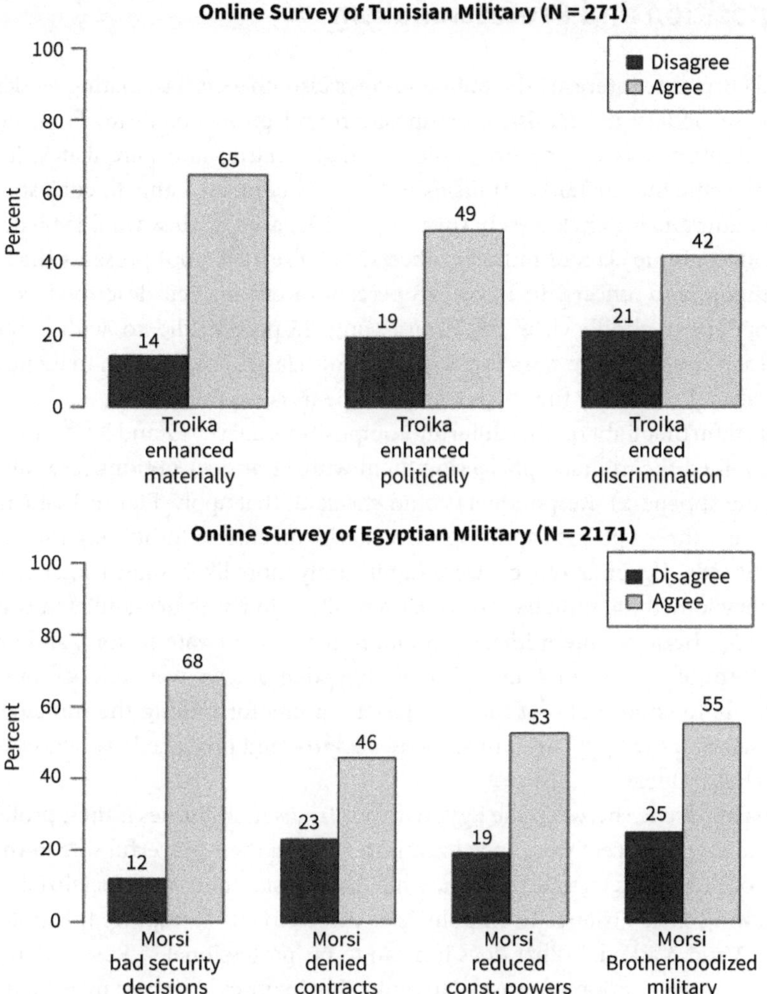

Figure 12.3 Corporate Interests under Democracy, Surveys 2 and 3

Figure 12.3 (bottom) presents their answers. Overall, 68 percent agreed that Morsi encroached on their security decisions, 53 percent on their constitutional prerogatives, and 46 percent on their economic contracts. Subsetting to officers, agreement was at 78 percent, 60 percent, and 57 percent, respectively. I likewise average these three variables into one, *encroached*. Finally, 55 percent of respondents believed Morsi tried to Islamize or Brotherhood-ize the military, including 69 percent of officers.

In short, in Tunisia, a military that was neglected and counterbalanced saw its fortunes improve, while in Egypt, a military that had been empowered saw its interests threatened. These differing corporate interests, I argue, should shape how these two militaries viewed the revolution and transition.

Composition and Professionalism

Beyond corporate interests, the online surveys also uncover fascinating evidence of the two secondary mechanisms: composition and professionalism. First, because Egypt's military was empowered, enjoying high salaries and perquisites, it could attract the elite into its ranks. Tunisia's military, by contrast, came to consist instead of the middle and lower classes. In surveys 2 and 3, I asked, "How would you describe the socioeconomic class of military officers?" Figure 12.4 (top) presents the results, subsetting just to officers. In Egypt, 78 percent of officers self-described as "upper class" or "upper-middle class." In Tunisia, only 25 percent did so, with 71 percent instead selecting "middle class" or "lower-middle class." The decision to empower or marginalize the military thus appeared to shape its composition.

To shed further light on this differing composition, surveys 2 and 3 also asked why officers joined the military, presenting them with 11 answer options (see full list in the online appendix). Respondents could check all that apply. Figure 12.4 (middle) presents the three options capturing the material incentives for joining the military. As can be seen, Egyptian officers were significantly more likely than Tunisian officers to say they joined the military "to secure a position in a military-affiliated company afterwards"; because "the military pays more than the private sector"; and because it "is a form of upward mobility." Overall, Egyptian officers were almost four times more likely to choose one of these material reasons for joining the military. With higher salaries, the Egyptian military appealed to—and produced—a relatively elite, upper-class military.

A final difference between the Egyptian and Tunisian militaries is their professionalism. In Egypt, officers were socialized into viewing their powerful role in the state as part of their professional mission, while in Tunisia, they were socialized instead into viewing their distance from politics as professional. To capture this difference, surveys 2 and 3 asked: "What does it mean to be 'professional'?" Respondents were shown six answer options and asked to rank them in order of importance. Figure 12.4 (bottom) plots what respondents from each country ranked as the most important factor. As can be seen, the biggest gap concerns "being apolitical." While 26 percent of Tunisian officers ranked being apolitical the #1 factor for professionalism, only 8 percent of Egyptian officers did the same ($p<0.001$). Likewise, while 45 percent of Tunisian officers ranked being apolitical within the top three most important factors, only 25 percent of Egyptian officers did the same ($p=0.015$).

In sum, the Tunisian and Egyptian militaries exhibit major differences in their corporate interests, composition, and professionalism. Each of these variables, in turn, should shape how these militaries view the revolution and democratic transition. Because the questions I could ask in each survey differ, I begin first with the survey of the Tunisian officers' association, and then turn to the online surveys.

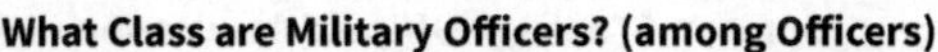

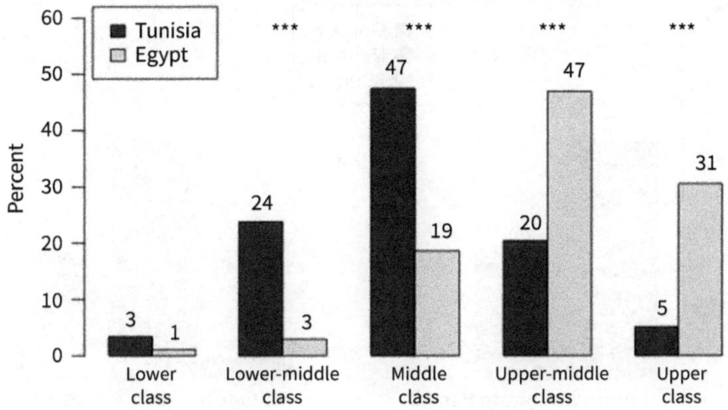

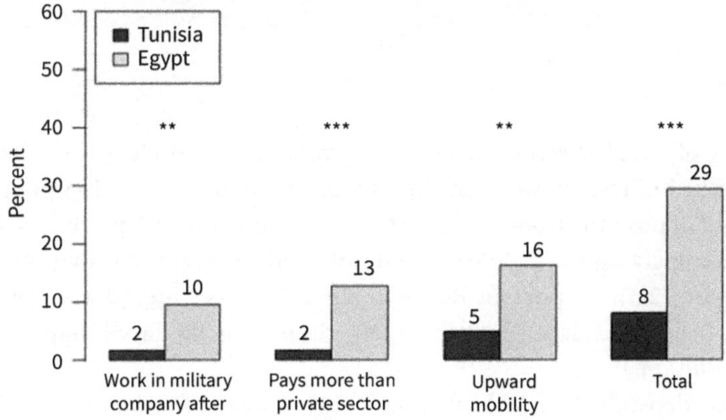

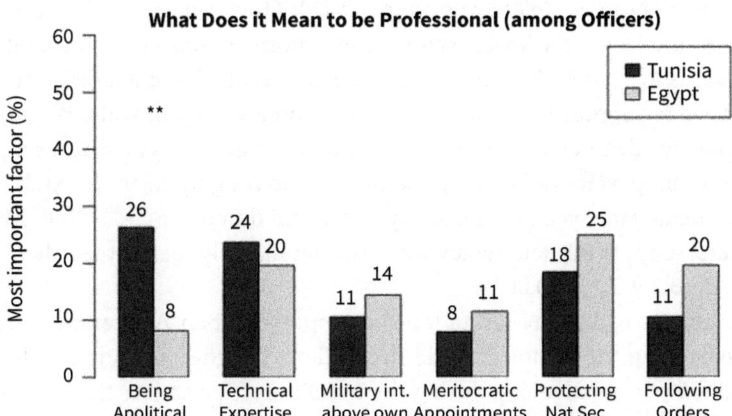

Figure 12.4 Military Composition and Professionalism, Surveys 2 and 3

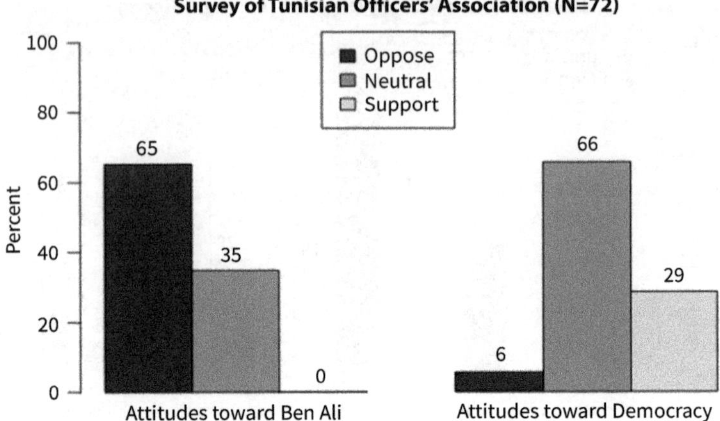

Figure 12.5 Support for Ben Ali and for Democracy, Survey 1

Survey 1

In the survey of Tunisia's senior officers, I examine two dependent variables. First, the survey asked officers how much they supported Ben Ali on a 1–5 point scale, from strongly oppose to strongly support. The vast majority, 65 percent, said they opposed or strongly opposed Ben Ali, and not a single officer said they supported him (see Figure 12.5). Support for Ben Ali on average was a mere 2.2 out of 5. That low support helps to explain why he was left without the military's support during the 2011 revolution.

The second dependent variable examines their support for democracy. Officers were asked how suitable democracy is for Tunisia, on a 1–5 scale from completely inappropriate (1) to completely appropriate (5). Only 6 percent of officers ranked democracy as a 1 or 2, the lowest values. The majority of officers, 66 percent, ranked democracy as a 3, while the remaining 29 percent ranked it as a 4 or 5. Overall, the average level of support for democracy was 3.2 on the 5-point scale. While modest, this support for democracy is significantly higher than the average Tunisian's at this time, whose support for democracy had dropped to roughly 2.2 in the Arab Barometer survey fielded that year, a statistically significant difference ($p<0.001$).[9] Moreover, the officers' support for democracy was also significantly higher than their support for Ben Ali (3.2 v. 2.2, $p<0.001$).

My argument is that the military's low support for Ben Ali stemmed from him counterbalancing the military, while the military's higher support for democracy stemmed from its rebalancing during the transition. To examine these correlations, Table 12.1 presents two regression analyses, the first predicting support for Ben Ali and the second support for democracy.

---

[9] The Arab Barometer Wave 4 asked the same question about the suitability of democracy, though has to be converted from a 0–10 point scale to 1–5 point one.

Table 12.1 Survey of Tunisian Officers' Association

	Dependent variable:	
	Support for Ben Ali (1)	**Support for Democracy** (2)
Ben Ali counterbalanced	−1.360** (0.624)	
Troika rebalanced		1.180** (0.470)
Ben Ali favored Sahel	0.464 (0.351)	0.646* (0.344)
from Sahel	0.451** (0.179)	0.257 (0.179)
Islamist	−0.035 (0.540)	−0.477 (0.559)
US Training	−0.181 (0.177)	−0.182 (0.175)
Army	0.086 (0.172)	0.077 (0.173)
Rank	0.095 (0.163)	0.221 (0.161)
Constant	2.531*** (0.605)	1.541*** (0.523)
Observations	66	68
R^2	0.231	0.204
Adjusted R^2	0.139	0.097

Note: *$p<0.1$; **$p<0.05$; ***$p<0.01$
Note: Model 2 also includes the priming experiment discussed below.

Model 1 shows that officers who believed that Ben Ali had neglected the military and favored the Ministry of Interior (*counterbalanced*) were significantly less supportive of Ben Ali. Figure 12.6 (top-left) plots the substantive effect size. As can be seen, officers who strongly agreed that Ben Ali counterbalanced the military were about a full point less supportive of Ben Ali than those who disagreed, dropping support for Ben Ali from a neutral 3 down to a more hostile 2 on the 5-point scale. While correlational, these patterns are consistent with Ben Ali's coup-proofing strategies breeding resentment towards him.

Model 2 then shows that the military's rebalancing during the transition produced support for democracy. Officers who believed that the military's position

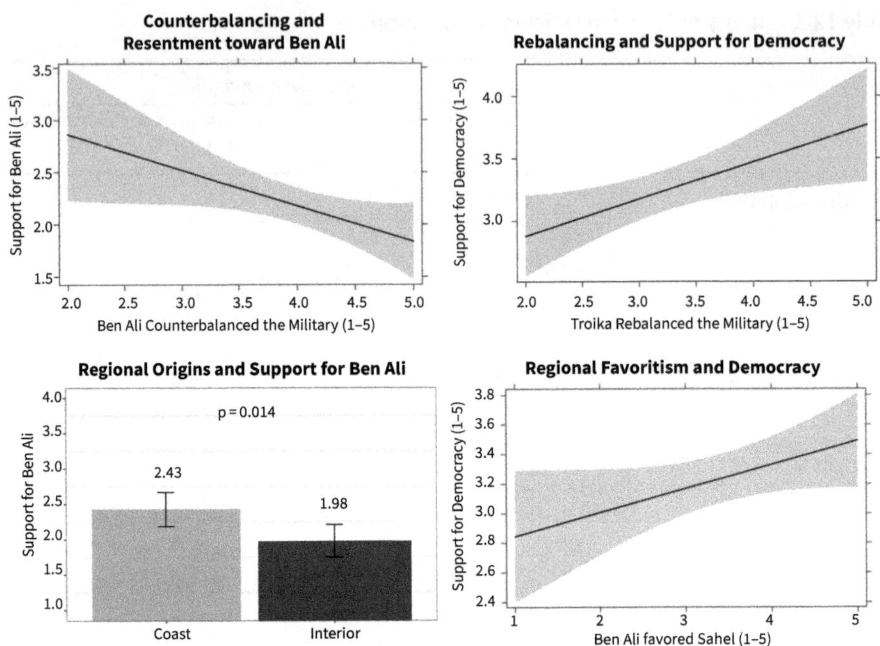

Figure 12.6 Coup-Proofing, Support for Ben Ali, and for Democracy, Survey 1

had significantly improved were almost a full point more supportive of democracy than officers who believed the military's position had worsened, moving support for democracy from a neutral 3 up to a supportive 4 (see Figure 12.6 top-right). The enhancement of the Tunisian military's interests under democracy appears to have bred goodwill towards the transition.

Both models also show support for the effects of regional discrimination. Ben Ali had privileged officers from the Sahel in promotions, and for good reason: model 1 confirms that officers from the Sahel were on average more supportive of him (see Figure 12.6, bottom-left). Yet, among other officers, those feelings of discrimination bred support for democracy: officers who believed Ben Ali favored the Sahel were about half a point more supportive of democracy (see Figure 12.6, bottom-right).

Each of these correlations are robust to controlling for a variety of potential confounders, as shown in Table 12.1. I control for rank, as officers who retired at a lower rank may harbor greater resentment toward Ben Ali. I control for branch, specifically the land army, which as the largest branch likely harbored the least resentment. I control for Islamism, measured as support for Ennahda leader Rached Ghannouchi, as Islamists might have been more supportive of the democracy that brought them to power. Finally, I control for having received US training, as a number of scholars have posited that that may have pushed the Tunisian military to abandon Ben Ali in 2011 and support democracy instead.[10] None of these controls, however, are significant.

---

[10] However, *all* of the officers in this survey trained in Western democracies, so the coefficient on US training compares those with US-training to those who trained in France.

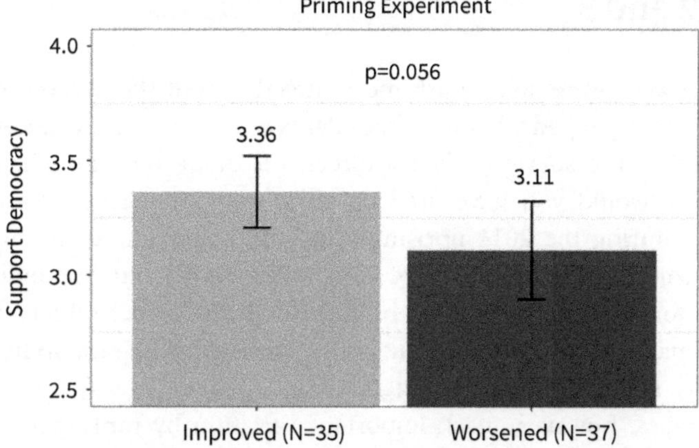

Figure 12.7 Priming Experiment, Survey 1

In short, Ben Ali's counterbalancing of the Tunisian military appeared to breed resentment toward him, while its rebalancing under democracy appeared to produce support for the transition. To determine whether these effects are causal, and not just correlational, survey 1 also included a priming experiment.[11] Prior to asking officers about their support for democracy, half of the sample was primed to think of how the military's situation improved under democracy, and half about how it has worsened:[12]

1. **Improved:** "Many officers claim that the position of the military has improved since the 2011 uprising, in terms of budget, weapons, salaries, and influence over national security decisions."
2. **Worsened:** "Many officers claim that the position of the military has worsened since the 2011 uprising, in terms of security threats and interference by political leaders."

Figure 12.7 presents the results. Officers primed to think that the military's situation has improved ranked democracy on average 0.25 points higher than those primed to think its position has worsened (3.11 v. 3.36, p=0.056 in a one-sided t-test). These results suggest that the military's improvement under democracy may indeed have had a causal effect increasing their support for democracy.

In sum, survey 1 provides strong evidence that the Tunisian military's corporate interests shaped its opposition to Ben Ali and support for democracy. To show the effects of the secondary mechanisms—composition and professionalism—and to trace out the effects on more sensitive questions, I now turn to the online surveys.

---

[11] For the online survey, the randomization was done through Qualtrics; for the handwritten surveys, I alternated the surveys in the stack handed to the association. The Online Appendix shows that the randomization succeeded in producing covariate balance across the two treatment groups.

[12] Given the small sample size, I could not also include in this survey a pure control group where no information was given. The primes are not perfectly parallel—in the sense of an increase in the budget v. a decrease in the budget—because such a lie would simply not be believed. Instead of parallel primes, I opted for primes that were both true, and thus did not involve any deception.

Surveys 2 and 3

The online surveys were able to ask more directly about the precise outcomes of interest. First, they gauged whether respondents wanted to repress the Arab Spring protests of 2011. The surveys asked a direct, yes or no question: "If ordered by your superiors, would you have fired upon protesters to protect President [Ben Ali/Mubarak] during the 2011 uprising?" In both countries, about 20 percent of respondents said yes they would have fired, while 80 percent responded no. That high support for defection could have been driven by social desirability bias and the retrospective nature of the question, but is also consistent with both militaries' actual behavior, since neither fired on protesters.

These averages, however, mask important variation by rank (See Figure 12.8, top).[13] In Egypt, the officers were about twice as likely as the lower ranks to say they would have fired (29 v. 16 percent, p<0.001). This is also consistent with their actual behavior: Egyptian officers only begrudgingly turned on Mubarak after their conscript soldiers began to sympathize with the protesters. Egypt's officers, moreover, were also significantly more willing to fire than Tunisia's (29 v. 18 percent, p=0.041), once again in line with reality: unlike Egypt's begrudging defection, Tunisia's officers more readily shirked when deployed, and even on occasion clashed with the police and presidential guard. While neither Egypt nor Tunisia's militaries fired, the surveys appear to capture the different processes by which they got there.

The second dependent variable is each military's level of support for a military coup in 2013 (see Figure 12.8, bottom). In Egypt, where a coup occurred, the survey asked a direct, yes or no question: "Did you support the military's intervention to remove President Mohamed Morsi on July 3, 2013?" Roughly 64 percent of Egyptian military personnel responded yes, including 82 percent of officers. While one may expect these results to be inflated by social desirability bias and/or fear of punishment, a list experiment (see online appendix) likewise produced high support, estimating 58 percent support for the coup overall, and 63 percent among officers.

In Tunisia, where a coup did not materialize, the survey instead asked a hypothetical question: "Hypothetically, during the political crisis in 2013, would you have supported General Rachid Ammar in ousting the troika government?" This question was answered on a 5-point scale from strongly support to strongly oppose. Just 29 percent of Tunisian military personnel said they would have supported or strongly supported a coup in 2013, including just 22 percent of officers.

These results suggest that Egyptian military personnel were far more supportive of a coup than their Tunisian counterparts (64 to 29 percent, p<0.001). This gap is even larger among the officers, with Egypt's officers almost four times more supportive of a coup than Tunisia's (82 v. 22 percent, p<0.001).

I argue that the officers' corporate interests, composition, and professionalism help explain their differing attitudes towards the 2011 revolution and 2013 coup. Let's

---

[13] I divide each survey sample into officers and non-officers. For simplicity I label the latter "soldiers," but in reality it includes soldiers, NCOs, and those who refused to reveal their ranks.

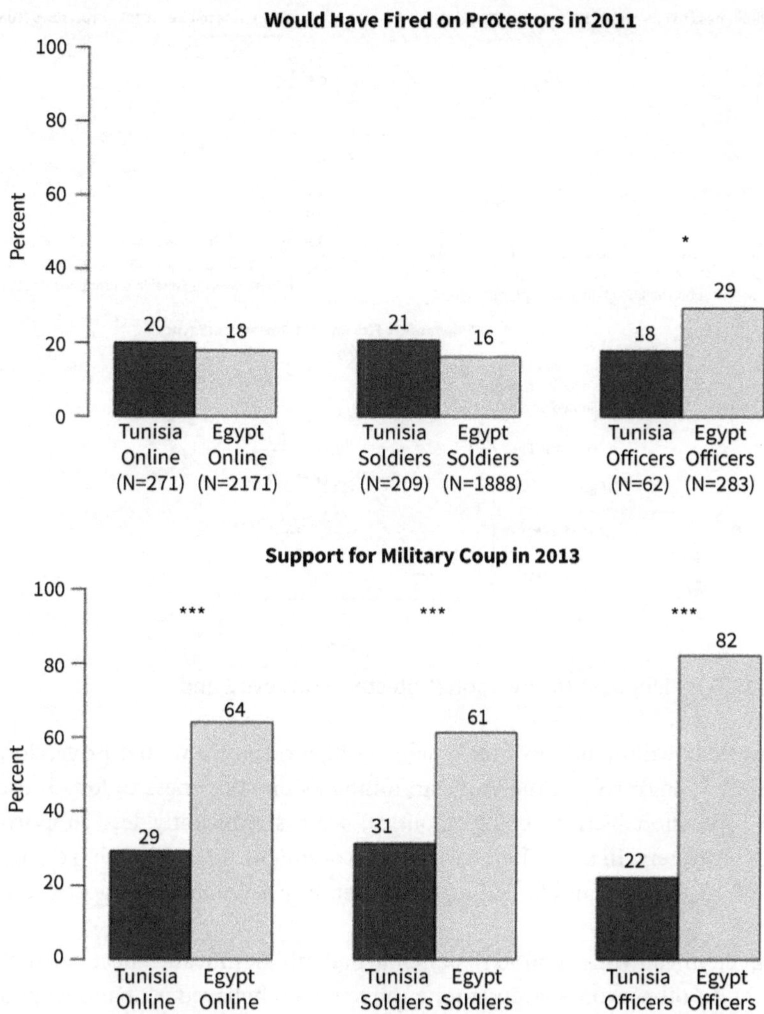

Figure 12.8 Support for 2011 Repression and 2013 Military Coup, Surveys 2 and 3

begin with the revolution. Table 12.2 examines how respondents' support for firing on protesters varied by a number of covariates. Models 1–2 focus on Tunisia, and 3–4 on Egypt.

In Tunisia, the results show that Ben Ali's counterbalancing of the military significantly reduced their support for firing upon protesters (model 1). As illustrated in Figure 12.9 (top-left), perceptions of counterbalancing cut their willingness to fire in half, dropping from roughly 33 percent to 14 percent. Model 2 then shows that Ben Ali's regional favoritism divided his military. As shown in Figure 12.9 (top-right), military personnel from the Sahel benefited from his favoritism, and thus were significantly more supportive of firing on protesters. However, the majority of the force—military personnel from the interior regions—resented their discrimination,

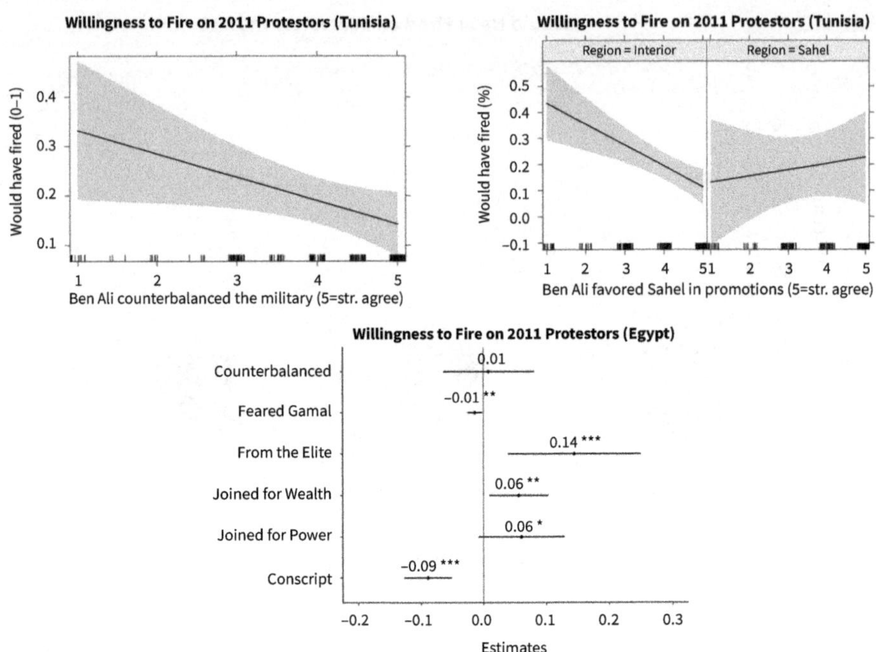

Figure 12.9 Willingness to Fire upon Protesters, Surveys 2 and 3

reducing their willingness to fire. Finally, both models show that professionalism also played a major role in the Tunisian military's unwillingness to fire. Those who defined professionalism as being apolitical were significantly less supportive of firing on protesters. In short, Ben Ali's coup-proofing strategies, keeping the military marginalized, divided, and far from politics, left him without its support in the 2011 revolution.

In Egypt, meanwhile, counterbalancing had no significant effect on defection (model 3). In other words, even among the few who believed Mubarak counterbalanced the military, this perception was not salient enough to influence their attitudes toward defection. Similarly, a belief that Gamal Mubarak was a threat to the military had only a minor effect breeding support for defection. Complementing our qualitative reading of these accounts (see Chapters 5 and 6), these factors do not seem highly salient in our survey, either.

Instead, the results in Egypt point to a vertically divided military. On the one hand, many factors were pushing the officers to be supportive of repression. Officers who self-identified as upper class or upper middle class (*elite officer*) were significantly more supportive of firing on protesters, as were officers who said they joined the military for material reasons (*joined for wealth*). Similar effects obtain for officers who said they joined the military "to secure a position in government afterwards" (*joined for power*). Empowered by Mubarak, Egypt's military attracted the elite and officers seeking power and wealth, who were significantly more supportive of repression.

On the other hand, however, those officers needed the soldiers below them to actually fire on protesters. Those soldiers were largely conscripts: forced to serve, and often mistreated. Indeed, the conscripts in our survey were significantly less

Table 12.2 Willingness to Fire on Protesters in 2011 Revolution

	Dependent variable: Would have fired to protect...			
	Ben Ali (Tunisia)		Mubarak (Egypt)	
	(1)	(2)	(3)	(4)
Counterbalanced	−0.24** (0.11)		−0.03 (0.03)	
Ben Ali favored coast		−0.32*** (0.09)		
Ben Ali favored coast*from coast		0.42** (0.19)		
from coast	−0.002 (0.07)	−0.30** (0.14)		
Gamal was threat				−0.05** (0.02)
Elite Officer	−0.05 (0.12)	−0.01 (0.12)	0.14*** (0.05)	0.14*** (0.05)
Joined for Wealth	0.02 (0.07)	0.01 (0.06)	0.06** (0.02)	0.06** (0.02)
Joined for Power	0.22** (0.09)	0.22** (0.09)	0.06* (0.04)	0.06* (0.04)
Apolitical	−0.12** (0.05)	−0.12** (0.05)	0.001 (0.02)	0.001 (0.02)
Covariates				
Conscript	0.01 (0.07)	0.001 (0.07)	−0.09*** (0.02)	−0.09*** (0.02)
Islamist	−0.18* (0.10)	−0.15 (0.10)	−0.05 (0.03)	−0.05 (0.03)
Prayer	−0.09* (0.05)	−0.07 (0.05)	−0.06*** (0.02)	−0.06*** (0.02)
Registered to Vote	0.04 (0.06)	0.07 (0.06)	0.01 (0.02)	0.01 (0.02)
Western Training	0.08 (0.06)	0.09 (0.06)	0.13*** (0.03)	0.14*** (0.03)
Joined to Defend Country	−0.10* (0.05)	−0.12** (0.05)	−0.05*** (0.02)	−0.05*** (0.02)
Joined for Thrill of Fighting	0.12* (0.07)	0.11* (0.07)	0.05* (0.03)	0.05* (0.03)
Deployed 2011	0.10** (0.05)	0.12** (0.05)	0.06*** (0.02)	0.06*** (0.02)
Active-Duty	−0.10* (0.05)	−0.10* (0.05)	0.03 (0.02)	0.03 (0.02)
Army	0.09 (0.10)	0.12 (0.09)	−0.05* (0.02)	−0.05* (0.02)
Navy	0.03 (0.12)	0.06 (0.12)	−0.03 (0.04)	−0.03 (0.04)
Soldier	−0.004 (0.07)	0.01 (0.07)	0.01 (0.02)	0.01 (0.02)
NCO	0.09 (0.07)	0.10 (0.07)	0.03 (0.02)	0.03 (0.02)
Jun. Officer	0.11 (0.09)	0.12 (0.09)	−0.06 (0.06)	−0.06 (0.06)
Sen. Officer	−0.11 (0.10)	−0.09 (0.10)	−0.12*** (0.06)	−0.12** (0.06)
Education	−0.01 (0.08)	−0.01 (0.08)	0.04 (0.03)	0.04 (0.03)
Rural	−0.11** (0.05)	−0.12** (0.05)	0.03 (0.02)	0.03 (0.02)
Constant	0.51*** (0.16)	0.50*** (0.14)	0.24*** (0.05)	0.25*** (0.05)
Observations	262	262	2,163	2,163
R^2	0.14	0.17	0.08	0.08
Adjusted R^2	0.06	0.09	0.07	0.07

Note: $^*p<0.1$; $^{**}p<0.05$; $^{***}p<0.01$

supportive of firing on protesters. That vertical division inhibited the ability of Egypt's empowered officers to repress the protesters, and ultimately forced them to begrudgingly defect from Mubarak.

A number of the control variables are also worth mentioning. First, while many have hypothesized that Western training helped to breed defection in the Arab Spring, our results suggest that Western training actually increased the likelihood of firing on protesters (and in Egypt, significantly so). Second, more religious and Islamist respondents were less supportive of repression, likely more supportive of the Islamists who would soon come to power. Third, respondents who joined the military out of "a sense of duty to defend the country" were less willing to fire on protesters, while those who joined seeking "adventure and the thrill of fighting" were more supportive. Finally, military personnel who were actually deployed during the 2011 revolutions were, interestingly, more likely to fire on protesters, perhaps having been selectively deployed by their leaders.

In short, each of our hypothesized factors—corporate interests, composition, and professionalism—helped to shape the military's attitudes toward repression and defection during the 2011 revolution. In Tunisia, a neglected, discriminated, and largely apolitical military had no qualms in abandoning Ben Ali. In Egypt, despite elite officers' desire to preserve Mubarak, they ultimately could not, limited by the conscript soldiers under their command. As a result, both Mubarak and Ben Ali were toppled, and Tunisia and Egypt embarked on transitions to democracy.

Support for a Coup

Egypt's transition, however, would soon fall to a military coup, while Tunisia's would not. To shed light on why Egypt's military was more supportive of a coup, Table 12.3 shows how support for a coup was shaped by a series of covariates in Tunisia (models 1–2) and Egypt (3–4).

In Tunisia, the troika government sought to reverse Ben Ali's coup-proofing tactics. The survey confirms that these efforts earned the troika goodwill from the military. First, military personnel who believed that the troika government rebalanced the military, increasing its budget and political influence, were significantly less supportive of a coup in 2013. Substantively, a belief that the troika rebalanced the military reduced support for a coup from roughly a neutral 3.3 to an opposed 2.3 on the 1–5 point scale (see Figure 12.10, top).

Second, the troika sought to reduce the favoritism of officers from the Sahel by elevating instead those from the interior. This reversal, as can be expected, generated mixed effects. Officers from the Sahel who believed the troika reduced their privilege became significantly more supportive of a coup, but those from the interior regions who believed the troika alleviated their discrimination remained opposed to a coup.

Finally, the apolitical professionalism the Tunisian military developed under autocracy likewise led it to oppose a coup. Respondents who defined professionalism as being apolitical were significantly less supportive of a coup, reducing support by about half a point.

Table 12.3 Support for a Military Coup in 2013

| | Dependent Variable: Support for Coup against | | | |
| | Troika (Tunisia) | | Morsi (Egypt) | |
	(1)	(2)	(3)	(4)
Troika rebalanced	-0.90^{**} (0.45)	-1.18^{**} (0.51)		
Troika elevated interior		1.88^{**} (0.88)		
Troika elev. interior*from interior		-1.87^{**} (0.94)		
from interior	-0.26 (0.26)	0.93 (0.65)		
Morsi encroached			0.38^{***} (0.05)	-0.03 (0.07)
Morsi Brother-hoodized				0.68^{***} (0.04)
Elite Officer	0.38 (0.50)	0.33 (0.50)	0.12^{*} (0.06)	0.08 (0.07)
Joined for Wealth	0.08 (0.27)	0.09 (0.26)	0.05^{*} (0.03)	0.04 (0.03)
Joined for Power	0.54 (0.38)	0.49 (0.38)	-0.08^{*} (0.04)	-0.08^{*} (0.05)
Apolitical	-0.57^{***} (0.20)	-0.50^{**} (0.20)	-0.07^{***} (0.02)	-0.03 (0.02)
Covariates				
Conscript	-0.11 (0.27)	-0.11 (0.27)	-0.08^{***} (0.02)	-0.06^{***} (0.03)
Islamist	-0.73^{*} (0.38)	-0.71^{*} (0.38)	-0.35^{***} (0.03)	-0.20^{***} (0.04)
Voted Shafik			0.26^{***} (0.02)	0.19^{***} (0.03)
Registered to Vote	0.23 (0.22)	0.24 (0.22)	-0.06^{**} (0.03)	-0.05 (0.03)
Western Training	0.24 (0.24)	0.25 (0.24)	0.01 (0.04)	0.03 (0.04)
Joined to Defend Country	-0.48^{**} (0.21)	-0.51^{**} (0.21)	0.06^{***} (0.02)	0.03 (0.03)
Joined for Thrill of Fighting	-0.03 (0.27)	-0.06 (0.27)	-0.06^{*} (0.03)	-0.07^{*} (0.04)
Deployed 2011	0.13 (0.20)	0.12 (0.20)	0.01 (0.02)	0.01 (0.03)
Active-Duty	0.41^{*} (0.22)	0.42^{*} (0.21)	0.05^{**} (0.02)	0.04 (0.03)
Army	0.61 (0.38)	0.63^{*} (0.38)	-0.02 (0.03)	-0.03 (0.03)
Navy	-0.18 (0.47)	-0.22 (0.47)	-0.02 (0.05)	-0.06 (0.05)
Soldier	0.38 (0.28)	0.40 (0.28)	-0.04 (0.03)	-0.03 (0.03)
NCO	0.34 (0.27)	0.32 (0.27)	-0.05^{*} (0.03)	-0.04 (0.03)
Jun. Officer	0.11 (0.35)	0.10 (0.35)	-0.05 (0.07)	-0.01 (0.07)
Sen. Officer	-0.41 (0.42)	-0.39 (0.42)	0.02 (0.07)	0.02 (0.07)
Education	-0.51 (0.32)	-0.52 (0.32)	-0.01 (0.04)	0.04 (0.04)
Rural	0.29 (0.21)	0.25 (0.21)	-0.01 (0.02)	-0.05^{*} (0.02)
Constant	3.10^{***} (0.70)	2.11^{**} (0.83)	0.56^{***} (0.07)	0.30^{***} (0.08)
Observations	229	229	1,931	1,197
R^2	0.19	0.21	0.23	0.36
Adjusted R^2	0.09	0.10	0.22	0.34

Note: $^{*}p<0.1$; $^{**}p<0.05$; $^{***}p<0.01$ All models include the priming experiments discussed below.

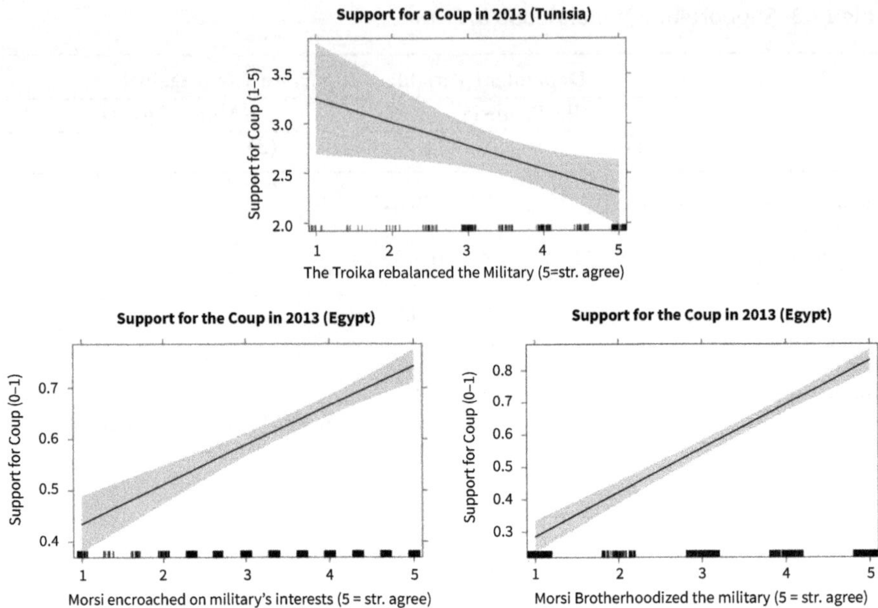

Figure 12.10 Support for a Coup in 2013, Surveys 2 and 3

Egypt, by contrast, saw the opposite dynamic. Given the military's empowerment under autocracy, democracy meant reining in its privileges, fueling support for a coup. Military personnel who believed that President Morsi encroached on the military's interests, clashing with it over security decisions, economic contracts, and constitutional powers, were significantly more supportive of a coup. The effect size here is massive (Figure 12.10, bottom-left), with a belief that Morsi encroached almost doubling support for the coup (from 43 to 74 percent).

Even more important were Morsi's attempts to alter the military's secular identity by lifting the ban on Islamists (Figure 12.10, bottom-right). Military personnel who believed that Morsi was trying to 'Brotherhood-ize' the military were almost three times as likely to support the coup (29 to 83 percent)—making it the strongest predictor of support for a coup in Egypt.[14]

Other elements of the military's composition and professionalism also played a role. Officers coming from the upper classes or who joined the military for material reasons were marginally more supportive of the coup. Likewise, the few who identified as apolitical were less supportive of the coup. In short, in both countries, the three hypothesized variables—corporate interests, composition, and professionalism—all emerge as important predictors of support or opposition to a coup in 2013.

One concern readers may have is whether respondents, particularly in Egypt, are being honest in their answers. There is likely to be considerable social and political pressure to say they support the coup even when they privately may not. Cognizant of this potential bias, the Egypt survey also embedded a list experiment prior to the

---

[14] This question was added late to the survey, and hence cuts the sample size in half.

direct question about the coup, which I detail in the online appendix. In the list experiment, the majority of respondents similarly said they supported the coup against Morsi, and more importantly, the same factors correlate with that support. A belief that Morsi encroached on the military's interests, and that he tried to Brotherhoodize the military, remain robust and significant predictors of support for a coup even in the list experiment.

Priming Experiments

A second concern is the one we discussed in survey 1: is this a causation or just a correlation? Regarding corporate interests in particular, Taylor (2003) and Lee (2008), among others, argue that corporate grievances can be found in every military, whether they stage a coup or not. They thus imply that corporate grievances may simply be a post-hoc justification for a coup, rather than the actual cause.

To demonstrate that corporate interests indeed have a causal effect on support for a coup, the online survey embedded priming experiments for both Egyptian and Tunisian respondents. Respondents were randomly assigned into either the control group, which received no text, or one of the treatment groups, which saw additional text designed to prime them to think about how the military's position either improved or worsened over the course of the democratic transition. The primes were:

1. **Control:** *No text.*
2. **Worsened:** "Many officers claim that the position of the military worsened between 2011 and 2013, in terms of security threats and interference by political leaders."
3. **Improved:** "Many officers claim that the position of the military improved between 2011 and 2013, in terms of budget, weapons, salaries, and influence over national security decisions."[15]
4. **[Tunisia only] Ended Disc:** "Many officers claim that the position of the military improved between 2011 and 2013, in terms of ending regional favoritism of officers from the coast in promotions."

In both countries, we see the same results (Figure 12.11): military personnel primed to think about how the military's position worsened under democracy were significantly more supportive of a coup than those in the control group. In Egypt, officers[16] in the "worsened" condition were 14 percentage points more supportive of the coup against Morsi (90 percent v. 76 percent, p=0.02). Similarly, in Tunisia, military personnel in the "worsened" condition were almost half a point more supportive of a

---

[15] The Egypt questionnaire did not include that final clause about security policy, given that it was not true in Egypt.

[16] Results do not hold for soldiers or NCOs, likely because they care less about the military's corporate interests.

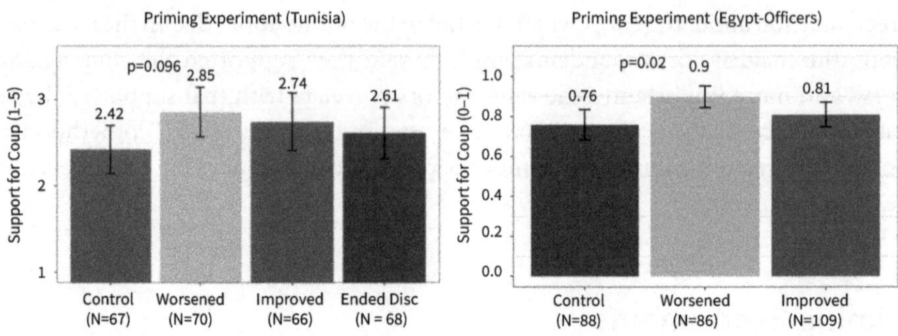

Figure 12.11 Priming Experiments, Surveys 2 and 3

coup against the Troika on the 1–5 scale (2.85 v. 2.42, p=0.096). The priming experiments thus provide causal evidence that corporate grievances have a causal effect
fueling support for a coup.

On the other hand, the various "improve" conditions had no effect relative to the
control. Military personnel primed to think of how the military's position improved
in terms of corporate interests, or in Tunisia, ending discrimination, were no less supportive of a coup. This suggests that at least in terms of survey experiments, losses
tended to be more powerful than gains in shaping coup support. In other words,
while we cannot conclude from the experiments that corporate gains necessarily
reduce coup support, we can conclude that corporate grievances have a causal effect
increasing coup support.

Conclusion

This chapter presented the results of three surveys of military personnel in Egypt
and Tunisia. The surveys confirm that each military's corporate interests, composition, and professionalism shaped how they responded to the Arab Spring uprisings
and subsequent transitions. In Tunisia, all three factors pointed towards supporting the democratic transition, while in Egypt, they pointed towards overthrowing it.
The survey results thus further validate the theory presented in this book, showing
how a dictator's coup-proofing strategy can create legacies that shape the process of
democratization.

Beyond these substantive contributions, the surveys presented in this chapter
also represent important methodological contributions. While militaries are generally black boxes, difficult to interview let alone survey, this chapter highlights two
methods of surveying militaries that might prove useful in other contexts. The first
involved building trust with retired officers over months of interviews until they felt
comfortable circulating the survey to their association. The second involved targeted
advertisements on Facebook, offering a route of recruiting military personnel on a
large scale and at a low cost. While each method has its own pros and cons, they are a
first step towards learning the opinions of a highly closed institution like the military.

13
Conclusion

The desire for democracy is universal and contagious. From Bahrain to Bolivia, Togo to Thailand, the masses have risen up, time and again, to demand democratic rule. But despite its normative appeal, democracy is by no means guaranteed to take root. Historically, about half of the world's democracies have collapsed, many in a rapid, spectacular coup d'état, others in a slow erosion of democratic backsliding, and still others into polarization and civil war. This book was motivated by the question of why some countries succeed in democratizing. What structural factors make democracy more likely to take root in some countries, but not others?

This, of course, is not a new question. Decades of political science scholarship have been written on this topic, with no shortage of candidate explanations. Yet what much of this literature overlooks is that the vast majority of democratic breakdowns—over 60 percent—have broken down in a military coup. Accordingly, we might expect that the military would be placed front and center in explanations of democratic breakdown. Existing scholarship, however, has largely neglected the military's motivations for overthrowing democracies. Perhaps because the military is one of the most difficult institutions to penetrate, existing literature has started with the premise that militaries always want to seize power, and thus the important variation is whether the opportunity exists. Scholars have thus highlighted certain conditions that create an opportunity, such as economic recessions, political polarization, security threats, and disillusionment with democracy.

The central insight of this book is that the opportunity for a coup is only half the puzzle. Even when the conditions are ripe, many militaries choose not to seize power. In Tunisia in 2013, for instance, each of the theorized conditions facilitating a coup were present. And yet, the military decided not to intervene. Some transitions appear to be blessed with "soldiers of democracy" who resist the temptations of power.

How do we explain why some militaries seize the opportunity to stage coups and others do not? The literature on civil–military relations provides an initial answer: militaries only stage coups when they have grievances that propel them to overthrow the status quo. Given the risks associated with a coup, as well as the uncertainty of what might come after, militaries are not always eager to seize power, and instead must be sufficiently aggrieved by the current system to outweigh these costs.

If grievances lead to coups, then the solution seems clear. New democracies must simply respect their militaries' interests. Indeed, Huntington (1991) suggested so much when advising new democracies to grant their militaries new toys to keep them satisfied. But satisfying the military during a transition is not as easy as it sounds. In some cases, democracy cannot proceed without curtailing the military's power. There

Soldiers of Democracy?. Sharan Grewal, Oxford University Press. © Sharan Grewal (2023).
DOI: 10.1093/oso/9780192873910.003.0013

are structural factors, I argue, that make the military more likely to gain or lose power under democracy. These are the military legacies from the previous regime. In most cases, transitions to democracy are not a blank slate. New democracies inherit a number of institutions from the previous autocratic regime, foremost among them the military. How the military had been treated under the previous regime, I argue, will create important legacies that shape whether new democracies are likely to enhance or curtail the power of the military.

For their own survival, dictators tend to pursue one of two coup-proofing strategies. The first is to empower their militaries, securing their loyalty through a share of power and wealth. The second is to marginalize their militaries, making a coup more difficult by neglecting and counterbalancing them. Both strategies are intended to prevent the military from ousting the dictator, and indeed they can be equally effective in helping a dictator survive.

But these two strategies have unintended, downstream consequences if and when the country were to democratize. New democracies that inherit empowered militaries have a difficult time consolidating, as democracy tends to encroach upon the military's interests and identity, sparking a coup. By contrast, new democracies inheriting marginalized militaries have a much easier time consolidating, as democracy tends to benefit these militaries, wedding them to the transition. At the same time, marginalized militaries also come with risks of their own. Weak and neglected, they are less able to fend off rebel threats, and thus more likely to descend into civil war. Moreover, just as they can be readily co-opted into democracy, they can also be readily co-opted into an incumbent takeover. An autocrat's choice of coup-proofing strategy thus creates important legacies, shaping both the likelihood of democratization and the forms by which it breaks down.

In this conclusion, I address two sets of lingering questions. First, are there any conditions under which democracy is still possible with an empowered military? I examine what structural factors can facilitate democratization even in these hard cases, and what role, if any, the international community can play. The second half of the chapter then turns to the second major threat to democratic transitions: incumbent takeovers. What strategies can domestic and international audiences pursue to discourage militaries from facilitating incumbent takeovers? The chapter thus aims to outline a set of policy recommendations to facilitate democratization no matter the type of military the transition inherits.

Escaping the Coup Trap

Most democratic transitions featuring empowered militaries end up breaking down in military coups. However, a sizable minority are still surviving today, particularly in Latin America. What lessons can we learn from these success stories? While a comprehensive analysis is beyond the scope of this chapter, a few initial patterns emerge.

First, many of these democracies had previous democratic breakdowns. In other words, even in these successful countries, democracy had previously failed. Rather than there being some country-specific factor that made these cases naturally amenable to democracy, even here, democratization proceeded in fits and starts. This is an optimistic finding, suggesting that even countries like Egypt may one day find their way to democracy.

Second, what facilitated democratization in most of these cases was that there was simply no opportunity for the military to intervene. Many of these successful transitions occurred immediately after their empowered militaries had been defeated in war, delegitimizing the military as a political actor, and in some cases, leading to their dissolution.[1] Japan after World War II was forced to disband its powerful military, Grenada and Panama followed suit after US invasions in the 1980s, and Costa Rica abolished its military after a deadly civil war. Yet even where the military remained, and may have wished to seize power, their defeat in war now deprived them of the public support needed for a coup. In Argentina, "following military defeat [in the Falklands War], the military government was about as discredited as it is possible for any government to be. [. . .] The unpopularity of the military is now so great that it should not [. . .] be too difficult for the government to suppress any disaffection from this quarter" (Philip, 1984, pp. 631–636).

Other successful transitions followed the military's "electoral defeat." In Uruguay, voters rejected the military's attempt to enshrine its powers and privileges in a 1980 constitutional referendum, signaling a declining popular support for military rule that facilitated a subsequent transition. In Bolivia, Nicaragua, Ghana, and Suriname, the military's preferred candidates were defeated in elections, signaling to these militaries that they lacked public support for a coup. In part because of the military's mismanagement of the economy under autocracy, and improved economic situation under democracy, voters rejected the military's attempts to return to the old ways. As Chapter 3 illustrated, when the economy is growing under democracy, even praetorian militaries will find it hard to intervene.

Finally, in a few cases, newly elected governments were able to effectively negotiate with their militaries to accept democracy. The "pacted transitions" described by O'Donnell and Schmitter (1986) demonstrate how through skillful bargaining—and a dash of luck—new democracies can on occasion successfully pace their reforms in line with the military's threshold for a coup. However, even when they do succeed, they typically produce a "tutelary" or "bounded" democracy,[2] where the military retains veto power or other political privileges, restricting civilian control and oversight and thus limiting the quality of the democracy produced. Moreover, as the case of Egypt demonstrates, such bargaining is rife with uncertainty, mixed signals, and miscalculations, more often than not leading to democratic breakdown.

---

[1] O'Donnell and Schmitter (1986, pp. 17–18), Barany (2012, p. 346).
[2] Shils (1960); Rabkin (1992); Tas (2015); Self (2022).

Policy Implications

Based on this analysis, what role can democracy promoters play in facilitating transitions in these difficult contexts? The framework presented herein suggests that the primary motivation leading empowered militaries to stage coups is a reduction in their power under democracy. International actors thus have two strategies: a) offsetting these domestic losses in power, and b) raising the costs of a coup.

The first strategy is to enhance an empowered military's power, thereby offsetting the losses they will incur domestically due to democracy. Allied governments, for instance, could increase military assistance upon initiation of a democratic transition. Military aid not only enhances the military's material resources—making up for that which will be redistributed under democracy—but such foreign engagements also enhance the military's prestige. Moreover, if such aid is targeted only to military officers who have demonstrated respect for democratic norms and human rights, as is legally required by US law, this may further incentivize reform.

Simultaneously, democracy promoters should increase the costs of a military coup. If there are credible threats to suspend military assistance in the event of a coup, military officers may think twice before intervening. Historically, Western governments have only selectively and inconsistently suspended aid after coups,[3] decreasing the credibility of this threat. Democracy promoters must also be internally consistent in signaling these threats ahead of time. If, as in Egypt, the US Department of Defense is sending a different message than the White House, then these mixed signals may serve only to heighten miscalculations in the new democracy's bargaining with the military.

While these recommendations provide guidance during a transition to democracy, a complementary strategy can occur under autocracy: encouraging dictators to pursue marginalization rather than empowerment in the first place. There are a number of factors that may lead dictators to invest in their militaries; among them are security threats.[4] If dictators need a powerful military to deal with internal or external threats, they are more likely to choose empowerment. Accordingly, democracy promoters should attempt to mitigate this insecurity. Providing strong, credible alliances and reducing the legal and illegal flow of weapons can help to lessen autocrats' reliance on their militaries, and thus encourage them to pursue marginalization.

Incumbent Takeovers

The second major threat facing democracies is an incumbent takeover. Such takeovers occasionally involve the use of the military, such as when Alberto Fujimori or Kais Saied deployed troops to close the parliament, or when Louis-Napoleon used them in 1851 to secure newspaper offices and then to repress opposition to his power

---

[3] Tansey (2017, 2018); Grewal and Kureshi (2019); Singh (2022).
[4] Goldsmith (2003); Digiuseppe and Poast (2018); Skogstad (2016); Yesilyurt and Elhorst (2017).

grab. How can domestic and international actors discourage militaries from playing these roles, while at the same time still ingraining civilian control? What is the proper response from a "soldier of democracy" when a president attempts to aggrandize his power?

In recent years, this tension has been on display in the United States, in ways that are useful for generating lessons for how professional militaries should behave. In 2020, in the wake of the Black Lives Matter (BLM) protests, former President Donald Trump sought to invoke the Insurrection Act to deploy the active-duty military to crush the protesters. "Can't you just shoot them?" Trump asked the Chairman of the Joint Chiefs, General Mark Milley. "Just shoot them in the legs or something?"[5] Milley and other advisors were able to talk Trump out of deploying the (regular) military, but Trump did deploy the DC National Guard, and governors across the country deployed (state) national guards, both of which are part of the US military. In total, 43,350 national guard troops were mobilized across 34 states in response to the protests.[6] In discouraging the deployment of the regular military, Milley had independently assessed the threat, and concluded that the national guard was sufficient. The role that Milley played here was widely viewed as professional and legitimate: offering his "best military advice" in discussions over the use of force. Yet, *had* Trump gone forward with invoking the Insurrection Act, it is likely that the US military would have had no choice but to obey such "awful but lawful" orders (although they could have crafted the rules of engagement in ways that minimized any potential for force). Had Trump gone even further, and directly ordered the troops to shoot protesters, the military "almost certainly" would have had grounds to refuse such "manifestly unlawful" orders,[7] but what they would have actually done is unclear.[8]

The episode raises at least four lessons for how militaries should behave as elected leaders consider the military for domestic missions. First, the military *should* independently assess the threat, and advise against deploying the troops when not necessary. In Tunisia in 2021, it appears the top brass did not do so, simply accepting Saied's premise that there was sufficient threat to warrant the military (and not just the police) "securing" the parliament. Given that a domestic deployment of the military can, even if unintentionally, represent a show of support for the president, and make it seem like all state institutions are on board with the takeover, it is important that militaries generally discourage their domestic involvement.

Second, if unable to discourage an order, the top brass should have a clear path by which to assess the legality of that order. It can be helpful if officers have training in what sorts of orders would be illegal or unconstitutional, but ultimately officers are specialists in violence, not constitutional law. In the United States, there are a variety of bodies that officers can in theory refer the order to: the legal advisor to the Chairman of the Joint Chiefs; the Department of Defense (DoD) general counsel;

---

⁵ Glasser and Baker (2022).
⁶ Glaser (2021).
⁷ Hodges (2022).
⁸ For initial thoughts inspired by Egypt and Tunisia, see Brooks and Grewal (2020).

the Department of Justice Office of Legal Counsel; and even the Supreme Court.[9] As an open letter by 13 former secretaries of defenses and chairmen of the joint chiefs emphasized: "Civilian control is [also] exercised within the judicial branch through judicial review of policies, orders, and actions involving the military."[10] Even if not regularly used, such channels must be in place, well developed, and widely known ahead of time.

Third, in case the order is found to be legal, the military must obey. Long term, refusing a lawful order can have negative consequences undermining civilian control. But, when troops are deployed domestically, it is important that they already have in place well-defined rules of engagement, and ideally have already conducted trainings in domestic uses of force, to limit any potential for escalation into violence. Given the increasing frequency of incumbent takeovers, and how detrimental an abuse of force can be for the military's image, it is imperative that militaries spend the time and resources to prepare for such an eventuality.

Still, the preceding discussion raises a central "paradox of professionalism," to borrow Brooks (2020)'s phrase: there are, in theory, lawful orders a president could give to the military whose second or third-order effects help to solidify an incumbent takeover. If the deployment of 43,000 national guard troops was legal in responding to BLM protests that were over 90 percent peaceful,[11] it is not hard to imagine a scenario where a president legally orders the military to help repress protesters he paints as violent or criminal. In many cases of incumbent takeovers worldwide, elected leaders invoke state of emergency clauses to legitimize and legalize military repression. In these situations, military officers might feel a professional duty to obey, even if the ultimate consequence is the weakening of democracy. The solution to this paradox is *not* to rely on the military to decide whether a lawful order is too detrimental to democracy to obey: that is a difficult and inherently political judgment call for specialists in violence to make. Instead, the solution is for officers to be able to refer the lawful but undemocratic order to qualified civilian actors to be able to weigh in on and block such orders. For added protection, it may be worth automatically requiring judicial and even legislative approval for any domestic use of military force.

Additional lessons can be derived from a second, even more serious, attempt at an incumbent takeover in the US. On January 6, 2021, Trump cajoled his supporters to storm the Congress in an attempt to disrupt its certification of Joe Biden's victory. In this episode as well, the US military ultimately helped to defeat the insurrection, sending national guard troops to clear the rioters. However, these troops arrived almost four hours after the DC mayor and chief of police requested their support, and well after most of the rioters had already dispersed. Milley downplayed the delay, claiming that the one hour it took for the Defense Secretary to approve the request and three hours to prepare and send over the troops was in fact "sprint speed" for the military.[12] By contrast, DC police and DC national guard officials both allege that US military officers at first refused or slow-rolled their requests, even calling

---

[9] Hodges (2022).
[10] Open Letter (2022).
[11] Beckett (2020); Chenoweth and Pressman (2020).
[12] Ryan and Lamothe (2021); Glasser and Baker (2022).

the protesters "peaceful" and noting that the optics of sending troops to the Capitol would not look good.[13]

The most charitable interpretation for why the military may have initially slow-rolled their response would be a reluctance to act without President Trump's approval. Trump had been refusing to send in the national guard, and ultimately the military decided to do so after speaking not with Trump but with Vice President Mike Pence, White House counsel Pat Cipollone, and Trump's Chief of Staff, Mark Meadows.[14] None of those figures, however, are in the chain of command and permitted to give the military orders. The Secretary of Defense did give them an order to deploy, but *had* Trump overruled him, how is the military to respond?

This hypothetical in turn illustrates a second paradox of professionalism: when the president is attempting an incumbent takeover, can the military take action to defeat it without his approval, let alone against his wishes? Here again, we have a potentially dangerous situation where a professional obedience to the president could have led the military to passively accept an incumbent takeover rather than actively resist it. In this particular case, the military decided to bypass this professional duty and send in the national guard, seemingly without Trump's explicit approval. Yet, it raises, once again, the importance of having qualified civilian actors make this judgment call about when professionalism can be overruled in favor of democracy. As Lindsay Cohn astutely notes, there is a line that "once crossed, means that civilian control as a value must be subordinated to some other value." But this is not for the military to decide: if it did, as Cohn continues, "the military becomes an arbiter of the political fate of the country and that's undemocratic and inappropriate."[15] It confirms, therefore, the need for other civilian actors, perhaps others in the White House or even the legislature or judiciary, to be legally permitted to overrule the president and give orders to the troops themselves in these narrow circumstances of incumbent takeovers. Such a reform would mark a radical departure from US history,[16] and no doubt will be difficult. But without it, an incumbent takeover may well succeed next time around. "Can you imagine what a group of people who are much more capable could have done?," Milley warned.[17]

In short, the events in the US in the past few years are helpful for generating lessons for how militaries can be properly discouraged from facilitating incumbent takeovers moving forward. The most important lesson is that this judgment call—of when to refuse lawful but undemocratic orders—should not be made by the military itself, a task which might politicize it and undermine its respect for civilian control. Instead, other civilian leaders must be empowered to make these calls and keep a president in check when they attempt to aggrandize their power. Only then can true "soldiers of democracy" be produced: militaries that neither stage coups nor facilitate incumbent takeovers, all while respecting civilian control. If this book has taught us anything, it is that keeping the military far from politics is typically the better option for democracy.

---

[13] Ryan and Lamothe (2021); Swan and McGraw (2021).
[14] Haberman and Cooper (2021); Mazzetti and Haberman (2022); Glasser and Baker (2022).
[15] Quoted in Ward (2022).
[16] See Cohn (2022).
[17] Quoted in Glasser and Baker (2022).

Bibliography

Abadeer, Caroline, Alexandra Domike Blackman, Lisa Blaydes, and Scott Williamson. 2022. "Did Egypt's Post-Uprising Crime Wave Increase Support for Authoritarian Rule?" *Journal of Peace Research* 59(4):577–592.

Abdalla, Ahmed. 1988. "The Armed Forces and the Democratic Process in Egypt." *Third World Quarterly* 10(4):1452–1466.

Abdel-Malek, Anouar. 1968. *Egypt: Military Society: The Army Regime, The Left, and Social Change Under Nasser.* New York: Random House.

Abdul Aziz, Muhammad and Youssef Hussein. 2001. "The President, the Son, and the Military: The Question of Succession in Egypt." *The Arab Studies Journal* 9(2):73–88.

Abid, Khaled. 2019. "*Trajiddiya dawla al-istiqlal: muhawala al-inqilab ala Bourguiba 1962* [Tragedy of the Independence State: The coup attempt against Bourguiba of 1962]."

Aboul-Futouh, Abdel Moneim. 2011. "Democracy supporters should not fear the Muslim Brotherhood." *The Washington Post* February 10. URL: http://www.washingtonpost.com/wp-dyn/content/article/2011/02/09/AR2011020906334.html

Aboulenein, Ahmed. 2012. "Morsi set to pick vice presidents, prime minister, and cabinet." *Daily News Egypt* June 26. URL: https://dailynewsegypt.com/2012/06/26/morsi-set-pick-vice-presidents-prime-minister-cabinet

Abrahamsson, Bengt. 1972. *Military Professionalization and Political Power.* Beverly Hills, CA: Sage.

Abul-Magd, Zeinab. 2012. "Occupying Tahrir Square: The Myths and Realities of the Egyptian Revolution." *The South Atlantic Quarterly* 111(3):565–572.

Abul-Magd, Zeinab. 2013. "The Egyptian Military in Politics and the Economy: Recent History and Current Transition Status." *CMI Insight* (2):1–6.

Abul-Magd, Zeinab. 2017. *Militarizing the Nation: The Army, Business, and Revolution in Egypt.* New York: Columbia University Press.

Abul-Magd, Zeinab and Elke Grawert. 2016. *Businessmen in Arms: How the Military and Other Armed Groups Profit in the MENA Region.* New York: Rowman & Littlefield.

Aburish, Said K. 2004. *Nasser, the Last Arab.* New York: St. Martin's Press.

Acemoglu, Daron, Davide Ticchi, and Andrea Vindigni. 2010. "A Theory of Military Dictatorships." *American Economic Journal: Macroeconomics* 2(1):1–42.

Acemoglu, Daron and James Robinson. 2006. *Economic Origins of Democracy and Dictatorship.* New York: Cambridge University Press.

Achcar, Gilbert. 2020. "On the 'Arab Inequality Puzzle': The Case of Egypt." *Development and Change* 51(3):746–770.

Aclimandos, Tewfik. 2011. "Reforming the Egyptian Security Services." *Arab Reform Initiative* June 1.

Adam, Mohamad. 2012. "Brute force: Inside the Central Security Forces." *Egypt Independent* November 11. URL: https://egyptindependent.com/brute-force-inside-central-security-forces

Afify, Heba. 2012. "Infighting in Constituent Assembly as draft articles presented." *Egypt Independent* July 25. URL: https://www.egyptindependent.com/infighting-constituent-assembly-draft-articles-presented

AFP. 2011. "Tunisia bars police from union activities." *Dawn* September 6. URL: https://www.dawn.com/news/657092/tunisia-bars-police-from-union-activities

AFP. 2013. "Tunisia leaders evicted from police memorial." *Al-Jazeera* October 18. URL: https://www.aljazeera.com/news/2013/10/18/tunisia-leaders-evicted-from-police-memorial

African Intelligence. 2021. "Kais Saied rules supreme but is more isolated than ever." October 15. URL: https://www.africaintelligence.com/north-africa/2021/10/15/kais-saied-rules-supreme-but-is-more-isolated-than-ever,109698780-ar2

Agence France-Presse. 2011. "Tunisia: New government fires top police officials." *GlobalPost* February 2. URL: https://www.pri.org/stories/2011-02-02/tunisia-new-government-fires-top-police-officials

Agence Tunis Afrique Presse. 2021. "Kaïs Saïed receives Director-General of National Agency for Intelligence and Security for Defence." URL: https://www.tap.info.tn/en/Portal-Politics/13556586-ka

Agence Tunis Afrique Presse. 2022. "July 25 Harak calls for salvation government including military." URL: https://www.tap.info.tn/en/Portal-Politics/15505730-july-25-harak-calls

Agüero, Felipe. 1995. *Soldiers, Civilians, and Democracy: Post-Franco Spain in Comparative Perspective.* Baltimore: Johns Hopkins University Press.

Ahmed, Ishtiaq. 2013. *Pakistan: The Garrison State.* New York: Oxford University Press.

Ahram Online. 2011. "Democratic Alliance (Freedom and Justice)." November 18. URL: http://english.ahram.org.eg/NewsContent/33/103/26895/Elections-/Electoral-Alliances/Democratic-Alliance.aspx

Ahram Online. 2012*a*. "Beleaguered Constituent Assembly votes on Egypt's draft constitution." *Ahram Online* November 29. URL: http://english.ahram.org.eg/NewsContent/1/64/59447/Egypt/Politics-/Beleaguered-Constituent-Assembly-votes-on-Egypts-d.aspx

Ahram Online. 2012*b*. "Egypt's 2012/13 budget a 'conspiracy' against next president: FJP official." *Ahram Online* June 21. URL: http://english.ahram.org.eg/NewsContent/3/12/45797/Business/Economy/Egypts–budget-a-conspiracy-against-next-president.aspx

Ahram Online. 2012*c*. "Egypt's Morsi draws up commission to look into protesters' deaths." *Ahram Online* July 6. URL: http://english.ahram.org.eg/NewsContent/1/64/47011/Egypt/Politics-/Egypts-Morsi-draws-up-commission-to-look-into-prot.aspx

Ahram Online. 2012*d*. "Egypt's SCAF forms National Defence Council without revealing its duties." June 18. URL: http://english.ahram.org.eg/NewsContent/1/64/45507/Egypt/Politics-/Egypt

Ahram Online. 2012*e*. "English text of Morsi's Constitutional Declaration." *Ahram Online* November 22. URL: http://english.ahram.org.eg/NewsContent/1/64/58947/Egypt/Politics-/English-text-of-Morsis-Constitutional-Declaration-.aspx

Ahram Online. 2012*f*. "English text of SCAF amended Egypt Constitutional Declaration." June 18. URL: http://english.ahram.org.eg/News/45350.aspx

Ahram Online. 2012*g*. "Morsi declaration hailed by supporters, deemed 'coup' by opposition." *Ahram Online* November 22. URL: http://english.ahram.org.eg/NewsContent/1/64/58950/Egypt/Politics-/Morsi-declaration-hailed-by-supporters,-deemed-cou.aspx

Ahram Online. 2012*h*. "Sabbahi, ElBaradei launch National Front to fight Morsi's decrees." *Ahram Online* November 24. URL: http://english.ahram.org.eg/NewsContent/1/64/59068/Egypt/Politics-/Sabbahi,-ElBaradei-launch-National-Front-to-fight-.aspx

Ahram Online. 2012*i*. "Unity project amongst Egypt presidential candidates, revolutionary forces to be announced before evening." June 22. URL: http://english.ahram.org.eg/NewsContent/1/64/45859/Egypt/Politics-/Unity-project-amongst-Egypt-presidential-candidate.aspx

Ahram Online. 2013. "Egypt opposition group criticises 'blatant interference' by US ambassador." *Ahram Online* June 19. URL: http://english.ahram.org.eg/NewsContent/1/64/74413/Egypt/Politics-/Egypt-opposition-group-criticises-blatant-interfer.aspx

Al-Ali, Zaid. 2012. "The New Egyptian Constitution: An Initial Assessment of Its Merits and Flaws." *Open Democracy* December 26. URL: https://www.opendemocracy.net/en/new-egyptian-constitution-initial-assessment-of-its-merits-and-flaws

al Anani, Khalil. 2015. "Upended Path: The Rise and Fall of Egypt's Muslim Brotherhood." *Middle East Journal* 69(4):527–543.

Al-Ashwal, Ismail. 2013. "Al-Ganzouri fi mudhakaratihi [Al-Ganzouri in his memoirs]." *Al-Shorouk* December 15. URL: https://www.shorouknews.com/news/view.aspx?cdate=15122013&id=0f0a4757-f86f-49f3-a7e5-427728f4c385

Al Aswany, Alaa. 2012. "What do we expect from the Muslim Brotherhood and the Salafists?" *Huffington Post* April 1. URL: https://www.huffpost.com/entry/what-do-we-expect-from-th_b_1245072?guccounter=1

Al Desoukie, Omnia. 2014. "Opposition leader calls protest law 'political suicide' for Sisi." *Al-Monitor* September 29. URL: https://www.al-monitor.com/pulse/originals/2014/09/egypt-opposition-figure-coup-morsi-sisi-brotherhood.html

al Ghanmi, Monia. 2018. "Tunisia's National Security Council to investigate Ennahda's 'secret apparatus.'" *Al-Arabiya* November 28. URL: https://english.alarabiya.net/en/News/north-africa/2018/11/29/Tunisia-s-National-Security-Council-to-investigate-Ennahda-s-secret-apparatus-.html

Al-Jazeera. 2011. "Three dead in Egypt protests." January 25. URL: https://web.archive.org/web/20121015000822/http://www.aljazeera.com/news/middleeast/2011/01/20111125 1711053608.html

Al-Jazeera. 2013. "Egypt warns Ethiopia over Nile dam." *Al-Jazeera* June 11. URL: https://www.aljazeera.com/news/africa/2013/06/201361144413214749.html

Al-Masry al-Youm. 2012*a*. "FJP in negotiations for cabinet formation, Baradei still a possibility." *Egypt Independent* June 30. URL: https://www.egyptindependent.com/fjp-negotiations-cabinet-formation-baradei-still-possibility

Al-Masry Al-Youm. 2012*b*. "Morsy orders formation of panel to review military detentions." *Egypt Independent* July 4. URL: https://www.egyptindependent.com/morsy-orders-formation-panel-review-military-detentions

Al-Masry al-Youm. 2012*c*. "Parliament committee sets maximum wage for government employees." *Egypt Independent* April 9. URL: https://www.egyptindependent.com/parliament-sets-maximum-wage-le50000-month-government-employees

Al-Masry Al-Youm. 2012*d*. "Political leaders deny involvement in SCAF's constitution supplement." *Egypt Independent* June 21. URL: https://www.egyptindependent.com/political-leaders-deny-involvement-scafs-constitution-supplement

Al-Masry Al-Youm. 2012*e*. "Politicians defend supplementary Constitutional Declaration." *Egypt Independent* June 21. URL: https://www.egyptindependent.com/politicians-defend-supplementary-constitutional-declaration

Al-Masry Al-Youm. 2012*f*. "Politicians divided on Morsy's new Constitutional Declaration." *Egypt Independent* November 22. URL: https://www.egyptindependent.com/politicians-divided-morsy-s-new-constitutional-declaration

Al-Masry Al-Youm. 2012*g*. "Presidential source: SCAF wants to keep four ministries in Qandil cabinet." *Egypt Independent* July 28. URL: https://www.egyptindependent.com/presidential-source-scaf-wants-keep-four-ministries-qandil-cabinet

Al-Masry Al-Youm. 2012*h*. "Update: Hundreds of thousands rally in Tahrir." *Egypt Independent* June 19. URL: https://www.egyptindependent.com/update-hundreds-thousands-rally-tahrir

Al-Masry Al-Youm. 2013*a*. "Opposition: outraged as Military Academy accepts Brotherhood recruits." *Egypt Independent* March 18. URL: https://www.egyptindependent.com/opposition-outraged-military-academy-accepts-brotherhood-recruits

Al-Masry Al-Youm. 2013*b*. "Sisi reaffirms independence of military; citizens petition for his rule in Port Said, Red Sea, Daqahliya." *Egypt Independent* March 1. URL: https://www.egyptindependent.com/sisi-reaffirms-independence-military-citizens-petition-his-rule-port-said-red-sea-daqahliya

Al-Masry al-Youm Staff. 2012. "Revolutionaries reject military council's martyr medallions." *Egypt Independent* January 22. URL: https://egyptindependent.com/revolutionaries-reject-military-councils-martyr-medallions

Albertus, Michael and Victor Menaldo. 2012. "Coercive Capacity and the Prospects for Democratization." *Comparative Politics* 44(2):151–169.

Albrecht, Holger. 2015. "Does Coup-Proofing Work? Political-Military Relations in Authoritarian Regimes amid the Arab Uprisings." *Mediterranean Politics* 20(1):36–54.

Albrecht, Holger. 2020. "Diversionary Peace: International Peacekeeping and Domestic Civil-Military Relations." *International Peacekeeping* 27(4):586–616.

Albrecht, Holger and Dina Bishara. 2011. "Back on Horseback: The Military and Political Transformation in Egypt." *Middle East Law and Governance* 3:13–23.

Alexander, David. 2013. "U.S. defence chief reaffirms military ties with Egypt." *Reuters* April 24. URL: https://www.reuters.com/article/uk-egypt-usa-defence/u-s-defence-chief-reaffirms-military-ties-with-egypt-idUKBRE93N1C420130424

Alexander, David and Phil Stewart. 2011. "U.S. sees Egypt's Tantawi as resistant to change." *Reuters* February 11. URL: https://www.reuters.com/article/us-usa-egypt-military-idUKTRE71A5KH20110211

Allen, Nathaniel. 2019. "Authoritarian Armies and Democratizing States: How the Military Influences African Transitional Politics." *Democratization* 26(2):247–268.

Allen, Nathaniel and Risa Brooks. 2022. "Unpacking 'Stacking': Researching Political Identity and Regime Security in Armed Forces." *Armed Forces & Society* OnlineFirst:1–21.

Alsharif, Asma and Yasmine Saleh. 2013. "Special Report: The real force behind Egypt's 'revolution of the state.'" *Reuters* October 10. URL: https://www.reuters.com/article/us-egypt-interior-specialreport/special-report-the-real-force-behind-egypts-revolution-of-the-state-idUSBRE99908D20131010

Amara, Tarek. 2011. "Tunisian minister talks of 'conspiracy' after attacks." *Reuters* February 1. URL: https://www.reuters.com/article/instant-article/idINTRE70J0IG20110201

Amara, Tarek. 2012. "Tunisia Islamist leader stirs fears of radicalism in video." *Reuters* October 11. URL: https://www.reuters.com/article/uk-tunisia-ghannouchi-salafis-idUKBRE89A16G20121011?edition-redirect=uk

Ammar, Rachid. 2011. "Testimony before the military court." *Available through Nawaat* April. URL: https://cdn.nawaat.org/wp-content/uploads/2011/11/302-312-Ammar.pdf

Amnesty International. 2009. "Tunisia: Behind Tunisia's 'Economic Miracle': Inequality and Criminalization of Protest." *June 17*. URL: https://www.amnesty.org/en/documents/mde30/003/2009/en

Amnesty International. 2012. "Egypt: A Year after 'Virginity Tests', Women Victims of Army Violence Still Seek Justice." *March 9*. URL: https://www.amnesty.org/en/latest/news/2012/03/egypt-year-after-virginity-tests-women-victims-army-violence-still-seek-justice

Anderson, Lisa. 1986. *The State and Social Transformation in Tunisia and Libya, 1830–1980*. Princeton, NJ: Princeton University Press.

Anisin, Alexei and Pelin Ayan Musil. 2021. "Resistance and Military Defection in Turkey." *Mediterranean Politics* Firstview.

Aouadi, Fathi. 2017. "Tunisie: Qui sera l'arbitre si l'armée est saturée? Appel à la rationalisation de son emploi." *HuffPost Maghreb*. URL: https://bit.ly/3T4HWoe

Arab Weekly. 2020. "Tunisia's Rear-Admiral Akrout: 'National security inseparable from intelligence.'" *The Arab Weekly*. URL: https://thearabweekly.com/tunisias-rear-admiral-akrout-national-security-inseparable-intelligence

Arriola, Leonardo R., David A. Dow, Aila M. Matanock, and Michaela Mattes. 2021. "Policing Institutions and Post-Conflict Peace." *Journal of Conflict Resolution* 65(10):1738–1763.

Arrow, Ruaridh. 2011. "Gene Sharp: Author of the nonviolent revolution rulebook." *BBC* February 21. URL: https://www.bbc.com/news/world-middle-east-12522848

Ashford, Douglas E. 1965. "Neo-Destour Leadership and the 'Confiscated Revolution.'" *World Politics* 17(2):215–231.

Ashour, Omar. 2015. "Collusion to Crackdown: Islamist-Military Relations in Egypt." *Brookings Doha Center* Analysis Paper(14).

Associated Press. 2013. "Behind Egypt's coup, months of acrimony between Morsi and top general over Sinai, policies." *Fox News* July 17. URL: https://www.foxnews.com/world/behind-egypts-coup-months-of-acrimony-between-morsi-and-top-general-over-sinai-policies

Astiz, Carlos Alberto. 1969. *Pressure Groups and Power Elites in Peruvian Politics*. Ithaca, NY: Cornell University Press.

Awad, Marwa. 2011a. "Egypt army officer says 15 others join protesters." *Reuters* February 11. URL: https://www.reuters.com/article/us-egypt-protest-officers/egypt-army-officer-says-15-others-join-protesters-idUSTRE71A12V20110211

Awad, Marwa. 2011b. "Egypt opposition says govt meeting inconclusive." *Reuters* February 6. URL: https://www.reuters.com/article/idINIndia-54692520110206

Awad, Marwa and Dina Zayed. 2011. "Army tries to limit Cairo protest camp space." *Reuters* February 6. URL: https://www.reuters.com/article/uk-egypt-protests-army/army-tries-to-limit-cairo-protest-camp-space-idUKTRE71527J20110206

Ayari, Yassine. 2011. "L'homme qui a dit non, et qui continuera à le dire: MOI." *Mel7it* July 19. URL: http://mel7it3.blogspot.com/2011/07/lhomme-qui-dit-non-et-qui-continuera-le.html

Banks, Arthur S. and Kenneth A. Wilson. 2017. "Cross-National Time-Series Data Archive." Databanks International.

Barany, Zoltan. 2011. "Comparing the Arab Revolts: The Role of the Military." *Journal of Democracy* 22(4):28–39.

Barany, Zoltan. 2012. *The Soldier and the Changing State*. Princeton, NJ: Princeton University Press.

Barany, Zoltan. 2016. *How Armies Respond to Revolutions and Why*. Princeton, NJ: Princeton University Press.

Baseera. 2013. "The President's Approval Rating After One Year In Office." *Baseera: The Egyptian Center for Public Opinion Research* June 25. URL: http://baseera.com.eg/EN/RecentPolls2.aspx?ID=24

Bayoumy, Yara. 2015. "In Egypt, ex-military men fire up Islamist insurgency." *Reuters* April 17. URL: https://www.reuters.com/article/us-egypt-militants-military-insight/in-egypt-ex-military-men-fire-up-islamist-insurgency-idUSKBN0MY1PR20150407?mc_cid=ec0e58fab4&mc_eid=0f03abde05

BBC. 2011a. "Egypt protests: Army rules out the use of force." January 31. URL: https://www.bbc.com/news/world-middle-east-12330169

BBC. 2011b. "Egypt unrest: Full text of Hosni Mubarak's speech." February 10. URL: https://www.bbc.com/news/world-middle-east-12427091

BBC. 2011c. "Fourteen killed in Tunisia unemployment protests." January 10. URL: https://www.bbc.com/news/world-africa-12144906

Beau, Nicolas. 2022. "Tunisie, des interrogations inquiètes sur le rôle à venir de l'armée." *Mondafrique.* URL: https://mondafrique.com/tunisie-des-interrogations-inquietes-sur-une-possible-intervention-de-larmee

Beckett, Lois. 2020. "Nearly all Black Lives Matter protests are peaceful despite Trump narrative." *The Guardian* September 5. URL: https://www.theguardian.com/world/2020/sep/05/nearly-all-black-lives-matter-protests-are-peaceful-despite-trump-narrative-report-finds

Be'eri, Eliezer. 1970. *Army Officers in Arab Politics and Society.* New York: Praeger.

Be'eri, Eliezer. 1982. "The Waning of the Military Coup in Arab Politics." *Middle Eastern Studies* 18(1):69–81.

Belkin, Aaron. 2005. *United We Stand? Divide-and-Conquer Politics and the Logic of International Hostility.* Albany, NY: State University of New York Press.

Belkin, Aaron and Evan Schofer. 2003. "Toward a Structural Understanding of Coup Risk." *Journal of Conflict Resolution* 47(5):594–620.

Bellin, Eva. 2004. "The Robustness of Authoritarianism in the Middle East: Exceptionalism in Comparative Perspective." *Comparative Politics* 36:139–157.

Bellin, Eva. 2012. "Reconsidering the Robustness of Authoritarianism in the Middle East: Lessons from the Arab Spring." *Comparative Politics* 44(2):127–149.

Bellin, Eva. 2018. "The Puzzle of Democratic Divergence in the Arab World: Theory Confronts Experience in Egypt and Tunisia." *Political Research Quarterly* 133(3):435–474.

Ben Bouazza, Bouazza. 2013*a*. "Thousands protest government at Tunisia funeral." *Associated Press* July 27. URL: https://apnews.com/d57fdabcbc0f40b6b75a1f2922b37a87

Ben Bouazza, Bouazza. 2013*b*. "Tunisia security blocks salafi conference." *Associated Press* May 19. URL: https://apnews.com/article/3171dd02ccd5421c970a7e669a64bd48

Ben Salem, Moncef. 2013. *Mudhakarat 'alim jama'i wa sajin siyasi: sanawat al-jamr [Memoirs of an academic researcher and political prisoners: The years of embers].* Tunis: Self-published.

BenKraïem, Boubaker. 2012. *Naisssance d'une armée nationale: la Promotion Bourguiba.* Tunis: Maison d'Edition de Tunis.

BenKraiem, Boubaker. 2015. "27 janvier 2015: il y a trente-cinq ans, l'affaire de Gafsa." *La Presse* January 27. URL: https://www.turess.com/fr/lapresse/95040

BenKraiem, Boubaker. 2017. "Quelles réformes pour notre pays, cette démocratie naissante?" *Leaders.* URL: https://www.leaders.com.tn/article/23501-boubaker-ben-kraiem-quelles-reformes-pour-notre-pays-cette-democratie-naissante

BenKraiem, Boubaker. 2020. "15 juillet 1960: La Brigade Tunisienne, avec les Casques Bleus, au maintien de la Paix à Léo et à Kitona (Congo) (3 partie/4)." *Leaders* July 19. URL: https://www.leaders.com.tn/article/30292-15-juillet-1960-la-brigade-tunisienne-avec-les-casques-bleus-au-maintien-de-la-paix-a-leo-et-a-kitona-congo-3-partie-4

Bermeo, Nancy. 2003. *Ordinary People in Extraordinary Times: The Citizenry and the Breakdown of Democracy.* Princeton, NJ: Princeton University Press.

Bermeo, Nancy. 2016. "On Democratic Backsliding." *Journal of Democracy* 27(1):5–19.

Bernhard, Michael, Christopher Reenock, and Timothy Nordstrom. 2001. "Economic Performance, Institutional Intermediation, and Democratic Survival." *Journal of Politics* 63:775–803.

Besley, Timothy and James A. Robinson. 2010. "Quis Custodiet Ipsos Custodes? Civilian Control Over the Military." *Journal of European Economic Association* 8(2–3):655–663.

Bhutta, Christine Brickman. 2012. "Not by the Book: Facebook as a Sampling Frame." *Sociological Methods & Research* 41(1):57–88.

Biddle, Stephen. 2004. *Military Power: Explaining Victory and Defeat in Modern Battle.* Princeton, NJ: Princeton University Press.

Biddle, Stephen and Robert Zirkle. 1996. "Technology, Civil-Military Relations, and Warfare in the Developing World." *Journal of Strategic Studies* 19(2):171–212.

Binnendijk, Anika Locke, and Ivan Marovic. 2006. "Power and Persuasion: Nonviolent Strategies to Influence State Security Forces in Serbia (2000) and Ukraine (2004)." *Communist and Post-Communist Studies* 39(3):411–429.

Bishara, Dina. 2020. "Legacy Trade Unions as Brokers of Democratization? Lessons from Tunisia." *Comparative Politics* 52(2):173–195.

Blair, Dennis C. 2012. "Military Support for Democracy." *Prism* 3(3):3–16.

Blair, Edmund, Paul Taylor, and Tom Perry. 2013. "Special Report: How the Muslim Brotherhood lost Egypt." *Reuters* July 25. URL: https://www.reuters.com/assets/print?aid=USBRE96O07H20130725

Bohmelt, Tobias, Abel Escriba-Folch, and Ulrich Pilster. 2019. "Pitfalls of Professionalism? Military Academies and Coup Risk." *Journal of Conflict Resolution* 63(5):1111–1139.

Bohmelt, Tobias and Vincenzo Bove. 2014. "Forecasting Military Expenditure." *Research and Politics* 1(1):1–8.

Boix, Carles. 2003. *Democracy and Redistribution.* New York: Cambridge University Press.

Boix, Carles and Susan Stokes. 2003. "Endogenous Democratization." *World Politics* 55(4):517–549.

Booth, John A. and Mitchell A. Seligson. 2009. *The Legitimacy Puzzle in Latin America: Democracy and Political Support in Eight Nations.* New York: Cambridge University Press.

Borsali, Noura. 2016. *Bourguiba wa almas'alat al-dimuqratia [Bourguiba and the Question of Democracy].* Tunis: Arabesques.

Bou Nassif, Hicham. 2012. "Why the Egyptian Army Didn't Shoot." *Middle East Research and Information Project* MER265. URL: https://merip.org/2013/01/why-the-egyptian-army-didnt-shoot

Bou Nassif, Hicham. 2013. "Wedded to Mubarak: The Second Careers and Financial Rewards of Egypt's Military Elite, 1981-2011." *The Middle East Journal* 67(4):509–530.

Bou Nassif, Hicham. 2014. Generals and Autocrats: Coup-Proofing and Military Elite's Behavior in the 2011 Arab Spring. PhD thesis Indiana University.

Bou Nassif, Hicham. 2015*a*. "A Military Beseiged: The Armed Forces, the Police, and the Party in Bin Ali's Tunisia, 1987–2011." *International Journal of Middle East Studies* 47:65–87.

Bou Nassif, Hicham. 2015*b*. "Generals and Autocrats: How Coup-Proofing Predetermined the Military Elite's Behavior in the Arab Spring." *Political Science Quarterly* 130(2): 245–275.

Bou Nassif, Hicham. 2017. "Coups and Nascent Democracies: The Military and Egypt's Failed Consolidation." *Democratization* 24(1):157–174.

Bou Nassif, Hicham. 2021. *Endgames: Military Response to Protest in Arab Autocracies.* New York: Cambridge University Press.

Bou Nassif, Hicham. 2022. "Why the Military Abandoned Democracy." *Journal of Democracy* 33(1):27–39.

Bouderbala, Taoufik. 2012. "The Report." *Republic of Tunisia* National commission to investigate the facts about the abuses and violations recorded during the period extending December 17, 2010 until their obligation ceases. URL: https://www.leaders.com.tn/uploads/FCK_files/Rapport%20Bouderbala.pdf

Boujellabia, Noureddine. 2004. *La bataille de Bizerte: telle que je l'ai vecue.* Tunis: Sud Ed.

Boularès, Habib. 2011. "Réponse de Habib Boularès au colonel Zoghlami et au lieutenant-colonel Mohamed Ahmed." *Realities.*

Brady, Thomas F. 1967. "Nasser prestige said to decline." *New York Times* October 19. URL: https://timesmachine.nytimes.com/timesmachine/1967/10/19/83637447.html?pageNumber=16

Brinks, Daniel and Michael Coppedge. 2006. "Diffusion Is No Illusion." *Comparative Political Studies* 39(4):463–489.

Brooks, Risa. 1998. *Political-Military Relations and the Stability of Arab Regimes.* New York: Oxford University Press.

Brooks, Risa. 2008. *Shaping Strategy: The Civil-Military Politics of Strategic Assessment.* Princeton, NJ: Princeton University Press.

Brooks, Risa. 2013. "Abandoned at the Palace: Why the Tunisian Military Defected from the Ben Ali Regime in January 2011." *Journal of Strategic Studies* 36(2):205–220.

Brooks, Risa. 2016. The Tunisian Military and Democratic Control of the Armed Forces. In *Armies and Insurgencies in the Arab Spring*, ed. Holger Albrecht, Aurel Croissant, and Fred Lawson. University of Pennsylvania Press chapter 10, pp. 203–224.

Brooks, Risa. 2017. "Military Defection and the Arab Spring." *Oxford Research Encyclopedia, Politics*. URL: https://oxfordre.com/politics/view/10.1093/acrefore/9780190228637.001.0001/acrefore-9780190228637-e-26?print=pdf

Brooks, Risa. 2019. "Integrating the Civil–Military Relations Subfield." *Annual Review of Political Science* 22:379–398.

Brooks, Risa. 2020. "Paradoxes of Professionalism: Rethinking Civil-Military Relations in the United States." *International Security* 44(4):7–44.

Brooks, Risa and Peter B. White. 2022. "Oust the Leader, Keep the Regime? Autocratic Civil-Military Relations and Coup Behavior in the Tunisian and Egyptian Militaries during the 2011 Arab Spring." *Security Studies* 31(1):118–151.

Brooks, Risa and Sharan Grewal. 2020. "Would the U.S. Military Repress Protesters? Lessons from the Arab Spring." *War on the Rocks* June 10. URL: https://warontherocks.com/2020/06/would-the-u-s-military-repress-protesters-lessons-from-the-arab-spring

Browers, Michaelle. 2007. "The Egyptian Movement for Change: Intellectual Antecedents and Generational Conflicts." *Contemporary Islam* 1(1):69–88.

Brown, Davis and Patrick James. 2018. "The Religious Characteristics of States: Classic Themes and New Evidence for International Relations and Comparative Politics." *Journal of Conflict Resolution* 62(6):1340–1376.

Brown, L. Carl. 2014. "The Tunisian Exception." *Informed Comment*.

Brownlee, Jason, Tarek Masoud, and Andrew Reynolds. 2015. *The Arab Spring: Pathways of Repression and Reform*. New York: Oxford University Press.

Bruce, Anthony P.C. 1980. *The Purchase System in the British Army, 1660–1871*. London: Royal Historical Society.

Buehler, Matt and Mehdi Ayari. 2018. "The Autocrat's Advisors: Opening the Black-Box of Ruling Coalitions in Tunisia's Authoritarian Regime." *Political Research Quarterly* 71(2):330–346.

Bueno de Mesquita, Bruce, Alastair Smith, Randolph M. Siverson, and James D. Morrow. 2003. *The Logic of Political Survival*. Cambridge, MA: MIT Press.

Business News. 2013. "Tunisia: Abbou veut la tête de Rachid Ammar [Abbou wants the head of Rachid Ammar]." June 7. URL: https://bit.ly/3hLpuip

Business News. 2019. "Les révélations incendiaires de Abdelkarim Zbidi." URL: https://www.businessnews.com.tn/les-revelations-incendiaires-de-abdelkrim-zbidi,520,90664,3

Cambanis, Thanassis. 2010. "Succession gives army a stiff test in Egypt." *New York Times* September 11. URL: https://www.nytimes.com/2010/09/12/world/middleeast/12egypt.html

Cambanis, Thanassis. 2015. *Once Upon a Revolution: An Egyptian Story*. New York: Simon and Schuster.

Camp, Roderic Ai. 2005. *Mexico's Military on the Democratic Stage*. Westport, CT: Praeger Security International.

Canache, Damarys. 2002. "From Bullets to Ballots: The Emergence of Popular Support for Hugo Chavez." *Latin American Politics and Society* 44(1):69–90.

Carter, Brett L. 2016. "The Struggle Over Term Limits in Africa: How International Pressure Can Help." *Journal of Democracy* 27(3):36–50.

Carthew, Anthony. 1967. "Double-think, Egyptian style." *New York Times* August 20. URL: https://timesmachine.nytimes.com/timesmachine/1967/08/20/107197891.pdf?pdf_redirect=true&ip=0

Casey, Adam E. 2020. "The Durability of Client Regimes: Foreign Sponsorship and Military Loyalty, 1946–2010." *World Politics* 72(3):411–447.

Cassese, Erin, Leonie Huddy, Todd Hartman, Lilliana Mason, and Christopher Weber. 2013. "Socially-Mediated Internet Surveys (SMIS): Recruiting Participants for Online Experiments." *PS: Political Science and Politics* 46(4):775–784.

Cavatorta, Francesco and Fabio Merone. 2013. "Moderation through Exclusion? The Journey of the Tunisian Ennahda from Fundamentalist to Conservative Party." *Democratization* 20(5):857–875.

Cebul, Matthew and Sharan Grewal. 2022. "Military Conscription and Nonviolent Resistance." *Comparative Political Studies* 55(13):2217–2249.

Chadbourn, Margaret. 2012. "Obama: Egypt neither enemy nor ally." *Reuters* September 13. URL: https://www.reuters.com/article/us-usa-obama-egypt/obama-egypt-neither-enemy-nor-ally-idUSBRE88C0S820120913

Cheibub, Jose A. 2007. *Presidentialism, Parliamentarism, and Democracy.* New York: Cambridge University Press.

Chenoweth, Erica and Jeremy Pressman. 2020. "This summer's Black Lives Matter protesters were overwhelmingly peaceful, our research finds." *The Washington Post* October 16.

Chenoweth, Erica and Maria Stephan. 2011. *Why Civil Resistance Works: The Strategic Logic of Nonviolent Conflict.* New York: Columbia University Press.

Cherif, Faysal. 2017. *Histoire de l'Armée tunisienne de l'indépendance: La genèse 1956–1960.* Manouba, Tunisia: Centre de Publication Universitaire.

Chin, John, Wonjun Song, and Joseph Wright. 2022. "Personalization of Power and Mass Uprisings in Dictatorships." *British Journal of Political Science* Firstview.

Chirambo, Reuben. 2004. "'Operation Bwezani': The Army, Political Change, and Dr. Banda's Hegemony in Malawi." *Nordic Journal of African Studies* 13(2):146–163.

Chollet, Derek. 2016. *The Long Game: How Obama Defied Washington and Redefined America's Role in the World.* New York: Public Affairs.

Chrisafis, Angelique. 2011. "Confusion, fear and horror in Tunisia as old regime's militia carries on the fight." *The Guardian* January 16. URL: https://www.theguardian.com/world/2011/jan/16/tunisia-gun-battle-army-tunis

Clinton, Hillary Rodham. 2014. *Hard Choices.* New York: Simon & Schuster.

CNN Wire Staff. 2011. "Obama: I told Mubarak he must deliver on his promises." *CNN* January 28. URL: http://www.cnn.com/2011/WORLD/africa/01/28/egypt.protests.u.s..response/index.html

Cohn, Lindsay P. 2022. To Execute the Laws of the Union: Domestic Use of Federal Military Force in the United States. In *Military Operation and Engagement in the Domestic Jurisdiction: Comparative Call-out Laws*, ed. Pauline Therese Collins and Rosalie Arcala Hall. Leiden, Netherlands: Brill chapter 3, pp. 57–90.

Cohn, Lindsay P. and Nathan W. Toronto. 2016. "Markets and Manpower: The Political Economy of Compulsory Military Service." *Armed Forces & Society* 43(3):436–458.

Collier, Paul. 2009. *Wars, Guns, and Votes: Democracy in Dangerous Places.* New York: HarperCollins.

Collier, Paul and Anke Hoeffler. 2006. "Grand Extortion: Coup Risk and the Military as a Protection Racket." *Working Paper.*

Cook, Steven. 2007. *Ruling But Not Governing: The Military and Political Development in Egypt, Algeria, and Turkey.* Baltimore, MD: The Johns Hopkins University Press.

Cooper, Mark N. 1982. *The Transformation of Egypt.* Baltimore, MD: Johns Hopkins University Press.

Copeland, Miles. 1969. *The Game of Nations: The Amorality of Power Politics.* New York: Simon and Schuster.

Cordesman, Anthony H. and Aram Nerguizian. 2010. "The North African Military Balance: Force Developments & Regional Challenges." *Center for Strategic and International Studies* pp. 1–124.

Cox, David R. 1972. "Regression Models and Life-Tables." *Journal of the Royal Statistical Society, Series B (Methodological)* 34(2):187–220.

Croissant, Aurel, David Kuehn, and Tanja Eschenauer. 2018. "The 'Dictator's Endgame': Explaining Military Behavior in Nonviolent Anti-incumbent Mass Protests." *Democracy and Security* 14(2):174–199.

D. 2022. "La fondation FIDA, qu'est ce que c'est?" *Tunisie Numerique* September 22. URL: https://www.tunisienumerique.com/la-fondation-fida-quest-ce-que-cest

Dahl, Robert A. 1989. *Democracy and its Critics.* New Haven, CT: Yale University Press.

Dahmani, Frida. 2013. "Tunisie : le général Rachid Ammar jette l'éponge." *Jeune Afrique* June 25. URL: https://www.jeuneafrique.com/170036/politique/tunisie-le-g-n-ral-rachid-ammar-jette-l-ponge

Davenport, Christian. 1995. "Multi-Dimensional Threat Perception and State Repression: An Inquiry into Why States Apply Negative Sanctions." *American Journal of Political Science* 39(3):683–713.

Davenport, Christian. 2007. "State Repression and Political Order." *Annual Review of Political Science* 10(1):1–23.

de Bruin, Erica. 2018. "Preventing Coups d'état: How Counterbalancing Works." *Journal of Conflict Resolution* 62(7):1433–1458.

de Bruin, Erica. 2020. *How to Prevent Coups d'Etat: Counterbalancing and Regime Survival.* Ithaca, NY: Cornell University Press.

de la défense nationale, Ministère. 2012. "Création du premier noyau de l'Armée nationale tunisienne." URL: http://www.hmp.defense.tn/index.php/fr/formation/formation-professionnelle/creation-du-premier-noyeau

Debs, Alexandre. 2016. "Living by the Sword and Dying by the Sword? Leadership Transitions in and out of Dictatorships." *International Studies Quarterly* 60:73–84.

Decalo, Samuel. 1990. *Coups and Army Rule in Africa.* New Haven, CT: Yale University Press.

Decalo, Samuel. 1997. Benin: First of New Democracies. In *Political Reforms in Francophone Africa*, ed. John F. Clark and David E. Gardinier. New York: Westview Press chapter 4, pp. 43–60.

Decalo, Samuel. 1998. *The Stable Minority: Civilian Rule in Africa, 1960–1990.* Gainesville, FL: Florida Academic Press.

Dee, Liz. 2012. "The Cairo Fire of 1952." *Association for Diplomatic Studies and Training* September 21. URL: https://adst.org/2012/09/the-cairo-fire-of-1952

Dennison, James and Jonas Draege. 2021. "The dynamics of electoral politics after the Arab Spring: evidence from Tunisia." *Journal of North African Politics* 26(4):756–780.

Diamandouros, P. Nikiforos. 1986. Regime Change and the Prospects for Democracy in Greece: 1974–1983. In *Transitions from Authoritarian Rule: Southern Europe*, ed. Guillermo O'Donnell, Philippe Schmitter, and Laurence Whitehead. Baltimore, MD: Johns Hopkins University Press chapter 6, pp. 138–164.

Diamond, Larry. 1999. *Developing Democracy: Towards Consolidation.* Baltimore, MD: Johns Hopkins University Press.

Digiuseppe, Matthew and Paul Poast. 2018. "Arms versus Democratic Allies." *British Journal of Political Science* 48(4):981–1003.

Diwan FM. 2021. "Al-Inqilab al-Askari fi Tunis Maza'a." URL: https://bit.ly/3AexFNw

Dworschak, Christoph. 2020. "Jumping on the Bandwagon: Differentiation and Security Defection during Conflict." *Journal of Conflict Resolution* 64(7–8):1335–1357.

Easton, Malcolm R. and Randolph M. Siverson. 2018. "Leader Survival and Purges after a Failed Coup d'etat." *Journal of Peace Research* 55(5):596–608.

Egypt Independent. 2010. "Brotherhood collects half million signatures for ElBaradei's reform demands." *Egypt Independent* August 18. URL: https://www.egyptindependent.com/brotherhood-collects-half-million-signatures-elbaradeis-reform-demands

Egypt Independent. 2011. "Democratic Coalition parties agree on supra-constitutional principles." *Egypt Independent* August 16. URL: https://www.egyptindependent.com/democratic-coalition-parties-agree-supra-constitutional-principles

Egypt Independent. 2012*a*. "Amendment stripping president of right to refer civilians to military trials approved." *Egypt Independent* April 10. URL: https://egyptindependent.com/parliament-approves-principle-amendments-code-military-justice

Egypt Independent. 2012*b*. "April 6 congratulates Morsy, holds him to his promise." June 18. URL: https://www.egyptindependent.com/april-6-congratulates-morsy-holds-him-his-promise

Egypt Independent. 2012*c*. "Morsy sends Tantawi to retirement, appoints Sisi military head." *Egypt Independent* August 12. URL: https://www.egyptindependent.com/morsy-sends-tantawi-retirement-appoints-sisi-military-head

Egypt Independent. 2012*d*. "Parliament's first legislation to increase compensation to revolution martyrs." *Egypt Independent* March 12. URL: https://egyptindependent.com/parliaments-first-legislation-increase-compensation-revolution-martyrs

Ehrenreich, Frederick. 1988. National Security. In *Tunisia: A Country Study*, ed. Harold D. Nelson. United State Government, Secretary of the Army chapter 5, pp. 267–316.

El-Din, Gamal Essam. 2012*a*. "Egypt fast-tracks constitution amid political turmoil." *Ahram Online* November 29. URL: http://english.ahram.org.eg/NewsContent/1/64/59412/Egypt/Politics-/Fasttrack-constitution-Voting-Thursday–months-bef.aspx

El-Din, Gamal Essam. 2012*b*. "Egypt PM Qandil makes some surprise, controversial ministerial choices." *Ahram Online* August 3. URL: http://english.ahram.org.eg/News/49380.aspx

El-Erian, Essam. 2011. "What the Muslim Brothers want." *The New York Times* February 9. URL: http://www.nytimes.com/2011/02/10/opinion/10erian.html?_r=1

El Fekih, Hassan. 2011. "Tunisia's new government purges police." *Sydney Morning Herald* February 3. URL: https://www.smh.com.au/world/tunisias-new-government-purges-police-20110203-1ae27.html

El-Gallad, Magdi. 2011. "Presidential candidate says constitution should give wide powers to the military." *Egypt Independent* July 3. URL: https://www.egyptindependent.com/presidential-candidate-says-constitution-should-give-wide-powers-military

El-Gamasy, Mohamed Abdel Ghani. 1993. *Memoirs of Field Marshal El-Gamasy of Egypt*. Cairo, Egypt: American University of Cairo Press.

El Gundy, Zeinab. 2012. "Morsi appoints new Egypt 'acting' spy chief." *Ahram Online* August 8. URL: http://english.ahram.org.eg/NewsContent/1/64/49967/Egypt/Politics-/BREAKING-Morsi-appoints-new-Egypt-acting-spy-chief.aspx

El-Hennawy, Noha. 2011. "Can Egypt's military be trusted to defend democracy?" *Egypt Independent* July 6. URL: https://www.egyptindependent.com/can-egypts-military-be-trusted-defend-democracy

El-Hennawy, Noha. 2012*a*. "Egypt's new People's Assembly swears in today, but powers are dubious." *Egypt Independent* January 23. URL: https://www.egyptindependent.com/egypts-new-peoples-assembly-swears-today-powers-are-dubious

El-Hennawy, Noha. 2012*b*. "The constitutional crisis: Morsy's chances and impasses." *Egypt Independent* November 25. URL: https://www.egyptindependent.com/constitutional-crisis-morsy-s-chances-and-impasses

El Materi, Moncef. 2014. *De Saint-Cyr au peloton d'execution de Bourguiba*. Tunis, Tunisia: Arabesques.

El Sisi, Brigadier General Abdelfattah Said. 2006. "Democracy in the Middle East." *U.S. Army War College* Strategy Research Project. URL: https://assets.documentcloud.org/documents/1173610/sisi.pdf

Eleiba, Ahmed. 2012. "The Brotherhood and the army." *Ahram Online* December 29. URL: http://english.ahram.org.eg/NewsContent/1/64/61449/Egypt/Politics-/The-Brotherhood-and-the-army.aspx

Eleiba, Ahmed. 2013. "F-16 deal redefines US relationship with Egypt's Morsi administration." *Ahram Online* January 14. URL: http://english.ahram.org.eg/NewsContent/1/64/62462/Egypt/Politics-/F-deal-redefines-US-relationship-with-Egypts-Morsi.aspx

Enloe, Cynthia H. 1980. *Ethnic Soldiers: State Security in Divided Societies.* Athens, GA: University of Georgia Press.

Eskandar, Wael. 2013. "Brothers and Officers: A History of Pacts." *Jadaliyya.* URL: http://www.jadaliyya.com/Details/27898/Brothers-and-Officers-A-History-of-Pacts

Espace Manager. 2011. "Garde Nationale Tunisie: des agents réclament le départ de Moncef Helali." *Espace Manager* September 6. URL: https://www.espacemanager.com/garde-nationale-tunisie-des-agents-reclament-le-depart-de-moncef-helali.html

Ezzat, Dina. 2012*a*. "Constitutional declaration leaves Egypt's Morsi with declining support." *Ahram Online* November 27. URL: http://english.ahram.org.eg/NewsContent/1/64/59302/Egypt/Politics-/Constitutional-declaration-leaves-Egypts-Morsi-wit.aspx

Ezzat, Dina. 2012*b*. "Egypt: The president, the army and the police." *Ahram Online* December 27. URL: http://english.ahram.org.eg/News/61344.aspx

F. K. 2019. "Moncef Marzouki: je me suis trompé en accueillant les partisans du terrorisme à Carthage!" *Realites Online* August 5. URL: https://www.realites.com.tn/2019/08/moncef-marzouki-je-me-suis-trompe-en-accueillant-les-partisans-du-terrorisme-a-carthage

Fadel, Leila. 2013. "As the Revolution Fades, Tunisia Begins to Splinter." *NPR* September 12. URL: https://www.npr.org/sections/parallels/2013/09/12/221798704/as-the-revolution-fades-tunisia-begins-to-splinter

Fahmy, Dalia F. and Daanish Faruqi. 2017. *Egypt and the Contradictions of Liberalism: Illiberal Intelligentsia and the Future of Egyptian Democracy.* London, UK: One World.

Faksh, Mahmud A. 1976. "Education and Elite Recruitment: An Analysis of Egypt's Post-1952 Political Elite." *Comparative Education Review* 20(2):140–150.

Farahat, Cynthia. 2011. "The Arab Upheaval: Egypt's Islamist Shadow." *Middle East Quarterly* 18(3):19–24.

Feaver, Peter. 1996. "The Civil-Military Problematique: Huntington, Janowitz, and the Question of Civilian Control." *Armed Forces and Society* 23(2):149–178.

Feaver, Peter. 1998. "Crisis as Shirking: An Agency Theory Explanation of the Souring of American Civil-Military Relations." *Armed Forces & Society* 24(3):407–434.

Feaver, Peter. 1999. "Civil-Military Relations." *Annual Review of Political Science* 2:211–241.

Fine, Jason P. and Robert J. Gray. 1999. "A Proportional Hazards Model for the Subdistribution of a Competing Risk." *Journal of the American Statistical Association* 94(446):496–509.

Finer, Samuel E. 1962. *The Man on Horseback: The Role of the Military in Politics.* New Brunswick, NJ: Transaction Publishers.

First, Ruth. 1970. *The Barrel of a Gun: Political Power in Africa and the Coup d'etat in Africa.* New York: Penguin Press.

Fish, M. Steven. 2002. "Islam and Authoritarianism." *World Politics* 55(1):4–37.

Fitch, J. Samuel. 1998. *The Armed Forces and Democracy in Latin America.* Baltimore, MD: Johns Hopkins Press.

FM, Mosaique. 2020. "La Tunisie réaffirme sa présence aux missions de maintien de la paix." July 15. URL: https://www.mosaiquefm.net/fr/actualite-national-tunisie/769569/la-tunisie-reaffirme-sa-presence-aux-missions-de-maintien-de-la-paix

Frankel, Sheera and Maged Atef. 2014. "How Egypt's Rebel Movement Helped Pave the Way For A Sisi Presidency." *Buzzfeed* April 15. URL: https://www.buzzfeednews.com/article/sheerafrenkel/how-egypts-rebel-movement-helped-pave-the-way-for-a-sisi-pre

Friedberg, Aaron L. 2000. *In the Shadow of the Garrison State: America's Anti-Statism and Its Cold War Grand Strategy.* Princeton, NJ: Princeton University Press.

Gaaloul, Badra. 2011. "Back to The Barracks: the Tunisian Army Post-Revolution." *Carnegie Endowment for International Peace* Sada. URL: https://carnegieendowment.org/sada/?fa=45907

Galey, Patrick. 2012. "Why the Egyptian Military Fears a Captains' Revolt." *Foreign Policy* February 16. URL: https://foreignpolicy.com/2012/02/16/why-the-egyptian-military-fears-a-captains-revolt

Gallagher, Tom. 1979. "Controlled Repression in Salazar's Portugal." *Journal of Contemporary History* 14:385–402.

Gallopin, Jean-Baptiste. 2019. "Dilemma and Cascades in the Armed Forces - The Tunisian Revolution." *Democracy and Security* 15(4):328–360.

Gandhi, Jennifer and Adam Przeworski. 2007. "Authoritarian Institutions and the Survival of Autocrats." *Comparative Political Studies* 40(11):1279–1301.

Gandhi, Jennifer and Ellen Lust-Okar. 2009. "Authoritarian Institutions and the Survival of Autocrats." *Annual Review of Political Science* 12:403–422.

Gandhi, Jennifer and Jane Lawrence Sumner. 2020. "Measuring the Consolidation of Power in Nondemocracies." *Journal of Politics* 82(4):1545–1558.

García-Ponce, Omar and Léonard Wantchékon. 2017. "Critical Junctures: Independence Movements and Democracy in Africa." *Working Paper.*

Gasiorowski, Mark. 1995. "Economic Crisis and Political Regime Change: An Event History Analysis." *American Political Science Review* 89:882–897.

Gates, Robert M. 2014. *Duty: Memoirs of a Secretary at War.* New York: Knopf.

Gaub, Florence. 2013. "The Libyan Armed Forces between Coup-proofing and Repression." *Journal of Strategic Studies* 36(2):221–244.

Geddes, Barbara. 1999. "What Do We Know About Democratization After Twenty Years?" *Annual Review of Political Science* 2:115–144.

Geddes, Barbara, Joseph Wright, and Erica Frantz. 2014. "Autocratic Breakdown and Regime Transitions: A New Data Set." *Perspectives on Politics* 12(2):313–331.

Geddes, Barbara, Joseph Wright, and Erica Frantz. 2018. *How Dictatorships Work.* New York: Cambridge University Press.

Ghanem, Dalia. 2019. "What will Algeria's military do next?" *Middle East Eye.* URL: https://www.middleeasteye.net/opinion/what-will-algerias-military-do-next

Gibler, Douglas M. and Jaroslav Tir. 2010. "Settled Borders and Regime Type: Democratic Transitions as Consequences of Peaceful Territorial Transfers." *American Journal of Political Science* 54(4):951–968.

Giglio, Mike. 2013*a*. "A Cairo conspiracy." *The Daily Beast* July 12. URL: https://www.thedailybeast.com/a-cairo-conspiracy

Giglio, Mike. 2013*b*. "Mahmoud Badr is the young face of the anti-Morsi movement." *The Daily Beast* July 2. URL: https://www.thedailybeast.com/mahmoud-badr-is-the-young-face-of-the-anti-morsi-movement

Glaser, April. 2021. "Who decides when there are helicopters? Experts weigh in on National Guard monitoring protests." *NBC News* January 10.

Glasser, Susan B. and Peter Baker. 2022. "Inside the War Between Trump and His Generals." *The New Yorker* August 15.

Gleditsch, Kristian S. and Michael D. Ward. 2006. "Diffusion and the International Context of Democratization." *International Organization* 60:911–933.

Gleditsch, Nils Petter, Peter Wallensteen, Mikael Eriksson, Margareta Sollenberg, and Håvard Strand. 2002. "Armed Conflict 1946–2001: A New Dataset." *Journal of Peace Research* 39(5):615–637.

Goldring, Edward and Austin S. Matthews. 2021. "To Purge or Not to Purge? An Individual-Level Quantitative Analysis of Elite Purges in Dictatorships." *British Journal of Political Science* Firstview.

Goldsmith, Benjamin E. 2003. "Bearing the Defense Burden, 1886–1989: Why Spend More?" *Journal of Conflict Resolution* 47(5):551–573.

Greitens, Sheena Chestnut. 2016. *Dictators and Their Secret Police: Coercive Institutions and State Violence.* New York: Cambridge University Press.

Grewal, Sharan. 2016. "A Quiet Revolution: The Tunisian Military After Ben Ali." *Carnegie Endowment for International Peace.*

Grewal, Sharan. 2017. "Tunisian Security Forces Rock the Vote." *Carnegie Endowment for International Peace* Sada. URL: https://carnegieendowment.org/sada/68021

Grewal, Sharan. 2018*a*. "Security Forces Balance Politics and Neutrality." *Carnegie Endowment for International Peace* Sada. URL: https://carnegieendowment.org/sada/76302

Grewal, Sharan. 2018*b*. "Time to Rein in Tunisia's Police Unions." *Project on Middle East Democracy* Snapshot:1–10.

Grewal, Sharan. 2019*a*. "Military Defection During Localized Protests: The Case of Tataouine." *International Studies Quarterly* 63(2):259–269.

Grewal, Sharan. 2019*b*. "Tunisian Democracy at a Crossroads." *The Brookings Institution.*

Grewal, Sharan. 2020*a*. "From Islamists to Muslim Democrats: The Case of Tunisia's Ennahda." *American Political Science Review* 114(2):519–535.

Grewal, Sharan. 2020*b*. "Tunisia's Foiled Coup of 1987: The November 8th Group." *Middle East Journal* 74(1):53–71.

Grewal, Sharan. 2021*a*. "How COVID-19 Helped Legitimate the Tunisian President's Power Grab." *Project on Middle East Democracy* August 23.

Grewal, Sharan. 2021*b*. "Why Sudan Succeeded Where Algeria Failed." *Journal of Democracy* 32(4):102–114.

Grewal, Sharan. 2022*a*. "Military Repression and Restraint in Algeria." *APSA Conference Paper.*

Grewal, Sharan. 2022*b*. "Norm Diffusion through US Military Training in Tunisia." *Security Studies* 31(2):291–317.

Grewal, Sharan and Drew Kinney. 2022. "What's in a Name? Experimental Evidence of the Coup Taboo." *Democratization* 29(7): 1332–1345.

Grewal, Sharan and Hamza Mighri. 2019. "Reforming Tunisia's Military Courts." *The Brookings Institution.*

Grewal, Sharan and Shadi Hamid. 2020. "The Dark Side of Consensus in Tunisia: Lessons from 2015–2019." *The Brookings Institution.*

Grewal, Sharan and Steve Monroe. 2019. "Down and Out: Founding Elections and Disillusionment with Democracy in Egypt and Tunisia." *Comparative Politics* 51(4):497–539.

Grewal, Sharan and Yasser Kureshi. 2019. "How to Sell a Coup: Elections as Coup Legitimation." *Journal of Conflict Resolution* 63(4):1001–1031.

Grimaud, Nicole. 1995. *La Tunisie a la recherche de sa securite.* Paris: Presses Universitaires de France.

Grira, Ridha. 2011. "Testimony before the military court." *Available through Nawaat* April. URL: https://cdn.nawaat.org/wp-content/uploads/2011/11/pdfGrira.pdf

Guiler, Kim. 2020. "From Prison to Parliament: Victimhood, Identity, and Electoral Support." *Mediterranean Politics* Firstview:1–30.

Haber, Stephen and Victor Menaldo. 2011. "Do Natural Resources Fuel Authoritarianism? A Reappraisal of the Resource Curse." *American Political Science Review* 105(1):1–26.

Haberman, Maggie and Helene Cooper. 2021. "Trump rebuffed initial requests to deploy the National Guard to the Capitol. Pence gave the go-ahead." *The New York Times* January 6.

Haddad, Mohamed. 2019. "National Security Council, 'a Think Tank Rather Than a Parallel Government' Says Kamel Akrout." *ResearchMedia*. URL: https://www.researchmedia.org/interview-kamelakrout-national-security-council-eng

Hafez, Sherine. 2014. "Bodies That Protest: The Girl in the Blue Bra, Sexuality, and State Violence in Revolutionary Egypt." *Signs: Journal of Women in Culture and Society* 40(1):20–28.

Haggard, Stephen and Robert R. Kaufman. 1995. *The Political Economy of Democratic Transitions*. Princeton, NJ: Princeton University Press.

Halawa, Omar. 2015. "Supporters of 3 July 2013: Where are they now?" *Ahram Online* July 3. URL: http://english.ahram.org.eg/NewsContent/1/151/133707/Egypt/Features/Supporters-of–July–Where-are-they-now.aspx

Hale, William. 1994. *Turkish Politics and the Military*. New York: Routledge.

Hamid, Shadi. 2014. *Temptations of Power: Islamists and Illiberal Democracy in a New Middle East*. New York: Oxford University Press.

Hamid, Shadi. 2016. *Islamic Exceptionalism: How the Struggle over Islam is Reshaping the World*. New York: St. Martin's Press.

Hamid, Shadi. 2022. *The Problem of Democracy: America, the Middle East, and the Rise and Fall of an Idea*. New York: Oxford University Press.

Hammami, Mohamed Dhia. 2022. "Unintended Consequences: The Civilian-Military March towards Tunisia's Coup." *2022 APSA Conference*.

Harb, Imad. 2003. "The Egyptian Military in Politics: Disengagement or Accommodation?" *Middle East Journal* 57(2):269–290.

Harkness, Kristen A. 2016. "The Ethnic Army and the State: Explaining Coup Traps and the Difficulties of Democratization in Africa." *Journal of Conflict Resolution* 60(4):587–616.

Harkness, Kristen A. 2017. "Military Loyalty and the Failure of Democratization in Africa: How Ethnic Armies Shape the Capacity of Presidents to Defy Term Limits." *Democratization* 24(5):801–818.

Harkness, Kristen A. 2018. *When Soldiers Rebel: Ethnic Armies and Political Instability in Africa*. New York: Cambridge University Press.

Hartshorn, Ian. 2019. *Labor Politics in North Africa*. New York: Cambridge University Press.

Hashim, Ahmed. 2011*a*. "The Egyptian Military, Part One: From the Ottomans Through Sadat." *Middle East Policy* 18(3):63–78.

Hashim, Ahmed. 2011*b*. "The Egyptian Military, Part Two: From Mubarak Onwards." *Middle East Policy* 18(4):106–128.

Hassan, Mai. 2020. *Regime Threats and State Solutions: Bureaucratic Loyalty and Embeddedness in Kenya*. New York: Cambridge University Press.

Hassan, Mai and Ahmed Kodouda. 2019. "Sudan's Uprising: The Fall of a Dictator." *Journal of Democracy* 30(4):89–103.

Hassan, Mazen, Jasmin Lorch and Annette Ranko. 2020. "Explaining Divergent Transformation Paths in Tunisia and Egypt: The Role of Inter-Elite Trust." *Mediterranean Politics* 25(5):553–578.

Hatab, Shimaa. 2020. "Threat Perception and Democratic Support in Post-Arab Spring Egypt." *Comparative Politics* 53(1):69–98.

Heikal, Mohamed. 1983. *Autumn of Fury: the Assassination of Anwar Sadat*. New York: Random House.

Hendawi, Hamza. 2012. "Gaza deal seals major role for Egypt's president." *Associated Press* November 22. URL: https://www.usatoday.com/story/news/world/2012/11/22/egypt-president-gaza-deal/1720759

Henry, Clement and Robert Springborg. 2011. "A Tunisian Solution for Egypt's Military: Why Egypt's Military Will Not Be Able to Govern." *Foreign Affairs*.

Hernandez, Carolina G. 1996. Controlling Asia's Armed Forces. In *Civil-Military Relations and Democracy*, ed. Larry Diamond and Marc F. Plattner. Baltimore, MD: Johns Hopkins University Press chapter 5, pp. 99–109.

Hill, Evan and Muhammad Mansour. 2013. "Egypt's army took part in torture and killings during revolution, report shows." *The Guardian* April 10. URL: https://www.theguardian.com/world/2013/apr/10/egypt-army-torture-killings-revolution

Hiltin, Paul and Lee Rainie. 2019. "Facebook Algorithms and Personal Data." *Pew Research Center* January 16. URL: https://www.pewinternet.org/2019/01/16/facebook-algorithms-and-personal-data.

Hodges, Doyle. 2022. "A Duty to Disobey." *Lawfare* August 19. URL: https://www.lawfareblog.com/duty-disobey

Holmes, Amy Austin. 2012. "There are Weeks When Decades Happen: Structure and Strategy in the Egyptian Revolution." *Mobilization* 17(4):391–410.

Holmes, Amy Austin. 2019. *Coups and Revolutions: Mass Mobilization, the Egyptian Military, and the United States from Mubarak to Sisi.* New York: Oxford University Press.

Holmes, Amy Austin and Kevin Koehler. 2020. "Myths of Military Defection in Egypt and Tunisia." *Mediterranean Politics* 25(1):45–70.

Horowitz, Donald L. 1980. *Coup Theories and Officers' Motives: Sri Lanka in Comparative Perspective.* Princeton, NJ: Princeton University Press.

Horowitz, Donald L. 1985. *Ethnic Groups in Conflict.* Berkeley, CA: University of California Press.

Horowitz, Donald L. 1993. "Democracy in Divided Societies." *Journal of Democracy* 4(4):18–38.

Hubbard, Ben. 2013. "Anger at Egypt's leaders intensifies in gas lines." *New York Times* June 26. URL: https://www.nytimes.com/2013/06/27/world/middleeast/anger-at-egypts-leaders-intensifies-in-gas-lines.html

Hubbard, Ben and David D. Kirkpatrick. 2013. "Sudden improvements in Egypt suggest a campaign to undermine Morsi." *New York Times* July 10. URL: https://www.nytimes.com/2013/07/11/world/middleeast/improvements-in-egypt-suggest-a-campaign-that-undermined-morsi.html

Human Rights Watch. 1992. "Behind Closed Doors: Torture and Detention in Egypt." *A Middle East Watch Report.* URL: https://www.hrw.org/legacy/reports/pdfs/e/egypt/egypt.927/egypt927full.pdf

Human Rights Watch. 2011. "Egypt: Retry or Free 12,000 After Unfair Military Trials." September 10. URL: https://www.hrw.org/news/2011/09/10/egypt-retry-or-free-12000-after-unfair-military-trials

Human Rights Watch. 2014. "All According to Plan: The Rab'a Massacre and Mass Killings of Protesters in Egypt." August 12. URL: https://www.hrw.org/report/2014/08/12/all-according-plan/raba-massacre-and-mass-killings-protesters-egypt

Hunter, Wendy. 1997. "Continuity or Change? Civil-Military Relations in Democratic Argentina, Chile, and Peru." *Political Science Quarterly* 112(3):453–475.

Huntington, Samuel P. 1957. *The Soldier and the State: The Theory and Politics of Civil-Military Relations.* Cambridge, MA: The Belknap Press of Harvard University Press.

Huntington, Samuel P. 1991. *The Third Wave: Democratization in the Late Twentieth Century.* Norman, OK: University of Oklahoma Press.

Hurewitz, J.C. 1969. *Middle East Politics: The Military Dimension.* New York: Praeger.

Hussein, Abdel-Rahman. 2011. "Egypt: Mohamed Morsi cancels decree that gave him sweeping powers." *The Guardian* December 8. URL: https://www.theguardian.com/world/2012/dec/09/egypt-mohamed-morsi-cancels-decree

Huweidi, Amine. 1992. *Al-Foras al-Da'i'a, al-Qararat al-Hasima fi Harbay al-Istinzaf wa-October.* al-Sharika al-'Arabiyya li-l-Tawzi' wa-l-Nashr.

Ibrahim, Arwa. 2015. "Egyptian politician lashes out at military in leaked tapes." *Middle East Eye* May 14. URL: https://www.middleeasteye.net/news/egyptian-politician-lashes-out-military-leaked-tapes

IkhwanWeb. 2011*a*. "34 Egyptian Parties Reject Supra-Constitutional Principles." August 15. URL: https://ikhwanweb.com/article.php?id=28939

IkhwanWeb. 2011*b*. "MB Chairman: A Leading MB Executive Bureau Member Will Resign to Head Freedom & Justice." March 21. URL: https://www.ikhwanweb.com/article.php?id=28263

IkhwanWeb. 2011*c*. "MB Chairman Confirms Group Will Take Part in Day of Rage March Despite Threats." January 23. URL: https://www.ikhwanweb.com/article.php?id=27905

IkhwanWeb. 2011*d*. "MB Chairman: Egypt Needs National Consensus." December 11. URL: https://www.ikhwanweb.com/article.php?id=29398

IkhwanWeb. 2011*e*. "Senator John Kerry and U.S. Ambassador Visit FJP, Discuss Egypt's Democratic Transition." December 10. URL: https://www.ikhwanweb.com/article.php?id=29395

IkhwanWeb. 2011*f*. "Text of Selmi's Controversial Supra-Constitutional Principles, in English and Arabic." November 4. URL: http://www.ikhwanweb.com/article.php?id=29360

IkhwanWeb. 2012*a*. "Al-Barr to U.S. Ambassador: Egyptians Demand US Respects Democracy, Protects Freedoms." January 26. URL: https://www.ikhwanweb.com/article.php?id=29596

IkhwanWeb. 2012*b*. "Badie to US Ambassador: Actions Not Words Will Help US Restore Its Credibility in Muslim World." January 19. URL: https://www.ikhwanweb.com/article.php?id=29568

IkhwanWeb. 2012*c*. "FJP Chairman Meets Former U.S. President Jimmy Carter." January 12. URL: https://www.ikhwanweb.com/article.php?id=29541

IkhwanWeb. 2012*d*. "FJP Chairman Meets with Assistant U.S. Secretary of State." January 12. URL: https://www.ikhwanweb.com/article.php?id=29538

IkhwanWeb. 2012*e*. "FJP Receives Assistant U.S. Secretary of State for Democracy and Human Rights, Discuss NGO." January 27. URL: https://www.ikhwanweb.com/article.php?id=29600

IkhwanWeb. 2012*f*. "Former U.S. President Jimmy Carter After Meeting With Badie: I Recognize Egyptian People's Love for the Muslim Brotherhood." January 14. URL: https://www.ikhwanweb.com/article.php?id=29546

Imam, 'Abdallah. 2001. *Al-Fariq Mohammad Fawzi, al-Naksa, al-Istinzaf, al-Sijn*. Cairo: Dar al-Khayyal.

Inkeles, Alex. 1966. "The Modernization of Man." *Comparative Politics* 44(2):138–150.

International Crisis Group. 2011. "Popular Protest in North Africa and the Middle East (I): Egypt Victorious?" *Middle East/North Africa Report* 101(February 24). URL: https://www.crisisgroup.org/middle-east-north-africa/north-africa/egypt/popular-protest-north-africa-and-middle-east-i-egypt-victorious

International Crisis Group. 2012. "Lost in Translation: The World According to Egypt's SCAF." *Middle East Report* (121):1–30.

International Crisis Group. 2013. "Marching in Circles: Egypt's Dangerous Second Transition." *Middle East and North Africa* Briefing 35.

International Crisis Group. 2015. "Reform and Security Strategy in Tunisia." *Middle East and North Africa Report* 161.

IVD. 2019. "The Final Comprehensive Report: Executive Summary." *Truth & Dignity Commission* (May). URL: http://www.ivd.tn/rapport/doc/TDC_executive_summary_report.pdf

Izadi, Roya. 2022. "State Security or Exploitation: A Theory of Military Involvement in the Economy." *Journal of Conflict Resolution* 66(4–5):729–754.

Jager, Kai. 2017. "The Potential of Online Sampling for Studying Political Activists around the World and across Time." *Political Analysis* 25:329–343.

Jamaal, Wael. 2012. "Soldier: Our projects (sweat) the Defense Ministry, and we will not let the state interfere in them." *Shorouk News* March 27. (In Arabic) URL: http://www.shorouknews.com/news/view.aspx?cdate=27032012&id=0de8ea0c-136a-4270-9a7c-79b576b91b51

Jamal, Amaney. 2007. *Barriers to Democracy: The Other Side of Social Capital in Palestine and the Arab World.* Princeton, NJ: Princeton University Press.

Jamal, Amaney. 2012. *Of Empires and Citizens: Pro-American Democracy or No Democracy at All.* Princeton, NJ: Princeton University Press.

Janowitz, Morris. 1960. *The Professional Soldier: A Social and Political Portrait.* New York: Simon & Schuster.

Janowitz, Morris. 1964. *The Military in the Political Development of New Nations: An Essay in Comparative Analysis.* Chicago, IL: University of Chicago Press.

Janowitz, Morris. 1977. *Military Institutions and Coercion in the Developing Nations.* Chicago, IL: University of Chicago Press.

Jebnoun, Noureddine. 2014. "In the Shadow of Power: Civil-Military Relations and the Tunisian Popular Uprising." *Journal of North African Studies* 19(3):296–316.

Jebnoun, Noureddine. 2022. "Cementing Saied's Sovereign Dictatorship in Tunisia." *DAWN MENA.* URL: https://dawnmena.org/saieds-sovereign-dictatorship-in-tunisia

Jeune Afrique. 2011*a*. "La général Ammar, l'homme qui a dit non." *Jeune Afrique* February 7. URL: https://www.jeuneafrique.com/192799/politique/le-g-n-ral-ammar-l-homme-qui-a-dit-non

Jeune Afrique. 2011*b*. "Tunisie: que mijotait Ali Seriati?" *Jeune Afrique* March 28. URL: https://www.jeuneafrique.com/192243/politique/tunisie-que-mijotait-ali-seriati

Jeune Afrique. 2012. "Tunisie: La veritable histoire du 14 janvier 2011." *Jeune Afrique* 25 January. URL: https://www.jeuneafrique.com/143296/politique/tunisie-la-v-ritable-histoire-du-14-janvier-2011

Jevon, Graham. 2017. *Glubb Pasha and the Arab Legion: Britain, Jordan, and the End of the Empire in the Middle East.* New York: Cambridge University Press.

Johnson, Paul Lorenzo and Ches Thurber. 2020. "The Security-Force Ethnicity (SFE) Project: Introducing a New Dataset." *Conflict Management and Peace Science* 37(1):106–129.

Jrad, Eya. 2021. "Constitutional or Unconstitutional: Is That the Question?" *Arab Reform Initiative* August 3. URL: https://www.arab-reform.net/publication/constitutional-or-unconstitutional-is-that-the-question

Kadivar, Mohammad Ali. 2018. "Mass Mobilization and the Durability of New Democracies." *American Sociological Review* 83(2):390–417.

Kadivar, Mohammad Ali. 2022. *Popular Politics and the Path to Durable Democracy.* Princeton, NJ: Princeton University Press.

Kamen, Al and Scott Armstrong. 1982. "Cost of transporting arms to Egypt probed by justice." *Washington Post* October 1. URL: https://www.washingtonpost.com/archive/politics/1982/10/01/cost-of-transporting-arms-to-egypt-probed-by-justice/03d986f0-e13b-4448-9cf7-cc9fc78c497c

Kamrava, Mehran. 2000. "Military Professionalization and Civil-Military Relations in the Middle East." *Political Science Quarterly* 115(1):67–92.

Kandil, Hazem. 2012. *Soldiers, Spies and Statesmen: Egypt's Road to Revolt.* New York: Verso.

Kandil, Hazem. 2015. *Inside the Brotherhood.* Malden, MA: Polity.

Kandil, Hazem. 2016. *The Power Triangle: Military, Security, and Politics in Regime Change.* New York: Oxford University Press.

Kapitalis. 2012. "Tunisie. Le gouverneur de Kébili rend le tablier." *Kapitalis* May 7. URL: http://www.kapitalis.com/politique/9733-tunisie-le-gouverneur-de-kebili-rend-le-tablier.html

Kapitalis. 2017. "Affaire Sidi Dhrif: Habib Ben Yahia condamné à 5 ans de prison." March 6. URL: http://kapitalis.com/tunisie/2017/03/06/affaire-sidi-dhrif-habib-ben-yahia-condamne-a-5-ans-de-prison

Karakatsanis, Neovi. 1997. "Do Attitudes Matter? The Military and Democratic Consolidation in Greece." *Armed Forces and Society* 24(2):289–313.

Kardi, Oussama. 2017. "Egypt coup plotters tried to overthrow Tunisian democracy, says ex-president." *Middle East Eye* August 11. URL: https://www.middleeasteye.net/news/egypt-coup-plotters-tried-overthrow-tunisian-democracy-says-ex-president

Karl, Terry Lynn. 1990. "Dilemmas of Democratization in Latin America." *Comparative Politics* 23(1):1–21.

Kasdallah, Mohamed. 2017. "Pourquoi tant de tension, tant de haine, tant de rancœ et rancunes contre l'armée?" *Leaders.* URL: https://www.leaders.com.tn/article/23292-ne-soyez-pas-sourds-car-nous-ne-sommes-pas-muets

Kechichian, Joseph and Jeanne Nazimek. 1997. "Challenges to the Military in Egypt." *Middle East Policy* 5(3):125–139.

Ketchley, Neil. 2014. "'The Army and the People Are One Hand!' Fraternization and the 25th January Egyptian Revolution." *Comparative Studies in Society and History* 56(1):155–186.

Ketchley, Neil. 2017. *Egypt in a Time of Revolution: Contentious Politics and the Arab Spring.* New York: Cambridge University Press.

Ketchley, Neil and Thoraya El-Rayyes. 2021. "Unpopular Protest: Mass Mobilization and Attitudes to Democracy in Post-Mubarak Egypt." *Journal of Politics* 83(1): 291–305.

Khalil, Ashraf. 2012. *Liberation Square: Inside the Egyptian Revolution and the Rebirth of a Nation.* New York: St. Martin's Publishing Group.

Khazbak, Rana. 2011. "As Tahrir returns to the spotlight, suspicion grows of Islamist intent." *Egypt Independent* November 17. URL: https://www.egyptindependent.com/tahrir-returns-spotlight-suspicion-grows-islamist-intent

Khazbak, Rana. 2012. "Morsy strikes a power-sharing deal to shore up presidency." *Egypt Independent* July 1. URL: https://www.egyptindependent.com/morsy-strikes-power-sharing-deal-shore-presidency

Kilavuz, M. Tahir. 2019. Authoritarian Persistence and Regime Change in the Middle East and North Africa: Autocrats, Opposition, and Coalitions. PhD thesis Notre Dame University.

Kim, Nam Kyu. 2021. "Previous Military Rule and Democratic Survival." *Journal of Conflict Resolution* 65(2–3):534–562.

Kimball, Anessa L. 2010. "Political Survival, Policy Distribution, and Alliance Formation." *Journal of Peace Research* 47(4):407–419.

Kingsley, Patrick. 2013. "Mohamed Morsi backs Egyptian military after malpractice allegations." *The Guardian* April 12. URL: https://www.theguardian.com/world/2013/apr/12/mohamed-morsi-backs-egyptian-military

Kinney, Drew Holland. 2022. Civilian Coup Advocacy. In *The Oxford Encyclopedia of the Military in Politics*, ed. William R. Thompson and Hicham Bou Nassif. New York: Oxford University Press.

Kirkpatrick, David D. 2011*a*. "Chief of Tunisian army pledges his support for 'the revolution.'" *New York Times* January 24. URL: https://www.nytimes.com/2011/01/25/world/africa/25tunis.html

Kirkpatrick, David D. 2011*b*. "Mubarak orders crackdown, with revolt sweeping Egypt." *The New York Times* January 28. URL: https://www.nytimes.com/2011/01/29/world/middleeast/29unrest.html

Kirkpatrick, David D. 2012*a*. "Backing off added powers, Egypt's leader presses vote." *New York Times* December 8. URL: https://www.nytimes.com/2012/12/09/world/middleeast/egypt-protests.html

Kirkpatrick, David D. 2012*b*. "Egyptian judge speaks against Islamist victory before presidential runoff." *New York Times* June 7. URL: https://www.nytimes.com/2012/06/08/world/middleeast/egyptian-judge-speaks-against-islamist-victory-before-presidential-runoff.html

Kirkpatrick, David D. 2012*c*. "Judge helped Egypt's military to cement power." *New York Times* July 3. URL: https://www.nytimes.com/2012/07/04/world/middleeast/judge-helped-egypts-military-to-cement-power.html

Kirkpatrick, David D. 2012*d*. "Recordings suggest emirates and Egyptian military pushed ousting of Morsi." *New York Times* March 1. URL: https://www.nytimes.com/2015/03/02/world/middleeast/recordings-suggest-emirates-and-egyptian-military-pushed-ousting-of-morsi.html

Kirkpatrick, David D. 2012*e*. "Secret recordings reveal Mubarak's frank views on a range of subjects." *New York Times* September 22. URL: https://www.nytimes.com/2013/09/23/world/middleeast/secret-recordings-reveal-mubaraks-frank-views-on-a-range-of-subjects.html

Kirkpatrick, David D. 2018*a*. *Into the Hands of the Soldiers: Freedom and Chaos in Egypt and the Middle East.* New York: Viking.

Kirkpatrick, David D. 2018*b*. "The White House and the strongman." *The New York Times* July 27. URL: https://www.nytimes.com/2018/07/27/sunday-review/obama-egypt-coup-trump.html

Kirkpatrick, David D. and David E. Sanger. 2011. "A Tunisian-Egyptian link that shook Arab history." *The New York Times* February 13. URL: https://www.nytimes.com/2011/02/14/world/middleeast/14egypt-tunisia-protests.html

Kirkpatrick, David D. and Mayy El Sheikh. 2013. "Morsi spurned deals, seeing military as tamed." *New York Times* July 6. URL: http://www.nytimes.com/2013/07/07/world/middleeast/morsi-spurned-deals-to-the-end-seeing-the-military-as-tamed.html

Kirkpatrick, David D. and Steven Erlanger. 2012. "Egypt's new leader spells out terms for U.S.-Arab ties." *New York Times* September 22. URL: https://www.nytimes.com/2012/09/23/world/middleeast/egyptian-leader-mohamed-morsi-spells-out-terms-for-us-arab-ties.html?pagewanted=all

Knights, Michael. 2013. "The Military Role in Yemen's Protests: Civil-Military Relations in the Tribal Republic." *Journal of Strategic Studies* 36(2):261–288.

Koehler, Kevin. 2016. "Political Militaries in Popular Uprisings: A Comparative Perspective on the Arab Spring." *International Political Science Review* Firstview:1–15.

Koehler, Kevin, Dorothy Ohl, and Holger Albrecht. 2016. "From Disaffection to Desertion: How Networks Facilitate Military Insubordination in Civil Conflict." *Comparative Politics* 48(4):439–457.

Koehler, Kevin and Holger Albrecht. 2021. "Revolutions and the Military: Endgame Coups, Instability, and Prospects for Democracy." *Armed Forces & Society* 47(1):148–176.

Kohn, Richard H. 1970. "The Inside History of the Newburgh Conspiracy: America and the Coup d'Etat." *The William and Mary Quarterly* 27(2):187–220.

Korotayev, Andrey, Leonid Issaev, and Alisa Shishkina. 2016. "Egyptian Coup of 2013: An 'Econometric' Analysis." *Journal of North African Studies* 21(3):341–356.

Kortam, Hend. 2013. "Morsi discusses Syria with Islamic scholars." *Daily News Egypt* June 14. URL: https://www.dailynewsegypt.com/2013/06/14/morsi-discusses-syria-with-islamic-scholars

Kuimova, Alexandra. 2020. "Understanding Egyptian Military Expenditure." *SIPRI* October. URL: https://www.sipri.org/sites/default/files/2020-10/bp_2010_egyptian_military_spending.pdf

Kurtzer, Daniel and Mary Svenstrup. 2012. "Egypt's Entrenched Military." *The National Interest.* URL: https://nationalinterest.org/article/egypts-entrenched-military-7343?page=0

La Presse. 2011. "Biographies des nouveaux gouverneurs." *Turess* February 21. URL: https://www.turess.com/fr/lapresse/23094

Lachapelle, Jean. 2020. "No Easy Way Out: The Effect of Military Coups on State Represion." *Journal of Politics* 82(4):1354–1372.

Lachapelle, Jean, Steven Levitsky, Lucan A. Way, and Adam E. Casey. 2020. "Social Revolution and Authoritarian Durability." *World Politics* 72(4):557–600.

Lafrance, Camille. 2021. "Tunisie: le rôle de l'armée dans la crise politique." *Jeune Afrique*. URL: https://www.jeuneafrique.com/1216944/politique/tunisie-et-larmee-dans-tout-ca/

Landler, Mark. 2011. "Obama cautions embattled ally against violence." *The New York Times* January 28. URL: https://www.nytimes.com/2011/01/29/world/middleeast/29diplo.html

Lasswell, Harold. 1941. "The Garrison State." *American Journal of Sociology* 46(4):455–468.

Lawrence, Adria. 2013. *Imperial Rule and the Politics of Nationalism: Anti-Colonial Protest in the French Empire*. New York: Cambridge University Press.

Le Monde. 2012. "Tunisie: des députés réclament la dissolution du parti islamiste au pouvoir." October 12. URL: https://www.lemonde.fr/tunisie/article/2012/10/12/tunisie-des-deputes-reclament-la-dissolution-du-parti-islamiste-au-pouvoir_1774301_1466522.html.

Leaders. 2011. "M. Mohamed Abdennaceur Belhaj, nouveau directeur général des Douanes Tunisiennes." *Leaders* July 8. URL: https://www.leaders.com.tn/article/5705-m-mohamed-abdennaceur-belhaj-nouveau-directeur-general-des-douanes-tunisiennes

Lee, Terence. 2008. "The Military's Corporate Interests: The Main Reason for Intervention in Indonesia and the Philippines?" *Armed Forces & Society* 34(3):491–502.

Lee, Terence. 2015. *Defect or Defend: Military Responses to Popular Protests in Authoritarian Asia*. Baltimore, MD: Johns Hopkins University Press.

Lerner, Daniel. 1958. *The Passing of Traditional Society*. Glencoe, IL: Free Press.

Levitsky, Steven and Daniel Ziblatt. 2018. *How Democracies Die*. New York: Crown.

Levitsky, Steven and Lucan A. Way. 2010. *Competitive Authoritarianism: Hybrid Regimes After the Cold War*. New York: Cambridge University Press.

Levitsky, Steven and Lucan A. Way. 2022. *Revolution and Dictatorship: The Violent Origins of Durable Authoritarianism*. Princeton, NJ: Princeton University Press.

Lieuwen, Edwin. 1961. *Arms and Politics in Latin America*. New York: Praeger Press.

Lieuwen, Edwin. 1964. *Generals v. Presidents: Neomilitarism in Latin America*. New York: Praeger Press.

Linz, Juan and Alfred Stepan. 1996. *Problems of Democratic Transition and Consolidation: Southern Europe, South America, and Post-Communist Europe*. Baltimore, MD: The Johns Hopkins University Press.

Linz, Juan J. and Arturo Valenzuela. 1994. *The Failure of Presidential Democracy*. Baltimore, MD: Johns Hopkins University Press.

Lipset, Seymour Martin. 1959. "Some Social Requisites of Democracy: Economic Development and Political Legitimacy." *American Political Science Review* 53(1):69–105.

Lipset, Seymour Martin. 1960. *Political Man: The Social Bases of Politics*. New York: Doubleday Press.

Londregan, John and Keith T. Poole. 1990. "Poverty, the Coup Trap, and the Seizure of Executive Power." *World Politics* 42(2):151–183.

Luciani, Giacomo. 2017. *Combining Economic and Political Development: The Experience of MENA*. Leiden, Netherlands: Brill.

Lutscher, Philipp M. 2016. "The More Fragmented the Better?—The Impact of Armed Forces Structure on Defection during Nonviolent Popular Uprisings." *International Interactions* 42(2):350–375.

Lutterbeck, Derek. 2013. "Arab Uprisings, Armed Forces, and Civil-Military Relations." *Armed Forces and Society* 39(1):28–52.

Lutterbeck, Derek. 2015. "Tool of Rule: The Tunisian Police under Ben Ali." *Journal of North African Studies* 20(5):813–831.

Luttwak, Edward N. 1979. *Coup d'état: A Practical Handbook.* Cambridge, MA: Harvard University Press.

Lyall, Jason. 2020. *Divided Armies: Inequality and Battlefield Performance in Modern War.* Princeton, NJ: Princeton University Press.

Lynch, Marc, Deen Freelon, and Sean Aday. 2017. "Online Clustering, Fear, and Uncertainty in Egypt's Transition." *Democratization* 24(6):1159–1177.

McCarthy, Rory. 2022. "Trangressive Protest after a Democratic Transition: The Kamour Campaign in Tunisia." *Social Movement Studies* 21(6):798–815.

Machiavelli, Niccolò. 1515. *The Prince.*

Mackey, Robert. 2011. "Social media accounts of violence in Cairo challenge official narrative." *New York Times* Replace in italics. URL: https://thelede.blogs.nytimes.com/2011/10/10/social-media-accounts-of-violence-in-cairo-challenge-official-narrative

McLauchlin, Theodore. 2010. "Loyalty Strategies and Military Defection in Rebellion." *Comparative Politics* 42(3):333–350.

McLauchlin, Theodore. 2015. "Desertion and Collective Action in Civil Wars." *International Studies Quarterly* 59(4):669–679.

McLauchlin, Theodore. 2023. "State breakdown and Army-Splinter Rebellions." *Journal of Conflict Resolution* 67(1):66–93.

McMahon, R. Blake and Branislav L. Slantchev. 2015. "The Guardianship Dilemma: Regime Security through and from the Armed Forces." *American Political Science Review* 109(2):297–313.

Maeda, Ko. 2010. "Two Models of Democratic Breakdown: A Competing Risks Analysis of Democratic Durability." *The Journal of Politics* 72(4):1129–1143.

Magued, Shaimaa. 2020. "Mobilization Structures and Political Change in an Authoritarian Context: The National Association for Change as a Case Study (2010–2011)." *Journal of North African Studies* 25(1):34–52.

Maher, Ahmed. 2014. "Lil-Asaf Kuntu A'lam [Unfortunately, I Knew]." *Masr al-Arabia* May 13. URL: https://bit.ly/3bcmp9o

Makara, Michael. 2013. "Coup-Proofing, Military Defection, and the Arab Spring." *Democracy and Security* 9(4):334–359.

Makara, Michael. 2016. "Rethinking Military Behavior during the Arab Spring." *Defense and Security Analysis* 32(3):209–223.

Mandraud, Isabelle. 2011. "La chute du régime Ben Ali racontée par le chef de la garde présidentielle." *Le Monde* April 2. URL: https://www.lemonde.fr/afrique/article/2011/04/02/la-chute-du-regime-ben-ali-racontee-par-le-chef-de-la-garde-presidentielle_1502095_3212.html

Marroushi, Nadine. 2012. "Renaissance man: Gehad El Haddad works as the Islamist project's pragmatist." *Egypt Independent* July 31. URL: https://www.egyptindependent.com/renaissance-man-gehad-el-haddad-works-islamist-project-s-pragmatist

Marshall, Shana. 2015. "The Egyptian Armed Forces and the Remaking of an Economic Empire." *Carnegie Middle East Center.* URL: https://carnegieendowment.org/files/egyptian_armed_forces.pdf

Marshall, Shana and Joshua Stacher. 2012. "Egypt's Generals and Transnational Capital." *MERIP Middle East Report* (262).

Masaki, Takaaki. 2016. "Coups d'Etat and Foreign Aid." *World Development* 79:51–68.

Masoud, Tarek. 2011. "The Upheavals in Egypt and Tunisia: The Road to (and from) Liberation Square." *Journal of Democracy* 22(3):20–34.

Masoud, Tarek. 2014. "Egyptian Democracy: Smothered in the Cradle, or Stillborn?" *Brown Journal of World Affairs* 20(11):3–17.

Masoud, Tarek. 2018. "Review Essay: Why Tunisia?" *Journal of Democracy* 29(4):166–175.

Masri, Safwan M. 2017. *Tunisia: An Arab Anomaly.* New York: Columbia University Press.

Massad, Joseph A. 2001. *Colonial Effects: The Making of National Identity in Jordan.* New York: Columbia University Press.

Matthews, Austin S. 2022. "Don't Turn Around, der Kommissar's in Town: Political Officers and Coups d'état in Authoritarian Regimes." *Journal of Peace Research* 59(5):663–678.

Mattingly, Daniel. 2022. "How the Party Commands the Gun: The Foreign-Domestic Threat Dilemma in China." *American Journal of Political Science* Firstview.

Mazzetti, Mark and Maggie Haberman. 2022. "A Jan. 6 mystery: Why did it take so long to deploy the national guard?" *The New York Times* July 21.

Meddeb, Mohamed. 2022. "La Neutralitè de l'Armée, un des préalables à la réussite de la transition démocratique!" *Leaders.* URL: https://leaders.com.tn/article/32871-mohamed-meddeb-la-neutralite-de-l-armee-un-des-prealables-a-la-reussite-de-la-transition-democratique

MEE Staff. 2015. "26 Egyptian officers allegedly jailed for plotting coup against Sisi." *Middle East Eye* August 17. URL: https://www.middleeasteye.net/news/26-egyptian-officers-allegedly-jailed-plotting-coup-against-sisi

Mekay, Emad. 2011. "Revolutionary Egypt Will Not Accept Military Junta." *Lobelog* February 10. URL: https://lobelog.com/revolutionary-egypt-will-not-accept-military-junta

Meng, Anne and Jack Paine. 2022. "Power Sharing and Authoritarian Stability: How Rebel Regimes Solve the Guardianship Dilemma." *American Political Science Review* 116(4): 1208–1225.

Middle East Monitor. 2017. "Marzouki: US military considered intervention in 2012." *Middle East Monitor* July 26. URL: https://www.middleeastmonitor.com/20170726-marzouki-us-military-considered-intervention-in-2012

Miller, Michael K. 2013. "Democratic Pieces: Autocratic Elections and Democratic Development since 1815." *British Journal of Political Science* 45(3):501–530.

Miller, Michael K. 2020. "The Strategic Origins of Electoral Authoritarianism." *British Journal of Political Science* 50(1): 17–44.

Mohamed, Khalid. 2013. "Army: 'Launching the beard' is a failed attempt and Sisi has ordered ban on talking about politics." *El-Watan* March 17. In Arabic. URL: https://www.elwatannews.com/news/details/148112

Mohsen, Manar. 2013. "Brotherhood supports calls for jihad in Syria." *Daily News Egypt* June 15. URL: http://www.dailynewsegypt.com/2013/06/15/brotherhood-supports-calls-for-jihad-in-syria

Moore, Barrington. 1966. *Social Origins of Dictatorship and Democracy: Lord and Peasant in the Making of the Modern World.* Boston, MA: Beacon.

Morency-Laflamme, Julien. 2018. "A Question of Trust: Military Defection during Regime Crises in Benin and Togo." *Democratization* 25(3):464–480.

Morrow, James D. 1993. "Arms Versus Allies: Trade-Offs in the Search for Security." *International Organization* 47(2):207–233.

Morsi, Mohamed. 2011. "This is Egypt's revolution, not ours." *The Guardian* February 7. URL: http://www.guardian.co.uk/commentisfree/2011/feb/08/egypt-revolution-muslim-brotherhood-democracy

Mosalem, Mahmoud. 2011. "Civil state is a matter of national security, says army chief of staff." *Egypt Independent* August 17. URL: https://www.egyptindependent.com/civil-state-matter-national-security-says-army-chief-staff

Nader, Aya. 2015. "Al-Sisi vows to 'go after' non-conforming Muslim Brotherhood." *Daily News Egypt* April 1. URL: https://dailynewsegypt.com/2015/04/01/al-sisi-vows-to-go-after-non-conforming-muslim-brotherhood

Narang, Vipin and Caitlin Talmadge. 2018. "Civil-military Pathologies and Defeat in War: Tests Using New Data." *Journal of Conflict Resolution* 62(7):1379–1405.

Nasr, Salah. 1999. *Muzakirat Salah Nasr (al-guze' al-awal): Al-Sou'd [The Memoirs of Salah Nasr (Part One): The Rise]*. Cairo: Dar al-Khayyal.

Nasser, Gamal Abdel. 1955. *Egypt's Liberation: The Philosophy of the Revolution*. Washington, D.C.: Public Affairs Press.

Nawaat. 2011. "14 janvier 2011 à Tunis: le jour où Ben Ali est tombé [Mediapart]." *Nawaat* November 12. URL: https://nawaat.org/2011/11/12/14-janvier-2011-a-tunis-le-jour-ou-ben-ali-est-tombe-mediapart

N'Diaye, Boubacar. 2002. "How Not to Institutionalize Civilian Control: Kenya's Coup Prevention Strategies, 1964-1997." *Armed Forces & Society* 28(4):619–640.

Needler, Martin C. 1964. *Anatomy of A Coup d'Etat: Ecuador 1963*. Washington, D.C.: Institute for the Comparative Study of Political Systems.

Neguib, Mohammed. 1955. *Egypt's Destiny*. London: Victor Gollancz Ltd.

Nepstad, Sharon Erickson. 2011. *Nonviolent Revolutions: Civil Resistance in the Late 20th Century*. New York: Oxford University Press.

Nepstad, Sharon Erickson. 2013. "Mutiny and Nonviolence in the Arab Spring: Exploring Military Defections and Loyalty in Egypt, Bahrain, and Syria." *Journal of Peace Research* 50(3):337–349.

Nepstad, Sharon Erickson. 2015. *Nonviolent Struggle: Theories, Strategies, and Dynamics*. New York: Oxford University Press.

Neto, Octavio Amorim and Pedro Accorsi. 2022. "Presidents and Generals: Systems of Government and the Selection of Defense Ministers." *Armed Forces & Society* 48(1):136–163.

Netterstrøm, Kasper Ly. 2016. "The Tunisian General Labor Union and the Advent of Democracy." *Middle East Journal* 70(3):383–398.

Newell, Jonathan. 1995. "An African Army under Pressure: The Politicisation of the Malawi Army and 'Operation Bwezani', 1992–93." *Small Wars & Insurgencies* 6(2):159–182.

Nordlinger, Eric A. 1977. *Soldiers in Politics: Military Coups and Governments*. Englewood Cliffs, NY: Prentice-Hall, Inc.

Norris, Pippa (ed.). 1998. *Critical Citizens: Global Support for Democratic Governance*. New York: Oxford University Press.

NPR Staff and Wires. 2011. "Defiant Mubarak Steps Back, But Not Down." *NPR* February 10. URL: https://www.npr.org/2011/02/10/133646320/spreading-labor-strikes-jolt-protests-in-egypt

Nugent, Elizabeth. 2020. *After Repression: How Polarization Derails Democratic Transition*. Princeton, NJ: Princeton University Press.

Obama, Barack. 2011*a*. "Remarks by the President on the Situation in Egypt." *The White House* January 28. URL: https://obamawhitehouse.archives.gov/the-press-office/2011/01/28/remarks-president-situation-egypt

Obama, Barack. 2011*b*. "Remarks by the President on the Situation in Egypt." *The White House* February 1. URL: https://obamawhitehouse.archives.gov/the-press-office/2011/02/01/remarks-president-situation-egypt

Obama, Barack. 2011*c*. "Statement of President Barack Obama on Egypt." *The White House* February 10. URL: https://obamawhitehouse.archives.gov/the-press-office/2011/02/10/statement-president-barack-obama-egypt

Obama, Barack. 2020. *A Promised Land*. New York: Crown Publishing Group.

Ocran, Albert Kwesi. 1969. *A Myth is Broken: An Account of the Ghana Coup d'Etat of 24th February 1966*. London: Longmans.

O'Donnell, Guillermo and Philippe Schmitter. 1986. *Transitions from Authoritarian Rule: Tentative Conclusions about Uncertain Democracies*. Baltimore, MD: Johns Hopkins University Press.

O'Donnell, Guillermo, Philippe Schmitter, and Laurence Whitehead. 1986. *Transitions from Authoritarian Rule*. Baltimore, MD: Johns Hopkins University Press.

Omer, Mohammed. 2013. "Foul sewage flooding raises Palestinian ire." *Al-Jazeera* March 9. URL: https://www.aljazeera.com/indepth/features/2013/03/201337135540513860.html

Onyszkiewicz, Janusz. 1996. Poland's Road to Civilian Control. In *Civil-Military Relations and Democracy*, ed. Larry Diamond and Marc F. Plattner. Baltimore, MD: Johns Hopkins University Press chapter 7, pp. 66–80.

Open Letter. 2022. "To Support and Defend: Principles of Civilian Control and Best Practices of Civil-Military Relations." *War on the Rocks* September 6. URL: https://warontherocks.com/2022/09/to-support-and-defend-principles-of-civilian-control-and-best-practices-of-civil-military-relations/

Osman, Dalia. 2011. "*Al-Liwa Mamdouh Shahin: Al-Rais al-Qadim mulazim bi-taghyer al-dustour* [Major General Mahmdouh Shahin: The next president is 'obligated' to change the constitution]." *Al-Masry al-Youm* March 16. URL: https://www.almasryalyoum.com/news/details/119538

Ozen, H. Ege. 2018. "Egypt's 2011–2012 Parliamentary Elections: Voting for Religious vs. Secular Democracy?" *Mediterranean Politics* 23(4):453–378.

Ozen, H. Ege. 2020. "Voting for Secular Parties in the Middle East: Evidence from the 2014 General elections in Post-Revolutionary Tunisia." *Journal of Norh African Studies* 25(2):251–279.

Pachon, Alejandro. 2014. "Loyalty and Defection: Misunderstanding Civil-Military Relations in Tunisia During the 'Arab Spring'." *Journal of Strategic Studies* 37(4):508–531.

Parker, Emily. 2013. "Deep Political Divide Over Calls to Dissolve Tunisian Government." *Tunisia Live* July 5. URL: https://web.archive.org/web/20130709201919/http://www.tunisia-live.net/2013/07/05/political-parties-split-over-nidaa-tounes-and-popular-front-statements

Perlmutter, Amos. 1974. *Egypt: The Praetorian State*. New Brunswick, NJ: Transaction Books.

Perlmutter, Amos. 1977. *The Military and Politics in Modern Times: On Professionals, Praetorians, and Revolutionary Soldiers*. New Haven, CT: Yale University Press.

Philip, George. 1984. "The Fall of the Argentine Military." *Third World Quarterly* 6(3):624–637.

Pierson, Paul. 2000. "Increasing Returns, Path Dependence, and the Study of Politics." *American Political Science Review* 94(2):251–267.

Pilster, Ulrich and Tobias Bohmelt. 2011. "Coup-Proofing and Military Effectiveness in Interstate Wars, 1967–99." *Conflict Management and Peace Science* 28(4):331–350.

Pinckney, Jonathan C. 2020. *From Dissent to Democracy: The Promise and Perils of Civil Resistance Transitions*. New York: Oxford University Press.

Pion-Berlin, David, Diego Esparza, and Kevin Grisham. 2014. "Staying Quartered: Civilian Uprisings and Military Disobedience in the Twenty-First Century." *Comparative Political Studies* 47(2):230–259.

Pion-Berlin, David and Harold Trinkunas. 2010. "Civilian Praetorianism and Military Shirking during Constitutional Crises in Latin America." *Comparative Politics* 42:395–411.

Pollack, Kenneth. 2018. *Armies of Sand: The Past, Present, and Future of Arab Military Effectiveness*. New York: Oxford University Press.

Poncet, Jean. 1959. "L'évolution géographique du peuplement tunisien à l'époque récente." *Annales de Geographie* 68(367):247–253.

Potzschke, Steffen and Michael Braun. 2017. "Migrant Sampling Using Facebook Advertisements: A Case Study of Polish Migrants in Four European Countries." *Political Behavior* 35(5):633–653.

Powell, Jonathan. 2012. "Determinants of the Attempting and Outcome of Coups d'état." *Journal of Conflict Resolution* 56(6):1017–1040.

Powell, Jonathan. 2014. "Regime Vulnerability and the Diversionary Threat of Force." *Journal of Conflict Resolution* 58(1):169–196.

Powell, Jonathan M., Christopher Faulkner, William Dean, and Kyle Romano. 2018. "Give Them Toys? Military Allocations and Regime Stability in Transitional Democracies." *Democratization* 25(7):1153–1172.

Powell, Jonathan and Clayton L. Thyne. 2011. "Global Instances of Coups from 1950 to 2010: A New Dataset." *Journal of Peace Research* 48(2):249–259.

Powell, Jonathan M., Trace Lasley, and Rebecca Schiel. 2016. "Combating Coups d'état in Africa, 1950–2014." *Studies in Comparative International Development* 51:482–502.

Prentice, R. L., J. D. Kalbfleisch, A. V. Peterson, N. Flournoy, V. T. Farewell, and N. E. Breslow. 1978. "A Proportional Hazards Model for the Subdistribution of a Competing Risk." *Biostatistics* 34(4):541–554.

Przeworski, Adam. 1991. *Democracy and the Market: Political and Economic Reforms in Eastern Europe and Latin America.* New York: Cambridge University Press.

Przeworski, Adam and Fernando Limongi. 1997. "Modernization: Theories and Facts." *World Politics* 49(2):155–183.

Quillen, Stephen and Campbell MacDiarmid. 2021. "Tunisian PM quits and military fall behind president as he cements power after 'coup'." *The Telegraph.* URL: https://www. telegraph.co.uk/world-news/2021/07/27/tunisias-prime-minister-military-labour-union-accept-presidents

Quinlivan, James T. 1999. "Coup-Proofing: Its Practice and Consequences in the Middle East." *International Security* 24(2):131–165.

Quinn, Andrew and David Alexander. 2012. "U.S. warns Egypt's military on ties after power grab." *Reuters* June 18. URL: https://www.reuters.com/article/us-egypt-election-usa/u-s-warns-egypts-military-on-ties-after-power-grab-idUSBRE85H19H20120618

Rabkin, Rhoda. 1992. "The Aylwin Government and 'Tutelary' Democracy: A Concept in Search of a Case." *Journal of Interamerican Studies and World Affairs* 34(4):119–194.

Rapanos, Grigorious. 2018. "The Role of Human Development in the Transition to Democracy after the Arab Spring." *Mediterranean Politics* 23(3): 364–386.

Reiter, Dan. 2020. "Avoiding the Coup-Proofing Dilemma: Consolidating Political Control While Maximizing Military Power." *Foreign Policy Analysis* 16(3):312–331.

Reuters Staff. 2011*a*. "Egypt fighter planes buzz Cairo protesters." *Reuters* January 30. URL: https://www.reuters.com/article/uk-egypt-warplanes/egypt-fighter-planes-buzz-cairo-protesters-idUKTRE70T1IL20110130

Reuters Staff. 2011*b*. "Egyptian Vice President Omar Suleiman speech." *Reuters* February 10. URL: https://www.reuters.com/article/us-egypt-suleiman-speech/egyptian-vice-president-omar-suleiman-speech-idUSTRE71990120110210

Reuters Staff. 2012. "Egypt Islamists: Military will not escape scrutiny." *Reuters* January 20. URL: https://www.reuters.com/article/us-egypt-brotherhood-army-idUSTRE80J1OW20120120

Reuters Staff. 2013*a*. "Egypt demands Ethiopia halt Nile dam, upping stakes." *Reuters* June 5. URL: https://www.reuters.com/article/us-egypt-ethiopia-dam/egypt-demands-ethiopia-halt-nile-dam-upping-stakes-idUSBRE9541EQ20130605

Reuters Staff. 2013*b*. "Egyptian armed forces chief sets ultimatum." *Reuters* July 1. URL: https://www.reuters.com/article/us-egypt-protests-army-text/egyptian-armed-forces-chief-sets-ultimatum-idUSBRE96014420130701

Reuters Staff. 2018. "Egypt's ex-army officers pose growing security threat." *Reuters* January 30. URL: https://www.reuters.com/article/us-egypt-security-military-insight/egypts-ex-army-officers-pose-growing-security-threat-idUSKBN1FJ1V8

Rial, Juan. 1996. Armies and Civil Society in Latin America. In *Civil-Military Relations and Democracy*, ed. Larry Diamond and Marc F. Plattner. Baltimore, MD: Johns Hopkins University Press chapter 4, pp. 47–65.

Rifai, Ryan. 2011. "Timeline: Tunisia's uprising." *Al-Jazeera* January 23. URL: https://www.aljazeera.com/news/2011/01/23/timeline-tunisias-uprising

Rodriguez, Linda Alexander, ed. 1994. *Rank and Privilege: The Military and Society in Latin America*. Wilmington, DE: SR Books.

Roessler, Philip. 2016. *Ethnic Politics and State Power in Africa: The Logic of the Coup-Civil War Trap*. New York: Cambridge University Press.

Roll, Stephan. 2013. "Egypt's Business Elite after Mubarak: A Powerful Player between Generals and Brotherhood." *SWP Research Paper* RP 8.

Roll, Stephen. 2016. "Managing Change: How Egypt's Military Leadership Shaped the Transformation." *Mediterranean Politics* 21(1):23–43.

Rose, Richard, William Mishler, and Neil Munro. 2011. *Popular Support for an Undemocratic Regime: The Changing Views of Russians*. New York: Cambridge University Press.

Ross, Michael L. 2001. "Does Oil Hinder Democracy?" *World Politics* 53(3):325–361.

Rouquié, Alain. 1987. *The Military and the State in Latin America*. Berkeley, CA: University of California Press.

Rozman, Stephen L. 1970. "The Evolution of the Political Role of the Peruvian Military." *Journal of Interamerican Studies and World Affairs* 12(4):539–564.

Russell, D.E.H. 1974. *Rebellion, Revolution, and Armed Force: A Comparative Study of Fifteen Countries with Special Emphasis on Cuba and South Africa*. San Diego, CA: Academic Press.

Rustow, Dankwart A. 1970. "Transitions to Democracy: Toward a Dynamic Model." *Comparative Politics* 2(3):337–363.

Ryan, Missy and Dan Lamothe. 2021. "Military reaction was 'sprint speed,' top officer says as Pentagon takes heat for Capitol riot response." *Washington Post* March 2.

Ryan, Yasmine. 2011. "Former Tunisia minister warns of coup risk." *Al-Jazeera* May 5. URL: https://www.aljazeera.com/news/2011/5/5/former-tunisia-minister-warns-of-coup-risk

S, Mourad. 2018. "Tunisie: Le syndicat de la garde nationale appelle à nommer rapidement un ministre de l'Intérieur." *Tunisie Numerique* July 10. URL: https://www.tunisienumerique.com/tunisie-le-syndicat-de-la-garde-nationale-appelle-a-nommer-rapidement-un-ministre-de-linterieur

Saati, Abrak. 2018. "Negotiating the Post-Revolution Constitution for Tunisia—Members of the National Constituent Assembly Share Their Experiences." *International Law Research* 7(1):235–246.

Sadat, Anwar. 1977. *In Search of Identity: An Autobiography*. New York: Harper & Row Publishers.

Safi, Omar. 2020. *The Intelligence State in Tunisia: Security and Mukhabarat, 1881–1965*. New York: I.B. Tauris.

Said, Atef. 2012. "The Paradox of Transition to 'Democracy' under Military Rule." *Social Research* 79(2):397–434.

Samuels, David and Cesar Zucco. 2014. "The Power of Partisanship in Brazil: Evidence from Survey Experiments." *American Journal of Political Science* 58(1):212–225.

Sanad, Maikel Nabil. 2011. "The army and the people wasn't ever one hand." *Blog Post* March 8. URL: https://rsf.org/sites/default/files/the_army_and_the_people_wasn_t_ever_one_hand–2.pdf

Sanborn, Howard and Clayton L. Thyne. 2014. "Learning Democracy: Education and the Fall of Authoritarian Regimes." *British Journal of Political Science* 44(4):773–797.

Sani, Giacomo andGiovanni Sartori. 1983. Polarization, Fragmentation, and Competition in Western Democracies. In *Western European Party Systems: Continuity and Change*, ed. Hans Daalder and Peter Mair. Beverly Hills, CA: SAGE Publications pp. 307–340.

Sartori, Giovanni. 1966. European Political Parties: The Case of Polarized Pluralism. In *Political Parties and Political Development*, ed. Joseph LaPalombara and Myron Weiner. Princeton, NJ: Princeton University Press pp. 137–176.

Satloff, Robert B. 1988. *Army and Politics in Mubarak's Egypt.* Washington Institute for Near East Policy.

Savage, Jesse Dillon and Jonathan D. Caverley. 2017. "When Human Capital Threatens the Capitol: Foreign Aid in the Form of Military Training and Coups." *Journal of Peace Research* 54(4):542–557.

Sayigh, Yezid. 2012. "Above the State: The Officers' Republic in Egypt." *Carnegie Endowment for International Peace.* URL: https://carnegieendowment.org/files/officers_republic1.pdf

Sayigh, Yezid. 2013. "Morsi and Egypt's Military." *Al-Monitor* January 8. URL: https://www.al-monitor.com/pulse/originals/2013/01/morsi-army-egypt-revolution.html

Sayigh, Yezid. 2015. "Missed Opportunity: The Politics of Police Reform in Egypt and Tunisia." *Carnegie Middle East Center.* URL: https://carnegie-mec.org/2015/03/17/missed-opportunity-politics-of-police-reform-in-egypt-and-tunisia-pub-59391

Sayigh, Yezid. 2019. "Owners of the Republic: An Anatomy of Egypt's Military Economy." *Carnegie Middle East Center.* URL: https://carnegie-mec.org/2019/11/18/owners-of-republic-anatomy-of-egypt-s-military-economy-pub-80325

Schmitter, Philippe C. and Terry Lynn Karl. 1991. "What Democracy Is and Is Not." *Journal of Democracy* 2(3):75–88.

Self, Darin Sanders. 2022. "Bounded Democratization: How Military-Party Relations Shape Military-Led Democratization." *Comparative Political Studies* Firstview.

Serrano, Monica. 1995. "The Armed Branch of the State: Civil-Military Relations in Mexico." *Journal of Latin American Studies* 27(2):423–448.

Shah, Aqil. 2014. *The Army and Democracy: Military Politics in Pakistan.* Cambridge, MA: Harvard University Press.

Shahin, Emad El-Din. 2012. "The Egyptian Revolution: The Power of Mass Mobilization and the Spirit of Tahrir Square." *Journal of the Middle East and Africa* 3:46–69.

Sharqieh, Ibrahim. 2013. "Tunisia's Lessons for the Middle East." *Foreign Affairs* September 17. URL: https://www.foreignaffairs.com/articles/tunisia/2013-09-17/tunisias-lessons-middle-east

Shenker, Jack. 2011. "Egyptians return to Tahrir Square to protest against military junta." *The Guardian* November 18. URL: https://www.theguardian.com/world/2011/nov/18/egyptians-return-tahrir-square-protest

Shils, Edward. 1960. "Political Development in the New States." *Comparative Studies in Society and History* 2(3):265–292.

Shorbagy, Manar. 2007. "Understanding Kefaya: The New Politics in Egypt." *Arab Studies Quarterly* 29(1):39–60.

Shukrallah, Salma. 2012. "Egypt's political forces and Brotherhood unite to counter military evasion of power handover." *Ahram Online* June 22. URL: http://english.ahram.org.eg/NewsContent/1/64/45889/Egypt/Politics-/Egypts-political-forces-and-Brotherhood-unite-to-c.aspx

Siddiqa, Ayesha. 2007. *Military, Inc: Inside Pakistan's Military Economy.* London: Pluto Press.

Singer, J. David, Stuart Bremer, and John Stuckey. 1972. Capability Distribution, Uncertainty, and Major Power War, 1820–1965. In *Peace, War, and Numbers*, ed. Bruce Russett. Beverly Hills, CA: Sage pp. 19–48.

Singh, Naunihal. 2014. *Seizing Power: The Strategic Logic of Military Coups.* Baltimore, MD: Johns Hopkins University Press.

Singh, Naunihal. 2022. "The Myth of the Coup Contagion." *Journal of Democracy* 33(4):74–88.

Skocpol, Theda. 1979. *States and Social Revolutions: A Comparative Analysis of France, Russia, and China.* New York: Cambridge University Press.

Skogstad, Karl. 2016. "Defence Budgets in the Post-Cold War Era: A Spatial Econometrics Approach." *Defence and Peace Economics* 27(3):323–352.

Slackman, Michael. 2011. "Choice of Suleiman likely to please the military, not the crowds." *New York Times* January 29. URL: https://www.nytimes.com/2011/01/30/world/middleeast/30suleiman.html?hp

Slater, Dan. 2010. *Ordering Power: Contentious Politics and Authoritarian Leviathans in Southeast Asia.* New York: Cambridge University Press.

Sorokin, Gerald L. 1994. "Arms, Alliances, and Security Tradeoffs in Enduring Rivalries." *International Studies Quarterly* 38:421–446.

Souaré, Issaka K. 2014. "The African Union as a Norm Entrepreneur on Military Coups d'état in Africa (1952–2012): An Empirical Assessment." *The Journal of Modern African Studies* 52(1):69–94.

Springborg, Robert. 1979. "Patrimonialism and Policy Making in Egypt: Nasser and Sadat and the Tenure Policy for Reclaimed Lands." *Middle Eastern Studies* 15(1):49–69.

Springborg, Robert. 1987. "The President and the Field Marshal: Civil-Military Relations in Egypt Today." *MERIP Middle East Report* (147).

Springborg, Robert. 1989. *Mubarak's Egypt: Fragmentation of the Political Order.* New York: Routledge.

Springborg, Robert. 2011. "Economic Involvements of Militaries." *International Journal of Middle East Studies* 43(3):397–399.

Springborg, Robert. 2013. "Sisi's Islamist Agenda for Egypt." *Foreign Affairs.* URL: https://www.foreignaffairs.com/articles/middle-east/2013-07-25/sisis-islamist-agenda-egypt

Springborg, Robert. 2014. "Abdul Fattah al-Sisi: New face of Egypt's old guard." *BBC News.* URL: http://www.bbc.com/news/world-middle-east-26188023

Spruyt, Hendrik. 2005. *Ending Empire: Contested Sovereignty and Territorial Partition.* Ithaca, NY: Cornell University Press.

Stacher, Joshua. 2012. *Adaptable Autocrats: Regime Power in Egypt and Syria.* Palo Alto, CA: Stanford University Press.

Steavenson, Wendell. 2011. "On the Square: Were the Egyptian Protesters Right to Trust the Military?" *The New Yorker* February 20. URL: https://www.newyorker.com/magazine/2011/02/28/on-the-square-wendell-steavenson

Stepan, Alfred. 1971. *The Military in Politics: Changing Patterns in Brazil.* Princeton, NJ: Princeton University Press.

Stepan, Alfred. 1988. *Rethinking Military Politics: Brazil and the Southern Cone.* Princeton, NJ: Princeton University Press.

Stepan, Alfred. 2012. "Tunisia's Transition and the Twin Tolerations." *Journal of Democracy* 23(2):89–103.

Stepan, Alfred. 2016. "Multiple but Complementary, Not Conflictual, Leaderships: The Tunisian Democratic Transition in Comparative Perspective." *Daedalus* 145(3):95–108.

Stepan, Alfred and Cindy Skach. 1993. "Constitutional Frameworks and Democratic Consolidation: Parliamentarianism versus Presidentialism." *World Politics* 46(1):1–22.

Sudduth, Jun Koga. 2017. "Strategic Logic of Elite Purges in Dictatorships." *Comparative Political Studies* 50(13):1768–1801.

Sudduth, Jun Koga. 2021. "Purging Militaries: Introducing the Military Purges in Dictatorships (MPD) Dataset." *Journal of Peace Research* 58(4):870–880.

Svolik, Milan. 2012. *The Politics of Authoritarian Rule.* New York: Cambridge University Press.

Svolik, Milan. 2015. "Which Democracies Will Last? Coups, Incumbent Takeovers, and the Dynamic of Democratic Consolidation." *British Journal of Political Science* 45(4):715–738.

Svolik, Milan W. 2013. "Learning to Love Democracy: Electoral Accountability and the Success of Democracy." *American Journal of Political Science* 57(3):685–702.

Svolik, Milan W. 2019. "Polarization versus Democracy." *Journal of Democracy* 30(3):20–32.

Swan, Betsy Woodruff and Meridith McGraw. 2021. "'Absolute Liars': Ex-D.C. Guard Official Says Generals Lied to Congress about Jan. 6." *Politico* December 6.

Tachau, Frank and Metin Heper. 1983. "The State, Politics, and the Military in Turkey." *Comparative Politics* 16(1):17–33.

Talmadge, Caitlin. 2015. *The Dictator's Army: Battlefield Effectiveness in Authoritarian Regimes.* Ithaca, NY: Cornell University Press.

Tang, Min, Narisong Huhe, and Qiang Zhou. 2017. "Contingent Democratization: When Do Economic Crises Matter?" *British Journal of Political Science* 47(1):71–90.

Tansey, Oisín. 2017. "The Fading of the Anti-Coup Norm." *Journal of Democracy* 28(1):144–156.

Tansey, Oisín. 2018. "Lowest Common Denominator Norm Institutionalization: The Anti-Coup Norm at the United Nations." *Global Governance* 24(2):287–306.

Tarek, Sherif. 2011. "Egypt's Muslim Brotherhood and ruling military: Deal or no deal?" *Ahram Online* September 28. URL: http://english.ahram.org.eg/NewsContent/1/64/22042/Egypt/Politics-/Egypts-Muslim-Brotherhood-and-ruling-military-Deal.aspx

Tarek, Sherif. 2012. "Egypt's next government remains anyone's guess." *Ahram Online* July 3. URL: http://english.ahram.org.eg/NewsContent/1/64/46766/Egypt/Politics-/Egypts-next-government-remains-anyones-guess.aspx

Tarhouni, Samir. 2011. "Press Conference." *Youtube* August 8. URL: https://www.youtube.com/watch?v=zQ6aHx6yrl8

Tartter, Jean R. 1991. National Security. In *Egypt: A Country Study*, ed. Helen Chapin Metz. Washington, D.C.: Library of Congress chapter 5, pp. 291–350.

Tas, Hakki. 2015. "Turkey—from Tutelary to Delegative Democracy." *Third World Quarterly* 36(4):776–791.

Taylor, Brian D. 2003. *Politics and the Russian Army: Civil-Military Relations, 1689–2000.* New York: Cambridge University Press.

Taylor, William C. 2014. *Military Responses to the Arab Uprisings and the Future of Civil-Military Relations in the Middle East: Analysis from Egypt, Tunisia, Libya, and Syria.* New York: Palgrave Macmillan.

Thelen, Kathleen. 1999. "Historical Institutionalism in Comparative Politics." *Annual Review of Political Science* 2:369–404.

Thompson, William R. 1973. *The Grievances of Military Coup-Makers.* Beverly Hills, CA: Sage Publications.

Toronto, Nathan W. 2014. "Military Recruitment Data Set, Version 2014.". URL: http://nathantoronto.com/research

Trager, Eric. 2011. "After Tunisia, Is Egypt Next?" *The Atlantic* January 17. URL: https://www.theatlantic.com/international/archive/2011/01/after-tunisia-is-egypt-next/69656

Trager, Eric. 2016. *Arab Fall: How the Muslim Brotherhood Won and Lost Egypt in 891 Days.* Washington, D.C.: Georgetown University Press.

Trew, Bel. 2012. "Morsi's counterpunch: A reading of Egypt latest Constitutional Declaration." *Ahram Online* August 8. URL: http://english.ahram.org.eg/NewsContent/1/140/50260/Egypt/First–days/Morsis-counterpunch-A-reading-of-Egypt-latest-Cons.aspx

Tukey, John W. 1977. *Exploratory Data Analysis.* London: Pearson.

Tuniscope. 2015. "Issam Dardouri: Rachid Ammar est un hèros en carton." *Tuniscope* November 9. URL: https://www.tuniscope.com/article/81958/actualites/tunisie/ammar-dardouri-carton-280817

Ulfelder, Jay. 2010. *Dilemmas of Democratic Consolidation: A Game-Theory Approach.* Boulder, CO: First Forum Press.

Vasquez III, Joseph Paul, and Jonathan Powell. 2021. "Institutional Arsenals for Democracy? The Postcoup Effects of Conscript Militaries." *Armed Forces & Society* 47(2):298–318.

Vatikiotis, P.J. 1978. *Nasser and His Generation.* London: Croom Helm Ltd.

Waldner, David and Ellen Lust. 2018. "Unwelcome Change: Coming to Terms with Democratic Backsliding." *Annual Review of Political Science* 21:93–113.

Ward, Alexander. 2022. "Did Milley Cross a Civ-mil Line?" *Politico* August 8.

Ware, L.B. 1985. "The Role of the Tunisian Military in the Post-Bourgiba Era." *Middle East Journal* 39(1):28–39.

Ware, L.B. 1988. "Ben Ali's Constitutional Coup in Tunisia." *Middle East Journal* 42(4):587–601.

Wehrey, Frederic. 2020. "Tunisia's Wake-Up Call: How Security Challenges from Libya Are Shaping Defense Reforms." *Carnegie Middle East Center.* URL: https://carnegieendowment.org/2020/03/18/tunisia-s-wake-up-call-how-security-challenges-from-libya-are-shaping-defense-reforms-pub-81312

Wejnert, Barbara. 2005. "Diffusion, Development, and Democracy, 1800–1999." *American Sociological Review* 70(1):53–81.

Wenig, Gilad. 2014. "Egypt's Army of God." *Foreign Affairs.* URL: https://www.foreignaffairs.com/articles/middle-east/2014-10-31/egypts-army-god

Werr, Patrick. 2012. "Egypt sees revenue in Suez Canal corridor project." *Reuters* October 10. URL: https://www.reuters.com/article/us-egypt-canal/egypt-sees-revenue-in-suez-canal-corridor-project-idUSBRE8990Y920121010

Weyland, Kurt. 2012. "The Arab Spring: Why the Surprising Similarities with the Revolutionary Wave of 1848?" *on Politics* 10(4):917–934.

Weymouth, Lally. 2011. "Egyptian generals speak about revolution, elections." *Washington Post* May 18. URL: https://www.washingtonpost.com/world/middle-east/egyptian-generals-speak-about-revolution-elections/2011/05/16/AF7AiU6G_story.html

Weymouth, Lally. 2013*a*. "Excerpts from Washington Post interview with Egyptian Gen. Abdel Fatah al-Sissi." *Washington Post* August 5. URL: https://www.washingtonpost.com/world/middle_east/washington-post-interviews-egyptian-gen-abdel-fatah-al-gen-sissi/2013/08/03/6409e0a2-fbc0-11e2-a369-d1954abcb7e3_story.html?utm_term=.3b3cc1a515f6

Weymouth, Lally. 2013b. " 'They are Incompetent': Tunisia's secular opposition leader Beji Caid Essebsi on why the Islamists must go." Slate, December 13. URL: https://slate.com/news-and-politics/2013/12/beji-caid-essebsi-interview-the-tunisian-leader-of-the-nidaa-touness-party-on-why-the-islamists-must-go.html

White House. 2011. "Statement by the Press Secretary on Recent Developments in Egypt." *Office of the Press Secretary* November 25. URL: https://obamawhitehouse.archives.gov/the-press-office/2011/11/25/statement-press-secretary-recent-developments-egypt

White, Peter B. 2017. "Crises and Crisis Generations: The Long-term Impact of International Crises on Military Political Participation." *Security Studies* 26(4):575–605.

Wiatr, Jerzy. 1968. Military Professionalism and Transformations of Class Structure in Poland. In *Armed Forces and Society: Sociological Essays*, ed. Jacques van Doorn. Paris: Mouton.

Wickham, Carrie Rosefsky. 2013. *The Muslim Brotherhood: Evolution of an Islamist Movement.* Princeton, NJ: Princeton University Press.

Wiking, Staffan. 1983. *Military Coups in Sub-Saharan Africa: How to Justify Illegal assumptions of power.* Uppsala: Scandinavian Institute of African Studies.

Willis, Michael J. 1997. *The Islamist Challenge in Algeria: A Political History.* New York: New York University Press.

Willis, Michael J. 2012. *Politics and Power in the Maghreb: Algeria, Tunisia and Morocco from Independence to the Arab Spring.* New York: Columbia University Press.

Wolf, Anne. 2017. *Political Islam in Tunisia: The History of Ennahda.* London: Hurst and Company.

Wong, Stan Hok-Wui and Kelvin Chun-Man Chan. 2021. "Determinants of Political Purges in Autocracies: Evidence from Ancient Chinese Dynasties." *Journal of Peace Research* 58(3):583–598.

Woo, Jongseok. 2011. *Security Challenges and Military Politics in East Asia: From State Building to Post-Democratization.* New York: Continuum International Publishing.

Woodberry, Robert D. 2002. "The Missionary Roots of Liberal Democracy." *American Political Science Review* 106(2):244–274.

Wright, Claudia. 1982. "Tunisia: Next Friend to Fall?" *Foreign Policy* (46):120–137.

Wright, Joseph. 2008. "Political Competition and Democratic Stability in New Democracies." *British Journal of Political Science* 38:221–245.

Yerkes, Sarah and Marwan Muasher. 2017. "Tunisia's Corruption Contagion: A Transition At Risk." *Carnegie Endowment for International Peace.* URL: https://carnegieendowment.org/2017/10/25/tunisia-s-corruption-contagion-transition-at-risk-pub-73522

Yesilyurt, M. Ensar and J. Paul Elhorst. 2017. "Impacts of Neighboring Countries on Military Expenditures: A Dynamic Spatial Panel Approach." *Journal of Peace Research* 54(6):777–790.

Yousfi, Hela. 2018. *Trade Unions and Arab Revolutions: The Tunisian Case of UGTT.* New York: Routledge.

Yukawa, Taku, Kaoru Hidaka, and Kaori Kushima. 2020. "Coups and Framing: How Do Militaries Justify the Illegal Seizure of Power?" *Democratization* 27(5):816–835.

Zaverucha, Jorge. 1993. "The Degree of Military Political Autonomy during the Spanish, Argentine and Brazilian Transitions." *Journal of Latin American Studies* 25(2):283–299.

Zhang, Baobao, Matto Mildenberger, Peter Howe, and Jennifer Marlon. 2020. "Quota Sampling using Facebook Advertisements." *Political Science Research and Methods* 8(3): 558–564.

Zielinski, Rosella Cappella, Benjamin O Fordham, and Kaija E Schilde. 2017. "What Goes up, Must Come down? The Asymmetric Effects of Economic Growth and International Threat on Military Spending." *Journal of Peace Research* 54(6):791–805.

Zoubir, Yahia. 2019. "The Algerian Crisis: Origins and Prospects for a 'Second Republic'." *Al-Jazeera Centre for Studies* Reports:1–16. URL: https://studies.aljazeera.net/en/reports/2019/05/algerian-crisis-origins-prospects-republic-190520100257161.html

Zoubir, Yahia H. 1993. "The Painful Transition from Authoritarianism in Algeria." *Arab Studies Quarterly* 15(3):83–110.

Index